The
Last
Romantic

A Biography of
QUEEN MARIE
of Roumania

Hannah Pakula

Simon and Schuster—New York

Published by Simon and Schuster
A Division of Simon & Schuster, Inc.
Simon & Schuster Building
Rockefeller Center
1230 Avenue of the Americas
New York, New York 10020
SIMON AND SCHUSTER and colophon are registered trademarks of
Simon & Schuster, Inc.
Designed by Rueith Ottiger/Levavi and Levavi
Manufactured in the United States of America

10 9 8 7 6 5 4 3

Library of Congress Cataloging in Publication Data
Pakula, Hannah.
 The last romantic.

 Bibliography: p.
 Includes index.
 1. Marie, Queen, consort of Ferdinand I, King of
Romania, 1875–1938. 2. Romania—Queens—Biography.
I. Title.
DR262.A2P35   1984   949.8'02'0924 [B]   84–20232
ISBN: 0-671-46364-0

For quotations which appear in this book the author would like to acknowledge and thank the following:
Thereza, Princess of Hohenzollern; the George I. Duca Collection, Hoover Institution Archives; the Hoover Presi-
dential Library; Robert Keedick and the Estate of Lee Keedick; Department of Special Collections, Kent State
University; The Maryhill Museum of Art; the Astor Papers, The Library, University of Reading; the Frank Polk
Papers, Yale University Library; Arhivele Statului Bucuresti, Romania Fond Casa Regala; and Charles Scribner's
Sons (as specified below). Also:
    George Allen & Unwin, Ltd., for Twenty Years in Roumania by Maude Parkinson, copyright 1921.
    American Review of Reviews for "Are Kings Useful?" by Charles H. Sherrill, May 1923.
    D. Appleton & Company for Some Royalties and a Prime Minister, copyright 1930, and Royal Portraits,
copyright 1928, both by Princess Marthe Bibesco.
    Atheneum for Edward VII, Prince and King by Giles St. Aubyn, copyright © 1977.
    B. T. Batsford, Ltd., for Roumanian Journey by Sacheverell Sitwell, copyright 1938.
    For For My Grandchildren by H.R.H. Princess Alice, Countess of Athalono, copyright © 1966; Dearest
Child, edited by Roger Fulford, copyright © 1964; and Your Dear Letter, edited by Roger Fulford, copyright ©
1971, all reprinted by permission of Bell & Hyman Publishers.
    Blue Ribbon Books for Athene Palace by Countess R. G. Waldeck, copyright 1942.
    For My Memoir, copyright 1938, 1939 by Edith Bolling Wilson, used by permission of the publisher, The
Bobbs-Merrill Company, Inc.
    The Bodley Head for The Emperor Alexander II by E. M. Almedingen, copyright © 1962.
    Books for Libraries Press for Downfall of Dynasties by Count Egon Corti, copyright 1934 (reprinted 1970).
    For Grace Coolidge and Her Era by Ishbel Ross, Dodd, Mead & Co., Inc., copyright © 1962 by Ishbel Ross,
reprinted by permission of Brandt & Brandt Literary Agents, Inc.
    Cambridge University Press for History of the Roumanians, copyright 1934, and Eastern Europe Between the
Wars, copyright 1945, both by Hugh Seton-Watson.
    Jonathan Cape, Ltd., and Amilcare SpA for Louisa, Lady in Waiting by Elizabeth Longford, copyright ©
1979.

(continued at back of book)

To Alan
who makes everything possible

Author's Note

This book was written to satisfy my curiosity about Marie of Roumania. I
wanted to understand why a woman, much less a Queen, who was a symbol
of success and beauty in her own generation, should have fallen into obscurity
and even disrepute within fifty years of her death. In the process of exploration
I have found a world close in time but social light-years away from our
own—a world of fixed values, predetermined lives, and extravagant romanticism. On the way I have been helped by people in both the East and the
West.

Queen Marie wrote one hundred diaries, dating from the time of her
husband's accession to the throne in 1914 until two weeks before her death
in 1938. Meant for eventual publication, they are now in the Archives of
the Casa Regala in Bucharest, along with approximately twelve hundred
personal and family letters. Until now all but a very small portion of this
material (a few diaries and fifty or so letters) has been unread and unknown
outside the Archives. I am most grateful to those who arranged for me to
do research there. I also wish to thank Mr. Vasile Arimia, Acting Director

of the Archives during my stay in Romania; Mrs. Sanda Racovicanu, a knowledgeable guide to the collection; and Mrs. Varvara Aioanei, a kindly monitor. Their cooperation made it possible to answer many questions about the Queen's life that were formerly a matter of conjecture.

I would like to express my gratitude to Her Majesty Queen Elizabeth II for gracious permission to publish portions of letters in the Royal Archives at Windsor Castle, copies of which were given to me by H.R.H. Princess Ileana of Roumania. I would also like to thank H.S.H. the Prince of Hohenlohe-Langenburg for permission to read and publish portions of letters written to his grandmother, H.R.H. Princess Alexandra; the Hon. Lady Bowes-Lyon for permission to read and publish extracts from letters written to her mother, Pauline Astor Spender-Clay; and H.R.H. the Prince of Hohenzollern-Sigmaringen for permission to do research in the Archives at Schloss Sigmaringen and publish extracts from material found there.

My special appreciation goes to the Reverend Mother Alexandra, the former Princess Ileana of Roumania, for her great assistance and friendship, as well as her permission to read and publish extracts from family letters. In pursuing the life of the mother, I have become a devoted admirer of the daughter. Other particular thanks are due to George Duca of the Hoover Institution at Stanford, who lent the benefit of his superb intellect to the project and allowed me to read and publish extracts from his unpublished manuscript on the Queen, as well as his private letters.

Many other people contributed to this book, so many that I can only list them by country and hope they will understand why I cannot devote a sentence of appreciation to each one. They are:

in Switzerland: H.M. King Michael of Roumania.

in Germany: Queen Marie's granddaughter, Baroness Alexandra Baillou, and her husband, Baron Victor Baillou; H.R.H. Princess Margaret of Hesse and the Rhine; H.S.H. the Princess of Hohenlohe-Langenburg; H.S.H. Princess Irma of Hohenlohe-Langenburg; H.S.H. Princess Beatrice of Hohenlohe-Langenburg; Madame Nadeje Flondor; and H.H. Prince Andreas of Coburg.

in France: H.I.H. Grand Duke Vladimir of Russia; H.R.H. Princess Paul of Yugoslavia; and H.R.H. Prince Alvaro of Orleans-Borbon.

in England: the Hon. David Astor; the Hon. Lady Bowes-Lyon; Mrs. Rosemary Cresswell; Prince Mircea Hohenzollern; and Prince Paul Hohenzollern.

in Romania: Ambassador David B. Funderburk, Samuel E. Fry, Edward McBride, Victor Jackovich, and Merrie Blocker of the United States Embassy; the Americas Division of the Romanian Ministry of Foreign Affairs; and friends who offered help when it was not easy to do so.

in the United States: Dr. Daniel J. Boorstin, Librarian of Congress, and Special Assistant to the Librarian, Janet Chase; Mr. John J. Schippe and Mr. Paul Shapiro of the United States Information Agency; Dr. Denton S. Cox; Mrs. Alfred Stern; Mr. Lee Keedick; Mr. John N. Rosekrans, Jr.; Prince

Alexander Romanov; H.R.H. Prince Andrej of Yugoslavia; H.R.H. Princess Elizabeth of Yugoslavia; Prince Marcus Clary; Mrs. Mica Ertegun; Miss Eleanor Harris; Mr. David Kahn; Mrs. Christa Armstrong; Mr. Dean H. Keller; and Mrs. Linda Brady Mountain.

In addition I wish to thank Lynn Nesbit, my agent, for her confidence and support, and Michael Korda and John Herman, my editors, for their superb direction. Appreciation is due to Claudia Craig-Potter, who shared research materials with me, and Elisabeth Hevner, who did the German translations. I also want to thank members of my family—Alan Pakula and Robert Boorstin, who gave valuable editorial assistance; Anna Boorstin, Louis Boorstin, and Gertrude Cohn, who accompanied me on research trips and copied research materials. Beyond specific help, they offered love and encouragement, which added to the joy of the work.

There is one person to whom I owe an incalculable debt of gratitude. Barbara Thompson Davis took time out from her own writing to advise me on mine. She accompanied me to Romania, where she helped read and digest the material in the Archives. And she engaged in endless discussions, supplying informed opinions, cogent suggestions, and friendship all along the way.

In conclusion I add a few words of explanation on dating and spelling in the text. Until the end of World War I, Romania followed the Julian calendar, which was two weeks behind the Gregorian calendar used in the West. On March 31, 1919, Eastern time was moved forward to April 14. Events occurring before this date have been conformed to the Western calendar.

I have taken the liberty of correcting Queen Marie's errors in spelling and punctuation. Marie spoke several languages fluently, and possibly because of that, never mastered spelling in any of them. Except for obvious mistakes, I have chosen to follow the Queen's spelling to eliminate discrepancies between quotations and text. Thus, in the book itself, I chose to use *Roumania*, the English spelling used by Marie and her correspondents at the turn of the century, rather than *Rumania* (the American spelling) or *Romania* (current usage); *Barbo* (Prince Stirbey), rather than the more common *Barbu*, to conform to the Queen's diaries; *Cantacuzène*, rather than *Cantacuzino*, to conform to her autobiography, and so forth. Other changes—like *Constantza* for *Constanta*—have been made to simplify pronunciation. Apart from clarification, I make no special claim for these choices. They are as idiosyncratic as the subject of the book.

Hannah Pakula
New York, 1984

Contents

List of Principal Characters and Their Relationship to Queen Marie

ALBERT, Prince Consort of England. "Grandpapa" (1819–1861). Born Prince of Saxe-Coburg-Gotha. Married Victoria, Queen of England. Marie's grandfather; her father's father.

ALEXANDER II, Tsar of Russia. "Grandpapa" (1818–1881). Married Marie, Princess of Hesse (1), Princess Catherine Dolgoruky (2). Marie's grandfather; her mother's father.

ALEXANDER III, Tsar of Russia. "Uncle Sasha" (1845–1894). Married Dagmar, Princess of Denmark (later known as Tsarina Marie). Marie's uncle; her mother's brother.

ALEXANDER I, King of Yugoslavia. "Sandro" (1888–1934). Married Mignon, Princess of Roumania. Marie's son-in-law.

ALEXANDRA, Princess of Hohenlohe-Langenburg. "Sister Sandra" (1878–1942). Born Princess of Edinburgh. Married Ernst, Prince of Hohenlohe-Langenburg. Third daughter of the Duke and Duchess of Edinburgh. Marie's sister.

ALEXANDRA, Queen of England. "Aunt Alix" (1844–1925). Born Princess of Denmark. Married Edward VII, King of England. Marie's aunt by marriage.

ALEXANDRA, Tsarina of Russia. "Alicky" or "Alix" (1872–1918). Born Princess of Hesse. Married Nicholas II, Tsar of Russia. Marie's first cousin.

ALFONSO de Orleans y Borbon, Infante of Spain. "Ali" (1886–1966). Married Marie's sister Beatrice, Princess of Edinburgh. Marie's brother-in-law.

ALFRED, Prince of England. "Affie" or "Papa" (1844–1900). The Duke of Edinburgh, later (after 1893) Duke of Coburg. Second son of Queen Victoria and Prince Albert. Married Marie Alexandrovna, Grand Duchess of Russia. Marie's father.

ALFRED, Prince of Edinburgh (1874–1899). Only son of the Duke and Duchess of Edinburgh. Marie's brother.

ANTON, Archduke of Hapsburg (1901–   ). Married Ileana, Princess of Roumania. Marie's son-in-law.

ANTONIA, Princess of Hohenzollern-Sigmaringen (1845–1913). Born Infanta of Portugal. Married Leopold, Prince of Hohenzollern-Sigmaringen. Mother of King Ferdinand of Roumania. Marie's mother-in-law.

ASTOR, Pauline (1880-1972). Married Colonel Herbert Spender-Clay.

ASTOR, William Waldorf (1879–1952). Married Nancy Langhorne Shaw.

AUGUSTA, Kaiserin (Empress) of Germany. "Dona" (1858–1921). Born Princess of Schleswig-Holstein. Married Wilhelm II, Kaiser of Germany. Marie's cousin by marriage.

BEATRICE, Infanta of Spain. "Baby Bee" (1883–1966). Born Princess of Edinburgh. Married Alfonso, Infante of Spain. Marie's sister.

BIBESCO, Princess Marthe (1888–1973). Born Marthe Lahovary. Married Prince Georges Valentin Bibesco. Writer.

BORIS, Grand Duke of Russia (1877–1943). Married Zinaida Sergeievna Rachevskya. Marie's first cousin.

BOYLE, Joseph Whiteside (1867–1923). Married Mildred Raynor (1), Elma Louise Humphries (2). Gold prospector in the Klondike and soldier of fortune.

BRATIANU, Ion (1822–1891). Roumania's first statesman; brought Prince Karl of Hohenzollern-Sigmaringen to Roumania. He died before Marie moved to Roumania.

BRATIANU, Ion, II (1864–1927). Married Princess Elise Stirbey. Prime Minister of Roumania five times and the major political figure during Marie's time.

CANTACUZÈNE, Maruka (dates unknown). Born Maruka Rosetti. Married Michel Cantacuzène (1), Georges Enesco (2).

CAROL I, King of Roumania "Uncle Carol" (1839–1914). Born Karl, Prince of Hohenzollern-Sigmaringen. Married Elisabeth, Princess of Wied. Marie's uncle by marriage.

CAROL II, King of Roumania (1893–1953). Born Carol, Crown Prince of Roumania. Married Jeanne Lambrino (1), Helen, Princess of Greece (2), Elena Lupescu (3). Marie's eldest son.

CHARLOTTE, Princess of Saxe-Meiningen. "Cousin Charly" (1860–1919). Born Princess of Prussia. Marie's first cousin.

CUZA, Prince Alexander Ion (1820–1873). First Prince of Roumania and immediate predecessor of King Carol I.

EDWARD VII, King of England. "Uncle Bertie" (1841–1910). Married Alexandra, Princess of Denmark. Marie's uncle; her father's older brother.

EDWARD VIII, King of England. "David" (1894–1972). Abdicated and assumed title of Duke of Windsor. Married Mrs. Wallis Simpson. Marie's first cousin once removed.

ELISABETH, Queen of Roumania. "Aunt Elisabeth" (1843–1916). Born Princess of Wied. Married Carol I, King of Roumania. Took pen name of Carmen Sylva. Marie's aunt by marriage.

ELISABETHA, Queen of Greece. "Lisabetha" (1894–1954). Born Princess of Roumania. Married George II, King of Greece. Marie's eldest daughter.

ERNST, Grand Duke of Hesse. "Ernie" (1868–1937). Married Victoria Melita (Ducky), Princess of Edinburgh (1), Eleonore, Princess of Solms-Hohensolms-Lich (2). Marie's first cousin and brother-in-law.

ERNST, Duke of Saxe-Coburg-Gotha. "Great-uncle Ernst" (1818–1893). Married Alexandrina, Princess of Baden. Marie's great-uncle; her grandfather Albert's elder brother.

FERDINAND I, King of Roumania. "Nando" (1865–1927). Born Prince of Hohenzollern-Sigmaringen. Married Marie, Princess of Edinburgh. Marie's husband.

FERDINAND I, Tsar of Bulgaria. "Uncle Ferdinand" (1861–1948). Born Prince of Saxe-Coburg-Gotha. Married Marie Louise, Princess of Parma (1), Eleonor, Princess of Reuss (2). Marie's distant Coburg cousin.

FRANZ FERDINAND, Archduke of Austria (1863–1914). Heir to the Austro-Hungarian Empire. Married Countess Sophie of Chotek. Assassinated at Sarajevo.

FRANZ JOSEF I, Emperor of the Austro-Hungarian Empire (1830–1916).

FRIEDRICH VIKTOR, Prince of Hohenzollern-Sigmaringen. "Friedel" (1891–1965). Married Margarethe, Princess of Saxony. Marie's nephew.

FULLER, Loie (1862–1928). American dancer.

GEORGE V, King of England. "Cousin George" (1865–1936). Married Victoria Mary, Princess of Teck (Queen Mary). Marie's first cousin.

GEORGE II, King of Greece (1890–1947). Married Elisabetha, Princess of Roumania. Marie's son-in-law.

HELEN, Queen of Roumania. "Sitta" (1896–1982). Born Princess of Greece. Married Carol II, Crown Prince of Roumania. Marie's daughter-in-law.

HILL, Samuel (1857-1931). Married Mary Frances Hill. American entrepreneur.

ILEANA, Archduchess of Austria. (1909–   ). Born Princess of Roumania. Married Anton, Archduke of Austria (1), Stefan Issarescu (2). Marie's youngest daughter.

JONESCU, Take (1858–1922). A major Roumanian statesman of Marie's time. Head of the progressive wing of the Conservative Party.

KIRILL, Grand Duke of Russia (1876–1938). Married Victoria Melita, Princess of Edinburgh (her second marriage). First cousin of Nicholas II, Tsar of Russia, who became the claimant to the Russian throne after the Revolution. Marie's first cousin and brother-in-law.

LAMBRINO, Jeanne. "Zizi" (1898–1953). Married Carol, Crown Prince of Roumania. Marie's daughter-in-law.

LEOPOLD, Prince of Hohenzollern-Sigmaringen (1835–1905). Married Antonia, Infanta of Portugal. Marie's father-in-law.

LUPESCU, Elena (1895–1977). Mistress, later wife, of King Carol II.

MARIE, Queen of Roumania. "Missy" (1875–1938). Born Princess of Edinburgh. Eldest daughter of the Duke and Duchess of Edinburgh. Married Ferdinand, King of Roumania. Subject of this book.

MARIE, Princess of England. "Mamma" (1853–1920). Born Grand Duchess of Russia. Daughter of Tsar Alexander II and Tsarina Marie. Married Alfred, Prince of England, and became the Duchess of Edinburgh, later (after 1893) the Duchess of Coburg. Marie's mother.

MARIE, Tsarina of Russia. "Grandmamma Empress" (1824–1880). Born Princess of Hesse and the Rhine. Married Alexander II, Tsar of Russia. Marie's grandmother; her mother's mother.

MARIE, Queen of Yugoslavia. "Mignon" (1900–1961). Born Princess of Roumania. Married Alexander I, King of Yugoslavia. Marie's second daughter.

MARIE, Tsarina of Russia (1847–1928). Born Dagmar, Princess of Denmark. Married Alexander III, Tsar of Russia. Marie's aunt by marriage.

MARIE, Grand Duchess of Russia (1890–1958). Married William, Prince of Sweden (1), Prince Sergei Putiatin (2). Marie's first cousin.

MARY, Queen of England. "Cousin May" (1867–1953). Born Victoria Mary, Princess of Teck. Married George V, King of England. Marie's cousin by marriage.

MIRCEA, Prince of Roumania (1913–1916). Marie's youngest child.

NICHOLAS II, Tsar of Russia. "Cousin Nicky" (1868–1918). Married Alexandra, Princess of Hesse. Marie's first cousin.

NICOLAS, Prince of Roumania. "Nicky" (1903–1977). Married Jeanne Doletti (1), Theresa Figueira de Mello (2). Marie's second son.

SAINT-AULAIRE, Count Charles de (1866–1954). French Minister to Roumania.

SOPHIE, Queen of Greece (1870–1932). Born Princess of Prussia. Married Constantine I, King of Greece. Marie's first cousin.

STIRBEY, Prince Barbo (1873–1946). Head of King Ferdinand's Household and principal adviser to the King. Married Princess Nadeje Bibesco.

VICTORIA, Queen of England. "Grandmamma Queen" (1819–1901). Married Albert, Prince of Saxe-Coburg-Gotha. Marie's grandmother; her father's mother.

VICTORIA, Kaiserin (Empress) of Germany. "Aunt Vicky" (1840–1901). Born Princess of England. Married Frederick III, Kaiser of Germany. Marie's aunt.

VICTORIA MELITA, Grand Duchess of Russia. "Ducky" (1876–1936). Born Princess of Edinburgh. Married Ernst, Grand Duke of Hesse (1), Kirill, Grand Duke of Russia (2). Marie's sister.

VOPICKA, Charles J. (1857–1935). American Ambassador to Roumania.

WILHELM II, Kaiser of Germany. "Cousin Willy" (1859–1941). Married Augusta, Princess of Schleswig-Holstein (1), Hermione, Princess of Reuss (2). Marie's first cousin.

WILHELM, Crown Prince of Germany. "Cousin Bill" (1882–1951). Married Cecilie, Princess of Mecklenburg-Schwerin. Marie's first cousin once removed.

WILHELM, Prince of Hohenzollern-Sigmaringen (1864–1927). Married Marie Therese, Princess of Bourbon-Sicily (1), Agelgunde, Princess of Bavaria (2). Marie's brother-in-law.

"Oh, life is a glorious cycle of song,
A medley of extemporanea;
And love is a thing that will never go wrong;
And I am Marie of Roumania."

Dorothy Parker

PART ONE
Royal Europe

Chapter 1

> The House of Hanover, like ducks, produce bad parents. They trample on their young.
>
> —*OWEN MORSHEAD, Librarian of Windsor Castle*

*I*f matters had been arranged as usual in the family of Queen Victoria—that is, exactly as the Queen wished—Marie of Roumania's father would never have married her mother. But the Queen's objections were overridden, and the union between her second son, Prince Alfred, the Duke of Edinburgh,* who was known in the family as Affie, and Grand Duchess Marie Alexandrovna, only daughter of the Tsar, took place on January 23, 1874.

The Queen had been trying to marry Affie off elsewhere for a long time. Twelve years earlier she had placed him firmly in the wings while setting the stage for the meeting of his older brother, Bertie (later Edward VII), with the lovely Princess Alexandra of Denmark. As Victoria wrote to her eldest daughter, Vicky, Crown Princess of Germany, "Affie would be ready to take

---

*The last person to hold the title before Prince Philip, the husband of H.M. Queen Elizabeth II, the current Queen.

her at once, and really if B. refused I would recommend Affie's engaging to marry her in three years. He will be very comfortably well off—and has a fine prospect, and is very charming."

The Duke of Edinburgh was only eighteen at the time. His prospect and comfort was to inherit the German duchies of Coburg and Gotha. Although the Queen preferred him at the moment to his older brother, she could not allow partiality to obscure dynastic priorities; the requirements of the heir to the throne came first. Victoria was relieved when the Prince of Wales married Princess Alexandra (Alix) of Denmark in March of 1863. She was less pleased that the young Duke of Edinburgh did not conceal his admiration for his brother's wife, and she confided her fears to his older sister, Vicky:

"In confidence I may tell you that we do all we can to keep him [the Duke of Edinburgh] from Marlborough House [residence of the Prince and Princess of Wales] as he is far too much '*épris*' with Alix to be allowed to be much there without possibly ruining the happiness of all three and Affie has not the strength of mind (or rather more of principle and character) to resist the temptation, and it is like playing with fire. Beloved Papa always said the feelings of admiration and even love are not sinful—nor can you prevent the impulses of one's nature, but it is your duty to avoid the temptation in every way. You may imagine how anxious this makes us. It makes Affie however anxious to marry and I hope he will be able to fix his affections securely even if he can't marry for two years."

The Duke of Edinburgh's anxiety to find a bride was not as compelling a motive for a quick engagement as was his mother's recent discovery—a "heavy blow" to her "weak and shattered frame"—that he could no longer be trusted with women. The Queen's obsession with purity was a legacy from her deceased consort, Prince Albert, combined with the awful example of her uncles. Since Affie had not inherited his father's unswerving belief in man's ability to withstand temptation, it was imperative to find him a wife. "The young Princess of Altenburg would be a very good match," said the Queen, "as well as the Hanoverian and possibly the eldest Weimar may turn out less ugly..."

Catherine, Princess of Oldenburg, boasted "very good teeth and skin," but did not catch the Prince's fancy. Although he found Princess Marie of Saxe-Altenburg "very pretty, very tall...with beautiful, large, thoughtful, grey eyes," his sister Vicky heard she was "sickly-looking, had bad teeth and very large bones, and large hands and feet!" Vicky also struck Princess Wilhemine of Württemberg off the list; she found her "very plain, not so much by her features as by the unwholesome and unkempt look she has—such untidy hair and a shocking complexion." Affie liked Frederika, Princess of Hanover, until the Queen vetoed her on the grounds of health and politics; not only was Frederika's father blind, but the Hanovers had been dispossessed of the English throne by the Coburgs, and a marriage between their two houses might be misconstrued as a restoration.

The most obvious candidate for the hand of the Duke of Edinburgh was a German princess, Elisabeth of Wied. Elisabeth's credentials were impeccable. The family had originally considered her as a possible consort for the Prince of Wales, but Vicky had objected to her then because "she does not look well-bred." "She has not a pretty nose and rather a long chin... she does not look very ladylike." Aside from physical shortcomings, Elisabeth cultivated intellectual and artistic aspirations that shocked her peers. Even Vicky, a young woman of considerable intelligence, was embarrassed by her: "She is so odd... says such things sometimes that I do not know which way to look—I get so hot—and she talks so much, and so long and laughs so loud."

Once the Prince of Wales was safely married, Vicky took a second look at the Princess of Wied. "I saw Elisabeth Wied... yesterday," she wrote the Queen in 1864, "and was much pleased with her. She is so much improved... Graceful and elegant her figure and her walk will never be, but she is a very pretty person now... Have you quite given up all thought of her for Affie?"

The handsome young Duke of Edinburgh was sent to Germany to meet Princess Elisabeth of Wied—a confrontation from which he beat a hasty retreat. Arriving at the Wied castle in the woods, he was introduced to a flushed, round-faced young woman who discovered that he played the violin and immediately insisted that he perform for her mother and her under the beechwood trees. Acutely embarrassed at being forced into this woodland recital, Affie did not wait for royal protocol but informed Elisabeth's mother on the spot that he would never under any circumstances marry her daughter.*

The Queen was clearly discouraged about her second son. "If he can only find a Princess likely to suit and please him," she wrote Vicky, "I would not mind who she was. The choice is becoming so narrow that I think we must get over the difficulties concerning religion—that is to say as regards the Greek religion [Orthodox Church]—and I believe it could be got over easily if there was a person likely to suit... I fear Elisabeth Wied (whom I should so much have liked) won't do—as he don't care for her... I cannot tell you how anxious I do feel about Affie."

Part of the Queen's anxiety had to do with the Duke of Edinburgh's position in the English royal family. Since he was only Victoria's second son, his future wife, whoever she might be, would rank below the Princess of Wales (Alix) and the Crown Princess of Germany (Vicky) in the order of precedence at Buckingham Palace. Precedence was a burning issue with

*Elisabeth of Wied did eventually marry—the man who became King Carol I of Roumania. She also won some recognition as a writer under the pen name of Carmen Sylva. More important to this story, she was to play a major role in the life of the Duke of Edinburgh's eldest daughter, Marie, who became the Crown Princess of Roumania, eventually succeeding Elisabeth as queen.

princesses of the day, and Affie's chances for a good match were jeopardized by his status.

Although the young Duke of Edinburgh had been offered the throne of Greece at the age of eighteen, a position which would have given his future wife a consort's crown, his mother had refused it for him. Not only had the Queen signed a pact with France and Russia not to touch the Balkan thrones, but she had agreed with Affie's father during his lifetime to place him elsewhere. Since the Prince of Wales would eventually inherit the English throne, Prince Albert had designated his second son to succeed to the duchies of Coburg and Gotha in Germany, titles and lands held by Prince Albert's childless brother, Duke Ernst. To the Queen, a directive from the deceased Albert was like a commandment from God. Affie would follow the course laid out by dearest Papa before his untimely death. In the meantime, he would pursue his career in the navy.

In 1866, at the age of twenty-two, the Duke of Edinburgh was given command of H.M.S. *Galatea,* one of the best-equipped and fastest ships of its day, in which he undertook a series of world cruises designed to convey the Queen's concern for her far-flung subjects. During the first tour, which culminated in Australia, Affie ate roast alpaca and grilled wonga pigeon at a banquet in Sydney, where, according to the Sydney *Mail,* "the tables were tastefully decorated with artificial flowers specially scented for the occasion." Extravagantly feted and offered an opportunity to unseat his mother by accepting the Australian throne, the Duke of Edinburgh survived a surprise attempt on his life. He arrived back in England in 1868, wounded and an object of unqualified hero worship, except to the Queen. Success aboard did not compensate for filial peccadilloes. "I fear little dependence is to be placed on him," she wrote Vicky a few months after Affie's return, "and I cannot trust or even feel happy or at ease when he is in the house. Marrying may improve him but I fear, without principle, that he may go on still as he does now—for how many do!"

Late that summer the Duke of Edinburgh met his future wife, Grand Duchess Marie, the daughter of Tsar Alexander II of Russia.

The meeting came about through Affie's sister-in-law, Alix, and *her* sister, Dagmar—two Danish princesses who had married the heirs to the thrones of England and Russia respectively. Devoted to each other and eager to ease tensions between their adopted countries, the young women invited members of the Houses of Hanover* and Romanov to the annual reunions of the Danish royal family. These were huge gatherings that included court attendants and personal servants. Politics was a forbidden topic of conversation. It was at one of these royal house parties in the summer of 1868 that the

---

*It was not until 1917 that the English royal house became known as the House of Windsor.

Duke of Edinburgh met the Grand Duchess for the first time. Although the Queen's son was twenty-four and the Tsar's daughter only fifteen, he decided to marry her. Since Marie was not pretty, her attraction for Affie may have had to do with her reputation as the richest princess in Europe. On her side, she was probably drawn to the glamour of an older man just home from exotic travels and recovering from a gunshot wound. Opposition to the match from both his mother and her father was so strong that four years elapsed before the Duke of Edinburgh dared make a formal request for the Grand Duchess's hand.

Even then the Tsar refused to give his immediate consent. Alexander II adored his only daughter. She was his assistant, reading his letters and ciphered correspondence to him every day. She sympathized with his problems with her chronically ill mother, while at the same time managing to remain on intimate terms with the ailing Tsarina. It is hardly surprising that the idea of marrying this daughter to Victoria's son and sending her to England was painful for both parents to contemplate. The Duke of Edinburgh's initial proposal, delivered through diplomatic channels, received only a lukewarm response and set the Russian court on a desperate search for another husband for their princess.

The Tsarina arranged for her daughter to meet every available candidate, explaining to her brother, "the Tsar is still *against* Alfred as a match...On the other hand, Marie inclines much more to him—and especially his position—than to Stuttgart, Strelitz, or Schwerin; but if you could find me a *charming Prince* who would be prepared to stay in Russia, I should prefer him to any of them." The alternatives to the Duke of Edinburgh proved disappointing, and by the spring of 1873 even the Tsar was reconciled to the marriage.

While the Romanovs agonized over the proposed union, Queen Victoria, a passionate Russophobe, did everything reasonable to prevent it. The possibility of a Russian grand duchess as a daughter-in-law swept away the Queen's resolution about surmounting religious differences if there was "a Princess likely to suit." The Queen appealed to Prime Minister Gladstone to take a position against the marriage. When Gladstone demurred, she responded with chilly dissatisfaction: "There is one thing w^h Mr. Gladstone does not mention w^h is the *only* one w^h the Queen, Ld Cairns, & Mr. Disraeli *really* fear viz: the event of P^ce Alfred's becoming King & his wife being a Greek [of the Orthodox faith]. This w^d be very objectionable."

When Gladstone refused to help, the Queen seized upon a rumor picked up by the English Ambassador to St. Petersburg, who told her that the Grand Duchess's indiscretion with at least one young man, Prince Golitsyn, had persuaded her parents to settle her into marriage. Vicky, who was as anti-Russian as her mother, wrote the Queen to tell her that the Tsar was saying unkind things about dear Affie all over Berlin. Egged on by the Crown

Princess of Germany, the Queen complained bitterly about a prospective daughter-in-law with *"half Oriental Russian notions."*

But the Tsar's daughter was as strong willed as her future mother-in-law. Spurred by the prospect of taking a place in one of the greatest courts of Western Europe, Grand Duchess Marie enlisted the help of an uncle, who invited the Duke of Edinburgh to lunch at one of his family castles in Germany. When Affie arrived, Marie was waiting for him. The proposal was offered and accepted, the betrothal arranged. The Tsar telegraphed to the Queen of England: "We implore with you God's blessing on our dear children and recommend to you our daughter, who kisses your hand."

"The murder is out," the Queen wired Vicky.

Victoria countered at once by demanding that Alexander II bring his daughter to England for her inspection. The Tsar refused even to discuss this. "Silly old fool!" he commented. The Tsarina cabled the Queen offering to bring Marie as far as Cologne, halfway between St. Petersburg and London. Victoria was incensed. To Vicky, always a willing ear, she complained that she, a "Sovereign & a lady," was being asked "to run after" the Tsarina— and "in three days" time! The Queen's second daughter, Princess Alice of Hesse, made the mistake of suggesting that perhaps her mama might go to Cologne. After all, the Tsarina, who was in precarious health, would feel the heat of summer even more than the Queen, and the trip would be a greater sacrifice for her. Victoria struck back:

"You have *entirely* taken the Russian side, & I do not think, dear Child, that *you* should tell *me* who have been nearly 20* *years longer* on the throne than the Emperor of Russia & am the Doyenne of Sovereigns & who am a *Reigning* Sovereign which the Empress is *not,—what I ought to do. I* think I know *that*. The proposal received on *Wednesday* for me to be *at Cologne*... tomorrow, was one of the *coolest* things I ever heard... How could I who am not like any little Princess ready to run to the slightest call of the *mighty Russians*—have been *able in 24 hours* to be *ready* to travel! I *Own every one* was shocked."

Behind petty concerns of status lay serious problems of state. In the eyes of England's Queen, Russia was the most dangerous of the rival Great Powers during the 1860s and 1870s. In 1873, the year of the Duke of Edinburgh's marriage, the Tsar signed a pact with the Emperors of Germany and Austria. In the face of this alliance and the recent collapse of France, England and her Queen found themselves politically and diplomatically isolated. The Russians wanted a free hand in Asia and had revived their age-old dream of capturing Constantinople from the Turks. Since the Crimean War, the Russian Army had been on the march through Central Asia, menacing British interests in India.

Nevertheless, the Queen managed to overcome her objections, and in

---

*In oversized numerals in the original.

July of 1872 wrote to her friend Kaiserin Augusta of Germany: "You know that I did not desire this alliance on various quite serious grounds. Principally on account of religion and politics, for these always seem to me precarious and undependable in Russia. But in spite of all difficulties, in spite of doubts and representations on both sides, it has nonetheless come to pass, and that through the decision of the young lady herself, hence I must believe that it is a dispensation of God."

It was characteristic of Victoria to grant the Almighty credit for what she had been unable to prevent. One thing she could and did do—urge her second son to be a good and faithful husband. He made her no promises.

The Queen did not attend her son's wedding, dispatching several trustworthy representatives in her place. Dean Arthur Stanley, sent by Victoria to perform the Anglican wedding service, was astonished by the size of the Winter Palace—sixteen hundred rooms, four thousand inhabitants—and delightfully surprised by its comfortable warmth in January compared to the dampness and drafts of Buckingham and Windsor. The Dean's wife—who had brought to Petersburg "all the diamonds that she ventured to accept the loan of!"—was aghast at the competition: ". . . really here, one almost gets tired of them—the Grand Duchesses are literally covered with them—belts, trimmings, skirts, bodies, heads—gigantic stones—and emeralds, and other stones besides." But for the rest of the English ladies, the unpleasantness of dirt superseded the joys of opulence. Lady Emma Osborne was distressed not only by the dust in the palace but by the lack of personal hygiene, dissolving into "fits" when she discovered that "when some Princess is presented that She is no better in that respect than a Mujik."

The bride herself did not live up to the visitors' expectations. Having seen some flattering pictures of Grand Duchess Marie, the English were disappointed. "One cannot (it is not fair to do so) call Her exactly pretty," said Lady Stanley. Short, dark-haired and round-faced, inclined to be plump and brusque, the Grand Duchess did not elicit easy admiration. Lacking good features or the ordinary bland courtesies of royalty, she seemed an odd choice for the Duke of Edinburgh. Anxious to find something good to report home, Lady Stanley noted that the Russian Princess was "practical, sensible and without caprice." Countess Tolstoy, the Grand Duchess's governess, explained the young woman's "abrupt manner" to the foreigners as a consequence of shyness and insecurity. It was old Countess Tolstoy herself, a nagging and hypercritical perfectionist, who had nurtured the self-dissatisfaction that appeared on the young woman's face in the shape of a permanent scowl.

Nonetheless, gowned in silver brocade studded with diamonds, trailing a mantle of silver and ermine, and wearing a gigantic diamond necklace and diamond crown, the daughter of the Tsar was a "truly regal" bride—and sadly touching. "She has been so very happy always that She has no misgivings," said Lady Stanley. "She... has always been so tenderly loved that it seems quite natural that it should continue so."

Curiously enough, the marriage of Affie and Marie was not the first instance of youthful attraction between the English and Russian courts. Victoria herself had become infatuated with Marie's father thirty-five years before, in 1839, when he was the tall, smiling twenty-one-year-old heir to the Russian throne on a visit to England and she was a diminutive girl of twenty, Queen for two years. Much to the annoyance of her court, Victoria had allowed herself to fall for the charming stranger whom she entertained with two concerts, a theatrical performance, a reception, and two balls. It was his grace in dancing that excited her. "The Grand-duke is so very strong that in running round, you must follow quickly, and after that you're whisked round like in a Valse, which is very pleasant." After the last ball she confided to her journal, "I never enjoyed myself more. We were all so merry... I got to bed by a ¼ to 3 but could not sleep till 5... I really am quite in love with the Grand-duke; he is a dear, delightful young man."

They met for the second and last time in their lives a few months after the wedding of their children, when Alexander II came to England on another visit of state. The "dear, delightful young man" had been on the Russian throne for nearly twenty years; Victoria had loved and lost her German consort; and England and Russia had fought each other in the Crimean War. In spite of the distrust that had built up over two decades, the Queen was moved. She found the Tsar "very kind but... terribly altered, so thin, and his face looks so old, sad, and careworn... It is just thirty-five years that I took leave of him, here, at Windsor, in June!"

Alexander was also touched with nostalgia. At a banquet in his honor, seated between the Queen and his daughter, he talked about the past and his first visit to England, recalling different rooms of the castle and the courtiers whom he had met before, now older and in some cases no longer alive. He told the Queen that "he did not see any reason why our two countries should not be on the best terms," and in case of difficulties suggested that he would write her personally. She agreed.

When he spoke about Marie, the Tsar's eyes filled with tears. "I thank you once again for all the kindnesses you have shown my daughter," he told Victoria; "I leave her in your hands: I hope she will always remain worthy." The Queen leaned across Alexander II to take her new daughter-in-law's hand in her own. The young woman, like her father, almost wept.

In spite of this sympathetic scene, Marie's early years as Duchess of Edinburgh were strained by tension over her position at court. Immediately after her wedding, the Tsar wrote the Queen to say that his daughter should be addressed in England as "Imperial Highness" rather than merely "Royal Highness." Victoria was infuriated by what she considered an assault on her rank; although she ruled an empire, she was still known by the title of Queen.* She reported that she didn't care if the title "Imperial" was used to address her new daughter-in-law, just so long as "Royal" came first, as it was the *English* title.

Since traditional court protocol stipulated that persons of imperial rank took precedence over those who ruled over simple kingdoms, the Russians argued that the new Duchess of Edinburgh, daughter of a tsar (i.e., emperor), should take precedence over the Princess of Wales, daughter of a mere king (of Denmark). Obviously, the Queen could not allow Marie, the wife of her second son, to rank above the wife of her eldest son, the future Queen of England, or her own daughter, the wife of the heir to the German Empire. Marie was placed in precedence squarely behind Alix, the Princess of Wales, and Vicky, the Crown Princess of Germany. Accustomed to a unique and exalted place as the only princess in her father's court, Marie of Edinburgh started life in England with considerable resentment at her new position.

The Queen dealt pragmatically with what she could not change. She made the most of her new daughter-in-law's virtues and accepted her shortcomings. Had the young Duchess of Edinburgh been more adaptable, her life in England might have been happier. "Between you and me," the Tsarina wrote a relative, "Marie thinks London hideous, the air there appalling, the English food abominable, the late hours very tiring, the visits to Windsor and Osborne boring beyond belief."

At the age of twenty the Duchess of Edinburgh either could not or did not want to fit into the more relaxed court life of England. An outsider, she suffered from a deadly combination of not belonging and feeling superior. Within the confines of her own home she insisted on preserving the strict etiquette of her youth. No one was allowed to turn his back on the twenty-year-old Duchess of Edinburgh. The only way to quit the august presence was by the traditional backwards walk. Those who didn't conform received an imperious stare and a mortifying lecture. A story circulated that one day while the Duke of Edinburgh was conducting his bride through the gardens of a country estate, the head gardener was summoned to accept the royal compliments. The gardener, anxious to leave, discovered that there were no gates within reasonable distance for him to make the required backwards retreat. Instead of allowing the poor man to exit with his dignity intact, Marie stood guard to make sure he backed off until he was completely out of sight.

As stories of the Duchess of Edinburgh's arrogance made the rounds,

---

*In 1876, two and a half years after the Duke of Edinburgh's marriage, Victoria had herself declared Queen-Empress by a Royal Titles Bill, but the title was seldom used.

the public, who fed on royal tidbits, compared her unfavorably to Alix, the Princess of Wales. It was unfortunate for Marie that she moved into a world in which her sister-in-law had already had eleven years to gain the love of the people. Alix was beautiful, Alix was graceful, Alix was unfailingly charming and courteous. Besides producing heirs, she did all the things royal princesses were supposed to do—she gave parties, she danced, she engaged in sports. What did it matter that she was not particularly intelligent?

The Duchess of Edinburgh's major attributes, on the other hand, were intellectual. According to Lady Randolph Churchill, the mother of Winston Churchill and one of the Duchess's few close friends, Marie was a woman of "rare intelligence and exceptional education... a fine linguist, speaking fluently several languages... [and she] wrote them equally well." Like the Duke of Edinburgh, the Duchess was a musician, and she played the piano much better than he played the violin.

All that counted little in the competition in which the young Duchess now found herself. Athletics and dancing were what impressed the English—and, of course, beauty. Marie wasn't even passingly good-looking, and with her rapidly expanding body she was hardly graceful. Nor was she gracious. She did little to endear herself to the public or even to the court.

Life in England was a shattering disappointment to the Duchess of Edinburgh. The gray stones of Buckingham and Windsor were dull compared to the gold and turquoise palaces of St. Petersburg. Not only was the court less elegant, she herself was a less awesome figure. Her fabulous jewels, which should have inspired admiration, merely made the Queen purse her lips. Her sapphires, a family treasure from Catherine the Great, were "too good" for a young woman, as were her "wonderful diamonds." And her husband, known for an inability to communicate with others, was no help.

Dark, blue-eyed, and handsome, the Duke of Edinburgh had a perpetually bronzed complexion from the sea air and the sun. Unlike his wife, he had had the good luck to be born with a face that camouflaged "an abominable temper" and "the most glaring want of tact." Having fought all his life against an embarrassing tendency toward tears, the Duke had succeeded in suppressing all outward emotion whatsoever. As his daughter Queen Marie of Roumania was later to write, "Papa... was a very quiet man, talked little, and was occasionally even somewhat taciturn. In fact, we were never entirely in touch with him." This hard-won emotional reserve opened up a chasm between Affie and his wife. Even when he was home from the navy, she was alone.

To the world, the Duke of Edinburgh was the perfect English

prince—a naval commander, an enthusiastic sportsman, an excellent shot. Within royal confines he was regarded with less admiration. "No officer knows his duty better or is more devoted to it—and yet—well no one likes him," said his older brother's secretary. "Uncle Alfred," commented one of his nieces, "loved ease and sport and was overfond of liquor."

The Duchess of Edinburgh blamed her husband's inability to get along with others on his "thoroughly English education." Intolerant of his wife's cultural and intellectual interests, the Duke was driven into temper tantrums over her passions for reading, serious conversation, and the theater. In later years the Duchess said that throughout her married life she had felt like no more than her husband's "legitimate mistress"—a "simply degrading" position for the daughter of the Tsar.

The Duke of Edinburgh was parsimonious. His own secretary, Sir John Cowell, said his concern with money "amounted to a disease." He was less cautious with his wife's money. Nor did he draw a fine line between his personal property and that of the British Empire. During his official tours of the colonies, undertaken at government expense, he was given a vast number of *objets d'art* to be presented to his mother, the Queen. The Duke of Edinburgh kept them in his private collection.

Choosing a wife for her fortune would not have been out of character for the Duke of Edinburgh, just as marrying a husband from an important court was in keeping with the personality of Marie. Their marriage was not a personal success nor a political one. It had been hoped that the alliance of the Queen's son and the Tsar's daughter would ease Anglo-Russian tensions, but it proved a mere dynastic irrelevancy. The union of the Duke and Duchess of Edinburgh succeeded only in placing them both in the middle of an international storm that built up during the early years of their marriage and threatened to pitch England and Russia into open warfare.

In 1877 Tsar Alexander II, under political pressure at home, took advantage of Christian uprisings in the Ottoman Empire to declare war on the Sultan. Under the guise of rescuing martyred Christians in the Balkan provinces of the Turks, Russia aimed at gaining control over the Balkans and conquering the Turkish capital of Constantinople. For a thousand years the Russians had coveted the city of domes and minarets lying at the exit from the Black to the Mediterranean Sea. Through the Bosporus, the Sea of Marmara, and the forty-mile straits of the Dardanelles lay access to warm waters and Western trade. The Russian Army began its march through Roumania, one of the Turkish provinces struggling to win independence from the Sultan.

The Queen of England took the Tsar's declaration of war as a personal affront. As the Russian Army advanced toward Constantinople, six British battleships, one of which was commanded by the Duke of Edinburgh, were ordered into the Sea of Marmara. This frightened the Tsar into bringing his army to a halt six miles outside the Turkish capital. It did not, however, prevent him from forcing a secret treaty on the Turks. The Treaty of San Stefano, which placed the whole Balkan peninsula under Russian domination, so incensed Victoria that she inflated a minor incident involving the Duke of Edinburgh and two nephews of the Tsarina into a near affair of state.

When the Russian Army reached the outskirts of Constantinople, foreign officers were given leave. Among them was Prince Alexander II of Battenberg (Sandro), a German nephew of the Tsarina. As was not uncommon in royal families of the day, Sandro's brother, Prince Louis,* was serving in the opposing British Navy on the *Sultan* with the Duke of Edinburgh. Invited on board by his brother Louis, Sandro was received by the Duke and his crew "with *extraordinary friendliness,*" taken on a tour of the British flagship, and introduced to the Commander of Her Majesty's Mediterranean Fleet.

The interlude would have been nothing more than a brief family reunion had word of Sandro's visit not reached the Queen of England at the same time as the terms of the treaty the Russians had imposed on the Turks. Infuriated at losing control of the East, Victoria accused the Duke of Edinburgh and Prince Louis of entertaining a "Russian spy." She ordered her son relieved of his command for as long as his ship lay off Constantinople and reprimanded by the Admiralty. Prince Louis was ordered back to England. One of Affie's sisters said that her brother could no longer show himself in England; another said she was ashamed of being related to him.

The Queen's fury did not last long, and she made appropriate amends. The Duke of Edinburgh was not to be reproved; Prince Louis's transfer was not a disciplinary one. Later it was discovered that the British Ambassador to Constantinople had been so miffed that the family meeting was arranged by the German Ambassador that he had worded his report of the incident purposely to incite the Queen.

This was not hard to do. Victoria continued to attack Russia in her letters to Affie, not realizing that everything she said was repeated in St. Petersburg. "The insulting things that the Queen says...about the Tsar and the Russian people are worthy of a fishwife," said the Tsarina, who thought little better of the Duke of Edinburgh: "It is a pity that her son has not got more character."

After nine months of grueling warfare, the Russians, depleted in

---

*Later Commander in Chief of Her Majesty's Atlantic Fleet and Marquess of Milford Haven, father of Earl Mountbatten of Burma.

forces and morale, were forced to submit their victory over the Turks to an international peace conference. Led by Otto von Bismarck of Germany, the Congress of Berlin met in 1878 to resolve the territorial differences between Russia, Austro-Hungary, and England raised by the outcome of the war. The terms of the peace were acceptable to everyone except Russia and the little kingdom of Roumania, newly liberated from the Turks. Russia complained that all she got for her lives and money was the return of lands that had previously belonged to her. Roumania, which had won the crucial battle of the war for the Tsar, was required to cede to Russia the rich province of Bessarabia. The Queen of England, who regretted "that Russia had got anything," still felt "vy triumphant."

It was during this international crisis that the Duke and Duchess of Edinburgh set up their home in England and started a family. Their eldest daughter, Marie, would one day become Queen of Roumania— one of the countries freed from the Turks and recognized for the first time as an autonomous state at the end of the Russo-Turkish War. Roumania celebrated its official birth in 1878. Marie, a granddaughter of the Queen of England and the Tsar of Russia, was born on October 29, 1875—just three years before her future country.

PART TWO

Childhood and Marriage

Chapter 2

I grew up an exceedingly royal little
person, full of my own importance, and
in the belief that our glory, like that of
the sun, was an unquestioned reality.

—*QUEEN MARIE OF ROUMANIA*

"*H*er Royal and Imperial Highness the Duchess of Edinburgh was safely delivered of a Princess at 10:30 this day. Her Royal and Imperial Highness and the infant Princess are doing perfectly well" read the dry little notice wired to the London *Times* from Eastwell Park in Kent. It was signed by the three doctors attendant at the future Queen Marie's birth.

The baby was named Marie Alexandra Victoria, Princess of Great Britain and Ireland. The Queen was not pleased. She thought Victoria should have been the child's first name rather than her third. Not that it made much practical difference. In the Hanover family everyone but the Queen was known by a nickname. The child would be called Missy.

Missy had been preceded by a brother, born the year of her parents' marriage and named Alfred for his father. She was followed by another girl. The second infant princess, born just thirteen months after Missy, gave the Duke and Duchess of Edinburgh another opportunity to please the Queen, and they named the child Victoria Melita; her nickname was Ducky. After Ducky came Princess Alexandra, Sister Sandra, born in 1878. Princess Beatrice, known throughout her life as Baby Bee, was born five years later.

For as long as the Duke was stationed with the Royal Navy in England, his family divided their time between several homes around the British Isles: Eastwell Park in Kent, where they spent the shooting season and Christmas; Clarence House in London, where they lived during the social months; and Osborne Cottage on the Isle of Wight, where they spent summers. There, in ducal palaces, insulated by layers of nannies, servants, and governesses, Missy grew up untouched by events in the outside world. Since she rarely saw her father, his irascibility did not ruffle her everyday routine. It was an impeccable childhood, unsoiled by even a hint of preparation for life.

Eastwell House in Kent was Missy's favorite home. A four-story gray mansion set in a magnificent park, it was surrounded by endless lawns, formal gardens, and an eleven-mile wall. Cattle grazed in the park and deer ran in the woods. The house itself was so huge that Missy and her siblings never finished exploring all its rooms.

Her attachment to Eastwell Park was matched by her dislike for Clarence House. The Duke and Duchess of Edinburgh's London residence offered nothing more enticing than a perfectly tidy garden. Outings were confined to the neat and therefore uninviting paths of Green Park, except for occasional visits to the Queen's gardens at Buckingham Palace, where there were some overgrown spots suitable for games of make-believe. Clarence House did hold two attractions, both public salons. The first, the Chinese Drawing Room, was filled with curios amassed by Missy's father on his foreign cruises. The second contained the Duchess's collection of Fabergé—those *objets de vertu* so dear to the Romanovs, carved from jasper, malachite, lapis, and rock crystal or enameled in jewel tones, mounted in gold, and studded with diamonds.

The most important person in Missy's childhood was her sister Ducky. Although she was born a year after Princess Marie, Ducky was taller and always was assumed to be the older of the two. She was not pretty like Marie, who, with her blond hair and pale-sapphire eyes, was the acknowledged family beauty by the age of five. Ducky was also more difficult—brooding, jealous, inclined to be resentful when corrected. But to Missy, Ducky's darker coloring indicated a passionate nature, and Ducky's moodiness seemed to be an asset. "I still remember the feeling of having my hair well brushed; I had a great mass of what my sisters called 'yellow' but what I loved to think of as 'golden' hair, of which old nurse Pitcathly . . . was tremendously proud. It would stand out in all its combed beauty, for indeed Nana groomed and cleaned and polished us up like pampered horses, and I can still feel in my shoulders the little twist I would give to be able to catch a glimpse of my own shining mane. But old Nana loved sister Ducky . . . best, and Ducky had brown corkscrew curls which Nana rolled over her finger."

Their nurse's preference for the temperamental sister made Missy uneasy about her own happy disposition. Nor could the young Edinburgh Princess help noticing how different she was from their mother, who seethed her way through married life in a state of continuous vocal resentment. Court life in England was not, in any case, particularly cheerful. It revolved around Queen Victoria in her unvarying costume of black silk and white widow's cap. Missy was taken to call on her grandmother with regularity.

"The hush around Grandmamma's door was awe-inspiring, it was like approaching the mystery of some sanctuary. Silent, soft-carpeted corridors led to Grandmamma's apartments...those that led the way...talked in hushed voices and trod softly...One door after another opened noiselessly, it was like passing through the forecourts of a temple, before approaching the final mystery to which only the initiated had access....

"When finally the door was opened there sat Grandmamma not idol-like at all, not a bit frightening, smiling a kind little smile, almost as shy as us children, so that conversation was not very fluent on either side. Inquiry as to our morals and general behavior made up a great part of it...I have a sort of feeling that Grandmamma as well as ourselves was secretly relieved when the audience was over."

Visits to the Queen were more fun when the Duchess came along to engage her in conversation. Excused from moral discussions, Missy and her sisters were free to explore their surroundings. The Queen's rooms, which always smelled of orange blossoms, were filled with fascinating treasures like their grandmother's feisty pet bullfinch and "mysterious photographs of dead people." Among these the most prominent were the likenesses of Missy's grandfather, Prince Albert: "Pictures and prints, statues, statuettes and photographs. There was Grandpapa in full general's uniform. Grandpapa in his robes of the Order of the Garter, Grandpapa in kilt, in plain clothes, Grandpapa on horseback, at his writing table, Grandpapa with his dogs, with his children, in the garden, on the mountains. Grandpapa with important-looking papers in his hands, Grandpapa with his loving wife gazing enraptured up into his face. Grandpapa," wrote Marie, "was certainly the first and foremost spirit of these rooms."

As had been agreed before the marriage, the Russian Orthodox Duchess raised her children in the Anglican Church, although she sometimes allowed them to enter her private chapel. It was no problem for the Duchess of Edinburgh to follow the dictates of her conscience, as she always kept in her personal employ an Orthodox priest and two Russian chanters. The combination of heady incense, antique icons, and "soul-stirring Russian chants" inevitably inspired awe in the Edinburgh children. Although Queen Marie later said she never wanted to exchange her faith for that of her mother, "standing beside her whilst she prayed and devoutly crossed herself" made the young girl "feel very near the Holy of Holies."

It wasn't only in religious observances that the Duchess of Edinburgh differed from other adults Missy observed around her. Her appearance set her apart from her contemporaries. She railed at current fashions, probably because no style really suited her, only to adopt them the moment they became *passé*. Since her figure was poor, she avoided showy gowns and made a virtue of serviceable jackets and skirts. She wore "funny-shaped" boots with small leather bows on the toes. These were ordered from St. Petersburg and were made precisely the same for both feet; the Duchess of Edinburgh believed it was "nonsense to imagine that you needed a left and right shoe, it was much more rational to have them both alike."

Even when she was young, Missy recognized that her mother's peculiarities "often isolated her from her neighbors." Although the Duchess of Edinburgh was a superb conversationalist, it was an art she considered wasted in the English court. Having with great difficulty conquered her own shyness, the Duchess insisted that her daughters learn to converse easily, directing them in dialogues with empty chairs as a form of training. There was nothing "more hopeless than a princess who never opened her mouth," according to the Duchess. "Besides, it is very rude."

Girls brought up in the Victorian Age were expected to occupy themselves continually with some sort of handwork. Knitting was the favorite of the Duchess of Edinburgh, and her daughters were required to knit stockings while their governesses read stories to them. Throughout her life, Marie of Roumania was never seen at leisure without some bit of work in her hands.

The children were taught to eat what was put before them, since it was insulting to a hostess to refuse any dish:

"But if they are not good, Mamma?"

"Then you must just behave as though they were good."

"But if they make you feel sick!"

"Then be sick, my dear, but wait till you get home. It would be most offensive to be sick then and there!"

Health was a major issue with the Duchess. "Children, don't let English people persuade you that certain foods are indigestible; everything is digestible for a good stomach, but English people spoil their digestion from earliest childhood by imagining that they cannot eat this or that. I always ate everything; in Russia no one ever spoke about their digestions, it's a most unpleasant subject and not drawing-room conversation."

The Edinburgh children were never permitted to be sick. "A headache must never be confessed or given way to, a cold did not keep you at home, a fever did not send you to bed." Minor annoyances like these were treated with pills and remedies, which the Duchess of Edinburgh ordered in prodigious quantities from Russia, explaining that English medicines were fit only for horses. She did not think much better of English doctors.

Out of place and unhappy in England, the Duchess of Edinburgh devoted herself entirely to her children. "It was Mamma who settled things," wrote

Queen Marie, "Mamma to whom we turned, Mamma who came to kiss us good night, who took us out for walks or drives. It was Mamma who scolded or praised, who told us what we were or were not to do. Mamma loved us passionately. Her whole life was given up to her children, we were the supreme and central interest of her existence."

She lived for them, but she was very difficult to please. To earn her mother's praise, Missy must never question her opinions nor deviate from her prejudices. "She was... the ruling sovereign of her household, the one who... let you feel that the power over good and evil was hers." The Duchess never lost this attitude, even when her daughters grew to maturity. "She need not have been so lonely," wrote Marie, "had she only trusted her children a little more."

There was one area in which the Duchess of Edinburgh was more successful than her peers in the English royal family. Victoria's other children and their spouses lived in awe of "'dearest Mamma'; they avoided discussing her will, and her veto made them tremble." Unlike the others, the Duchess was not intimidated by the Queen and reported to her own mother that "you only have to give her a good fright to make her draw in her horns." This bravado may have been based on financial independence. Whatever its origin, the Duchess of Edinburgh was known to outsiders as "the sole member of the British royal family over whom Her Majesty does not attempt to domineer."

The Edinburgh children grew up amid a profusion of uncles, aunts, and cousins. Missy's favorite was Aunt Alexandra, the Princess of Wales. Her first memory of the family beauty dated back to a shooting party at her parents' home in Kent. It was teatime, and the Edinburgh children had been brought downstairs to be seen by their elders. Suddenly there appeared a magnificent creature in a red velvet gown with a long, sweeping train. "She dazzled me utterly," recalled Queen Marie. "I was speechless with adoration and my enchantment can be imagined when this velvet-clad apparition, who called herself Aunt Alix, volunteered to come up to the nursery to see us in our bath! There she sat in her glorious crimson gown, and fascinated, I gazed at her over my sponge, spellbound, fearing that the enchanting vision might suddenly fade away."

The Prince of Wales (later King Edward VII) was another matter. "We were never quite sure if we liked Uncle Bertie; he was too patronizing... and we were not yet old enough to come under the influence of his charm." Nor was Missy particularly fond of Aunt Vicky, Crown Princess (and later Kaiserin) of Germany. There was "something of a bite" in Aunt Vicky's ready smile that put her niece on guard. The English uncles and aunts were generally not very satisfactory, owing to a peculiar quality of indifference they displayed toward the young. "Even our father had this absentmindedness, characteristic of the family; he sometimes simply looked through you."

The Russian side of the family was entirely different. Missy's Romanov uncles were enormous men who smelled of cigarettes and leather and, unlike the Hanovers, paid special attention to the children of the family. "They were, if anything, too aware of your existence and teased you mercilessly; always, on all occasions, public or otherwise, they teased."

The chief tease was Uncle Sasha (later Tsar Alexander III), her mother's brother. Uncle Sasha, whom history remembers less fondly than his niece, was a Herculean giant, leading the young members of the family on excursions and silly pranks. When Missy was small, he invented a wonderful game using a gigantic net stretched taut above the ground. The object was to jump on the net and gain as much height as possible, like a modern trampoline. With his tremendous weight Uncle Sasha would chase his little nieces until he cornered them, bounce down hard, and send them laughing and flying into the air. It was, said Queen Marie, "a game for the gods."

As to the rest of Missy's Russian relations, "was there ever a nobler, more imposing company, men more huge, women more beautiful and more gorgeously attired, and where in the whole wide world could one see such jewels?" It didn't take unusual insight for the young Edinburgh Princess to realize that this was where her mother belonged. The Duchess was "curiously at home in that radiant assembly, much more at home than she is in London or Windsor." Even her style of dress improved in the gold-pillared salons of the Winter Palace. "Her gown is deep gentian blue, trimmed with sable, and the rubies she wears are like enormous drops of blood."

When the Duchess was in Russia without her children, she wrote them long descriptions of life in St. Petersburg and Tsarskoye Selo, the Tsar's summer home. Her delight was contagious. Missy grew up believing in her mother's homeland as a magical place where the sun lit the snow, servants never protested against work, and life was a series of sleigh rides and other innocent pleasures. Missy's mother never missed an opportunity to compare St. Petersburg with London, which she dismissed as foggy and dirty, an appropriately disagreeable setting for the dissolute pleasures of its inhabitants.

As often as she could, the Duchess took her children to Russia with her—along with a lady-in-waiting, an equerry, four nursemaids, four ladies' maids, four footmen, a courtier, and a page. Missy enjoyed these migrations thoroughly. When the children arrived, "everybody loved you and spoilt you and gave you good things to eat or hung lovely little crosses or lockets set with precious stones around your neck." In Petersburg and Pavlovsk, the servants kissed Missy's hand, and she and her sisters were given their own sailor to keep them amused and take them on outings.

In May of 1880, when Missy was four, the Duchess of Edinburgh was summoned home to see her mother before her death. When the Duchess arrived at the Winter Palace, she was appalled to find Catherine Dolgoruky, the Tsar's beloved mistress, installed with her children in apartments on the floor directly above the dying Tsarina. She and her father had an enormous row over this, the first argument of their lives. Afterward the Tsar fled with Catherine to Pavlovsk. He was not in St. Petersburg when his wife died shortly thereafter in the arms of their daughter.

Six weeks later the Tsar married his mistress, justifying his defiance of convention by the constant attempts on his life. He showed tragic foresight. On March 13, 1881, less than a year later, Alexander II was blown up by a bomb thrown by the Nihilists. Missy was five at the time and was shocked to find her mother, that paragon of self-control, in tears. She accompanied the Duchess to Russia for the funeral. "I still have a dim recollection of standing at a window of the Winter Palace and seeing an endless and gorgeous funeral procession pass by, but was it Grandpapa's or Grandmamma's funeral? I really do not know." What no young member of the family ever forgot was the sight of the funeral processions themselves. Imperial Romanov corteges wound their way along the shores of the Neva to the Fortress of Peter and Paul, led by the "Herald of Death," a man garbed head to foot in black, bearing a six-foot sword before him.

Queen Marie's memories of her grandfather when he was alive were limited to brief encounters dimly recalled. She remembered the Tsar entering the night nursery at Tsarskoye Selo one evening at bedtime when the other Edinburgh children were down with the measles. Missy was still well and therefore eligible for his good-night kiss. "I can still see . . . Grandpapa bending towards me, the tall, tall man to the wee little girl, and how absurdly proud I was that I could still be kissed."

She recalled seeing her maternal grandmother only once, on a train that was taking her to the south of France. The Tsarina was ill—"a pale emaciated woman" in a bed draped in blue. The Edinburgh children could see nothing of her but a "thin, waxen face and long, white, beautiful hands." Taken from their tea, the grandchildren stared unsympathetically at the "sad-looking" creature. "She had already been an invalid for several years," wrote Marie, "and, as I have heard since, had more reasons than ill health for being sad."

In 1886, when Missy was eleven, her father was named Commander of Her Majesty's Mediterranean Fleet and the Edinburgh family moved to Malta. It was a nice solution to the Queen's problem of what to do with the Duchess. Away from the English court, Missy's mother was in a position to enjoy her precedence undisturbed. The move to Malta was good for Missy as well.

"A walled-in oasis, Eastern and secret-looking" was her first reaction to the San Antonio Palace, where the Edinburghs were installed. Beneath the elegant shuttered windows and colonnaded porches of the palace were vast gardens, rampant with Mediterranean flowers. Beyond the fragrant gardens were the stables, and horses soon took over Missy and her sisters' lives. Riding was certainly not unusual for Victorian princesses; equestrian competence was an expected accomplishment, like dancing, drawing, and smiling. What was unseemly was their style. "Our ideas about riding were anything but civilized. We were entirely fearless and our chief pace was full gallop." Racing down the stone-walled roads of Malta with officers from her father's fleet, Missy learned to handle the high-spirited Arabian horses of the island. It was her first lesson toward becoming one of the most accomplished horse-women of her day.

Unlike other children of her caste who respected their parents but loved their nannies, Missy preserved a certain aloofness from that special group trained to raise the members of the ruling class. This was because the Duchess was such an attentive, if eccentric, parent. She was also a poor judge of character when it came to hiring surrogates.

The servant who meant the most to young Marie was her first nurse, Nana Pitcathly, a stern old Scotswoman who kept two straps (one black, one brown, neither used) at the foot of the nursery cots. Nana kept her charges "in almost military subjection," but Missy admired her physical courage— a discipline that kept her walking the floor night after night comforting Missy's baby sister, Beatrice, although she herself was suffering from cancer. In contrast was Mlle. Heim, a "dry, shivering spinster," ruler of the schoolroom. Ungainly, with large spreading features and mousy hair, Mademoiselle didn't have Nana's aristocratic bearing. Nor was she loyal. Mademoiselle was only too happy to add her complaints to those of the Duchess of Edinburgh's English suite, who constantly criticized their employer for her foreign ways.

A happy childhood influence was Maurice Bourke, a young man who came into the life of the Edinburghs on Malta, where he served as captain of the Duke's yacht. An Irishman with dark wavy hair, blue eyes, and a sense of humor, Bourke was a healthy contrast to the carping ladies surrounding the Duchess. "I can honestly say that Maurice Bourke was my first love," wrote Queen Marie. "He was indeed a hero to me, and I have even known fits of agonizing jealousy when I was afraid he might care for one of my sisters more than for myself."

Another male friendship that started on Malta, one of far greater future significance for Marie, was the relationship with her first cousin George, later King George V of England. Following the pattern set by Victoria and Albert, George, the second son of the heir to the throne, had been enlisted by his parents in the Royal Navy. Short, with a bearded face, full of energy and good cheer, George was serving in Malta under his uncle, the Duke of Edinburgh, Commander of the Mediterranean Fleet.

Cousin George was included in all the Edinburgh family outings, and there was a room kept ready for him at all times in the San Antonio Palace. Although his mother worried about the effect of the unconventional Edinburgh girls on her son and his sisters always referred to their Edinburgh cousins as "poor little" or "dear little," George enjoyed the entire Edinburgh family. The Duke of Edinburgh, who had little to do with his own son, was close to this nephew, as was the Duchess. In his diary, George V described his aunt as "kind, honest & straightforward & so true." When she died he said she had been "like a second mother" to him.

But the big attraction of the San Antonio Palace was Missy herself. In her memoirs Queen Marie referred to George as her "beloved chum" and said that he was the only person capable of managing the three older Edinburgh girls. "He called us 'the dear three,' but I proudly remember that in the case of Cousin George I was a decided favourite, there was no doubt about that whatever."

When George was away at sea, they corresponded avidly. "I am so longing to see you my darling Missy," he wrote her from England in January of 1888. "I never show your letters to anybody & I hope you don't show mine." "You are always in my thoughts darling Missy," he wrote from Spezzia, and in October of 1889 sent "a great big kiss" for her "sweet little face."

It was obvious to everyone in the English royal family that Prince George, already in his early twenties, was waiting for the girl of his heart to grow up.

In 1889 the Edinburghs moved again—this time to the little German duchy of Coburg, which the Duke was due to inherit along with the neighboring territory of Gotha. Coburg was a small picturesque town, the home of "simple burghers, uncritical and loyal." Ruled over by Missy's great-uncle Ernst, the childless elder brother of her grandfather, Prince Albert, it was not unlike other provincial German capitals of the period—simple, old-world, and full of its own importance. The social climate of feudalism that still clung to these little duchies was vastly appealing to the autocratic Duchess.

In town, the Edinburghs occupied the Palais Edinburgh, a trim home overlooking the central square across from the official residence of the reigning Duke. But it was the Rosenau, the cheerful country *Schloss* where her grandfather Albert was raised, that Missy really loved. And no wonder. It was and is an enchanting castle with bright ocher, false Gothic walls, studded with leaded windows under a stair-step roof. To one side of the façade is a small tower enclosing a spiral staircase. On the other side, a stream tumbles noisily over rocks before meandering off into the woods. From tiny dormer windows spotted haphazardly under the eaves, the young Princess and her sisters could see out past their private park to the surrounding farms and all the way down to the village itself.

At the top of the tower was the sort of room in which the Edinburgh girls imagined Sleeping Beauty must have pricked her finger. The Duchess gave it to her daughters to furnish for themselves. Missy, in the middle of her teen-age hearts-and-flowers period, decorated it accordingly. Fortunately for ladies' magazines of her day, the Queen of Roumania's passion for interior decoration never waned, although her style evolved over the years from Bavarian Primitive to Royal Byzantine.

Being raised in the middle of a fairy tale suited Missy's budding sense of drama. The role of wicked witch was played by her new governess, Fräulein von Truchsess. With her soft-spoken manner, Fräulein had at first seemed more promising than Mademoiselle. "Those who have not known her," related the Queen, still angry after forty-five years, "cannot picture to themselves how perfectly she could counterfeit the guileless, almost innocent girl telling a harmless little story to amuse the Duchess.... She spoke without accentuating her words, she made them smooth, like beautifully woven silk.... Little by little we came to loathe this gentle relating of innocuous stories... knowing that someone's reputation was going to be attacked, some servant was going to lose his place, some friend was going to be undermined.... It was torture to watch her ways."

The governess soon convinced the Duchess that the character of her daughters would be better served if they wore less becoming, less elegant clothes. Silk underwear and nightgowns were tossed away in favor of harsh calico. Teen-age vanity was countered by "ugly gowns, hats and cloaks, badly shaped shoes—in fact anything that could 'uglify' us in any way.... Fräulein, the moment she spotted which was the pattern of stuff we most disliked, would choose it for us with a sort of evil delight."

Fräulein worked with and eventually married Dr. Wilhelm Rolfs, a pompous martinet whose high intellect and erudition appealed enormously to the Duchess of Edinburgh. But Dr. Rolfs, according to Marie, was a product of "German 'Kultur' at its worst, arrogant, masterful, overruling everyone else, turning the best into ridicule, laying down the law, intolerant, tyrannical." Like his mistress, Wilhelm Rolfs was an Anglophobe. "His object," according to Marie, "was to uproot in us the love of England and to turn us into Germans." The Germanizing of Marie was never a success, probably because it was presented as expiation for the sin of being born and raised in the placidity of English wealth.

Missy's older brother, Alfred, had been given over entirely to Dr. Rolfs in 1883 when he was nine years old. This was done in order to prepare the boy—only son of the Duke of Edinburgh and second in line to the duchies of Coburg and Gotha—to take up his German inheritance. The Duchess "rejoiced" to have her son sent out of England to be brought up as a German, but Missy was incensed by Dr. Rolfs's treatment of her brother. Alfred had problems even without Rolfs: he was "eager, blundering, a little swaggering, always getting into trouble, always being scolded." Rolfs delighted in ridiculing his pupil in front of others, and his insensitivity helped destroy young Alfred's life.

Although the Duke of Edinburgh disliked Dr. Rolfs and Fräulein as much as his children did, he could not prevail upon his wife to dismiss them. The Duchess found in Dr. Rolfs a cultural substitute for her nonintellectual husband, and Fräulein was the first governess in the household who did not ally herself with the couple's English suites against her mistress. It was four years—most of Missy's adolescence—before the Duke finally succeeded in forcing the German academic out of his lucrative sinecure. Unfortunately for Missy, this did not occur until eight months after her marriage.

For all her intelligence, the Duchess of Edinburgh had a curiously patronizing attitude toward the education of her children. She did not consider them particularly bright or gifted and did little to improve their minds. Reading aloud was the only quasi-educational habit she bothered to instill in her daughters. Even in drawing and painting—one area in which the girls all inherited Queen Victoria's talent—they received only pedestrian instruction. As to religion, the Duchess refused to even discuss it with her daughters, turning them over completely to a local priest to prepare them for a German Protestant confirmation.

Missy's mother did believe stongly in the moral and physical benefits of nature and outdoor activity. When the children were young, she took them for long walks, picnics, and mushroom hunts; as they grew older, she encouraged riding, bathing, lawn tennis, and ice skating. It was from the Duchess that Missy learned to observe the change of seasons, the smell of the air, the budding of trees and flowers. As the oldest daughter in the family, she was expected to write letters when the Duchess was away, giving details on the weather and their activities. Writing came easily to Missy, and she quickly graduated from descriptions of the flowers at the Rosenau to anecdotes about the household and its visitors. Although a poor student, Missy was an acute reporter on the appearance, manners, and peculiarities of those around her.

There was a lot to observe in Coburg. For amusement there were outings twice a week to the Coburg theater, a "self-righteous little institute" subsidized by the ducal court. For sheer curiosity there was wicked Great-uncle Ernst: "An elderly man . . . heavy, ponderous, but at the same time an old beau. . . . The jaw of a bulldog, the lower teeth protruding far beyond the upper and with a pair of bloodshot eyes alive with uncanny, almost brutal intelligence."

Even in his youth Ernst had never been considered handsome or virtuous like his younger brother, Albert. Soon after Albert married Queen Victoria and moved to England, Ernst contracted syphilis, which did not deter him from marrying Princess Alexandrine of Baden. Forty years later Missy met Great-aunt Alexandrine, a "drooping, sad-looking old lady in shabby black . . . with a flat and stayless body. A weak, grisly beard covered her chin and two kindly bleared eyes protruded above a depressed-looking nose, hopelessly pear-shaped." The Edinburgh children resented the way their Great-uncle Ernst treated his wife, "as no one else would dare to treat a servant." Her devotion to the old man mystified them.

Alexandrine's capacity for martyrdom was noteworthy. She always referred to her degenerate husband as *der Lieber, Gute Ernst* [Dearly Beloved, Good Ernest]." When he died, in 1893, she took his current mistress, the last of a long line, under her protection and declared that their love nest—a villa in the park he had used for his other women as well—must never be touched or inhabited again "because it was there that her beloved Ernst had lived such happy hours!"

A terrible husband, Ernst was an able and well-liked ruler. Unlike his frugal brother, Albert, Duke Ernst spent lavishly. This worried Victoria, who knew that the Duke of Edinburgh would have to pay for his uncle's extravagances when he inherited the duchies. Ernst's peers did not share his subjects' enthusiasm for him. The Tsarina's brother, an archconservative who loathed Ernst's political ideas "if indeed he can be said to have any," referred to him as "that clown from Coburg." Arthur Stanley, the Dean of Westminster, who married Missy's parents, met Duke Ernst once in Egypt. If anything in the world could have increased his respect for Prince Albert, the Dean said, it was the thought of what would have happened to England had Victoria married his older brother.

The Edinburghs were no more enthusiastic about Uncle Ernst than his other relatives. The Duchess of Edinburgh stipulated that diplomats with young or pretty wives not be accredited to the court of Duke Ernst. As her husband prepared to take over his uncle's duchies, the ladies of Coburg who had been living on Ernst's generosity began looking around for husbands or other means of support. Duke Ernst, it was observed in the early 1890s, was aging quickly.

Before he inherited the duchies of Coburg and Gotha, the Duke of Edinburgh was appointed Naval Commander in Chief in Devonport. The Duchess followed her husband back to England in 1891, leaving the older children behind in Coburg to finish their studies with Dr. Rolfs and Fräulein. Late in the year, however, Missy was allowed to accompany her mother to Russia for the funeral of the wife of one of the Duchess's younger brothers. Missy's aunt had died in childbirth, and the Romanovs gathered in the church in the Fortress of Peter and Paul to lay her to rest.

The sixteen-year-old English Princess was impressed by the burial cathedral of her Russian family. Massive pillars stood like blue and gold sentries over the marble sepulchers of her ancestors, and huge sapphire glass chandeliers glowed with light from hundreds of tapers. Most awesome of all was the mammoth iconostasis that separated worshipers from priests—a sculptured screen of pure gold on which Christ appeared in the robes of the Tsar. "Russia..." Marie wrote many years later, "had glamour [and] prestige for me, especially in my unthinking days... when I saw only the magnificence of it."

The Duchess of Edinburgh knew this. She used the funeral in Petersburg to reintroduce her eldest daughter to the East and her Russian cousins, one of whom, Grand Duke George Michaelovitch, asked for Missy's hand in marriage. The boys both fascinated and frightened Missy; they were charming, kind, and generous to the point of lavishness. "We too had Russian blood in us, so we were strongly attracted, but the English side seemed on guard...And yet I think at that time it would have needed but little persuasion to keep me in Russia altogether."

This was not her mother's plan.

Chapter 3

No one in the English royal family understood why Princess Marie of Edinburgh was not given to her cousin Prince George of England, who wanted her for his wife. In an era when even the plainest princess of Missy's lineage would have qualified for a major alliance, the sacrifice to a minor throne of one of the memorable beauties of the House of Hanover still calls for an explanation. In her autobiography the Queen of Roumania herself was discreetly vague on the subject, but nearly all the other books about her, King George V, and his wife, Queen Mary, as well as letters of the English royal family, point to George's desire to marry Missy.

Queen Victoria, their mutual grandmother, was anxious for the match and strongly recommended his enchanting blond cousin to George. He graciously, if ungrammatically, refused to be hurried into matrimony. "I quite... understand your reasons for wishing Eddy [George's older brother] & I to marry as soon as possible," he wrote the Queen. "But still I think marrying too young is a bad thing... Then again," he added, alluding to the fact that Missy was only fifteen at the time, "the wife ought not to be too young."

Both George's and Missy's fathers, the Prince of Wales and the Duke of Edinburgh, declared themselves early for the marriage. It was their mothers who fought the idea. The Princess of Wales's prejudice against her niece can be attributed largely to Missy's German upbringing. Ever since Prussia and Austria had taken the duchies of Schleswig and Holstein away from her father, the King of Denmark, Missy's Aunt Alix loathed everything to do with the Germans. When George told her that he would like to marry Missy, but was in no hurry to do so, she wrote back: "I quite agree with you it certainly wld be too soon in every way!! particularly as the bride is not in long petticoats yet!!! *Entre nous,* talking about *her*! it is a pity those children shld be entirely brought up as Germans. Last time I saw them they spoke with a very strong foreign accent—which I think is a great pity as after all they are English."

The Princess of Wales's main objection was not Missy herself, but her mother. In April of 1891 she again wrote her son George in her inimitable style: "Well & now about yr Matrimonial prospects!!! ha ha ha! You are *quite* right to think Grandmama has gone mad on the subject—& it is too *ridiculous*... the girl being a perfect baby yet—altho Aunt Marie begging her pardon does *all* she can to make her *old before her time*... and what do you say to Aunt Marie having *hurried* on the *two girls confirmation*—& in Germany too so that now they won't *even know* that they have ever been English—particularly as they have been confirmed in the German church."

While the Princess of Wales tried to discourage George from marrying Missy, the Duchess of Edinburgh prepared for the inevitable English proposal by keeping Missy away from George and hurrying her off to St. Petersburg with Ducky for the funeral of their aunt. From Russia she took the girls to Germany, ostensibly so Missy could make her social debut at the court of Kaiser Wilhelm II, eldest of Aunt Vicky's children.

Unlike the Princess of Wales, the Duchess of Edinburgh was a fervent Germanophile who blamed the failure of her own marriage on the temptations of London society. "I simply hate it [London]..." she wrote Missy in 1893, "it is an impossible place, people are mad of pleasure... All your feelings seem to be stifled in people by... passion for dissipation. No, this life is not made either for me or all of you."

There was also the matter of pride. The Duchess had determined not to allow her daughter's future, like most things in the English royal family, to be dictated by the Queen. To thwart her mother-in-law she had already started negotiations toward what she wanted for Missy—a marriage with the Kaiser's cousin Ferdinand, Crown Prince of Roumania. The successful arrangement of such an alliance would gain the Duchess the gratitude of her own family, the Romanovs, who wanted to extend Russian influence in the Balkans, as well as that of the German Hohenzollerns, anxious for an appropriate wife for the heir to the Roumanian throne. It would also be the final revenge on the Hanovers for not treating her with sufficient respect. What is clear now, nearly a hundred years later, is that it was the Duchess of Edinburgh's resentment of her husband's family that prevented her eldest daughter from living up to her royal potential.

The Duchess carefully concealed her plans from Missy. Royal brides were traditionally kept in ignorance of the dynastic schemes of their elders. Coded inquiries and discreet intermediaries were the accepted preliminaries to marriages of state. Meetings between future spouses were arranged as if by chance; only the young man knew why he was there. As for the bride, it was necessary to keep her from suspicion and premature rebellion. In Missy's case, this meant steering her firmly away from her cousin in the direction of her mother's choice. Toward that end, she was seated next to Crown Prince Ferdinand of Roumania at dinner the evening of her first adult appearance in society.

Ferdinand's full name and title was Ferdinand Victor Albert Mainrad, Prince of Hohenzollern-Sigmaringen. He was born on August 24, 1865, ten years before Missy, the son of Prince Leopold and Princess Antonia of Hohenzollern-Sigmaringen. On his father's side, he was descended from an ancient branch of the German royal family, the Hohenzollerns. On his mother's side, he was related to the Portuguese ruling house and the Coburgs.

Prince Ferdinand was born with protruding ears, which his parents instructed his nurse to pin back with bandages when he was still an infant. The remedy failed. Throughout his life, Ferdinand's ears sat at right angles to his face, making him a difficult subject for court photographers and an easy target for satire. Apart from this and legs too short for his trunk, he was considered a fine-looking young man, although rather ungraceful.

His parents' second son and his mother's favorite child, Ferdinand was intensely shy and painfully inarticulate. Although he attended the War Academy in Cassel and served two years in the German Army, he was far more devoted to the Catholic Church and his books. His obsession was botany. "How he loved flowers!" an admirer said. "With him it was more than a taste, more than a fancy or mania—it was a profound and reasoned passion. His knowledge of botany surpassed the ordinary knowledge of a professor."

Ferdinand would probably have been happiest spending his life in the tranquillity of the family castle in Germany, reading, hunting, and taking long botanical walks with his dogs. But in 1874 his uncle, King Carol of Roumania, lost his only child, and it fell to the King's older brother, Prince Leopold, to provide the succession to the Roumanian throne. Prince Leopold had three sons. Ferdinand's older brother, Wilhelm, tried life in the Balkans for a year, but found it unrewarding; Wilhelm, who preferred living in Germany as a Prince of Hohenzollern, handed down the Roumanian honors to his younger brother. Ferdinand, who conducted his life largely by default, was too weak to refuse a position that he disliked and for which he was eminently unsuited.

In the spring of 1889, the new Crown Prince of Roumania embarked on a lonely and incompatible existence in the Balkan peninsula. He passed his days reviewing the army and overseeing government functions, neither of which particularly interested him, and giving formal audiences to strangers—an excruciating ordeal for a painfully shy man. Evenings were spent reading the newspapers and playing billiards with the King. Occasionally there was an opera or a concert to attend. Because of intrigues and power plays among the Roumanian aristocracy, King Carol allowed his heir no friends.

Ferdinand's sole companion in Roumania was his unremitting uncle, who drummed politics into the heir apparent and drilled him interminably in his duties. The only other contact allowed Ferdinand was Carol's artistic consort, Queen Elisabeth (the former Princess Elisabeth of Wied). More than anyone else, the Queen knew how difficult the King could be. Ferdinand's friendship with Elisabeth meant many hours in the company of her favorite lady-in-waiting, Helene Vacaresco. Helene was brilliant, witty, and a talented writer; she was unattractive but temptingly plump. Prompted by Aunt Elisabeth, Ferdinand fell in love with her and decided to marry her.

But Ferdinand had forgotten why he was brought to Roumania in the first place. The Roumanians did not want one of their own sitting on or even next to the throne. After centuries of infighting between princely families vying for the ultimate power, they had imported the German Hohenzollern dynasty to avoid just that. The love-sick nephew had a terrible scene with his uncle, and his "poor little attempt at romance" dissolved before the wrath of the King. To emphasize the lesson, King Carol sent his Prime Minister to remind the Crown Prince of the facts of royal life: "Your Royal Highness could not make a better choice than Mademoiselle Vacaresco.... But the Heir Presumptive to our throne must marry a foreign Princess, equal in rank and birth, who can be his future Queen. The Constitution is quite definite on this matter."

Ferdinand was given an ultimatum: Helene or the throne. He did not want to rule, but, apologizing to his parents for "the manifold sorrow and heartaches" he had caused them, he made the honorable Hohenzollern decision and gave up the girl. He was sent away with a list of eligible princesses from which to choose a wife.

The Crown Prince of Roumania traveled through Holland and Belgium and all over Germany. He met Missy of Edinburgh, whose name was first on his list, in Cassel. Having been informed through the Duchess that Missy was available, he had requested her photograph before their meeting. Attracted first by her beauty, then by her charm, he urged his parents to act "quickly." "I cannot wait until they all have been grabbed away in front of my nose..." he wrote home, "quick action has to take place, before someone else engages her, better today than tomorrow." Learning of Queen Victoria's plans, he expressed the fear that George of England might "interfere" with his suit. As the months passed and Ferdinand was informed by Missy's mother that he would be successful, he explained to his parents why he was in such a hurry to marry. "I have few pleasures enjoyed by my peers. I therefore have the greatest desire for my own happy home, which would help me to content myself with the serious way of life and the lack of amusements of any kind" in Roumania.

Missy, of course, knew none of this. The Duchess told her only that she might be allowed to attend her first adult party, given by the Kaiser at an eighteenth-century château in Cassel. Although she did not like her thirty-two-year-old cousin the Kaiser—"there was something about him that roused antagonism"—she was flattered to be included in the formal celebration of the Kaisermaneuver, an important military event in pre–World War I Germany. Her mother gave her a new mauve dress for the party and coached her in keeping up a conversation. "A princess who does not talk to her neighbour is a nuisance to Society," said the Duchess of Edinburgh. Seated next to Ferdinand of Roumania, Missy did her best to be amusing. Ferdinand spoke no English, but he was refreshingly unpretentious in the stiff pomposity of the Kaiser's court.

Missy attached no importance to her meeting with Ferdinand, nor did she realize why her mother hustled her off almost immediately to Berlin to visit Cousin Charly, Princess Charlotte of Saxe-Meiningen. Charly was the daughter of Aunt Vicky and sister of the Kaiser; she was the intermediary between the Duchess of Edinburgh and the Hohenzollerns, and it was she who had arranged the meeting between Ferdinand and Missy. Older than Missy, Charly was a constant visitor to Coburg, where she was on excellent terms with Dr. Rolfs. Small in stature and engaged in a perpetual war against weight, the Kaiser's sister moved with deliberate grace and spoke in a soft, melodic purr. Like a cat, Charly bared her claws at unexpected times.

As a child Missy had had an enormous crush on Charly, which withered away in the light of reality: "She was flattered by our admiration, and she could be more charming than anyone I have known," Queen Marie wrote many years later. "She knew things, though not as many as she gave you to believe; she spoke always as a connoisseur, be it about horses, music, flowers, cooking or army equipment, and for many long years I bowed down before her superior knowledge."

The Duchess of Edinburgh's plan to throw her daughter and Ferdinand together under Cousin Charly's roof aborted rather quickly. In Berlin the Kaiser's sister was the center of a sophisticated set, one which sixteen-year-old Missy and fifteen-year-old Ducky were clearly too young to join. "We looked on and suffered the cruelest pangs of jealousy, watching our idol exposing a side of her character we had never before dreamed of; whilst for us, uninteresting *Backfische* [teen-agers] to whom she had promised a glorious time, she had hardly a word or a look."

Crown Prince Ferdinand was among Charly's more favored guests: "... if we had continued meeting in her house I do not think that today I should be where I am," Queen Marie wrote later, "for it was only too natural that the grown-up German prince... should be much more amused in her ex-hilarating company than searching for topics of conversation in keeping with our *Backfisch* innocence."

The Duchess soon realized that she had overplayed her hand, that Missy did not appear to advantage against a backdrop of Berlin's smart young royalties. After only a week in Berlin, "one of the most painful memories of my young life," Missy was taken back to Coburg.

While the Duchess of Edinburgh was plotting Missy's German alliance, Queen Victoria and the Wales family were still planning for her to marry George of England. In early 1892, George's future unexpectedly changed. His older brother, Eddy, stricken with flu, died of pneumonia on January 14. Suddenly George was in line for the English throne. The Prince and Princess of Wales tendered a tentative proposal of marriage on his behalf to the Edinburghs. Their offer was refused outright by the Duchess. She told the Wales family that Missy had just been confirmed in the German Protestant Church and that she "would for nothing in the world, influence" her daughter to change her religion back to the Church of England.

Unaware of his aunt's intrigues, George did not understand why he had not seen Missy for two years, ever since he and his father had visited Coburg in April of 1890. "What fun we had... when we danced," George had written his cousin after the family reunion. Seeing their fun, Missy's mother and Fräulein had made plans to keep them apart. When the Duchess took Missy back to England later in 1890 and 1891, she made sure George was away at sea. "... it is nearly 9 months since I have seen you now, but you are constantly in my thoughts..." George wrote "darling Missy" in January of 1891, begging her not to "quite forget yr most loving & devoted old Georgie."

George did not rely on his parents to do his proposing for him. Having heard of Missy's Russian suitor (George Michaelovitch), but ironically not about Ferdinand, he wrote her a personal letter, hoping to prevent her from promising herself to anyone else before they could speak face-to-face. In the letter he said that he had always understood that the two of them would one day, when she was old enough, marry. Missy's answer, written from Coburg, was dictated by her mother. It said that although she was fond of George, "he must not think that there was anything definite in the friendship that had sprung up between them at Malta."

The Edinburgh refusal sent shock waves through the Queen's family. The

Duke of Edinburgh blamed Fräulein. The Queen complained that "Georgie lost Missy by waiting & waiting." The Prince of Wales stopped speaking to his brother and sister-in-law. The Princess of Wales was delighted.

Family loyalties—to her mother, King George V, and his wife, Queen Mary—prevented Queen Marie from fully explaining the circumstances that kept her from marrying her cousin. While other members of the family provided various explanations* for the Duchess's actions, only once in her autobiography did Marie allude in writing to what had really happened to her. Citing her mother's theory that princesses should marry very young before "they begin to think too much and to have too many ideas of their own," Marie said that her own premature appearance on the European marriage market annoyed other royal matriarchs with eligible daughters. "But, she added, "the young princes seemed to be of another opinion and before I was sixteen more than one gave me to understand that I was entirely to his taste.

"No names need be mentioned, but. . . it must be told that there came a period when my heart was touched by two suitors of the same name** but belonging to far different corners of Europe, and I knew many a pang because each in his own way let me feel that it was in my power to make him either happy or miserable. . . I did not want to make anyone miserable; but the heart is such a troublesome organ and at that early age anything definite seemed so far off. Besides, one could not make up one's mind all by oneself!"

Whether Missy would or would not have preferred to be Queen of England, she was hurried off to Munich in the spring of 1892 by her mother to be courted by Ferdinand of Roumania. The Duchess made plans for Missy and Ferdinand to be together constantly—excursions, visits to art galleries, theater parties, shopping. "Munich is the town of towns for this sort of thing. . . we were both young, there was love in the air, it was springtime, and Mamma had a happy, expectant face."

*Royal history offers two reasons for the nonalliance of George and Marie. The first and more commonly cited explanation is that George was a second son; by refusing to allow Missy to marry him, the Duchess of Edinburgh hoped to save her daughter from the unhappiness of her own life. This overlooks the fact that the Wales proposal was not advanced until after the death of George's older brother, when George was already in line for the throne. The second reason comes from Princess Ileana, youngest daughter of Queen Marie: "It was only because they were first cousins. And my grandmother [the Duchess of Edinburgh] disapproved terribly of cousins marrying. . . she [Marie] did want to marry him. But she was only sixteen. . . I don't think my mother was aware of the proposal. In fact, I'm convinced she wasn't. . . it was her mother who made the decision." This explanation, which justifies the Duchess's refusal on religious grounds—the prohibition by the Russian Orthodox Church of marriage between first cousins—is unsupportable in the light of sister Ducky's marriage one year later to a first cousin on her father's side of the family, to say nothing of a second marriage to a first cousin on her mother's, the Russian Orthodox, side.

**Prince George of England and Grand Duke George Michaelovitch of Russia.

Never before had the young Edinburgh Princess been given such an opportunity to please her mother. Throughout her childhood she had listened to Mamma's constant complaints about England, Missy's father, and the Queen. Suddenly the Duchess was cheerful and enthusiastic, letting her eldest daughter know that she was being presented with a future worthy of her mother's illustrious past. If Russia was the only country where Mamma said that royalty lived as it ought, Roumania, just next door, must be a delightful place to settle, especially as the wife of a cultivated German prince due to inherit a throne. All that was required of her was acquiescence.

Prince Ferdinand was bashful. His timidity attracted her. "It gave you a longing to put him at ease; . . . it aroused your motherly feelings, in fact you wanted to help him." But for all her gaiety, charm, and conversational ability, Missy herself was painfully naïve. "We had been kept in glorious, but I cannot help considering dangerous and almost cruel, ignorance of all realities . . . it was cruel, yes, cruel is the only word which really describes it; it was . . . a deliberate blinding against life as it truly is, so that with shut eyes and perfect confidence we would have advanced towards any fate."

The engagement followed quickly at the Neue Palais in Potsdam. "Mamma was radiant and it was, I believe, Charly who . . . actually led the timid prince up to the crucial moment. How he ever had the courage to propose is . . . a mystery to me; but he *did* and I accepted—I just said 'Yes,' as though it had been quite a natural and simple word to say. 'Yes,' and with that 'Yes' I sealed my fate."

The exultant Duchess of Edinburgh cabled relatives all over Europe to proclaim her triumph. Their reactions were less than enthusiastic.

"We have been much startled lately to hear of *Missy's Engagement* to *Ferdinand of Roumania*," Queen Victoria wrote one of her other granddaughters. "He is nice I believe & the Parents are charming—but the Country is very insecure & the immorality of the Society at Bucharest *quite awful.* Of course the marriage would be delayed some time as Missy won't be 17 till the end of Oct.!"

And to her daughter Vicky: "Missy's engagement . . . had us all by surprise . . . it seems to have come very rapidly to a climax. The Country is vy insecure & the Society—dreadful—& she is a mere Child, & quite inexperienced! . . . Missy herself wld *not* have Georgie. . . . It was the dream of Affie's life. . . ."

Lady Geraldine Somerset, known for her acerbic court diary, wrote more bluntly: "Disgusted to see the announcement of the marriage of poor pretty nice P. Marie of Edinburgh to the *P. of Roumania*!!! it does seem too cruel a shame to cart that nice pretty girl off to semi-barbaric Roumania and a man to the knowledge of all Europe desperately in love with another woman . . . too bad."

In response to such outcry, the Duchess of Edinburgh announced that she had really wanted Missy to marry George all along. Clearly a ploy, her about-face was staged to obscure her previous machinations and to pacify her husband and his brother. The Queen was briefly taken in: "I fear Bertie is very angry—but he is unjust & wrong. Affie and Marie wished for Georgie & fm a worldly point of view it was so much better & gter a match than this one! There was no *running* after this as Bertie says—& Marie [Duchess of Edinburgh] did *not* go to Potsdam for *that*, but because *Dona* [Kaiserin of Germany] had pressed her so much & *wished* Missy for *odious Gunther*! [the Kaiserin's younger, scandalous brother]...Poor Georgie...is not bitter."

But to everyone else it was obvious that the Duchess of Edinburgh had chosen Missy's husband; it was Mamma, not Missy, who wore the "happy, expectant face." The Queen's eyes were eventually opened to the truth, and ever after she spoke of Missy as "a great victim...to be enormously pitied."

After the excitement of the engagement, Marie was left wondering how to deal with her father, who had never met Ferdinand, and Queen Victoria. "Papa had not been there at the engagement and somehow my conscience was not quite easy; I felt, almost knew, that Papa had had other dreams. And then there was Grandmamma Queen, she would have to approve of my future husband; none of her granddaughters married without her approval. We should have to go to Windsor and be inspected, a rather formidable ordeal."

Besides her English family there were Ferdinand's German relatives, particularly King Carol of Roumania. "You could not be long in the company of Ferdinand, Crown Prince of Roumania, without discovering that '*der Onkel*,' as he called him, loomed almost oppressively large in his life. When he spoke of him something very like anxiety and not far removed from dread came into his eyes; one felt that a shiver ran down his spine."

King Carol was first. The meeting was set to take place at Sigmaringen Castle, home and birthplace of the Hohenzollern dynasty. A huge feudal edifice dominating the green Swabian countryside, the castle is reflected in the still waters of the Danube, only a quiet, narrow stream at this point very near its source in southwestern Germany.

Seen today, the old *Schloss*, built on a steep hill and rising anywhere from five to ten stories in height, seems rather welcoming. The jumble of brick-red turrets and roofs is friendly; the grayed-out stone is peaceful. There is a cheerful multitude of irregular chimneys and steeples, courtyards and passageways, softened by sinuous vines, ancient trees, and softly moving water below.

But once inside, the visitor knows—as the Duchess must have known—that Sigmaringen Castle was then and still is the domain exclusively of men. From its low vaulted entry, hung with war-torn banners of the Hohenzollerns' own regiment, to vast trophy halls studded with thousands of antlers, there is little to suggest the presence of women among the warriors. An occasional French salon or a fanciful Venetian mirror appears out of place in the castle's somber interior. Unlike the cheerful clutter preferred by her English family or the gilded French preciosity adapted by the Russians, this German castle spoke commandingly if silently of the role Missy's future in-laws would expect her to fill. Princess Marie of Edinburgh was being delivered by her mother into the Hohenzollern clan purely for purposes of breeding.

The Hohenzollern-Sigmaringen family is the oldest branch of the Hohenzollern dynasty that ruled Germany until 1918. Unlike their relatives who sat on the throne, they are Catholic. During the revolutionary wave that swept through Europe in the late 1840s, Ferdinand's grandfather, Prince Karl Anton, renounced his sovereignty in favor of his cousin, the King of Prussia. Karl Anton sired four sons, of whom Prince Leopold, Missy's future father-in-law, was the eldest, and Prince Karl, who became King Carol of Roumania, was the second. When Missy entered the family, Prince Leopold was Head of the House.

Missy liked her future father-in-law immediately. With his long, sensitive face, light eyes, and fading blond beard, Prince Leopold was decidedly handsome. The same, Missy felt, could not be said of her future mother-in-law, Princess Antonia. "Having heard that she had been a great beauty, I was all eagerness to see her, but I could not reconcile myself to this pale-faced, pale-lipped, Grecian-nosed woman with the too-small bust and too-long legs. These proportions can occasionally be beautiful, but in her case, the hips being enormous, there was something about her figure which made you feel positively uncomfortable."

An invalid, Princess Antonia was always dressed and jeweled magnificently for her prearranged family appearances, and she welcomed Missy although she disapproved of her favorite son marrying a Protestant princess. She was currently angry at the wife of Ferdinand's older brother and found it convenient to shower Missy, her future daughter-in-law, with extra affection designed to hurt the daughter-in-law she already had. Although she was beautifully educated, Princess Antonia lived, according to Marie, "in a small circle of rules, prejudices and conventions which she considered perfection... hedged in by her Church, nursing her delicate health, everybody serving her, caring for her, spoiling her." Portraits of Princess Antonia bear out Marie's description of a judgmental and discontented woman.

Missy's own mother was happy at Sigmaringen. The pomposity of the Sigmaringen court suited her well, and she reveled in the erudition of its inhabitants. The Duchess of Edinburgh had brought along all her children and her entire household, including Dr. Rolfs and Fräulein. Only Missy's father was absent.

After several placid country days, the other members of the family grew noticeably anxious as the time approached for the arrival of Prince Leopold's younger brother, King Carol of Roumania. Even the unflappable Duchess appeared "a little excited and nervous" as she inspected her children before the great event. The entire family drove in state through the provincial German village, decked in red, yellow, and blue Roumanian flags for a formal reception.

With all the buildup King Carol in the flesh had to be disappointing. His pictures had conveyed a correct impression of austerity and discipline. But his piercing eyes, hawk nose, and aggressively pointed black beard demanded an imposing stature, and King Carol's body was not large enough for his face. Missy was not impressed: "He simply seemed to me rather a short man with somewhat incurved knees, his feet in thick-soled boots exceedingly firmly planted on the ground . . . His movements were slow and deliberate, with a sort of conscious majesty . . . the movements of a man who, having himself completely under control, can also control and master others. But for all that, the first sight of *der Onkel* did not at all come up to my young expectations."

There was one problem of life at Sigmaringen that outweighed Missy's initial contact with an entire clan of people who would play major roles in her future—the competition between her fiancé and her sister Ducky for her affections. She was torn by two loves, each equally important in her adolescent mind. Nando (she adopted his family's nickname for Ferdinand) could not bear to let her out of his sight. "He always wanted to be alone with me and suffered because of the many others who claimed their share."

Choosing a date and location for the future wedding presented difficulties that were aggravated by the resentment of Queen Victoria and the Duke of Edinburgh over the marriage itself. After some discussion it was decided to postpone the ceremony until January of the following year (1893) so that Marie should have attained the age of seventeen. By marrying a Catholic, Marie was giving up all rights to the English throne. Moreover, the proposed union between a Catholic prince and a Protestant princess who would then raise their children in the Roumanian Orthodox Church— the official religion of their future country—had strained the Catholic Hohenzollerns' standing with the Pope. While envoys were sent to mollify the Pontiff, the family set about to choose a place for the festivities.

Queen Victoria wanted Missy married in St. George's Chapel at Windsor Castle like all her English grandchildren. But since there had to be two ceremonies, one to satisfy each religious persuasion, and since neither church would relinquish the honor of celebrating its rites first, plans for a Windsor wedding had to be abandoned. Missy was disappointed. Her mother was delighted. The Duchess would have liked to stage the wedding at Coburg, where she would soon be reigning lady, but Missy's English relations refused to attend ceremonies in wicked Uncle Ernst's court. It took several months before everyone agreed to Sigmaringen Castle—"a solution," said Marie, "I personally did not really care about."

Since the first meeting between Edinburghs and Hohenzollerns passed successfully, it was decided there should be a second one hosted by the Kaiser. Wishing to show his good will toward the more ancient, if less powerful, branch of the ruling house of Germany, Wilhelm II chose as the site the Burg Hohenzollern. One of the ancestral homes of the dynasty, it was shared equally by all members of the clan and seemed an ideal spot for another family gathering.

Rising suddenly and dramatically out of the flat plains of Swabia, the castle dates back to the eleventh century. By the time Missy saw it, however, it had been restored with so much false Gothic that its position—looming out of the fog—was its most impressive feature. To enter this bastion of battlements and parapets, it was necessary to negotiate a nearly perpendicular spiral road. Greeted by two life-size stone guards in medieval battle dress, the Edinburghs had to pass over a drawbridge, through a long, dark tunnel and under a defense tower before arriving at the castle itself. Once inside, the sterile military architecture was relieved suddenly and improbably by a fanciful, green-leafed family tree sprawling from floor to ceiling of the entryway. Clearly the Burg Hohenzollern was maintained less as a residence than a family memorial. No one, in fact, had ever lived there.

The castle was filled with innumerable reminders of Ferdinand's illustrious ancestors—portraits, tapestries, uniforms, flags, and sarcophagi. Unmoved by all the panoply, Missy was upset by her fiancé's reaction at one banquet to a toast offered by the King of Roumania. The King rose to speak, "superbly aware of his importance" in the lives of Missy and Ferdinand. "Let me drink," he said, looking at the young couple, "to your 'honey day' (*Honigtag*)."

Ferdinand turned pale. Although he raised his glass politely, his gaiety had been visibly punctured, and his hand was trembling. "Thoroughly miserable," he drew his fiancée into a corner as soon as the meal was over. "Did you hear?" he demanded, nostrils quivering.

"Hear what?"

"He said a '*Honigtag*.'"

"Well, why not? He seemed very kind and full of goodwill."

"Why not? Don't you understand what he means? He means that instead of a honeymoon he will only allow us a honey day! That's just how he is—he does not care for or understand other people's feelings. With Uncle it is all work and no play, year in and year out, all through the seasons. He never cared about a honeymoon for himself. . . he is all duty and no weakness and expects everybody to be the same. It's always like that; everything has to be sacrificed. He has no feeling nor understanding for the wants and desires of the young. When it is a question of state he is absolutely pitiless!"

At the time, her fiancé's tears of frustration confused Marie. "Later," she wrote, "I understood."

As soon as the German introductions were over, the Duchess of Edinburgh and Missy took Nando to meet her family in England. In spite of Ferdinand's shyness, his presentation to the Queen was negotiated successfully, thanks to Victoria herself. Missy's grandmother spoke to the young man in German of his parents and told him she always kept a picture of his mother in her personal apartments. (Like Missy's English grandparents, Princess Antonia was a Coburg.) When Ferdinand committed the social gaffe of breaking his breakfast roll into his coffee, the Queen announced that he must come to breakfast with her another day soon, so that together they could dunk their rolls "in the good old German fashion."

King Carol of Roumania also had a bad moment during the visit to Windsor. When Queen Victoria asked him if it was true that Ferdinand had been engaged to another girl before Missy, Carol prevaricated, saying that the romance had been nothing more than a figment of his wife's, Queen Elisabeth's, lively imagination. The Queen of Roumania was famous for her flights of fancy, and this was one time when her renowned peculiarities served her husband well.

The Crown Prince of Roumania in Windsor was like a child on holiday from school. Although King Carol took advantage of his visit to England to tour financial establishments, trying to raise foreign capital for Roumania's underdeveloped resources, his nephew refused to accompany him. "He was never in love himself so he does not understand; I am here to be happy— not to be dragged about looking at State institutions."

Missy was not as lighthearted as her fiancé. "All the time I had a sad little feeling... that Papa would be disappointed and perhaps others as well. My betrothed was a complete stranger, and... quite foreign to that life that was once mine, a stranger to all the beloved Malta atmosphere, to all, in fact, from which I had sprung. I felt a little bit of a traitor somehow, so that all Nando's loving ardour and Mamma's smiles and reassurances could not make me feel entirely happy... I hid my inner desolation as best I could, bracing myself for each new meeting; Papa, Grandmamma, all the uncles, aunts and cousins, with George in particular, George, most cherished chum of the beloved Malta days."

The meeting with Prince George took place in the broad curved corridor of Windsor under the eyes of their common family against a backdrop of beloved treasures, paintings, and statuary. "I have my best dress on... guests have arrived at the Castle, amongst others Cousin George. I believe Uncle Bertie was there also, but I only remember Cousin George.... It is the first time we meet since I have decided for the new harbour; since I have burnt my boats behind me. My heart is beating... I have always that sick feeling at heart that I am in some ways betraying all the things I had loved....

"'Well, Missy?' Cousin George is very kind and very sweet and I have a lump in my throat. We avoid speaking of the dear Malta days, for I could not have stood it just then, not at that moment when I had set my face towards a far, far land."

Missy, her mother, and sisters spent the summer and fall of 1892 traveling back and forth between England and Germany, where they were often joined by the Crown Prince of Roumania. Ferdinand clearly preferred meeting his fiancée in his native country. Although he wrote his older brother that Queen Victoria was "in general... very gracious toward me," he complained of "an air of envy and nastiness" at Windsor—doubtless due to family disappointment. Back in Coburg he pronounced himself "in seventh heaven with my dear little one."

The "dear little one" was less ecstatic. Careful to say and write all the correct things, Missy soon began to realize that she and Nando were not superbly matched. "My mother... was almost absurdly anxious that I should understand nothing about the realities of life," said Marie. "I was to be led utterly innocent up to the altar... But there were occasional moments when it suddenly came to me that Nando and I had not perhaps exactly the same tastes about everything."

Missy of Edinburgh was a child of England; physical prowess and winning at games (or losing with verve) were natural to her. Ferdinand, on the other hand, could not understand why, if they were out riding and it started to rain, she insisted on remaining in the saddle when he had the good sense to climb into a warm, dry carriage and leave his mount to those hired for that purpose. While sportsmanship was important to Missy, it was intellectual refinement that counted with Nando. He was surprised by her indifference to the superiority of German culture and did not hesitate to join the Duchess, Dr. Rolfs, and Cousin Charly in lampooning her adorable ignorance.

Despite rumblings of fundamental disparity, Missy played hard at the game her mother had set up for her. In answer to a letter from Queen Victoria, she wrote, "I will try and follow your good advice dear Grand'Mama and though my task may at first seem difficult, I am sure that both Ferdinand and the King will do all they can to make it easy for me. I am not at all frightened to go away so far, and to a land so different from what I have been accustomed to... I am rejoicing on seeing You now in a very short time, and I am delighted that Ferdinand can also come as of course I always feel very sad when we are separated."

Missy was attracted in a puppyish way to her fiancé. She exchanged kisses with him when they were together and answered his love letters when they were apart. These came at the rate of nearly one a day, reiterating the Crown Prince's loneliness and the conviction that never before had there been any two people who "loved each other more and were more happy than we two." Ferdinand told Missy that they "must show our dear parents how grateful we are to them that they... let us find each other and be so happy," and he promised his parents that he and his bride would be "good and obedient children."

When Missy admitted nervousness about the future, Nando tried to comfort her. "You write to me that sometimes you feel very sad at the thought that in a few months you shall leave your old home forever for a new and quite unknown one. Oh I understand the feeling so well, and I know it myself." "It will be indeed funny for you to have no Mama but then I shall try to be all for you... you shall be my baby and I shall guide you. Then of course my evenings will be no more dull as you are here and after I finish my game of billiards we can go to our rooms." A comically inarticulate lover, consumed by passion, the Crown Prince described himself as "jumping around like a mouse at childbirth... I have such great yearning and am so sentimental."

Before the Edinburgh Princess could marry the heir to the Roumanian throne, there was one more presentation required—to Queen Elisabeth of Roumania. King Carol's wife was the former Elisabeth of Wied, the girl whose artistic fancies had frightened off Missy's father thirty years before. Queen Elisabeth, whose pen name was Carmen Sylva, was currently living in disgrace in Germany, banished from Roumania by the King for her role in the Ferdinand–Helene Vacaresco romance. Missy was not told this. She was led to believe that the Queen of Roumania, temporarily invalided, would be unable to attend her wedding in person, and therefore she must call on the Queen at her family home in Germany.

Met at the door of the castle in Neuwied by an alarming assortment of the blind, the deaf, the dumb, and the lame, Missy soon discovered that Queen Elisabeth's mother was a psychic healer and that these people lived with her in hopes of miraculous cures. The old Princess of Wied herself was charming, hospitable, and an excellent conversationalist—until the Duchess of Edinburgh inquired about the health of her daughter, the Queen of Roumania. The mother threw up her hands and told them what a great burden Elisabeth was, how she had been lame or paralyzed or imagined she was for several months, how she could neither walk nor stand. "Ach! my Elisabeth is very fantastic... the real poet temperament, inclined to be tragic always, but now, alas, there has been enough to be tragic about."

"Shall we have the pleasure of seeing your daughter?"

"Ach, Gott, yes! She is prepared, she will receive you, she is painting in her bed, she is always painting. Sometimes it is poetry, only poetry, or then it's music, but now it is painting, and such large paintings, so difficult in bed. But Elisabeth likes difficulties."

Queen Elisabeth of Roumania had carefully arranged the setting for this first meeting with her unwanted future successor. The situation invited dramatization, and Queen Elisabeth was an enthusiastic tragedienne. Light poured down on the invalid, dressed in white, propped up among white pillows on her bed of pain to receive the "one who was usurping the place of the girl she had chosen." She clasped Missy to her breast and called her "*lieb Kindchen* [dear child]," while she allowed her eyes to cloud with emotion and ran her hands over Missy's young face and blond hair. Later the invalid was wheeled in to lunch in a high chair. Wrapped in white cashmere, her white hair flowing around her shoulders, she gazed down on the group "like some sort of high priestess expounding strange creeds too confusing for the ordinary mind."

The trip to Sigmaringen for Missy's wedding was made in great discomfort, since the Duchess of Edinburgh did not like saloon carriages and had refused all offers of more luxurious transport. The party traveled in old, rickety coaches, innocent of the most elementary creature comforts. Compartments were completely cut off from each other; there were no beds and no hot water. Missy and Ducky were billeted together and slept on a cold, dirty floor.

Bouncing along with her sister on the trip south, the bride must have had time to speculate on her uncertain future. Like other girls of her day, she was sexually unaware and uninformed. Unlike them, she could not rely on a rapport with her future husband. Much as Ferdinand loved her, his shyness and desperate need to please his elders kept him from building any emotional bridge between them. A beautiful young Princess-bride, Missy should have been at her loveliest on her way to the fairy-tale castle in the snow. But her blue eyes, normally bright with fun, were dimmed by the prospect of the unknown and a new docility, brought on by Nando's worried looks.

Although Marie tried in her best English manner to put a gallant face on the proceedings, she appeared "small, awkward and lost" throughout the many banquets, receptions, and balls in her honor. All dressed up in new gowns and beautiful jewelry—her mother gave her many of her own Russian stones—she had nothing to say to the overwhelming company of royalties and future subjects gathered to greet her. The Duke of Edinburgh certainly did nothing to liven things up. A few days before the wedding he called Missy into his apartments to tell her about her dowry of one million French francs. Taking her in his arms, the Duke burst into tears, explaining that he had cherished other dreams than this for her future.

Of the many royalties present, the most important was Kaiser Wilhelm II, who arrived with "an embarrassingly numerous suite composed of embarrassingly huge gentlemen in blazing uniforms." The Kaiser changed uniforms as many times each day as the ladies changed their gowns and with the same attention to sequence of colors. This display climaxed in a grand nighttime finale, when the Kaiser burst forth in blazing white with huge gauntlet gloves, boots polished to a shimmer, and a "Lohengrin-like" helmet topped with an eagle. His aides, being tall and handsome, looked far better in their uniforms than the All Highest himself. Cousin Willy's white knight was more of the comic-opera variety.

On the morning of January 10, 1893, Missy was awakened by the sound of wedding bells. It was a cold wintry day. The ceremony was celebrated three times—civil, Catholic, and Protestant. The Catholic ceremony was the most impressive, as Ferdinand was devoted to his faith. The service was interminably long, but the bride took some comfort in the monotonous Latin chants. "They enveloped me in a sort of protective trance which calmed fear and allowed hope to filter into my anxiously throbbing heart."

The Anglican rite took place in a small anteroom of the Ancestors Hall of Sigmaringen Castle. It was conducted by a chaplain of the British Navy. Missy passed through the ceremonies and wedding banquet "as though it were a dream, a very far-off dream in which I played a dream part."

The dream Princess was gowned in heavy, corded white silk with the stiffly belled skirt and exaggerated sleeves of the early 1890s. Her gown was embroidered in pearls, crystals, and tiny silver sequins. Because she disliked lace veils, she was permitted to wear tulle, caught by a diamond tiara wrapped around a small wreath of orange blossoms. It was the only concession granted. Otherwise Missy's own romantic ideas of bridal finery lost out to the ponderous taste of her mother. In her memoirs she described herself as a "thin, flat little maiden with very fair hair frizzled Queen Alexandra–wise on the forehead" and said she felt she lacked the dignity to live up to the overpowering weight of her clothes and the occasion.

Nor did she have any reactions of a happy bride off on a honeymoon. Ferdinand's father gave them the hunting castle of Krauchenwies in the woods not far from Sigmaringen for their seclusion. A friendly house as castles go, Krauchenwies is only two stories tall and built in the shape of a U. With its yellow walls, green shutters, and faded red roof, it was, wrote Marie, "more picturesque than comfortable, but quite a romantic setting for a honeymoon." But the hours and days, as indicated by the great clock over the entrance, passed achingly slowly for the new bride. "It was winter, we were shy and still strangers to each other and there was absolutely nothing to do. Nando was not a man of high spirits, nor was he imaginative, so he was quite at a loss how to entertain so childishly young a wife."

Physically too, the honeymoon was a failure. Missy left her marriage bed disillusioned, lonely, and in search of storybook romance. Nando left feeling awkward and boorish. Marie's own delicate explanation was that her husband "was terribly, almost cruelly in love. In my immature way I tried to respond to his passion but I hungered and thirsted for something more... There was an empty feeling about it all; I still seemed to be waiting for something that did not come." Years later she told a friend, "I married so young, nothing in me had awakened... marriage came as a bad shock to me and I could but very slowly adjust my... mind... to accept it."

Before embarking on the long journey to Roumania, Missy was allotted a few days in Coburg to say goodbye. The night before her departure she was ill. The Duchess, who refused to recognize even a possibility of weakness or sickness in her daughter, sent her to bed early and came to kiss her good night.

"We both tried to be brave; I knew that Mamma disapproved of outbursts of sentiment... so I swallowed down every cry of fear and grief that welled up within me at the thought of tomorrow's farewell. I did give her an extra hug, though, but no word was spoken."

The Duchess left the room to give a few words of last-minute advice to her new son-in-law. Missy didn't try to listen to their conversation, but did hear her mother say, "'I must just have a last look at her...' and there, peeping round the edge of the door, was her dear face and tears were actually running down her cheeks! Seeing I was awake, she managed a brave smile, and we nodded to each other; I longed to throw my arms round her, to nestle my face against her damp cheeks and have a good cry, but Spartan training made all such effusion impossible.... I did not dare, so we simply smiled at each other and of course I was not supposed to have seen the tears. But for months and months afterwards, devoured by loneliness and homesickness in that far land, the vision of Mamma's brave face all wet with tears, peeping round the corner of the door, came back again and again, filling me with intolerable pain... so that often I had to smother my mouth in my pillow not to call out with grief and longing—Mamma... Mamma ... Mamma!"

1

Queen Victoria, Prince Albert and their five older children, 1846, in the famous painting by Winterhalter. Prince Alfred (Affie, the Duke of Edinburgh), father of Marie of Roumania, is the child standing in a skirt on the left. The Prince of Wales (Edward VII) is next to the Queen; the Princesses Alice and Victoria are admiring baby Helena.

2

Tsar Alexander II (seated left), Tsarina Marie Alexandrovna (seated right) and their six children in the Winter Palace, around 1871. Their only daughter, Grand Duchess Marie, the mother of Marie of Roumania, is standing among her brothers. Seated in the middle is Marie Feodorovna (Dagmar), wife of the future Tsar Alexander III, with her son, the last Tsar, Nicholas II. She and her sister, Alexandra, wife of the future King of England (Edward VII), introduced Marie of Roumania's parents to each other.

3

Marie of Roumania's parents, Prince Alfred of England (the Duke of Edinburgh) and Grand Duchess Marie of Russia, in a classical Victorian engagement picture, 1873.

The four older children of the Duke and Duchess of Edinburgh, 1882. "Missy" (Princess Marie) is seated on the right, next to her older brother, Prince Alfred. "Ducky" (Princess Victoria Melita) is seated in the foreground, while "Sister Sandra" (Princess Alexandra) is seated in back. "Baby Bee" (Princess Beatrice) was not yet born.

4

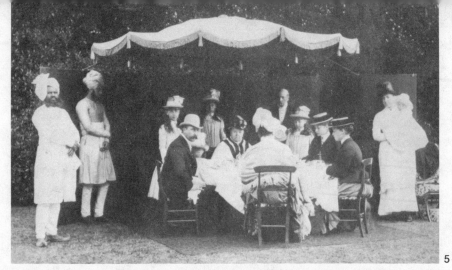

Missy and her sisters visiting their grandmother, Queen Victoria, at Osborne in 1887, when Missy (standing left) was twelve. The Queen (seated center) had breakfast and tea served on the lawn under a gigantic beige umbrella, fringed in green. She was usually attended by white-turbanned Indians, gray-and-green-kilted Scotsmen, and one or two of Missy's nervous aunts.

The Duchess of Edinburgh and Missy, 1887. Missy's mother was "the ruling sovereign of her household, the one who...let you feel that the power over good and evil was hers."

"Cousin Charly," Princess Charlotte of Saxe-Meiningen, 1885. The Kaiser's sister, a constant visitor when Missy was a child, would attempt to sabotage her throughout her life.

8

Great-uncle Ernst and Great-aunt Alexandrine, the Duke and Duchess of Coburg, 1893. Alexandrine always referred to her degenerate husband as "der Lieber, Gute Ernst [Dearly Beloved, Good Ernst]," but he treated her "as no one else would dare to treat a servant."

9

Fraulein von Truchsess, governess to the Edinburgh Princesses. Fraulein was in league with the children's tutor, Dr. Rolfs, to turn them forcibly into good little Germans.

10

A family gathering in Coburg in 1890 on the occasion of Missy's brother Alfred's coming of age. On the left is Uncle Bertie, the Prince of Wales (Edward VII), and on the right, Missy's father, the Duke of Edinburgh. Missy is in front of him; behind her is Cousin George. Missy's mother, the Duchess of Edinburgh (center) was determined to prevent George from marrying Missy.

11

The Duke of Edinburgh with his son, Prince Alfred (foreground), and his nephews, Prince George of England (center) and Grand Duke Ernst of Hesse, Coburg, 1890. The Duke wanted Missy to marry George and Ducky to marry Ernie.

Crown Prince Ferdinand of Roumania. A shy and frightened young man, he was forced to break off his first engagement to one of Queen Elisabeth of Roumania's ladies-in-waiting. After he became engaged to Missy, he promised his parents that he and his bride would be "good and obedient children."

12

14

Princess Antonia of Hohenzollern-Sigmaringen, Missy's future mother-in-law. Born an Infanta of Portugal, she lived "in a small circle of rules, prejudices and conventions... hedged in by her Church, nursing her delicate health, everybody serving her, caring for her, spoiling her."

Prince Leopold, Missy's future father-in-law, in his robes of the Black Eagle. The Head of the House of Hohenzollern-Sigmaringen, he was King Carol I of Roumania's older brother.

13

15

The official engagement picture of Princess Marie of Edinburgh (Missy) and Crown Prince Ferdinand of Roumania, 1892. Standing from left to right are Ferdinand; his father, Prince Leopold; and her father, the Duke of Edinburgh. Seated are Missy; her mother, the Duchess of Edinburgh; and King Carol of Roumania, the groom's uncle.

The Princess of Wales (right) set the styles for a generation of ladies, royal and otherwise. The gowns in Missy's trousseau (inset of sketches as they appeared in *The Illustrated London News*) were more flattering to Aunt Alix than to Missy.

16

17

18

Sigmaringen Castle in southern Germany, Ferdinand's family home. Pictured at right is the all-important Hall of Ancestors.

19

20

Missy on the day of her marriage to
Crown Prince Ferdinand of Roumania.
Her husband kept this picture in its gold
frame on his desk throughout his life.

PART THREE

The Crown Princess

Chapter 4

s the honeymoon train pulled out of Coburg station,
the new Crown Princess of Roumania gave in to despair. Unaccustomed to
depression, Missy wanted to confide in Lady Monson, one of her mother's
ladies-in-waiting sent along to accompany her. Having been raised by a woman
who represented herself as the ultimate authority in everything, the seventeen-
year-old bride was lost when separated from the source of wisdom. She needed
to fill the void with another mentor, but her husband disapproved. Ever since
his experience with Helene Vacaresco, he had weaned himself forcibly from
the luxury of trust. Missy would be allowed no intimacy but his.

Their journey was interrupted by an official visit to Vienna where the
young couple were to pay their respects to the Austrian Emperor, Franz
Josef. Everything in Missy's new life was now to be done with a purpose—
King Carol's purpose. This visit was aimed at strengthening the ties between
little Roumania and the vast Austro-Hungarian Empire, still in 1893 one of
the powers that controlled Europe. There was also a personal reason.

Five years earlier Franz Josef had referred to King Carol as a "vain and short-sighted gasbag." As proof of Carol's mismanagement of Roumania, the Emperor pointed to the King's negligence in providing heirs to his throne. That was in 1888, one year before Ferdinand was officially declared the heir apparent. Now that Ferdinand was married to a granddaughter of Queen Victoria, and a beauty at that, it was obvious that Carol knew very well how to manage dynastic affairs. This, he knew, would not be lost on Franz Josef.

During the visit Marie was the guest of honor at a state dinner at the Hofburg Palace. "The table," she reported "was one mass of beautiful flowers and superb gold plate; we ate off exquisite, rare old china; there was excellent music and a great deal of light." The light at the Hofburg was provided by elongated silver-and-crystal chandeliers that crashed down with some regularity, endangering the Emperor's guests. Another risk of dining at the palace was hunger. Since Franz Josef hated small talk, he had his staff trained to serve and clear a twelve-course feast in less than an hour— the next course being brought in the moment the Emperor finished eating the last one. This often resulted in guests at the bottom of the table finding their plates whisked away before they had a chance to attack them. Seated next to Franz Josef, Marie noticed none of this. For her the evening was spoiled by the embarrassment of a large grease stain on her pale-pink gown.

Emperor Franz Josef regarded the new Roumanian Crown Princess with interest tinged with pity. "You sent something much too beautiful to Roumania. I don't understand how the Duchess of Edinburgh could make up her mind to do so," he told Lady Wallpurga Paget, wife of the British Ambassador, during the evening.

Lady Paget: Perhaps, as a Russian, she feels more sympathy with those semi-barbarous people than the German mind is capable of feeling.

Franz Josef: Semi-barbarous—they are unfortunately much too civilized. Politically we cannot be sufficiently grateful to the Duchess of Edinburgh.... I only trust the King of Roumania won't wish to governess them too much. I don't like the young couple living in the same palace with him.

Lady Paget: I suppose he feels lonely and I fear the Queen's illness shows no sign of amendment and that her legs are quite paralyzed.

Franz Josef: She is stark mad...

When Franz Josef said that the Austrians could not be sufficiently grateful to the Duchess of Edinburgh, he was expressing more than courtly courtesy. He was voicing a hope, common to many lesser Europeans, that Marie's presence in the Balkans would ease international tensions. Contemporary opinion, as expressed by a pair of English commentators, was optimistic on the subject. "It is the Duchess to whom belongs the credit of having negotiated the marriage between the Crown Prince of Roumania and her eldest daughter, Marie—a matrimonial alliance that will contribute more than anything else to the peaceful settlement of the ever-smoldering Eastern question... It invests the court of Bucharest with ties of close and intimate relationship with that of Russia and of Great Britain, which cannot fail to impart strength and solidity to the hitherto perilous Roumanian throne."

This attitude was echoed with enthusiasm by the Roumanians. Their new Crown Princess was the niece of the Tsar, whose army had always threatened Roumania. She was also the granddaughter of the Queen of England, whose might had for years stood behind Roumania's other historical enemy, the Sultan. Moreover, Marie's lineage and wealth removed her from any temptation to engage in the political and financial intrigues that had plagued Roumania since her earliest beginnings.

The history of the Roumanian people starts in the district of southeastern Europe called Dacia, whose inhabitants were conquered by the Romans under Trajan in A.D. 101.* This date is usually assigned as the beginning of Roumanian history, since the name "Roumania" was thereafter used to describe that particular portion of the Roman Empire. The Roumanians (at least in their pre-Communist days) took enormous pride in what they considered their pure Roman descent and Latin-based language, but they themselves were actually the result of a century and a half of Roman legionnaires impregnating Dacian women, followed by hordes of barbarians—Goths, Huns, Bulgars, Slavs, and Tatars—doing the same.

The political history of modern Roumania begins about the end of the thirteenth century when the Vlachs, as the mixed populace was now called, inhabited two principalities on the Danube River known as Wallachia and Moldavia. Both fell to the Turks, who did not, however, interfere with their Christian religion or their native dynasties. Princes, called hospodars, followed each other in rapid succession. They rarely lasted long and usually died before their time, since the sole qualification for a royal title was sufficient funds to buy it from the Sultan. In return for his rank, the hospodar rendered tribute back to the Sublime Porte.

The most infamous of these hospodars, Vlad IV, called Vlad the Impaler, lived in the fifteenth century. Incorrectly credited by history as the model for Dracula, Vlad was a savage warrior against Turks and corrupt officials.

---

*The Roman victory over the Dacians was commemorated in a triumphal column erected in Trajan's Forum in Rome; the figures carved on the column wear clothing like that worn by the Roumanian peasants of the twentieth century.

His specialty was impaling without killing quickly, and he often dined outdoors surrounded by his screaming victims dangling from their stakes.

The most famous hospodar was Michael the Brave, who succeeded in uniting the three provinces of Wallachia, Moldavia, and Transylvania in 1600. The unification of this triple kingdom, which corresponds roughly to present-day Roumania, lasted less than a year, but it served as inspiration for centuries of Roumanians. Three hundred years later, in 1918, the three territories were once again joined under a single autonomous government— an achievement for which Queen Marie can be given much of the credit.

After 1711, native Roumanians were no longer permitted to hold the title of hospodar in either Wallachia or Moldavia, and the privilege of purchasing princely sovereignty fell to a particularly grasping group of Greeks. Called Phanariots, they came from the Phanar (lighthouse) quarter of Constantinople and served as the Sultan's bankers. Predictably worse than their Roumanian predecessors, the Phanariots exploited the native population in direct proportion to the fabulous sums they had to bid to buy the throne and the speed with which they had to recoup their investment. In the words of an Italian envoy, "the land sweated blood."

The Phanariot prince kept a representative, called a Bash-Kapukihaya, to watch over his interests in Constantinople. This meant distributing baksheesh (Turkish bribe) in meaningful places to counter the intrigues of the representatives of other would-be princes. If he negotiated poorly and lost the throne for his prince, the Bash-Kapukihaya tried to warn his master in time for the prince to empty the treasury before the arrival of his successor. Paintings of Phanariot princes show swarthy potentates dressed in long velvet mantles trimmed with fur and fastened with jeweled clasps. Some wear turbans with diamond aigrettes, others high fur bonnets. "What is remarkable about these despots," wrote an eighteenth-century historian, "is that all their riches, money, jewels, hoards and furnishings, are always in trunks and travelling coffers, as if they had to leave at any moment."

The Roumanian boyars (landed gentry) were forced to prove submission to the current Greek prince by carrying him in their arms from room to room, even from bed to chair. During the prince's siesta all traffic, business, church bells, and audible voices were silenced. The local aristocracy, required to submit to these indignities, took out its frustration and greed on the peasants. The lot of the Roumanian peasant was so miserable, the tribute exacted so exaggerated, that he was known to kill his cow or destroy his house to avoid paying the cow tax or the so-called chimney tax. By skimming off all the profit from their labors, the Turks destroyed the Roumanians' motivation to work, and the rich resources of the principalities remained undeveloped. Wallachia and Moldavia, one Russian general noted, were "favoured by nature, but persecuted by fate."

The Turks were not alone in exploiting the Roumanians. From 1768 to 1854 Wallachia and Moldavia were overrun by Russia six different times.

As the Turks struggled to maintain the profitable *status quo* against the Russians, the Austrians, who had already appropriated the Moldavian province of Bukovina, schemed to add the rest of Moldavia and Wallachia to their possessions. The Austro-Hungarian Empire coveted all of Roumania in spite of the fact that it was already having serious trouble with the Roumanians living in the Hungarian province of Transylvania.

Transylvania, a natural alpine fortress of agricultural and mineral wealth encircled by protective mountains, had been settled by the same Dacians who farmed the neighboring provinces of Wallachia and Moldavia. So rich was Transylvania that when Trajan conquered it, he made off with enough gold to cancel all taxation in the Roman Empire for one year and bestow a gift of 659 denarii on every Roman citizen. When the Romans fell before the invading hordes moving westward, the Daco-Romans retreated into caves, emerging to farm their meadows hidden away high in the Transylvanian Alps and to mine the salt and gold from their mountains.

These Daco-Romans were eventually overrun by the Magyars, whose nomadic ancestors had swept out of Asia. Finding the province thinned out by centuries of invasion, the Magyar kings encouraged settlers. By the middle of the fifteenth century, there were three recognized groups of citizens in Transylvania: the Magyar nobility, the Hungarians of the mountains, and the German townspeople. Only the Roumanians, the descendants of the original Daco-Romans who comprised the bulk of the population, were disenfranchised and prohibited from practicing their Orthodox religion. Although they enjoyed one hundred and fifty years of independence from Hungary starting in the middle of the sixteenth century, the Transylvanians fell under Austrian rule at the end of the seventeenth century, and the Roumanians of Transylvania spent the next hundred and fifty years struggling against the Magyars for their rights.

From the middle of the eighteenth to the middle of the nineteenth century, the Roumanians—Wallachians, Moldavians, and Transylvanians alike—were trapped, spiritually between East and West and geographically between the three great Eastern Powers of the day: Turkey, Russia, and Austro-Hungary. A brief look at a map of southeastern Europe illustrates their predicament. Seen together, Wallachia and Moldavia form a backwards letter L, with the plains of Wallachia, the east-west province, lying under and to the west of the more mountainous terrain of Moldavia, which runs north and south. Surrounded by great empires, guarded only by the Danube to the south and the Prut to the east, the Wallachians and Moldavians were cut off from their Transylvanian brothers by the 8,000-foot peaks of the Carpathian Mountains. Unprotected by natural frontiers, blessed with fertile soil, pine-laden forests, and important mineral wealth, Roumania was an easy and tempting conquest.

Geographically defenseless, the Roumanians developed an unerring instinct for survival and a high degree of intellectual sophistication. Respect for French culture, introduced by the Phanariots, led to the practice of sending the sons of the aristocracy to Paris for their education. Echoes of the February Revolution in Paris (1848) reverberated through Roumania as Roumanian intellectuals agitated for independence and the unification of Wallachia and Moldavia.

After the Crimean War (1853–1856), Wallachia and Moldavia were placed under the collective guarantee of the six nations* represented at the Congress of Paris, and elections were ordered to determine their future governments. In the second of two plebiscites (the first was so corrupt it had to be discounted), the Roumanians voted unequivocally for the unification of Wallachia and Moldavia; at the same time an international commission unanimously recommended joint government for the two principalities under a foreign prince. Ignoring both the will of the people and the findings of their own commission, the Great Powers, motivated by their respective imperialistic designs, ruled that each principality was to be governed by its own native prince and maintain a separate legislature. But the Powers left a loophole in their scheme for keeping Wallachia and Moldavia separate and powerless; nowhere did they specifically state that the two principalities could not vote in the same prince. This they did, electing Colonel Alexander Ion Cuza to serve as their common leader. On December 23, 1861, Cuza proclaimed, "The Roumanian nation is founded." A native son, Cuza was required to pledge to abdicate should the opportunity arise for closer union under the rule of a foreign dynasty. "Gentlemen," said the foresighted Prince at the time of his election, "I fear you will not be satisfied with me."

Well-meaning but self-indulgent, Cuza's lack of experience made him an easy mark for parasites and crown followers. His poorly planned land reforms earned him the hatred of boyar and peasant alike; he gave away concessions that enabled foreigners to exploit Roumania's resources; and his private life was considered scandalous in a society practically free of moral restrictions. Power quickly corrupted Cuza, and by the end of his reign he functioned almost entirely at the mercy of dishonest advisers. Government finances were nonexistent; salaries went unpaid. The much-hoped-for union of Wallachia and Moldavia, which should have simplified the government, only increased its instability. The Conservative and Liberal parties were forced to band together to depose Cuza. While the other conspirators organized a coup, the leader of the Liberals and Roumania's first statesman, Ion Bratianu, journeyed to Western Europe in search of a foreign prince. The scion of a powerful royal house, it was hoped, would bring prestige to the new political entity; moreover, a wealthy foreign prince would be above local clan intrigues.

*Austria, Britain, France, Russia, Sardinia, and Turkey.

The take-over itself was easy, thanks to Cuza's choice of companion for the night, a lady whose identity had to be shielded. When a group of prominent army officers entered the palace around midnight, they found the Prince with his mistress. Since Cuza could not call for his guard or sound an alert, the officers were able to force him to sign an act of abdication on the spot. By the next morning a Regency had been proclaimed.

The Roumanian Assembly immediately offered the position of Prince of Roumania to the younger brother of the King of Belgium, but he was frightened off by the threats of the Powers. Their second choice, Prince Karl of Hohenzollern-Sigmaringen, was not so easily deterred. When the Provisional Government of Roumania proclaimed him their leader, he hurried through several countries in disguise in order to take up his new position.

It is not surprising that this particular prince was willing to cross Europe for a throne. Ambition had been bred into Karl by his ancestors. In the days of his grandfather, who ruled Schloss Sigmaringen with a Teutonic fist, the castle was not the seat of refinement that enchanted Missy's mother. It was a fanatically run household where the Prussian patriarch wound his watch every night at precisely 9 P.M. and by 10 P.M. all the inhabitants of the castle had fallen obediently into silence. From his grandfather, Karl learned promptness, will power, and moral rectitude.

This emphasis on righteousness, one of Prince Karl's least appealing traits, was offset by his most salient virtue, political acumen. Karl was good enough at what he did to make up for being a machine of a man. With her lands coveted by the empires of the East and her government in disarray, Roumania did not need a prince with charm or a sense of humor. What the country needed was what she got—an indefatigable taskmaster with enough patience and drive to guide her through her political birth and adolescent growing pains.

Prince Karl (later King Carol I of Roumania) was born in Sigmaringen in 1839, the second son of the reigning family of Hohenzollern-Sigmaringen. A plodding but retentive student, he was commissioned in the Prussian Army and stationed in Berlin. Karl is said to have enjoyed the high life of an officer in the capital, but from what we know of him, the availability of wine and women titillated him far less than proximity to power. In Berlin Karl enjoyed a close association with his cousins King Wilhelm I and Crown Prince Friedrich (Aunt Vicky's husband).

On Good Friday of 1866, Ion Bratianu arrived in Prussia to offer the Kingdom of Roumania to Prince Karl. Prompted by his ambitious father, Karl readily accepted, but told Bratianu that he could do nothing without the permission of his cousin the King. While Wilhelm I hesitated over allowing his kinsman to defy the Powers interested in suppressing Roumanian autonomy, Chancellor Otto von Bismarck called Karl to a secret meeting in which he advised the young Prince to bypass Wilhelm I.

"Proceed at once to the country, to the government of which you have been called!. . . you have no need for the direct permission of the King. Ask the King for leave—leave to travel abroad. The King (I know him well) will not be slow to understand, and to see through your intention. You will, moreover, remove the decision out of his hands, a most welcome relief."

Afraid of being recognized and stopped on the way, Prince Karl made his way across Europe in the discomfort of second-class accommodations. After a nervous train trip through Austria, a miserable passage up the Danube, and two days in a bumpy, dusty carriage across the Roumanian plains, the Prince reached his new capital of Bucharest. Greeted by enthusiastic citizens, he was escorted with some pomp to a house with a guard posted outside When Prince Karl asked where he was, he was told he had reached the royal palace. Looking at the building and thinking he had not heard correctly, Karl asked, "*Where* is the Palace?" His informant could only point in embarrassment to the low building that looked out on an undistinguished guardhouse and a gypsy camp, with its group of pigs wallowing in the mud.

Primitive conditions aside, the twenty-seven-year-old Hohenzollern Prince faced the gargantuan task of organizing a country left by the Turks no less than a century behind Western Europe. The peasants were hungry, angry, and illiterate; the aristocracy, greedy and unconcerned beyond momentary pleasures; the soldiers and police, proficient only in baksheesh and graft. The treasury was empty; the army, badly disciplined and ill equipped. There were no railways; communications were nonexistent.

To deal with these problems, Karl tried to secure recognition of his position from the Powers. There was no help from that quarter. Refusing to decide for or against him, the Congress of Paris left Roumania in diplomatic limbo and Karl under the nominal sovereignty of the Turks. The Sultan, arguing that the Hohenzollern Prince's presence in Roumania was illegal, immediately massed his soldiers along the Danube. Within a week of his arrival in Roumania, Prince Karl was forced to review his troops with the possibility of leading them off to war. The army was not encouraging. One battalion mutinied straight off, since there was not enough powder in its arsenal for more than a few rounds per soldier.

To calm the Turks, Karl made a trip to Constantinople, where the Sultan offered him a sword and a belt of diamonds and gold, receiving him with ceremonies usually accorded a head of state rather than a vassal of the Sublime Porte. Karl knew that the magnificence of his reception was due to his Hohenzollern parentage rather than his position of Prince of Roumania. When Ali Pasha offered him Turkish orders to dispense to Roumanian soldiers, the wily Prince graciously declined and gained the Porte's permission to strike his own medals for his own army.

Certainly Karl needed all the diplomatic cunning he could muster to steer Roumania through the shoals of international animosity. Apart from Turkey, it was Austria that had most strongly opposed the unification of Wallachia and Moldavia and now, because of Transylvania, continued to fight Roumanian autonomy. Transylvania had been incorporated into the Austro-Hungarian Empire the previous year (1865). Determined to gouge every trace of nationalism out of the Roumanians of Transylvania, the Hungarian Magyars intensified their political and religious persecution—a policy in which they were supported by Emperor Franz Josef. Although his new countrymen constantly agitated for war to save their three million kinsmen in Transylvania, Karl knew he was in no position to help anyone. "My sole task," he said, "is to revive by good administration a country which has been utterly ruined, morally and financially."

To do this he needed a constitution. By July 11, 1866, just fifty days after his arrival in Roumania, Karl had a document that paid lip service to the liberties of conscience, press, education, assembly, and equality under the law. The new Roumanian Constitution was a skillful work, designed to favor the aristocracy with an artificially large percentage of the vote. The only people not allowed (at least on paper) a say in their own destiny were the Jews, since only those "belonging to Christian persuasions" could be naturalized.

The Constitution settled the throne on Karl and his heirs; if he produced no offspring, the dynasty would fall to his brothers and their children. The Prince was appointed Commander in Chief of the Army. He was empowered to make treaties with foreign states; to be legal, however, the treaties must be approved by the legislature—a condition that Karl never felt the slightest obligation to fulfill. Legislative power was shared by the ruler and two houses of Parliament, a Senate and a Chamber of Deputies.

In 1869, at the age of thirty, Prince Karl set out to find a wife. Passing up Missy's mother, the sixteen-year-old Grand Duchess Marie, whom he met in Livadia, Karl returned to his fatherland, where his cousin Crown Prince Friedrich urged him to marry Elisabeth of Wied. Friedrich's wife, Vicky, was still determined to find Elisabeth a husband; if brother Affie hadn't found her attractive before, maybe Karl would now.

Elisabeth was already twenty-five, perilously close to spinsterhood, when Karl arranged to see her. They had met once before in Berlin when she tripped and fell down the palace staircase and he caught her. "I was sincerely glad to meet the Prince again," said Elisabeth of Wied, "for I was full of admiration for the adventurous spirit and strong sense of duty with which he had entered on his task in his new country. . . . I said to myself, he hardly knows me, he cannot love me, he only happens to have heard how well and carefully I have been brought up, and thinks I may prove the suitable companion, the fittest helpmate for him in the work he has set himself."

It was the idea of a mission in life that attracted Elisabeth. She accepted Karl's proposal, delivered the very day of their second encounter. The wedding was celebrated a month later, on November 15, 1869. The text chosen for the ceremony came from the Book of Ruth: "Whither thou goest, I will go..." After a three-day honeymoon they left for the Balkans. Met on her arrival in Bucharest with a 101-gun salute and cheering crowds, Elisabeth was thrown into panic: "One of the hardest things in the world [is] for a foreign princess to make her entry into the capital of her new country. The faces surrounding you show nothing but a cold curiosity."

When Missy arrived in Bucharest to confront a similar scene twenty-four years later, Queen Elisabeth, the only person who could—not necessarily would—have helped her, was not there, banished by a husband who had long ceased to trust her. The relationship of Karl and Elisabeth hit its high point the evening he proposed to her. After that it plummeted.

As did Karl's popularity in Roumania. Financial repercussions from the Franco-Prussian War (1870–1871) undermined Roumania's grain exports and her economy. At the same time Karl's pet project, the building of railways, came under suspicion when government officials were caught mishandling the funds raised through bond sales. While antidynastic agitators spread tales of malfeasance in high places, the Queen of England and the Crown Princess of Prussia, safe in their imperial bastions, looked eastward in self-satisfied horror:

"I believe Charles Hohenzollern's affairs are going on as badly as possible—" Vicky wrote her mother, "he makes one mistake after another which I suppose he cannot help, cannot keep a single German or reliable person about him—and is said to be very much out of spirits." The Queen agreed. "I am very sorry indeed for the bad accounts from Roumania.... How can any people long for such thrones?"

Almost unseated by the Francophile Roumanians during the economic crisis created by the war, Karl developed a method of ruling based on distrust of both his government and his people. In this system Karl used the battles between the Liberals, who represented emerging middle-class materialism, and the Conservatives, the party of the landed gentry (in Roumania no one spoke for the peasants), to play them off against each other. Since it was customary to change the entire personnel of the government when a new party came to power, it was easy for Karl to placate the incoming faction with "access to the manger" while pursuing policies based purely on his own judgment.

In 1877 Prince Karl seized on the last of the Russo-Turkish Wars* to wrest Roumania's independence from Turkey and win the title of King for himself. In the ten years he had commanded the Roumanian Army, he had whipped a dispirited rabble into a crack fighting force. Now, as the Tsar and the Sultan stalked each other for battle, Karl concluded an agreement with Russia allowing the Russian Army to cross freely through Roumanian territory. At the same time, he declared his country's independence from the

---

*See Chapter One.

Sultan and entered the war voluntarily on the side of the Tsar. Fighting under Karl, the combined forces of Russia and Roumania won the decisive battle of the war, defeating Osman Pasha at Plevna. Both the Tsar and the Kaiser decorated Karl after his monumental victory. The biggest prize of all, however, was the full independence of Roumania, granted by the Congress of Berlin, which met to draw up the terms of the peace in 1878.

As the price of independence, the peacemakers forced two provisions on Roumania that left her feeling, much like Russia, that she was badly treated in Berlin. In the first place, Roumania was required to cede the fertile territory of southern Bessarabia, the richest part of Moldavia, to Russia. In return for Bessarabia, Roumania was given the arid wastes of the Dobruja, a much less desirable area bordering the Black Sea, known in history as the setting for Ovid's exile. Russia, according to England's Lord Derby, "turned a devoted and submissive ally into an enemy."

Secondly, before it agreed to recognize Roumanian independence, the Congress of Berlin insisted that Roumania enfranchise her Jews. The situation of this minority had long been a problem to the Western Powers, and this was their chance to force Roumania to change her anti-Semitic ways. Denied the vote, excluded from owning property, farming, making contracts, or selling food, the Roumanian Jews held mortgages and lent money in bad times at exorbitant rates. They were loathed by both landowners and peasants, who pressed Karl for further suppression. Prince Karl was no more anti-Semitic than others of his class—that is to say his anti-Semitism was as unquestioning and ingrained as most other aspects of his world view. For the Prince of Roumania, the question of enfranchising the Jews posed a problem in finances, not humanity. Karl feared that if he did not comply with the demand of the Congress, the rich Jews of Western Europe would use their influence to stop the flow of much-needed capital to his developing country.

The Congress of Berlin forced Roumania to admit Jews to the franchise, but since a special act of Parliament was required for *each individual case*, citizenship was merely theoretical.* By forcing Roumania to comply nominally with their demands, the Powers, however well meaning, succeeded in redoubling the persecution of Jews in Roumania.

Having ceded Bessarabia with all the grace he could muster and having complied theoretically with the Powers' demands for the Jews, Prince Karl declared Roumania a fully independent kingdom and made plans for his Coronation. This event, which took place on May 22, 1881, was a moment of supreme triumph for the man who would henceforth be known as King Carol I of Roumania.

It was not a happy day for his Queen. Riding in a flower-bedecked coach,

*Because the compliance was so glaringly unjust, the Chamber of Deputies did vote the naturalization of nine hundred or so Jews *en masse*—families of the men who had fought for Roumania in the Russo-Turkish War and survived.

Elisabeth was noticeably strained. To quote an account of the day: "The lips of the Queen...seemed compressed and drawn together to repress a sob, which every moment threatened to escape her." What galled Queen Elisabeth was the King's nephew Ferdinand, recently advanced as the probable successor to the throne and riding opposite her in the state coach. Since her arrival in Roumania, the Queen had given birth to only one child—a daughter who died at the age of four—and Ferdinand was King Carol's replacement for the heirs his Queen had been unable to provide. The efforts to put a good face on her situation cut deeply into the Queen's reserves of good will.

After his Coronation, King Carol returned to serious concerns of state, the most urgent of which was the development of Roumania's backward economy. In this he was aided by Ion Bratianu, who had risen to the post of Prime Minister from a background in the merchant class rather than the landed gentry. Bratianu considered himself a political realist and built the Roumanian economy on the greed of a burgeoning middle class. During his lifetime he was Roumania's most prominent politician. He died before Marie's marriage to Ferdinand.

In 1884 the Constitution was changed to create a Royal Domain—lands whose revenues were paid to the Crown—making King Carol the biggest boyar of them all. These farms served as models of peasant housing, hygiene, and cottage industry. They also made a fortune for Carol I. Although he professed to like the peasants, the King did nothing to improve their lives. The Roumanian peasants had learned through centuries of exploitation the same instinct for survival as had their aristocratic owners. Distrusting innovation, they clung tenaciously to the land, the actual spot of their ancestors, and engaged in periodic uprisings serious enough to frighten the government into occasional agrarian reforms.

In foreign affairs King Carol continued to seek support for his kingdom from his German cousins in spite of the Roumanians' professed dislike of Germany. The King knew he needed a powerful ally. France, the natural choice of his countrymen, had not recovered from its loss of the Franco-Prussian War. The experience with Russia in 1878 left the King very bitter over Bessarabia. Britain was remote. And Roumania's relations with the Austro-Hungarian Empire constantly threatened to break down over the Roumanians of Transylvania.

In 1879 Bismarck made a new alliance with Franz Josef. Realizing he needed a geographical bulwark against the Tsar, Bismarck set out to court King Carol. Because of the Roumanian King's strong personal attachment to his fatherland and deep-seated fear of Russia, Bismarck gained him easily as an ally. In 1883 Carol signed a treaty with Germany and Austria-Hungary. By the terms of the treaty, both major powers promised Roumania support against aggression from any source. Roumania was responsible for helping

Germany and Austria, but only if the aggressor was Russia or Serbia. Italy joined in 1888.

The most important thing about the treaty was its secrecy. Only three men in Roumania knew of its existence: King Carol, Ion Bratianu (who died in 1891), and the Foreign Minister. There was only one copy of the agreement in the entire country, and it was locked up in Carol's private safe in his summer home in the mountains. No duplicate existed, not even in the Foreign Office.

In 1888 when the treaty was renewed, the King, still fearful of letting others in on his secret, took foreign policy completely into his own hands. Thus, while a generation of politicians promised revindication for the persecuted Roumanians of Transylvania, King Carol clung to an alliance with their Hungarian tormentors; while successive premiers and foreign ministers publicly pledged Roumania to neutrality, their King held a document which, under certain circumstances, committed Roumania to war against Russia and/or Serbia.

In 1889 Ferdinand was officially proclaimed the heir apparent. By 1893, when Marie journeyed to Bucharest, Roumania had been an autonomous kingdom for just fifteen years. It is not hard to sympathize with Queen Victoria's apprehension over what was going to happen to Missy in such an "insecure" country where the society was so "dreadful."

Chapter 5

Our youth is a long tale of abnegation.

—QUEEN MARIE OF ROUMANIA

*T*o all outward appearances, the girl on the train bound for the Balkans was just what a princess should be—a pretty blond cipher. At seventeen, Missy's pink cheeks were still too plump with youth for much character to show. Only her eyes, a penetrating ice-blue, hinted at internal strength.

The new Crown Princess's natural beauty was not enhanced by the fashions of the day. Curls pulled down over Marie's forehead in stylish imitation of the Princess of Wales only distorted the younger woman's more regular features. The cumbersome gowns of the 1890s hung loosely on her athletic figure. An observer might have said that Marie and her body had been lost in the preconceptions of her elders.

Her voyage across the bleak winter landscape of Eastern Europe was made in the stuffy splendor of King Carol's private carriage. Missy cried her way through the first day of the trip. Anxious to learn something about where she was going, she plied her husband with questions, but Nando, hopeless at descriptions himself, guarded her jealously from their traveling companions who might have satisfied her curiosity. "It was a long journey and the days too seemed long," the bride complained. As her normal high spirits ebbed under the strain, Marie found comfort in sleep.

Sweet and solicitous as he was, the Crown Prince had not grown more amusing in their several days of intimacy. Beneath his impressive uniforms Ferdinand was even more anxious about their life in Roumania than his bride. Desperately in love, comforting her tears and arranging her physical comforts, Ferdinand was unable to admit his concerns. He spoke to Missy in measured tones, allowing himself only premeasured ideas, and kept his thoughts to himself. What might have been a shared adventure became a dreaded ordeal as Marie prepared to make her formal entry into Roumania.

From the time the train crossed the border at Predeal, a resort town nestled under fifty-foot pines in the Carpathian Alps, and began its descent to the capital in the flat plains below, Marie and Ferdinand were overwhelmed by hordes of peasants gathered in the stations, cheering and clamoring for a glimpse of their new Crown Princess. Missy had no idea how she ought to respond to these short, swarthy men and women smothered in colorfully embroidered greatcoats, brandishing the red-yellow-and-blue flags of her new country. Nando didn't know what to do either. The timid young couple stood at the window of their train looking down blankly on all the curious faces staring up at them.

"We shall be arriving in half an hour, you had better dress," the Prince ordered his bride.

The Duchess of Edinburgh had chosen the clothes for her daughter's entry into Bucharest with the same disregard for congruity with which she had selected her husband. The violet-and-gold cape, lined with white fur and worn over a green velvet gown, was excellent protection against the winter cold, but the collar was so huge that Marie's head almost disappeared into its depths. The *pièce de résistance* provided by the Duchess was a tiny gold toque studded with amethysts; the hat was so "ridiculously small" that it too nearly disappeared in Missy's blond hair, which had been painstakingly frizzed up by her maids for the occasion. "Clothes," the Duchess had warned her daughter before sending her out on her own, "play a great part all over the world and more especially in Southern countries, so never forget to dress carefully for festive occasions, it belongs to a princess's duties."

As their train pulled into Bucharest station, the new Crown Princess tried her best to concentrate on the faces of the cheering soldiers. In their gray coats and long-plumed hats, they seemed less forbidding than the elegantly gowned women and top-hatted men gathered on the platform to greet her. But it was official Roumania Marie was expected to meet. Bucharest society waited impatiently to be presented.

The triumphant King stretched up his short arms to help the Crown Princess down from the train and held her against his chest. She could feel that he was trembling. The Mayor of Bucharest gave up trying to shout his welcoming speech over the roar of the crowd and had to content himself with a mute offering of the traditional bread and salt. Carol I led the bride into a reception salon, built for the occasion and decorated with pink and white roses. The government officials stepped up one by one to be presented to her. They were ranged in precise order, starting with the current Prime Minister, followed by the members of his Cabinet, the President of the Chamber of Deputies, the President of the Senate, representatives of the Orthodox Church, the army, the university, the law, and the police. As each stepped forward, he or his wife presented the Crown Princess with a bouquet, which she tried to pass quickly to someone standing behind her. "Rather bewildered" by the continuing cheers, overwhelmed by pounds of flowers that threatened to stain her new clothes, Marie began to comprehend her importance to the nation.

Outside the station the crowds were lined up several deep, and the windows, trees, and balconies were hung with tricolored flags. The black-and-gold state coach, "simply embowered in flowers," stood waiting behind six horses with huge colored plumes on their heads. Marie was handed in to the seat of honor next to the King; her husband was forced to sit alone. Preceded by mounted police and a detachment of cavalry, the royal family was drawn in procession to the Metropolitan (State) Cathedral for a *Te Deum* mass in honor of the new Crown Princess. Although she was relieved to take refuge in the dim interior, the heat was intense and the service lasted nearly an hour.

Marie was surprised that the state coach which took them to the palace was closed. Since the Duchess of Edinburgh had never allowed her daughters to ride behind glass, even in bitter cold, the Crown Princess thought they must be slighting the thousands of onlookers standing in the streets and hanging out the windows. Because of the densely packed crowds, she couldn't see much of Bucharest. This was just as well, for the capital of Roumania in 1893 was little better than an overgrown town. Although there were huge villas in the rich residential neighborhoods, the commercial center was largely unpaved and always muddy from the waters of the River Dimbovitza, on which the town was built.

Even the Calea Victoriei, the principal boulevard of the city and site of all the important buildings, including the royal palace, was so poorly paved that it was impossible to conduct any sort of conversation above the noise of the carriage as it rumbled over the rough cobblestones. Not that Missy had much to say. Catching sight of a Union Jack fluttering next to the flag of Roumania, the Princess realized that she was locked into a "glass case" with two men she barely knew—a stranger condemned to spend the rest of her life in this alien land.

The first sight of her new home did not cheer her. "Not a very imposing building, squat, low and of no distinctive style" was her description of the Palatul Victoriei, the Roumanian royal residence. It was an ordinary two-story structure covered in stucco with a mansard roof—a far cry from the palaces of Missy's childhood. Three-sided, built around a fountain, her new home was enclosed by a high iron fence where the sentries were stationed. Inside, beyond a red marble rotunda, were dim, high-ceilinged rooms paneled in black marble and dark woods. On the walls were religious paintings of tragedy and suffering.*

The Palatul Victoriei had one fine feature, a monumental staircase, and it was up these stairs that the King, clanking his sword, conducted Roumania's future queen. Black-eyed, black-haired schoolgirls with dark complexions and white dresses had been lined up on either side of the stairs to strew flowers before the blond Princess. Ferdinand, relegated once again to a position behind his uncle and his bride, seemed anxious to finish with the official ceremonies.

What most depressed Missy were her personal apartments, which she knew had been carefully arranged by her husband and his uncle in her honor. Their idea of interior design was heavy, somber, and self-consciously regal. Marie was ushered into "rich, dark, pompous, unhomelike, inhospitable rooms, all windows, doors and fixtures and nowhere a cosy corner, nowhere a fireplace, nowhere any flowers, nowhere a comfortable chair!" The King embraced her, made a little speech about happiness in her new home, and left. She sat down. Nando came over and put his arm around her.

"You are tired?"

"Yes, a little..."

"Those hateful official ceremonies?"

"Yes, they were rather long."

"You must have a rest now, there will be a big dinner this evening."

"Yes...a big dinner...."

The dinner for elderly ministers and their wives was followed next day by thirty-two peasant weddings timed to coincide with that of the Crown Prince and Princess. The grooms and their brides, who arrived in carts drawn by huge oxen with gilded horns, were presented with money by the King and the Crown Prince and were allowed to kiss the hand of their new Crown Princess. There was also a spate of charity balls. Missy wrote her mother that the charities of Bucharest hoped to "get a great deal" that season because of her. "I am such a new attraction for everyone that they all want to see

---

*Among these were several El Grecos, purchased by King Carol as part of a collection with no regard for their value. El Greco was then a forgotten artist, and the King had bought them along with some indifferent Italian paintings simply to cover the walls of his palace.

me. At the last ball, I rather felt like some show animal, but if it can give them any satisfaction in looking at me I really don't mind."

What she did dislike were the official parties given for her at the palace by King Carol. After a reception for one thousand, she complained about the "hideous lot of old uninteresting monsters" she was required to meet, commenting that after two solid hours of presentations, the room before her seemed only "a mass of grey and black greasy heads with black watery eyes and backs, and orders and white waistcoats." At a ball for two thousand, the King refused to allow her to dance with any of the young men, only with the old ones. "So at the end," the seventeen-year-old Princess wrote home, "I did not want to dance anymore."

Along with these entertainments there were gifts for the heirs to the throne: native embroideries, brightly flowered carpets, carved and painted chests, and icons from the peasants, as well as more elaborate presents from the aristocracy. From the ladies of the Liberal Party, currently out of power, Marie received a chased gold casket filled with money to start a worthy charity; from the Conservatives, a large silver centerpiece for the royal table.

Each group, regional and national, sent a representative to the palace with a present. There was even a delegation from the coachmen of Russia, a mysterious sect known as the Skoptzi. The Skoptzi neither drank nor smoked and, as proof of their ultimate devotion to God, had themselves castrated after siring two children. Hounded out of Russia for their fanaticism, they had become the coach drivers of Roumania. Huge blond eunuchs with hair cut like Dutch boys', dressed in long black cloaks sashed in pink or blue satin, the Skoptzi presented the Crown Prince and Princess with a silver platter.

But when Marie wasn't the living centerpiece for one of King Carol's formal functions, there was nothing for her to do. The King, afraid that the Crown Prince and Princess might ally themselves with one or another political party, had decreed that his heirs were to have no outside acquaintances. Ferdinand submitted meekly. Missy was informed that friends were dangerous. She and her husband were forbidden to visit private residences, including legations.

King Carol did not even trust Mme. Grecianu, the middle-aged woman he appointed as Marie's Roumanian lady-in-waiting, and she was allowed to come to the palace only when specifically invited by the King. Unlike other transplanted young royalties, Missy had not been permitted to bring a lady-in-waiting of her own age and nationality with her from home. Lady Monson, who served as lady-in-waiting to the Duchess of Edinburgh, had been allowed to accompany Marie, but only long enough to settle the Crown Princess in her new home and report on Bucharest society to the Duchess before returning to England. Lady Monson had lived abroad much of her life and was most enthusiastic about social life in the capital. But when she told Missy about the dinners and balls given for *her*—the magnificence of the homes, the wit of the guests, the elegance of the parties—the Crown Princess grew more depressed.

The Duchess's lady-in-waiting did take one afternoon off from society to visit Marie before going home to England. She found the Crown Princess collapsed in the middle of her boudoir, a "disastrous rococo room," surrounded by half-unpacked wedding gifts with which she was trying unsuccessfully to enliven her quarters. "Everything was out of place in this heavily pretentious setting; my dearest possessions took on a forlorn and reproachful aspect; they were as homesick as I was."

Lady Monson, "always voluble," rushed into Missy's room: "My dear child! you do not look very cheerful, and all your pretty things on the floor! Are you feeling seedy? You're so pale."

"Yes. I'm not feeling well, I can't understand what's the matter with me. I feel giddy, everything makes me sick, food disgusts me, and I, who never felt the difference of climate, cannot get accustomed to this one. Everything makes me feel sick; smells, noises, faces, even colours. I'm altogether changed, I don't recognize my own self!"

"Oh! but my dear, this is an excellent sign, how delighted everybody will be!"

"Delighted? Why? Because I'm feeling sick and miserable?"

"But, my dear, you surely know what it means when a young wife begins feeling sick?"

Missy did not know. "What should it mean?"

"You don't mean to say no one ever told you?" Lady Monson was incredulous.

"Told me what?" asked the frightened girl. "Told me what?"

The Englishwoman seated herself on the floor next to the Crown Princess and tried to explain the facts of life, emphasizing the importance of Marie's role in the future of her new country. Aware for the first time of her real function, Missy burst into tears and blurted out her miseries—her loneliness, her boredom, her confinement to the palace. Lady Monson offered little sympathy. These were no more than the expected vicissitudes of royal life. The Duchess of Edinburgh's lady-in-waiting advised Marie not to inflate small discomforts into major tragedies. Informed of his wife's condition, the Crown Prince advised her to write to her mother.

Part of Marie's problem was purely physical. Pregnant within two weeks of her marriage, she, who had never been unwell, was suddenly subject to nausea, fainting attacks, and severe headaches. "This condition, with the continuous throwing up is very trying and tiresome, but I guess one has to go through this," she wrote her mother-in-law. "I know, later the joy will be so great, that I will quickly forget all these little unpleasantnesses."

But the weeks crawled by "uniform, grey and depressing." Up early to breakfast with her husband, the Crown Princess spent her mornings alone while the Crown Prince visited his regiment. The palace was a somber zone of silence in the middle of the lively capital. Missy wandered from room to room, hall to hall, trying to fill the hours. Lunch and dinner were taken with the King and Nando, who discussed local politics and the army during meals and afterward smoked strong cigars that made her ill. The only other human contacts allowed the Crown Princess were her German maids and a language master, sent to the palace to teach her Roumanian. Apart from Mme. Grecianu, who was occasionally called in to sit with Missy while Ferdinand played his nightly game of billiards with the King, she was permitted to see and speak to no one else.

If King Carol allowed no one near the young couple, he himself rarely left them alone. He ate all his meals except breakfast with them and sat with them in their apartment after dinner. "It is not always very amusing," Missy wrote home, "but one must not be selfish, he has so little pleasure, and he likes so much to come to us." Once in a while the King left the newlyweds to themselves. ". . . we generally sit and kiss and are foolish till it is time for bed," Missy told her mother. ". . . we are. . . just as foolish as ever I can assure you. It is the best thing to be, if we were not childish together we would become two old creatures before our time as otherwise there is no fun here in any way. One might even call it a very tiresome life."

Having grown up in a large family, Marie did not know how to entertain herself. Used to abundant physical exercise—riding, tennis, ice skating—she had to content herself with promenades with the King and sedate carriage rides with the Crown Prince. Trained to jump out of bed very early, she was surprised by her husband's lack of energy. "He is a lazy old chap, my Nando," she confided to her mother. Even at 8 A.M., Missy had to prod the Crown Prince to face the day. "It is rather late," she admitted, "but as Nando told me beforehand it is not easy to get up here."

Knowing her mother would have little patience with complaints, Marie tried to make the best of things. Alone in her apartment, she wrote dutiful letters to Ferdinand's parents, reiterating her love for her husband and reassuring her mother-in-law that she was not endangering the future heir by "dressing too tight." In letters home she emphasized the King's kindness and Nando's love and concern. "You will not think that I am discontented will you?" she begged her mother shortly after her arrival in Bucharest. ". . . you must not think that I am depressed," she wrote a month later. "Sometimes perhaps I feel a little sad. . . But I assure you, I do not let myself go, anyhow I try hard not to and really when one has a husband like mine, it would be a sin to complain." But when Marie tried to describe the events of her days, she had nothing to report. "Give yourself a little trouble to write amusing descriptions of your life," the Duchess of Edinburgh admonished her daughter.

The first person to take notice of the Crown Princess was Mme. Grecianu, her Roumanian lady-in-waiting. Mme. Grecianu, who had raised three daughters herself, realized that the mother of the future ruler of Roumania was being subjected to a routine that was not only bad for her but perhaps damaging to the unborn heir as well. Armed with this, she approached King Carol. "Our Princess is moping, in her state of health this is not a good thing... It is not right that she should be exclusively left to her homesickness and to the company of her maids."

After lengthy deliberations with his ministers, the King decided that the best form of diversion, one which would not give Marie "undue illusions about freedom," would be a series of formal tea parties. These were organized like royal presentations, at which guests lined up on either side of an aisle through which the royalty advanced to a seat on a small dais; after everyone had made a low bow, individual guests were brought forward to be presented.

Marie's tea parties took place in a dark-red reception room decorated with paintings of King Carol at war and were attended by the middle-aged wives of eminent men. Because of her poor French, the Crown Princess dared not start a conversation. Moreover, Marie had never before seen ladies who wore makeup and did not know if they were proper. Worse was her physical discomfort. She felt ill when she tried to stand, but was humiliated by what she considered an unmentionable condition.

In the English court no one referred directly to pregnancy. The most that could be said was that a lady was "in a delicate health." This was never said in front of a child, which Missy was considered up until the day of her wedding. In Eastern Europe, courtiers did not suffer the same reticence. Marie was bombarded with questions that she was not only too embarrassed but too poorly informed to answer. One brave guest, surveying the Crown Princess dressed in a gown grown too tight across her waist, finally offered congratulations loudly and directly. "Your Royal Highness, since your condition is no longer a mystery, may we felicitate you upon it?" Marie burst into tears.

At Easter she gamely wrote her in-laws that "it does not help to be sad, and it is not right." Nevertheless, it was "very depressing to be so alone" at holiday time, particularly thinking "back to Coburg where they are all sitting together in our good old church." While Nando and the others went off to celebrate the Resurrection in the Metropolitan Cathedral, Missy, alone except for Mme. Grecianu, attended services in the German Protestant Church. In the middle of the Lord's Prayer, the girl who was carrying the hope of the country fell into a dead faint. Mme. Grecianu brought her home to King Carol, who was frantic at the thought that the fall had undone his plans for the dynasty. But Missy was sturdier than he imagined. When it became clear that nothing untoward had happened to the future heir, Mme. Grecianu took the opportunity to point out once again to His Majesty that something should be done to improve the life and state of mind of the Crown Princess.

After this there were a few outings to religious and military landmarks. On one of these, Marie was taken to visit Cernica, a monastery rising out of the huge swamp on which Bucharest itself is built. Cernica, with its gray-bearded monks in tall headdresses and thick black veils, fascinated Marie. Although they were "hideous," "dirty-looking," and smelled "most tremendously of garlic," their chapel was old and their gardens ran down to the swamp, filled at that time of year with waving reeds and wild yellow iris. "I sensed that behind the deadly ennui of the life I was condemned to live, there was something else... that might even be tinged with some of that poetry I had imagined I should find in this far land," she said.

In June the court moved to Sinaia, a fashionable resort of elegant hotels and tall alpine villas 2,900 feet high in the Carpathian Mountains. Here the rich boyars and their wives, joined by Western diplomats on assignment to the Balkans, fled the terrible heat and humidity of Bucharest in the summer. They rode, played tennis, or promenaded during the day and gambled in the casino at night. "An agreeable feature of this Casino," said the Canadian wife of a Roumanian naval commander, "was the absence of the shabby crowd which so often elbows the *élégantes* at Monte Carlo and similar resorts. Everyone was of the same world, and nearly all acquainted."

Everyone was acquainted except the Crown Princess, still in social quarantine. Sinaia was nonetheless a happy change. An outdoor girl, Missy took sustenance from the deep green forests of pine and the cool air of the resort. The alpine meadows were filled with wild flowers, which she and Nando picked together.

While a home was being built for them the young couple lived with the King at Castle Peles. Peles stands on a green knoll on what was once a wooded hill; in the days of the monarchy, it was reached by a romantic road winding through the pine trees with magnificent vistas of Transylvanian peaks in the distance. The setting of the castle was then and still is far more successful than its façade. As one visitor commented, "It is a vision of enchantment which, like some women, loses much of its attractiveness when you come up close." Aunt Vicky called Peles a "gimcrack affair." "Oh! dear," she wailed when King Carol showed her pictures of his castle, "to think of six million francs spent on so ugly a building."

A miscegenation of styles—German Renaissance, Neo-Gothic, Byzantine, and Transylvanian—the 150-room castle epitomized King Carol's taste. He was exceedingly proud of his creation and saw no inconsistency in a façade that featured a Turkish loggia directly above an alpine porch, the former outlined by Byzantine arches, the latter by a brown wooden balustrade. Turreted, pinnacled, and ornamented down to the last square meter, Peles had taken the King ten years to construct. He continued to fuss with it for the rest of his life, adding a room here or a terrace there, enclosing the reception hall, originally planned as an inside courtyard, with a retractable roof.

Inside, Castle Peles seemed to groan under the weight of too many columns, arches, and balconies. There was too much carving and gilding, too many escutcheons, crowns, and statues, and far too much furniture, mostly Gothic Revival. The public rooms were decorated in every conceivable style: a Renaissance dining hall, a Turkish room, a Moorish room, and a huge music room hung with glass chandeliers from Venice. Either through affinity of taste with his uncle or simple fear, Ferdinand hailed the throne room and library as "true works of art."

Like its master, the palace was dreary. The windows were made of stained glass. "Everything seemed to have been planned to shut out the sky, the sun," Marie complained. Even the interior color scheme—Queen Elisabeth favored old gold and moss green—added to the gloom.

Life at Castle Peles was not much of a holiday, for King Carol enforced the same rigid court schedule in the country as he did in Bucharest. Marie spent her days alone and her evenings watching her husband and his uncle play billiards. Fortunately, it was not too long before the Duchess sent Ducky from Coburg to amuse her sister. Although she still had to conform to the restrictions of the court, Missy now had someone her own age with whom to share her frustrations. Ducky also provided an excuse to explore the countryside.

While Marie was showing her sister the little she knew of Roumania, their mother was settling into a new role in Coburg. Uncle Ernst died that summer (1893), and Missy's father finally assumed his position as the reigning Duke of Coburg and Gotha. "For Uncle Alfred this is a difficult time," Aunt Vicky wrote her daughter, "he will have to give up dear old London for good, and devote himself to his German home and his new duties. But... Aunt Marie will love being No. 1 & reigning Duchess, I am sure."

With the new Duchess permanently ensconced in Coburg and wicked Uncle Ernst's mistresses out of the court, the old embarrassing social problems gave way to new financial ones. Uncle Ernst died leaving his economic affairs in disarray, and Missy's mother was forced to pay off her husband's inherited debts out of her own personal fortune. Liabilities notwithstanding, Aunt Vicky said that "the fortune is in fact a very fine one, & if properly managed and looked after, ought to be very large."

In October, just two months after her husband's accession, the new Duchess of Coburg traveled to Roumania to preside over the birth of Missy's child. "I hope that I can await my big day in Sinaia," the Crown Princess wrote her mother-in-law. "I would much rather have it that way, but until now, Uncle is very much against it. When Mamma comes, she has to convince him to give permission."

For King Carol all occasions, great and small, had to be subjected to painstaking study over possible political ramifications. The birth of a future heir was clearly no minor event. It was composed of endless decisions starting with the most propitious location—"doctors, wet nurses, dates, names, hours of the day, and even rooms." The King scrutinized each item, balancing the pros and cons and their future effect on the history of the nation. Everything was full of portent. There were traps lying in all directions to catch the unsuspecting.

Practical and high-handed, the Duchess of Coburg swept through the King's arrangements like the imperious Romanov she was. Not only had she borne five children herself, she was living in a home where there was no woman besides her daughter to share female prerogatives. While the exiled Queen Elisabeth of Roumania drove her mother mad in Neuwied, the Duchess reigned supreme at Castle Peles. Missy withdrew from the discussions, leaving Ferdinand buffeted between two of the most autocratic royalties of the day, battling over the birth of the first native heir to the Roumanian throne.

Even Queen Victoria entered the fray by recommending appropriate medical attendants. "I had terrible fights with Granny dear about an English. . . . nurse for you," the Duchess had written her daughter before her arrival, "but will not give up the admirable one I have already engaged and will bring her with me, instead of the old gossip Granny wants you to have." Along with the Russian nurse who attended Marie in this and future labors, the Duchess brought her own personal physician, Dr. Playfair, brother of one of Victoria's lords-in-waiting and hence acceptable to the Queen. Accompanying Dr. Playfair was a telegram from Missy's grandmother demanding that King Carol accept the English doctor's services: "We want to be on the safe side," the Queen directed, "so near the East you know . . . most uncertain."

Unsuspected by Missy, Dr. Playfair was actually the solution to a major conflict, a fight over the use of chloroform in the delivery of the child. In demanding the pain-killer for Missy, the Duchess of Coburg and the Queen of England were combating the religious and scientific beliefs of their day. Roumanian clergymen objected vehemently: women must pay in agony for the sin of Eve. Roumanian doctors agreed.

The subject was so delicate that the teen-age mother was kept in complete ignorance of both the controversy and Queen Victoria's role in it. Almost two years later, when she was visiting her grandmother in England, Missy was asked by the Queen if she had been given chloroform to help relieve the suffering of childbirth. "I felt the blood rush to my cheeks, felt my throat become dry," she reported. "Courage! Confess that you had been given a whiff of chloroform, that Mamma and the English doctor had insisted upon this. . . . And now for the scolding, for the sermon, for the expression of the royal lady's scorn; for Queen Victoria, no doubt, was a Spartan and would wholeheartedly despise me for my cowardliness. But what was my astonishment when I heard a sweet, crystalline peal of laughter, and Grandmamma . . . declared: 'Quite right, my dear, I was only given chloroform with my ninth and last baby, it had, alas! not been discovered before, and I assure you, my child, I deeply deplore the fact that I had to bring eight children into the world without its precious aid!'"

Missy's labor pains began at dinner and by one o'clock on Sunday morning, October 15, 1893, in the Great State Bedroom of Castle Peles, she had given birth to a son. The infant was named Carol after his great-uncle.

Furious at Dr. Playfair, who had the insensitivity to say that she had "a very easy time," Missy "felt like turning my face to the wall, unwilling to take up a life again in which such pain could exist." "Listen to the cannon," the Duchess cajoled, "think of how delighted the people will be when they hear the hundred and one salutes." But the Crown Princess was indifferent to the hopes of the Roumanians. Insulated from the people, she felt no joy in giving them a prince. She felt more like the helpless victim of a conspiracy in which Nature and those who supposedly loved her had taken part. She was not mistaken.

Chapter 6

Oh, I was meant to be a mother!

—QUEEN ELISABETH OF ROUMANIA

*W*ithin three months of the birth of her son, the Crown Princess of Roumania was pregnant again. She was very unhappy and grew "thin as a thread." Pregnancy was never easy for Marie. She felt personally responsible for being sick and fat: "One feels so humiliated at being so ugly," she wrote her mother. "I don't know if all women suffer so much under it as I do! Perhaps it is not right but I cannot help it."

She also began to speak openly about the restrictions placed on her life. Her mother's visit had given Missy courage. Angered by the routine King Carol imposed on the Crown Princess, the Duchess of Coburg wrote letters to both the King and his older brother, Prince Leopold, to protest her daughter's isolation and her son-in-law's failure to stand up for his wife. Thereafter, Missy was permitted to attend one or two parties at the homes of government ministers. The Duchess was delighted. "You will teach Uncle that there are in this world *gay young people*... that the Roumanian constitution will not suffer from your going to balls and even dancing with young officers instead of old ministers."

Missy's new pregnancy soon put a stop to these liberties. "Life has nothing to offer for us here..." the Crown Princess wrote her mother-in-law in the spring, "it is of the utmost importance that I get away more frequently... be among happy people."

For the Crown Princess and her husband, regular holidays came in the summer, lasted precisely six weeks, and were carefully divided between his family and hers. Life at Sigmaringen revolved around Nando's increasingly demanding and hypochondriacal mother, who soon began to shower attentions on a younger, more favored daughter-in-law in hopes of making Missy jealous. Although Marie never lost her early fondness for her father-in-law, she grew to dislike his wife. It irritated her to watch Princess Antonia fawn over Nando. Home in Sigmaringen, the Crown Prince of Roumania strode through the family castles smoking huge cigars. "Nando looks happy, eats quantities and gives way to as many ugly sounds... [as] he likes before his indulgent Mamma," Missy wrote the Duchess of Coburg a few years later.

The Crown Princess could scarcely wait to get home to Coburg, where she settled happily into old routines—tea in the garden of the beloved Rosenau, lawn tennis, excursions on horseback or by carriage, and long evenings of reading aloud. There was always local theater, as the Duchess of Coburg was an enthusiastic patron, reading new plays, supervising their production, and even encouraging her daughters to try acting with the ducal company.

In April of 1894 Marie was allowed to return to Coburg for the wedding of sister Ducky to Grand Duke Ernst of Hesse. In royal terms Ducky's marriage was considered the best of all the Edinburgh alliances. It was not a particularly happy wedding, however, as neither the bride nor the groom was enthusiastic about the match.

Ducky and her Russian cousin Grand Duke Kirill Vladimirovitch had been in love for three years, but Ducky's mother and Kirill's father were sister and brother and the Russian Orthodox Church forbade marriage between first cousins. Unfortunately for Ducky, the Protestant Church had no such restrictions. Prohibited from marrying her cousin on her mother's side, with whom she was in love, she could and did marry her first cousin from her father's family. Ernst, Grand Duke of Hesse, was the eldest son of her father's sister Alice.

Queen Victoria and the Duke of Coburg had insisted on this match. While the Duchess of Coburg was busy in Roumania presiding over the birth of Missy's son, the Duke went to England to arrange Ducky's alliance with his mother. The Queen, who "had it out" with the Duchess, pushed her reluctant grandson into a proposal of marriage. The Duke was delighted. "Your and my great wish has been fulfilled this evening," he wired his mother in January of 1894. "Ducky has accepted Ernie of Hesse's proposal."

It was everyone's wish except the bride, the groom, and the bride's mother. Ducky was in love with another man, Ernie was not attracted to Ducky, and the Duchess of Coburg feared that her daughter would now be drawn into the English camp. "I had a long talk with Ernie... about the English family," she wrote Marie, "about Granny and explained to him why we could not really like them and how often they had been nasty and spiteful to me... he must not always be dragging Ducky to England in perpetual adoration of Granny and... [he must] understand the reasons why *we* can *never* adore her."

Ducky and Ernie's wedding was the major social event of the year, attended by Queen Victoria herself and a host of other royalties. "I never saw so many," quipped the Queen's private secretary. Among these was the bride's older sister, nearly four months pregnant, dressed in white satin embroidered in gold. "Little Missy of Roumania," said Aunt Vicky, "was looking pale and thin."

After Ducky's wedding and a brief interlude in London, the Crown Princess returned to Roumania to await the birth of her second child. For this confinement, the eighteen-year-old was left to manage on her own. This time there was no English doctor, no anesthetic, and no Duchess of Coburg, whose arrival was delayed. Worse, Missy had to contend with Queen Elisabeth of Roumania, just returned from her exile in Germany. Now that his dynasty was increasing according to plan, King Carol could afford a certain generosity toward his wife. The arrival of the Queen signaled problems for Marie. Like her father, the Crown Princess of Roumania quickly discovered that she had nothing in common with the former Princess of Wied.

Elisabeth of Wied, who became Queen Elisabeth of Roumania, had grown up surrounded by suffering. Her father, a scholarly gentleman of the German ruling class, was a consumptive; her mother, a chronic invalid. Since medical science could not help them or her young brother, who died in agony at an early age, Elisabeth's mother had turned to faith healing. From the age of twelve, Elisabeth was encouraged to participate in table turnings, mesmerisms, and spirit writings.

As a child Elisabeth of Wied was extremely hard to manage, hyperactive and ultrasensitive. To teach her restraint, she was taken to the local lunatic asylum to observe the inmates. This, coupled with years spent in bedside attendance on suffering members of her family, did not minimize an overwrought nature. During her mother's stepmother's death struggles, Elisabeth was required to remain kneeling at the old woman's bed without food for most of a day and night.

This was the background of the girl who had frightened off Affie when he came looking for a wife. Elisabeth was in her middle twenties, no longer hoping for a husband but desperate to have children, when she met the future King Carol of Roumania. The loss of their only child was the personal and political tragedy of her life; she never conceived again and spent the rest of her childbearing years consulting specialists. The Queen also listened to quacks, one of whom got her to eat a pregnant rabbit complete with its young inside.

Gowned in white mourning for her little girl, Queen Elisabeth took the pen name of Carmen Sylva and gathered around herself a coterie of neo-phytes—the Tragic Muse attended by her handmaidens. She dressed these young women in Oriental robes, referred to them as her children, and led them in the pursuit of beauty. Her favorite was Helene Vacaresco. Carmen Sylva convinced herself that the soul of her dead daughter had returned in Helene's body.

When Ferdinand arrived at court in 1889, the Queen decided that this surrogate daughter would make the perfect consort for him. She began by seating the Crown Prince next to Helene at family dinners, then arranged more intimate encounters, and finally wrote a poem about the young lovers. Queen Elisabeth believed that she was doing Roumania a favor by trying to unite native and royal blood.

The Roumanians didn't look at it that way. When the story of the Crown Prince's romance came out, they raised an enormous outcry against their Queen. Their anger was fueled by the King, who needed a scapegoat, po-litically to cover Ferdinand, and privately to screen an attachment he had developed for one of his wife's maids. He exiled the Vacaresco girl and sent the Queen to her mother in Germany, where Missy first met her at the castle in the woods.

The Queen of Roumania was banished for two years. During that time Marie was married and gave birth to the heir to the throne. "Poor Elisabeth!" the Empress Frederick wrote Queen Victoria on the occasion of Prince Carol's birth. "I had not the heart to telegraph to her, as I feel the joy cannot be without great bitterness for her." The Queen of Roumania, who wrote Marie before Carol was born to say that she hoped the child would be a girl, was reported to be "furiously angry" when told the baby was a boy.

Queen Elisabeth returned to Roumania just in time for Marie's second confinement. Aching for the calm of her mother, Marie was subjected to the histrionics of the Poet Queen. "Aunty, overcome by the poignant mem-ories of her own maternity and of her many frustrated hopes, was much agitated and moved by this family event, and kept exhorting me to realize that this was the most wonderful, glorious, blissful hour of my life. Torn to pieces by excruciating pain I could in nowise rise to the height of her enthusiasm and wept with longing for my mother, who only appeared on the scene a few days later."

Marie was attended by a Roumanian physician who joined with Queen Elisabeth in refusing to give her anesthetic. The pain was intensified by the emotional stress; the experience was agonizing. The baby was a girl, named Elisabetha after the newly reinstated Queen.

The birth of this second child was a turning point in Marie's life. Years later she would write exotic tales of romance and fantasy. One of these, *Crowned Queens*, is the story of two female sovereigns, one young, one old, both thinly disguised portraits of the author herself. In this book, the mythical young queen describes the effects of childbirth on her attitude toward herself and her husband: "It was after the birth of the second that I suddenly felt firmer ground under my feet, that I was no more the chattel in the hands of one man—something in the pain I had had to bear gave me the right to look into my master's eyes with the knowledge that we were equals, that the tender infant lying against my breast was as a shield against further surprises that could overtake me no more."

After the birth of Elisabetha, Marie decided she need not have a child every year. It was not easy to convince her husband, subject to Catholic and dynastic pressures, of her right to a life outside perpetual motherhood. In her campaign she was spurred on by the Duchess, who declared that in these matters all men were completely selfish. Missy disagreed: "...you must not think Nandchen [Nando] so selfish," she wrote to her mother, "he is not, he is quite contented with the present state of affairs & does not torment me at all about it."

Queen Elisabeth was not as manageable as the Crown Prince. No sooner did she arrive than she began to reclaim her position as mistress of the palace—a maneuver that required the downgrading of her successor. The Queen considered herself an authority on children and nurses. "Everyone feels he has the right to interfere in my business and I get quite aggravated at times," Marie wrote her father-in-law.

The Crown Princess's only comfort during her long postpartum recuperation was her sixteen-year-old sister, Sandra, left behind by their mother. Realizing that Missy was under attack, Sandra asked King Carol to let her go home to Coburg for Christmas. The King refused. Queen Elisabeth had just returned from Germany. If the Crown Princess left now, it would look to the world as if the two women did not get along; Marie must return with the court from Sinaia to Bucharest so that people would not talk. "It is just a rest from all of you that she needs," Sandra warned, "or her nerves will go to pieces!"

Carol eventually relented, but only on condition that Marie move back to Bucharest before going home and leave her babies behind in Roumania. The Crown Princess fought over this with the Queen and lost her temper when Elisabeth told her that the children did not belong to their mother but to the King and Roumania.

The King always raised objections when Marie tried to leave Roumania, with or without her children. The Duchess of Coburg did not understand this and blamed Missy for not being able to assert herself: "...with Uncle be firm," she advised her daughter, "and whenever he has been obstinate and disagreeable, be cold and rather *stiff* and show him that you owe him a grudge for some days...I know best how to deal with this sort of self-willed and obstinate people. If you give way you *are lost* and they regularly trample upon you and stamp out every bit of life and pleasure out of you."

The Duchess often missed the point. Disagreements over travel were only a reflection of deeper differences in attitude among the King, the Queen, and the Crown Princess. (The Crown Prince expressed no opinions.) King Carol, who had sacrificed his entire life for Roumania, believed that he could continue to hold his country together by sheer force of will and attention to duty. He could not understand why his nephew's wife had not arrived in Roumania as he had, prepared to make it her entire *raison d'être*. According to Carol I, personal happiness was not a legitimate goal for a Hohenzollern prince or an Edinburgh princess.

Accused by the King of apathy to duty and by the Queen of insubordination, the young Crown Princess of Roumania was written off by her Western European relations as shallow and insensitive. Aunt Vicky described Marie and her husband in a letter written during the second year of their marriage, while they were on a visit to Germany: "Yesterday evening Missy and Ferdinand of Roumania came to see us, she looking sweetly pretty & quite a baby, & very transparent & delicate, & he, poor dear, more unprepossessing than ever. She seems quite happy, but she is so young & inexperienced & cannot compare people with one another. At sweet 18, she rejoices in life & change & beauty. She has all the buoyancy of youth, & luckily for her no very deep feelings, I suppose."

Marie would never have accepted this evaluation of herself. Raised in the courts of England, Germany and Russia, where the tedium of royal duties was relieved by large families and social diversions, she had been totally unprepared either for Roumania or its King: "...in the new country...I was merely a little wheel in a watch which was keeping Uncle's time but a little wheel which had to do its part, relentlessly, and no one tried to surround that part with any glamour or make it seem worthwhile...Everything I did seemed always to be wrong and no one understood that when you were young and life runs like fire through your veins, you wanted to be gay sometimes, to laugh, be foolish with companions of your own age...to be a separate entity, someone with a mind of her own, with her own thoughts, her own habits, tastes, ideals, desires."

The Queen, Missy felt, understood her even less than the King. After her exile, Elisabeth returned home chastened, determined to confine herself publicly to charity and personally to the arts. As before, she gathered about herself a group of women who sat at her feet while she wrote and recited poetry, painted, and played the piano. It was the Queen's conviction that creative work was good only if it was spontaneous, untouched by criticism or revision, and she was therefore able to discover new talents in herself and others every day.

Young as she was, Missy realized that the Queen's salons were exercises in the glorification of mediocrity. "According to my appreciation, good taste was not one of Aunt Elisabeth's specialities, and to make matters worse it was a loud, assertive, eccentric, not-to-be-ignored taste . . . as Aunt was . . . very much convinced of the merits of all she did, you were always being called upon to admire and approve."

What the Almighty had failed to give Elisabeth in talent, he had more than made up for with determination, and the Queen never stopped trying to overwhelm her niece into artistic submission. If Missy ventured into Elisabeth's rooms, she was immediately brought to heel. "Sit down here at my feet and listen, darling," the Queen commanded, throwing out her arms to bring the Crown Princess into the fold. Marie would obediently take a seat while all the ladies, old and young, who had risen to their feet at the approach of royalty, took their places again, "their eyes glued upon the poet-queen's face."

"The air," Marie reported, "was always vibrant with tense excitement over some topic, some new hobby, some bit of music, of embroidery, some painting or the marvellous discovery of some new book. Nothing was ever taken calmly, everything had to be rapturous, tragic, excessive . . . Aunty . . . needed a continual audience, and this audience was trained to hang on her every word, to follow her every mood, they had to laugh or weep, praise or deplore according to the keynote given."

Considered an absurd figure outside her tight little circle of sycophants, Elisabeth's methods of dispensing charity were apt to be as tasteless as her art. During the visit of a Hohenzollern cousin, Missy was appalled to see the Queen fling open a window of the palace overlooking the Calea Victoriei and pose "in affectionate positions" while waiting for the crowd she knew would gather below. When an old beggar approached the window, the Queen nearly threw herself out of it, stretching out her arms to him "like Elsa von Brabant." She had the old man brought up to her, clothed, and fed, commenting repeatedly to her visitor on the "lovely effect this will have on the lookers-on." What upset Missy most was that the charade produced exactly the result the Queen expected.

Clearly not cut out to join the followers of the Queen, Marie's only antidote to the severe regime imposed on her by the King was travel. In the spring and summer of 1895, she managed to get to England for Ascot Week and a month's holiday with Ducky and their children on the Isle of Wight. Ducky had given birth to a daughter in March of that year. It was a joyous vacation in which the two sisters reinforced each other in delayed adolescent rebellion. Ducky, it turned out, was at least as miserable in her new married life as Missy was in hers.

After her marriage to Grand Duke Ernst of Hesse, Ducky moved to his duchy in southern Germany. Never pretty, she acquired a "certain regal magnificence" that made her look every inch the Grand Duchess. She refused, however, to play the role.

The customs of provincial life aroused Ducky's hostilities. She seemed to go out of her way to defy local custom, invariably causing offense at official receptions by speaking only with the amusing guests, never the important ones. Like Marie she adored riding. Ignoring her husband, she galloped off frequently on her untamed black stallion, forgetting to come home to pay official calls or answer important letters. When Ernie admonished her, she threw china at him. Once she let her stallion loose in the castle courtyard where he tore up the flower beds, frightened the guests, and chased the young Grand Duke, tearing a sizable piece of cloth out of his trousers. She often had the palace grooms bring her favorite mount around from the stable to a spot under her bedroom window so that she could climb down a ladder onto his back and dash off into the woods while her husband stayed home writing poetry or pursuing his activities as patron of the arts.

Given her temperament—manic highs dropping swiftly to brooding lows—Ducky had seemed a reasonable match for the charming, artistic Grand Duke. Once married, however, they lived essentially like brother and sister. It was a difficult life for the passionate young woman.

In April of 1896, the third sister, Sandra, married Prince Ernst of Hohenlohe-Langenburg, a grandson of Queen Victoria's half sister, and went to live in Schloss Langenburg, not far from Hesse. Both Marie and her father were against this marriage, which was considered less than brilliant. But the new Princess of Hohenlohe, according to the Duchess, was "the most uninteresting specimen" of her four daughters. Often ill, Sandra suffered from headaches and jealousy.

The month after Sandra's wedding, Marie and Ferdinand were invited to Moscow to celebrate the Coronation of her cousins Nicholas II and Alexandra. The summer of 1896 was a watershed for Marie, a final blow to her assigned role of passive, conventional, turn-of-the-century princess. If Elisabetha's birth gave Marie a sense of her own worth and the weeks spent with Ducky in England bolstered her will, this trip to Russia taught her just how pretty and desirable she was. It did not take her long thereafter to decide that she had the right to make her own rules, many of which appalled her relations.

The Coronation of Nicholas and Alexandra, "more like a dream than reality," was the supreme moment in Marie's young married life. Gowned in gold lamé, standing with her relatives inside the Uspensky Cathedral in the Kremlin, she was mesmerized by ancient ceremonies that had once consecrated her ancestors and now, in 1896, seemed to deify her cousins. Painfully aware that she herself was stuck in a shabby royal corner of the world, Marie was shocked at the attitude of the young Tsarina, resplendent in diamonds and glory. "Nothing ever seemed to give her pleasure," Marie said, "she seldom smiled, and when she did it was grudgingly as though making a concession." The twenty-four-year-old Tsarina found everything fatiguing. "I can still see how Alix's never very happy face became more and more pathetic as the hours lengthened," said Marie, for whom the experience was exhilarating.

Victim of her mother's dynastic prejudices, Marie had never experienced any social life before being whisked off to Roumania. There, she had encountered nothing for three years but restraints and disapproval. In Russia her natural high spirits, anathema in the court of King Carol, were considered an asset. As she waltzed down the white marble Hall of the Knights of St. George, the light from gigantic crystal chandeliers reflected in her blond curls, Marie was irresistible. Immediately she captured a whole squadron of impassioned admirers, "most of them... officers, brilliant, dashing, sentimental, daring, full of Russian ardour mixed with that almost intolerable melancholy so characteristic of the Slav, a melancholy which tore at your heartstrings and disturbed your peace." The most ardent was her cousin Grand Duke Boris, with his laughing smile and husky voice. Missy was not daunted by his reputation as a Casanova. "Russians," she said, "catch fire easily, and Slav tongues are soft."

For sister Ducky and Boris's older brother, Kirill, the Russian Coronation provided an opportunity for more than a dance-floor flirtation. Fed by her marital frustrations, their mutual passion grew more demanding during those weeks in Russia. "Ducky and I were striking contrasts," Marie said, "I so fair and she so dark and somewhat sombre and melancholy, whilst I was gay and always amused."

Ferdinand was not as delighted with the holiday as his wife. Romanovs made him nervous. Except for the new, mild-mannered Tsar, they were troubling men, enormous and sure of themselves. Loud-voiced, teasing, and autocratic, Missy's Russian uncles and cousins swept everything before them, including the timid, repressed Crown Prince of Roumania, haunted by King Carol's admonitions against enjoying himself.

After Moscow the royal guests were invited to the country "to recover from the fatigues of the Coronation festivities." While the older and duller royalties (a designation that included the newly crowned Tsar and Tsarina) recuperated elsewhere, Missy, her husband, and the other young ones were guests of Prince and Princess Yusupov at their country estate, Archangelskoye.

Archangelskoye, like many great Russian palaces, owes its architectural inspiration to eighteenth-century France as interpreted by Italians under the influence of Russian prodigality. In spite of its huge columned halls and frescoed ceilings, the Yusupov country home was considered more livable than other palaces due to a happy profusion of old furniture, plants, and flowers scattered beneath the Tiepolos. A columned rotunda used for receptions opened on to a park and woods beyond. Two huge terraces outlined with statues stretched down to a river; the gardens were laid out in imitation of Versailles; there was a private theater and a zoo. It was a brilliant setting for fireworks, riding, boating, picnics, and nightly dancing to the music of

Tziganes. In honor of his guests, Prince Yusupov sent to St. Petersburg for the Italian opera company. In honor of the Crown Prince and Princess of Roumania, he brought in a Roumanian gypsy band, then very popular in Moscow.

Felix Yusupov, the murderer of Rasputin, was only nine years old in 1896. Years later he described Marie's effect on him: "Princess Marie was already famous for her beauty: she had wonderful eyes of such a rare shade of grayish-blue that it was impossible to forget them. Her figure was tall and slender as a young poplar, and she bewitched me so completely that I followed her about like a shadow. I spent sleepless nights conjuring up her lovely face. Once, she kissed me; I was so happy that I refused to let my face be washed that night."

Among the guests at Archangelskoye was a Prince Wittgenstein, an officer in the Cossacks of the Imperial Guard, known for his extravangance and dash. With "a waist as slim as a woman's," he dressed in a purple Cossack caftan, high leather boots, and a tall fur cap. A magnificent silver dagger was plunged into his belt.

Prince Wittgenstein and Princess Marie both liked being the center of attention and were not overly fond of each other. Nevertheless, he admired her daring horsemanship. The Prince owned a fierce, unkempt Cossack horse, untrained and skittish, "exactly the sort of horse which you would expect young Wittgenstein to ride," according to Marie. Claiming that this animal could beat at a trot any other horse at full gallop, Wittgenstein dared Missy to try him—a contest that terrified Ferdinand, but which he was powerless to stop.

"That ride remains one of the most glorious memories of my youth..." wrote Queen Marie. "The moment I was on his back that untamed horse and I understood each other absolutely and I was ready to accept any wager. I was given a few hundred yards' start and then off flew all the other riders in wild pursuit. What a race that was!... Having reached the point set as our goal, I remember turning my horse to face the onrush of my pursuers who came pounding up the small hillock on which I stood awaiting them. Cheers and exclamations! I had won my bet and bending down I threw my arms round my horse's neck and kissed him in exultant gratitude."

She was not unaware of her effects. "I rejoice in my beauty," she once told an admirer. "Men have taught me to."

In the fall of 1896, Missy's brother, Alfred, and their cousin, Grand Duke Boris of Russia, came to Sinaia to visit. Enrolled in the German Army at Potsdam after the dismissal of Dr. Rolfs, Alfred had begun to make up for the deprivations of his childhood with women and alcohol. He was well on his way to destroying his health when his parents sent him to his sister. "I certainly will talk to him as you wish it," Missy assured her mother, "& I am sure I shall find words enough, because I find the whole thing so loathsome." In spite of a loving relationship with her brother, Marie was unsuccessful in her attempts to reform him: "... how will one ever be able to do anything as long as those horrible things are... found quite natural by most, and encouraged," the Crown Princess wrote her mother.

Although Alfred was a worry to Marie, Boris was an amusing companion. Unlike her brother, Boris was not her responsibility. Unlike her husband, he was full of energy. Boris, she said, is "not as lazy as Nando who sits and yawns." But her cousin's lengthy stay and obvious adoration started royal gossip and drew admonishments from her mother. What was Missy thinking of? Did she prefer Boris to her husband?

The Crown Princess was surprised and hurt. She tried to explain how lonely her life was with Nando, how "very different" their temperaments were, and how much, because of that, she enjoyed her guests. "Perhaps," she admitted to her mother, "I have not been as nice to Nando as I ought to have been, and am too easily irritated... What is so difficult is that he always first says no to everything... Don't think that I do not love him! I don't think I am anymore very 'in love with him'... don't think for a moment that there is any other man I would prefer as husband! as you very rightly said... if one was to belong to them one would not like them at all... the pleasant thing... with other men is just that they have no right over you."

The Crown Princess hated being owned, even by a man who was so obviously as kind as her husband. "... all intimate life with a man is difficult for me," she wrote in later years. "I am born with a desperate desire of my own physical bodily liberty." "My husband sees me cry," she wrote her mother, "he is awfully sorry, he wants to console me, he has every intention to do so, his heart is full of love, he begins to kiss me then he forgets that, and tries to console me by giving way to just that, that I dread most on earth."

Marie had entered marriage expecting to find a male companion. "What does one find, a man intensely in love with you, & who has the right to ask everything of you, when you ask him to read to you in the evening he hurries over it only to get to bed for other amusements which he does not perhaps think is a one-sided amusement, when one wants to talk with him, he is reading the newspapers, when one says one is lonely, he says you have the children, he is perfectly devoted to you, and yet he will not give up even a cigar to sit a moment with you!"

Marie's sense of isolation was not helped by the hostility of the Queen, who seized on her friendship with Boris as an example of the girl's unworthiness. Joining in the criticism of the Crown Princess was Olga Mavrojeni, the most powerful lady-in-waiting at King Carol's palace. Spare and intelligent, invariably gowned in black satin and veils, Olga Mavrojeni had been brought to court by the King to watch over his injudicious Queen and make sure her fantasies did not lead to any more politically embarrassing situations. Unaware of this, Marie was convinced that Mme. Mavrojeni's sole mission in life was to stir up trouble against her, and she dubbed the older woman the Chief Inquisitor.

A third member of a new clique that sprang up in the King's palace was Cousin Charly, destined to crop up to sabotage Marie throughout her life. The Kaiser's sister was known in royal circles as the lady who "always had to have a king 'up her sleeve.'" Having progressed from the old King of Saxony to the King of Sweden, she arrived in Roumania in 1896. King Carol was completely taken in by Charly's assumptions of secret political information, as well as her whispered stories about the Crown Princess.

Variously motivated, the three ladies agreed on two things: Marie was far "too English" and "too frivolous." They called her the "Young Light" and worried that she might develop ambitions to shine on her own. Certainly she could not be relied upon to supervise her own children. Cousin Charly and Mme. Mavrojeni stood solidly behind Queen Elisabeth as she maneuvered to take over young Prince Carol and Princess Elisabetha.

Although the Crown Prince and Princess moved to their own home, Cotroceni Palace, on the outskirts of the city in 1896, the Queen kept her hand in their household by staffing it with servants loyal only to herself. For a woman who had so passionately wanted children of her own, the proximity of Marie's brood was an irresistible temptation. With opportunities for meddling came occasions for martyrdom. Invited to spend Christmas at Cotroceni, the Queen found little Carol and Elisabetha playing around the tree. "God of mercy," she cried at the sight of Marie's babies, "do not forsake me...I cannot! It is more than I can bear."

The only place the Crown Princess could escape the weight of resentment was outside with her horses. "Riding played an enormous part in my life; to some this may appear trivial, but I had an instinctive sense of self-preservation." Ignoring the old wives who warned that horseback riding would endanger her ability to continue the dynasty, she put on a dark blue and scarlet riding outfit sent by one of her Russian admirers, took off her ladylike sidesaddle, and mounted her horse astride. In the summertime at Sinaia she defied court rules by riding alone into the mountains. Soon even *"der Onkel* got accustomed to seeing me on a horse and would greet me with a kindly smile when I came riding towards him through the woods. In his steely makeup there was some corner which was in sympathy with this Anglo-Saxon girl whose will he could not break. He did not approve of me, I was a constant anxiety, but he liked me in spite of himself." In the autumn of 1897, "in an hour of weakness," King Carol appointed Marie Honorary Chief of a regiment of cavalry, the Fourth Rosiori (Hussars). She could hardly wait to order bright-red tunics with black braid and gold buttons to match her soldiers.

Back in Bucharest, the Crown Princess took daily gallops on a large exercise field behind her new palace. "My soldiers were always on the lookout for me and each time I galloped past them I was greeted with lusty cheers. There was a giddy sort of exultation in this...I felt absolutely at home amongst

our soldiers; I had the happy sensation that they accepted me uncondi-
tionally... I was not on approbation... They admired me for my iron nerve
on horseback... I was *their* princess, my ways were not found fault with."

While the old palace clucked in disapproval, the Hussars offered simple
adoration. The Crown Princess was grateful. "Each man saluted me as he
saluted his flag; a warm feeling came over me, I was at home."

Chapter *7*

*O*ne of the major concerns of monarchs at the end of
the nineteenth century was the correct and opulent entertainment of their
royal counterparts from other countries. When Emperor Franz Josef of Austro-
Hungary came to Roumania on a state visit in September of 1896, King
Carol was particularly anxious to impress his mighty neighbor, feudal lord
over some fifty million disparate souls living next door. Crown Prince Ferdinand was more nervous than ordinary, afraid that Missy might disgrace
him by taking the occasion too lightly.

The King wanted to receive Franz Josef in the baroque halls of Castle
Peles, of which he was very proud, rather than the Palatul Victoriei in
Bucharest, which was notoriously uncomfortable. But since it was essential
to put sovereigns on parade in capital cities where there were enough people
to gawk and cheer them, the visit started in Bucharest and moved to Sinaia
only after the official festivities were over. In Sinaia, the Emperor was treated

to a series of elaborate bucolic entertainments, designed to convey the joys of simple Roumanian country life.

Marie's father had also chosen this particular time to pay his daughter a visit. To avoid a congestion of royalties, King Carol asked the Duke of Coburg to postpone his journey. The Duke refused. He said he would be delighted to see Franz Josef again, as it had been some time since their last meeting.

The arrival of the Duke of Coburg was a big event for Queen Elisabeth, who had kept a vision of the handsome blue-eyed violinist alive in her heart for more than thirty years. "It was my one little romance," she told the Crown Princess. Although Missy tried to explain that her father was no longer young and beautiful and that it had not been his "everyday habit to play under the trees of the forest," the Queen was convinced that the Duke loved music above everything else and planned a woodsy concert in his honor. For this she procured the services of a painter who claimed he could sing tenor, baritone, or bass on demand.

Marie was caught between the Queen, who dragged the party through the forest to a rocky spot she had chosen for the performance, and her father, best known at this time of his life for shortness of temper and high consumption of alcohol. For the concert Carmen Sylva had gathered a motley group of hangers-on, primed to appreciate and applaud.

The Duke, as Marie expected, did not "particularly relish being dragged up steep mountain paths, nor did he find either pleasure or repose on his rocky seat." The Crown Princess was nervous. "I watched him anxiously.... Papa's British conventionality was going to receive something of a shock."

When the "pseudo-singer" materialized dramatically from behind a rock, "striking an heroic attitude considered in keeping with the mountain background," Missy promised her father she would find an excuse to make an early exit. With Carmen Sylva clasping her hands in adoration of her protégé, the Duke of Coburg and his daughter slipped away.

"Is that what you call singing here in Roumania...?" Missy's father grumbled, stubbing his toes as they climbed down the steep rocky path. "I had the feeling of being in a lunatic asylum!"

The Poet Queen's comment on the afternoon was that she could find nothing in the portly, middle-aged Duke to remind her of the slim violinist of her youth. "Such a pity," she sighed, "nothing at all, not even his love for music."

A few months later Ducky and Ernie arrived in Roumania for a prolonged visit. At this point in her life Marie depended on her sister and brother-in-law for amusement, and she hoped that Ernie's "infectious" sense of fun would overcome Nando's inability to enjoy himself. In spite of, or perhaps because of, their incompatibility, the Grand Duke and Duchess of Hesse were known as the party givers among the young European royalties of their day. The Crown Princess's happiest weeks were those spent at Schloss Wolfs-garten, Ernie and Ducky's summer residence near Darmstadt, where Missy met cousins of her age from all the capitals of Europe.

Wolfsgarten, the center of Marie's social activities in the late 1890s, is a two-story, red stone castle built entirely around a sunny courtyard. The main building, which then housed the Grand Duke of Hesse and his wife, formed one of four wings; the guest quarters, where Missy stayed, a second; the wing for children and nannies, a third; and the stable, of great importance to the mistress of the house and her sister, the fourth.

There was no court etiquette observed at Wolfsgarten, and no distinctions made in rank. Most important, none of the guests was over thirty. All the old, respectable courtiers who thrived on issues of precedence were left to natter unheeded in town. Even the royal children, models of disciplined manners elsewhere, were given their own playhouse in the woods. Adults were strictly forbidden to enter this miniature blue cottage built by Grand Duke Ernst for his adored daughter, Princess Elisabeth. Frantic royal nurses and tutors were often found pacing up and down the walk outside the play-house, barred from entering or stopping the raucous laughter and plebeian games taking place inside.

Many members of Europe's ruling houses came to Wolfsgarten at one time or another, and most could not wait to return, scratching their names, in accordance with eccentric royal practice, on a windowpane in the main salon. "It was the jolliest, merriest house party to which I have ever been in my life," Prince Nicholas of Greece said about his trip to Wolfsgarten in the late 1890s. "We were all closely related; young and healthy; like school-children on a holiday. . . . The two sisters, Queen Marie of Roumania and our hostess, the Grand Duchess of Hesse. . . one fair and the other dark, were as beautiful as they were charming. The Queen of Roumania, then at the height of her beauty, with eyes like sapphires, with golden hair, a faultless complexion, and a perfect figure, was a picture; but what I admired then, as now, was her extraordinary vitality."

Led by Ducky and Missy, the guests took long horseback rides and picnics in the woods. In the evenings there were games or private theatricals, arranged by Ernie and attended by a few privileged friends from town. If it rained, the entire house party painted or did decorative wood carving and wood-burning in the current style of Art Nouveau, while one of the party, often Tsar Nicholas II, read aloud from some thriller like *Dracula*.

When Ducky and Ernie paid Missy a return visit in Roumania in the spring of 1897, the Crown Princess was determined to make their stay as lively as possible. With "the fighting Grand Duchess"* to back her up, Marie broke through most of King Carol's restrictions and got her initial taste of social life in Bucharest.

---

*One of Ducky's nicknames at the German court. The other was "the little spitfire."

Court society—whether in London, St. Petersburg, or Berlin—had been no preparation for life among the Roumanian nobility, where the two major preoccupations were love and politics. Always ardent, often violent, the aristocratic Roumanian made no attempt to curb his desires or temper their immediate gratification. According to one prominent member of the aristocracy, there was no word in the Roumanian language for self-control—"the term and idea being equally untranslatable and alien to a Roumanian mind."

Such luxuriant permissiveness in the rich leisured class bred love affairs "so numerous and intricate" that the uninitiated had difficulty keeping track of them. Western European sexual morality was not an issue in the Roumanian *haut monde*. Life was not a pilgrimage toward character development, but a game of intrigue played with a nimble mind and a passionate heart.

One of the chief factors in marital freedom was the facility of divorce. In other countries Church and State closed ranks to keep a curb on the ruling class through the threat of social and religious excommunication. In Roumania there were few legal or social taboos. The Roumanian Orthodox Church sanctioned three marriages per person; all three weddings could be held within its sacred walls, the only stipulation being that with each succeeding celebration the ceremony grew shorter.

When Queen Elisabeth first arrived in Roumania, she had been faced with the decision of whom to receive at the palace, as in any other European court of the day, divorced women would have been automatically barred. After canvassing the situation, the Queen compromised with local convention by admitting any woman who had not been divorced more than once. This apparently caused some confusion, as Elisabeth did not keep track of the affairs of the nobility. The aristocrats themselves were no help, for they moved freely among former spouses and current lovers with equanimity. "It is quite bewildering to a stranger when she meets the past, present and future husband of a pretty woman in the same drawing-room!" complained the Canadian wife of a Roumanian naval officer.

The second most salient characteristic of the Roumanian nobility was a generally high and usually irreverent quality of intellect. Unlike the descendants of most other European aristocracies, whose forebears were primarily fighters, the ancestors of the Roumanian boyars had won status not by bald courage but through artful survival. The former Wallachians and Moldavians had kept their heads and lands by learning to outsmart the Turk—to grovel when necessary, bribe when expedient, and intrigue all the time. Intermarriage with the Greek Phanariots had increased the canniness and greed of the class. These traits, combined with outsized pride in their Roman origins and slavish imitation of the French, had produced a class of aristocrats unlike any other in Europe.

This highly charged atmosphere, intimidating to even the most educated diplomat, frightened the twenty-one-year-old Crown Princess. The Roumanians whom she met all spoke four or five languages fluently, while she wasn't even comfortable in French. Fortunately, English nursemaids were the rule among the best families, so most upper-class Roumanians spoke English before they learned their native tongue. Aside from linguistic superiority, the Roumanians were loudly conversant in politics, a subject on which Missy's mother told her she was too young to have opinions. For her early forays into society, the Crown Princess depended exclusively on her looks and her rank.

Like aristocracy at the turn of the century everywhere, the descendants of the old boyars kept ancestral holdings in the country and villas for the season in town. Their thickly walled country estates recalled the days of the Turks, while their town houses resembled homes in the suburbs of Paris. Both were scaled in the grand manner and were nearly self-maintaining. Beyond the stately villas of Bucharest, which were often Mediterranean in style and set in flowered parks, there were laundries, kitchens, and walled gardens housing chickens, pigs, and cows. To man these sprawling establishments required many devoted, well-trained servants. Armies of chefs, butlers, footmen, maids, and laundresses, saved from the Asiatic slums of Bucharest by domestic servitude, kept the homes operating smoothly and producing the sparkling dinners and balls Princess Marie quickly learned to love.

The return of the boyars from their country estates and the start of the social season in the capital coincided with the opening of Parliament in the middle of November. Society balls started after Christmas and lasted into the spring. For these gatherings, the Roumanians transformed their homes into fantastic winter gardens. Sweet-smelling flowers appeared from the Riviera; vintage wines, champagnes, truffles, and pâtés arrived from France; cotillion favors came from Paris on the *Orient Express*. Only the guests and the music were local; gypsy bands were engaged to play Western waltzes and current dance numbers, along with stirring, sentimental Roumanian folk songs.

Marie adored dancing, and once liberated from King Carol's restrictions, she became the most enthusiastic guest and hostess in Bucharest. Princess Anne-Marie Callimachi, a member of the prominent Vacaresco family, describes the Crown Princess as she appeared at the time:

"She was known to come early, which set the family on tenterhooks lest she arrive before the other guests, and to leave last. 'One more dance, Madame Vacaresco, please, I want to have a waltz with Radu [her host known as le Beau Radu]' she was known to plead at five o'clock in the morning, when Granny felt near collapsing, while my father had already secretly gone down to the kitchen to order breakfast for the royal party. . . . She was always very well, but most spectacularly, dressed in light tulles or muslins, sequined, embroidered, or covered with feathers. She wore marvellous jewelry, but was supposed to rush quite frequently to rigid King Carol . . . begging for payment of the bills which she could not meet because of her very limited dress allowance."

In spite of the tight financial rein the King kept on his successors, it would not have occurred to Missy to cut down in matters of dress. With Ducky, every bit as vain as her sister, she now joined fashionable Bucharest in late-afternoon drives on the Chaussée Kisselev. The Chaussée was a large open parklike area at the end of the Calea Victoriei, the main street of the capital. The streets of Bucharest are unusually wide and bordered by trees and flowers. The Chaussée Kisselev was, in those days, the most splendid of all. Shadowed by four rows of lime trees, surrounded by villas with black and gold railings, and enlivened by several outdoor cafés, the Chaussée was to the well-off inhabitants of turn-of-the-century Bucharest what the Bois de Boulogne was to Parisians.

Every day between the hours of 5 and 7 P.M., society gathered to drive up and down, back and forth in open carriages drawn by magnificent horses. Those without their own transport hired carriages driven by the Skoptzi and drawn by black Orloff trotters. Competing with the women and horses for attention were officers of the Roumanian Army, often trussed up in corsets worn under brightly sashed tunics. With "every shining perfumed hair in place, an occasional monocle fixed immovably to the eye," and cigarettes dangling from their lips, these Ruritanian dandies surveyed the passing show, smiling and clicking their heels in appreciation of the prettiest girls.

"Ducky and I often took part in this late-afternoon parade and would dress up in consequence, careful that our gowns, hats, cloaks or parasols would be in pleasant harmony," wrote Queen Marie. "We liked being as smart as possible; often we dressed alike and were not above certain eccentricities of attire."

Their originality in dress often got the sisters into trouble with the Duchess of Coburg, who also worried about her daughters' behavior: ". . . you are both only too ready to get rid of your husbands . . ." she wrote Missy and Ducky during Ducky's visit. "Flirt, amuse yourself, but don't lose your heart, men are not worth it and if you could, *really* could see their lives, you would turn away in disgust, for you would find there dirt and nothing but dirt, even in the lives of those who seem to you good and noble."

When she and Ducky were not in society, the Crown Princess arranged riding picnics and excursions outside Bucharest to explore peasant towns and gypsy encampments. Marie's delight in the country villages with their "wee churches" and "wee houses with their over-large roofs heaped with maize-leaves" was that of a tourist rather than a future sovereign. It did not occur to her at the time that life inside these mud huts might be less than idyllic. She found the gypsies even more fascinating than the peasants and wrote with some pride that she and her sister "would leave our carriage and penetrate undismayed among the tents, climbing over heaps of indescribable refuse, gazing about us full of interest but not without a shudder."

Even more picturesque than the naked brown children begging for pennies and "impudently handsome girls, scantily draped in filthy rags" were the old gypsy crones, models for the witches who would appear later in the Queen of Roumania's fairy stories. "Crouching above mysterious black pots, standing motionless at the dark mouths of their tents, leaning on their staves, gazing with bleared eyes at visions of their own or coming slowly towards us through the dust, wrinkled, toothless, crooked, they were almost too good to be true," she said.

The Edinburgh Princesses enjoyed riding and local color in the mornings, fashionable drives in the afternoons, and dancing at night—until, early in May of 1897, Crown Prince Ferdinand was struck down with typhoid fever.

Three doctors were put on duty at his bedside twenty-four hours a day, but in spite of best medical efforts, Missy's husband nearly died. "I feel dazed and weary..." she wrote Sister Sandra in the middle of June, "Nando often is delirious." The Crown Princess's burden was not eased by Queen Elisabeth, who insisted on pantomiming the dismal news of the patient's condition from a window in Missy's palace to the public in the streets below.

"Sickness had a strange effect upon her..." Marie reported. "Her imagination saw, and to a certain degree even revelled in, the tragedy that it would be if the young Crown Prince were to die... a child of four becoming heir to the throne, a young widow, foolish, inexperienced, unworthy of bringing up her own children, and she, Carmen Sylva, as saviour, in her element, with large motherly gestures, sweeping the bereaved into her embrace. She imagined it all, she lived it through in thought, and as her thoughts became words, she, so to say, forced us to live it with her, for she spoke of nothing else. Each time she mounted the high Cotroceni stairs leaning upon the arm of a servant—and she came twice a day—it was as though for a funeral and the swish of her long robes over the carpets was pregnant with disaster.... She would settle down in one of my rooms, assembling around her as many women of the household as she could gather together, and then in a deep, grief-laden voice she would gloat over every tragic story of sickness or death that she or others had ever witnessed. Curiously enough she was always hungry, so food had to be set before her at odd hours. I can still see her eating large ham sandwiches whilst she kept discoursing upon these lamentable subjects."

In the middle of one night, Missy was summarily awakened to say goodbye to her husband. She knelt down next to his bed, holding his hand. Emaciated, glassy-eyed, his breath coming in gasps, the Crown Prince lay immobile while the three doctors, who had given up hope of saving him, stood at the foot of his bed. The King and Queen were called in—he bowed with anxiety, she bloated with incipient tragedy. A priest started to drone the final rites in Latin. In the middle of the prayers the dying man began to breathe more quietly. One of the doctors took his pulse and nodded to his wife. The crisis was over.

The convalescence, however, was "long and wearisome." There were several relapses and flare-ups of high fever. The doctors finally said that the patient seemed well enough to be moved up to the healthier air of Sinaia, but once there, they kept him in bed for another six weeks. He seemed "almost a stranger" to his wife—"pale, exhausted, with a brown beard, terribly changed, with gaunt waxen face, sunken cheeks and skeleton-like hands."

Ferdinand never regained his looks. Even Princess Marthe Bibesco, one of his most ardent admirers, was appalled by the physical transformation of the Crown Prince. She described him during his convalescence as still "pale and haggard, his face old with suffering. His cap was jammed over his ears, but could not hide his baldness... it was despairing to look at him... I tried to persuade myself that I would again see him as he was... once he was cured." But the bland, aristocratic well-being of Ferdinand's face was gone. At thirty-two, Missy's husband resembled a rather touching, bearded scarecrow.

Ducky left Roumania in the middle of June 1897 for Queen Victoria's Diamond Jubilee in London, which Marie and Ferdinand had planned to attend. In spite of a renewed fondness for her husband, Missy was "terribly, terribly disappointed" not to be able to go. Her mother did not understand. The Duchess of Coburg's letters to Sinaia from London were filled with complaints—about the English royal family, the dizzying schedule of festivities, the inferiority of English theater versus German, and the unseasonable heat in June. Only Ducky's flirtations seemed to amuse the Duchess.

Meanwhile in Sinaia, summer dragged on for the near-widow. "I am much worried... just now because people are so tiresome and one never seems to do the right thing," she wrote her mother. "If I go out for rides or drives, they say, she is heartless to go out when her husband is ill, if I remain the whole day at home, they say I begin to look ill and must take exercise!"

In August King Carol and Queen Elisabeth left for their annual water cure in Switzerland. Since her husband was still unwell, the King appointed an aide-de-camp to the Crown Princess. Lieutenant Zizi Cantacuzène, an officer in Marie's regiment of Hussars, was the illegitimate son of a member of the princely Cantacuzène clan. Small and dark, not good-looking but amusing, Zizi dressed with panache and rode exceedingly well.

After the King and Queen left, the Duchess of Coburg arrived in Sinaia with Missy's fourteen-year-old sister, Beatrice. The Duchess, who liked to see young people active, volunteered to sit with her invalid son-in-law so that his wife could get out a bit. With the Duchess rather than the King and Queen in residence, there were fewer restrictions, and Marie, Baby Bee, and Lieutenant Cantacuzène rode happily through the forests and up into the mountains around Sinaia.

"After the long strain my youthful spirits gained the upper hand again..." Marie wrote in later years. "High spirits are a dangerous possession for a royal lady as there come hours when everything is unimportant but the joy of the moment. Caution is thrown to the winds and the spirit of fun and mischief is allowed full sway, mostly with disastrous results, for... there are jaundiced eyes ready to see things as they are not, ready to make mischief, to tear a reputation to pieces."

When the King and Queen returned to Roumania, the Queen's lady-in-waiting, Mme. Mavrojeni, had prepared a list of criticisms and innuendos for their consideration. Before the King had a chance to remonstrate with the Crown Princess for spending too much time with her A.D.C., he was told that the doctors had ordered Ferdinand to the south of France for the winter to recuperate. Carol was not pleased. Missy was thrilled. The Duchess of Coburg owned a villa in Nice, and although Missy had been invited to join her mother and sisters there every winter, King Carol had always refused to let her go. Faced with the court doctors, the King made it plain to Nando and Missy that they were on leave for matters of health, not fun.

When the subject of appropriate escorts for the trip came up, however, Zizi's name was immediately struck from the list by King Carol, who said that there was talk of the Crown Princess's being on too friendly terms with "this absolutely insignificant person." Marie wrote her father-in-law, begging him to intercede. "To my greatest regret I learned that... Nando will be deprived of this joy, because ugly rumors are arising about me. Dear Papa, I *beg* you, I implore you to do whatever you can to influence Uncle to give his permission and appoint him, so that all bad tongues will be silenced... if Uncle does not go along with it, he puts us in the wrong before the entire world, and, Papa, I do not know if I can accept this quietly."

Not even the King's older brother could make him change his mind, and the Crown Prince and Princess were sent to Nice with "safe guardians" whose job it was to report back daily and secretly on their activities.

They stayed at Château Fabron, the villa belonging to the Duchess of Coburg. The sunshine, flowers, and ocean views delighted Ferdinand. His health improved, and Missy's intentions of living a sedentary life dissolved in the face of fun-loving members of other royal families who came to the south of France every year to enjoy themselves. King Carol was informed that the Roumanian Crown Prince and Princess appeared at Carnival with Marie's Uncle Arthur and Aunt Louise of Connaught,* who lured them out of their official box down into the ordinary crowds. He was told that they visited Cannes and attended a Bal Masque, although they did not mask themselves or mingle with the people. "But," wrote Marie, "all our poor little frivolities were carefully noted by the spies specifically attached to our heels, and were then passed on to Uncle to brood over to his heart's content."

Marie also heard complaints from the Duchess of Coburg about her clothes, her companions, and the fact that she had tried gambling and liked

*The Duke of Connaught was Queen Victoria's third son.

it. At the same time, the Duchess was extremely grateful to Missy for spending much of her vacation with her father, whose yacht was moored at Villefranche. "If you only knew how easy and comfortable life is without him," the Duchess wrote her daughter from Coburg. She begged Missy to keep the Duke where he was, to watch over him, "feed him well and in a joky way, prohibit his taking spirits." Missy did what she could and enjoyed being with her father. When the Duke returned to Coburg, he told his wife that he was "simply enchanted" with their eldest daughter, her children, and her "success at Nice."

Ferdinand and Marie returned to Roumania in the spring. Zizi was reinstated at Cotroceni Palace as a temporary gymnastics instructor for Carol, and his flirtation with the Crown Princess started up again. When Marie went to Germany for a cure, the Lieutenant followed. Roumanian society, where such things were expected, looked on and smiled.

Missy's relations, privy to royal gossip, were not as broad-minded. Aunt Vicky wrote to her daughter Sophie, Crown Princess of Greece, comparing Sophie's life in Greece with Marie's in Roumania: "I think Missy of Roumania is more to be pitied than you. . . . The King is a great tyrant in his family, & has crushed the independence in Ferdinand so that no one cares about him, & his beautiful & gifted little wife, I fear, gets into scrapes, & like a butterfly, instead of hovering over the flowers, burns her pretty wings by going rather near the fire!"

Closer to home there was Queen Elisabeth, eager to find an excuse to take Marie's children away from her. By the winter of 1898 the Queen had convinced the King that the Crown Princess was irresponsible and that he must hire a governess for Prince Carol. Her choice was Miss Winter, a great friend of the Wied family, who had worked for Elisabeth's cousin the Queen of Holland. Marie, who smelled a plot hatching, agreed to interview the governess, but only on the proviso that if she did not like her, she would not be forced to take her into her home.

". . . the moment I set eyes on her all hope vanished. . . . The woman was just everything that could not be borne, thick-set, heavy with staring, goggle-eyes, a large fleshy nose and repulsive mouth; she was common, with a commonness that only one of her own nationality could rightly appreciate. Also, her speech was common and throaty, her expressions were second-rate, unrefined. . . . The very sight of her was a shock and her speech completed the repellent exterior."

The Crown Princess announced that she could not accept this woman as governess to her son, but the Crown Prince would not stand up to the King and Queen. Marie was forced to concede, but "with the express understanding" that Miss Winter would not come until the spring of 1899. Suddenly, on the eve of a trip to Gotha for her parents' silver wedding anniversary in January, she was told that Miss Winter was arriving that evening to stay with her children while she was away.

Marie demanded that her children be permitted to travel with her. "I could not consent to leave the children here, under these circumstances..." she explained in a letter to her father-in-law. "I was against the idea of a governess in general... and, in addition, I thought Aunt could manipulate Miss Winter.... This, I am certain, is not going to be the last problem which we will encounter."

When the Crown Princess arrived in Gotha, she found her brother, Alfred, "pale and emaciated... his young life wasting away." It had been a tragic year for Alfred. The heir to the dukedom was suffering from venereal disease. During the summer he had been discharged from his regiment. Missy had last seen him in the fall, when their mother, disgusted and embarrassed by his disease, had sent him to Roumania. Since then he had vastly deteriorated. "He hardly recognizes anyone and often does not know what he says, poor boy," Missy wrote Sandra in despair.

Shortly after Missy's arrival, her brother was moved to a rest home in Merano, Italy, where he died almost immediately, attended by only his French tutor and a servant. Marie Mallet, one of Queen Victoria's ladies-in-waiting, claimed that the doctor had warned the Duke and Duchess that "the boy would not live a week," but that they "packed the poor youth off to Meran [Merano] and now lament and weep at his having died quite alone.... How strange Royalties are," Victoria's lady-in-waiting said, "their children seem to lack the ordinary care bestowed on our own humblest middle class. Such a thing could never have happened to any of the boys I know and if it had the parents would be blamed by the whole of society."

Aunt Vicky said that her nephew should never have been put in the German Army and wrote her daughter Sophie to that effect: "It is true that he was giddy & wild, as many young men alas are, & that he contracted an illness, of which I know next to nothing, as I have never asked or heard anything about it, one dislikes thinking about it, & still more speaking or writing about it. This was neglected & the poor boy led a dissipated life besides. Potsdam!—*that* was not the place for him."

Alfred's death raised the question of the succession to the duchies of Coburg and Gotha. The Duke no longer had a son to inherit and, according to Lady Mallet, his own life was "not one that would be accepted at any Insurance office." After a number of conferences with Queen Victoria, Coburg and its 130,000 pounds annual income was settled on another English grandson, fifteen-year-old Charles, the Duke of Albany, who was promptly removed from Eton and sent to Coburg to be Germanized.

After her brother's funeral, Marie returned to Roumania. Within two months she was pregnant again. "May God give that it is another son," the happy Crown Prince wrote his mother. Ferdinand was also pleased with Miss Winter, now in full control of young Carol. Marie was not. As she had feared, the new governess was Queen Elisabeth's personal watchdog installed in Cotroceni Palace to save Carol, aged five, from his mother.

Incited by the Queen, Miss Winter was turning the boy against Marie and had even succeeded in removing "God bless Mamma" from his nightly prayers.

With Miss Winter in residence, Marie traveled more frequently. Her home was no longer a refuge and she was not its mistress. She remained in Bucharest only a short while before fleeing to the seaport of Constantza, where she spent several days on a yacht moored off the coast of the Black Sea.

Some weeks earlier, the Crown Princess had received a letter from Queen Elisabeth, asking her to invite Zizi Cantacuzène's cousin, a teen-age orphaned girl who had done social work with the Queen, to spend the summer. Scandal erupted when Marie appeared in Constantza with Zizi and his cousin constantly at her side. It was said that the Crown Princess drove through the town with the Roumanian lieutenant, accompanied only by the thirteen-year-old girl. Instructed by the King to keep him informed of the activities of the Crown Princess, the members of Marie's suite reported that she was with Zizi from morning to night and that he spent hours in her cabin with her. They said that the Crown Princess offended district officials and members of the consular corps by bidding her official goodbyes to the town with the young lieutenant at her side. Queen Elisabeth and Miss Winter accused Marie of inviting a motherless girl for the summer to screen her relationship with Zizi.

The King laid the indictment before the Crown Princess on her return. She admitted her romance with Zizi, but denied inviting his cousin to conceal it. "Aunt asked me to invite her," she told Carol. But Queen Elisabeth denied her role in the summer plans, and Marie was unable to find the Queen's letter. King Carol's reaction was entirely in character. "We of course all know that Nando may not be so very entertaining. But that does not mean that you may find your entertainment elsewhere." To make sure of this, Cantacuzène's regiment was changed and he was sent out of the country.

This was the chance for which Queen Elisabeth had been waiting. With Miss Winter's assistance, Missy's fling in Constantza was exploded into a major scandal, which the two ladies recounted in vivid detail in letters sent to friends and relatives around Europe. When the story reached England, Queen Victoria, accustomed to discretion in such matters, wrote King Carol to register her displeasure over the spread of the gossip. Back in Roumania the Crown Princess continued to search frantically and unsuccessfully for Queen Elisabeth's letter. Meanwhile, she and the Crown Prince lived noticeably apart. Since it was almost time for their annual vacation, King Carol sent the young couple on to Coburg to quiet things down.

On the day they were to leave Roumania, Marie was waiting for her carriage on a chair in the entrance hall of her palace. Edgy and jittery, she put her hand down behind the seat cushion, where she felt a piece of paper. It was the famous letter the Queen had denied writing. Although it was too late to stop the tornado of gossip touching down all over Europe, Marie and Ferdinand were reconciled. When they arrived in Coburg, they told the Duchess that they had had a fight with the King over a matter of no consequence.

After their vacation, Nando returned to Roumania while Missy stayed in Germany. She was still there when their son, Carol, came down with typhoid fever. Ferdinand sent her an urgent wire, and she hurried home. When she arrived at Cotroceni Palace, she ran upstairs, but Miss Winter stepped out to bar the entrance to her son's room. "It would be dangerous to admit anyone to the baby's bedside," she announced. "The doctor's instruction—" For perhaps the first time in his life, the Crown Prince stood up for his wife. "Stand aside," he told the governess. "The Crown Princess is the child's mother."

Happily for Marie if not his country, Prince Carol survived. His mother was doubly grateful. "I pray to the Lord that I am not again to be separated from my darling..." she wrote her father-in-law at the end of October. "Thank you for all your love and kindness, which you have shown me during this trying and sad time...I...suffered terribly...because of the knowledge that all of you suffered because of me...I hope to be permitted to rectify everything again...through my love to Nando."

But it was not so simple. With the story of Marie's transgression flying around Europe, the Duchess learned the truth about her daughter. Shocked but loyal, bristling with imperial pride, Missy's mother wrote to the King of Roumania. Her daughter was guilty of a "serious and unpardonable fault," but so were the King and the Crown Prince.

First, there was Ferdinand's character—"his laziness, his indolence, his antipathy for all work, for any serious endeavor and...worst of all, his sensual passion for Missy [which] finished by...repulsing her. Nando," the Duchess wrote the King, "will himself avow that he treated his wife like a mistress, caring little for her emotional well-being in order to constantly assuage his physical passions." There were also his own extramarital lapses, which the Duchess knew of "as a positive fact."

Secondly, there was the King himself. "I can never understand why you did not try to keep the deplorable story within the family. But alas! it has become the public property of all sorts of ruling families...the Empress Frederick [Aunt Vicky]...Charlotte Meiningen [Cousin Charly]...all my Russian and English sisters-in-law, my brothers know all the details of this terrible story, hinting that they learned it from gossip and letters coming directly from Roumania and evidently spread to blacken the reputation of my daughter!...I can never pardon you, my dear Cousin, for not having...wanted to restrain the scandal." Added to all this, the Crown Princess's children had been purposefully taken away from her. Spies had been attached to her suite. "As culpable as she is *nothing* will excuse the indignity of such procedures," declared the Duchess of Coburg.

It was noble wrath, answered by a *"very feeble"* letter from the King. The

Duchess pressed her advantage. The Crown Princess must be sent home for her confinement. If this was not agreed to at once, the Duchess herself would come to Roumania to fetch her. Miss Winter, who "was permitted to write all the details of this terrible story about Missy to the Queen Mother of Holland," must be fired.

The Duchess of Coburg offered Missy some advice by mail as well. "Your old Mama grieves but will never abandon you," she wrote. "You have greatly sinned, but it is time still to become a good steady woman." The Crown Princess must pull herself together, get rid of Miss Winter, never show her mother's letters to Nando, never tell her husband "the whole truth" about her "iniquitous behavior," and get herself as quickly as possible to Germany.

Marie returned to Gotha with daughter Elisabetha a week before Christmas, and on January 9, 1900, gave birth to a baby girl. A pretty towhead with a Cupid's bow mouth, she was named Marie after all the Maries in the family, but nicknamed Mignon* after the opera the Crown Princess attended the evening of her birth. For whatever reasons—a quiet existence away from her enemies, a peaceful birth, the near death of her firstborn—Marie adored this baby, lavishing on it more love than she had felt for the first two. "I could not let her out of my sight," she said, "she was a message of peace and hope."

Ferdinand came to Gotha to see his new daughter. He promised to dismiss Miss Winter on his return to Bucharest and meet his wife for a vacation with their son in Italy. But once back in Roumania, the Crown Prince was too cowed by the governess to fire her and repeatedly put off the family vacation. With each postponement he sent another letter begging Missy to come home before his prestige was destroyed. "I hope you also thought sometimes of your poor worried old husband here who can't be happy if he has not his little darling wify with him," Ferdinand wrote two months after the birth of their new daughter. "You forget... that the wife owes her husband obedience," he threatened a day later. "Your Nando... is more serious and has thrown his laziness overboard... I will pay more attention to you and when you are asking me for something, I will not come with all kinds of excuses just so I do not have to do it," the desperate Crown Prince promised.

Life in exile was no punishment for the errant Princess. She lived with her mother and seventeen-year-old sister, Beatrice, at Schloss Friedenstein, a huge castle built around a courtyard "large enough," in the words of a cousin, "to act as a parade ground for a battalion of infantry." The castle itself, overlooking the town from an elevation of one thousand feet, had its own museum, theater, library, and picture gallery; it was so huge that Missy's family occupied only one floor. The three women spent the long winter days

*She will be known as Mignon throughout this book in order to distinguish her from her mother.

in a central living room, painting, embroidering, and reading. "It was a blissful, harmonious and busy family life," Marie wrote.

With the Duchess of Coburg fighting for her daughter's rights, an eventual agreement was reached on the subject of Miss Winter. The Crown Princess would return to Roumania, but not until Miss Winter was dismissed. Even then, the King and Queen took some time before they could bring themselves to part with the governess. "Her only crime," said Carmen Sylva, "was her being deeply devoted to my family... I had hoped she would make a man of the child." It was April before Miss Winter was finally sent away—four months after Missy left Roumania. "Mamma had won the day, but from then onwards she and Uncle were only polite, but never more on really friendly terms," Marie later wrote.

While the Crown Princess was in Germany with her family, a Miss Ffoliet, the price of her return, was installed at Cotroceni Palace. A "long, thin" Irish woman, Miss Ffoliet was timid and withdrawn to the point of self-effacement. "Exceedingly shortsighted, she had a somewhat vague and watery look and gave a very limp hand in greeting, but I liked her," said Marie. Even now the Crown Princess had not been allowed to select a governess for her son. As King Carol had written the Duchess of Coburg the previous fall, "The education... of my future heir rests with me... it is my duty and my right as head of the family and as King." No more than a resident cipher, the new nanny was still the best of all the mentors ever provided by King Carol for the education of the heir to the throne.

With Miss Ffoliet in residence, Missy "had at last to tear myself away from Gotha and all those of the beloved family circle to join my husband and Uncle and Aunty." Ferdinand, taking no more chances, came to Gotha to collect his wife and two daughters.

Chapter *8*

Only the frivolous consider youth the best years of life.

—*KING CAROL I OF ROUMANIA*

*T*he Crown Princess returned to Roumania in the spring of 1900. It was not a pleasant homecoming. Marie found her six-year-old son, Carol, rude and demanding. She complained that his father had not disciplined the boy in her absence, but, as she told her mother, Ferdinand "*never* would have the courage to do anything by himself!"

Spurred on by the Duchess, Marie started a campaign to clean up the drainage system at Cotroceni Palace. After two cases of typhoid in the family, it was frustrating to be told that these improvements were too expensive. She also arranged for Carol and Elisabetha to start instruction in the Roumanian Orthodox Church. "Nando," she wrote the Duchess, "will again sit down to his stamps and 'règlements militaires', leaving the children's education to the person who will first insist on it. With him the terror of doing anything incorrect prevents him doing the things he ought to."

At twenty-four Marie was disillusioned and chastened: "At first one thinks that if one does not find happiness at home one can find it on crooked paths, but I have had to learn that it is not possible and that it is bitterly punished," she told her mother. If the romance with Zizi was over, the gossip was not. Nor would it be for some time to come. More than a year later Cousin George, still trying to douse the fires of criticism blazing through royal circles, wrote Missy a sympathetic letter. His kindness unleashed waves of self-pity: "Yes, I have been through hard moments, partly through my own fault I know, but also because many things have been very difficult and above all because I have been dreadfully lonely—I know one must not expect too much of life, Georgie dear, but... all was so different to what I thought... I very soon found out that down here one has to be very strong to stand the loneliness of it all, & I was not always strong, and expected too much— and wanted to be happy—and of course I had to learn by bitter experience all that one cannot have, and may not expect!—You will try and understand me, won't you—and when one speaks unkindly about me—will you some- times take my part... The brightest times I ever had were those Malta days."

Three months after her return home, the Crown Princess received word that her father was dying of cancer of the throat. When he refused to receive her or anyone in his immediate family, she sent Nando to Coburg. Ferdinand found his father-in-law being fed from a tube. The doctors had given him up; they told the Crown Prince that even if they removed the Duke's tongue, he could not be saved. Since the Duke and Duchess had been living apart for some time, it fell to their eldest daughter to re-establish contact between them. Missy asked her mother to write her father a cheerful letter, but not to try to see him. A visit from the Duchess, said Missy, "would only excite him more." Three weeks later the Duke of Coburg died at the Rosenau.

"Oh, God, my poor darling Affie gone... It is hard at eighty-one!" cried Queen Victoria, who had not been told until the week before of her son's condition. Within six months (January 1901) the Queen herself was dead.

Marie was angry at not being allowed to attend her grandmother's funeral with her husband. She wrote her mother to say that she was "quite dreadfully upset and unhappy about it!" She said she realized that the Duchess would not understand "because you never loved England," but she had still "kept an awful awful longing to see it all again if only for a day or two, to have a last peep at the old house.... with our dear old Granny the last link is cut off!—And now the thought that Nando goes there, sees you all whilst I am here all all alone, I tell you it is an inconceivable sorrow for me."

The loss of England was more painful for Marie than the loss of her grandmother, whom she had seen infrequently over the past ten years. Except for his one visit to Roumania and hers to Nice, she had not spent much more time with her father. Marie's primary concern over the Duke's demise was its effect on her mother, who had "barely recovered" from the death of her only son the year before. Whatever the Duchess of Coburg's mistakes in directing her daughter, she was still the most important person in Missy's life. It was her happiness or unhappiness, her approval or disapproval that registered most strongly with the Crown Princess. The Duchess was also Missy's major link with other members of the family scattered among the thrones of Europe.

Unlike her relatives in the royal network, who wrote unceasingly about births, deaths, and marriages in their caste, the Crown Princess of Roumania was absorbed almost exclusively during her twenties with her own problems. But for her relations in Germany, England, and Russia, Missy's life and that of sister Ducky were fruitful sources of conversation. It was clear that both girls had been glaringly mismated. Even ingenuous Cousin George, England's future king, recognized this. As his wife, May, wrote him toward the end of 1901, "after what you told me the other day of the sad lives of poor Missy & Ducky, we should be even more grateful to feel that so much sympathy exists between us 2 in our married life."

If Marie had to put up with a bad marriage to acquire a throne, Ducky was not in the same position. She and Ernie had begged Queen Victoria during her lifetime to allow them to divorce, but the Queen had always refused. Victoria knew she had made a mistake: "I arranged that marriage. I will never try and marry anyone again." Still, she remained adamant that Ducky stay with the husband chosen for her.

Queen Victoria's death cleared the way for the young Grand Duchess of Hesse to leave the Grand Duke, and in December of that year she divorced him to marry Grand Duke Kirill of Russia. Ducky's action was met with opprobrium throughout the courts of Europe. For once, Edward VII and his nephew, Kaiser Wilhelm II, found something about which they agreed. Their censure was benign, however, compared to the vindictive fury of Tsarina Alexandra of Russia.

Alexandra (known in the family as Alicky or Alix) was Ernie's youngest sister. A strangely isolated and haughty young woman, she had served as hostess in her brother's court until his marriage. Although she was in love with the future Tsar Nicholas II of Russia, Alicky had hesitated to convert to Orthodoxy to marry him. The arrival in Hesse in 1894 of the colorful, self-assured Ducky encouraged Alicky to leave home. Eight years later, the young Tsarina still resented Ducky for marrying Ernie and usurping her position in Darmstadt. Presented with a chance to destroy an old adversary in the name of righteous indignation, Alicky took full advantage of the situation. The Tsar was the tool of his wife's vengeance. Although he was fond of his cousin Kirill, he forebade the Grand Duke to marry the divorced Ducky. There was nothing for Ducky to do but retire to Coburg in hopes that the Tsar would change his mind.

Of all the members of Europe's royal houses, Queen Elisabeth of Roumania offered the most original solution to Ducky's problems. "God," the Queen declared, "had moulded" Ducky "for sorrow . . . and . . . she must fulfill her destiny." She "must not run after happiness anymore, but give up her life" to help others. She must "go and learn how to nurse, form a sisterhood of her own, wander about the world in search of all the suffering, all the misery, all those that life has treated hardly. Lead a life of continual sacrifice, that her grand nature was destined for this."

These pronouncements, outlined in a thirteen-page letter to Marie, made Ducky's sister smile, but did not divert her from what she saw as Ducky's real problem—the nature of her beloved Kirill. Marie worried that if Kirill defied the Tsar, gave up his country, his career, his wealth, and his family to marry Ducky, he would eventually regret his decision and take it out on her. Marie did not trust her sister's fiancé, whom she referred to as "the marble man." "I don't think you would like K.," she confided to an English friend, "he is an extraordinary cold and selfish man, you never can feel really happy and jolly with him, he seems to freeze you up, has such a disdaining way of treating things and people."

Very tall and aristocratic, with a small moustache, cool gray eyes, and a cleft in his chin, Grand Duke Kirill was the leader of the young royal set in St. Petersburg—"the idol," claimed one of his uncles, "of all women and the friend of most of the men." Contemporary pictures, however, justify Marie's lack of enthusiasm. Kirill looked down on the world from his great height with an expression of fastidious contempt.

In the summer of 1902, while the disgraced Ducky was in retreat with Kirill, Marie and Ferdinand traveled to London for the Coronation of Edward VII. Uncle Bertie, ordinarily not Missy's favorite uncle, had endeared himself to her by officially requesting her presence at the celebrations, and King Carol could not refuse to honor King Edward's request.

Since her return to Roumania more than two years before, the Crown Princess had been allowed no privileges. Although she had finally obtained the King's permission to eat lunch and dinner in her own palace, there had been few other concessions granted. Marie did not feel she could ask for much. "Nando," she wrote her mother, "shuts me up completely, perhaps I am paying for former mistakes, but it is almost unbearable... It really is an exile down here... It's a prison, Mama... And there is not only one jailor, they are all jailors."

The invitation to England could not have come at a better time. Edward VII was to have been crowned in late June, but an emergency operation postponed the festivities for six weeks. Although most of Europe's other heads of state returned to their countries, the Crown Princess settled down in the British Isles for the summer, earning the title among local wags of "Marie Remained Here."

It was during this period that she met Waldorf and Pauline Astor. "My dearest friends of all," Marie said, "were the Astors... We were asked down to Cliveden for lunch on the classical Sunday when everyone leaves town. It was an invitation like any other, a mere politeness, but it was the starting point of a very dear friendship which has meant much in my life." The party was such a success that Waldorf and Pauline invited the Crown Prince and Princess and their suites back to Cliveden to await the Coronation.

Cliveden soon took the place of Wolfsgarten as Marie's favorite vacation spot—a home where she could find good friends, compatible conversation and a civilized life. The original house, built in 1661 but destroyed by fire in 1795, had been replaced in 1848 by another one, designed by the architect of the Houses of Parliament. Laid out on a huge terrace surrounded by rolling lawns and groves of trees, the mansion, which is twenty miles from London, resembles a baroque Italian palazzo; it is flanked on one side by the original two-hundred-yard balustrade, complete with statues and fountains, which was brought from the Villa Borghese in Rome. In the early years of this century, Cliveden was decorated in the Italian Classical style with cracked leather furniture and serious tapestries. "The keynote..." said a later occupant, "was splendid gloom." Houseparties in the Astor home were normally dismal affairs, conforming to rigid timetables enforced by its cantankerous owner, William Waldorf Astor.

William Waldorf was the man who inherited the largest fortune in America from his father, John Jacob Astor III. When John Jacob died in 1890, the London *Spectator* suggested that he was possibly the richest man in the world except for Marie's father-in-law, Prince Leopold of Hohenzollern-Sigmaringen, and her cousin the Tsar of Russia. When John Jacob's $200 million failed to buy his son, William Waldorf, the social deification he considered his due or a seat in Congress, he left America, declaring that the United States was "not a fit place for a gentleman to live." Contentious and autocratic, William Waldorf Astor lived in England in a state of perpetual dudgeon, determined to avenge himself on his fellow Americans by buying a British peerage. His wife died in 1894, leaving the two older children, Waldorf and Pauline, to deal with an irascible father, a younger brother at Eton, and a little sister dying of tuberculosis.

When Missy met Waldorf and Pauline, they were both in their early twenties, younger than she, isolated, and as much in need of sympathy and friendship as the lonely Crown Princess. At twenty-one Pauline was in charge of her adolescent sister, who required constant nursing. With her easy familiarity, Missy endeared herself to the young Astor woman early in the Cliveden visit by staying behind one day, while the rest of the house party went off to London, to see how young Gwendolyn would survive an emergency operation. When Pauline emerged from her sister's room, she found the Crown Princess pacing up and down the hall. "I had no idea she was there. When I asked her why she'd stayed, she said she couldn't have left without knowing how the operation had gone. I was deeply moved at such sympathy from one we barely knew."

"A more charming couple than Waldorf Astor and his sister Pauline it has never been given me to meet," Marie wrote years later. "By some happy chance there was a perfect affinity of taste between us, somehow we looked at life in the same way; the same things amused or bored us, we had much the same opinions and ideals.... Those few weeks at beautiful Cliveden belong to the most perfect memories of my life. It was pure bliss. Rather starved of those things I had been born to, I found at Cliveden a healthy life of freedom in superb surroundings with young companions entirely congenial."

The Astors were as attractive as they were hospitable. Pauline, a slim and graceful brunette with a small face, was more engagingly appealing than pretty. Her huge brown eyes looked quizzically out at the world "as though everything came to her as a surprise," said Marie. The Crown Princess added that "Waldorf... too had large velvety brown eyes and a charming smile."

Waldorf Astor was tall and unusually handsome. His quiet manner masked a determination to live a life of public service. When Marie met him, he had just been graduated from Oxford, where he had served as captain of the polo team. Forced to quit polo because of a weak heart and an injured knee, he could still give Missy "many a useful hint about riding." They rode together through the Cliveden woods, around the local countryside, and in the Great Park at Windsor Castle. "The degree of enchantment this free, easy English country life brought me is impossible to describe," she wrote. "It was absolute happiness."

One day they visited Blenheim Castle unannounced. Ferdinand was with them. It was Tourist Day and the Duchess of Marlborough, the former Consuela Vanderbilt, had retreated into her private apartments, where the Groom of the Chambers ferreted her out: "I thought Your Grace should know... that the Crown Prince and Princess of Roumania accompanied by Mr. Waldorf Astor are touring the Palace."

When the Duchess found her "uninvited guests," they were in "fits of laughter"; the housekeeper of Blenheim, not knowing who they were, had been identifying for them the royalties pictured in photographs on the palace tables. The young Duchess of Marlborough was annoyed at the interruption, the gaiety of her visitors, and Marie's lack of what she considered appropriate regal sedateness: "The Crown Princess..." said the American-born Duchess, "was... a very beautiful woman. Dazzlingly fair, with lovely features, the bluest of eyes and a luscious figure, she was at that time at her zenith. Remembering that she was Queen Victoria's granddaughter, I was not prepared for the disconcerting bohemianism she affected; nor did her evident desire to charm successfully replace the dignity one expected.... I thought her eagerness indiscreet, and was conscious of a theatricality usually associated with a prima donna rather than with a bona fide princess...

"The Crown Prince, on the other hand, was a most unprepossessing person. He was ugly, and his ears protruded at an extraordinary angle. Waldorf Astor, who accompanied them, was my childhood friend. With his curly hair and flashing smile, he was as opposed to the Crown Prince as an Adonis."

There is little doubt that Marie fell in love with Waldorf Astor and that he to some degree reciprocated her affection. According to legend they had a passionate affair, but the truth seems to be that their relationship remained platonic. In a society in which the nobility patterned their love affairs on those of Edward VII, the American-born Waldorf Astor was an aristocratic Puritan, straitlaced and contained, not the sort of man to try to make love to another man's wife.

"My father," said David Astor, "was quite the most honest man in the whole world and the least capable of anything clandestine.... He was a very handsome young man and very nice, and totally safe. You could have had a sort of verbal romance with him without risk." Further testimony to the innocence of their relationship lies in Queen Marie's autobiography. Her memoirs abound in tender descriptions of the second Viscount Astor—an indiscretion she never would have committed had he been more to her than a friend.

The Crown Prince and Princess of Roumania returned to London in early August to attend Edward VII's Coronation and the attendant festivities. A ball given at Grosvenor House by the Duke and Duchess of Westminster symbolized for Marie everything she had left behind in England. The blue pavilion, built for the occasion, laid with quantities of Georgian silver and decorated with blue hydrangeas, pinpointed her loss:

"This enormous... room was a feast for the eye, complete harmony such as only the most perfect English taste and tradition could achieve... rich but not ostentatious, consummate refinement. Perfectly liveried footmen with that stately deportment peculiar to English servants, every one of them picked out for their fine figures and good looks, prodigious flowers, exquisite china, glass and silver, clever lighting, flattering to the complexion; in the distance soft music. Always an artist at heart, I sat there drinking in all this beauty rendered possible only by generations of civilization and wealth. Fate had taken me to a country where all was in the making, where everything meant effort, and here I was, come back to the land of my birth, to that beauty most kindred to my soul."

Immediately after the Coronation, Marie and Ferdinand hurried home. Shortly thereafter, Waldorf and Pauline's young sister died, and Missy invited her new friends to spend October with the royal family at Sinaia. This was the first of a series of annual visits, and from 1902 to 1906 the Crown Princess counted heavily on the Astors to enliven the Roumanian scene. They fell in love with Roumania and taught its Crown Princess to recognize and savor its unique charms. Formal ceremonies and local festivities, formerly only tolerated, became "a source of amusement" when seen through Waldorf's deep-brown eyes. Waldorf Astor was the first person to suggest that the Crown Princess establish closer contact with her people. The Duchess of Coburg's advice, based on her training in the Russian court, was all aimed at maintaining Marie's position with the aristocracy. Waldorf concerned himself with the people as well. When Marie wrote that she was finally learning Roumanian, he was delighted. "I'm *sure* that it will do more to ensure popularity than almost anything else. If when visiting a small village one can talk to them fluently without accent & perhaps even with a bit of slang thrown in one wins more sympathy than you w^d imagine. This is a well-known historical everyday fact," Waldorf wrote back.

King Carol appreciated the Astors' interest in his country; because of them, he changed his attitude toward Marie. Carol had always directed his demands to Ferdinand, assuming that it was he who carried them out. Pauline tactfully explained that it was Marie who ran Cotroceni Palace, since Ferdinand was unable to make decisions or give orders. The King learned the truth of this in the winter of 1903 when the Crown Prince and Princess ran into serious debt. Marie was the person who undertook an investigation of palace finances and confessed their plight to the King; her husband was too frightened to do it. This act of courage impressed the monarch. He bailed them out—though rumor says he charged interest—and thereafter showed new respect for the Crown Princess.

Raised by a difficult father in a trying environment themselves, Waldorf and Pauline had learned to approach their problems with finesse. Watching them in touchy situations, Missy began to do the same. More sophisticated than the Crown Princess, they taught her the expediency of moderation. Because they were beautiful and witty, she accepted the lessons.

Certainly Nando was neither. He had lost his looks and, worse for his wife, had started to play the fool. A master of languages, ancient and modern, as well as a first-rate botanist, Ferdinand chose to hide his learning from others. His great apologist, Princess Marthe Bibesco, said that "he played the ignorant . . . so as not to offend others who were not equally erudite." To Marthe, the Crown Prince was a displaced savant, too intelligent and sensitive for his uneducated English wife.

It is possible that Princess Bibesco's assessment of Ferdinand is entirely accurate. He may well have been a true intellectual aristocrat who "understood the difference between himself and those closest to him, the unattainable distance that separates people of high culture from the others. Sad for having measured the distance in his favor, he hid himself to offend nobody." According to George Duca, son of Jean Duca, a Roumanian Premier of later date, "Ferdinand was a very great personality intellectually, and practically no one knew it. Those who knew it, like my father, were absolutely full of admiration."

Another aristocratic Roumanian writer, Princess Anne-Marie Callimachi, looked at Marie's husband differently. "Prince (later King) Ferdinand of Roumania was a shy, somewhat clumsy man . . . who never seemed at ease with society women, although he was reputed to frequent, without reluctance, less commendable ones." Britain's Military Attaché during World War I concurred. He reported to the Foreign Office in London that Ferdinand was popular but weak, with "no vices but one, which, when practiced by Royalty, commends the good-humoured approval of the worst prude . . . a taste for somewhat indiscriminate fornication."

Withdrawn at home, frightened by society, the Crown Prince was still an object of considerable female attention, and he counted among his conquests at least one of his wife's closest friends and one of her ladies-in-waiting. "Being the great gentleman that he really was," said a friend, "he did everything quite discreetly. . . . At military manoeuvres, it was easy for him to have affairs with certain ladies of bad repute."

If military gatherings away from home provided surcease for Ferdinand, those that took place in Bucharest were socially hazardous. An inept horseman in a world in which parades signified power, any military review in which he took part offered an opportunity for the Crown Prince of Roumania to make a fool of himself in public. During one particular parade, Ferdinand failed to execute a simple trotting maneuver, easily managed by all the officers preceding him, and he fell off his horse in front of the reviewing stand. All Bucharest stared as the police rushed forward to grab the animal and help the Prince to his feet. Coldly ignoring his nephew, King Carol continued to review the troops while one or two observers clapped their hands in derision. "In those days the crowd did not care for him or admire him," said a member of the aristocracy.

Ferdinand's incompetence with horses was matched by his gracelessness with people. He was so shy that even as king, his hand shook when he greeted visitors. Often he stammered or repeated meaningless phrases—a habit about which strangers were warned before being presented to him. The story is told that one outspoken American wife of a British Minister, frustrated by Ferdinand's incessant repetition of her inane pleasantry, finally interrupted him. "Now, Sir, let us have a serious talk, and don't repeat what I say."

If he didn't stammer, he was often struck dumb. George Duca, son of a prime minister, recalls going through the reception line at Cotroceni Palace. A young man, the guest at the palace had just entered the army and was appearing in uniform for the first time. As King and Commander in Chief of the Armed Forces, it was imperative that Ferdinand say something appropriate to the boy in uniform: "And so he looked at me and he pushed me aside and he looked at me again and then he started giggling and then he turned around and then he pushed me again. He wanted to say something, but he couldn't say it. And I, of course, was petrified. I was a corporal, I was nothing, and I was in my uniform and I didn't dare to talk. . . . He wanted to say something and it didn't come out. I thought, 'I must help the poor man, but what can I say?' And by the time that I had decided that I couldn't say anything, he had decided that he couldn't say anything whatsoever, so he started smiling and laughing and nodding his head and going to the next guest. And that was typical."

In contrast was the dazzling Marie, described at this period of her life by

Princess Callimachi as she appeared arriving at the opening of a provincial charity. Dressed in a long, dark simple gown with a scarlet cape tossed dramatically over her shoulders, she was wearing a large black picture hat of feathers that set off her blond hair and pale skin:

"Framed in the doorway of the royal coach, her luminous beauty lighting up the dullness of our drab railway station, she remains an unforgettable vision. Her magnificent blue eyes sparkled; her vivid complexion glowed ... She was simply breath-taking. To radiant beauty she added intelligence, wit, passion."

Princess Callimachi thought Marie was superb. "I knew her all my life, was devoted to her, believe she was the most beautiful woman I ever saw, held her in total admiration, and, whatever her shortcomings, no word of real criticism could fall from my pen. Even her faults, moral or physical, turned out to her advantage... Her love affairs and caprices were never considered a grievance by the people. On the contrary, I believe the Roumanians, with their natural lack of morality, felt relieved at not having a saint for their Queen."

The Roumanians, for whom infidelity was a way of life,*ascribed many more love affairs to their Crown Princess than she had. This created problems for Marie in her relationship with Waldof Astor. Waldorf and Pauline were due to arrive in Roumania in the summer of 1903, shortly after the time Marie expected the birth of her fourth child. The baby was late; the days ticked by, bringing nearer the date set for the yearly visit of the Astors. Aware of the gossip about herself and Waldorf, Marie wrote Pauline:

"I am dreadfully troubled to know what to do... I would like to say come on... if it's over with me or not! but would it do? W. has the wretched

---

*In her memoirs, Princess Anne-Marie (Vacaresco) Callimachi tells a story which illustrates the Roumanian attitude toward extramarital love. It is the story of her grandfather's birth:

"Constantine Vacaresco had ... begun his political service as Prefect of ... a province not far distant from the capital. One late night he was driving home from Bucharest ... and in order agreeably to surprise his young wife, he silenced the loud cries of his post carriage and proceeded to the front door of the residence, only to find it closed and everything dark and silent. Astonished and curious, he went round the single storied house; not a sign of life. Helen must have gone to bed. So he would go and knock at her window. But stop! a ray of light was filtering through the curtains of that one and only window. He drew nearer, hesitating to give her a fright. Peeping quietly through the panes, he received a shock ... his wife was not alone. . . .

"Just as silently as he had come, he withdrew, went back to his postilions and coach, entered it, and gave orders to drive full speed, all bells ringing and men shouting, thrice around the main streets of the small, sleepy town. When, an hour later, he alighted at his front door, the house was fully lit up, the servants were on duty, and his wife awaiting him in evening dress. A son was born some time later." (Callimachi, *Yesterday Was Mine.*)

quality of being 'un jeune homme'... and though between us right-thinking ones it is all perfectly natural, and I know he would be the dearest kindest most restful companion even on the second day, others might not see it in that light... I cannot come to another conclusion but that it would not be wise to have W. here, till at least 8 days *after* the event.... You know how I love and trust him... but there is the world and its stupid conversation."

The Crown Princess finally gave birth on August 7, 1903, to her second son. Of all her babies, this one, with his blue wolf's eyes and hawk nose, most resembled the Hohenzollerns. Marie and Ferdinand named him Nicolas and asked Nicholas II of Russia to be his godfather, hoping to influence the Tsar in favor of Ducky and Kirill. It didn't work. Tragedy struck Ducky that November when her eight-year-old daughter, vacationing with the Grand Duke of Hesse and the Russian royal family, fell desperately ill in Poland. Although the doctors warned the Tsarina that the child's mother should be called at once, the telegram was not sent until too late. Ducky's child died of typhoid fever before Ducky could reach her.

But for Marie, these were good years. Waldorf and Pauline Astor filled the void caused by the separation from her sisters and intensified by her husband's neglect. For the first time since leaving home ten years before, Marie found companions outside the family circle, friends with whom she could share her loneliness as well as her enthusiasms for horses, home decoration, and her newest passion, photography. Letters filled with detailed descriptions of the weather, her children, their nannies, her trips, and the tedium of court life flew from Roumania to England, often several a week. As did gifts. No sentiment or object was too trivial or too heartfelt that Waldorf and Pauline, her friends of the soul, would not understand.

Neither of the young Astors was healthy. "Delicate" was the word Marie used to describe Waldorf's angina and Pauline's nervous depressions. She worried about them both, nagged them in person and by post to be sure they got enough rest. When Waldorf left on a trip to the United States, Missy sent his valet enough letters so Waldorf could be given one every day he was away.

On their visits to Roumania, Marie took her friends galloping into the mountains on her favorite horses. Back at the palace they read out loud or spent quiet hours burning and carving wood to be made into Art Nouveau furniture. They recorded their activities in hundreds of photographs, exaggeratedly romantic pictures in the style of overprivileged Pre-Raphaelites: Waldorf on a restive mount, framed by the rugged Transylvanian Alps; Missy in lace, reclining languorously in one of her baroque rooms, a lily in her hand; little Elisabetha and Mignon lying on two fur rugs, their childish chins resting on the heads of the animals—Mignon on a tiger, Elisabetha on a bear.

As Waldorf and Pauline spent more time in Roumania, they came to understand and share Marie's irritation with her husband and his family—

their pomposity, humorlessness, and insensitivity to others. In one satirical letter, Waldorf characterized the Crown Prince as a man "who through his talents, character, and temperament is eminently fitted to be a Royal Personage and nothing else." His family was described by young Astor as "the illustrious, undivorceable... skittle-loving, cigar smoking (4 penny extra specials for own consumption and six a penny mal de mers for subjects & unroyal friends) House of Hohenzollern."

Not surprisingly, Marie lived from visit to visit, impatient with anything that threatened to keep the Astors away. In her letters to England she assigned aliases to members of the Roumanian court so that she might write more openly about them. King Carol was named Dombey from Dickens' *Dombey and Son*, a cruel, cantankerous old man who lived only for his work and his male heir. Ferdinand was known as Dombey's Nephew. Lonely and frustrated, the Crown Princess proved too ardent a correspondent and friend. Even in an era of throbbing hearts, her letters reek with what one Astor descendant terms "sentiment laid on with a spatula."

The young Astors could not devote themselves forever to Marie. Both married within the next four years and set about pursuing their own lives. For obvious reasons Pauline's marriage, which came first, did not cause Marie the same turmoil as her brother's. In 1904 the young Astor woman disgusted her upward-striving father by marrying a commoner, captain Herbert Spender-Clay, later a Conservative M.P.*

Marie was not permitted to go to England for her friend's wedding, but made up for her absence with many letters of good wishes and advice. In one of these, addressed to Spender-Clay himself, she begged the future groom not to be jealous of her devotion to his wife, to remember that Pauline's health was not good, and to "be very gentle with her, because it all seems very strange to a woman at first, to some, it's hard. She is a little bit my child," added Marie, probably embarrassed at her own frankness, "that is why I say this."

Her reaction to Waldorf's marriage was more ambivalent.

In 1906 he met and fell in love with Nancy Langhorne Shaw, an American divorcée with a young son. Faced with the inevitable, Marie responded gallantly, writing Mrs. Shaw that "it is the greatest joy... to think that such happiness is now soon in store for him. I know that his dream is to create a happy home with a woman he loves, and I am sure he will be able to make her happy—as he is so truly good, so clean-minded, and has remained so unspoilt amidst temptations and flatteries."

Missy did wish Waldorf happiness, but she also wanted desperately to be

---

*William Waldorf Astor did not live to know that Pauline and Herbert's daughter would one day be sister-in-law to the Queen of England, H.M. Queen Elizabeth, now the Queen Mother.

included in his future life. Hence an avalanche of letters from Cotroceni Palace, detailing her loneliness and the importance of the Astors in her life, begging the lovers to come to Roumania for their wedding trip.

It became quickly apparent that the bride and groom did not intend to share their first days with a third party, and the Crown Princess gave in gracefully. "How full of emotion you must feel at the idea of the wedding," she wrote Nancy a month before the event. "I wish I could be there, but it will be nicer still to receive you here soon after—only have your honeymoon first, one must not spoil one's honeymoon by the presence of anyone else."

But when Marie learned that Roumania was not on the Astors' foreseeable itinerary, she lost all self-restraint. "I longed so to hear from you both as I have been feeling desperately lonely," she wrote the new Mrs. Astor four weeks after her wedding. "But indeed it's a very very great disappointment that you are not coming. I clung to the hope of your coming with all the strength of my poor worried old heart. . . . I know you *would* have come if you had been able and that consoles me in a sort of little way. But I want just to tell you openly *why* I mind so very much . . . you will build up your life and get into your habits and have other friends and poor lonely me will have to get on as best I can with nothing to look forward to. You see, I felt so *sure* in my heart that when you knew me, you would like me."

One of Marie's fears was that her reputation had preceded her, and Nancy might not care to become her friend. In England the Crown Princess of Roumania was known for flamboyance and, thanks to Queen Elisabeth, indiscretion. "You have probably heard the world say unkind things about me, but you who have gone through hard times yourself, will know how seldom the world leaves a woman alone," she wrote her friend's new wife.

There is an Astor family story, based on no less an authority than Lady Astor herself, that throughout their honeymoon Waldorf received daily letters from Marie, and in order to stop the correspondence, Nancy had to threaten to leave him. One of Lady Astor's recent biographers* claims that the letters were a figment of Nancy's aged and failing memory and that, although there were far too many notes from Marie on the honeymoon, they were sent not to Waldorf but to his bride, reiterating the Crown Princess's overbearing eagerness to meet her.

The name on the envelope does not matter. Judging from letters that have survived, in which Waldorf begs Marie time and time again "not to send too many notes," Marie reached new heights of self-defeating fervor toward *both* bride and groom. Pitiable in her efforts to be included, she had to be eased firmly and swiftly out of their new life. Given the commanding ego and highly competitive nature of Nancy Astor, the blow fell within a few months of the marriage and nearly severed the relationship for good. Waldorf had warned Marie repeatedly. Now he just stopped writing. She was stunned: ". . . it was not as if he had been my lover (don't be horrified at my

*Christopher Sykes, *Nancy: The Life of Lady Astor.*

frankness)," she wrote Waldorf's sister Pauline, "it is not... as if I had tried to catch him, I had quite simply and quite naturally loved him with all the *very best* my nature had to give... he was the breath, air & spirit of my life and *he knew it*. Yet the moment he was married he gave me up entirely, mercilessly, in fact... and he *knew* what it meant to me to suddenly lead a life without him.... You will remember *all* we were to each other, even perhaps more than you know, because you have not read all his letters, you don't know how till every smallest detail I shared his life, and he mine.... Don't be afraid little Pauline, I have given him up now entirely, I see she has him in her hand... little W. that was—*he is no more....*"

In spite of Marie's emotionalism, the relationship was not dead. Nor was the real Waldorf Astor. Within a few months they started corresponding again—occasionally and not so personally, as befitted Astor's married state. With Nancy the Crown Princess exchanged holiday gifts and solicitudes over the discomforts of pregnancies. One special present, probably a peace offering, arrived at Cotroceni for Christmas in 1906, the year of Waldorf's marriage. A gray crocodile motoring bag with solid-gold fittings, it was Marie's favorite gift of the season in spite of the fact that King Carol presented the Crown Prince and Princess with a large dark-blue automobile in which she might carry it.

Marie soon accepted her new status as friend of the family with courteous resignation, if not total grace. "I won't try to keep him, not even to remind him of former days," she vowed in a letter to Pauline, "but I shall always keep up a correspondence from time to time so that we should not feel strangers when we meet." It was 1911, in fact, before she finally did see Nancy for the first time. By then the Crown Princess was prepared to love her friend's wife without trying to devour her and quickly became one of Nancy Astor's greatest admirers.

Whether the respect was mutual is open to question. Nancy Astor was known for her acerbic tongue, and Marie was almost too easy a mark. Nonetheless, the intensity of the early intimacy with Waldorf and Pauline provided a basis for lifelong trust. Whenever the Crown Princess, later Queen of Roumania, was in trouble, she turned instinctively to the Astors, the friends of her youth, confident of finding ready help and support for herself and her family. She was never disappointed.

Chapter 9

I was brought up by my mother's iron
principles and one was never to give way
to anything, neither to love, emotion or
illness!—I stuck to the illness.

—*QUEEN MARIE OF ROUMANIA*

As Waldorf and Pauline Astor withdrew from Marie's life, the Crown Princess began to look around for companions to take their place. By 1906 the King had relaxed most of his early prohibitions. Marie responded by grasping every chance to move out into the world of Roumanian society.

The life of an unmarried girl of aristocratic Roumanian descent was bound by almost feudal restrictions. Marriage, on the other hand, brought astonishing freedom to girls often still in their teens. Rich, attended by numerous servants, the young society matron was not only urged to exercise her intellectual predilections, but tacitly encouraged to follow her passions as well. Stupidity, not infidelity, was a Roumanian sin. This social climate created a class of unusual, often eccentric young women, some of whom grouped themselves around their Crown Princess.

Of these the most important in early years was Maruka Cantacuzène, wife of the Mayor of Bucharest. "A sudden friendship which has sprung up between me and Mme. Cantacuzène... gives me pleasure," Missy wrote Sister Sandra early in 1907. "We motor about together even in the snow.... When Nando goes out shooting I sometimes even go to her after dinner, this is not really admitted but sometimes one *must* take a little freedom if none is given.... It makes a difference in my life as... I was feeling very friendless."

Maruka was of Moldavian descent—dark, striking, and strong-minded. Married to the eldest son of the wealthy leader of the Conservative Party, she was rich enough to cultivate her peculiarities. Maruka was afraid of light and crowds, and refused to go to other people's homes, but became famous for her own parties. These took place in a large salon, half lit by soft flames floating on the surface of mammoth jars of oil. The hostess received her guests from a low couch on which she spent the entire evening, not even rising to greet royalty, but occasionally sending a scribbled rapturous note to some favored soul. Regulars spoke of the hazards when an outsider ventured into this dimly lit den; the uninitiated invariably stumbled over a piece of furniture or stubbed his toe on an oil jar, while the habitués, all of whom were young, laughed at his confusion. "Once I even made Nando dine there..." Missy wrote in triumph, "a till now absolutely unheard-of thing." A frequent guest at Maruka Cantacuzène's was Georges Enesco, whose violin, according to Marie, "never sang more beautifully than in her presence." Years later, after the death of her husband, Maruka married the great musician.

Another member of the inner royal circle was Princess Marthe Bibesco, well on her way to becoming an author of international repute. Marie had originally met Marthe when the Crown Princess first came to Roumania and Marthe was just a child. "I liked to have her with me..." Queen Marie later recalled. "The adoration she had for me was pleasant to my young vanity. I had a great name and two long rows of ancestors from the opposite sides of Europe looked down upon me; all this Marthe knew, knew it even better than I did."

Born into a clan of Conservative Party ministers, Marthe Lahovary was married at sixteen to Georges Bibesco, scion of one of the great princely families of Wallachia. One of her contemporaries describes the young bride as "strikingly handsome, with a scheming nature, faulty ankles, great intelligence, steady will power, and an incomplete education." Her new mother-in-law spirited Marthe off to an isolated country villa in the Carpathian Mountains, where the young woman was put on a diet of reading, writing, and grace.

Two years later Princess Bibesco burst on the literary scene with the publication of her first book, *Les Huit Paradis*, crowned by the French Academy when its author was only eighteen years old. Marthe left at once for Paris, where she was lionized by French literary society. Marcel Proust fell into the long line of her admirers, and Paul Claudel said he considered her second only to Colette in French prose style. "French salons of quality..." said Princess Callimachi, "instantaneously opened wide their doors to this girl, so young, so ravishing, and so gifted.... Her looks, her wit, her impeccable French, her enormous emeralds exotically set, her talent, her skillful quotations, the retinue of beaux surrounding her—she was the marvel of the city."

Marthe Bibesco's great flaw was wanton ambition, an inexorable need to be in the center of the social and political scene. As one of her acquaintances put it: "She *had* to be right there with the right people on the right spot at the right moment.... She was ready to compromise any kind of situation just because she wanted to be on the right side no matter *who* was on the right side and what the right side was." This obsession eventually led the Roumanian Princess into an affair with the Kaiser's eldest son, Crown Prince Wilhelm of Prussia, and once having committed herself, to misjudge the outcome of World War I. It also carried her into a liaison with Ferdinand after he became king. But in the early days of the Crown Princess's ascendancy, Marthe Bibesco was one of Marie's liveliest friends.

Neither Maruka nor Marthe, however, could take the place of Ducky. In spite of their temperamental differences, Marie had a special feeling for this sister that lasted throughout her life. They shared the same background and interests. Both loved painting and interior design. When Marie set out to decorate Cotroceni Palace, it was Ducky who came to Bucharest to help her realize her exotic visions.

Marie's first venture into decorating set the pattern for a lifetime of homes. Whatever her current taste—Byzantine, Renaissance, or Art Nouveau— Marie's domestic environments were always theatrical. Coffered ceilings, fanciful walls, painted friezes—these were only the background elements of rooms overflowing with carved and gilded furniture, animal-skin rugs, silk cushions, silver picture frames, and jades. There were masses of flowers everywhere—at least one or two vases on every table and large containers on the floor.

Cotroceni Palace was originally a seventeenth-century monastery, converted by Prince Cuza into a summer residence for himself. Three stories high, standing outside the city of Bucharest on a hill in the middle of a large wooded park, it was built on the foundations of the old monks' cells around three sides of a courtyard. Within the courtyard among ancient trees stood the old basilica, a small sanctuary filled with glowing icons, gold and silver lamps, and ancient evocations of austere saints.

Having just discovered the glories of Byzantium, the Crown Princess began at some expense to reproduce them in her personal apartments. Queen Elisabeth reacted to her successor's alterations by donning sackcloth. "I have still got the same old things, even some furnishings of Cuza's time!" the Queen complained to a friend. "Instead of admiring the Princess for her inventions, they ought to admire me for bearing so long the old things.... I have nearly as good taste as the Princess! The ideas are not wanting in my head! But I never dared ask for anything from the hour I ceased to be a mother."

Carmen Sylva envied Marie's newly decorated salon, where the Crown Princess began to give parties. "It is something between an Indian temple and a fairy tale, so lovely... marvellously beautiful, and so original," the Queen said. Princess Anne-Marie Callimachi drew a different comparison, remarking that the new room reminded her of "both a church and a Turkish bath."

Marie's turquoise salon rarely left visitors indifferent. Its colorful walls were nearly obscured by yards of cascading ribbons and hedge roses, carved from wood and gilded. In the middle of the room stood a bronze statue of a girl holding a brightly lit cross. The coverings on the furniture were embroidered with peacock feathers, worked by the Crown Princess herself. Bronze chandeliers hung from the vaulted ceiling, while huge jars of flowers and exotic plants were scattered around the green tile floor. "Crossing its threshold, one hesitated between horror and laughter," said Callimachi, "and then decided to concentrate on the hostess, beautiful in brocaded silks, or floating gauzes, wearing heavy barbaric jewelry designed to fit the setting, which suited her to perfection."

Marie's "beloved church bedroom" was done in silver, its cathedral ceiling carved with branching trees. The woodwork, painted ivory, was executed by Missy and Ducky themselves. There were silver braziers on the floor filled with lilies; antique silver lamps hung over the massive silver-leaf furniture. Marie's bed was a low couch on a platform, backed by a headboard in the shape of a Greek cross; it stood under an elaborate canopy and was covered with fabric shot in silver, purple, and gold. Across from the bed was a fireplace and over the mantel, a picture of white anemones painted by Ducky for her sister and lit by concealed lighting. Beneath the picture there was an inscription, "Once it was always springtime in my heart."

In October of 1905, four years after her divorce, Ducky and Kirill defied the edict of the Tsar and married secretly in the Duchess of Coburg's private chapel. Since many Russians had looked on Kirill as their future Tsar, the couple had waited to marry until the birth of Nicholas and Alexandra's only son in 1904.* Kirill's near death during the Russo-Japanese War made up their minds. Since no one could find a Russian priest who would risk disobeying the Tsar to perform the service, the ceremony was conducted by the Duchess's private confessor. Marie was not present.

The Crown Princess of Roumania, though "very pleased it's done," was still dubious. "I hardly know to what sort of happiness it will lead," she

*As the eldest son of the eldest Grand Duke, Kirill was closely in line to the throne; married to his divorced cousin, he would have been ineligible.

confided to Pauline (Astor) Spender-Clay. Her apprehension was justified. Pressured by the Tsarina, Nicholas II struck Grand Duke Kirill's name off the list of imperial allowances and stripped him of all his titles, decorations, and privileges. Kirill, who hurried off at once to Russia to confess his marriage and ask the Tsar's forgiveness, was given forty-eight hours to get out of the country.

Life in exile was not hard on the young couple, as both his parents and her mother stepped in to support them. Although they had an apartment in Paris, Ducky and Kirill spent summers in Tegernsee, the Duchess of Coburg's new home outside Munich, and winters at Château Fabron in Nice. Kirill devoted his energies to golf, which, according to his mother-in-law, he treated "as seriously as others would sitting in Parliament."

In the summer of 1906 Ducky and Kirill emerged from discreet obscurity to attend their first public function, the Roumanian International Exhibition, held in Bucharest. During the Exhibition it was fashionable to dine in festive pavilions hung with flags and lit with Chinese lanterns, overlooking a lake awash in floating lights. Every night for a week the Crown Prince and Princess and the Grand Duke and Duchess Kirill, flanked by important members of the aristocracy, came to drink champagne, eat caviar, dance to the music of the gypsies, and watch fireworks.

The Roumanian International Exhibition of 1906 was planned to commemorate the first forty years of the reign of King Carol I. "Not an anniversary habitually celebrated," remarked Princess Callimachi, who explained that the exhibit was really designed to display Roumania's burgeoning economy. There was some cause for national pride. Over the years since 1866, Roumania had acquired at least the external trappings of Western civilization.

Oil was being produced in large quantities. There were nearly two thousand miles of railway crisscrossing the land. The Iron Gates—rapids feeding into the Danube at the point where the river enters Roumania—had been blasted for navigation. A bridge had been completed over the Danube at Cernavoda, uniting Constantza, Roumania's port on the Black Sea, with the rest of the country and opening up the heretofore unused wastes of the Dobruja. The nation's once empty treasury now earned sufficient credit to borrow from European financiers at 4 percent. Roumania, the road between Berlin and Constantinople, had become "the Belgium of Southeastern Europe."

There would have been much to celebrate had this been the whole story, which it was not. Eighty percent of the population still farmed for a living, but about half the land remained in the hands of a few rich boyars. These aristocratic landlords kept the peasants enslaved by continually raising their rents and then requiring them to borrow money at high interest, payable in hard labor. The peasant who owned his own land was not much better off, for ignorance of modern farming techniques and poor health from malnutrition kept him from using it to advantage.

King Carol and Queen Elisabeth appeared at the Exhibition in their honor only once, on opening day, when, in the words of Princess Callimachi, "correct and stiff, the pale, bearded King read his inaugural speech in perfectly worded Roumanian rendered practically unintelligible by his strong German accent." The King and Queen were not popular, according to Callimachi. "They were a highly moral couple, in a serious, stolid manner, commanding the Roumanian people's respect and perhaps admiration, but not its gay, lighthearted love—that all went to the princely couple, the Heir Apparent and his lovely wife."

The Crown Princess was now in her early thirties, the Crown Prince in his early forties, and they had been married nearly fourteen years. In her twenties Marie had complained to her mother, "I don't love my husband." At thirty-one she was resigned. "At least Nando and I are very good friends now," she wrote the Duchess, "and I hope that we may work together in spite of what is missing." Fortunately for them both, the Crown Prince was named Inspector of the Cavalry, which gave him a specific job to do. He spent more time away from home on troop inspections and hunting trips. Shooting was Ferdinand's favorite sport, particularly wolves and bear. Occasionally Marie joined him on these excursions, but as she wrote Sister Sandra from the Prince's shooting box near Bucharest, "Certainly there is no duller companion than Nando!"

Moreover, when they were together, Ferdinand always seemed to be scolding his wife, collecting grievances to tot up against her. "We know certain characters and it is better not to do things they would always be able to dish up against me in times to come!" Marie wrote Pauline Spender-Clay, peeved that the Crown Prince had refused to let her go on a country weekend with friends pending the imminent death of a friend of the Hohenzollern family.

A stickler for form, Ferdinand still lived in awe of his uncle and in terror that Marie or someone from their palace might do something wrong. More than six months after the death of his father in 1905, the Crown Prince refused to allow his gentlemen-in-waiting to attend the theater. He had difficulty instructing them in the simplest matters, such as when to order his carriage, but was furious if Marie did it for him. Enslaved by convention and infuriated by his own indecisiveness, Ferdinand took out his frustrations on his wife. The fact that he could not control her increased his agitation. The relationship cannot have been easy for either of them.

Nevertheless, the Crown Princess had developed a personal routine for coping with life in the Balkans. Winters were the hardest. The weather was harsh; the days were short and often bleak. Visitors from Western Europe rarely braved the long trek to Roumania, preferring to join the royal exodus to the Riviera. In spite of the freezing cold, Marie rode every day, expending on her favorite horses some of that surfeit of energy that never seemed to desert her. Attacked by wild dogs on one of her rides she shrugged off the danger: ". . . when one rides a lot one must just take the chances of an accident or two, because after all a horse is never an armchair."

When she wasn't galloping in the mountains, teaching her children to ride, or visiting her regiment on maneuvers, she attended to the many schools, theaters and charitable institutions she was expected to patronize— planning bazaars, arranging exhibitions, lending her name and efforts to worthy projects. In the winter of 1906–1907 Marie was president of six charities. Although she hated giving public balls on winter nights "because of the poor coachmen and horses,"* she had started giving large teas at Cotroceni Palace in order to meet as many of her future subjects as possible. "You can't even know *how* in spite of all my faults and my so-called flightiness the *whole* country counts upon me & looks up to me as the strength of their future!" the Crown Princess wrote her mother.

The Duchess was difficult to impress. Consciously or unconsciously she punished Marie for her good health, cheerful disposition, and efforts to triumph over a difficult life. In letters from St. Petersburg, Coburg and Nice, she accused her eldest daughter of being a "disappointment" and wrote that she "shed tears of humiliation" over what she called Missy's selfishness and desire to be amused. Ducky's conversion to the Russian Orthodox Church in early 1907 provided a new point of attack: "I had so hoped that you would also one day turn Orthodox, especially on account of the children!" Missy's mother wrote. "But no, it is better so, as one must take it seriously and your life is not like that."

Although the Duchess refused to recognize Marie's growth, the Crown Princess was gaining respect from an unexpected quarter. During the fall of 1906, King Carol fell ill and took to his bed for several weeks. The deterioration of his health marked an improvement in his relationship with Marie. She paid him daily visits, usually at teatime, when she perched at the foot of his bed with her handwork to listen to him discourse on politics. As the King came to know Marie better, his admiration for her native intelligence increased, and a genuine affection sprang up between them. This bond grew stronger during the political crises that preceded World War I.

In the middle of March 1907, an uprising of the Roumanian peasants led to an even more important change in the life of their Crown Princess. The revolt started as another pogrom, of little concern to the monarchy or nobility. The Roumanian aristocrats had chosen to ignore all previous indications of unrest, including the abortive uprising of the neighboring Russian peasants two years before. Still feudal in his outlook, the boyar pursued love

---

*The Crown Princess's concern for the comfort of her servants was not the norm among royalties of her day. When Marie first moved to Cotroceni Palace, her mother advised her to be sure her maids slept two to a room so as not to spoil them. At the Kaiser's court one unventilated toilet was provided for every twenty-six servants.

and local politics, oblivious to the privations of those whose lives paid for his luxuries. The monarchy was not much better. Marie claimed that it was only King Carol's illness that had kept him out of touch with the people. "There seemed contentment and happiness all round," she wrote a friend, "there was a wonderful harvest and everyone was rich and well off... Certainly it is due to socialistic influence, but of course the peasants *are* badly off & a great deal remains to be done for them."

The peasants soon turned from burning and looting the homes of the Jews, who acted as middlemen for the nobility, to those of the large tenant farmers and absentee landlords. Within a few days they had leveled whole sections of the countryside, setting fire to the estates of the boyars and destroying their country palaces as well as the flammable crops stored in their granaries. The Roumanian peasant was not ordinarily bloodthirsty, at least not vis-à-vis the boyar, but there were certain landowners, long hated by their tenants, who were found savagely murdered.

As the revolt fanned out over the country and Austrian troops began to mass along the Transylvanian frontier, King Carol moved into action. Although he issued a royal proclamation pledging agrarian reform in keeping with the usual monarchical practices of the day, his actions were anything but conciliatory. The King mobilized 120,000 soldiers with orders to shoot without mercy; Bucharest was declared under state of siege and cordoned off. More than ten thousand peasants were reportedly killed within three days. Whole villages were razed, and criminal charges were brought against anyone even suspected of peasant sympathies. No one will ever know exactly what was done to suppress the revolt, as all the pertinent files were taken from the Ministries of War and Interior. Ironically, Marie reported to her English friends that "the only consolation out of it all was that not a single word was uttered against the royal family, on the contrary they looked upon us as their help."

Once the revolt was crushed, the Liberal Party took up the agrarian cause, primarily for its political value. Led by their new Minister of the Interior, Ion Bratianu II, the Liberals passed legislation to promote the transfer of land from the boyars to the peasants. Since execution of the law rested with the landowners themselves, peasant gains were kept to a predictable minimum.

The Revolt of 1907 seriously damaged Roumanian prestige abroad. Marie said it was a "miserable humiliation" for the King, but for the Crown Princess herself, March and April of 1907 was a season of discovery: "I have more than one reason for remembering that spring... when my eyes were opened to several truths and when I began to go more deeply into the interests of my country. Much that I had not understood, or had overlooked through ignorance or lack of perception, became comprehensible to me; my horizons widened, I came together with more interesting people.... The days of acute loneliness were over."

The awakening was due to Prince Barbo Stirbey.

During the worst of the peasant riots many nervous boyars sent their wives and children to the mountain resorts away from the dangers of Bucharest. Among the emigrants was Princess Marie, taken to her home in Sinaia along with her four children. There were very few people in the summer resort that early in the year. One of these was Marie's friend Marthe Bibesco, whose English country house, Posada, was nearby. Marie spent five days in the gray fieldstone mansion. Another houseguest was Nadeje Stirbey. Nadeje was married to Prince Barbo Stirbey. A contrast to many Roumanian women of her class, Princess Stirbey was more typical of her generation elsewhere in Europe, a woman content with her home, her servants, and the sort of work—painting, embroidery, gardening—sanctioned by the gods of domesticity.

A third guest during the emergency was Jeanne Vacaresco; her stepdaughter, Princess Callimachi, later told the story of the romance that developed between Crown Princess Marie and Prince Barbo Stirbey:

"With male company grievously lacking, visiting husbands were undoubtedly welcome, above all so intensely attractive a specimen of virile masculinity as Barbo Stirbey . . . Stirbey must have been seriously concerned with the state of his properties and recent industrial ventures, badly mauled by the rioters, and Princess Marie's delightful sympathy surely brought relaxation from anxiety. That the attraction went a little further soon became visible. Since he was reputed a devoted husband and loving family man, it took the public a long while to awaken to this budding affair. Anyhow, within a short span of time his feelings and attachment were so conspicuous that no doubt was possible for those who knew him. Riding the clouds, his wife remained blissfully oblivious."

Barbo Stirbey came from one of the great ruling families of Roumania. His grandfather, a prince of the Bibesco clan, reigned over Wallachia before the Hohenzollerns. Born two years before Princess Marie, Barbo Stirbey was educated, like most aristocratic Roumanians, in Paris, where he studied law at the Sorbonne.

Stirbey was tall and slim. He carried himself with great authority, although his manner was deceptively self-effacing. Mysterious, elusive, he was said to be impervious to flirtations. Nevertheless, the ladies of Bucharest spoke of his charm and the "strange hypnotic quality" of his dark-brown eyes. He could have had any number of women, but had chosen to marry at the age of twenty-two his not outstandingly pretty cousin, Nadeje Bibesco. With the death of his father shortly thereafter, Prince Stirbey inherited the family estate of Buftea, an hour or so outside Bucharest. Five years later he won a seat in Parliament, but his concern with agrarian reform did not sit well with his colleagues in the Conservative Party, and he withdrew from active political life. From then on he devoted himself to building a financial empire.

Stirbey turned his gigantic farm into a profitable agrarian conglomerate— growing, processing, and transporting the products of his orchards and fields on a private railway to his own shops in town, where they were sold to the public. His name became synonymous with excellence; the best Roumanian wine was known simply as "Stirbey." By channeling his profits into venture capital and banking, Prince Stirbey grew to be one of the richest and most powerful men in his part of the world.

Seductive to women, in his own home Barbo Stirbey was the adored papa, a young patriarch who showed his temper only if one of his four daughters dawdled after the ringing of the dinner gong. His peers were impressed with his quiet, unassuming attitude and his talents for persuasion and speaking to the point. "In a country of fast-talking people," one contemporary recalled, "I have not encountered a man of fewer words; in a society preoccupied with appearances, I did not meet a man of greater modesty."

The Crown Princess had never known a man like Stirbey. Unlike the Crown Prince, he had no pedantic pretensions or nervous assumptions of superiority. A social being at ease in the world around him, Stirbey was quiet because he was confident. More important to Marie, he had no rights over her.

Although the Roumanian Prince made it clear that he was passionately attracted to the Crown Princess during their sojourn together at Posada, she took some time to return his affection. Stirbey was used to the women of his world who thought nothing of a casual affair. Still recuperating from Waldorf Astor, Marie was not an easy conquest. Barbo demanded what Waldorf had not, an adult relationship. In return he offered total commitment.

Marie must have shown more than just politeness, for in May, off on a shooting trip alone with Nando, she wrote Sandra that the glorious weather made her "long for nice cheery companions to enjoy things with, but alas that is never to be my lot in this country, the moment I get fond of anybody, jealousies arise... and *sie werden weggebissen* [they are driven away]!"

In spite of this, the Crown Princess began to visit Buftea frequently. A fine horseman, Stirbey took Marie on long rides through the sun-dappled woods around his estate. To give her pleasure, he had long bridle paths cut through the towering white oaks. When their duties kept them apart, Stirbey wrote the Crown Princess graceful letters, homages to her beauty and his joy conveyed through opaque layers of courtly formalities.

For Barbo Stirbey this was the great love of a lifetime. "His speech was short and straight to the point," Marie wrote years later in *Crowned Queens*, describing a man partly modeled on Prince Stirbey, "and no one had ever guessed what passions lay beneath his unbendable pride."

Chapter 10

... mothers getting ready to be
queens... have so many thousands of
things to see to that they cannot be
perpetually watching over those under
their protection.

—*PRINCESS MARTHE BIBESCO*

*P*rince Carol was thirteen when Prince Stirbey and his mother fell in love. Tales of violent confrontations were invented to explain the enmity that eventually grew up between Marie's eldest son and the Roumanian aristocrat. They are not true. If Carol resented Stirbey at this early age, it was only a brief manifestation of his Oedipal love for his mother and an acknowledgment that Prince Stirbey was one of the few men the young heir to the throne could not order about.

Marie was an adoring but ineffectual parent. She could not bring herself to discipline her offspring and took pride in the fact that the palace nurseries were always happy places, undisturbed by harsh words. "I hated the feeling of any sort of tyranny or coercion, and had an insurmountable aversion from scolding... I confess that many of the failures, even the disasters of my life, can be brought back to this fundamental inability to scold or reprove," she admitted. In spite of her enormous attachment to Carol, Marie would have been the first to agree that he was the greatest disaster of all. In his case, it was not entirely her fault.

Carol's problems began on the day he was born. The first child and heir to the throne, the baby Prince was spoiled by everyone from the King and Queen down to the servants who waited on him. His father was weak, his grand-uncle tyrannical. From an early age little Carol was led to believe that whatever he ordered would be carried out.

A bright boy, a voracious reader and memorizer, Carol was blessed with enormous natural curiosity, which soon turned into spiteful pedantry. "He was unusually interested in all things pertaining to rules, laws, proscriptions and interdictions..." his mother wrote, "this came probably from being a great deal with Uncle, whose specialty was to instruct." Young Carol developed a passion for things military, particularly uniforms and discipline. He set up rules to tyrannize his younger siblings—games that annoyed but amused his mother, who found her young son's purposefulness more manly that his father's passivity. Marthe Bibesco, who frequented the royal household, said that Marie's eldest son was "absolutely convinced that he knows everything, that he is superior to humanity in general."

King Carol and Queen Elisabeth took Carol out of his parents' hands as early as possible, installing what they considered safe surrogates in the young palace. These preceptors were not, as might be guessed from their unsuitability, carelessly chosen. Like everything to which King Carol I put his mind, tutors for the heir were hired only after far-flung research, intensive consultations, and minutely detailed recommendations. The choice of a German master was considered so momentous that Prince Carol lived for years ignorant of the beloved language of his father and great-uncle because a person of sufficient caliber had not been located to instruct him.

At the age of five Carol was turned over to Miss Winter. At six he was delivered into the insipid care of Miss Ffoliet. Well meaning though she was, Miss Ffoliet was little help to the Crown Princess when it came to reestablishing the boy's respect for parental authority, undermined by her predecessor. When crossed, Carol flew into "fits of rage and anger." It was obvious to Marie that the young Prince needed strong male guidance. After a long search the King appointed a tutor for the boy. M. Mohrlen was a morose Swiss homosexual devoted to botany, the Bible, and the republican ideals of his homeland.

As far back as Marie's ancestor Catherine the Great, members of ruling houses had imported Swiss intellectuals to tutor their heirs. The object was to apply a liberal veneer over a firm sense of the royal calling. Mohrlen failed on both counts. Had he been a man of clear convictions, he might have trained an enlightened Prince, anchored in the democratic realities of his time; had he been a man of emotional strength, he could have taught Carol self-discipline. Mohrlen was neither. He gave the young Prince no political precepts on which to hang his future crown. Worse, he fell in love with the boy, allowed him to have his own way, and in his anxiety to keep the love object to himself, alienated Carol from his family. Together and alone, teacher and pupil trudged off on long botanical expeditions during which the melancholy tutor passed his persecution complex on to the future King of Roumania. From Mohrlen, Carol learned the easy lesson of self-pity.

At first Marie noticed only Mohrlen's dour face and lack of energy. Although she referred laughingly to her son and his tutor as "two old maids," she acknowledged that the Swiss was an excellent linguist and "profoundly moral, which is a good thing for here." It took some time before she or Ferdinand began to suspect that Mohrlen was a bad influence on their son and was "filling his [Carol's] mind with disturbing doubts, especially about being a prince and a soldier."

In 1909, when Carol was sixteen, Marie and Ferdinand tried but failed to have Mohrlen dismissed. The King, having chosen the tutor with Germanic thoroughness, refused to admit he had made a mistake. In the presence of His Majesty, Mohrlen was "humble and unpresuming," and King Carol mistook mousiness for harmlessness. With her penchant for misjudgments, Queen Elisabeth supported Mohrlen to the end, declaring that "one so well versed in the Bible must be a good and holy man."

Eventually the two court doctors came to the parents' aid and insisted on Mohrlen's dismissal. Carol was nearly eighteen. He was sent to England with General Perticari, an A.D.C. to the King. Weeping hysterically at being left behind, Mohrlen ran off and hid in the woods for three days after his pupil's departure. When he finally reappeared, he "went to pieces with remorse," volunteering to Marie that in the early years he had been consumed with desire at the sight of young Carol kneeling by his bed at night saying his prayers. The Crown Princess sent him away, but touched by his misery, continued to send him money when he needed it.

Marie's sister Beatrice saw Prince Carol when he arrived in London in 1911 with General Perticari and wrote a letter about him to his mother: "I found... Carol rather inclined to try and settle things over the general's head [,] quite jolly and amiable but I am sorry to say inclined to be rude to the general... It is difficult with him as he gets most violently rude if one only differs in opinion from him [,] he is evidently accustomed to completely lay down the law... He seems quite astonished that everybody is not of his opinion, especially... girls... as they... treat him as if he were anybody else... He puts himself... on a most satirical and superior footing, smiling down on the rest of humanity as if they were half-wits."

Faced with severe disciplinary problems with her eldest son, Marie conceived the idea of sending Carol to Potsdam to join his father's regiment. The young Prince's outward behavior improved at Potsdam, although it was too late to undo years of emotional damage. Carol never outgrew his adolescent adoration of his beautiful young mother, and Marie continued to be flattered by his attachment. Convinced that her son would eventually learn to use his intelligence for the good of his country, the Crown Princess regarded her great, strapping boy with pride, blinded by his serious psychological problems.

Marie adored her eldest son, but she had difficulty liking her eldest daughter, Elisabetha. In this she was not alone. Aunts and uncles, nursemaids, and friends of the family had great trouble warming to this enigmatic child, whose birth had caused her mother more physical and emotional pain than any other single event in Marie's early life. Like her brother Carol, Elisabetha was taken over by the King and Queen. In the girl's case, however, the Crown Princess was allowed to supervise some activities, and Marie enjoyed horseback riding and exploring with this spunky if unaffectionate daughter.

As a baby, Elisabetha was remarkable to look at and a source of pride to her mother. "Since she came into existence she has had that irreproachable face, as perfect as it is classic, so classic as to inspire much the same feelings as... a wonderful piece of sculptured marble," said Marthe Bibesco. Withdrawn and unsociable as a little girl, at puberty Elisabetha began to put on excessive weight, which humiliated the slim and graceful Crown Princess. While Carol sprouted up, his sister got fat. "I feel as if I wanted to prune my two eldest children," Marie wrote Sister Sandra in 1908, "they seem to grow out on all sides and need tidying." "Carol... would be good-looking if he had not those awfully fat lips. Lisabetha is spreading dreadfully and decidedly is not pretty just now." Nor was she interesting. "Mamma thinks her decidedly dull," Marie admitted.

Unloving and haughty, Elisabetha was another product of too many authorities and too little discipline. Like Carol, she was highly intelligent; unlike him, she was intellectually lazy. Queen Elisabeth taught her namesake that she was superior to her mother, the Crown Princess, that hers was a "deeper, more artistic and much [more] interesting nature." To pull her into line, Marie hired Leile Milne, former governess to the English Connaughts. In a letter arranging the details of Miss Milne's employment, the Crown Princess discussed frankly her problems with the child and difficulties with her meddling great-aunt:

"It is more important for you to have a good influence upon Lisabetta than to give her lessons... she loves all that is beautiful, but she... has little ambition.... You will find that the Queen will be quite charming to you and, alas, I have never found a governess yet who did not prefer her to me— as she is much more charming, but it does not lead to real happiness in the end. Try to have the force to resist her charm and remain heart and soul devoted to my house—two courts alongside of each other are always a danger and a difficulty unless there is absolute faithfulness to the real master."

The advent of Miss Milne was a boon to Marie. In a household where courtiers, nannies, and servants all jockeyed for recognition from the old palace, Leile Milne remained loyal to her employer. Still, she had trouble getting through to Elisabetha. "Lisabetha is a curious rather cold reserved nature and she seems able to keep people at a distance in such an uncomfortable way," Marie complained to a friend.

When Elisabetha reached eighteen, the Kaiser wanted to marry her to one of his sons. Marie was afraid that her eldest daughter, accustomed to the freedom of life in Roumania, would balk at the rigidity of the German court. Nevertheless, pressed by her husband and the King, who were flattered at the prospect of such a match, Marie arranged for Princess Elisabetha to meet Prince Adalbert in Munich. The Kaiser's son was unimpressed. Marie was not surprised. As she told her mother, "... young men don't get very fond of Lisabetta, she is too sharp and too silent, not gay enough, a sort of living statue." The only time Elisabetha expressed any enthusiasm was over clothes and jewels, which she avidly collected.

Mignon, the third of Marie and Ferdinand's children, was the opposite, a girl with virtually no malice and no material desires. The Roumanian Crown Princess was in disgrace when Mignon was born, shunted off for her indiscretion to her mother in Germany. "I used to predict," she said, "that this third child I was carrying would be a child of tears, because in those days there was not a night that I did not weep myself to sleep, but my previsions were wrong. When my little daughter was born in Gotha on January the 9th, 1900, she was from her first day a child of joy and sunshine."

Marie was also a different parent. She had always adored her babies, but as time passed she learned to assert herself in caring for them. Lavishing on her infants great physical affection, Marie defied royal custom and insisted on nursing them herself. When Prince Carol was born, he had been placed with his nurses at some distance from his mother's apartments in King Carol's palace; to visit her infant son, the young Princess had been forced to run from one end of the palace to the other. By the time Mignon came along, Marie and her family had moved to their own home, where Marie had easy access to her babies.

A placid contrast to her older siblings, Mignon was sweet-tempered, happy, and unjudging. She was, said her mother, "born to be the *souffre-douleur* [butt] of all the others." Mignon admired her older brother and sister but could not compete with them. They teased her unmercifully. "She is pretty and she does not know it," said Marthe Bibesco. "How could she know it? Elisabetha is so beautiful—more beautiful than she is and than all the world. Carol is so very much more intelligent than she and tells her so every minute."

The Crown Princess often sent Mignon to visit her unprepossessing Aunt Sandra (Princess Hohenlohe) at Langenburg Castle. Sandra, whose married life was less harried than that of her older sisters, sometimes took Missy's children when they needed a vacation from the stresses of court life. More than any of the others, Mignon flourished in the simpler, less competitive household of her aunt, away from her brothers and sisters. Mignon loved the warmth of the old German Renaissance *Schloss* perched high on a green mountain ridge overlooking storybook valleys below. "She is a friend with every servant, knows the people in the village and has a special pet name for Uncle Erny [Prince Ernst of Hohenlohe]. . . . Unfortunately the Langenburg food is too excellent, Mignon gains weight, but she is so happy, she loves everybody and everybody loves her," said her mother.

As she grew up, Mignon grew increasingly heavy and passive. Seemingly devoid of ego, she dressed herself in Elisabetha's castoffs. For her mother, who planned every outfit with minute attention, Mignon's disregard for fashion was an annoyance, her lack of feminine vanity an enigma. The least demanding of Marie's children, Mignon had to be protected from being bullied by the older two and forgotten in the concern for the babies.

Prince Nicolas was born in 1903 in the middle of Marie's Waldorf Astor period. The Crown Princess, innocent of wrongdoing and aware of the rumors, was feeling noble, put upon, and secure enough in her adopted country to realize her worth. Motherhood was the one thing that always gave the Crown Princess, subject to Balkan attitudes, a sense of importance. She was feeling so indispensable that during the pregnancy she threatened to leave Roumania as she had in 1900, only this time her exodus would be voluntary and permanent.

Her threat grew out of a complaint lodged against her by one of her ladies-in-waiting, all of whom answered not to the Crown Princess but directly to the Queen. "This gave them the whip hand," she explained, "as they soon understood that in matters of conflict they would always be upheld." This particular lady was waiting on the Crown Princess on May 10, Roumanian Independence Day. Pregnant with Nicolas, accompanied by three-year-old Mignon, Marie arranged her carriage for the celebratory parade, inadvertently insulting the woman by directing her to the seat opposite rather than next to herself, thus forcing her to ride backwards. "I was so occupied acknowledging all the ovations. . ." said Marie, "that I had little leisure to observe my lady's face." Next day the Crown Princess received a written reprimand from King Carol saying that the lady-in-waiting had tendered her resignation on the grounds that Marie had "offended and humiliated her in public." The King considered the charge "entirely justified" and demanded an explanation. The press got hold of the story, the public took sides, and the incident mushroomed into a *cause célèbre*.

Besieged by the King, the Queen, and her clucking ladies, Marie wrote the Duchess of Coburg for support. There was little sympathy from that quarter. "The ladies want always to be one's friends and confidantes. . ." her mother wrote back; "you are too awkward and too little experienced to know how to hold in hand your surroundings. Having so much Miss Astor with you is a grievance that *no* lady will ever get over." Nando, though more sympathetic than her mother, was no more of a comfort. "What of course no one can understand," Marie wrote Pauline Astor, "is that Nephew [Ferdinand] is no good! I can't talk to him...or ask him to help, because I know he would not even try to, couldn't in fact. Where is he...to find courage...Nephew's only system is to heap discouragement upon discouragement upon me, and after a talk with him I always feel worse."

Pushed to the wall, Marie sent for the current Prime Minister. Six months pregnant with Nicolas, she received the head of the government sitting in bed, framed against her pillows, angry, imperious, "very much Queen Victoria's granddaughter and daughter of Marie Alexandrovna, Grand Duchess of Russia." Quivering with fury, seesawing between French and German, she threw out the ultimate threat: "I have decided to leave the country if this sort of thing continues; I shall shake its dust off my heels, return to my mother, taking with me the unborn child, boy or girl, which was to have been my fourth gift to those whose only sport it has been to suspect, calumniate and willingly misunderstand me....I am indifferent to the outcry there will be, to the scandal; you can explain my desertion as you will."

It was pure blackmail, and it worked. The Prime Minister, terrified that Marie's spasms of indignation might upset Roumania's hopes for another prince, stood horrified while the Crown Prince patted his wife gingerly on the back and promised that the Premier would speak to the King if only Missy would calm down. Later, the lady-in-waiting's resignation was accepted, but on Marie's terms and not before the Crown Princess had verified for herself that Roumania needed her more than she needed Roumania.

Prince Nicolas was born three months later. His birth delighted the Roumanians. His charm, as he grew, enchanted his mother. Nicky was funny and independent and could get away with things allowed none of the other royal brood. Thin, wiry like a monkey, he was irresistible to the King and soon superseded his older brother, now a hostile adolescent, in their great-uncle's affections. Marie was pleased with herself: "With this son they will leave me more alone and I shall carefully avoid the faults which have so much spoilt Carol," she wrote her mother.

Unlike Marie's other babies, Prince Nicolas was rather ugly. The long hawk nose of the Hohenzollerns sat strangely on his pinched child's face, and his blue eyes reminded his mother of a wild beast. Sickly, prone to respiratory infections, he was hard to treat, working himself up into "blind furies" against the doctors, kicking and flailing at them, trying to defend himself against further pain, and having finally to be subdued by force. To avoid these unhappy episodes, he was sent away from the freezing cold of Roumania to his Aunt Sandra, who, because of her own precarious health, spent winters in the Duchess of Coburg's villa at Nice.

A hyperactive child, Nicky was the most difficult of all the Crown Princess's offspring, but still to Marie "quite the most amusing creature alive." She admired his fearlessness and agility, both lacking in his older brother. He was almost impossible to discipline, for those detailed to control him fell quickly under his spell. On visits to the Duchess of Coburg he mixed water with the gas for her cars; his grandmother, a stern old lady unaccustomed to being crossed, said he ought to be whipped, but could not bring herself to order or administer the punishment. On visits to Langenburg he rode his bicycle round and round the inner courtyard, exhausting his nannies without tiring himself. "Here as everywhere he... establishes for himself a special freedom no one dares curtail," laughed his mother.

Prince Nicolas' sense of freedom eventually blossomed into irresponsibility. But in his early years, he was considerably more appealing than his brother and, next to Princess Ileana, his mother's favorite among her children.

Ileana, "the child of my soul," was not born until 1909—a time when the Crown Princess, aged thirty-three, had started to pay more attention to her duties. The arrival of a new baby in the household created some excitement among the older children. Carol was Ileana's favorite, and the fifteen-year-old, normally withdrawn, returned her love, smiling openly and allowing her to tug at his hair. Mignon quickly became Ileana's second mother, while Nicky guarded her crib "like a jealous little dog." Only Elisabetha was "indifferent" to the baby, refusing to pick her up. "She has no maternal feelings at all," Marie complained to Sandra.

With dark-blue eyes, a tiny nose and mouth, Princess Ileana looked to her mother as if she might turn into a beauty. As active as Nicolas, she was also the easiest of Marie's children to raise. "Ileana was naturally well-behaved; Ileana, as is so seldom the case, was born with the law within her, it was never necessary to teach Ileana the difference between right and wrong; Ileana knew."

Ileana had another gift that appeared at a young age and delighted her mother—social *savoir-faire*. Although extreme courtesy was part of the code of royal behavior, Ileana was the only one of Marie's three daughters who inherited their mother's ease and gift for smoothing out the vicissitudes of court life. At luncheon one day, noticing that the officer on duty had no one to talk with, Ileana excused herself from "the more royal part of the table" to pull up a chair beside him and engage him in conversation. She was seven years old at the time.

Because of her favored position with her mother, Ileana confronted enormous jealousies as she grew older. Being younger, she also benefited from her mother's earlier mistakes. She was better educated; more attention was paid to her. By the time this child was born, the King and Queen were too old and too tired to interfere, and Marie had gained self-confidence.

Ileana was born two years after Prince Stirbey became an intimate friend of the household, and it was rumored that she and her younger brother were Stirbey's children. In the case of Ileana, Stirbey's letters to Marie disprove the gossip. He writes about Ileana in the same way and with the same degree of concern as he writes about her older brothers and sisters; it is the interest of a kindly uncle or a trusted family friend. In the case of Marie's youngest son, however, there is a marked difference in tone.

Marie's last child was born in January of 1913 and named Mircea after a Wallachian hero of the fourteenth century. He survived only a few years, succumbing to typhoid fever two months before his fourth birthday.

Unlike most of her royal counterparts, Marie spent a great deal of time with her children. Court life in Roumania offered few of the diversions that tempted her peers in Western Europe or St. Petersburg. The Crown Princess not only turned to her offspring for simple companionship, but expressed open irritation when their lessons interfered with outdoor games. Childlike herself, full of bubbling enthusiasms and recklessness, she was more playmate than mother—delighting in their pranks, leading their adventures, revolting against their and her authority figures: the King, the Queen, and the stodgy monitors thrust on Cotroceni from the old palace.

This quality of youthful rebellion was related less to Marie's chronological age than to her basic makeup, an unusual blend of free spirit and *noblesse oblige*. There is no question that Marie of Roumania was monarchical to the core. She believed absolutely in the rights and duties of her lineage, but not in the dreary minuets of court protocol that often enslaved her peers. Although she accepted the disappointment of her marriage with resignation (and later grace), she felt justified in looking for ways to escape the tedium of Carol's court and believed she had the right to find amusement elsewhere, after she had performed the dynastic duties imposed on her by birth.

The most acceptable form of entertainment was the ceremonial royal visit, and the Crown Princess of Roumania seized every invitation with alacrity. In 1910 she and the Crown Prince were invited to Germany to celebrate the Kaiser's birthday. Accompanying them was Marthe Bibesco, currently in favor with the Kaiser's son.

Deeply loyal to the Hohenzollerns, Ferdinand never passed up a chance to return to his family and homeland. Although Marie enjoyed living in Frederick the Great's magnificent blue-and-gold rococo bedroom during her stay in Berlin, she was peeved by the condescension shown her by Dona, the Kaiser's wife, who held "a very decided bad opinion" of her. She was also put off by the Kaiser's brusque superiority and contempt for women in general.

Cousin Willy seemed to enjoy sparring with Missy, and his habit of parading the male plumage brought them to an open clash one evening during the festivities. Used to being unreservedly admired, Marie was incensed when the Kaiser, eyeing her gown of silver sequins, inquired if she imagined she was Lohengrin or the Lorelei. "I was always perfectly able to hold my own with him," she commented later, "but must admit that he roused in me a certain pugnacity... all conversation with him was like crossing swords."

The Kaiser was not fond of Marie. This she knew from remarks he made behind her back. Unknown to the Crown Princess, she had an ally in Uncle Bertie (King Edward VII). In a conversation with his nephew a few years earlier, the King of England had spoken of Missy "with great affection," saying he could never understand the Kaiser's attitude toward her. "A little coquetry and a flirtation every now and then were surely permissible in a young and pretty woman. Moreover rumours were always exaggerated," commented the King of England. As to Missy's husband, he got what he deserved. "It is not wise to play the schoolmaster everywhere," said Uncle Bertie.

If Marie was tolerated in Berlin and liked in London, she was adored in St. Petersburg, where she took Ferdinand for the marriage of one of her young Russian cousins to the Prince of Sweden in 1908. The wedding was held at Tsarkoye Selo where the Tsar and the Tsarina had retreated, rarely if ever appearing in town. As a member of the Romanov clan, Missy was included in family discussions of what was wrong with Nicholas and Alexandra.

Marie blamed Nicky's withdrawal from the family solely on his wife. In spite of a spectacular chain of shilling-sized diamonds worn by the young Tsarina as other royalties wore pearls, Alexandra, said Marie, preserved "the face of a martyr... convinced that it is the style which suits her best." Marie avoided Alexandra during her Russian visit. "I can't say that I have much desire to be with Alix and she probably has none to be with me..." she wrote her mother.

The only reigning sovereigns of whom Marie wholeheartedly approved were the English. In 1911 she and Ferdinand attended the Coronation of Cousin George (George V), a ceremony that brought back memories of the Coronation, nine years before, of his father, Edward VII. Both their consorts, Marie felt, were fortunate women: "Queen Alexandra and Queen Mary: two serene figures, imbued with all the dignity of Royalty, lovely faces of calm assurance; their crowns, although weighted by a hundred gems, did not seem to oppress them, nor to be unduly heavy, there was an established security about these queens which made you feel glad for them, not afraid."

In one way Marie was better off in Roumania, where there were outlets for her excess energies and power drive. If there were fewer luxuries and social rewards, there were other compensations. The wife of the King of England had to confine herself to established charities and ceremonial appearances. The wife of the Crown Prince, later King, of Roumania had practically no traditional restraints. Only the second person to hold her position, she could shape it to the extent of her capabilities.

While Marie observed her peers already sitting on thrones around Europe, King Carol prepared for the inevitable transfer of power to the younger generation in Roumania. Impatient with older, more intransigent ministers, the King had already turned to Ion Bratianu II, aged forty-two, to help him steer Roumania through the peasant revolt of 1907 and the political and economic upheavals that followed in its wake. "Bratianu... is receptive, he follows up my ideas, quickly understands my desires... He is eager to please me," the King told the Crown Princess.

"Thus," Marie said, "did Ion Bratianu's star begin to rise."

As the eldest son of the deceased Ion Bratianu, Bratianu II was a natural choice for leadership in the second generation. It was his father who had brought Prince Karl of Hohenzollern-Sigmaringen to Roumania and worked with him to create a stable government. Now King Carol turned easily to the son.

Ion II had been carefully prepared for his role. Like most upper-class Roumanians, he was educated in France. Unlike some others, he had emerged with a command of the French language admired by the most snobbish Parisians, who ignored the whine in his voice to admire the purity of his syntax and the beauty of his accent. Superbly conversant in history and the French literature so dear to his countrymen, he possessed one of the best libraries in Eastern Europe. "He was a very great politician," said one member of the aristocracy, "a great historian, a man who was very aloof, who considered himself in many ways (and he was certainly justified) superior to those around him."

Secure in his destiny, Bratianu wrapped his intellectual arrogance and inflexible will in wheedling, insinuating charm. A stocky Don Juan with a leonine head, black eyes, and black beard, he was idolized like a Turkish pasha by the women of his milieu, who cast themselves quite successfully before him. Even Bratianu's enemies marveled at his power over women. From their initial introduction, when she was seventeen and he was twenty-eight, it was clear to Marie that Bratianu "had a way with ladies."

When the Crown Princess arrived in Roumania, Bratianu was the only man under forty whom she was "occasionally allowed to see!" Ion II never made the mistake of the elder statesmen of his day, who discounted or patronized the girl destined to be their queen. On the contrary, he made it his business to show Marie what an "eminently agreeable companion" he could be.

After a short, unhappy first marriage, Bratianu had married Elise Stirbey, Barbo Stirbey's sister. A tall, imposing woman, an aristocrat of lineage and the mind, Elise Bratianu was an awe-inspiring figure to young Marie. The Crown Princess hesitated to approach her in the early years, but as time passed she overcame her shyness. When they got to know each other better, Marie often referred to Elise laughingly as "my severe old lady."

Elise Bratianu once asked Marie why she did not do more serious things with her time. "Because I am not intelligent," the Crown Princess replied. "You have no right to say such a thing!" countered Elise. "You are full of intelligence but you are too lazy to use it; just try and see the things you could do, if you gave up being lazy!"

Guided by Barbo Stirbey and goaded by his sister, Marie began to look more carefully at her adopted country. Although politics was not a consideration in the first attraction between Barbo and Marie, Stirbey was above all a patriot, and it was natural for him to inspire in Marie his own passion for Roumania. The Stirbeys, brother and sister, were the first people in Marie's life to allow or demand more from her than beauty and charm. It had suited the Duchess to keep Marie uneducated and under her control. As to the Crown Prince, his ego demanded that he regard his wife as his inferior. Marie understood all this. Long after her political awakening she continued to intone ladylike disclaimers. "I don't mix in politics," she wrote Sandra, "but I have my ears open and begin to understand things more."

For a man like Stirbey, who relished pulling strings behind the scenes, Maries was an ideal pupil. Inherently bright but innocent of preconceptions, she accepted the ideas he believed in but had been unable to effect on his own. She was headstrong, but he learned to reason with her. With his careful, analytical mind and her rapid powers of comprehension, they soon grew to be a formidable team.

Not an intellectual, Prince Stirbey had an intuitive grasp of economic realities and a great facility for getting things done. "I never met a more perfect common sense and a more perceptive political instinct," one admirer commented. Looking at the world around him, Stirbey had come to the conclusion that democracy, not autocracy, was the wave of the future. From this he had concluded that "it was by far more sensible not to go against the current."

The Crown Princess was temperamentally disposed to accept Stirbey's ideas. During the abortive 1905 revolt of the peasants in Russia, Marie had written her mother advocating reform. She was pleased when the Russians acquired a constitution and told her mother so. "No doubt, for many it was a hard moment," she wrote the autocratic Duchess, "but remember that your Father [Tsar Alexander II] had meant to give it out when he was murdered!"

Slightly astonished that she could fathom the conversations between her husband and King Carol, Marie now followed their discussions of "all that was vital to the country: agriculture, industry, army, internal and foreign politics, the desire for expansion." The King, disappointed in his heir, had already begun to realize Marie's potential. He took her into his confidence, explaining the central issue of Roumanian foreign policy—the ill-treatment of the Roumanians of Transylvania. Marie listened patiently as he grumbled about politics in the Austro-Hungarian Empire. The Hungarians, King Carol told her, were "severely trying his loyalty towards the Triple Alliance."

By now Roumania's treaty with Germany, Austro-Hungary, and Italy was an open secret. As was, or soon would be, Princess Marie's relationship with

Prince Stirbey. In 1913 the King appointed Stirbey Superintendent of the Crown Estates. Roumanian society noted that the post of Superintendent threw Barbo Stirbey and the Crown Princess together on a daily basis. "No admirer could have been more tactful and efficiently influential at the same time," observed Princess Callimachi. "His shrewd judgment and diplomatic abilities made him a valued negotiator in home politics and almost a power behind the throne well before the accession of Marie and Ferdinand." In placing Stirbey in this position, King Carol sanctioned his relationship with the Crown Princess. The King also laid the foundation for the triumverate— Ferdinand, Marie, and Prince Stirbey—that would guide Roumania when he was gone.

Crown Princess Marie as a bride, dressed in a Roumanian costume given her by her husband's uncle, King Carol of Roumania.

21

22

The Palatul Victoriei, King Carol's palace in Bucharest. Led up the monumental staircase by the King, the new Crown Princess was shown into her rooms, which were dark and dreary and furnished in *altdeutsch* rococo —"nowhere a cosy corner, nowhere a fireplace, nowhere any flowers, nowhere a comfortable chair."

23

Crown Prince Ferdinand with his first son, Prince Carol. Ferdinand was always uncomfortable holding babies.

24

25

The new Crown Princess jumping her hunter, "Wheatland." The only place she could escape the Germanic court was outside with her horses. "Riding played an enormous part in my life; to some this may appear trivial, but I had an instinctive sense of self-preservation."

King Carol I of Roumania. He did not allow Ferdinand or Marie to have friends or attend any functions outside the palace. According to the King, personal happiness was not a legitimate goal for a Hohenzollern prince or an Edinburgh princess.

Queen Elisabeth of Roumania in her salon. It was the Queen's conviction that creative work was good only if it was spontaneous, untouched by criticism or revision. She was therefore able to discover new talents in herself and others every day.

26

27

Marie's only antidote to the severe regime imposed on her in Roumania was travel. This picture was taken in Coburg at the time of sister Ducky's wedding to Grand Duke Ernst of Hesse—the major royal social event of 1894. Seated in front is Queen Victoria flanked by her daughter, the Empress Friedrich of Germany, and her grandson, Kaiser Wilhelm II. In back of the Kaiser are the future Tsar Nicholas II of Russia and Alexandra, who announced their engagement during these festivities. Marie, pregnant with her second child, is standing in the center back; Ferdinand is in front of her to the right.

29 At the Coronation of Nicholas II and
Alexandra, Moscow, 1896. Marie is
seated on the left with her mother
(center) and sister Ducky (standing).
In back are (left to right) an attendant, Ferdinand, Ernie (Ducky's husband), another attendant, Marie's
father, Marie's brother and a third
attendant. This event, "more like a
dream than reality," was the supreme moment in Marie's young
married life. For the first time she
had a chance to discover just how
pretty and desirable she was.

Three young royal couples in 1896.
Back row from left to right: Cousin
George of England, Ernie of Hesse,
and Ferdinand of Roumania. In
front: Princess May, who married
George in 1893; sister Ducky; and
Marie.

31   The Crown Princess in a room of her palace decorated with the help of her sister, 1907.

Pauline (circle) and Waldorf Astor in the early 1900s. "My dearest friends of all were the Astors." Waldorf is posing with Mignon, Marie's third child; he titled the photograph, "The Dwarf and the Giant."

33

Prince Barbo Stirbey. Tall and slim, he carried himself with authority, although his manner was self-effacing. The ladies of Bucharest spoke of the magnetism in his dark brown eyes. For Stirbey, Marie was the love of a lifetime.

34

King Carol and Crown Prince Ferdinand at the Danube River during the Second Balkan War, 1913.

The Russian and Roumanian royal families at Constantza, June 1914. The object of this meeting was a marriage between Ferdinand and Marie's son, Prince Carol, and Nicholas and Alexandra's daughter, Grand Duchess Olga, but the young people were not attracted to each other. Had they married, Olga would have escaped the tragic end met by the rest of her family. Seated left to right: Grand Duchess Marie of Russia, Tsarina Alexandra, Grand Duchess Olga (with Princess Ileana on her lap), Marie, and Grand Duchess Tatiana holding Prince Mircea. Standing: King Carol I, Grand Duchess Anastasia, Princess Mignon, Prince Carol, Crown Prince Ferdinand, Queen Elisabeth, and Tsar Nicholas. The two boys in front are the Tsarevitch and Prince Nicholas.

Tsar Ferdinand of Bulgaria, Marie's sybaritic
Coburg cousin, was defeated in the Second
Balkan War and came to Bucharest to sue King
Carol for peace.

37

38

Marie of Roumania in a photograph used by the English press in October
1914, just after she became Queen.

H.R.H. PRINCESS ELIZABETH OF ROUMANIA, ELDEST DAUGHTER OF KING FERDINAND.

H.R.H. PRINCE NICHOLAS: SECOND SON OF THE KING OF ROUMANIA.

H.R.H. PRINCESS MARIE, SECOND DAUGHTER OF KING FERDINAND

H.R.H. PRINCE CHARLES, HEIR TO THE THRONE; ELDEST SON OF KING FERDINAND.

H.M. QUEEN MARIE OF ROUMANIA: WITH H.R.H. PRINCESS ILEANA, HER YOUNGEST DAUGHTER

A page from *The Illustrated London News*, August 1916. The Allied press made much of Roumania's decision to enter World War I on its side, citing Roumania's choice as a certain indicator of victory.

39

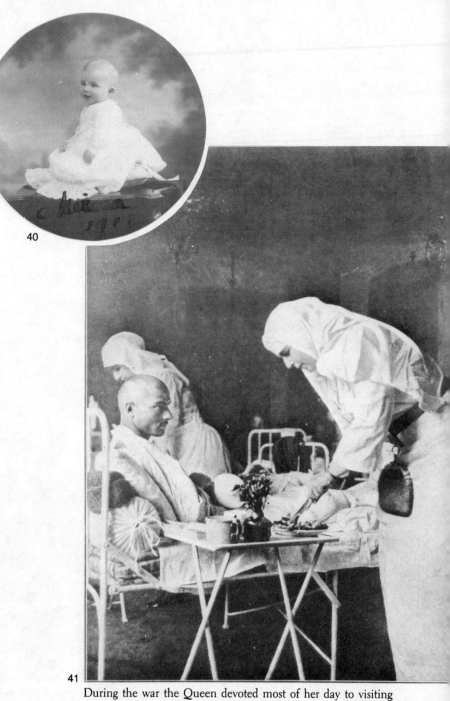

40

41

During the war the Queen devoted most of her day to visiting wounded soldiers. Although she was able to help the hospitalized men, she could do nothing for her youngest child, Mircea (top left), who died of typhoid at the age of four shortly after Roumania entered the war.

Colonel Joseph Boyle, as he appeared when Queen Marie met him. "... he clasped my hand promising that neither God nor man would make him forsake me as long as I and my country needed him, and to this promise he stuck with a single-mindedness characteristic of his nature."

42

43

The four Allied Foreign Ministers at Jassy. From left to right: Sir George Barclay of England, Charles J. Vopicka of the United States, Count de Saint Aulaire of France, and Baron Fasciotti of Italy. Thanks to Marie's charm and determination, envoys sent to Roumania invariably ended up supporting Roumania's cause with their own governments.

44

45

Princess Marthe Bibesco, an authoress of international repute, whose great flaw was an inexorable need to be in the center of the social and political scene. This obsession led her into an affair with the Crown Prince of Germany, and once having committed herself, to misjudge the outcome of World War I.

Jeanne Marie Valentine (Zizi) Lambrino. Crown Prince Carol deserted his military post to elope with her. The marriage was a godsend to the enemy.

46

King Ferdinand and Queen Marie's triumphal entry into Bucharest after the war. With them is General Henri Berthelot, the Frenchman who successfully reorganized the Roumanian Army.

Ion Bratianu II. Highly intelligent but far too Byzantine for the delegates to the Peace Conference, he mishandled Roumania's case at Versailles and was forced to call on Queen Marie to come to Paris to help him.

Queen Marie with Princess Elisabetha and Princess Mignon walking on the Place Vendôme outside the Ritz Hotel, 1919.

Take Jonescu, the diplomat Clemenceau called "un grand Européen," should have represented Roumania at the Peace Conference.

AN IRRESISTIBLE CLAIM.

Roumania. "I HOPE, WHILE THEY'RE FEEDING THEIR STARVING ENEMIES, THEY WON'T FORGET THEIR STARVING FRIENDS."

Cartoon appearing in *Punch* when Queen Marie arrived in London to plead for famine relief in Roumania.

50

The Warrior Queen.

51

53

52

"Mother-in-law of the Balkans."

54

55

Top left: Princess Elisabetha of Roumania and Crown Prince George of Greece on their wedding day. Center: Princess Helen of Greece and Crown Prince Carol of Roumania at their wedding. (The two young attendants are Princess Ileana, sister of the groom, and Princess Catherine, sister of the bride.) Bottom: Princess Mignon and King Alexander of Yugoslavia as they appeared at the time of their engagement.

Chapter *11*

I was born a leader.

—*QUEEN MARIE OF ROUMANIA*

*I*n January of 1913 the Crown Princess gave birth to her last child. The pregnancy had been a difficult one, and after her confinement, she was kept in bed with phlebitis. In April she was sent to Spain for a cure. After weeks of mud baths, steam, strong massage, and exercises, Marie was pronounced fit and allowed to go to Madrid to visit her youngest sister, Beatrice. Baby Bee had married the Infante Alfonso in 1908 and moved to Spain. A charming man, half French, half Spanish, Ali quickly became Marie's favorite brother-in-law. On her way home, the Crown Princess spent two weeks in Paris at Ducky's apartment. Because King Carol regarded France as a "place of perdition" Marie had never before been allowed to go to Paris. She enjoyed her trip immensely and returned home "stimulated and refreshed... ready to take up my life and duties again in the eternal old round."

But the old round was changing. Ever since the early 1900s there had been a gradual shifting of power among the Balkan nations, one with which Marie was only partially acquainted, but which was to catch her and all her

European relations in its backlash. These local changes reflected a larger power struggle, as the Austrians, Russians, and Turks—and to a lesser degree, the Germans and English—jockeyed for control of Eastern Europe.

In 1903 Serbia had declared its independence from the Austro-Hungarian Empire. To punish the Serbs, Emperor Franz Josef annexed the Serbian-speaking provinces of Bosnia and Hercegovina in 1908. King Carol was deeply disturbed. Not only did Franz Josef condone the mistreatment of the Roumanians of Transylvania, but he seemed bent on destroying Serbia, Roumania's traditional bulwark against her "historical rival and enemy" to the south, Bulgaria. In the summer of 1909, the Archduke Franz Ferdinand, the ill-fated heir to the Austro-Hungarian throne, came to Sinaia with his wife to soothe the Roumanian monarch.

Franz Ferdinand's well-publicized concern for the subject peoples of his future Empire made him an ideal emissary, and King Carol issued orders that the Roumanian royal family "must in all ways manifest...good will" toward the Habsburg heirs. Coached by Barbo Stirbey and the King, Marie was well aware of the political implications of the endless round of stiff little dinners and luncheons, claustrophobic musicales, and dreary excursions into the countryside. "I am not looking forward to it," she wrote her mother, "as I know the dullness of the way we entertain visitors." The Crown Princess was frequently embarrassed by the provincialism of the Roumanian court. "I feel what real savages we become down here [;] we are absolutely out of contact with the rest of the world [.] Uncle has remained a naïve old baby...living in ideas forty years back, Aunt is absolutely unnormal, and I am certainly not conventional [,] Nando is terribly timid."

In spite of these shortcomings, it was the most gracious meeting imaginable. Queen Elisabeth received the Archduke's morganatic wife, the Duchess of Hohenberg, with "almost royal honour." The Queen of Roumania reveled in the romance of morganatic marriage. Although the Duchess of Hohenberg, accustomed to the punctilious slights of the Viennese court, was "quite bewildered" by Elisabeth's effusions, Franz Ferdinand was touched. No one had ever treated his wife so well before. "Always afterwards," said the Austrian Minister to Bucharest, "Roumania, in his eyes, was endowed with a special charm."

While Missy watched Carmen Sylva flutter over the Archduke's wife, the Archduke, King Carol, and Prime Minister Bratianu held serious conversations, talks in which Crown Prince Ferdinand was "occasionally allowed to take part." During these meetings Franz Ferdinand expressed his disapproval of the Hungarian persecution of the Roumanians of Transylvania. Although nothing more definitive than "a friendly mutual understanding" came out of the visit, it was considered a fine success at the time. In the long run, it was only a small, misleading prelude to the conflagration about to erupt around the Roumanian royal family, their subjects, and their neighbors—an example of a misguided belief, prevalent among monarchs of the day, in the efficacy of family conferences to ward off international aggression.

In 1912 Italy defeated Turkey in the Tripolitan War, signifying to Turk watchers that the "sick man of Europe," the Ottoman Empire, was on the wane and the time had come to divide up Turkish holdings. In the fall of 1912, Bulgaria, Serbia, and Greece declared war on the Sultan. Known as the First Balkan War, it was a nasty defeat for the Turks, who avenged themselves by setting fire to the Christian villages through which they retreated. During the peace conference that followed, the Turks played for time, rightly assuming that while they stalled, their Balkan enemies would start quarreling among themselves over the territorial spoils.

"The Bulgarians have gone off their heads because of their successes and want to be the only power in the Balkans," Marie wrote her friend Pauline Spender-Clay after the First Balkan War. The prevailing belief in Western Europe was that of all the Balkan countries, it was Bulgaria, not Roumania, that was destined for territorial and cultural preeminence. Infuriated by Bulgarian gains, the Roumanians demanded that the Great Powers restore the balance of power by giving Roumania a slice of the southern (Bulgarian) Dobruja—the long, narrow province between Roumania and Bulgaria on the Black Sea. As her countrymen agitated for war against Bulgaria, the Crown Princess, bedridden after the birth of her last child, grew frantic. "I only pray with all my soul that war shall not break out before I am up and about," she wrote Pauline in January of 1913. "The Roumanians have become terribly pugilistic & the King is dead against war, only public opinion is driving him horribly."

In utter defiance of public opinion, King Carol renewed Roumania's secret alliance with Austro-Hungary and Germany in February of 1913, thus lining up his country with the Habsburgs, who supported Bulgaria's territorial claims. Not surprisingly, Carol I was reported to be in a state of nervous exhaustion. Although the Great Powers awarded part of the disputed Dobruja to Roumania in May of 1913, it was not sufficient to extinguish the war fever raging through Roumania and the rest of the Balkans.

The ink was barely dry on the treaty that ended the First Balkan War when the Bulgars launched a surprise attack on their former allies, the Serbs and the Greeks. Serbia and Greece retaliated by joining with their old enemy, Turkey, to fight Bulgaria. Pressured by the frenzied militancy of his people, King Carol and his government issued a call for mobilization and declared war on Bulgaria. "Bucharest," said the Crown Princess, "went mad with delirious excitement." Men registered for the army in unprecedented numbers. Driving through the capital with her husband, Marie was taken aback by the "unreasoned delight" of the crowds that clustered around the royal car, cheering, throwing their caps into the air, even climbing on the running boards to be as near the royal couple as possible.

It did not matter that Roumania was too late to join in the fighting. Undaunted by an absence of resistance, the Roumanian Army crossed the Danube and marched through Bulgaria. The Second Balkan War, a simple Bulgarian rout, lasted about a month. "For Roumania," Princess Callimachi said, "it was an unglorious walkover." For King Carol, it was triumph pulled from the jaws of disgrace. The King moved once again into public favor by proving that the Austro-Hungarian Empire, however destructive to its other small neighbors, had no control over Roumanian foreign policy.

But for Roumania's landowners, the victory had repercussions that would haunt them forever. Progressing through the countryside, the Roumanian peasant soldier saw just how well his Bulgarian counterpart lived. The country south of the Danube was alive with small, thriving farms where superior methods of cultivation yielded better crops. There were no aristocratic land-lords or their middlemen waiting to skim off the hard-earned profits of peasant labor. The alternatives to Roumanian feudalism were prosperity and pride. Although King Carol missed the implications of this lesson, Bratianu, the new leader of the Liberal Party, embarked on political programs geared to placate the peasants.

The soldiers encountered little armed resistance in Bulgaria, but they marched straight into a cholera epidemic sweeping through the countryside. The contagion was spread by the Bulgars themselves, who threw the corpses of men who had succumbed to cholera into water wells in the districts through which the Roumanians must pass.

It was this aspect of the Second Balkan War that opened up new vistas of activity for the Crown Princess. In wartime it was the practice for rich and fashionable ladies to organize hospitals, nurse the wounded, and equip personal ambulances at their own, rather than government, expense. Among the women leading the war on cholera was Elise Bratianu, who told Marie that she could be of enormous help if she was serious about the job to be done. Although Roumanian ladies, royal princesses included, were forbidden to visit the Bulgarian side of the Danube, Marie crossed the river to look at the hospital conditions for herself.

"I saw sights which made my blood run cold. Cholera brings panic in its wake... I found many of our soldiers almost abandoned and dying for the want of nursing and proper care... Looking about me I felt that what was wanted was a leader, an encourager, and one high enough placed to have authority, and who by remaining calm and steady could become a rallying point for those who were beginning to lose their heads... Something never before felt rose from the very core of my being, an immense urge towards service, a great wish to be of use, even to sacrifice myself if necessary, to put myself entirely at the disposal of my people. I cannot help looking upon that sudden contact with cholera as a turning point in my life."

Devoid of physical fear herself, the Crown Princess obtained permission from the King to personally administer one of the cholera camps. Because of her position, her appeals for provisions were answered not only by the authorities but by rich friends as well. "My hands were always full and I could appear everywhere as a dispenser of those 'extras' unobtainable in military camps." Marie soon proved she could stand up to the strains and horrors of ugly death. Never self-effacing, she reported her triumphs in detail. "Soon doctors, orderlies, soldiers, officers and sisters of charity became my most ardent adherents; I was never tired or discouraged, I would allow no difficulty to beat me, the harder the work the more strength did I find, and in a few days I had become the pivot around which everything revolved."

Conditions were appalling. The heat was fierce, broken only by torrid rains which turned the camp into a muddy morass. Hospital wards were wooden barracks; the soldiers lay on damp pallets of straw; the paths between the bodies were mud. There were no mattresses, almost no linen. Lighting was primitive and dangerous. The Crown Princess waded through the filth in her riding boots, talking to the doctors, encouraging the soldiers, and passing out provisions.

Soldiers not already stricken with cholera were angry at being isolated and examined for infection before they were allowed to return home to their families and unreaped harvests. Marie took up their cause, making regular forays to the detention camps, bringing cigarettes and cheerful conversation to keep up their spirits. "They began to count on my visits and the moment they saw me coming from afar, they would all rush to meet my car, with shouts and excited welcome." Prince Carol, aged nineteen, asked permission to join her. "He was a good and steady worker and liked being my keeper," she said, proud of her son's ability to get on so well with the soldiers.

Skeptical at first, the doctors came to rely on Marie's gift for helping without interfering or growing "unnecessarily sentimental when I am of no use." The sisters of charity, whom she brought with her to do the actual nursing, became friends. Seated on an upside-down box, watching the nuns "paddling about with bare feet in ankle-deep mud, the rain dismally dripping down upon the beds," Marie discovered a sense of deep camaraderie with her people; "my life & interests have changed..." she wrote her mother. "I don't feel myself at all, I am a changed person."

The Crown Princess returned to Roumania with a sense of purpose and an enhanced reputation; "in 1913 things had definitely changed and my work in the cholera camp had suddenly brought me before my people in another light... I was better informed than I used to be and certain newer influences around Uncle had made him understand that I could become useful if handled in a tactful way."

Much to Missy's delight, Cousin Charly's voice at court had finally been replaced by those of Barbo Stirbey and the Bratianus, anxious for King Carol to bring the Crown Princess into the inner circle. Pointing to her basic intelligence as well as her recently proved efficiency, the Liberal power clique convinced the King that Marie was his rightful heir. "He spoke to me... no more as a schoolmaster to a pupil but as to a co-worker able to understand."

The first lesson Princess Marie learned was that Roumania's adherence in any future conflict to Russia, her neighbor to the east, or to the Austro-Hungarian Empire, her neighbor to the north and west, was of paramount geographical importance to both sides. As a secret member of the Triple Alliance (Germany, Austro-Hungary, and Italy), Roumania was currently allied to Austria, but the major factor holding her there was King Carol's allegiance to his beloved fatherland. The issue of loyalty boiled down to whom the Roumanians distrusted most: the Russians, who had stolen Bessarabia in 1878, or the Hungarians, still oppressing the Roumanian minority in Transylvania.

In the summer of 1913 Tsar Ferdinand of Bulgaria came to Roumania to sue for peace. A large man, heavyset and coquettish, the Tsar of Bulgaria had little eyes placed close together over an enormous nose, which he himself never missed a chance to ridicule. Ferdinand was a true sybarite, famous even among royalty for a fabulous collection of unset gems that he fondled through his long, white fingers like worry beads. An irreverent wit, the Tsar of Bulgaria was particularly fond of Marie, whom he had regaled over the years with jabs at his more serious, less soigné rival, King Carol of Roumania. Now he arrived in Bucharest to beg Carol to save Bulgaria from ruin.

If there was any role the King of Roumania relished, it was that of the wise monarch. "Uncle is both a diplomat & a gentleman so he knows how to resist the temptation of humiliating a fallen enemy," Marie wrote. A happy Solomon, Carol I called a conference of the five Balkan nations (Roumania, Bulgaria, Serbia, Greece, and Montenegro) in Bucharest to arrange the terms of the peace and the division of Turkish spoils. Under threat of imminent intervention by the Great Powers, Bulgaria was forced to cede the southern Dobruja to Roumania, Albania was granted independence, and the Serbs and the Greeks were awarded chunks of land formerly controlled by the Turks.

The Roumanians were delighted with the Treaty of Bucharest. Not only had they acquired the southern Dobruja, but their Macedonian kinsmen (Kutzo-Vlachs), long under Turkish oppression, were now to live under the flag of Albania. The Roumanians hoped for good things from the Albanians, because the new Prince of Albania was a nephew of their own Queen Elisabeth.

The settlement of the Balkan Question greatly enhanced Roumania's prestige at home and abroad. Even the Kaiser, anxious to pacify King Carol, considered honoring his kinsman with a personal visit, but he abandoned the idea for fear of offending the Tsar. Left to woo the King of Roumania without the Kaiser's help, Franz Ferdinand secured the appointment in the fall of 1913 of one of his closest advisers, Count Ottokar Czernin, as Austrian Minister to Bucharest. Czernin arrived in Roumania with instructions to convince Carol of Austria's good will and to persuade the King to disclose

Roumania's alliance with Austria, Germany, and Italy—now twenty-five years old and still a secret from the Roumanians.

Count Czernin was an excellent choice of representative. Aristocratic, beautifully mannered, arrogantly witty, he was known to be highly critical of the Magyar policy toward the three million Roumanians of Transylvania. After a short time in Bucharest, Czernin reported home that it would be impossible to publicize Roumania's treaty with the Triple Alliance in the face of the anti-Hungarian feeling in the country.

For the first time in her life and with proper apologies, Marie of Roumania began to talk and write directly about the political situation, which, she said, "underwent certain changes" in the last years of King Carol I's reign. Marie admitted knowing that Roumania had renewed its treaty with Germany, Austro-Hungary, and Italy, adding that "most of the political world knew, or anyhow guessed, that Roumania was a fourth in the Triple Alliance." In order to downplay her own role in the shifting of Roumania's allegiance, the Crown Princess explained her country's estrangement from its former friends purely in political and economic terms:

"In spite of repeated warnings sent by King Carol to Vienna, the persecution of our people under Hungarian sway never lessened and this filled Roumanian hearts with bitterness. Besides, Hungary invented every possible economic and administrative chicane [trick] against our country and was insufferable on the Danube question." According to Marie, King Carol warned Berlin that if the Germans permitted the Austro-Hungarians to assume the upper hand in the Triple Alliance, he could no longer answer for Roumania's adherence. Carol also informed his Hohenzollern cousins that French and Russian propaganda was turning the Roumanians against Germany. "Although this warning came straight from the Head of State himself, Berlin paid little attention," said Marie. The King, "deeply offended" at being ignored, "began to let things go." With no opposition to the propaganda emanating from the other side, the question of Transylvania soon eclipsed that of Bessarabia.

Marie disclaimed any responsibility for the shift away from Germany. She had to. If Ferdinand accepted his wife's fledgling involvement in politics, he didn't want it known outside court. Letters to his older brother, Wilhelm, now the reigning Prince of Hohenzollern-Sigmaringen, bristled with assurances of Missy's political virginity. The Crown Princess held up her end of the charade. To talk of politics "is not a woman's affair," she wrote her brother-in-law in 1913, adding that "Aunt and I are kept busy with the Red Cross."

In February of 1914, the Crown Prince and Princess of Roumania were invited to St. Petersburg. The object of the trip was a match between Prince Carol of Roumania and Grand Duchess Olga, eldest daughter of Tsar Nicholas II. For almost two years Marie had been investigating the possibility of this alliance. She consulted with King Carol, who thought it would be popular with the Roumanians, and Izvolski, the former Foreign Minister of Russia, who believed it would be politically advantageous for both sides.

Before going to Russia, Marie and Ferdinand journeyed to Potsdam to pick up Carol for the trip eastward. The Crown Princess was pleased with her eldest son, who seemed happy in the German Army. After Potsdam, the Kaiser invited his cousins to Berlin, ostensibly for a happy family get-together. Cousin Willy had heard rumblings of the Russian project. If he ordinarily ignored Roumania's rulers as falling beneath his proper sphere of attention, the Kaiser still did not like the idea of a possible blood alliance between them and the Romanovs.

When they arrived in Berlin, the Kaiser's wife was not there. Missy was delighted. Cousin Willy was in excellent spirits and spoke to the Crown Princess for the first time "as though I really existed." Aware that this was due less to her charm and beauty than to international pressures, Marie still enjoyed the attention of the formerly chilly monarch. "Conversation at meals was gay and animated and my husband looked pleased. Being overmodest and shy, Nando could seldom create an atmosphere, but he felt hurt when William treated him with indifference."

The opening of a new library had been scheduled to take place during the Roumanian visit to Berlin. Since his wife was away, the Kaiser asked Marie to be his partner in the grand procession. "As I solemnly walked down the great hall beside my cousin, I felt rather as though I was on the stage; the grand entry in *Tannhäuser*, or *Aida* . . . too-long, too-loud silver trumpets were being sounded as if for the Last Judgment over our heads by too-tall buglers. . . . Too tall to be real were also the white-clad officers who stood rigid like statues behind the red velvet chairs we had finally reached. Bold and upright sat my triumphant kinsman, his field-marshal's staff held like a sceptre on one knee, staring around him with the gaze of a conqueror. . . . I felt towards him somewhat as I had felt in former days towards my small son when he considered himself a conqueror because he was brandishing a toy sword."

From Germany Marie and Ferdinand traveled on to Russia with their son. The contrast between Cousin Willy's bombast and Cousin Nicky's passivity was enormous. By 1914 Nicholas and Alexandra had shut themselves off completely in their country palace, Tsarskoye Selo, not only from the seething masses but from other Romanovs as well. Passing through the endless procession of armed Cossacks circling the park of Tsarskoye Selo, Missy, who loved the trappings of her caste, was annoyed to discover that all the imperial pomp "ended at the front door . . . stepping over the threshold you entered suddenly into a quiet family life, uniform, exclusive and rather dull."

Nicky was kind and welcoming, but lived "in a sort of imperial mist." His wife was as chilly as ever. "She managed to put an insuperable distance between her world and yours . . . She made you . . . feel an intruding outsider

... The pinched, unwilling, patronizing smile with which she received all you said as if it were not worth while answering, was ... disheartening ... Although there was little difference in age between us, she had a way of making me feel as though I were not even grown up!"

The Crown Princess could scarcely wait to escape from Tsarskoye Selo to St. Petersburg, where Ducky and Kirill, finally forgiven by the Tsar, had been reinstated to Romanov wealth and glory. There, bombarded with family gossip about Nicholas and Alexandra, she learned that "Tsarskoye Selo was looked upon as a sick man refusing every doctor and every help. And it was always Alix's name which was mentioned as the chief stumbling block. And of course also the name of Rasputin was on every lip ... I never saw Rasputin."

Before leaving Russia, the Crown Princess of Roumania initiated a conversation with the Tsarina on the reason for the visit—the possible alliance of their children. Given the personalities of their respective husbands, it is not surprising that the women were left to carry out this exchange. "In all fairness towards Alix," said Marie, "I must say that on this occasion she did not make conversation difficult and talked very quietly, like a reasonable mother." They agreed that as parents they would make no promises in the names of their children, that they would confine themselves to creating "occasions" on which Olga, a bright-looking but not very pretty girl, and Carol might meet. "Alix was as pleasant as was possible for her, but I quite realized that these 'occasions' for meeting would never come about, as it did not in the least look as though our son or their daughter were attracted to each other."

Nevertheless, on June 13, 1914, the Romanovs paid a return visit to the Roumanian royal family at Constantza, the Roumanian port on the Black Sea. Marie was delighted to have the Tsar present himself to King Carol. If his visit did not result in marriage between their houses, at least it would go far to "wipe out the old offense" of Bessarabia. The King was even more pleased than his niece, to whom he was "unusually affectionate." No reigning sovereign of a major power had so honored him since Franz Josef, eighteen years before. Carol nearly shook with emotion as the Tsar's yacht, accompanied by guns and flags, cheers and music, steamed into the port.

It was a standard royal visit. After the usual *Te Deum* and a public drive through Constantza, there was a military review led by the King past the Tsar. "Family lunch" was followed by a rest period based on the ill health of the seventy-five-year-old King of Roumania and the forty-two-year-old Tsarina. Tea was served on the imperial yacht, and at the end of the day there was a gala banquet in a hall built especially for the occasion. Nicholas II was placed between Queen Elisabeth and Crown Princess Marie in the center of a long, narrow table of eighty-four guests. The Queen of Roumania had forgotten to put on her orders. The Tsarina removed hers. Marie did not. Grand Duchess Olga was seated next to Prince Carol; his attentions to her were halfhearted, and her replies to his questions unenthusiastic.

While the royalties plowed through a day of formalities, the Russian

Foreign Minister, Sergei Sazonov, and Prime Minister Bratianu drove off together on a private excursion into Transylvania. Like his predecessor, Sazonov had been promoting the match between the heir to the Roumanian throne and the eldest daughter of the Tsar. He knew that the Roumanians were wary of the Russians and was well acquainted with King Carol's loyalties, if not with his secret treaty. By the time the two politicians arrived at the banquet in the evening, they seemed to be "on very good terms."

But the marriage project failed. Prince Carol was obviously not attracted by the Grand Duchess Olga, and she was adamant about not leaving Russia. "Who could have foreseen that if the marriage had taken place she would have escaped the dreadful fate in store for her!" her brother's tutor lamented in later years.

Count Czernin, the shrewd Minister from Austria, observed the Russian visit with much interest. He had recently warned his government that the Roumanian foreign policy might soon depend not on Ferdinand, the future King, but on his consort, Marie, with her Russian ties and leanings. "Her character and mentality is one of the most important reasons for putting relations with Roumania on quite another basis," Czernin wrote home.

Meanwhile, Archduke Franz Ferdinand and Kaiser Wilhelm II conferred on how best to bring Roumania closer to the Triple Alliance. Their last meeting took place on June 13, 1914, precisely the same day that the Romanovs visited the Roumanians at Constantza. As usual, the heir to the Austro-Hungarian Empire decried the treatment accorded the Roumanians of Transylvania by his Hungarian subjects. The Kaiser promised to instruct the German Ambassador to Austria that whenever the diplomat ran into Istvan Tisza, the Hungarian Premier, he was to greet him with the words, "Lord, remember the Roumanians!"

It was with this in mind that Franz Ferdinand, the last hope of the Roumanians of Transylvania, left on the fateful trip to Bosnia that ended his life and plunged the world into war.

Chapter *12*

God has called us to civilize the world.
We are missionaries of progress.

—*KAISER WILHELM II*

*T*he assassination on June 28, 1914, of the heir to the Austro-Hungarian Empire and his wife at Sarajevo shook the provincial court of Bucharest as it did governments throughout the Western world. The members of the royal family were at the Sunday races when a telegram announcing the tragedy was delivered to King Carol. The King, the Queen, the Crown Prince and Crown Princess immediately withdrew, followed by an anxious crowd of somber diplomats. Carol I told the American Ambassador that the murder would lead inevitably to world war.

One month later, much of Europe had chosen up sides. Crown Princess Marie and the majority of Roumanians were on the side of the Entente.* This put them in direct opposition to their King and Queen, who were

*The Entente (also known as the Allies) originally included Great Britain, France, Belgium, and Serbia in Europe and Russia in Asia. They were later joined by Italy (1915), Portugal (1916), the United States (1917), and Greece (1917). (Partial listing only.)

violently pro-German and consequently for the Central Powers.* Carmen Sylva, for years the self-appointed high priestess of French and English culture, reverted vociferously to her homeland and original loyalties.

"Aunty... suddenly found herself *die Rheintochter* [daughter of the Rhine] with a vengeance: it was all the time *Deutschland über Alles, Gott mit uns,* and all the rest of it," Marie wrote. "I was told that I must look upon the downfall of England as a certainty; that it was Germany's day, the beginning of the Teuton era, they *must* become lords of the world for the good of humanity. She even said... that England *had* to fall because her women had become immoral!"

While a rift with the Queen might ruffle Marie's feathers, a break with the King was far more troubling. The unity of purpose they had achieved was falling apart in the face of old loyalties. Carol I and Marie preserved all outward appearances and were "careful not to hurt each other's feelings"; this did not, however, prevent the King from insisting that the moment had arrived for the rest of the world to bow before German superiority. "We still came often together and I listened," Marie said, "but I was mute."

Austria formally declared war on Serbia on July 28, 1914. Four days later, on August 1, Germany declared war on Russia. On August 2 the Kaiser invaded Luxemburg and demanded that Ferdinand's first cousin King Albert of Belgium open his frontiers to the German Army on its way to the invasion of France. King Albert refused. King Carol, who was very fond of his nephew, said he was a fool.

On that same day, August 2, the Germans appealed to King Carol of Roumania to mobilize immediately against Russia. The seventy-five-year-old King was shaken. His health was weakening, and his physical ills were intensified by the moral dilemma in which he now found himself. Terrified of having his clandestine diplomacy exposed publicly, but prodded by Germany and Austria to declare war on their side, Carol could do nothing more definitive than summon a meeting of the Crown Council, a conference at which he promised to advocate mobilization toward supporting his friends.

That this was the best he could do for the fatherland humiliated the old autocrat. The Austrian Minister to Bucharest, Count Czernin, reported that each time he appeared at court to remind the King that "*his honour* obliged him to unsheathe his sword," his verbal blows cut "like the lash of a whip" into Carol's back. It was not without some gratification that Czernin recalled a "particularly painful" interview in which the King, "weeping bitterly, flung himself across his writing-table and with trembling hands tried to wrench from his neck his order *Pour le Mérite.*"

As important to Carol as his loyalty to the Hohenzollerns and the secret

---

*The Central Powers originally designated Germany and the Austro-Hungarian Empire. They were joined in 1914 by Turkey and in 1915 by Bulgaria.

treaty was his conviction that Germany was headed for immediate and total victory. Trained in the Prussian Army, the King believed that no one could stop Germany's men in arms. If for nothing more sacred than enlightened self-interest, he felt that Roumania must declare herself for the Central Powers quickly, before it became too late.

But the mood of Carol's countrymen was one of indecision and distrust. Roumanians had based their irredentist hopes on Franz Ferdinand, the anti-Magyar heir to the Austro-Hungarian Empire. The shots that killed the Austrian Archduke had shattered their dreams of a peaceful union with their Transylvanian brothers. And if adherence to the Central Powers implied strengthening the Hungarians, a switch to the Entente meant exposure to certain danger. Roumania did not trust Russia, and Russia's allies in Western Europe (England and France) were too far away to represent realistic help or security.

Although neutrality had its drawbacks in the loss of valuable friendships and the possibility of isolation, most Roumanians were inclined to watch and wait and stay clear of diplomatic or military entanglements. Moreover, Italy, the fourth country in the secret alliance and weather vane for smaller nations, had yet to declare for either side. Roumania's immediate worry was the inevitable shift in the balance of power achieved after the Balkan Wars. It was assumed that Serbia would now be destroyed by Austria, Bulgaria thereby enlarged, and Roumania's territorial position endangered.

The Crown Council was due to convene on August 3 to decide Roumania's fate. The day before the meeting, Take Jonescu, the leader of the liberal wing of the Conservative Party and an influential spokesman for the pro-Entente faction of the government, arrived from London and was summoned to luncheon at Castle Peles.

The atmosphere in the castle, according to Jonescu, was that of "a house divided against itself." The King, he said, "was more than worried... the Queen was more bellicose than the King, and... the Crown Princess... was dead against the policy of her uncle and aunt, and did not conceal it from them. It even seemed... that tears had recently been shed in that Royal Palace."

Queen Elisabeth spoke out at once in favor of going to war on the side of Germany. Jonescu answered that victory for Germany meant victory for Hungary and was therefore "not compatible" with the aspirations of Roumania. But the Queen, who was in Jonescu's words, "not sufficiently versed in politics to understand a word," remained unconvinced.

The Crown Princess asked Jonescu if he thought that England would remain neutral in the coming conflict. The statesman replied that Marie knew as well as he that England "would go into the war with her last man and her last shilling." The Crown Princess cast her steely blue eyes on the Queen. "You hear what he says, aunt." Turning back to Jonescu, she announced bitterly, "That is what I tell them all the time, and they refuse to understand it. They understand nothing in this house."

The Crown Council, which met at the castle the next day, took place in the same atmosphere of high drama and emotional intensity. The resort of Sinaia, ordinarily peaceful, was described by one inhabitant as "a boiling cauldron of passion and political intrigue." While the people waited anxiously to hear their fate, members of the government and leaders of the opposition wound their way up the long, pine-bordered road to Carol's summer palace.

King Carol, noticeably pale, opened the proceedings with a declaration in French. As he almost always made the extreme effort of using Roumanian for official speeches, this was seized upon as indicative of great nervousness. In his opening statement the King condemned what he called a "policy of sentiment," but his own arguments rested largely on blind Teutonic loyalty. Public opinion, he alleged, would never stomach an alliance with Russia, and Russia was a member of the Entente. Neutrality, he claimed, would destroy the position Roumania had finally won for herself among the nations of Europe. Therefore, he argued, both honor as regarded the treaty of alliance and self-interest required the Roumanians to join the war at once on the side of Germany and the Austro-Hungarian Empire.

His speech was met with disapproving silence. Among all his ministers, there was no one except Peter Carp, Roumania's most violent Germanophile, who spoke in support of his sovereign. One Conservative politician went so far as to remind his King that neither he nor most of the gentlemen present had ever even *seen* the treaty His Majesty proposed to honor; the secrecy with which the treaty had been signed, he said, rendered it unconstitutional, since no engagement with foreign states was valid without the sanction of both political parties. A second minister warned the Council that any decision to wage war on the side of the Austro-Hungarian Empire might well provoke civil war. Even Alexandru Marghiloman, leader of the Conservative Party and pro-German by economic conviction, argued for neutrality.

While others spoke, the heir to the throne sat quiet and withdrawn, a nonparticipant in the decision that would irrevocably alter his life. His loyalties, like those of his uncle, lay with Germany. "May God guide you to a victory," he wrote his older brother just days after the Crown Council. Since his sentiments echoed those of the King, it might be argued that Ferdinand ought to have supported the old man under fire. But the Crown Prince was bound by more than one allegiance. The object of an intense pro-Entente campaign waged by the Crown Princess, Ferdinand was submitted to pressure from government ministers as well. "We all have confidence in the patriotism of Your Royal Highness," one of the Conservative members of the Council warned him before he left the room. Frightened of opposing either his uncle or his wife, aware of the ultimate expectations of his government, the unhappy Ferdinand was reduced to impotent observation.

The forty-eight-year-old heir to the throne was a sad contrast to Prime Minister Bratianu, aged forty-nine and at the height of his political power. Having carefully orchestrated his entrance into the debate, Bratianu waited patiently for the others to finish their speeches. He had already laid out Roumania's future course of action, but tradition dictated that the King and the members of his Council be given a chance to be heard. Restrained and confident, Bratianu finally took the floor. He advocated armed preparation and announced the government's official decision to remain neutral while preparing public opinion toward eventually entering the war on the side of the Entente.

The meeting was almost at an end when a messenger broke into the Council chamber saying that the Italian Minister to Bucharest, Baron Fasciotti, requested an audience immediately on a matter of some urgency. King Carol left the hall. He returned a few minutes later, forced to admit that Italy had also just that morning decided for neutrality. "Gentlemen," said Carol I by way of closing the meeting, "you cannot imagine how bitter it is to find oneself isolated in a country of which one is not a native." His ministers were unmoved. "In peacetime," one said, "it was possible for Your Majesty to follow a policy contrary to the sentiment of the country, but to make war in defiance of that sentiment is impossible."

Outside the Council chamber, Queen Elisabeth walked back and forth, up and down the gloomy red-carpeted corridors of the castle "like a great animal in a cage," pulling the Crown Princess along with her, talking continuously. "It was incredibly painful," Marie wrote, "to be pacing thus arm and arm with Aunty, each of us with a separate fear or hope in our hearts." Over the past few years Marie had come to appreciate the Queen's devotion to the ailing King, and she was touched by the late rapprochement of this old couple, previously so at odds with each other. Nonetheless, when the King emerged from the meeting, "a broken and saddened man," she observed that the Queen reacted entirely in character. "Aunty..." Marie noted, "became dramatic, and, as was her way, almost revelled in the grand tragedy of the situation: the old King denied by his people after a long life of hard work for his country."

After the Crown Council, King Carol's popularity waned steadily as his people saw in him only an obstacle to declaring war on Hungary and rescuing the Roumanians of Transylvania. Under these circumstances, the pro-German Minister, Peter Carp, said he expected Carol I to offer his abdication. The Queen too urged her husband to "shake the dust of his ungrateful country from his feet." Many thought Carol was holding that threat in reserve, just in case Roumania undertook the unthinkable and entered the war on the side of the Entente.

Whispers of possible abdication sent waves of panic through the Crown Princess. Foreseeing imminent accession to the throne and knowing that it was she, not the King, the Queen, or the Crown Prince, whose loyalties coincided with those of the people, Marie was frantic at the possibility of losing now, at the eleventh hour, the only recompense that life with Ferdinand had promised her. In her autobiography she couched her anxiety carefully:

"I was not initiated into what was actually being discussed between uncle and nephew . . . I had no feminine curiosity . . . I never tried to make my husband speak when he desired to be dumb, but this was not only a political question, it meant our very existence. What understanding had the King and Crown Prince which I was not to know? If Uncle abdicated would he persuade my husband to do the same? Would it mean that . . . I was to be torn away just at the hour when our people might really need me? How could I today stand this awful fear without trying to make my husband confess if he had made any fatal promise? But he was dumb, cruelly dumb; nothing would induce him to give me a hint about what secret understanding he had with his uncle, of what they were preparing for us, over our heads, without consulting our feelings or allowing us to raise any protest . . . Finally, unable to stand the strain, I sent for Prince Stirbey . . . and asked him if he knew anything definite. No, he had not been told nor consulted: he, too, was anxious, but he could neither confirm nor abate my fears."

Marie was stunned that even Barbo, eternal source of information, had not been able to ferret out the King's intentions. Ferdinand's maddening silence was probably based on the fact that the Crown Prince knew no more than the Crown Princess. It is unlikely that the autocratic King would have consulted his heir on his future plans, and it would have been hard for Ferdinand to admit that to his wife. It was easier for him to play the wise mute.

While Marie was trying vainly to break through the wall of silence and mystery that had risen around her, she received a surprise visit from the Minister of Finance, who said he had come with the express purpose of asking the Crown Princess not to leave Roumania under any circumstances. "Even if the Prince . . . feels bound to follow his uncle into self-imposed exile, promise that you will remain with us with your son Carol, if possible with all your children . . . it is not possible nor fair that you should forsake us at this crisis when we know you are with us with all your heart." Never was a promise more readily given.

In spite of political defeat and intimations of approaching mortality, the King continued to exercise incomprehensible influence on his soon-to-be heir. On September 23, 1914, Carol was too ill to receive the Austrian Minister, and Count Czernin asked to see Ferdinand in his place. After the interview Czernin characterized the Crown Prince as "irresolute, shifting his point of view, making unreliable statements, being evasive, having little authority, having little self-confidence or energy . . . impulsive and weak . . . using ambiguous language." Although Ottokar Czernin was capable of modifying his perceptions to fit his desires, his interpretation of Marie's husband as merely a "passive instrument of his surroundings" was echoed by most people who came into contact with Ferdinand.

In contrast to the indecisive Crown Prince was the fanciful Queen, who announced that the Roumanian royal family must join hands and rise up together to heaven to escape the misery around them. The King told the Queen that he had no wish to leave earth at the moment, as he was far too curious about the outcome of the struggle. To Marie he added that, considering the course the war was taking, they could not "hope for peace before Christmas." He died long before the holidays, suddenly and quietly in his sleep.

Marie and Ferdinand were both absent from Sinaia on October 9, 1914, the night of the King's death. Although they were seldom away, the Crown Prince and Princess had gone to Bucharest to show themselves in public. During the autumn season the aristocracy gathered at the racetrack, not so much to watch the horses as to gossip and be seen. There was no better place for the royal couple to appear to squelch rumors that they were leaving Roumania.

After the races Ferdinand retired to Cotroceni for the night. Marie, who had promised to dine with Marthe Bibesco, was driven out to Mogosoaia, Marthe's seventeenth-century villa outside Bucharest. Mogosoaia was one of Marie's favorite spots. A large brick palace of beautiful proportions, its stone balconies and balustrades were reflected in the waters of its own private lake. Marie loved to paddle a small boat through the tall reeds, watching the colors of sunset and listening to Marthe weave exotic tales. After a quiet and peaceful night in Mogosoaia's famous Empire bedroom, the Crown Princess was awakened by the telephone early on the morning of October 10, 1914. It was Prince Stirbey to tell her that the King was dead. "I was Queen," she said. "I felt wholly capable of being a Queen."

The new Queen of Roumania hurried back to Sinaia. By the time she arrived at the little railway station that evening, everyone had gathered to kiss her hand and acknowledge her new position, even the ladies of Carmen Sylva's entourage. She was touched by their obeisance, but left quickly to pay her respects to the body of the old King.

Marie knelt by the side of Carol I's bed and took silent vows, which she repeated for posterity in her memoirs. "Have no fear, Uncle, we shall bravely carry on. Your hand was heavy, often you tortured my youth, but according to your lights you were fair and just. I shall not forget the lessons you taught me . . . here, kneeling beside you . . . I feel that you still have a message for me, your once so troublesome niece; yes, Uncle, I shall try to be, as you were, faithful unto death, loving your country as you did for so many long years. If God wills, bravely and fearlessly we shall carry on your work. —Amen."

The rhetorical extravagance is characteristic of the era. The determination was Marie's own. She ordered a bowl for Ferdinand made of gold and inscribed, "Tomorrow may be thine if thy hand be strong enough to grasp it." Before retiring that night, Marie called Barbo Stirbey and Maruka Cantacuzène to come to see her. "I need my friends around me," she noted in her diary, "my real friends."

When King Ferdinand took his oath in Parliament the next afternoon, the new Queen, covered with a long, black mourning veil, stood to one side with her four elder children. During Ferdinand's message to the nation his voice broke with sobs several times; when he descended from the dais his eyes were "red," his feet "unsteady." After acknowledging the new King, the crowd turned to cheer Marie. "It was like a great wave of applause, gratifying, touching[,]" she wrote in her diary, "but as I looked into their approving, admiring, enthusiastic faces, I could not help wondering if their affection for me will survive the mistakes I am sure to make sooner or later."

Nevertheless, hearing the crowd cry "Regina Maria," the new Queen raised her black veil. "I suddenly felt that I must bare my face before the whole house, that I must turn towards them with no veil of mourning between them and myself. A great clamour mounted to the vault above, something long drawn out and tremendous that came irresistibly from many hearts! 'Regina Maria!' And we faced each other then, my people and I. And that was *my* hour—mine—an hour it is not given to many to live; for at that moment it was not only an idea, not only a tradition or a symbol they were acclaiming, but a woman; a woman they loved."

The ovation given the new Queen in Parliament was sincere. The public was aware that it was Marie's unyielding loyalty to the Allied cause that had bolstered and would continue to steady her German-born husband. "As Crown Princess she had been popular: as Queen she was even better loved," said Princess Callimachi.

According to law, Prime Minister Bratianu tendered his and his Cabinet's resignation immediately upon Ferdinand's accession. Ever the loyal heir, the new King responded by swearing in exactly the same men who had served his uncle. "Poor Nando," Marie wrote one of her sisters, "it is hard for a character like his to take up such heavy responsibilities, and having been so long the humble follower it's difficult for him to realize that he is master."

Certainly Ferdinand exhibited less than enthusiasm for the job ahead and complained bitterly about it in letters to his brother Wilhelm in Sigmaringen. Four months after he assumed the crown, he called it a "legacy which I would not wish on my arch enemy."

King Carol I, said a member of the aristocracy, "was given a grand funeral, many speeches of official praise . . . not one sincere regret." He was buried in a thirteenth-century basilica at Curtea de Arges, a small village in the Carpathian foothills. On the day of the funeral the new Queen appeared on the steps of her palace, carefully draped in trailing black crepe, looking her most beautiful. Forgetting the solemnity of the occasion, the crowd burst into cheers. Jean Duca, a young minister and friend, reported that Marie could barely suppress a smile as she climbed into her coach for the ride to the station.

The death of King Carol caught the royal family by surprise, and for the first weeks of their reign Ferdinand and Marie's living arrangements were anything but comfortable. Cotroceni was in the middle of renovation, and Marie lived in a small corner of the palace by herself. While workmen rushed to finish the job, Ferdinand moved into the old palace on the Calea Victoriei with the Dowager Queen; the children were sent to Sinaia. A few weeks after her accession, Marie wrote to her sister Sandra to complain that she had "not even a cook" at Cotroceni and, in order to eat, had to "drive to the palace [Palatul Victoriei] in solemn loneliness to lunch and dine with his Majesty my husband and the old lady."

In spite of the inconveniences, Marie reveled in her new power. She also enjoyed the improvement in finances. The new Queen said that it was hard for her husband, "who had always been so passionately careful about every penny he spent, in trembling fear of Uncle's disapproval," to realize that he was "suddenly a rich man." As the months passed and Carol I's estate was divided up in gifts and bequests, Marie understood that they would never be "so rich as Uncle." With a quarter of the fortune going to the country, a quarter to the widow, and "enormous" income taxes to pay, the new Queen lowered her sights. Still, she and her husband were much better off than before, and for the first time in their lives, masters of their own purse strings.

Soon after Carol I's funeral his widowed Queen moved into the Episcopal Palace at Curtea de Arges across from the church where her husband was buried. From there she continued to expound her theories on the war. To one caller Elisabeth spoke of the influence that the general massacre then taking place would have on the science of the occult, in which she was a strong believer. "Think of all the mothers who have lost their sons, of all the women who have lost the man they loved!" Elisabeth said. "It is certain that communication with the other world must make immense progress now. So many people will want to speak with their dead!" To Queen Marie, Elisabeth reported frequent conversations with the archangels, especially Raphael, explaining that all her wisdom and advice came directly to her from that faraway source.

In later years it pleased Queen Marie to recall how well she treated the widowed Elisabeth during the year and a half she survived her husband. "I . . . was keen to demonstrate . . . that the trouble we had had together was not of my making. The moment power passed into my hands and the ordering about fell to my share, all quite naturally became peace and good will; no more intrigues and never a harsh or ungracious word, only kindness and harmony, and pleasant understanding." This magnanimity enveloped not only the Dowager Queen but her ancient ally, Mme. Mavrojeni, the Chief

Inquisitor of Marie's youth: ". . . true to my principles I did not pay her back in kind; it was hard enough for her to have to kiss her victim's hand."

After Carol I's death, Helene Vacaresco, who had submitted to voluntary exile in France, returned home to Roumania. No longer an Oriental seductress, Ferdinand's first love had grown extremely fat. Admired for her writing skill, treasured for her wit, Helene Vacaresco conducted one of the most successful salons in turn-of-the-century Paris. Before leaving France, she met the new French Minister to Bucharest, Count Charles de Saint Aulaire. Saint Aulaire was concerned about his Roumanian assignment in light of King Ferdinand's German birth. Helene told him not to worry about Ferdinand. "I know him well," she said, "he is above all a man of duty and, if necessary, of the most painful duty."

Although Queen Elisabeth knew better than anyone else that Helene was back in Bucharest, she did not ask to see her. Puzzled, the former lady-in-waiting and surrogate daughter felt she could not ask for an audience, sending her respects instead through a mutual acquaintance. "Oh," said Elisabeth, her old cataractous eyes filling with tears, "I wish I could see Helene." The visitor told her that Helene was in Bucharest. "In Bucharest! So near to me! . . . Tell her that I never forget her—that my life has never been the same since we parted; and thank her for keeping silence. Tell her I should like to see her—but ask her to forgive me."

They never met again. The presumption is that King Carol had years before extracted a promise from his wife that she would never again receive her former lady-in-waiting. Even after his death, the old Queen stuck to her word.

The Dowager Queen survived her husband by only seventeen months. Tormented by a constant fear of suffocation, Elisabeth got into the habit of going out on her balcony in her nightgown or opening her windows wide to the freezing winter air. In this way she caught pneumonia and died early in the morning of March 2, 1916. Queen Marie was with her during her last night and reported that even at the end, Carmen Sylva was aware of her literary efforts. "You are supposed—to say—beautiful things—and you can't—", the old woman rasped out with her last conscious breath before she fell into a coma and died.

Queen Elisabeth was buried under a white marble slab beside King Carol at Curtea de Arges. Between them was placed the tiny coffin of their daughter, exhumed from its former crypt. The chief mourner was King Ferdinand, who spoke of "the great void" that the death of his "revered aunt . . . a German-thinking and German-speaking human," had left in his life. "Without doubt," the King wrote his brother Wilhelm, "it was a great, a very great loss . . . especially for me . . . since she was actually the only human with whom I could freely and openly speak in these trying times."

PART FOUR

The Queen

Chapter 13

*I*n spite of pressures, financial and moral, from both the Entente and the Central Powers, Roumania clung to neutrality throughout the first two years of World War I.

She was not prepared for war. Although her ammunition supply was scarcely dented by the Second Balkan War of 1913, it was still pathetically insufficient for large-scale combat. Because of King Carol's belief in the fatherland and his conviction that conflict would never arise between his old and new countries, he had imported virtually all his military equipment from Germany. After his death the Roumanians found they had no munitions factories of their own and, not surprisingly, Germany and Austria exhibited an ever diminishing inclination to ship those armaments already ordered and paid for. By December of 1914, with the end of war nowhere in sight, King Ferdinand could count only enough ammunition for a campaign of three months with no guarantee of supplies from the Entente.

Hospitals, another necessity of war, were inadequate, antiquated, and improperly staffed by ignorant peasant women paid an average of eight dollars a month. No trained nurses existed; hospitals relied for the most part on the irregular if well-meaning ministrations of society ladies. In Roumania, the wealthy had always gone to Switzerland for their operations.

Geographically too, Roumania lay uncomfortably exposed. Her borders were long. Her only fortifications were natural ones—the Carpathian Mountains and the Transylvanian Alps on the Hungarian side (north and west) and the Danube River, which separated her from Bulgaria, to the south. To the east lay the Russian Bear. Although King Carol I had inaugurated his forty-plus years on the throne by providing the country with its first railway, he had died leaving it with few militarily strategic tracks, none closer than fifty miles to any frontier.

A major deterrent to Roumania's declaring for the Entente was Great Britain. Although Roumania now boasted an English-born Queen, the prevailing theory in government circles in the early months of the war was that England's leaders secretly supported Count Tisza, the intransigent Magyar Premier of Hungary and *bête noire* of Roumanians everywhere. According to this hypothesis, England was planning after the war to back a Greater Hungary, strong enough to take Austria's place as the eastern counterweight to Russia. Although Russia was now Britain's comrade-in-arms, the English did not trust her.

Nor did the Roumanians. The one prize Russia had always coveted and would surely demand from an Entente victory was the city of Constantinople, guarding the world's only exit from the Black Sea. Roumania's one seaport, Constantza, also lay on the Black Sea. The Roumanians did not want Russia in control of their commerce.

But what really prevented Roumania from entering the war in its early phase was Bulgaria. The Roumanian bogey was the Bulgar lying in wait, ready to pounce from the south the moment the Roumanian Army marched northwestward into Transylvania. When the Bulgarians turned on their former allies in the Second Balkan War, they lost the last bit of credibility with their neighbors.

Eyeing each other across the Danube River, King Ferdinand of Roumania and Tsar Ferdinand of Bulgaria held two tenets in common: belief in absolute monarchy and faith in the German Army. Like the Roumanians, however, the Bulgarians preferred the Entente. For as long as Bulgaria and her Tsar vacillated between the two sides, fear of what she might do in the south prevented Roumania from committing her troops to the north and west.

Queen Marie did not like neutrality. It obliged her to watch "every word," which, as she said, was "entirely out of keeping with my character." If there was no one in Roumania less temperamentally suited to holding her tongue, there were other uneasy neutrals among the ruling class. Chief among these were Take Jonescu and Nicolas Filipescu, two prominent politicians who left the Conservative Party to form, along with a group of Transylvanian exiles, the National Action Party. The main thrust of this coalition was to demand immediate entry into the war on the side of the Entente. Although Jonescu was admired as a man of diplomacy, his combative colleague Filipescu was not. A former Minister of War, Filipescu insulted King Ferdinand in the press, called him a traitor and a coward, and blamed him for Roumania's neutrality.

In contrast to his dislike of Ferdinand, Filipescu harbored a genuine admiration for his Queen. Marie was therefore nominated to meet with the outspoken patriot to "try and tame" him. To avoid any semblance of officiality, the Queen and the politician met for an early evening ride in the woods of Prince Stirbey's estate, Buftea. Using all her "feminine tact" to disarm the "belligerent gentleman," Marie explained her husband's position. The King, she said, could not rush headlong into war without an understanding with his future allies. This must include military aid as well as firm commitments as to territorial spoils. "The ride," she said proudly, "was a success."

During the two years of neutrality—from August 1914 to August 1916—much of the work of the Roumanian government was carried on at the Stirbey home. Under the guise of a simple country retreat, Buftea was the operations center of the power establishment. According to Princess Callimachi, a close observer of the political scene, "Queen Marie was constantly there, often the whole day in a riding habit to justify her presence. Thus dressed I once saw her remain for dinner with the King, important Allied envoys, and the Prime Minister... later casually dropping in. After the meal they disappeared one by one into a secluded sitting room for a meeting to be kept from spying ears. The whole procedure had a flavor of Eastern mystery I much enjoyed."

The Queen spent a great deal of time at Buftea. Hardly a graceful architectural achievement, the Stirbey home, a three-story amalgamation of German and Eastern influences, seemed nonetheless to gather in everyone who ever visited it. Its unpretentious atmosphere appealed to Marie's love of cozy corners, while the breathtaking park surrounding the house delighted her passion for nature. Huge trees—sycamores, chestnuts, maples, and oaks—spread their branches over fragrant undergrowth, and wild flowers bloomed on the edges of soft paths. "Prince Stirbey had cut long avenues through his forest along which we could gallop for miles on good ground," Queen Marie wrote. "The Prince and three of his daughters were excellent riders, and we were happy all together... With steaming horses and glowing cheeks we would return full of *joie de vivre* to the... old-fashioned house where Nadeje, fresh and radiant, would be awaiting us on the threshold inviting us in for a welcome meal, tea or supper according to the hour of the day."

Barbo Stirbey's relationship with Marie did not seem to intrude on his family life. The Prince was absolutely respectful toward the Queen, and Nadeje Stirbey loved and admired her. According to one young relative, "If no one had known the truth, it was just the Queen of the country arriving to visit the family of very dear and old friends." Indeed, it was always that as well.

The most painful aspect of the war was for Marie, as it was for many European royalties, the split in her personal family. The Queen's main concern was her mother. The Duchess was living in Germany with Sister Sandra and her husband, Prince Ernst of Hohenlohe-Langenburg, who had been named Regent of Coburg for the duration of the war. Marie knew that the Duchess was being subjected to intense German propaganda. To counteract this, she wrote her mother frequently, declaring her unchanging filial devotion and justifying her personal allegiance to the Entente in terms of the Roumanian desire for Transylvania. At forty years of age, Marie still dreaded displeasing her mother.

The Queen also worried about her sisters. "Who knows what bitterness will remain and if we won't all have grey hair before we can peacefully come together once more," Marie wrote Sandra. "You and Ducky on opposite sides and each of you vibrant with your own country, each hoping for final victory." Marie was under constant pressure from Ducky to break neutrality and declare for Russia and the Allies. "Ducky is furious that we have not joined them," Marie told Sandra in the spring of 1915, "and sends me insulting messages through the people who come here as only Ducky can produce in which she considers her rightful wrath against 'those cowards!'"

While Ducky prodded Marie to join the Entente, Ferdinand's family attacked him from the German side. Having sworn allegiance to his new country, the King continued to hope against hope for miraculous accommodations from the Hungarians. He personally did not believe that the Roumanians had a historical right to Transylvania. "It never belonged to Roumania like the Bukovina or Bessarabia," he wrote in confidence to his brother Wilhelm. But Ferdinand knew the temper of his people and wrote to his cousin the Kaiser outlining the situation in which Roumania found herself. Ferdinand explained that whatever his own personal sympathies, he was first and foremost King of a nation agitating for the deliverance of her kinsmen living under harsh Hungarian masters. In the case of general warfare, he warned, he would be unable to prevent the Roumanians from claiming Transylvania as their God-given right. He put Cousin Willy on notice that if Italy broke neutrality toward Germany, he would be hard put to prevent Roumania from following suit. The Kaiser, high-handed to the point of self-destruction, paid no attention.

The Kaiser's indifference to King Ferdinand made matters easier for those who advocated joining the Entente. The Queen's role in the rapprochement of Roumania and the Allies was outlined by Bratianu. Being everyone's relative warmed diplomatic waters. She plunged in, pausing only to pay lip service to traditional feminine reticence. "The Emperor of Russia and the King of England being both of them my first cousins, it was easy for me to keep in touch with them unofficially, and of course I was ready to serve my country in every way. Being entirely trusted by both the King and his Prime Minister, I was more initiated into State affairs and secrets than is usual for queens. I was considered a valuable asset and therefore expected to do my share."

This involved writing to King George and Tsar Nicholas—letters styled in her own breezy prose with its eccentric punctuation and spelling, but dictated as to content by Prime Minister Bratianu. On March 13, 1915, Marie wrote an introductory letter of ten pages explaining Roumania's position to Cousin George:

My dear George...

Being neutral I get news from all sides... each... tries to persuade us, that defeat for them is impossible... Promises and threats being dangled over our heads.

Poor Uncle's death came at a very hard moment for us... the last months of his life were saddened by a feeling of conflict between him and his people, because all their sympathies were French and always will be French and consequently English, Russian and furiously anti-Hungarian... therefore against Austria-Germany.

Even before Uncle's death the country began to worship in me what they considered the supporter of their national ambition which is Transylvania, and when we came to the throne my popularity was great. This put me in a particularly delicate position, which although flattering I did not allow to turn my head, for what is more odious than a woman making politics on her own hook. But it was impossible not to see how always more and more public feeling turned towards the side where my heart really is... Italy and Bulgaria play of course a great part for us. Bulgaria hates us, Italy pretends to be our friend and considers herself our leader...

We well realise that the position of our country down here is of importance for either side... I for one am very happy to see England take at last some interest in Roumania.

Nando is placed in a very difficult position... but he is a man of duty and I *know* that nothing will count for him but the good of this country, but of course he cannot launch into an adventure cutting himself away from all the old moorings unless he can absolutely count upon the new, and Russia can be a big bully if *England* and France don't countersign her promises... Till now Germany has been a better friend to Roumania than England has...

I hope that in spite of hard times you and May are well and that both of you will be able to feel sympathy for me and my struggling little country...

Your
Affectionate cousin...

The Queen of Roumania received a "very kind answer" to this; the response delighted Bratianu, who "begged" her to write again with specific demands. Knowing that the intricacies of Balkan territorial disputes would only confuse and bore the King of England, who had struggled through his geography lessons as a child, Marie added her own comments to Bratianu's claims, remarking that "these geographical explanations must be Chinese to you, but the places *can* be found on a map." Nor did the Queen (perhaps out of old loyalties) ever admit to her Prime Minister the truth about King George's ignorance of the layout of Eastern Europe.

The message to England was clear: the price of Roumania's allegiance to the Entente included Transylvania; the Banat, a region southwest of Transylvania known for rich mineral deposits and fertile plains; and Bukovina, a mountainous territory of natural forests northwest of Moldavia. All three of these provinces had at one time, however briefly, belonged to Roumania and been wrested from her by the Austro-Hungarian Empire.

It was Marie's first venture into geopolitics, and in spite of the fact that the terms and explanations were dictated by the Prime Minister, the presentation—all sixteen pages of it—was pure Marie. Armed by Bratianu with a barrage of historical and geographical data—rivers, treaties, economic needs, and ethnic distribution—the Queen of Roumania bolstered the facts with subtle references to their common background and a direct appeal to "England's feeling of justice." If Roumania asked for Transylvania, Bukovina, Bessarabia, and the Banat, it was no more than her due. The Allies had "already reaped great advantages" by Roumania's neutrality. "It would therefore be a pity to discuss at this late hour our rights," Missy told George. "Our geographic and military situation is such that we can be of great help to hurry the end of this horrible war."

Writing to Cousin Nicky required more tact. Marie sent a letter to the Tsar of Russia, which he answered at the end of May 1915 in a state of unhappy surprise. Although Nicholas II congratulated "dearest Missy" on pleading Roumania's cause "in a wonderfully clear way," he and his government, he said, were "deeply amazed by your country's *enormous* demands." He questioned both the size and the validity of Roumania's claims, but told the Queen that he had instructed his Foreign Minister "to bring the negotiations between our governments to a speedy and successful conclusion by making some concessions, *provided* Roumania takes an active part at once."

Most of Marie's letters to Russia were addressed to her aunt, the influential Grand Duchess Vladimir (Ducky's mother-in-law), who was "very eager" that Roumania enter the war on the Russian side. They kept up a large correspondence over the exchange of prisoners of war and the possible alliance of Roumania with the Entente. With her aunt, not a reigning sovereign, Marie allowed herself more candor. She suggested that the Russians stop wasting money on propaganda vilifying Roumania's German-born King. Her husband, she said, "is first of all the King of Roumania, and an excellent patriot...Nando may not be very energetic, but he has a curiously strong dose of resistance, and the more he is coerced and threatened, the less will he move; he is not what one may call a man of action, *mais on ne peut pas l'intimider* [but he cannot be intimidated]. Besides I am there to help him fight his battles, and I am a good watchdog I can assure you!"

After twenty-two years of marriage, Marie had learned to handle her husband, but she was still not absolutely sure of what he would do. If her own loyalties were so thickly rooted in the long ago, his must be as well. Given his tendency to dig in his feet under assault, Ferdinand had to be approached with delicacy. His wife knew she was the only person who could help him when the time came for the ultimate sacrifice.

Amazingly enough, Ferdinand seemed totally unaware of Marie's influence over him. "Missy is not one bit interested in politics," he asserted to his brother Wilhelm only seven months before Roumania's entry into the war. In her autobiography Queen Marie explained how her husband could have believed this. The King, as she put it, was "exceedingly hazy about details of everyday life," and his "habit of counting upon me for his material comforts had been unconsciously extended also to brainwork. I grasped things easily, even those not really within my province, and my old attitude of not taking myself overseriously allowed him to ignore how great a help I really was...All this, to explain how warily I had to go."

During the early stages of the war there was little change in conditions of life in Roumania. The harvests of 1914 and 1915 yielded excellent crops that sold at very high prices; Bucharest was a speculator's paradise where the Central Powers and the Entente both threw away huge sums of money trying to keep supplies away from the other side. Along with the speculators the boyars made fortunes, but as always the peasants remained outside the charmed circle of profit. To improve their lot, they tried to drive their cattle across the Carpathian Mountains to sell them in the Austro-Hungarian Empire at inflated wartime prices, but they were soon stopped by the government. Meat rationing was enacted, and meat was allowed to be sold in markets and restaurants only four days each week.

This cut into the normal schedule of lavish diplomatic entertaining. One by one the foreign contingents withdrew from the social scene, each nationality staking out its own, oddly appropriate, preserve in the city. The Germans took over the Athene Palace, Bucharest's grand hotel patterned after the Paris Ritz—a setting that offered, according to one diplomat, "enough of gilding and enamel to make a fit frame for a Prussian officer." The French gathered in the "faintly Bohemian atmosphere" of the Café Moderne, while the English favored Capsa, a restaurant known in prewar days for superb cuisine, exorbitant prices, and a clientele of Roumanian dandies.

During the days of neutrality, Bucharest resembled nothing so much as a giant Oriental bazaar, patronized by everyone from Eastern or Western Europe with something to sell. The local black market dealt indiscriminately in commodities and loyalties, and it was frequented with equal enthusiasm by representatives of both the Entente and the Central Powers.

For those who were waiting to enter the war on the winning side, a major consideration was the outcome of the British attack on the Dardanelles. If successful, British control of the straits would have solved the Entente's supply problem in the Balkans. Launched in February of 1915, the offensive failed; Britain was forced to withdraw in May and again at the end of the year. This was one factor that discouraged Bulgaria from joining the Entente. Another was money. When England, France, and the United States all refused to grant Bulgaria the loans she sought, she began to look to the Central Powers. In June of 1915, the Bulgars turned to the Germans for financing. Four months later, on October 14, 1915, Bulgaria joined the Central Powers by declaring war on Serbia. Serbia, attacked by the combined forces of Austro-Hungary, Germany, and Bulgaria, was overcome.

With Bulgaria gone and King Constantine of Greece leaning toward Germany, Roumania found herself isolated from her neighbors during the last year of her neutrality. Encouraged by their victories in the Balkans, the Central Powers treated the royal family and the Roumanian government with increasing disdain. King Ferdinand's older brother, Prince Wilhelm, now Head of the House of Hohenzollern-Sigmaringen, wrote the King a "harsh" letter on the subject of loyalty. In his reply Ferdinand cited in his defense the sale to Austria of fifty thousand truckloads of grain, a transaction he said he had personally insisted on and one that "overjoyed" him. But when Roumania concluded a similar sale of corn to Britain, the Germans told King Ferdinand that Berlin would have no future dealings with his government.

In a last, desperate attempt to gain Roumania for the Central Powers, the Ministers of both Germany and Austria approached Queen Marie. It was obvious by now to both sides that the Queen controlled the King. Although Marie made no secret of her feelings, each Minister thought he might sway her—one with an appeal to her sense of the pragmatic, the other with an attempt to vilify her friends.

During his audience with the Queen, Count Czernin of Austria accused her of playing fast and loose with the fate of her country. Did she realize "what a fearful responsibility" she was taking "by pushing Roumania towards the side of the Allies?" As an old friend he offered her "a last chance" to bring her country into the war on the side of the winners. Pleading, threatening, and flattering Marie, Czernin, a skillful diplomat, "made promises, dangled victory and triumph . . . played the adviser, the accuser, the tempter." But the Queen, firm in her belief that "England always wins the last battle," could not be budged. "I should die of grief," she told him in parting, "if Roumania were to go to war against England."

Herr von dem Busche, the German Minister, was even less successful. Gauche in dress and manners, von dem Busche was the wrong man to send to Queen Marie. He treated her "rather in the style of a very patronizing schoolmaster," putting his hand in the pocket of his poorly fitting frock coat and pulling out a pack of dumdum bullets: "Would Your Majesty like to see the sort of bullets the English use against the Germans?" he asked.

She stood up and turned her back on him.

In the spring of 1916 Roumania watched eagerly while the Russians gathered for a massive assault on the Eastern Front. The Great Brusilov Offensive, due to roll in July (to coincide with the Somme offensive in the West), was pushed forward in Galicia in June to draw Austrian troops away from the Italians. Advancing without sufficient preparation or warning, the Russians overran both the Austrian Fourth and Seventh Armies. By late June they were nearing the Carpathian Mountains; in July, they stood at the crest. The Entente informed Bratianu that to be useful to the Allies, to upset the balance of power in the East during the Battle of the Somme in the West, Roumania must enter the war at once.

This was Bratianu's moment, the crisis for which he had waited to force Roumania's demands on the Entente and raise the territorial ante. "Performing like a peddler in an oriental bazaar," Roumania's Prime Minister negotiated with obvious and irritating relish, hawking his soldiers' lives like so many bolts of cloth. Known as the "belle odalisque," Bratianu gained undreamed-of concessions for Roumania, but in the process forfeited his standing as a man of honor and Roumania's good will among her future allies.

As the price of Roumania's adherence to the Entente, her Prime Minister insisted that when the time came for peace negotiations, Roumania be admitted to the community of Allied nations on an equal footing with the Great Powers. The Russians refused, citing the fact that Belgium and Serbia, which had entered the war in 1914, were not considered primary powers. Bratianu countered by raising a distinction between nations such as Belgium and Serbia, which had submitted to war, and Italy, which had joined the Entente voluntarily and been accepted as an equal with the major Allies.

Secondly, the Roumanian Premier demanded an unconditional guarantee of three territories—Transylvania, the Banat, and Bukovina. Russia, which wanted Bukovina for herself, equivocated, but the President of France wrote the Tsar to say that "immediate Roumanian intervention will enable us to break the military stalemate to our advantage." The Tsar allowed himself to be convinced, although, unbeknown to him, his ministers and generals had other plans for Roumania.

In August of 1916 Bratianu concluded two years of haggling with the Entente, and Queen Marie informed King Ferdinand that the moment was at hand. In Hungary Premier Tisza complained that Transylvania was so denuded of troops as to invite the hated Roumanians to a "military promenade"; in Austria Czernin warned his government that Roumania would move as soon as the crops were in. They were both correct. The Roumanians should have joined the Allies in early summer, but remained home to reap the harvest and further their military preparations, inadequate even now.

For the first time in many years, royal and diplomatic Roumania stayed in Bucharest during the summer of 1916 to swelter in the humid heat of the capital and swat mosquitoes. The King, tormented by buzzings of old Hohenzollern loyalties, suffered from insomnia. "What he needed," said the Queen, "was the constant presence of someone who knew his trouble without trying to talk about it, and who was all the same there if he wanted to discuss the approaching events." To divert Ferdinand, Marie took him to Copaceni, a small farm left to her a few years earlier by a rich old Roumanian with no descendants. At Copaceni they planted flowers, fruits, and vegetables and picnicked on their own produce. Ferdinand loved to drive, so Marie tempted him out for long early-evening rambles over the countryside. She left the King alone as little as possible, knowing "there could be but one solution, all his hopes and desires could not, dared not, count against that...the going against the country of his birth, against his brothers, his friends, against all that he had loved and believed in."

Aptly termed the Allies' "best ally," Queen Marie had compassion for her husband's agony, but this did not stop her from turning him against the land of his birth. "Only I and one other," she said, referring to Barbo Stirbey, "know what he [Ferdinand] has been through." "Thank God," she wrote in her diary in August of 1916, "there was a good friend who watched with me."

Without Stirbey, Marie might not have had the strength. Nine years had passed since she met him. She had come a long way from the young woman of thirty-one, asking her mother's permission to have a good time, to a middle-aged consort, willing to take responsibility for hundreds of thousands of lives. Stirbey not only loved Marie, he believed in her. Her political Pygmalion, he had recognized her intelligence and given her the tools of statesmanship. Unlike the Duchess of Coburg, who regarded her daughter as a pawn, Stirbey honored Marie as a viable political force.

"I like being queen," Marie wrote her mother during that difficult summer, "and people like me in that part. I don't make it heavy, and yet I feel how they count upon me...Forgive my occasional outbursts of sincerity, but amidst so many people who complain and are aggrieved with fate, perhaps it will refresh you to hear of someone satisfied with her lot. I always cared to be loved, admired, appreciated, was miserable when I was not...I believe in myself, others believe in me, which is most useful for all sides. I don't mind in the least if you smile at me! I smile at myself!"

The Queen also tried to prepare her mother for Roumania's entry into the war against the Duchess's beloved Germany. "I would have much to say but I can't," she wrote toward the end of August. "I *only* want to tell you all that I love you and think of you and long for you whatever happens, and that my heart cannot change."

On August 17, 1916, Roumania signed a treaty of alliance with the Entente. In it she undertook to declare war with all available force on Austro-Hungary no later than August 28. Her price: all of Transylvania, Bukovina to the River Prut, the Banat, and other lands for which, as Seton-Watson observed, "there was no shadow of ethnographic or strategic excuse." But the Allies were prepared to offer any territory that belonged to someone else. They also promised to admit Roumania as an equal to any future peace conference; behind Bratianu's back, Sturmer (for Russia) and Briand (for France) agreed between themselves to bypass Roumania when the time came for peace negotiations.

Militarily, it was agreed that Roumania's entry into the war would be preceded by one week with a French offensive from Salonika, and that in this way, the Allies would keep the Bulgars busy on their side of the Danube. Russia also agreed to send one cavalry and two infantry divisions to the Dobruja to fight Bulgaria, while continuing her offensive along "the whole Austrian front" with special attention to Bukovina. As a further provision, Roumania was to be supplied "uninterruptedly with at least three hundred tons a day of war material."

Queen Marie had arranged with Barbo Stirbey to inform her when the treaty with the Entente was signed. Late in the evening of August 17, 1916, the Prince telephoned a message in code to Sinaia, where Marie was staying. The message was delivered to the Queen by her small, round, cheerful lady-in-waiting Simky Lahovary, who had not the slightest idea of what she was transmitting. When Simky gave her the note, Marie had already retired for the night. "I simply said 'Thank you,' as though it had been a quite simple message. There I sat in my bed alone and knew, knew that it was war—war! That ten days after the signing we were to come into the great struggle, that we were to live or die! . . . Next day I got up with my heavy secret and the whole world seemed changed."

Chapter *14*

There is no country dearer to her
children than Roumania. They love her
because she is sweet, laughing, maternal
and fecund. But they love her less for
what she gives them than for what she
costs them.

—*COUNT CHARLES DE SAINT-AULAIRE*

*I*n celebration of the King's fifty-first birthday, which
fell on August 24, 1916, Ferdinand and Marie received the ministers of their
government in the large gold salon at Cotroceni Palace. The day was hot
and humid. Marie dimmed the lights to camouflage Nando's pallor and
visible disquiet. She stood next to him for support while Prime Minister
Bratianu, carefully emphasizing the confidence Roumania held in her King,
presented the government's congratulations. Although "every sentence was
heavy with significance," nothing specific was said. War would not be officially declared for three more days.

August 27 was the day set for the decisive meeting of the Crown Council.
Aware of the importance of the deliberations, the public milled about the
steamy streets of the capital, peering excitedly into the black limousines
as they drove members of the government into the entrance of Cotroceni
Palace. During the meeting Queen Marie sat upstairs, "knowing that down
below Nando was facing all his ministers and statesmen, was standing up
for a cause that went against his instinct." She waited for three hours.

In the Council chamber gathered much the same group as had met two years before with King Carol: Premier Bratianu and the Liberals, currently in power; Alexandru Marghiloman, the elegant, ingratiating leader of the Conservative Party, whose studies in economics had led him to favor the Germans; Peter Carp, the truculent Germanophile; Take Jonescu and Nicolas Filipescu, representing the pro-Entente, pro-war National Action Party. At 10 A.M. the King entered the hall to receive his ministers. After a moment of silence, Ferdinand spoke.

His face, according to one account, was white, "ravaged by an interior struggle...his voice cut with sobs, his hands trembling." Only a month before, the King had written to warn his brother Wilhelm that he could no longer "think and act as a German, but must think and act as a Roumanian." He told the Council that victory for the Central Powers now seemed impossible, that after due reflection and an inner struggle—which the attendant gentlemen would surely understand—he had agreed on the necessity for entering the war on the side of the Entente. "Although I am a member of the Hohenzollern family, I am the King of Roumania first, and therefore I have to do what my subjects wish me to..." he announced, adding "May Roumania conquer her enemies, as I have conquered myself."

The King's declaration threw the pro-German ministers into disarray. Marghiloman, skeptical of the Allies' chances, said that he could not in good conscience endorse this declaration of war, but would style his objections so as not to alienate himself from his government. "If things go badly," he announced in a moment of tragic foresight, "I shall be there to help." Peter Carp attacked the King. "It is not possible, Sire, to vanquish the Hohenzollerns," he said. "Pardon, dear Monsieur Carp, you are wrong," Ferdinand answered. "I have just vanquished one—myself!"

Queen Marie was waiting outside when her husband emerged from the Council chamber. "Gentlemen," she said, taking his hand in front of his ministers, "no one of you realizes so well as I what this has cost him. I am proud of him. And Roumania should be."

Ferdinand's decision was, according to the October issue of *Current History*, the *New York Times* monthly magazine, "the Chief Military Event" of August 1916. By entering the war on the side of the Entente, the Roumanians brought more with them than their army. They were, in fact, serving "notice to the neutral world that the most formidable uncommitted nation of Europe after two years of investigation feels sure that the cause of the Central Powers is lost."

Roumania declared war on the Austro-Hungarian Empire at 5 P.M. on the evening of the Crown Council meeting. One hour later the declaration of war was handed to the Austrian Foreign Office in Vienna; at the same time Roumanian troops streamed over the border into Transylvania to liberate their brothers.

The public reacted to the evening headlines with joy. "It's all right," announced one of the Princesses Cantacuzène, calling in to see a friend on her way home from the Sunday races, "we're going in—and on the right side!" Within a few hours of the declaration, bands of university students gathered to parade before Cotroceni Palace, yelling out lusty patriotic songs. The crowds spilled from the sidewalks into the streets, halting the flow of traffic. But at midnight the frantic tolling of church bells, signaling enemy bombardment, put a stop to the rejoicing.

Although Roumania did not declare war directly on Germany, the quickest response to her challenge to the Austro-Hungarian Empire came from Berlin. Within a few hours German planes began bombarding Bucharest, flying in from the Bulgarian border, which was twenty-three minutes away. The German press launched an attack on the Roumanian people, calling them Latin traitors and claiming that by their reversal they proved to be descended not from the noble soldiers of Rome but from the criminals deported in ancient days to the outposts of the Roman Empire. The Kaiser immediately struck King Ferdinand's name from the House of Hohenzollern. Ferdinand was characterized as a degenerate and compared most unfavorably to the Kaiser's pro-German brother-in-law, King Constantine of Greece. Word was spread, rightly or wrongly, that the King of Roumania's brothers had donned elaborate mourning, which they flaunted as if their kinsman were dead. Only the outbursts of enthusiasm from his people helped the King of Roumania over the first repercussions of his sacrifice.

Queen Marie, on the other hand, "embraced war as another might embrace religion." Since it was no longer safe for the royal family to remain at Cotroceni Palace, the Queen moved with the five younger children to Prince Stirbey's home at Buftea, while the Prince and his family withdrew to a smaller house on the estate. (King Ferdinand had taken Crown Prince Carol with him to Army Headquarters at Scroviste, outside Bucharest.) From Buftea the Queen drove back and forth every day, leaving at 8 A.M. to visit Army Headquarters and tour various hospitals throughout Bucharest. She began to prepare her own hospital in King Carol's Palatul Victoriei, ordering the old banquet halls whitewashed and equipping them at her personal expense.

The early news from the front was exhilarating. In one of the first communiqués, the Queen received word that her old friend Zizi Cantacuzène had distinguished himself on the battlefield. "I was sure he would," she wrote in her diary, "he is brave and decided and rather mad." Since the Roumanian Army began its march over the Alps to Transylvania at the moment when the Austro-Hungarian Empire was busy digesting her declaration of war, the army advanced well into Transylvania before the enemy had time to gather itself.

Even with minimal resistance, the progress of the Roumanian Army was disappointingly slow. This, said the Roumanian Chief of Staff, was the fault of the Russians, who had promised to press their offensive in the north but failed to "advance a single yard." In the south the situation was worse. Although the French had agreed in the treaty with Roumania to distract

Bulgaria with an offensive from Salonika, the promised action never materialized, and Roumania's southern flank lay naked and exposed to her archrival and now declared enemy, Bulgaria.

On September 1, five days after Roumania declared war on Austria, Bulgaria declared war on Roumania. With the bulk of their army on the offensive in Transylvania, the Roumanians had retained only six divisions in the south, three to guard the Danube River and three to defend the Dobruja. On September 5, Field Marshal August von Mackensen, the German general who defeated Serbia, stormed the fortress that guarded the Danube, thirty miles from Bucharest. In one day the Germans decimated the three divisions left to protect the river. Instead of pushing her way into Transylvania with as many men as possible, Roumania had now to divert soldiers to the south to shore up her defenses. The Russians, who had promised to send fifty thousand men to the Dobruja, sent only twenty thousand.

Anxious about the failure of the Allies to keep their promise of a southern offensive, Queen Marie shot off a letter to Cousin George in England. After the amenities and a recapitulation of Ferdinand's sacrifice and Roumania's good faith, she voiced her country's predicament:

> ...our people are so enthusiastic for the Transylvanian side they are inclined to overlook the great danger of the Bulgarians, who are good soldiers and hate us with a deadly hate. I only hope Russia will keep her promise and not leave us in the lurch: it would be disastrous for us as well as for the Entente, if the Bulgarians were not beaten... I want you to understand that at this moment I am considering the *general* cause. The Bulgarians must be beaten: that would mean the fall of Constantinople, Serbia saved, the Allies' armies on the Danube...
>
> This letter is just a confidential letter from cousin to cousin, written badly, written in haste, because my hands are full, and there is so much to do and see to which one must do oneself. Once more let me tell you that I am happy we are together in these great and terrible times, and let me have the feeling that we can always turn to you when in need, as there may be very hard times to face. I am not afraid but I am anxious.
>
> My best love to May.
>
> > Your affectionate Cousin,
> >
> > > Missy

King George's response did not arrive until a month after the campaign was over. Having acknowledged "the sacrifice made by Nando," he offered some specific military advice, which, however sensible, did not take into account Roumania's primary reason for entering the war. "I urge you," he wrote Marie, "to send more troops to Dobruja making it your first and most important objective and Transylvania can be dealt with when Bulgaria is defeated. I feel keenly for you," he added gently, "in your anxiety."

With the outbreak of war, Queen Marie changed her daily routine. Impatient with long meetings at which "everybody talks at once," she moved about quickly, "indifferent to rules and appearances," unencumbered by ladies-in-waiting and accompanied only by her A.D.C., Colonel Ballif. She concentrated on those friends on whom she could rely—Maruka Cantacuzène, who forgot her fear of crowds in the face of wartime emergencies; Nadeje Stirbey, whose chronic headaches disappeared as she plunged into war work; and Barbo Stirbey, who was appointed A.D.C. to the King and whose presence at Army Headquarters reassured the Queen.

To raise funds for British Red Cross work in Roumania, the Queen wrote her first book, which was published in England. A slim collection of sketches of Roumanian country life, it was entitled *My Country*. Marie's quaint portraits of gypsies and peasants are sentimental in the extreme, and her convoluted sentences are reminiscent of Carmen Sylva at her most flowery, but the book brought in money and help for the troops.

The Queen devoted most of her day to visiting hospitalized soldiers. The hospitals around Bucharest were a prime target of German bombers, who bombed them so continuously that the Roumanians were forced to erect prisoner-of-war camps next door to which they transferred German prisoners. This information, forwarded by the spy network back to Berlin, eventually persuaded the bombers to move on to other objectives.

Following the pattern she had developed in the Balkan Wars, Marie did no nursing herself, but passed out food, candy, cigarettes, and cheer to the hospitalized soldiers. The Queen wore a Red Cross uniform in which she had her picture taken to give away to her subjects. Prince Nicolas often accompanied his mother on her rounds, while her "fat daughters," as she called twenty-two-year-old Elisabetha and sixteen-year-old Mignon, handed out lunch and dinner trays and chatted with the soldiers.

The Roumanian soldiers, most of them peasants, believed they were fighting a "holy war," undertaken to rescue their Transylvanian brothers. Asked if he suffered from his wounds, the Roumanian soldier invariably answered, "What matter my suffering as long as you become Empress of all the Roumanians!" Stepping outside the hospitals, Marie was surrounded by their women, who echoed the same sentiment. Enshrined by the masses, the Queen took her symbolic role personally. "Why should they have to suffer, to give their lives so that I should rule over many, and amongst which, if really there is to be a day of victory, these simple creatures will probably be no more... They all keep looking at me when I enter a room as though all their eyes took possession of me; a strange weight to carry, the look of so many eyes—I never knew it would be so heavy."

Hospital work and writing used only a part of Marie's seemingly inexhaustible vitality. She despaired that she was not living in the "heroic" times of Joan of Arc. "I am desperate not to be able to help," she said; "I feel I ought to be doing something, something useful, something energetic. But what can a woman do in modern war?... I only know that if I were at the head of things I would not sit down and mope; I should want to be everywhere at once and see everything with my own eyes."

Visits to Army Headquarters did not improve her state of mind. She guessed rightly that the "little vices" of peacetime Roumania were hindering the war effort. Accustomed to the spoils system, politicians and generals continued to base appointments on patronage rather than qualifications. Bratianu, said the Queen, "has no military spirit. He is a man of ruse but not a man of action." "I think he is a very clever politician and I think he is a good patriot, but he is no soldier... war is too fearfully serious a thing to try it with favourites!"

Marie was irritated by the King's lassitude. "Oh! he could break through if he would have the courage... I feel I ought to help and yet how can I! How can I, the woman, come and say... Your generals are incapable and would rather *se couler naturellement* [go along as they are] than save the country!" Ferdinand, she said, ought to go out to the front lines to see things for himself or send the Crown Prince. "People begin to wonder why neither of them have been seen amongst the troops yet—and no wonder," said the frustrated Queen toward the end of September.

Had the passivity of the King or the incompetence of his generals constituted Roumania's major problems, Marie might have taken heart. But the country's military efforts were foredoomed.

In the first place, Roumania had waited too long to enter the war. By the time the Roumanian Army moved into Transylvania, the Great Brusilov Offensive had mired down in mud; the Russians stopped moving just when the Roumanians counted heavily upon them to keep the enemy occupied in the north. On the southern front, the help that was supposed to be dispatched from Salonika came late and small, "half-hearted and bungling" and, according to British historian Seton-Watson, "never deserved the name of a real offensive."

Secondly, even when Roumania finally joined the Entente, she was not adequately prepared for war. Starting in the summer of 1914, she had had only two years to increase her forces from 180,000 men to 820,000, 560,000 of whom had to be ready for combat. The inadequacy of her manpower was aggravated by her lack of equipment. According to the American Ambassador to Bucharest, "The bulk of the Roumanian army was made up of inexperienced soldiers, who to a great extent were not well officered. Many generals whom I knew personally, were not able men, and some were even strong German sympathizers... The Roumanian army lacked artillery... There was also a great scarcity of hand grenades."

Moreover, the Roumanians entered the war under a diplomatic cloud.

France and Russia had long disagreed about Roumania. The French wanted her in the war as a counterbalance to Russia, whom they did not trust. The Russians worried that ill-trained Roumanian troops might prove a liability and thought Roumania's territorial demands excessive, particularly when they conflicted with Russia's own. A major element in the confusion was an unfortunate change in St. Petersburg of Foreign Ministers. Sazonov, a man loyal to his country's best interests, negotiated Roumania's entry into the war. Just before the treaty was to be concluded, Sazonov was pushed out by Empress Alexandra and Rasputin, who replaced him with a provincial flunky, Boris Sturmer.

There were many people, not all of them Roumanians, who accused Sturmer of treachery toward Roumania. The Roumanian Chief of Staff claimed that Russia forced Roumania to enter the war at the worst possible moment "because of the unfair plan of the Germanophile party in Petrograd to sacrifice Roumania." That there was such a scheme is corroborated by the French Minister to Roumania, the Count de Saint Aulaire. In his memoirs, Saint Aulaire said that although the Tsar himself was unaware of it, his ministers and generals under Sturmer had devised a plan for a separate peace with the Germans and had decided how to partition Roumania between them—Wallachia to go to Germany, Moldavia to Russia. Along with many others, the French Minister attested to the fact that ammunition and desperately needed supplies sent from France to Roumania via Russia—the only open road between Roumania and the West—were purposely detained by the Russians, eager to sabotage the Roumanian war effort. At the very least, it must be said that Sturmer's arrival on the scene undermined Russia's ability to undertake the promised offensive on the battlefield.

Early in the war Queen Marie met Stanley Washburn, an American war correspondent with the London *Times*, covering the Transylvanian front. Washburn, who had "made all the Russian retreats," confided to the American Ambassador that "Poor Roumania is lost." To Queen Marie he stressed the seriousness of Roumania's military predicament and urged the Queen to appeal to the Tsar personally for the promised military aid. On September 24, 1916, less than a month after Roumania's entry into the war, Marie wrote Cousin Nicky, the only Allied leader with whom she could still make direct contact, begging for help:

My dear Nicky,
If I write you today, it is not as cousin but as Queen of a country I dearly love. We have bravely entered this war, well knowing what we were doing and that our resources are not beyond a certain limit. From all sides our Allies assured us that when we came in, such tremendous efforts would be made on all fronts at once that we would not find ourselves fighting against forces quite beyond what we could cope with. Now we have come to the realization that we are facing tremendous and immediate

danger, and that unless we are helped *at once,* it may be too late...it is not a question of weeks but of days...if we are not to be destroyed we must be helped, and you alone can help us and must help us, Nicky!...

Your loving cousin,
Missy

But Tsar Nicholas II, struggling to maintain his crumbling empire in the face of treacherous ministers, dispirited troops, and an angry populace, was in no position to help anyone.

As the enemy vise tightened around Roumania, Marie's frustration with the King increased. "If only he could really be a master, our country needs it so much just now. Oh! why am I not King! I would go everywhere and see everything and talk to the troops...they would adore me...I would be a reality amongst them not a name!"

If the King's passivity irked Marie, Prince Stirbey's quiet strength supported her. She relied on Stirbey's ability to define and cope with the problems facing Ferdinand at Army Headquarters. Stirbey, the Queen said, "has time for everything, takes all in hand without fuss...If Nando were left to himself, nothing would be done." At the end of his long days, Stirbey journeyed back to Buftea to take tea with the Queen and listen patiently to her ideas.

Another member of Marie's inner circle was Colonel Ballif, her A.D.C. Tall, with graying fair hair and hanging moustaches, Ballif was obstinate and severe, not a man "for amiable conversation or lighter talk," but responsible. "He does not discuss my orders, but none, not even the smallest is ever forgotten. He recognizes no master except me. I like that feeling of dog-like devotion that asks nothing, absolutely nothing in return, and that will accept neither thanks nor money." Ballif gave the Queen "solid military advice, sometimes hard and dreadful but always terribly to the point." When she sent him to talk to the King, Ferdinand, accustomed to the equivocations of his General Staff, got "furiously angry." Nonetheless, the Queen said that her husband "must listen! The country must be saved!"

There was little chance of that as the Germans responded to Hungarian Premier Tisza's call for help in the north. In early October they sent ex-War Minister General Erich von Falkenhayn with more than 900,000 soldiers, including the Bavarian Alpine Corps, experts in mountain warfare, along with quantities of ammunition to save the Hungarians. Forced to halt its Transylvanian campaign in order to send troops south, the Roumanian Army was driven back bit by bit over every foot of ground won just weeks before. On October 9 the Transylvanian city of Brasov, less than thirty miles from Sinaia, was captured. The defeated Roumanian soldiers began their retreat, struggling home through the 7,500-foot-high passes, straggling down into the Wallachian plains, followed by thousands of Transylvanian refugees, barefoot and homeless, fleeing Magyar reprisals.

With much of the Dobruja already in German hands, Field Marshal

Mackensen now set out to secure the great Carol Bridge at Cernavoda, the one bridge spanning the lower Danube in six hundred miles. Beyond the bridge lay Constantza on the Black Sea, Roumania's only seaport and her principal line of communication with her Russian allies. Attacking Cernavoda was a consortium of Germans, Turks, and Bulgars; defending it was what could be scraped together in the way of Roumanians, Russians, and Serbs. Although the Germans admitted that "fierce and fluctuating battles have taken place, the enemy defending himself with great stubbornness," they reported the capture of Constantza on October 22. The Dobruja, object of years of contention between Bulgaria and Roumania, was nearly all in the hands of the Central Powers by late October.

To stop Germany from eating Roumania alive—and Russia from offering her the spoon—Paris sent General Henri Berthelot as military adviser to the Roumanian Army. A man of monumental girth, Berthelot had, according to the French Minister, Saint-Aulaire, "as much finesse as rotundity." This savoir-faire along with a dogged optimism and a "calm, smiling, inflexible will" endeared the French General to Roumania's Queen.

Berthelot arrived in Bucharest on October 18, 1916, with twelve hundred French soldiers, forty-four of whom were well-trained officers. He entertained no illusions about the job to be done. He had traveled to Roumania via Russia and had stopped for an audience with the Tsar and meetings with Sturmer and Russian military leaders. Nicholas II assured Berthelot in all sincerity of Russia's steadfastness toward her ally. "Tell King Ferdinand that I am in back of him with my armies[,] all my armies, and that I will support him to my last man and last kopeck." But the language of the Tsar's Foreign Minister Sturmer "rang with the sound of treason and a separate peace." Sturmer's attitude was underlined by the Russian Chief of Staff. Scarcely polite during their encounter, the Chief of Staff showed Berthelot a map that he hit vigorously over and over to emphasize the line between Wallachia, which the Russians planned to evacuate, and Moldavia, which he treated like part of Russia and which they meant to defend. Berthelot's subsequent arrival in Roumania provoked a secret directive sent from St. Petersburg to the Russian Mission in Bucharest: "Do not forget our basic object is to keep the French Mission from succeeding."

During October Roumania's Queen struggled with another, more personal tragedy. A few days before the Wallachian retreat, Mircea, her youngest child, took sick and was put to bed. "I am not an anxious nor a fussy mother," she wrote, "but...I looked with uneasiness at my beloved little boy, though at first I would not believe that he was really very ill." By October 23, the day after the fall of Constantza, the doctors confirmed her suspicions. Mircea had typhoid fever.

The next day he was clearly sinking. He stopped talking and expressing his childish likes and dislikes. October 25: "Day of struggle and anguish;

three times my Mircea nearly slipped away... Saw General Berthelot and had a long earnest conversation with him, as I consider he is the man who must help us save our country... Told him my child was dying, that perhaps God would ask this cruel sacrifice of me; but in spite of this terrible thing which was now completely absorbing me I wanted to speak to him of my country, so that I should not lose both child and country at once!... Berthelot is beginning to understand that although a woman, I know what I am talking about, and that I count for something in this country."

At 12:30 the following night Marie was called to her son's room. She found Mircea half dead with his pulse waning and the doctors working frantically over him with stimulants and artificial breathing. The King and Prince Carol arrived. After a long vigil, Prince Stirbey suggested that the Queen go to bed. "I have no will to rise from my chair—I feel I must sit there on and on as long as he breathes. The doctors bend over him, feel his pulse, say that it is less weak, that it can last... probably will last..."

Mircea was still alive in the morning, and his condition improved slightly during the week. Marie took a chance and left him one day to visit her regiment, on its way to the front lines. Another day she and Stirbey took a long walk and brought roses and four-leaf clovers back to the child's room. They lit a "holy taper," which they put beside him.

From Stirbey's constant presence in the sickroom, it seems likely that he was Mircea's father. Marie never clarified the boy's paternity, but often spoke with pride of his dark-brown eyes. (All the other children were blue-eyed, like Ferdinand and herself.) Whatever Stirbey's real relationship to the dying child, he was the only person to whom Marie could turn for comfort in this time of desperation. Her husband had never been a support. Although she begged her mother to write, she had heard nothing from the Duchess since Roumania's entry into the war. It was Stirbey who sustained Marie during the personal and national tragedies that now engulfed her.

On Sunday, October 29, 1916, "after a terrible night passed between anxiety and hope," the Queen turned forty-one. Early in the morning she found Mircea slipping away. Once more the doctors brought him back to life. She spent the day running between the child's bedside and public appearances. "The moment I can escape, I dash up to see how he is... always that ghastly cry, those terrible sightless, upturned, bloodshot eyes... I had to go up somewhere to be 'congratulated' by the ministers... the room is full of flowers, beautiful flowers, but my only thought was 'perhaps they will be laid on a grave.'" Each time she returned to her son's room, Marie was confronted with the same scene: Mircea "nearly gone... once more the doctors... forced the poor little sufferer back to life!... He cannot live and he cannot die... I cannot sit in his room and hear him scream."

The struggle lasted four more days. The Queen asked the doctors to bandage Mircea's eyes; she could not look at them any longer. On November 2, he stopped screaming, although he still ground his teeth and clacked his jaw. At noon the Queen knew it was almost over. "I think he is sinking. The doctors say nothing, but I think he is sinking." By midafternoon Marie was sure. The King was informed at Headquarters that "the end was near." During the final hours, Marie begged her family to leave her alone with the dying child. Prince Stirbey waited with her. By 9:30 that night, Marie's youngest was dead. Stirbey "lifted his little head whilst I attached his little cross and chain around his neck." They laid a holy picture on his chest "so that it should go down with him into the grave." "We carried him away from Buftea and the Stirbeys were angels of kindness. The Prince had a quiet way of doing things, never many words, only efficient help, but you feel that he is suffering with you. Silence alone could make me bear my grief."

Mircea was buried in a tiny coffin, which his mother wrapped in a piece of old red-and-gold brocade, in the little chapel at Cotroceni. The church, decked in white chrysanthemums and lit with white tapers, was filled to overflowing.* "I recognized no one," said the Queen. "The little coffin...was let down beneath the stones...I knelt beside the gaping hole. Everything was dead in me, and when I stepped out again into the daylight I felt like a ghost, and all the faces looking at me were the faces of ghosts. The whole world was dead."

Immediately after Mircea's death, the Queen undertook a tour of Moldavia to visit the wounded. Riding in an open car from hospital to hospital, she was impressed with the Russian soldiers whom she saw quartered among the Roumanian peasants. At the end of October 1916, the Russian Army in Moldavia numbered more than half a million men. In their gray astrakhan hats and volumnious belted tunics, the Russians were well off, well dressed, well mounted, and well organized. They kept busy by cooking their food, grooming their horses, and cleaning their rifles.

Referring to the treaty that had promised a Russian offensive, General Berthelot and the Roumanian General Staff asked for these Russian soldiers to be sent in to relieve the exhausted Roumanians and hold the Transylvanian line. The Russian General Staff refused. Bombarded by wires from Paris and Bucharest demanding the pledged reinforcements, the Russian Chief of Staff wired the Chief of the Russian Military Mission in Roumania: "Not a man, not a gun!" This, said the French Minister, was "military treason," conforming to the statement made to Berthelot on the necessity of abandoning Wallachia. He said it was also "political treason" on the part of Foreign Minister Sturmer, conforming to his secret plan of signing a separate peace.

---

*During Mircea's funeral the enemy had a chance to kill everyone of importance in Roumania, but it is said that the Kaiser refused to bomb Cotroceni. This sort of gallantry fits with royal practice. During World War I it was customary for members of royal families to send condolence messages to their relatives on the enemy side, although these family courtesies in no way diminished the progress of the war between them. Within days of Mircea's funeral, the Germans, who had finally discovered where the Queen was living, sent bombers specifically to raid Buftea.

While the Roumanians and the French negotiated desperately with Russia, the Germans and the Austrians had ample time to surge over the mountain passes between Transylvania and Roumania. By mid-November all the passes through the Transylvanian Alps were in German hands, and von Falkenhayn was starting downward into the plains of Wallachia eastward toward Bucharest. This signaled the next move in the south, where Mackensen switched his main thrust to the west. On November 23, 1916, Mackensen and his troops crossed the Danube River close to Bucharest. Germans, Austrians, Bulgars, and Turks now converged on the capital.

Rumors of imminent evacuation did not stop the Queen in her daily hospital rounds. "Cruel news was reaching us from every side, daily it grew worse..." she wrote, adding not unproudly, "I worked relentlessly, hardly ever knew an hour's rest." The work consisted of personally visiting as many of the wounded and dying as she could reach in as wide an area as possible. Although the news had reached crisis proportions, Marie had received no instructions from the King. On November 24, 1916, she confided to her diary that "although [the] situation is desperate, he never sent me a message of any kind, has taken no measures for our evacuation, has let me know nothing about what I am to do. Luckily," she added, "I have Barbo and Ballif so there are chances that I should not be taken prisoner."

That same evening, Prince Stirbey and Colonel Ballif returned from Headquarters to tell Marie she must leave Bucharest the next day for Jassy, the provincial capital of Moldavia. They outlined a plan of escape. The Queen must say nothing to anyone but go into town early the next morning, leaving Ballif to pack up her house. Marie's mood was not improved by a letter from Carol. The twenty-three-year-old Crown Prince told his mother that Headquarters would not allow him to go to the front.

At nine o'clock the next morning Marie set off for Army Headquarters, prepared to do battle with the King. She found Ferdinand surprisingly calm in the face of defeat. She said she had been told she must leave Bucharest. Had Nando decided where she might "rest" her "royal head" and those of their children? Although all the necessary plans had been made to move Army Headquarters, it was obvious that the King had not even considered what would become of his family. Fumbling and hesitating, Ferdinand answered that he thought "Stirbey and Ballif had arranged" something. The Queen responded with icy calm. "I prayed him not to make any efforts, that I was accustomed to look after myself—at which he seemed relieved, little realising what my words really meant."

By this time Marie had begun to focus her hopes for the dynasty on Carol, who was infinitely more energetic than his father. She attacked the King on the subject of the Crown Prince, accusing her husband of "behaving criminally" and "playing with his son's future" by not sending him to the front. Turning to Carol, she advised him to act immediately and on his own. "You must go tomorrow, if not today!... go from troop to troop, from general to general, indifferent to weather, or roads, or hardships, share their life with them, be their friend [,] their help, let them have the feeling that you are everywhere [,] that no exertion is too great [,] no sacrifice too heavy."

The Queen's impatience grew out of months of frustration. "I can do all the work, think out each detail but the order must be given by the King," she had once complained to her diary. It was up to Ferdinand to send the heir to the dynasty out among their soldiers. This was Carol's great opportunity to gain the confidence of the army. His father must not be allowed to let it dissipate out of sheer inertia. The war was nearly over: "As things now stand..." she told her husband and son, "if you lose time perhaps you will no more have any army to go to!"

Before returning home, Queen Marie visited her hospital, where the soldiers were in various stages of panic. Some of the wounded had already been evacuated; the remainder were terrified of being transported or, worse, being left to fall into enemy hands. From the hospital she went on to Cotroceni Palace, "the house which had been mine for twenty-three years, the house I had improved and decorated, been proud of and loved. And yet all had to be done unemotionally as we were not supposed to say that we were there for the last time." "The hardest parting," she wrote in her diary, "was still to come. Barbo had promised to come to be with me... Barbo who more than any other shared with me sorrow and pain and joy... the parting from my poor little grave."

She dined with the Stirbey family in their small house on the Buftea grounds. She asked Prince Stirbey to go with her into Mircea's room: "We went there together, we two alone and lighting a candle we stood on the spot where his bed had stood—and then silently, wordlessly we remembered the days of agony when a battle of another kind had been fought and lost."

The Prince accompanied the Queen, her children, and his own wife and family to the Jassy train. "The last person I said goodbye to was Prince Stirbey; he was returning to Headquarters to be with the King. As we clasped hands we wondered when and where we would meet again. There were no words with which to express our despair."

Chapter *15*

The friendship of Russia has been more unfortunate to the Roumanians than the enmity of all the other peoples combined.

—*FRENCH HISTORIAN*

*T*he Queen's getaway train was packed with members of the royal family, ladies-in-waiting and their families, Princess Stirbey and her daughters, everyone's servants, and "endless, endless luggage. . . . I do not know where we are going," Marie said. "Nothing is settled, never in my life have I gone out thus into the unknown."

As soon as they arrived at the station near Jassy, the Queen's A.D.C., Colonel Ballif, left to go into town to find her a house. Prince Stirbey, "who always foresees," had taken a house in Jassy for his family a few months earlier. The King had arranged for himself and the Crown Prince to live at Army Headquarters in Zorleni, outside Jassy, and had ordered his new home furnished with things from Sinaia. But it was two weeks before Ballif was able to locate a suitable home for the Queen and her four younger children. Once found, it had to be equipped with bathtubs, washtubs, and ovens.

Meanwhile Marie lived on her train. Cut off completely from Bucharest, her life hung in limbo. She received no word from the King and only an occasional message from Stirbey. Most of her energies were directed toward combating panic in those around her; she did this by relieving their confinement with long, energetic tramps into the foothills around the station.

One piece of news finally reached the Queen—the fall of Bucharest. The King, the Crown Prince, and the Roumanian Army were said to be retreating into Moldavia. Six days later Barbo Stirbey arrived with confirmation of the defeat.

The King fled the capital on December 2, 1916. The next day Bratianu and the other officials of the government escaped from Bucharest for Jassy, leaving the wealthy citizens (those with their own transportation) to follow as best they could. The less fortunate were left behind to face the enemy. Some thirty thousand refugees thronged the railway station, vainly hoping for a train to spirit them off to Moldavia and safety. As much as six hundred dollars was paid to hire a taxi, although the line of cars stretching from Bucharest into Moldavia was a favorite target for German bombers.

Diplomats complained about the "indescribable confusion" following the exodus of the King. The Roumanian government had made no contingency plans in case of defeat. "The idea of being obliged to evacuate the capital had never entered their heads," complained a member of the British Legation, forced to burn his government's papers before catching the last train out of Bucharest.

Charged by the fleeing English, Russian, Italian, and Serbian ministers with the interests of their respective countries, the American Ambassador, Charles J. Vopicka, who had already taken over the representation of Germany and Turkey, was left to conduct the affairs of the Roumanian government-in-exile as well as those of his own country. The nominal representative of eight sovereign nations, Vopicka observed the "panic" that followed the flight of Ferdinand and his ministers: ". . . the people were very nervous, and feared that the enemy would murder many inhabitants and commit all manner of crimes. I gave them assurance that their fears were groundless."

The Ambassador was wrong. The arrival of an envoy from General Mackensen, demanding the surrender of Bucharest, marked the beginning of two years of systematic rape by the Central Powers. On December 6, 1916, a little over three months after Roumania entered World War I, the Germans took over her capital.

Inflated with the ease of their victory and eager to extract the spoils, the enemy raced toward the valleys of the Prahova and Dimbovitza rivers. Here, barely an hour's ride from Bucharest, lay the oil fields of Ploesti, Roumania's most valuable resource.

But the Germans might have guessed that neither the Roumanians nor their allies would allow them easy access to the richest oil deposits in Europe. To confound the enemy, the British had sent Colonel Sir John Norton-Griffiths, an M.P. and a renowned engineer, to Ploesti ahead of the Germans.

Norton-Griffiths, who came to be known respectfully as "the man with the sledge-hammer," led a crew of men in hacking up oil equipment like derricks, tools, pipes, and pumps. Underground pipes were force-fed with scrap iron, drilling bits, even mud and rocks to choke them off. Reserve tanks, holding all that was left of Roumania's wealth, were set on fire, and the resulting explosions pitched gigantic flaming steel drums out over a radius of a hundred yards. The largest petroleum tank in Europe, holding ten thousand tons of oil, was ignited just an hour or so before the enemy arrived. In place of the thriving oil industry the Germans expected to find, they were met with a pyrotechnic phenomenon which, when it eventually subsided, had reduced the valley of Ploesti to a blackened, charred wasteland lying under clouds of asphyxiating gas.

Once in possession of Bucharest, the enemy tried to make up for material disappointments elsewhere. The citizens of the capital were ordered to turn in two-thirds of their stores to German Headquarters. Shortly thereafter they were forced to make a further division of their goods, offering up substantial portions of what was left. All soldiers of the Central Powers were entitled to send home parcels of five kilos of provisions, thus depleting the city of remaining supplies.

Members of the aristocracy who remained in Bucharest, most of whom were pro-German, set about entertaining the officers of the occupation. Among them was Marie's friend, Princess Marthe Bibesco. Marthe had told the Queen that she wanted to stay behind in order to "taste every experience for the sake of literature, even occupation under the Germans." Marie was not fooled. "I am sure Marthe would manage to have a very good time," she wrote in her diary, "and her 'amitié' with the [German] Crown Prince would certainly be exploited in every way." Princess Bibesco had doubtless played on old Hohenzollern loyalties in her efforts to comfort King Ferdinand, with whom she had become romantically involved before the evacuation of Bucharest. "She must be very proud to have a King even in wartime," said the Queen. Marie never begrudged Ferdinand his ladies, but she had come to recognize her old friend as a "born adventuress."

While cooperative Roumanians like Princess Bibesco were deprived of some luxuries, the poor of Bucharest were left with none of the basic necessities for winter survival—heat, food, or the means of obtaining them. "One can imagine how the people lived and suffered," remarked the American Ambassador, "as they had no fuel to prepare their meals." Houses abandoned by their owners were stripped down by the soldiers. The only homes left undisturbed were the royal palaces; out of respect for the deceased King Carol I, friend of the Germans, these were ruled out of bounds for spoilers.

There were dozens of complaints of robbery and rape within the first few days of occupation, but no satisfaction could be gained from the authorities. The Germans blamed the Bulgarians, who pointed the finger at the Austrians, who accused the Turks. It was not possible to identify the guilty soldiers, as they stayed in the city only a day or two. The fact that the captain of the German police in charge of maintaining order was the same man who had gained a reputation for unusual cruelty in Belgium did not reassure the local citizenry.

With the Germans in possession of Bucharest, the Roumanian government was forced to establish a temporary home at Jassy. Lying only ten miles west of the Russian border, Jassy was the former capital of Moldavia. A town of 70,000 inhabitants, the provincial city strained to accommodate some 230,000 refugees. Before the exiles arrived, most of the large buildings had been commandeered by the Russians for hospitals and military quarters. The Russian officers lived exceedingly well; they dressed in warm uniforms, rode sleek horses, and hoarded all available fuel. They had even thought to bring their own cows.

Roumania's other allies had not been so farsighted. The English could not find housing and after a few weeks were short of food. Even the French Minister, billeted in the home of one of the great princely families of Roumania, discovered with horror that his servants were cutting down trees from the public park for fuel. When he confessed this to the Mayor of Jassy, the latter seemed remarkably unperturbed. "You are not the first to cut the trees in the public gardens," the Mayor told him. "The members of our own government did it before you."

As the only member of the royal family readily available to her subjects, Queen Marie had a difficult time during her first days in Jassy. "Everybody came to me, the Jassyites as well as the foreigners, and each one had something to protest or complain about... it was all I could do not to lose my head... I was myself a refugee with no house of my own, most of my worldly possessions left at Cotroceni, and what I had with me still packed away in great cases in the train... I, the Queen, had nowhere to go, so how could I help?"

Marie's diary, usually an example of spirited optimism under stress, deteriorates at this stage of the war into a series of lamentations, culminating in an invocation to the Lord, entitled "A Queen's Prayer." Proud of her rhetoric, the Queen included the entire prayer in her autobiography. It is interesting to read today, not for the moral or literary value she thought she achieved, but for what it tells us about the Queen of Roumania and her royal relations around Europe—those men and women who sincerely believed that the Almighty had reached down from heaven to personally install them on their thrones and might, if properly entreated, keep them there:

"... Thou hast made my face to shine before the lowly of this world, Thou hast placed purple on my shoulders and a crown on my head, and Thou has bidden me wear these as though they were not a burden... Therefore, do I cry unto Thee, O my God! Give me the strength to face every fate, to overcome every fear, to breast every storm...And if any remember me on earth, O Lord, may they see me with a smile on my lips, a gift in my hand, and in my eyes the light of that faith which removeth mountains."

Fortunately for Roumania, such excessive concern with her regal image gave impetus to Marie's wartime efforts. If the Queen's style was high-flown, her actions were hardheaded and earthbound. In spite of Roumania's near total devastation, it never occurred to Marie that the Entente would not eventually triumph. To that end she set herself personally to keep the King bolstered, the government intact and right-minded, and Roumania's allies sympathetic.

She embarked on a campaign to strengthen the defeated King's image by diluting Bratianu's power. The Prime Minister must be forced to take some pro-Entente members of the Conservative Party into the Liberal government; the King must open Parliament himself. Prince Stirbey helped Ferdinand draft a letter to that effect. When Bratianu received it, he hurried to see the Queen. They spent "an excessively uncomfortable hour and a half" together, during which Bratianu let Marie know that he was "accustomed to power and means to keep it...I quite realized that he had come to crush me, the woman, with his superiority and to make me understand that if we were to be opponents, mine would be the losing hand."

The Queen did not back down, and Parliament, which reconvened in exile at the end of December, was opened by the King. The theme of his address, carefully discussed if not actually dictated by Stirbey and Marie, was the need for a coalition government and the necessity of distributing land to the suffering peasant soldiers. With Prince Stirbey working behind the scenes, a compromise Cabinet was formed; it included Take Jonescu and three men from other political parties.

From the political arena Marie moved to the military. To counteract the corruption of the Liberal Party, she tried to increase the power of the army and recommended General Prezan, an early hero of the Transylvanian campaign, to replace Bratianu's Chief of Staff: "To my mind, only a real honest military rule could put some order into our rather rotten administration," she said. By the middle of December, Prezan was Roumania's new Chief of Staff.

The winter of 1916–1917 was the coldest in fifty years. With well over three times the normal population of Jassy competing against one another and the Russians for supplies, even privileged representatives from the diplomatic community struggled for heat and food. "After a few months," said a member of the British Legation, "there was no more tinned food to be had, and people began to die like flies of starvation. Typhus, smallpox, and other epidemics were soon raging, and...more than three hundred thousand deaths from these causes took place in the district...Owing to the lack of transport, and the state of the roads—feet deep in snow—wood fuel soon gave out; there was never any coal. The climax came in February 1917, when, with the temperature almost at zero, we had no fuel and nothing of any kind to eat but beans."

Beans were the staple of the royal family as well. Princess Ileana, eight years old at the time, developed vitamin deficiencies from which she never completely recovered. Sixty years later she still remembered "clearly wishing one could live without eating because it was so unpalatable." Visitors to Army Headquarters were disgusted by midday dinner, which never varied: soup with scraps of horseflesh and cabbage, maize, a bit of black bread, and black coffee made from dried acorns.

But the members of the diplomatic community, the generals, and the royal family were the lucky ones. Horse-drawn carts moved regularly up and down the streets of Jassy, piled with the bodies of men, women, and children who had frozen or starved to death on the sidewalks because, according to Red Cross observers, "there was no room for them to die indoors." The rate of mortality among soldiers was even higher. Discharged as convalescents from overcrowded hospitals, they wandered disconnectedly about the icy streets, "mere shadows of men waiting for the relief of death."

When Queen Marie arrived in Jassy in December, she found the hastily organized hospitals in chaos with soldiers dying not from their wounds but from pneumonia caught in the freezing cold of unheated wards. Since there was no wood to heat the water to wash their linen, the unfortunate men were left lying half uncovered, their wounds dressed in sawdust, or in such filth that they readily contracted new infections. Often there was nothing for them to eat, as the mills had no fuel with which to bake bread. Outside Jassy there was wood, cut and ready to bring into town, but political torpor stood in the way of transportation.

The irate Queen called together a group of ministers and General Prezan, who promised that the government and military would cooperate to hasten transport of the life-giving fuel. This left the problem of sanitation and the accompanying threat of infectious disease, particularly black typhus, traceable to fleas brought in by Mongolian trench diggers who had arrived earlier with the Russian Army. With only a 17 percent recovery rate, this germinating epidemic threatened to render all other emergencies insignificant.

After some difficulties with the Bratianu party, Queen Marie managed to have an old friend from the Balkan Wars, Dr. Jean Cantacuzène, named head of a sanitary organization, but it was too late to stop the virulent typhus. The epidemic had already started to decimate military ranks, as underheated, overcrowded hospitals piled the wounded three to a bed regardless of infection. By February, typhus was raging, aggravated by the fact that sanitation supplies sent to Roumania by France were, like military equipment, detained in Russia. The sanitation equipment did not arrive in Jassy until trains escorted by officers detailed from the French Military Mission were sent into Russia to get them.

Jassy itself, according to the French Minister, Saint-Aulaire, was "only the first circle of hell." On the Moldavian front one of the officers of the French Mission counted a Roumanian regiment of twenty-two hundred men of whom eighteen hundred were ill. These soldiers seldom recovered, for they were short of food and lived in wooden huts and trenches crawling with lice.

The Russian soldiers, who had been immunized against typhus, suffered mainly from venereal disease. They marched through Moldavia in regiments. Their officers, accompanied by wives and mistresses outfitted as nurses and nuns, followed in cars. Along with the cars were trucks piled with cases of champagne and delicacies, and for Chiefs of Staff, their own table service.

The Russian military leaders took advantage of the Roumanian defeat in Wallachia to take over the defense of Moldavia. In spite of superior numbers, they immediately evacuated the Dobruja. "Without firing a shot," said the embittered French Minister, "they abandoned positions covered by three lines of trenches and fifteen rows of barbed wire." By giving the enemy the Dobruja, the Russians surrendered the Danube River as well, Roumania's only supply route to her starving people.

In early December Queen Marie received her first word from the Duchess of Coburg since Roumania's entry into the war. Throughout Mircea's illness, his death, and the downfall of Bucharest, the Duchess had remained silent in spite of her daughter's constant pleas for some communication. A week after her arrival in Jassy, the Queen finally received a letter—a cruel, accusatory diatribe of eight pages in which the Duchess announced that she had "determined not to write" Missy for the duration of the war and would have kept to her vows except for the "terrible sorrow" of Mircea's death. "Oh! why, why did you begin this war?" railed the Duchess. "...the worst of all, is that they specially accuse *you* of having been the chief element of bringing it about!...I can hardly believe in my old days, that a daughter of mine is at the head of such a movement, my former little beloved peaceful, fair Missy, the sunshine in the house...But all Germany says it was you, you who pushed on towards the war from insane, blind confidence in the Entente."

"Can she really believe I am responsible for this war!" the Queen cried. "And she, a Russian, minding so terribly that we should have turned to the side of her former *patrie!*"

Her mother's cruelty was offset by the arrival of sister Ducky. The Grand Duchess Kirill, who brought much-needed medical supplies and provisions, came when the Queen was "all but desperate, when misfortune was crushing in upon us from every side." Marie thoroughly enjoyed a brief moment of warm companionship with her favorite sister.

The Queen's sister was also welcomed by Roumania's Premier/Foreign Minister* Bratianu, who used the Grand Duchess to carry messages directly

*He had taken over both positions in the current Cabinet.

to the Tsar. It was obvious that Roumania's future now depended entirely on the Russians—those big, strapping mujiks who melted away at the approach of the enemy. "Everybody seems to agree that our greatest hope lies in Nicky..." said Marie, "from all sides they continue pressing in upon me declaring that I must remain in close, affectionate contact with him." Marie sent her sister back to Russia with instructions from Bratianu and a "weighty" personal letter to give to the Tsar.

Official requests for military cooperation sent by Queen Marie to the Russian Tsar included indignant descriptions of the inequalities existing between her soldiers and those of Nicholas II. Your Russians, Missy told Nicky, don't fight but ransack our warehouses, where they get one kilo of bread and six hundred grams of meat per day; my men, who fight for two, are allowed only three hundred grams of flour a day and three hundred grams of meat twice a week.

A group of Marie's close friends decided that the Queen herself should journey secretly to Russia to beg the Tsar to force his troops to hold their ground. Prompted by the news that in the middle of a recent and crucial attack the Russians had retreated without a fight, they besieged Marie to confront Nicholas II in person. When, on Christmas Day, the Russians fouled another military operation, the King, the Queen, and Prince Stirbey sent for Bratianu and Jonescu to discuss the plan with them. Jonescu declared himself in favor of the idea; Bratianu spoke against it on the grounds that it would not be in keeping with the Queen's dignity. Marie responded that "a queen was never humiliated unless she *felt* humiliated." The Prime Minister reluctantly agreed to send a wire to see if a visit by the Queen to St. Petersburg would be in order.

But by the next day rumor reached Jassy that there was trouble at the Russian court; Rasputin had been murdered, and the imperial family was in revolt against the Empress. "... something uncanny & dreadful is going on," Marie wrote in her diary, "it will certainly be a difficult moment for me to arrive." She interviewed the Russian Minister, who confirmed the death of Rasputin. He warned Marie that even though she might appeal to the Tsar, "the Empress was a danger because she has a quite marvellous way of throwing cold water upon all his enthusiasms." Two days later Ducky wrote to say that this was not a propitious moment for Marie to go to Russia. The family situation was "too strained." It was decided to send Bratianu and the Crown Prince instead.

Their trip was not a success. Whereas in previous dealings with the Entente, the wily Roumanian Premier had always had something to trade—his country's adherence to the Allied cause—he was now reduced to begging, and Bratianu in the position of suppliant was an angry incongruity. He tried to convince the crumbling Tsarist government to renew its offensive; he used an Inter-Allied Conference that opened in St. Petersburg in February to try to rouse sympathy for his countrymen and improve his own blighted prestige at home. He failed on both counts. The Russians were hostile in the extreme, and the delegates to the Conference were too busy worrying about the apocalyptic domestic crises in Russia to pay attention to Bratianu's pleas.

Indifferent to the fate of Roumania but mindful that the loss of Moldavia would endanger Russia itself, the Russian General Staff finally issued the order to send in troops to hold the Sereth Line—a 500-kilometer front extending in an arc from the junction of the rivers Sereth and Danube, in the south, northwestward through the Carpathian Mountains. New Year's 1917 saw the Roumanians huddled back into the northeast corner of Moldavia, protected by the Danube River in the south and the snowbound, wolf-infested peaks of the Carpathians to the west. But a line had finally been drawn, the enemy held in check. Roumania sent her gold reserves, archives, and crown jewels to Moscow for safekeeping. The Germans, having reduced the Roumanians to many months of military impotence, were free to send their troops elsewhere.

With the threat of immediate battle removed, Queen Marie turned to a personal problem that had been disturbing her for some time. Two years earlier, at the beginning of World War I, Crown Prince Carol had returned from his military training in Potsdam. His stint in the German Army had improved his outward manner, although it had not lowered his inflated opinion of himself. He had recently fallen in love with Zizi Lambrino, a girl of aristocratic Roumanian background. This romance, like that of his father and Helene Vacaresco a quarter of a century before, must come to nothing in the end. The writers of the Roumanian Constitution, fearing that one Roumanian clan or faction might gain control of the throne, specifically prohibited marriage between members of the royal house and their subjects. With Roumania teetering on the brink of total defeat and the enemies of the dynasty blaming the English-born Queen for the debacle, it was supremely important for the entire royal family to conduct itself according to the law. To that end, Marie had packed Carol off with Bratianu to St. Petersburg, where the Prime Minister had revived the possibilities of a Russian marriage. Now she was faced with what to do with Carol on his return.

Like other members of the privileged class, Zizi Lambrino and her mother had emigrated to Jassy. They lived in a one-room apartment from which Prince Carol rescued his beloved for long drives in his Rolls-Royce and games of bridge with friends. To see more of Carol, Zizi joined the group of ladies working in Marie's temporary palace. The former ballroom of the Queen's new home had been converted into a workroom, where women of the nobility sewed underwear and knitted socks for the soldiers. Zizi worked from 5 to 7 P.M. At the end of her daily stint, the Crown Prince met her in a little garden near the entrance.

Marie must have been aware of these arrangements, for in the middle of February she asked the King's permission to bring Carol to live with her where she could keep an eye on him, instead of at Army Headquarters with his absentminded father. The Queen had high hopes for her son. She knew he was spoiled and pompous, but admired his practicality and persistence. "He is a worker and knows how to organize... He has the tenacity that his father always lacked, he has a much greater opinion of his own capabilities."

To take advantage of his virtues, the Queen arranged to send the Crown Prince around Moldavia, "inspecting, inquiring, looking into things." She made sure he was "laden with gifts; I wished my son to be better known and better loved." But when Carol finished running his mother's errands, he hurried back to Zizi. In the spring, word reached the Queen that the Crown Prince was being widely criticized for lack of personal involvement in the war. She was not surprised: "with all my might I have been trying to get Carol to do his duty & I get so very little help," she said. Since the King would not take a stand, Marie sent Prince Stirbey to speak to the Crown Prince. She was pleased with the results of their conversation; "at dinner Carol announced... that he was leaving Monday for Botosani [a town north of Jassy]. I hope that by degrees Carol will... get into the way of steady hard work."

Like many others Marie came down with the flu during the winter and was forced to spend several weeks in bed. Prince Stirbey also took sick. "Am very sad to be shut away from him," Marie wrote in her diary, "he is always my helper and counsellor." Marie counted on Barbo's evening visits—quiet hours when they discussed the day's news, planned the King's program, and read aloud to each other over a cup of tea. Robbed of Stirbey's calming influence, Marie found herself involved in long, "fruitless" arguments with her husband: "With Nando one talks & talks, finally he flies into a rage about everybody & everything & nothing is done!" she complained to her diary.

During her long convalescence, the Queen had time to reflect on the situation outside Jassy, which was becoming progressively worse. The Roumanian Army, forced to abandon one village after another in its retreat, had left its supplies behind, which were quickly "devoured" by the Russians. "Their money was always forthcoming," Marie wrote, "and their appetite was huge. The peasants, little realizing that in a short time money would be completely useless as there would be nothing more to buy, gave their all without reserve!... Like the locusts of old, these slow-moving, well-fed, steady-going, earth-coloured Russians... who had been greeted as saviours turned into a mighty danger none had anticipated."

How dangerous these Russian soldiers were to become, not even the Queen had yet begun to realize.

Chapter *16*

A foreign dynasty is a delicate plant.

—*JEAN LAHOVARY*

*A*t this stage of the war, Roumania's meager chances to recoup her losses depended totally on the cooperation of Russia, her only undefeated ally in the East. But this was 1917, the year of the Russian Revolution. From the overthrow of the Tsar in March to the Bolshevik coup in November, the breakdown of the old order, which changed the course of history, also undercut Roumania's hopes for a military comeback and nearly destroyed the Roumanian monarchy as well.

At the beginning of 1917 the Tsar was still in power, serving as Commander in Chief at Russian Army Headquarters. Left to her own devices in the capital, the Tsarina had placed the Foreign Ministry in the hands of Boris Sturmer, a reputedly pro-German minion of Rasputin, lending credence to rumors of treason in the upper echelons of government and in the palace itself. The morale of Russia's soldiers and civilians had been undermined by heavy losses on the front and terrible shortages at home, traceable to the inefficiency and corruption of the Tsar's government. Even the assassination on December 30, 1916, of the Tsarina's evil genius, Rasputin, had not been enough to compensate the dispirited troops and angry people.

On March 8, 1917, strikes and riots broke out in Petrograd.* "Some disorders occurred today," the British Ambassador advised London, "but nothing serious." The Ambassador was not the only Westerner to misread the onset of the Revolution. Assuming that the uprising was only a protest against Tsarist repression and hoping that a new government in Petrograd would produce a more efficient military machine, Russia's Western allies welcomed the upheaval, little realizing that the Russians were demonstrating against the war itself. Lloyd George sent a congratulatory wire to the revolutionaries. Woodrow Wilson, about to bring the United States into the conflict, greeted the events of March 1917 as "heartening news." The Roumanians did not share their allies' enthusiasm. "What would happen to us if things went wrong in Russia is not even to be contemplated," Queen Marie wrote. "It would mean utter and complete disaster, it would mean the end of everything!"

On March 15 the Tsar abdicated for himself and his hemophilic son. The King and Queen of Roumania sent a wire of condolence to which they received an immediate response. "I thank you both from my heart for your touching message..." said the fallen Tsar. "May God bless you and the Roumanian people and grant you the final victory and realization of all your aspirations."

Marie was moved by Nicky's response. "He was losing everything... but in a last cry of friendship he wishes for us a better fate." Her sentiments toward Alexandra were no more charitable than they had ever been. "What an hour for that woman, who because of her fanaticism has brought about this crisis; she who would listen to no one except Rasputin."

Since no one yet envisioned the tragic end of the Tsarina, it must have been a great release for Marie to express her hostility toward this cousin, who had always made her feel inferior. Moreover, the Queen of Roumania was aware of the parallels drawn by others and must surely have heard Barbo Stirbey referred to as "the Rasputin of Roumania." The chain of command in Roumania was similar to that in prerevolutionary Russia: from the Queen's adviser through the Queen to the King. The difference lay in the prime movers. Marie knew she had chosen a better mentor than her cousin. Prince Stirbey was an aristocrat with an acute sense of self-preservation, not a mystical scoundrel.

On March 16 the Provisional Government took over the power in Petrograd. In Jassy the lesson was not hard to infer. The Roumanian monarchy must initiate reform "from above" so the people would not import revolution from across the border. Within three weeks of the Tsar's abdication, Marie, Stirbey,

---

*St. Petersburg was renamed at the beginning of the war to remove any taint of the German language.

and Ferdinand had prepared a speech for the King to deliver to his soldiers announcing agrarian and political reforms. Ferdinand left for the front to proclaim the message in person. It was simple, eloquent, and years overdue:

"Sons of peasants who, with your own hands, have defended the soil on which you were born, on which your lives have been passed, I, your King, tell you that besides the great recompense of victory which will assure for every one of you the nation's gratitude, you have earned the right of being masters, in a larger measure, of that soil upon which you fought. Land will be given you . . . and you will also take a larger part in public affairs."

The King was also "persuaded" to "act quickly" in the matter of Roumania's Jews. These people, long an object of intense persecution, were natural supporters of the revolutionary movement. Shortly after his speech to the soldiers, the King received a delegation of Jews to whom he promised that "all those who spilt their blood for their country would be treated alike when the War was over."

These timely proclamations helped neutralize the numerous threats to the dynasty that hung like clouds over defeated Roumania, and they undercut ambitious politicians tempted to use revolutionary fever to increase their own power. "Prince Stirbey . . ." Marie wrote, "was the one who chiefly encouraged the King to speak to his troops . . . before others could take the initiative out of his hands."

To combat her own "ever-growing uneasiness" and pay her dues as a sovereign, the Queen expanded her inspirational and organizational work among the sick and wounded. "I think," she wrote, "there are few queens who have seen such sights, who have been in places of such abject, unimaginable misery."

Unabashedly immodest, Marie was as omnipresent as she claimed. She cleaned up the triage at the Jassy railway station—a dark, freezing, stench-ridden barracks where wounded soldiers lay on the floor, covered with lice, until room could be found for them in one of the overcrowded hospitals. When she wasn't at the triage, she visited the hospitals. Dressed in the white uniform of a nursing sister, the white enamel Cross of Marie hanging on an orange ribbon around her neck, the Queen advanced up and down the rows of cots, stopping at each one to offer a pack of cigarettes, a selection of prayers, or for the worst cases, a piece of bread she cut herself and spread with jam. For the wounded or dying who wanted crosses or icons, Marie carried a ready supply in the huge front pocket of her apron. She herself bathed the eyes of one soldier whose face had been "shot to pieces" and whose lids had stuck fast.

The Queen made herself famous by refusing to wear rubber gloves like the nurses in the typhus wards. Nor did she hesitate to offer her bare hands to the dying to hold or press to their lips. When a timorous lady-in-waiting reminded her that the doctors required gloves, she sniffed, "I really cannot ask them to kiss India rubber!" Returning home at night, she stood fully clothed in her rubber boots in a pail of boiling water into which she shed her clothes to kill the virulent lice.

Marie also wrote articles of encouragement for the newspaper most popular with the troops, as well as completing a second volume of her sentimental travelogue of Roumania, *The Country That I Love*. In April she published a message in several American magazines appealing for sympathy and supplies.

Writing was beginning to interest the Queen more and more. For some time she had been publishing fairy stories for children. Now she directed her talents to public relations and propaganda. She always wrote quickly and impulsively. Although her impassioned portrayals of Roumania's wartime calvary might have profited from a second, more critical glance, Marie seldom failed to find the poignant detail that gave life to her picture and insistence to her story.

She usually wrote in the very early morning, although she occasionally returned to her work in the evening with supper on a tray in bed. By 8 A.M. she was always on her way, visiting soldiers in and out of the city. She moved about constantly, nervously—flying trips to the front, to towns with names like Bacau, Onesti, Roman—spending whole days in makeshift hospitals where the guns boomed only yards away. She saw that her car was kept loaded with provisions so as to be able to offer immediate help en route. As food, clothing, and medicines began to come in from the Allied Red Cross, Marie took obvious pleasure in giving on a direct, personal basis to prisoners of war encountered on the road or to thc starving Jews of Jassy as well as to her own soldiers. When the spring thaw opened the roads, the Queen traveled into the mountain villages with provisions for the peasants and soldiers who had miraculously survived the winter.

As spring and the Russian Revolution progressed, the problems of hunger and typhus were superseded by the danger of the Russian soldiers quartered in Moldavia. Passive on the battlefield, the Russians had grown cocky, undisciplined, and increasingly belligerent in the demilitarized zones. Hostile, marauding bands of men roamed seemingly at will through what was left of unoccupied Roumania.

To celebrate May Day, Russian soldiers marched on the Jassy prisons to release "martyrs to the people's cause." Having freed the prisoners, both political and criminal, they moved on to the temporary palace to demand the overthrow of the Hohenzollern dynasty. Fortunately for Ferdinand and Marie, their shouts were not followed by actions, for the Cabinet in exile had voted to offer no resistance even if the building itself were attacked.

Five days later another attempt to unseat the King and Queen was discovered. This one was instigated by the Workers' Committee in Petrograd, which ordered Russian extremists in Jassy to storm the palace and seize or massacre the sovereigns and their children. Take Jonescu, acting as Roumania's Premier in the absence of Bratianu, turned to the Foreign Ministers who secured the intervention of Allied officers quartered in Jassy. These soldiers, "strengthened by certain well-directed generosities," disarmed the would-be assassins.

In the middle of May the Queen, who had had no word about Ducky since the Revolution, received a long, sad letter from her. Marching at the head of his Naval Guards to the Tauride Palace, Ducky's husband, Grand Duke Kirill, was one of the first to pledge his allegiance to the new Provisional Government. Nevertheless, it had become quickly apparent that there was no longer any room in Russia for relatives of the fallen Tsar. Ducky was furiously embittered.

Marie was also aware of how her own prestige had fallen with the abdication of Nicholas II. "This makes a great difference for Nando & me, especially for me...I* was the one who could most easily obtain things from the Tsar. I could be a real aid for my country, that is now over."

Later in the summer the Queen received a letter from her mother, who had heard that the Tsar and his family had been "bundled off in the middle of the night to some unknown destination! May God have mercy on them!" the Duchess of Coburg wrote. Since Roumania's defeat, the Duchess had softened toward her daughter, assuring "Darling Missy" that she thought of her all the time. "God bless and protect you in your terrible trials," she wrote, "I pray for you and love you!" The Duchess said she admired her daughter's "courage to visit all the nests of infection and misery," but warned her to keep her children at a safe distance from possible contamination.

Marie did just the opposite, encouraging her children to share the misery of the people and the soldiers. She was particularly pleased with the development of daughter Mignon, aged seventeen. Mignon had started working at a hospital near the front lines, where she was happy and content. The Queen visited her and was enormously pleased with this child who worked well with the other nurses and seemed to take pleasure in doing the most menial jobs.

The same could not be said of Mignon's older sister, Elisabetha. Although the Queen's eldest daughter accompanied her mother on errands of mercy and even had a hospital nominally under her charge, she had little interest in good works. Debilitated first by a weak knee, then jaundice, and finally a "breakdown," Princess Elisabetha filters through the pages of Marie's diary, available for dutiful charity, but with no enthusiasm for the job.

Certainly it would have been hard for the Queen's daughters to compete with her in vitality or warmth. Nor did Marie ever underestimate her own role in the accomplishments of the Roumanian soldiers. "I had been with

*Underlined twice in the original.

them everywhere—in the hospitals, on the front, right into the trenches; I had seen them gradually turn again from half-starved skeletons into healthy human beings. I had sustained [them] with all my energy ... Looking into the eyes of their Queen, they had sworn to stand up like a wall to defend the last scrap of Roumanian territory which was still ours. Many a dying soldier whispered to me with his last breath that it was for me that he was fighting, for was I not his home, his mother, his belief and his hope?"

During the winter and spring of 1917, a period of military quiescence, the French Mission under General Berthelot started the reconstitution of the Roumanian Army, weeding out the corrupt, the incompetent, and the political untrustworthy, replacing musty old generals with young officers already experienced on the battlefield. New recruits were drilled by French officers in Western-style warfare and equipped with French guns and ammunition steered through revolutionary Russia by armed French guards. By April of 1917, the Roumanian Army, although significantly reduced in size, was a competent, well-drilled, even formidable fighting force. By that summer the Roumanian soldiers constituted, in the words of the American Ambassador, "one of the best fighting organizations in Europe."

July of 1917 was the target date for a much heralded Russian offensive against the Germans and Austrians. The Russian Provisional Government, which had been in office for four months, had been trying to revitalize the waning enthusiasm of its people for the war; by unifying soldiers and citizens behind the war effort, Kerensky hoped to combat the disruptive elements in the Russian Army fostered by Lenin and the Bolsheviks. To coincide with the Russian assault, the Roumanians planned a simultaneous drive through the Austro-German lines between the Danube and the mountains toward Bucharest.

Before the joint offensive there was talk of giving Crown Prince Carol a major command. Queen Marie was completely opposed: ". . . a boy who has not made a real military career! if it turns out badly all the fault will fall back upon him, and he is not a simple general who can be put on one side and forgotten . . . I am never sure here that for selfish reasons or for reasons of personal revenge or jealousy . . . one will not give Nando bad advice."

Both the King and the Crown Prince were at the front during the historic summer offensive, although Carol did not join the fighting, nor was he given a command. The Crown Prince moved from regiment to regiment by car, visiting with the soldiers and encouraging them. His mother, who was just behind the front lines working in the forward hospitals, missed out on the Battle of Marasti, one of the landmarks of the Eastern campaign. "I did not at the time exactly realize the importance of this battle," she confessed. What the Queen did perceive with clarity was the unreliability of her Russian ally.

At first the Roumanian soldiers met with brilliant success, advancing more than twelve miles on a twenty-mile front, capturing five thousand prisoners and many guns. Suddenly the operation fell apart. The Queen's diary for July 13 records the reason. "Day of growing anxiety. Nando appeared unexpectedly for breakfast, called back from the front by Headquarters, who had stopped our offensive, as something terrible seems to be going on in Russia. It appears that they are giving way all along the front before an enemy only a quarter their number; they simply retreat in masses without fighting... Misfortune pursues us; if the Russians will not fight we can be invaded in a few days... The Russians cut our throats."

There was nothing the Roumanian soldiers could do as their Russian counterparts, prey to Bolshevik propaganda urging immediate peace, gave in to the Germans. The Roumanians were forced to abandon hard-won gains in order to send troops north to shore up the collapsing Russians. A resounding victory at Marasti, which should have opened the way to a southern offensive, was followed instead by a series of desperate holding actions, designed to save what was left of northern Moldavia and its capital, Jassy, from the enemy. As the Russians retreated without a fight, Roumania's last frontiers were reached. "There are no words to express our indignation," said Marie as she and Prince Stirbey looked up on a map possible places for escape.

Although the Queen made plans for evacuation, she relied on the King's promise that whatever happened she should be allowed to stay with him and their army on Roumanian soil until the last possible moment. Many of her friends left for Odessa. "I think it reasonable that people should evacuate by degrees so that there should not be a rush if danger comes," she said, but she herself refused to leave.

The last struggle took place a month later. In the Battle of Marasesti, in Herculean fighting that lasted from August 12 to 19, 1917, the Roumanian peasant soldiers, armed and trained by the French, defeated the combined forces of Germany and Austria, saving Odessa from occupation—and perhaps Moscow itself. Even General Mackensen voiced ungrudging admiration for his opponents. From England, Lloyd George promised that the Allies would never forget how brilliantly Roumania carried out her duty to the common cause.

The Queen was proud of her men. "In spite of the bad example of the Russians, who had mostly turned Bolshevik and were daily abandoning their positions by the thousand, our soldiers, underfed, insufficiently armed and hardly ever relieved, remained staunch to a man, unshaken amidst the débâcle of their erstwhile allies."

On this point British historian Seton-Watson was quite specific: only the "full disintegration" of the Russian Army prevented the Roumanians from following up their triumph with offensive action. "Indeed," said the Balkan expert, "the frequency of fraternisation between the Russian and German trenches often left the Roumanians in an extremely precarious position."

After the Battle of Marasesti, there was no more discussion of a Roumanian offensive. Without the Russians, the Roumanians could not advance. The Germans, who had been providing financial support, propaganda, and arms to the Bolsheviks, had helped complete the demoralization of the Russian Army. Within a few months Lenin would take command, and Roumania and her Queen would find themselves totally isolated from their allies.

Chapter 17

There is only one man in Roumania and
that is the Queen.

—*COUNT CHARLES DE SAINT-AULAIRE*

*B*y the middle of September 1917, Roumania's
active role in World War I had ceased. When the American Ambassador
arrived in Jassy in the fall, he was warned by King Ferdinand not to unpack
his bags. The royal family, the government, and the diplomatic corps all
might have to evacuate to Russia at any moment. The prevailing opinion
in Jassy was that the Russian soldiers who were still on the front lines would
abandon their positions around the beginning of October.

Accompanying Ambassador Vopicka to Jassy were forty members of the
American Red Cross: doctors, engineers, hygienists, and sanitation experts.
Queen Marie welcomed them and their chief, Colonel Henry Anderson,
an aristocratic old gentleman from Virginia. "They came with full hands
and a magnificent supply of provisions of every kind, which seemed quite
dazzling at this time of dearth... besides, they were magnificently practical
and efficient, and went about things in the right manner."

To make sure that her Roumanians did not turn American largess into personal profit, she insisted that the Minister of the Interior prepare detailed plans for the equitable distribution of supplies. Oriental baksheesh presented an ongoing problem to the Anglo-Saxon Queen, who often upset herself "to the pitch of despair" over her ministers' moral turpitude. Unable to reconcile herself to Roumanian ways, she usually called for Prince Stirbey, who listened patiently to her righteous angers, calmed her, and tried to teach her to live with the realities around her.

The defeat and frustrations of the summer had worn Marie down. Autumn and the first anniversary of Mircea's death loomed like an impassable milestone. For her forty-second birthday on October 29, Marie received money from the King, four ducks from Ileana, and a huge pig from the rest of her children for the canteens she had started in needy villages. Four days later came the dreaded "death-day." Late in the afternoon Stirbey came to see her. "We were very still and sad...we...hardly dared speak of what was uppermost in our hearts."

Less than two weeks later, word came through that Lenin and his followers had overthrown the Russian Provisional Government on November 6 (1917). The Bolsheviks were said to be suing the Germans for peace and threatening to imprison the Roumanian government and royal family if they did not agree to lay down their arms as well. On November 17, Lenin and Trotsky broadcast a proposal for a general armistice on worldwide radio and announced that they wished to start negotiations with the Germans. Prince Stirbey came to discuss what position the Queen and her family would take in case the Russians made peace with the enemy over their heads. There was no question in Marie's mind of what was right. She got the King and the Crown Prince to agree that "the last thing we could do, was to treat for peace with the Germans, that our Country could do it if it wanted, but *we* could not." Her alternative was escape. "Part of our army would probably have to surrender... but we should all the same try to cut ourselves a way with a small armed force through Russia to a safe place. Of course it all sounds fantastic... But for all that it is for this solution that I vote."

Speaking out against the Queen's bravado was General Averescu, commander of the only organized army Roumania still possessed. "We know too well the egoism and the hostility of the Russians to have any illusions on the hazards that await us. We don't even know how we could get [to Russia]," he said, pointing out that the new People's Commissars had commandeered all the saloon cars of the Grand Dukes for themselves, their wives and mistresses.

Although King Ferdinand and Queen Marie asked for help from the Entente, their allies could not assure safe-conduct for them through or even into Russia. Ever since the end of July, the Foreign Ministers of France, England, Italy, and the United States had been cabling home from Jassy asking their respective governments to put pressure on Russia to hold the front and, in case exodus proved inevitable, to guarantee King Ferdinand's position as head of his country wherever he fled. But while the Allies equivocated, Russian troops seized all means of transportation that might have made the Roumanian flight feasible. Events on the Eastern Front moved faster than the decision-making processes in the West. Marie's march was at first postponed, then abandoned by practically everyone except Marie.

The only word coming out of Western Europe was a "very warm" telegram that arrived on December 2, 1917, for the Queen. Sent directly by King George V of England to his cousin, it assured Missy that she and her children would be welcomed in England whenever they chose to come. At first flattered, the Queen soon realized that George's cable signaled Allied recognition of the hopelessness of her position. She wired back thanking George "with all my heart for your telegram. Your kind words come at a moment when we are facing tragic facts owing to Russia's failure, so tragic indeed that it will perhaps be impossible to profit by your kind offer of hospitality."

On the same day that the Queen received an offer of asylum from England, the Roumanian government learned of another threat to the lives of Ferdinand and Marie. Russian soldiers were reported to be plotting to arrest or kill their officers, attack the Roumanian government, destroy the telephone, telegraph, and railways systems, and "violently remove" the royal family and the Foreign Ministers. They planned to start the mayhem by burning the home of General Tcherbatcheff, Commander in Chief of the Russian Army on the Roumanian front. The Russian general appealed to Prime Minister Bratianu for help.

"I cannot mobilize a single Roumanian soldier to defend you against your own troops," Bratianu told him, "without taking part in the interior struggle of Russia and provoking a fight with your new masters [the Bolsheviks]... Surely you have a regiment?"

"I regret to admit to Your Excellency that I have not one," Tcherbatcheff said.

"Do you have a battalion?"

"If I had a battalion, I wouldn't be asking for help."

"A company?"

"Not any longer. I have not a single sure man, not even my A.D.C. nor my orderly. I sent everyone good to Kerensky, which, however, served only to disarm me without saving him."

Fortunately for Tcherbatcheff and the Roumanians, the Russian soldiers, hearing that members of the French Mission had been recruited to guard their commander, reneged on the planned assault. The next day General Tcherbatcheff was given another opportunity to serve the Roumanians, when the Russian soldiers under his command declared an armistice with the Germans and replaced all their generals with Bolshevik lieutenants. Faced with the choice of yielding his post to one of the revolutionaries or standing in the way of peace, Tcherbatcheff declared the armistice himself. Thus he enabled Roumania to keep her troops fighting at the front for a few crucial days and saved her from a turncoat army on a rampage within her borders.

The following day news reached Jassy that the Russian Army, now in a state of chaotic breakdown, had thrown off the last vestige of discipline. The Bolsheviks had taken over Russian Army Headquarters at Stavka and had murdered General Dukhonin, their former chief, by cutting him to pieces on their upturned swords. In Moldavia, the Russian soldiers responded to this news by killing their officers, deserting their positions on the front, and splintering off into violent bands that terrorized the countryside, burning, raping, and devastating whole Roumanian villages. Sweeping eastward toward Russia, they traveled empty-handed, stealing what they wanted, leaving their guns and ammunition for the Germans.

Up to this time Premier Bratianu, fearful of provoking the Russians into official conflict, had avoided using Roumanian soldiers against their nominal allies. Now he had no choice. With the approval of Tcherbatcheff, General Berthelot, and a hastily summoned Crown Council, a Roumanian police force composed of army reserves (the regulars were still trying to hold the front against the Germans) was mobilized and placed under a Russian officer. Equipped with the best arms and tanks available, it headed out of Jassy to disperse the marauders. The reservists were so effective that they helped provoke new Bolshevik threats against the Roumanian government.

These mass desertions of Russian soldiers left the Roumanian Army with huge gaps in its lines through which the enemy now began to pour. There was little the Roumanians could do to hold them back. What is astonishing is that the Roumanian peasants themselves did not succumb to the revolutionary frenzy raging around them. Thanks in part to King Ferdinand's promises of reform and Queen Marie's popularity, they remained faithful, displaying unusual fortitude under anarchic conditions.

It was obvious that Roumania must soon capitulate and sign some sort of armistice. One British diplomat described Roumania's position in December 1917 as that of "an island surrounded on all sides by the enemy, with no hope of assistance from the Allies. On the north, west, and south lay the Germans, Austrians, Bulgarians and Turks. At her back was revolutionary Russia, no whit less hostile than the former. There was but little ammunition, and the stock of food was almost entirely exhausted." But Roumania's Western allies either misread their maps or chose to ignore their representatives in Jassy. They informed Prime Minister Bratianu that they were opposed to an armistice and that the Roumanian Army must continue to fight.

From the eye of the hurricane Queen Marie agreed. "I was terribly unresigned and could not believe that we were destined to give up." She fell back on her plan of marching through southern Russia with a part of her army to the land of the "still faithful" Cossacks. "To sit still and die, suffocated between Russian traitors and German haters is really too poor a death! To this I would prefer la Grande Aventure." Barbo Stirbey did his best to reason with the Queen, but even he could not convince Marie that the war was over for Roumania.

The Queen's chief worry was that the Entente would use a separate peace to slide out of territorial commitments. "If we are to die," she said, "let our Allies at least know that we do not die like blind fools, but as conscious heroes, knowing that we have been sold and betrayed, and that at the moment when, through the failure of others, our front is becoming useless, our big protectors begin to haggle and bargain with us, as to whether they will be able to keep any of the promises given to us when we were still prosperous, before the Russian revolution cut our throats!"

Although she could not prevent the laying down of arms, Marie managed to extract telegraphed promises from the British government to "uphold Roumania's interest and 'revindications,' regardless of how much she will presently be forced to give way." And, on insistent urging from Bratianu, the Allied Foreign Ministers in Jassy signed a letter stating that "Roumania, having battled heroically to the extreme limits of the possible, found herself driven back by the betrayal of the Russians to the extent where it was absolutely necessary to dispose provisonally of her weapons and that, therefore, the armistice should not affect the allied agreements with her."

On December 6, 1917, hostilities between Roumania and the Central Powers ceased. Three days later the armistice was signed.

Within two weeks peace negotiations between Russia and the Central Powers opened at Brest-Litovsk. Trotsky came to represent the Bolsheviks— a job that did not prevent his sponsoring a scheme to seize Ferdinand, Marie, and the Roumanian government in order to extend the revolution into Moldavia. Once again Roumanian troops were called out to intercept the revolutionaries. General Tcherbatcheff, who stood between the Russians and the royal family, was saved by a Cossack guard who dispersed the marauders with his gun. Bratianu, learning that Socola, a town on the outskirts of Jassy, was being used as headquarters and ammunition cache for the Bolsheviks in Roumania, occupied the town with police troops, disarmed five thousand Russians, and sent them home.

This did not stop the attempts to murder the Roumanian royal family. Returning from the theater one evening less than two weeks later, the Queen was asked to receive Captain Laycock of British Intelligence, "a simple, cold-blooded, unemotional little man" who had once offered to get her younger children out of Roumania. The Captain informed the Queen that his agents in Russia had uncovered yet another assassination plot, this time against Ferdinand and his two sons. The "ugly news" was corroborated by letters intercepted by British agents in Russia which Laycock offered to Marie so that she might read them herself.

On January 5, 1918, Lloyd George dealt Roumania a major political blow. England's Prime Minister announced that Russia's defection from the Entente called for a revision of Allied treaties. Countermanding his vows to honor Britain's promises to Roumania, Lloyd George said that under present circumstances the dismemberment of Austria-Hungary was no longer consistent with British policy. Three days later President Wilson pronounced his famous Fourteen Points, two of which demolished Roumanian hopes for territorial expansion after the war. Point one, "open covenants openly arrived at," denounced secret diplomacy, thus compromising Roumania's Treaty of 1916 with her allies; point ten recommended that after the war Austria-Hungary be reorganized to give its people an opportunity for autonomous development and a return to the territorial status quo, rather than a rearrangement of borders and nationalities.

During the same week Marie and Ferdinand celebrated their twenty-fifth wedding anniversary. "I wonder if you will have thought of that cold winter morning 25 years ago when you sent off your eldest daughter into the world..." the Queen wrote her mother; "how young I was, how full of hope." Marie mused over her relationship with her husband. "Nando and I, hand in hand, confess to each other that at this hour, in spite of our misfortunes, or should I say because of them, we have become the firmest possible friends, attached to our country in a way not often given to sovereigns." Twenty-four years after the fact, glossing over her youthful ignorance of biological processes, Marie gave herself full credit for presenting her people "at the earliest possible date...the heir they longed for."

It was a festive day. Early in the morning a committee of ladies brought the Queen a braided crown of silver thread to wear in place of her jewels, which had been sent for safekeeping to Moscow. The King and Queen entertained the members of their official household at luncheon. At dinner the Chief of Staff presented the Queen with a medal for bravery, and Premier Bratianu gave a "very fine speech" to which the King replied. "Nando," said Marie, "had to make seven speeches today and spoke perfectly each time."

Three weeks later, on the last day of January 1918, the Bolsheviks declared war on Roumania and expropriated the Roumanians gold and crown jewels in their possession. During their evening tea, Prince Stirbey asked Queen Marie to help him compose a wire for King Ferdinand to send King George of England. When Stirbey read back the wire, which "cruelly summed up our desperate and hopeless situation," Marie burst into tears.

A week later the Germans put extra troops on the Roumanian front and delivered an ultimatum: Roumania had four days to begin peace talks. The announcement toppled the Liberal government. Since the Conservatives were not strong enough to form a Cabinet, the King asked General Alexandru Averescu, the hero of Marasesti who had declared himself in favor of peace negotiations, to form a government. The result was a Cabinet of second-rate politicians, since all the better men refused to deal with the Germans.

King Ferdinand had a good reason for bringing in a Prime Minister amenable to making peace with the Central Powers. He had recently received a secret visitor sent by Emperor Karl of Austria, the thirty-year-old Emperor who had succeeded his great-uncle, Franz Josef, a little over a year before.

Karl, an earnest, peace-loving young man who had inherited a splintering empire, had sent his envoy to inform Ferdinand that Vienna did not agree with Germany's avowed intention of inflicting "punishment for treachery" on the King of Roumania. On the contrary, Austria wished to arrange a fair peace with Ferdinand, a member of the illustrious Hohenzollern dynasty.

This was not the attitude of the Kaiser. On a tour of occupied Roumania the previous summer, Cousin Willy had boasted to his troops that he would unseat King Ferdinand. The King's pro-German enemies in Bucharest were delighted by this. Led by old Peter Carp, the die-hard Germanophile politician, they had been scheming since the beginning of the war to depose Ferdinand and his English-born Queen. Now they suggested that the Central Powers refuse to negotiate with the King, as they had already voted to bring in a new German dynasty.

Queen Marie could not bring herself to compromise with the political facts which were threatening her throne and her very existence. Her English morality was shocked by the Phanariot approach to bargaining and the ease with which Roumanian politicians adjusted their beliefs toward the ultimate goal of survival. She railed at General, now Premier, Averescu for accepting the role of peace mediator "instead of... organising a glorious resistance in keeping with the heroism of all our wonderful steely little soldiers." The Queen realized she was behaving irrationally, but could not control herself. Not even Barbo Stirbey could get through to her. "I began to feel cruelly lonely, almost an outcast, because of that impossiblity of resigning myself to our fate. The idea that the Allies would forsake us and that we should be left alone, strangled, done away with, drove me to the verge of madness."

In spite of Roumania's Queen, peace negotiations proceeded. These talks were modified by events in two Russian provinces, Bessarabia and the Ukraine—changes that improved Roumania's position vis-à-vis her enemies and Russia. As Queen Marie put it, "Each part of Russia seemed to have a different ideal and to wish to set up independently. The Tsar had been the string upon which *toutes les Russies* were threaded: the string had been cut through."

In Bessarabia, a long, narrow province lying lengthwise between Roumania and Russia, the fall of the Tsar in 1917 had led to the formation of the National Democratic Party, a group whose goals were autonomy and unification with Roumania. After the fall of Kerensky's Provisional Government, the Bessarabians proclaimed their independence and appealed to their Roumanian neighbors for help in their struggle for self-determination. Under the guise of protecting the railways, Roumania sent in troops to help the Bessarabians drive out the Bolsheviks.

The Ukrainians, who inhabited the large Russian province on the other side of Bessarabia, also sought freedom from the Bolsheviks. On January 24, 1918, they declared their independence as a People's Republic, and two weeks later concluded a separate peace with the Central Powers. The Roumanians, seeing a friendly alternative to Lenin next door, cultivated diplomatic relations with them. The Ukrainians responded by sending a deputation to Jassy, where they were received by the King and Queen.

With Bessarabian autonomy and Ukrainian independence as new givens, the peace talks between the Central Powers and Roumania got under way in the capital. Roumania was represented by Alexandru Marghiloman, a clever negotiator, and the new Prime Minister, Averescu.

At the same time, the Austrian Minister, Count Ottokar Czernin, asked King Ferdinand for an audience in Bucharest. Ill prepared for this kind of ordeal, the King could not refuse. Czernin held a low opinion of Ferdinand's ability to bargain, as did Marie: "Prince Stirbey has worked up point for point all that the King will have to say to Czernin. We pored over these points with the utmost care and anxiety. The future of the country is at stake!"

While the King faced the Austrian Minister in Bucharest, Marie, at home in Jassy, received news of Ducky. The first word in nine months, it came not from her sister but from England. The Grand Duchess, her husband, and two daughters had fled over the border to Finland,* where she had given birth to a son in August of 1917. Caught in the middle of the civil war raging between Reds and Whites in the former Russian province, Ducky, Kirill, and their children had thus far not been molested, although they lived in constant danger from Bolshevik sailors in the area. The Swedish royal family was trying to get them out.

The Queen's fears about the King's interview with Czernin were realized on Ferdinand's return from Bucharest. The Austrian Minister had been "barely polite," and Emperor Karl's promises of "an honourable peace" had lost out to German revenge. "The peace conditions are absolutely inacceptable," said Marie. But the alternatives were unthinkable. If Ferdinand refused, Roumania would be wiped off the map of Europe, hacked up between Austria, Bulgaria, Germany, and Turkey. "If Nando does not want to accept peace now and at the terms they dictate, then the two Emperors wish him to know that they will pursue him with relentless resentment and never more lift a hand to protect him or any member of his family."

With Vienna demanding an immediate answer, the King called an emer-

---

*There is a story of Kirill and Ducky's escape from Russia which, although commonly accepted, is untrue. This version had Kirill fleeing his homeland on foot carrying his pregnant wife in his arms over the Finnish border. According to the Grand Duke's memoirs, he obtained permission to leave Russia from Kerensky and departed Petrograd calmly by train with his two daughters. Their life in Finland has also been subject to exaggeration. The most romantic authors picture Kirill keeping his family warm by sawing the door and window frames of their tiny wooden house into logs. According to their son, Grand Duke Vladimir, Ducky and Kirill left Russia with several servants, and although they were subjected to food and fuel shortages, they spent the winter on the estate of old family friends.

gency meeting of the Crown Council for March 2, 1918. Knowing her husband was unprepared to make a quick decision, Marie debated what position she should take to protect him. "I tried... to inspire him with all the courage possible... Tragic moments when I wish I were a man! Nothing would have induced me to go unprepared and unprotected to preside at that terrible sitting."

Marie and Stirbey waited together for Ferdinand to emerge from the Crown Council, but when he finally came out, his responses to their questions were "completely unsatisfactory.... Nando was very weary, so I hardly dared press him to give me a clear description of what had taken place; besides, Nando is never very lucid when summing up a situation, for words do not come easily to him." All the Queen and Prince Stirbey could determine was that there was to be a second meeting the next morning, brought about by the receipt of a German cable demanding further concessions.

The postponement of the final decision gave Marie time to line up resistance. Early the next morning she called in Crown Prince Carol, who was to attend the Crown Council, to plead with him to speak out in her name and the name of all the women of Roumania against signing the peace. While she was talking to him, his father arrived. There was a "terrible scene," in which the Queen told the King that "he was selling his soul, his honour and with it the honour of his family and country... not because he was a fool but because a man with his character is always the instrument and the dupe of those stronger than he."

The King flew into a "towering rage." Had her husband been "a man of the people," Marie said, "he would have certainly beaten me." Nonetheless, she continued her attack. "You shall hear it once... for those around you... have caught you in a net of dishonour after having systematically sapped your faith and energy, till you are nothing but a lifeless instrument in their dirty hands... As we are anyhow to die, let us die with head high without soiling our souls by... putting... the signature to our death warrant."

When Prince Stirbey appeared, the Queen repeated her accusations for his benefit and mediation. "Barbo," she wrote in her diary, "is always absolutely calm." Stirbey said that although the Queen "judged quite rightly" in some things, she was being unfair to the King by expecting him to "stand alone" for resistance. Stirbey explained that His Majesty could not function unless he was "upheld by... responsible men." Marie retorted that there were "no men in this country" and that she was "ashamed of being the Queen of nothing but cowards!"

Later, after the Crown Council, Carol threw his arms around his mother, thanking her for giving him words "to express his own feeling." "But it is all over now," Marie admitted, "no one rallies for resistance... Nando and I could hardly face each other, he was a completely broken man. I did not try to argue any more; I knew that all was over; I knew that I was defeated."

She decided that there was only one road to honor left in face of an infamous peace, and that was abdication. She prevailed upon Carol to try to persuade his father "to do what we consider right and honourable." She asked Generals Berthelot and Prezan to speak to the King. She badgered Prince Stirbey as well. "Nando *cannot* sign that peace, he *cannot*, let him abdicate," she said.

But all the Queen's heroism paled before the fact that the Russians' rejection of peace terms at Brest-Litovsk had only rejuvenated the German Army and triggered a new offensive. The enemy was in a position to extort whatever it wanted. "The character of the Austro-German demands," said the American Ambassador, "plainly indicates a disposition to reduce Roumania to a condition of slavery."

The preliminary peace was signed at Prince Stirbey's estate of Buftea on March 8, 1918. The final Treaty of Bucharest, signed two months later and described by a Munich newspaper as a "model of the peace to be imposed on all our enemies," outlined the details necessary to execute enslavement. When one of the Roumanian delegates to the conference complained about the severity of the treaty to the President of the German Delegation, the German was unmoved: "A harsh peace?" he retorted. "Just wait till you see what we are preparing for France and England!"

There were five major points: (1) Roumania was forced to cede the Dobruja. (2) Substantial changes in favor of Hungary were made all along the Transylvanian border in order to put all strategic defense points in enemy hands. (3) Roumania's oil was turned over to an Austro-German company for ninety years, while her agricultural output fell to the enemy for nine years. (4) An enemy army of occupation was set up in Wallachia to be maintained at Roumanian expense. (5) All Allied Missions were ordered to leave the country at once.

For all of this, the Roumanians secured permission to keep the dynasty on the throne and the right to annex Bessarabia if its citizens desired.

The Allied Missions all came to say goodbye. The King gave a large luncheon on March 7 at which General Berthelot spoke. "We all sobbed," said the Queen, "whilst he himself could hardly talk because of the tears that were rolling down his chubby cheeks." That evening the Queen gave a party for the French, English, and Americans who were leaving. Colonel Anderson of the American Red Cross came to bid Marie a private farewell and threw himself at her feet, kissing the hem of her dress. On March 8, the Queen gave a luncheon for the English and Italians. The English, said Marie, "swore to me that... my poor, torn mutilated country would not be forgotten." To make sure, the Queen took this last opportunity to send King George a letter with one of the officers of the British Military Mission:

My dear George,
    ... Our agony has been fearful: cut off, betrayed, encircled by enemies,

we have had to give up, in spite of the high spirit of our troops, in spite of our unshakable fidelity to our mutual cause, in spite of our fortitude in the face of impossible odds. I for one did all that was in my power... You will fight and win, and on the day of victory do not forget us. Until that blessed hour, goodbye, George, I am going out to meet a fate, almost too dark to be conceived. Rather would I have died with our army to the last man, than confess myself beaten, for have I not English blood in my veins?

Your loving cousin,
Missy

On March 9, 1918, the Missions departed. Queen Marie persuaded the King to defy the government and go with her and their children to see General Berthelot and his French Military Mission off on the last train. A Canadian, Colonel Joseph Boyle, dined with the royal family that evening. A member of a transport mission in Russia, Boyle, said the Queen, was "a curiously fascinating man who is afraid of nothing... a real Jack London type." Since the French Mission was not due to leave until after midnight, the Queen and the Canadian Colonel sat up talking until it was time to leave for the station. "I tried to let myself be steeled by the man's relentless energy, tried to absorb some of the quiet force which emanates from him. I poured out my heart to him during those hours he sat with me. I do not know all that I told him, the memory is a blur, but I made a clean breast of all my grief and when he left me and I said that everyone was forsaking me he answered very quietly 'But *I* won't,' and the grip of his hand was as strong as iron."

Later at the station, lit by moonlight on the snow and torches carried by Roumanian soldiers, everyone sang the "*Marseillaise*" and cried. The King kissed Berthelot goodbye. From his window the indomitable French General called "À *bientôt, à bientôt*" as five coaches, armed with machine guns, rubles, francs, and pounds disappeared on their way into revolutionary Russia. This roundabout and dangerous route was still, as it had been since the beginning of the war, the only way to get from Roumania to Western Europe.

The next day Queen Marie took to her bed. She stayed there for two days.

With the departure of the Allied Missions and the enemy take-over of the telephone and telegraph, Ferdinand and Marie were forced into ever-narrowing isolation. On March 15, the Germans sent the Queen a list of people they expected the court to banish from Roumania. As a gesture of defiance, the Queen countered by sending three cables—one to King George, one to the President of the American Red Cross, and a third to an American who had visited Roumania the previous summer. She begged them not to forget her, her family, and her country "even if a dreadful and deadly silence were from now onwards to cut us off from the living... It is not peace; it is foreign occupation, it is living death, it is strangulation." She called for Prince Stirbey, whom the Germans had threatened to send away as well. "We sat contemplating a future we do not understand, nor do we know how long we shall still be together."

One of the court's last links with her allies was the French Minister to Roumania, the Count de Saint-Aulaire. The Queen confided in Saint-Aulaire that both she and the King had wired King George requesting guarantees of Ferdinand's sovereignty in case of deposition or abdication and Roumania's participation in the peace talks after the war—"formal assurances which his [King Ferdinand's] dignity did not permit him to explicitly request and which he could not demand from his allies without seeming to doubt their good faith; we were, in fact," Marie said, "astonished that they were not accorded us spontaneously... Well," she concluded, "we have never had the slightest response."

"That is an answer..." the sympathetic Minister told her, "that King George, in spite of his affection for Your Majesties, cannot give."

Aware that Premier Averescu had not dealt as cleverly as he should have with the Central Powers at the bargaining table, the King called on Alexandru Marghiloman to form a new government. Despite German pressure to retain the opportunistic Averescu, Marghiloman accepted, forming a Cabinet of what the American Ambassador called "very ordinary men." Marie, forced to accompany her husband to the swearing in of the pro-German ministers, "could hardly bear" the ordeal. "I do not," she declared, "in the least consider myself a beaten Queen... but... the leader of a glorious army which has *not* been vanquished, but had to submit to a fearful and preposterous peace because it was betrayed by its Ally, Russia."

The Allies applauded. The Queen of little Roumania had turned out to be the consummate propaganda heroine. The English claimed her as their own. The American *Literary Digest* ran an article on Roumania's martyrdom, entitled "Marie, Queen of Conquered Roumania, Defies the Kaiser." "Declaring that she would rather abdicate than rule over a country under German domination," the story read, "Marie, Queen of Roumania, beloved of her people, refused to recognize the peace treaty between her little country and Germany."

Not being descendants of Queen Victoria or objects of worldwide admiration, Roumanian politicians had to seek consolation for defeat elsewhere. They found it in the annexation of Bessarabia, the province that they had lost in victory forty years before* and had now regained in defeat. It was clear that the Bessarabians could not survive alone against the Bolsheviks, and the Bessarabian National Assembly voted for union with Roumania on

---

*At the Congress of Berlin in 1878.

April 8, 1918. A few days later a large delegation from the Assembly visited Jassy. They proclaimed Ferdinand "King of the Peasants" and insisted on "carrying off" Marie's sons and daughters to dance in the streets with the crowd. "Nando," wrote Queen Marie, "actually allowed it and my two fat daughters found themselves suddenly the centre of violent acclamations, dancing a hora in the strada Lupucianu with these enthusiastic quite unknown Bessarabians! What is the world coming to!"

She was amused but not consoled. "The annexation of Bessarabia is, no doubt, a great event for our country...For me all possibility of rejoicing is smothered by the misery of this abominable peace, and by the anxiety with which I am watching the politics of our new Government." The Queen did not give up trying to convince her husband to abdicate and devised a plan whereby Carol could be named "Vice-Roy" for the duration of the war.

It was becoming apparent that Queen Marie was excess baggage. To the enemy she had become an unsilenceable irritant; to the Roumanians who believed in the final victory of the Central Powers, a vocal menace; and to the rest of her government, a nuisance. She was even an embarrassment to herself, scrawling long, angry passages in her diary and then blacking them out. The month of April was "a very dark one." "Sometimes I have the feeling that I am going out of my mind," she wrote. When Easter came, Marie asked the King's permission to go live in a little wooden house built for her during the war at Cotofanesti, near the old front lines. "Nothing," she claimed, "would induce me to go to church with the actual Government; no prayers would have been possible for me in their presence." Furious with her, Ferdinand finally relented.

On and off for the next few months the Queen took her youngest daughter and withdrew into the country with her convalescent soldiers and the local peasants of Moldavia. She was soon joined at Cotofanesti by her new friend Colonel Joseph Boyle, the man she met the evening the Allied Missions left Roumania. "Colonel Boyle, the brave and adventurous Canadian..." Marie wrote, "was a refreshing personality and his quiet, almost insolent, strength seemed to me as a rock amidst tumultuous seas...At the hour of darkness when our Allies had to leave us, abandoning us to the enemy, he...clasped my hand promising that neither man nor God would make him forsake me as long as I and my country needed him, and to this promise he stuck with a single-mindedness, characteristic of his unyielding nature."

Chapter *18*

"*J* have acquired a contempt for Aladdin," an
English journalist wrote about Joseph Boyle in the early 1900s. "I have met
a man who enslaves genii a million times mightier than those of *Arabian
Nights*. He rubs the lamps of the genii and palaces of mechanical wonder
spring forth overnight. He gives orders and changes the course of rivers . . . His
jaw is iron and his eyes blue steel . . . He knows what he wants and how to
demand it."

The figure who entered Queen Marie's life in March of 1918 was big,
straightforward, and arresting; his presence was as commanding as his phy-
sique. An exaggeration of a man, Colonel Boyle reads today like a fictional
hero created by his contemporaries to lighten the frustrations of defeat. Were
it not for the corroborating memoirs of his partner, Captain George A. Hill
of the British Secret Service, we would write Boyle off as the wish fulfillment
of a desperate queen looking for a twentieth-century Lancelot.

Canadian by birth, Joe Boyle had worked as a sailor, prizefighter, and fight promoter before joining the Klondike Gold Rush of the 1890s. There, he acquired the rights to more than six miles of the richest gold creeks in the Yukon, which he operated with the world's largest dredge. By World War I, Joe Boyle was a rich soldier of fortune with a current wife, a former wife, and four children.

Boyle responded to the news of the war by raising and equipping at his personal expense a machine-gun battery and sending it off to Europe. In 1916 he left the Yukon and crossed the Atlantic to London, where he offered himself and his knockabout talents to the Allied war effort. Snubbed by the bureaucrats in the Foreign and War offices, Boyle secured a place on a private transport mission sent by the American Society of Engineers to Russia. For this appointment he had made for himself the uniform of a British Army colonel, embellished by lapel badges of pure, glistening Klondike gold.

Colonel Boyle arrived in Russia in the summer of 1916. After two years of war, the Russian generals blamed their military defeats on the legendary inefficiency of the Russian railway system—a labyrinth of tracks, crosstracks, switches, and spurs in which men and supplies languished entrapped, often for weeks. Utilizing strong-arm tactics learned in driving men and animals over mountains of ice in the Yukon, the Canadian succeeded in disentangling motors, soldiers, and ammunition and dispatching them speedily to the front. The grateful Russians decorated Boyle with the Order of Stanislaus and asked the Allies' permission to send him to try to relieve the food crisis in Roumania. With more than a million Russian soldiers, the entire Roumanian Army, and all the Roumanian refugees crowded into a corner of Moldavia, the railroads were paralyzed and food was running out. Boyle managed to divert stalled provisions from railway cars to boats, temporarily alleviating the threat of famine, and was awarded the Russian Order of St. Vladimir for his efforts.

Boyle did not stay in Roumania long. He was reported back in Russia reorganizing construction work on the Bessarabian railways before the Bolshevik coup of November 1917. It was at Stavka, Headquarters of the Russian Army, that Colonel Boyle first met Captain George A. Hill. Hill, who was attached to the British Artillery Mission, had discovered a plot by German agents to incite the local Bolsheviks into dispatching by train or by murder all the members of the Allied Military Missions in the area. He enlisted Boyle's help, and together they foiled the German plot.

From Russia, Boyle and Hill headed for Roumania, the last Allied holdout on the Eastern Front. Stopping in Petrograd on the way, they saw the Roumanian Minister to Russia, Constantine Diamandi. He informed them that his country's entire gold reserve, paper currency (about $20 million worth), crown jewels, and Foreign Office archives, which had been sent to Moscow for safekeeping during the evacuation of Bucharest, had been impounded by the Bolsheviks. Diamandi held out little hope that the Russians would release the Roumanian national treasure, and even if they did, that anyone could get it safely out of Russia past the revolutionary gangs roving the country. Boyle and Hill managed to get hold of a large part of the currency and the archives, which they drove fifteen hundred miles in a train and delivered to Jassy in December of 1917. For their services, King Ferdinand conferred the Grand Cross of the Order of Roumania on Boyle and the Star of Roumania on Hill.

The two men were not in Roumania long before they were asked by the Roumanian government to return to Russia to try to secure a peace treaty between Russia and Roumania.* In pursuing their goal, Boyle and Hill fell into a German trap involving the sailors of the Russian Imperial Black Sea Fleet, men who had just mutinied, disemboweled their officers, and thrown them, feet in chains, into the ocean. German agents, eager to keep Russia and Roumania at war with each other, had informed the sailors that Boyle and Hill were advance men for a British fleet of warships on its way to bring reprisal for the slaughter. Arriving at the railway station in Sevastopol, Boyle and Hill were met by members of the Fleet "surging around the station, swarming over the platform, crowding the tracks, a mob," in Hill's words, "frenzied with the blood lust and baying for our lives." Boyle was known for his ability to talk to crowds. At the end of his impromptu harangue, translated by Hill, history records that the sailors of the Black Sea Fleet, the leading revolutionary body in southern Russia, were converted back to the Allied camp. With their help, Boyle and Hill secured a peace treaty between Russia and Roumania, the first of World War I. The two men then separated.

Hill, who remained in Russia, later wrote about Joe Boyle in his memoirs. "He was born a fighter, a great talker, and blessed with an exceptional amount of common sense. He was independent to a revolutionary extent. Etiquette and procedure meant nothing to him, especially if a job had to be done. He was in Russia to get on with the war, to harry the Germans, and to help the Allies, and in so doing he cared not whom he rode roughshod. Such was Colonel Boyle, a man whose equal I have encountered neither before nor since."

Treaty in hand, Boyle flew back to Jassy. He arrived on March 9, 1918, the night the Allied Missions were forced to leave Roumania. Queen Marie described him as he appeared to her then as "an elderly man of heavy build, with strong, rugged features, almost ugly in fact, but his eyes, which were deep blue and keen, sometimes even fierce, could on occasion become gentle, almost tender, and his smile was kindly and reassuring."

It is popularly contended that this evening "marked the fall of Prince Stirbey as the Queen's favorite and Klondike Boyle's ascendancy to his place." Like many tales related about Marie of Roumania, this is an exaggeration that fails to take into account the nature of the Queen or, for that matter, Joe Boyle. Marie was an ultraromantic, a woman who had learned by middle

*The Bolsheviks declared war on Roumania twice in the course of sixteen months—on January 31, 1918, and again on May 18, 1919.

age how to sidestep unwanted physical entanglements. Joe Boyle was a natural aristocrat, a man too proud to ask for personal favors. Far more important than the attraction the Queen inspired in Boyle was the quality of their friendship. Whatever course this friendship eventually would take, Boyle came to Jassy at a time of crisis and left on another mission for Roumania within forty-eight hours of his arrival—scarcely time for more than a recognition of common sympathies and goals.

During the German advance a number of Bucharest's prominent residents had fled to the Russian city of Odessa on the Black Sea. In January of 1918, when the Bolsheviks declared war on Roumania, Christian Rakovsky* was the leader of the Bolshevik organization in southern Russia. Rakovsky, a former Roumanian citizen who had been imprisoned for subversive activities, was an avowed and embittered enemy of the Roumanian government. He arrested the Roumanian leaders—ex-ministers, senators, industrialists, members of the aristocracy—as hostages in the struggle between Russia and Roumania over Bessarabia. Word reached Jassy that these prisoners were in imminent danger of mass execution. Boyle flew to Odessa. There he discovered that Rakovsky had confiscated the prisoners' private fortunes, as well as Roumanian state funds earmarked for Roumanian relief, and had fled with the money the night before Boyle's arrival. At the same time the Roumanian prisoners had been packed on a death ship with Bolshevik guards. Queen Marie relates the rest of the story:

"He [Boyle] had rushed down to the harbour to find that the ship was just leaving its moorings. Unarmed as he was and companionless, he had sprung on board, and for a fortnight, although he could not speak a word of Russian, had kept the Bolsheviks at bay whilst they moved the ship from harbour to harbour: a fantastic and incredible voyage, comparable only to adventurous tales from out of the past. Finally, single-handed, with almost hypnotic force of will, this courageous Canadian obliged the lawless revolutionaries to run the ship with its frightened cargo of prisoners into a Roumanian port."

The story of the bizarre voyage reached Roumania ahead of Boyle and his flock, and by the time the Canadian made his second triumphal entry into Jassy, the streets were packed with cheering crowds. "People had given up the prisoners and their saviour for dead," said the grateful wife of one of those rescued. At a celebratory luncheon the next day, March 25, 1918, Boyle received the Star of Roumania. The former hostages also presented him with a scroll attesting to their gratitude, and a plaque in his honor was placed in a local church. Two days later Boyle was back flying over Bessarabia, doing intelligence work for the British and French and scouting provisions to ease the starvation imposed by the German occupation on the Roumanians.

*Later (1926–1927) the Soviet Ambassador to France.

• • •

Queen Marie's fears about peace under the Germans were proving sadly prophetic. Marghiloman, the new Prime Minister, believed that the Central Powers would win the war, and he conducted his government under the occupation on the principle that Roumania's only chance for the future lay in placating the Germans. But the victor was insatiable, a voracious monster whose appetite only grew the more he was fed. Before, during, and even after peace negotiations were completed, throughout the entire remainder of the war, the Germans piled further demands on the Roumanian economy and people.

Having taken over the oil fields, rivers, and farms, they seized the railways, postal service, telegraph, and telephone, completely cutting off Roumania's contact with the outside world, and demanded the prosecution or deportation of all politicians who had supported the Entente. They distributed incendiary pamphlets condemning King Ferdinand, Queen Marie, and their government in an effort to foment revolution and strengthen their hold on the country—a formula reminiscent of tactics highly successful in Tsarist Russia. Male and female peasants, aged fourteen to sixty, were subject to forced labor; disobedience resulted in deportation, imprisonment, or death.

Ambassador Vopicka, a conservative diplomat, described the occupation as "systematic robbery . . . anything that can be used," he said, "is being taken and sold . . . Where the Germans expect resistance of the enraged population, they surround the village with machine guns and compel them to deliver their food under threats of general massacre." "They make a prison of Roumania, where all the people are condemned to hard labor for the profit of the enemy."

Queen Marie did what she could to bolster national morale. She made excursions to the "ex-front" to review her soldiers. With the King she led a Requiem for the Fallen, a celebration conducted over government protest in the inimitable style of the Queen of Roumania: "I stood before my high throne-chair dressed in my white Red Cross uniform, a candle in my hand . . ." She found food for the beleaguered peasants of Moldavia. Inside, she was seething:

"I thought I was destined to be a happy, brilliant successful queen; all within me seemed to promise this, and I seemed made for that part. But perhaps, on the contrary, my lot is to be tragic, vanquished queen, ever so much more tragic than Carmen Sylva ever was with all her talk of a martyr's crown. I had no vocation for a martyr's part, and yet it looks as though God had singled out Nando and myself to bear a cross which at times seems almost too heavy."

Marie spent as much time as possible in her wooden cottage at Cotofanesti. Here she could physically remove herself from having to condone the actions of the hated Marghiloman government. "The King," as she put it, "at last realized that it was better for me not to be too much in Jassy." Once out of the way, she worried about what was taking place behind her back and spent the early summer of 1918 traveling back and forth anxiously between her provisional retreat and the capital. "I hated going back to Jassy, but... I was the watchdog." The Queen urged her husband "not to be weak with his government" and "always to talk over things with Barbo first." When Prince Stirbey was with the King, Marie could relax and concentrate on the House of Four Winds at Cotofanesti.

Decorating was excellent therapy; the style, Moldavian Bucolic. "I mean to make a treasure of this little house, with nothing but rustic things in it; I shall only bring the beds from Jassy, because they, of course, must be good." She had muslin dyed bright orange for curtains; the effect was eminently satisfying. She was particularly proud of her bedroom, where the walls, ceiling, and floor were stained dark brown. On the darkened paneling behind her bed—"a broad couch heaped up with cushions in every shade of orange"—she hung an old piece of gold brocade from a Russian church and over it an antique icon framed in silver. On the floor was a muted Turkish rug. Instead of vases, Marie put her flowers in empty shell cases of all sizes and calibers, "heavy and rusty brown." To complement the autumnal color scheme she added the odd bit of pottery in bright green and an occasional brass dish.

"Undeniably my wooden abode was an adorable retreat and everyone who saw it loved it as I did. Many came to visit me in my solitude, especially those who, like me, were sick of what was going on in our official world. My doors were hospitably open to every visitor, and my table stretched according to the number of my guests."

Chief among these was Colonel Boyle, whose generosity and ingenuity in helping her people impressed the Queen. "No one will ever know how much Boyle has done here, nor the money he has spent. I never saw anyone so ready to help." Colonel Boyle bought a cow for one village so the children would have milk; in another village he bought an abandoned house, rebuilt it, and gave it to three refugee families in the name of Princess Ileana. He supervised repairs, ferreted out supplies, and gave away untold amounts of money. He frowned on useless complaints. Boyle, said Marie, "made all wailing seem paltry, almost cowardly... In times of depression he was an extraordinarily refreshing and invigorating companion, and an unexpected touch of early Victorian Puritanism added much to his quaintness." The Queen, who loved to shock people by smoking, was surprised to discover that Joe Boyle neither smoked nor drank. She was pleased with his influence on Ileana; he gave her nine-year-old daughter "strong and healthy maxims which later she carried with her out into life."

Early in June the Queen was distressed to hear that Boyle had suffered a stroke while flying over Bessarabia reconnoitering supplies. The pilot of his small plane had landed at Kishinev, where the Canadian was put into a hospital. Marie had grown dependent on Boyle. If that overwhelming presence could so easily be felled, what else might collapse around her? Prevented by her position from going to help her friend, she badgered the King and Prince Stirbey to keep in contact with the hospital. In early July she was relieved to hear that the Canadian Colonel was resting comfortably, assisted by a young English-speaking Georgian. With the knowledge that he was in good hands, Queen Marie returned to Jassy.

Prime Minister Marghiloman was due to present for the King's signature a general amnesty for all Roumanians who had supported the Germans. "He *must* not sign this paper," Marie wrote on July 6, 1918, "I implored him to be strong and resist Marghiloman's coercion, but he gave me no positive assurance." Knowing that Nando usually followed the advice of the last person who spoke with him, the Queen wrote a "fearfully energetic little note" that she entrusted to her fourteen-year-old son, Nicky, to give his father "*during* his audience with his premier." Later, in the privacy of the royal train, Ferdinand told her that he had followed her wishes and refused to sign.

Putting spine into the indecisive King, which was never easy, was harder during the occupation: "... he resented it when people... found in me a resolution they did not always find in him, and in spite of the displeasure he often showed me, I *had* to stand firm... it kept him steady and frightened those who wanted to coerce him to do the wrong thing. It was my unshakable belief that I was right, which gave me the sad strength to be such a termagant... But certainly I was not a *pleasant* companion at that period; of this I was well aware."

The war, which had popularized the King with his people and brought husband and wife together in adversity, was currently threatening to drive them apart. "I am too violent, much too violent and then he gets angry," Marie admitted to her diary. "He is also angry because people come to me. I try to explain to him *why* they all come to me even the generals." But the last thing Ferdinand wanted to hear was that he was indecisive or that his temper put people off. "Poor man he is terribly harassed, but his own ways & character make it all so much worse," said his wife.

To lessen domestic strain and get out of the Germans' way, Ferdinand and Marie moved to Bicaz, one of the Crown Estates in the mountain valley of the Bistritza River. They settled with their children into a house at river's edge, a quiet home with a cool veranda and large white rooms furnished with oversized tables and chairs; there were blue curtains at the windows and blue Persian vases, which Marie filled with flowers. While the King puttered about the garden, the Queen, dressed in native clothes, organized food and medical help for the local peasants.

Marie had gained weight during the war. In spite of her athletic prowess and boundless energy, expressed in daily gallops on her horses, her body had grown slack. During her days of hospital work, she had worn Red Cross outfits—long, white, nunlike garments that camouflaged her figure. Now she dressed herself in elegant versions of the colorful Roumanian peasant dresses, which also disguised imperfections.

Middle age and an excess of worry had begun to take their toll on the Queen. Her hair, although still blond, had started falling out; each morning a woman arrived to massage her scalp back to health. Her famous skin had lost the resilience of youth. When Lavillère came to copy her face for a medal, she was depressed by the results. "My face is tired-looking, my eyes are weary," she wrote in her diary. "I give a false impression of youth because I am animated and move quickly, but when I sit quite still... my face falls into a middle-aged immobility which is certainly unbecoming... looking at Lavillère's medal, one would never take me for a pretty woman."

Up to this point in her life, Marie had always relied heavily on her beauty, rationalizing that it was one of her "royal duties" to please the plebeian eye. The time was clearly coming when her features and figure would no longer ease her way. "I have never been specially vain," she prevaricated a few months later, "but my face has been like a friend, and if it changes it will be like living with someone who is a stranger to me, and it will be horrid!"

Prince Stirbey also moved his family to Bicaz for the summer. He and the Queen continued to take tea together every day. Marie felt that the strain of war was beginning to show on Barbo as well: "... he has carried the load of all our changing fortunes more than any other and now he is suddenly tired," she wrote in her diary. A chronic worrier, Stirbey kept in constant touch with Jassy, bypassing the official government, which he did not trust, to bring uncensored information to the King and Queen. Although Marie genuinely loved Nadeje Stirbey, she knew that Nadeje was not strong enough to bear the weight of the family while Barbo occupied himself with more urgent matters. Prince Stirbey's wife and daughters, the Queen said, "suck his energy."

On August 1, 1918, Queen Marie arranged for Joe Boyle to be brought to Bicaz to recuperate from his stroke. Determined to overcome the physical damage, Boyle stood for hours before a mirror forcing the defective muscles on one side of his body to imitate the unimpaired ones on the other. The stroke had destroyed his confidence, which had been based largely on his tremendous physical strength, and the Queen set about to rebuild his image of himself. If their relationship ever moved beyond friendship, as some claim, it was only for a brief moment, brought on by Marie's sympathy for the suffering man. Nevertheless, Boyle fell in love with Marie, and that love changed his life. Three months later he wrote her to say that she had become the "central figure" of his life. For the first time in his fifty-one years, Joe Boyle found someone to live for, and from then on he devoted himself to the Queen and her family. "I who gambled each day or hour or minute with all I had... and laughed at people who were afraid of anything... I pray God to teach me to appreciate and to make me a man worthy in every way of you," he wrote.

In spite of his physical problems, Marie found Boyle's judgment as perceptive as ever. She had her supper brought to his peasant hut in the evenings so they could talk. As Boyle gained strength, he renewed his intelligence operations and famine relief. Marie brought him into her consultations with Barbo Stirbey. Boyle was like Marie herself—full of noble ideas and pronouncements. Stirbey was Oriental and subtle. An odd triumvirate, the Queen, the Prince, and the Colonel stood guard to make sure that the King did not compromise himself with the forces of the occupation.

During the summer word came that the Tsar and his family had been murdered. In defiance of their government, the Roumanian royal family held a requiem for the Romanovs in the village church. "Poor Nicky!..." wrote Marie, "if you had died on the throne what a fuss they would have made, what pompous ceremonies there would have been in every church, in every country! But today because you are fallen from power, an exile, they try to ignore you."

Near exiles themselves, Ferdinand and Marie saw little of their government during their stay in Bicaz, although ministers did appear every so often "to worry the King with their different, sickening demands." The gentlemen usually traveled all night and arrived in time for breakfast, during which the Queen, eyeing them suspiciously with a glacial stare, shored up the King's unsteady defenses.

For the first time since the beginning of the war, Marie had time in Bicaz to think about her children. Although she was pleased with the development of the three younger ones, Carol and Elisabetha continued to worry her. The Crown Prince was as attached as ever to Zizi Lambrino. After the Treaty of Bucharest, Marie had arranged for him to be put in command of a regiment of Chasseurs at Targu-Neamtz, a camp in the Carpathian Mountains. Military drill suited Carol well, and his mother hoped to get his mind off Zizi. But the young Roumanian girl followed the Crown Prince and moved in with friends to be near him. Carol's occasional visits to Bicaz underlined Marie's anxiety. Early in the summer the Queen found her twenty-four-year-old son "crying like a child," but he refused to confide in her. All Carol would say was that he would never do "anything" to make his mother "ashamed of him."

Elisabetha was also a problem. She pursued men with "cold-blooded persistence... She is always the same, wherever she is, with whoever she is... one can never trust her," the Queen wrote in her diary. "Poor child, poor child... she needs some love all to herself, but one cannot allow her to dash after every caprice of the moment!"

It was not that Queen Marie did not wish members of her family happiness in love. When Aristitza Dissescu, the King's faithful mistress, came to Bicaz to see him, the Queen was pleased. "She really loves Nando and not because he is King. She is absurd, provoking and touching and with me, knowing that I might be annoyed, not having a very clear conscience, she is desperately nervous although I have never been anything but kind and nice with her, but occasionally I have smiled."

As news of Allied victories on the Western Front filtered through the censors, the Germans occupying Roumania grew increasingly belligerent. The fortunes of war, which had seemed to belong to the Central Powers in April of 1918, took a sharp turn in favor of the Allies in August. With three-quarters of Roumania still in enemy hands, the King and Queen had to guard against any premature signs of joy that might bring down upon their countrymen further brutalities.

Marie was never as easily intimidated as Ferdinand. One day in August she raised a political storm by visiting villages due to be transferred to Hungary as part of the peace settlement. An article in a Magyar newspaper accused the Queen of spreading propaganda against the Central Powers by arriving with a car full of supplies and allowing the peasants to kiss her hand. The article came to the attention of Marghiloman, who journeyed to Bicaz to register his disapproval with the King. Marie was subjected to "a certain amount of reprimand," which did not bother her. "When the weeping peasants flocked around me kissing my hands and deploring their fate," she told Marghiloman, "I... said to them that I did not consider this a definite goodbye; that hope lay still before us, and the last word would be spoken by the guns of the Allies."

Marie felt that Premier Marghiloman often "profited unduly by the King's predicament" to obtain concessions to the occupying forces. Marghiloman was a gentleman of the world, a smooth and skillful negotiator, but to Marie he was "quite like a butterfly... pink, smiling, gliding over all that was disagreeable, in an eternal state of admiration about the Germans and their stupendous organization... even when it was to the detriment of our Roumanians." When Marghiloman's charm failed him, he resorted to threats of resignation. These were usually effective, since the King had no alternative premier acceptable to the enemy other than radical pro-Germans who had sworn to unseat him. When the occupation demanded the arrest and trial of Bratianu and other members of the government who had voted to support the Entente, Marghiloman used the resignation threat. Ferdinand was saved by Bratianu, who sent word that he wished His Majesty to acquiesce, since he believed that a trial of that nature would eventually redound to the benefit of the accused.

Throughout the summer and early fall of 1918, Germany's demands increased in direct proportion to its loss of power. "It is the apparent intention of the Germans to reduce this country to a state of absolute helplessness before it becomes necessary to withdraw any considerable number of the occupation troops," said the American Ambassador. When the demands could no longer be met, the King and Prince Stirbey left for Jassy to try to negotiate with the enemy.

While Nando and Barbo were in Jassy, Marie enjoyed a peaceful country life of long rides, walks and drives, visits to the peasants, conversations with Joe Boyle, and excursions with him and Ileana to ancient monasteries and tiny villages. Fed by news of Allied gains, the Queen's mood reflected her increasing hopes and the resurgence of old energies and enthusiasms. Then, without warning, on September 15, 1918, "an almost insurmountable grief" struck her and the King—"a staggering family tragedy which hit us suddenly, a stunning blow for which we were entirely unprepared."

The heir to the throne, Crown Prince Carol, had eloped with a commoner.

ANNO 1922

REGINA TUTUROR ROMÂNILOR

Queen Marie, the official Coronation poster, 1922.

57

King Ferdinand and Queen Marie on a state visit to England, shown with King George V and Queen Mary, 1924.

58

Carol "Craiman" (the name the Crown Prince adopted after he abdicated the succession), and Elena Lupescu, his mistress, on the Riviera.

59

Time magazine, August 4, 1924. The caption reads "Marie Windsor Hohenzollern, 'A regular, regular, regular, regular royal queen.'"

59a

Loie Fuller in a poster after Bac, 1892. Her devotion to Marie began when they were both young and the Roumanian Crown Princess helped the dancer over one of her life-long financial embarrassments. Marie's disastrous United States tour in 1926 was Loie's idea.

60

Queen Marie with President and Mrs. Coolidge in Washington, D.C., 1926. The President, terrified of being engulfed in the frenzied publicity accompanying Marie's American tour, tried to avoid having this picture taken with her.

62

61

The ticker-tape parade in honor of Queen Marie's arrival in New York, 1926. Inset: closeup of the Queen and Mayor Jimmy Walker on their way from City Hall after the Mayor presented her with the gold medal of the City of New York.

63

The body of King Ferdinand lying in state, 1927. "Such a beautiful face with his noble features frozen into a stillness which gave him a grandeur which was not his in life."

64

King Michael I of Roumania and his mother, Princess Helen. With the abdication of his father and the death of his grandfather, Michael became King at the age of five.

Two pictures of Queen Marie and her sisters, the first taken around the turn of the century, the second immediately after the death of King Ferdinand. Top, from left to right: Sister Sandra (Princess of Hohenlohe-Langenburg), Baby Bee (later an Infanta of Spain), Ducky (Grand Duchess of Hesse), and Marie (Crown Princess of Roumania). Bottom, from left to right: Sister Sandra, Marie, Baby Bee (standing), and Ducky (then Grand Duchess Kirill of Russia).

65

66

67   68   69

(*top left*) Juliu Maniu, the Jesuitical leader of the National Peasant Party who brought King Carol II back to Roumania.

(*top center*) Ion Duca, the incorruptible head of the Liberal Party who declared war on the fascistic Iron Guard and paid with his life.

(*top right*) Corneliu Z. Codreanu, "Capitanul" of the Iron Guard, the terrorist organization supported by Hitler and Mussolini.

Prince Barbo Stirbey. He was exiled by King Carol II. The mere existence of Stirbey, the man who knew the truth about him, was an offense in the eyes of the King.

70

71

Queen Marie with her grandson, eleven-year-old King Peter of Yugoslavia, coming out of the Ritz Hotel in London after the assassination of his father, 1934.

72

Queen Marie with King Carol II, who returned to Roumania in 1930, and her grandson, Crown Prince Michael, at a national celebration in Bucharest, 1936.

73

The Queen Mother of Roumania.

74

The burial church of the Roumanian royal
family at Curtea de Arges.

The funeral of Queen Marie of Roumania, July 1938.

75

Chapter 19

> It is a fact that the presence of a romantic
> character on the stage of history
> frequently upsets the balance of the
> whole plot.
>
> —*ANTONIA FRASER*

*T*he Crown Prince's bride was Jeanne Marie Valentine Lambrino, known as Zizi. She claimed as her forebears a ninth-century emperor of Constantinople married to a daughter of Charlemagne. Other less notable Phanariot ancestors settled in the small Moldavian town of Roman, where Zizi and her brothers grew up. An obstinate child by her own admission, Zizi was sent away to a convent school in France, where the "charming anarchy" of Roumanian country life was forcibly surrendered to a regimen of rules, compulsory silences, and study. In 1910 she was brought home to Bucharest, launched on a program of English, piano, painting, and singing, and soon became part of the aristocratic society that revolved around the court.

Zizi's father was a friend of the Conservative stateman Marghiloman, who gave a ball at which Zizi first met Carol. Oddly enough, it was not Carol but his father who first noticed the graceful young brunette. "Paternal and gallant at the same time," Ferdinand showed a decided preference for dancing with Zizi, offering her a carnation each time he guided her around the ballroom. His attentions filled the young girl, as she put it, with "pride and excitement" but "did not succeed in diverting" her from her real interest, Carol. Their romance dated from Zizi's formal debut, which took place at Cotroceni Palace. Although Carol was sent off to Potsdam shortly thereafter, they corresponded until his return at the beginning of the war.

At twenty-four the Crown Prince resembled an overgrown schoolboy— big and blond with a soft face and pedantic ways. Zizi was a striking contrast. Small and dark, blessed with pronounced gifts of phrase, subtlety, and imagination, she was the acme of a Byzantine ingenue subjected to the rigors of a French education. Ignoring the war, "drunk with youth and dreams of the future," the young couple lived in a world of their own, whipping off on excursions into the countryside in the Prince's Rolls-Royce. In spite of Queen Marie's attempts to keep them apart, the romance blossomed. "The common people sometimes wonder how the important of this world love..." Zizi wrote in her memoirs, "with as much delicious simplicity as others, with the same bad lyric taste for sentimental romance... The loves of princes are like those of the most humble."

After several months, Carol asked Zizi to marry him. Although she accepted at once, it took the Crown Prince some time to research his constitutional position. "It is necessary to weigh everything... to hit with a strong blow..." he explained to his would-be bride. "The great difficulty is the legal question." But all Carol's investigations into obscure legalities only proved that there was no way around the law of the land: the Roumanian Constitution specifically forbade the heir to the throne to marry any but a foreign princess of equivalent rank. The legal question was the same one that had dogged Carol's father more than a quarter of a century before; Zizi Lambrino, like Helene Vacaresco, was excluded from becoming the wife of the future King of Roumania. Zizi was in despair; Carol said he would renounce the throne. He worked out a plan to cross the Russian border incognito. Once married, they could proceed to France, where Carol could continue fighting for Roumania.

On the last day of August 1918, a nervous Crown Prince, his fiancée, a friend, and Carol's chauffeur left Jassy for the border. They had no difficulty passing the Roumanian border guard, but on the Russian side, which was reinforced by German police, the Crown Prince was recognized, stopped, and told he might proceed only as far as Odessa. Booked into the Hotel Bristol with Carol and Zizi was a German officer, sent along to keep the Crown Prince under surveillance. The Prince's German escort must have had orders if not to actively help the runaways, certainly not to put any obstacles in the way of their union. An unconstitutional marriage for the heir to the Roumanian throne would be a political godsend to the Germans, whose armies were losing ground daily. Carol and Zizi found a priest who agreed to marry them on September 14, 1918. The night before, the bride was taken ill with food poisoning. She went ahead with the ceremony, dizzy with fever, dressed in a homemade gown of white crepe de chine, described by her as "a poor honest dress of a marriage of love where it scarcely mattered that the man I married was called to rule."

Queen Marie did not learn that her son had deserted his military post— an act of treason punishable by death—until after his marriage. Barbo and Nando broke the news of Carol's disappearance to her, saying that Carol had left three letters, one addressed to his father, one to his sister Elisabetha, and a third to Zizi Lambrino's brother. The Queen spent an anxious evening pacing up and down her garden with Prince Stirbey and Joe Boyle, waiting for two of the letters to be brought from Carol's camp. They did not arrive until 4:30 A.M., when Nando brought them to her room.

In Carol's letter to his father, he claimed that the situation in Roumania had rendered him "unable to do his duty as a soldier," and he was therefore leaving the country "for political reasons." The Crown Prince told his father that since he had "taken no oath," he was "breaking no vows." He never mentioned Zizi. The letter to Elisabetha instructed her what to do with his possessions in case he should not return; Carol mentioned his first girl friend and his dog, sent a special greeting to his sister Ileana, and begged everyone "to think kindly of him."

Queen Marie was crushed: ". . . for me nothing *nothing*, not a word, not a sign, not a message, not a greeting, not a thought—and I am his mother, I have always been his defender, to me he has always turned in all important moments in his life... I would understand his desire to go off as soldier, he knows I would understand it, but perhaps he has gone off with the girl & that he knows I would find wrong!"

Her suspicion was confirmed the next day when Carol's A.D.C. arrived in Bicaz with the letter the Crown Prince had sent Zizi's brother. In this letter Carol, who said he was "hated and persecuted by the Boches [Germans]," admitted that he had run off with Zizi. On the following day word was telegraphed from Berlin by the Germans that the Crown Prince of Roumania had married Zizi Lambrino in Odessa.

The news hit Ferdinand and Marie like a tidal wave, undermining the precarious pilings of their dynasty, already weakened by defeat and revolution. Over the years both King and Queen had accepted the anomaly of their own marriage with grace, and they had expected their children to follow their example. Ferdinand was devastated by his son's weakness. If he sympathized with Carol's problem, remarkably like his own at a similar age, he could not accept the Crown Prince's solution. Marie vacillated between fury at what she considered Carol's treachery and hurt that he had not confided in her. Unwilling to admit that Carol was responsible for his own actions, she chose to see her beloved firstborn caught in the trap of a scheming young woman. Her immediate thought was to release him. She sent her A.D.C., Colonel

Ballif, to Odessa with the royal train to bring the Crown Prince back. Then she joined the King and Prince Stirbey on an official appearance in Jassy.

The atmosphere in the temporary capital was hostile to the dynasty. Premier Marghiloman and his pro-German party demanded the immediate removal of the Crown Prince from the succession; Carol was openly attacked in the Senate; the public clamored for his head. Aware that "all eyes were upon me to criticize my son, and to condemn him," the Queen felt that she must "hold up my head for two." Prince Stirbey advised the King to play for time and try to find support for the Crown Prince in the opposition parties and the military.

From Odessa Ballif brought the Queen a letter Carol had asked him to give her in private. In it the Crown Prince said he had not contacted his mother before because to her he "could write *nothing but the truth*," and the success of his plans depended on total secrecy. Carol told Marie that he had a "wonderful plan of getting through to the French front," and, since he would not be able to return, he was taking along "the woman he loved."

A day or two later the Queen boarded the royal train, now circling Moldavia going nowhere, to speak alone with the Crown Prince. Carol repeated what Marie called "his incoherent, absurd and yet touching tale," begging his mother for sympathy and comprehension. "And you, you can understand, you were my best friend, you always understood, you will understand now!" he told her. The Queen asked Carol to give up Zizi temporarily until the war was over. She promised him that then he would be free to go away with his love, but "not at a moment when his flight was a desertion."

Beset by friends who told her she was "endangering the whole dynasty" by not casting her son out, Marie broke down only when she was alone. "God! what a mess he has got himself and us and the country into," she confided to her diary. "But I must try and save him if I can, I and those who love him and us." Foremost among the tight circle closing around the royal family was the "relentlessly faithful" Barbo Stirbey, who outmaneuvered the pro-German parties and helped Ferdinand withstand the pressure to remove Carol from the succession. In this he was joined by Bratianu, who was, Marie said, "all for saving the boy by all means if possible." With these men, Joe Boyle, and a few others, Marie and Ferdinand battled their government for two months' grace in which to bring the Crown Prince "back to his senses."

Acting as Commander in Chief of the Army (a position that since the armistice he no longer legally held), the King sentenced his son to two and a half months' imprisonment for leaving his command and crossing the frontier without permission. Embarrassed by the rebuke and afraid of looking foolish, Carol complained that this punishment would destroy his prestige. His mother disagreed. "Faults can be lived down," she told him. "I know it myself. Once when I was young and got into a mess, the world wanted to break me and cast me adrift, but I lived it down." On September 22, an army general led the sobbing Prince off to Horaitza, a monastery in the mountains near Bicaz. One of Marie's ladies-in-waiting took Zizi back to her family in Jassy, where the young woman searched the newspapers in vain for an announcement of her marriage to the Crown Prince.

Although Marie visited Carol at Horaitza several times, it was Joe Boyle who finally talked the Crown Prince into accepting a temporary annulment of his marriage. "His heart is breaking over it, but he agrees to the inevitable, but I do *not* know how he will stand it," said his mother, who called her triumph over Carol "a cruel and sickening victory." Although Carol lived in comfort with his books and his dog at Horaitza, Marie was deeply distressed every time she saw him; "he simply howls for her," she wrote in her diary after one visit.

When word reached Zizi of the proposed annulment, she refused to sign and consulted lawyers. One eminent practitioner told her that she was without doubt the legal wife of the Crown Prince, but that in Roumania "there was no justice against power." "The King. . ." he assured her, "would get whatever judgment he wished."

He did. In the absence of both parties, the marriage was legally annulled.

More pressing than the reversal of Carol's marital status was the immediate danger posed to the dynasty. Roumania's enemies, about to lose the war, seized this chance to try to remove the Crown Prince from the succession, force abdication on Ferdinand, and proclaim fifteen-year-old Nicolas a boy king in order to introduce a pro-German regency. It was even suggested that the Kaiser's son-in-law be brought in to rule Roumania. Caught between the Germans and the royal family, Prime Minister Marghiloman was eventually persuaded to support his King and Queen.

Starting in midsummer of 1918 and corresponding with the Allied counteroffensive, cautious hopes for victory had begun to filter through the Queen's dynastic frustrations. By fall, with victory seemingly only weeks away, even the Carol crisis was not enough to quench Marie's excitement over military successes.

In December of the previous year the Allied forces at Salonika, long dormant, had been strengthened and reorganized by a French general, who had finally convinced the Allies of the need for a major Balkan offensive. In the middle of September 1918, some 700,000 French, English, Serbian, and Greek soldiers advanced on the Bulgarians. Within two weeks Bulgaria surrendered. "After a fatal delay of two years," said the embittered Minister from France, "the offensive which was stipulated in our treaty with Roumania as a prerequisite of their entry into the war [came about]."

"Cambrai has fallen!" the ecstatic Queen wrote on October 1, only a week after her elder son was imprisoned. "The Bulgarians have accepted the sweeping peace conditions of the Allies. We must hope that Turkey will also have to give in."

For the Roumanians it was a glorious irony that the Bulgarians, their traditional Balkan rivals, were the first of the Central Powers to capitulate. Three days later Marie received the "sensational news" that Uncle Ferdinand, the Tsar of Bulgaria, had abdicated in favor of his son and fled to Hungary. On October 7, she took a long walk to the Stirbeys' house. Her conversation with Barbo left her "almost giddy" with expectation. "There is a tense excitement in the atmosphere," she wrote in her diary, "events are precipitating themselves and other horizons are opening before us."

By mid-October it was obvious that the collapse of Turkey, and with it the enemy's control over the Dardanelles and the Eastern sector, was imminent. The Germans, who could see as well as anyone else what was coming, swung with dizzying rapidity between intimidation and appeasement. Having added continual demands to their peace agreement with the Roumanians, they now found themselves with a treaty yet to be ratified by a nation eager to resume hostilities against them. Toward instant ratification they now offered territorial bribes including the whole of the Dobruja, the re-establishment of the old Hungarian-Roumanian frontier, and formal approval of the union of Bessarabia with Roumania. After a secret conference with the American Ambassador, Ferdinand ordered Premier Marghiloman to accept nothing from the enemy, to avoid exchanging signatures, and above all to play for time.

Meanwhile, Bratianu started nagging the American Ambassador for President Wilson's personal guarantee of the territorial promises held out to Roumania when she joined the Allies. At first all Ambassador Vopicka could secure was a promise that Roumania, if she remained true to the Allies, would lose none of her present territory. This, according to the Ambassador, was piddling compensation for the loss of nearly 360,000 soldiers and about as many civilians—practically one-tenth of Roumania's population. Later Washington sent a telegram confirming the 1916 treaty guarantees. Ferdinand wired immediate thanks to Wilson, and Marie expressed her gratitude to Vopicka with an elaborately autographed picture of herself. Crowds of enthusiastic citizens and military bands stationed themselves in front of the American Legation to serenade the Ambassador and cheer for the United States. Subsequently there appeared a large number of streets, restaurants, and hotels, as well as infant Roumanians, bearing the name of Wilson.

Even before Vopicka heard from America, Marie had received a note from George V in answer to her latest and most desperate appeal. The response from the King of England, written on a very small scrap of paper, dated three months earlier and delivered somewhat dramatically by a French aviator flying over from Salonika, promised that England would not forget Roumania. The King of England added that he hoped to find the Roumanians "ready" when their allies "give the sign from over there."

The Queen, who had been regarded as a nuisance six months earlier, now qualified as her country's best spokesman. She was asked to send Premier

Clemenceau of France, an outspoken critic of Roumania's separate peace, a personal wire to try to win him over. The message, duly sent off, was written in her "own energetic and somewhat drastic style."

On the last day of October 1918, the Turks surrendered, and the Strait of the Dardanelles was opened to Allied ships. "We are no more cut off from everything, suffocated; there are hopes now that we shall not starve!" the Queen wrote the next day, adding that "Austria is rapidly falling to pieces." On November 1, the Hungarians declared their independence from the Habsburgs. Three days before, the Yugoslavs* had done the same, while the Czechoslovaks had proclaimed their autonomy even earlier. The dismemberment of the Austro-Hungarian Empire was already a *fait accompli* when on November 3, 1918, Austria concluded an armistice with the Allies, agreeing to complete demobilization, withdrawal of her troops, and evacuation of the territories still under her occupation.

But the Germans, unlike the Austrians, Bulgars, and Turks, did not give up. They launched a double-edged attack, aimed at throwing Roumania if not into Lenin's hands at least into chaos. They intensified the dissemination of Communist propaganda, even going to the trouble and expense of opening Communist schools. At the same time they deliberately starved the peasants. Roumanian mothers, unable to feed their children, committed suicide in the presence of German officers. Germany's aim was to force King Ferdinand to ratify the Treaty of Bucharest before the end of hostilities, to render remobilization of the Roumanian Army impossible, and to confound the inevitable take-over by the Allies.

Prince Stirbey outlined the situation to Ferdinand and Marie, explaining that Roumania might yet fall to the Communists unless Allied forces and food got through to them immediately. Beaten in war, exploited by the conqueror, bombarded by Communist slogans, the Roumanian peasant was still ripe for revolution. The Queen and Stirbey pushed the King to declare the universal suffrage and land reform he had promised a year and a half before. He must do it quickly, before the deadly combination of German agents and Communist agitators could persuade the people to join the Russian mujiks in revolt.

Added to the domestic crisis was the uncertainty of what Roumania's allies would do once the war ended. If, in spite of assurances coaxed out of King George and President Wilson, the Entente should fall under the influence of Clemenceau and renege on its territorial promises, the Roumanian monarchy would be vilified as the dupe of the Allies and would surely fall. With the heir to the throne in disgrace, a starving populace, slippery allies, and vengeful enemies in league with powerful revolutionaries, Marie of Roumania knew she was sitting astride a difficult horse. She watched the King and

*Yugoslavs: The Serbs, Croats, Slovenes, and Montenegrins, who had declared their unity fifteen months earlier.

Prince Stirbey go off to Jassy together to prepare a pro-Entente take-over of the government. In the four years her husband had been King, he had grown completely dependent on Stirbey. "Nando cannot do without him," Marie wrote in her diary, "there is something touching and pathetic in the way he clings to him."

The Queen herself leaned heavily on Joe Boyle, now completely recovered from his stroke. Although she tried to launch him as an adviser to the King, the results were unsatisfactory. Where Barbo led Nando gently, Boyle attacked him like a bulldog. "This brings Nando to the verge of fury, he resents being coerced... He has a morbid terror of action."

Boyle's manner appealed to Marie, but not to those around her. "I am terribly in sympathy with his methods which would exactly be mine if I were a man and free," she wrote in her diary. "Fundamentally we understand each other [,] that is the explanation of our extraordinary friendship, which seems queer to some and even makes them sneer." Marie had stopped trying to explain her Canadian hero to her Latin friends. "They can hardly understand... that a man can put *all* his energy, *all* his heart in a thing that brings him *no* profit whatever."

The Queen thrilled at Boyle's exploits, admired his ability to get things done, and realized that he was an excellent influence on her as well. At an official requiem for King Carol I in October, Marie was surprised by her own vindictiveness, an unseemly and unqueenly emotion. Looking down from her throne on those who had scorned her in their rush to collaborate with the Germans, she was filled with contempt, which she later admitted to Boyle. Looking at her "squarely in the eye, and with a very grim mouth," he admonished her, "Your Majesty, you have been a good loser, let me also find you a good winner."

Under increasing pressure from all sides, Premier Marghiloman resigned on November 6, 1918. He was replaced by a temporary ministry of generals and functionaries, whose task it was to prepare for immediate mobilization and pave the way for Bratianu and a pro-Entente Cabinet to take over the government. Although the King and Prince Stirbey stayed in Jassy to supervise the rapid changes taking place, the Queen was instructed to remain in Bicaz. Her refusal to recognize the peace disqualified her from taking part in this change of government. She must not be the one to officially welcome the Allies; it must be the German-born Ferdinand, whose sacrifice would underline Roumania's own and improve the country's standing with the victors.

Marie was still in Bicaz when she heard that Ferdinand had proclaimed universal suffrage and land reform for the peasants. "I am pleased he has done this without either Bratianu or Averescu in power, so that it should be his name alone which will remain attached to these reforms," she said. Chafing at being kept away from all the excitement, the Queen finally defied orders and left to join the King and Prince Stirbey in Jassy. She doubted that her dream of Roumania taking up arms again before the general armistice would be realized. "Germany," she noted in her diary, "seems to be giving in too quickly for that. Yet perhaps there is a plan on foot of which I know nothing. I cannot help hoping that there is."

Marie's wish was fulfilled. On November 9, 1918, King Ferdinand ordered mobilization of the Roumanian Army. The King's decision, reflecting the advice of the American Ambassador and Prince Stirbey, was met with enthusiasm that erupted into jubilation when the people heard that Allied troops under General Berthelot had just arrived at the Danube. "We realized," the American said, "that in the present miserable state of Roumania, the immediate value of the mobilization was mainly its moral effect."

Coupled with the order for remobilization was a proclamation by the King which gave the Germans twenty-four hours to leave the country. At the end of this time the Roumanians would consider themselves once again formally at war with their captors. This declaration seems to have surprised the Germans occupying Bucharest. They stormed through the city, commandeering the last of the spoils in preparation for a hasty departure.

Queen Marie's joy at news of mobilization was tempered by word of the Kaiser's abdication. Vengeance was not so satisfying as she had anticipated. Monarchy had suffered a personal blow. "Perhaps it is the solidarity of caste," she wrote, "for certainly there was no love lost between us." "I, for one, like a country to stand and fall with its ruler, its King, a father with his family. Kaiser Wilhelm tried to destroy us, but I did not want to see him destroyed... beaten: yes, that I passionately desired because he wished to have this country wiped off the face of the earth... But... I do not like to hear of his abdication."

The Queen arrived in Jassy on Armistice Day, November 11, 1918. Unbeknown to her a "tremendous reception" had been prepared in her honor. She "tumbled out of the train" straight into the arms of the King. Behind him were members of the new government and the representatives of the Allies. In the midst of the clamor the French Minister stepped forward. He asked for silence and presented the Queen with the Croix de Guerre, citing her as "an unshakable, loyal and faithful friend, as firm in the hour of disaster as in the hour of success." A true Ancien Régime royalist, the Count de Saint-Aulaire demurred at the climactic moment, hesitating to compromise Marie's rank. The Queen, deeply touched and close to tears at being decorated like a soldier, had not lost her sense of humor.

"Why are you waiting to kiss me?" she asked.

"She didn't have to ask me twice," said Saint-Aulaire, as the crowd broke once more into cheers and, singing the "Marseillaise," escorted Marie in triumph to her car.

The Queen spent the remainder of Armistice Day receiving well-wishers—

generals, foreign ministers, and the ministers of her new government. One of the first who came to congratulate her was Prince Stirbey. "In the morning Barbo came to me and I tried to thank him for all his faithful work but he never *will* be thanked, he is too modest... His name may disappear in the history of his country but... at least these pages shall testify the truth."

Late that afternoon the general armistice was announced. People poured into the streets of Jassy in spontaneous victory parades. Bands appeared as if by magic. The entire population, well and wounded, streamed onto the streets, cheering and singing, as the Roumanian Army marched through its wartime capital.

Among the joyous throngs was Zizi. The Crown Prince, freed from imprisonment in order to lead his regiment into Jassy, saw his wife standing in his path with the police behind her. Before the victory march, Carol had been told that he would be allowed no contact with her. The Crown Prince had appealed to his mother in frantic letters and tearful visits to intercede on his behalf.

Although Marie thought Carol was headed for a breakdown, there was nothing she could do. The King was intransigent. Even Barbo Stirbey begged her to stand firm in order to "save him [Carol] from complete ruin." Bratianu met with the Crown Prince to tell him some hard truths about his position, but it was Prince Stirbey who finally persuaded Carol to sign a paper, demanded by his father, agreeing to the annulment of his marriage; in exchange for acquiescence, Stirbey said that Carol would be allowed to see Zizi to say goodbye. The Crown Prince met his wife at the house of one of the Queen's ladies-in-waiting. The interview, as reported back to Marie, was "long & painful" and "somewhat stormy" on Zizi's side. The following day the Crown Prince returned to his regiment.

Marie could scarcely wait to participate in the triumphal re-entry of the sovereigns into Bucharest, an event that had to be delayed because the Germans had blown up all the bridges around the capital. The celebration finally took place on the morning of December 1, 1918. The day was gray and overcast, the buildings were ransacked shells, but the exhausted, ragged citizens who had survived German occupation were incredibly gay. As was their Queen. Her husband had invited her to ride at his side at the head of the Roumanian and Allied troops. "I would never have asked for this," she said, "but it is... by far the greatest honour that could be done me, because if ever a queen was one with her army, I was that queen! This I say," she added, "without any modesty!"

Dressed in a military tunic, a long, fur-collared military cape, and leather vest made for the occasion, Marie added a gray astrakhan bonnet strapped under her chin, giving her, as she put it, "the look of a healthy, chubby youth." Preceded by their children—Carol riding at the head of his regiment, their daughters in a carriage drawn by four horses—the King and Queen were the last to start. Flanked by General Berthelot on one side and Prince Nicolas (promoted to sublieutenant for the occasion) on the other, followed by dozens of generals and officers, they advanced down the Chaussée Kisselev.

As they entered the city and started down the Calea Victoriei, they were met by a "town . . . gone absolutely mad." It seemed to the Queen "as though the houses as well as the pavement were cheering with the crowd." Flags flew from windows, rooftops, and lampposts; every child seemed to have been given his own miniature banner. Mixed in the undulating sea of red, yellow, and blue were the French tricolor, the Stars and Stripes, and the Union Jack. As the horses and riders wound their way to the square with the statue of Michael the Brave brandishing his sword, Marie thought of the processions she had witnessed here—twenty-five years of them now, but "never a parade such as this one."

With only ten minutes to transform herself from Victorious Soldier to Reigning Monarch, the Queen disappeared to change clothes while guests assembled for a thanksgiving service in the Metropolitan Cathedral. As they emerged from the dim church into the daylight, General Grigorescu, a hero of Marasesti and the new Minister of War, came forward to beg King Ferdinand on behalf of the Roumanian Army to accept the staff of Field Marshal. Marie had suggested this to the generals. It came as a complete surprise to the King, and the Queen was happy to see how "deeply touched" he was.

At the end of the festivities, Marie and Ferdinand drove to Cotroceni Palace. After almost two years as a refugee, the Queen returned home.

Chapter *20*

... the thought of Roumania and
especially of M. Bratianu aspiring to the
status of a Great Power was an agony to
the soul.

—*HAROLD NICOLSON, MEMBER OF THE
BRITISH DELEGATION TO THE PARIS PEACE
CONFERENCE*

*A*s the cheers subsided, the privations of life after
the Armistice emerged. What the Germans hadn't stolen from Roumania
during the occupation they had seized on the way out. Representatives of
the worldwide Council of Relief and Rehabilitation, sent in to survey the
destruction, said it was "difficult to describe the minuteness of the German
despoliation. Every town, house and farm was visited...[The enemy] removed table linen, silver, kitchen utensils, furniture, blankets, clocks, metal
articles, wagons, work animals, livestock... [all] packed and sent to Germany." Dressed in rags, barefoot in the icy cold, the surviving peasants were
now in no less danger of starvation than before the Armistice.

Members of the middle and upper classes were slightly better off, but the
wanton looting of the railways made it difficult for them to return home.
Only a handful of working engines and a few thousand third- and fourth-
class railway cars were left in the entire country. There was no glass in the
windows of most of these carriages; travelers stuffed the jagged openings with

whatever rags they could spare from their own bodies. To protect themselves from freezing rains, they packed their legs in straw up to the knees. Able-bodied men kept warm by walking home alongside the moving trains. It was not hard for them to keep up, so slowly did the rusted, wheezing engines proceed and so often did they have to stop while the passengers cut wood to keep them fueled.

Once they reached Bucharest, former residents faced bomb-scarred homes, stripped by the occupiers. "Disorder, dirt, rubbish—the sight made me choke with anger," said the wife of a naval commander returning to her former mansion. "Furniture was stained, soiled, broken; drawers and bureaus and tables missing; no china, glass, bibelots, linen, pictures, books or brasses left." This particular lady was surprised to find fourteen trouser stretchers, all marked with the same name, in her closet, her cellar full of empty champagne bottles, and corks in all the drawers in the house. The last occupant, she was told, was the director of the German opera.

Even for the well-off, the necessities of life were unavailable. Ladies unraveled heirloom lace for thread to mend more substantial clothing. "We are now burning dried corncobs and files of old newspapers in order to keep warm..." said the naval commander's wife. "We are reduced to living principally on beans and musty cornmeal porridge."

Unlike other countries where demobilization followed peace and the joys of family reunions mitigated postwar deprivation, Roumania's politics kept her army in the field long after the soldiers of other countries had gone home. Fearing that the Entente would not honor its territorial promises of the Treaty of 1916, Prime Minister Bratianu, whom King Ferdinand summoned back to power in December, ordered Roumanian troops to occupy Transylvania, Bessarabia, Bukovina, and the Dobruja.

The addition of these four provinces was a mixed blessing. With postwar Roumania doubled in size and her population increased from 7.5 million to 16 million people, there were 8.5 million more mouths to feed, 8.5 million more Roumanians susceptible to revolution. The food and transport crisis seemed tailored to Communist agitation. "During the German occupation we had bread, now we have none," gibed the revolutionaries, while Premier Bratianu sent desperate appeals to the Allied governments for quick relief. "The Allies do not take into consideration the fact that the worst situation among all the Allied nations exists in Roumania," the American Ambassador wrote home, "as she was entirely devastated by the Germans and the Russians... We urge and we beg in the name of humanity, as well as for the political and economic interest of our countries, that... relief be sent as soon as possible."

Famine in Roumania was not a priority among Western leaders. "It is rather hard to... read about how comfortable old gentlemen sit round a green table and discuss... the 'League of Nations[,]' how medals are being stamped in honour of Wilson 'The World's Liberator[,]' whilst one cannot obtain a single engine that would help us to feed our starving population!" wrote Queen Marie.

A riot broke out in front of the royal palace in late December of 1918; the mob called for the end of the monarchy and the birth of a republic. When the police arrested the demonstrators, they recognized many of the same German and Russian agitators left over from the war. Confronted with threats of revolution, Marie wrote a friend that it was "not physical fear that... takes hold of me, or the horror of what might happen to me and mine, but the thought that all my work should end in final failure."

In December Joe Boyle left for Western Europe to expedite famine relief to Roumania. He caught Herbert Hoover, chairman of the Allied Food Council, in Paris. Boyle had known Hoover before the war when the American was a free-lance engineer and the Canadian was gold king of the Klondike. He prevailed upon Hoover to send three cargoes of food to Roumania. In London Boyle helped negotiate a $25 million loan to Roumania from his native Canada to be paid in Canadian-made goods. Dubbed by the English press the "Duke of Bucharest," Boyle returned to Roumania some months later as head of a Canadian Mission for Roumanian relief.

It was Hoover's opinion that since England and France held large oil and railway interests in Roumania, they should be the countries to offer aid to ease the famine. Emissaries sent to study the situation demanded more commercial concessions as the price of relief. The Roumanian Minister of Interior, no stranger to bribery in high places, said that his country "would rather starve" than accept the conditions offered by England and France. The English finally came through by diverting shipments en route home from Australia and adding to them surplus army provisions from Salonika. But no food was forthcoming from the French, who responded only with army equipment and cosmetics for sale.

While he was in England, Boyle arranged to put fifteen-year-old Prince Nicolas in school at Eton. In London he took Nicky to Buckingham Palace to see his Uncle George and Aunt May. King George was impressed with Colonel Boyle, whom he had heard of but never met: "... he is a remarkable man & seems utterly fearless," the King wrote Marie. George promised Missy that he and May would "keep an eye on Nicky & are proud you have sent him to England to finish his education." According to the King, "school life in England always turns out the best men."

The months immediately following the Armistice were intensely busy ones for the Queen. Before the war she had established a precedent of being readily available to the public. "All day long people call at the palace," said one of the royal governesses, "and if Queen Marie is at home she will see them at once." This policy of easy accessibility, more feasible in a static, feudal society, now nearly overwhelmed Marie as the rigors of postwar life brought malcontents by the droves to Cotroceni Palace. Among these were representatives of the occupied areas of Transylvania and Bukovina, Bulgars from the Dobruja, and Bessarabians. The Queen soon discovered that she had gathered under her loving wing some rather disparate and quarrelsome new subjects: "... it was all very well to talk of the brothers beyond the mountains," she wrote; "these certainly had the same language, the same aspirations, but they also had their own habits, their pride, their susceptibilities... they were super-sensitive, easily suspicious, very much on their guard, ready to see offense in every brotherly approach."

Nonetheless, Marie was thrilled with her new role. Her delight was observed by a young Russian cousin, the Grand Duchess Marie, who had been rescued with her husband from Odessa by Joe Boyle and brought to Bucharest to live with the Queen. "Rumania was on the point of becoming a very much larger country than she had been before, and the ambitions of her Queen had been gratified beyond expectation," the Grand Duchess later wrote. "Queen Marie already saw herself being invested with a Byzantine tiara and mantle at the old city of Alba Yulia, although the new borders of her enlarged realm had not yet been defined. It was a moment she had been dreaming of all her life."

While the King occupied himself implementing the agrarian reforms he had promised the peasants, the Queen concentrated on helping disabled veterans, widows, and orphans. As usual, Marie rose very early, capturing a private hour or two for her writing before launching into more queenly occupations. Unable to budge what she called the "wall of real Roumanian inertia," she imported foreign experts to help her put her projects into action. These and any number of other guests were invited to join the royal family and their suites for lunch at the palace.

The Queen used her afternoons to visit destitute villages in the countryside around Bucharest; her personal car was always followed by a second one loaded with food and clothing. Due to winter weather, the poor condition of the roads, and the distances, these trips were fairly hazardous. The Grand Duchess Marie, invited to move into Cotroceni with her husband, accompanied the Queen on these excursions. Although they were often stuck in the mud and sometimes stopped by blizzards, the Queen, said the Grand Duchess, "would let nothing stop her. We came home long after dark," the young Russian woman reported, "cold and wet."

After changing their clothes the two ladies gathered for tea in the Queen's study, where Marie, lying on a sofa, often read to her guest from her work in progress. Like her predecessor, Carmen Sylva, the Queen had adopted the practice of reading what she had written aloud to reap the praises of her audience. Marie treated her writing like her beauty—as an impersonal phenomenon to be admired by everyone, including herself. Although she continued to write propaganda pieces for her country, she had progressed in her fiction from fairy stories written during the war for Ileana to legends of romance and magic. Tales of perfect love and passionate longings, they are made more palatable by her natural gift for humorous characterization.

Queen Marie seldom joined her husband and children for the evening meal, preferring a tray and a book in her own apartments. "Great parcels of books arrived at regular intervals from England and France," reported Grand Duchess Marie, astonished that the Queen managed to keep herself current in reading in spite of her other responsibilities. After dinner the family came to the Queen's rooms for coffee. Ferdinand usually retired early to his own quarters, leaving his wife, his daughters, and their Russian guests to play the piano, embroider, or read until bedtime.

This routine can hardly have satisfied Elisabetha and Mignon. The Princesses, aged twenty-four and eighteen, had no social life outside an occasional visit to the theater or a government function at the palace. There was little Marie could do to dress up what the Grand Duchess called the "monotonous" life of her daughters. No doubt there were marital plans germinating in the Queen's mind, but these would have to wait until the girls could be shaped up and introduced to their peers in Western Europe.

Much to her mother's distress, Elisabetha had grown fatter and lazier during the war. Although she occasionally indulged in a brief enthusiasm for some sort of handwork like embroidery or beading, Elisabetha's "real passion" remained clothes, a fancy utterly foreign to Mignon. Although she too was overweight, Mignon was more attractive than her older sister. Mignon took herself with humor and was cheerfully easygoing. Writing to their old governess, Leile Milne, the Queen despaired of finding someone energetic enough to rouse either of her elder daughters out of the slough of inactivity. "My daughters, being so lazy... need a person to bustle them about... I want to get rid of Oriental habits in my house."

The Queen, the Grand Duchess observed, loved her children dearly "but seemed at a loss what to do with them... At the moment she was very much worried over the conduct of... Carol, for whom she had a special fondness." The Crown Prince, who fulfilled no real functions outside his regiment, had plenty of time to dwell on his marital frustrations. In public he was sullen; in private he indulged in temper tantrums, during which he cried and threatened to renounce his family and his future throne. "He is trying to behave himself but he suffers horribly, and my heart aches over him," said his mother, who decided that the only way to rehabilitate her son was to put him to work in famine relief. When no one else could find Carol "a real job," the Queen started a small motor transport service with personal funds and put him in charge of it.

During his enforced separation from Zizi, Carol had taken a mistress, a young milliner sponsored by an older man who hoped to make his fortune off the Crown Prince. This frightened the King and Queen into letting Zizi come to Bucharest. After her arrival, the young couple led a cozy family life. Carol left each morning for his regiment and returned to spend the afternoons walking or driving with Zizi. In the evenings they invited friends for singing and bridge. But, according to Zizi, "a shadow... fell across that second honeymoon" when she discovered she was pregnant. She was unhappy; Carol was delighted. She wanted an abortion; he forbade it.

• • •

In spite of what the Grand Duchess Marie considered the Queen's unwarranted timidity toward her children, she greatly admired her cousin. The younger woman was amazed to find Marie, even in her forties, full of youthful enthusiasm and remarkably unspoiled. "The more I saw of her," said the Grand Duchess, "the more she attracted me. She was sincere in everything she did and said... Even in her childish vanity she was sincere, the vanity of a very beautiful woman. She admired herself enormously and often when speaking about herself she would sound as if it were some other supremely beautiful and fascinating creature she was seeing and describing."

No one who knew Marie well was surprised when a young relative discovered a piece of paper lying on a table in Cotroceni Palace that read, "Marie of Roumania—one of the most wonderful women in the world. A woman like that is born once in a century." The handwriting was unmistakably that of the Queen herself. Princess Irma of Hohenlohe, the youngest daughter of Marie's sister Sandra, recalled in later years that Aunty Missy, who believed in reincarnation, had explained that she, the Queen of Roumania, would not return to this world again, as she had already in this life reached the ultimate perfection toward which all her previous embodiments had been aimed.

Marie was, as one friend expressed it, "the most out of the ordinary example of narcissism" he had ever encountered. But, he explained, "her vanity was counter-balanced by such a naive simplicity that it rarely irritated people, only made them smile, often with a kind of affectionate indulgence." "I never met a woman who could talk so much about herself and so frankly, and yet with such freedom from any disagreeable egotism," said one American visitor to the palace. "She is always so clever and amusing in her accounts of herself that one forgets that it is the first person of whom she is talking."

Ferdinand, on the other hand, was still uncomfortable with himself at fifty-three. Over the years he had gained weight and wore his graying hair in an ugly German brush out from under which his ears "protruded in a most disconcerting fashion." Having not seen the King for ten years, the Grand Duchess Marie was shocked to find him aged, exhausted, and "extremely anxious to conceal this fatigue even from himself." Although she liked him and felt he was conscientious and kind, the Grand Duchess was "struck by his lack of external charm." Short, with his disproportionately large body grown heavier over his spindly legs, the King was still as awkward in his behavior as his body. "He lacked eloquence and ease in speech, had little poise, and his manner was shy and nervous. Knowing his own deficiencies he never attempted to step into the limelight, leaving this entirely to Queen Marie, who by her charm, beauty, and ready wit could obtain anything she desired," the Grand Duchess noted.

It was obvious to many that Marie of Roumania had an extraordinary gift for dealing with people, and in early 1919 it occurred to some that this talent might be used to help her country. Roumania's official representatives to the Peace Conference, currently underway in Paris, were acquitting themselves poorly. As a result, Roumania's plans for postwar expansion were in jeopardy.

Although it had been strongly suggested that Bratianu go to Paris immediately after the Armistice to prepare the way for the peace negotiations, Roumania's leading spokesman had elected to stay home to solidify his power, while Take Jonescu, "his chief colleague, and... only serious rival," left for Western Europe to plead Roumania's cause. Take Jonescu realized that the Great Powers could wriggle out of their 1916 Treaty of Alliance with Roumania simply by pointing an accusatory finger at the separate peace Roumania had been forced to conclude with Germany. Bratianu had been gifted with no such foresight.

Of all Roumania's territorial claims, the major area of contention was the province of the Banat—eleven thousand square miles of highly prosperous agricultural and mining lands bound on three sides by navigable rivers in the southwest corner of Transylvania. Since almost 25 percent of the people of the province were Serbs and since the treaty between the Allies and Roumania had been kept secret from Serbia, Jonescu negotiated an agreement with the Serbian Prime Minister that partitioned the Banat between their two countries on the basis of nationality. He also laid the groundwork for a Balkan alliance, under which Roumania and her neighbors would resolve their own differences and present a unified front to the Big Five (England, France, the United States, Italy, and Japan) at the Peace Conference.

Before the agreement between Roumania and Serbia could be presented for parliamentary approval in Bucharest, however, it leaked out in the Roumanian press, where it came under attack. This gave Bratianu the opportunity to jettison his major political rival, and he withdrew his original plan of including Jonescu as the second delegate to the Peace Conference. In place of the man Clemenceau called "*un grand Européen*," Bratianu substituted Nicolas Misu, an able diplomat but not a forceful one. Bratianu knew his associate would neither outshine him nor question his authority.

Bratianu was supported in this by the King and Queen. Marie said that Bratianu was "the only man *really* capable of treating abroad" and wrote King George to disavow Jonescu. She also pressed the King of England to support Roumania's territorial claims at the Peace Conference: "... disquieting rumours have reached us that... our treaty of alliance is not to be respected," she wrote George. "Personally I have always had faith in our Allies... even when most about me doubted—I would laugh in their faces and tell them that they did not know England if they could imagine that she could go back on her word because our misfortune had made us helpless."

Marie had the wit to appeal to George's sense of honor. Bratianu did not. His personal lack of commitment to humanity at large colored his vision and undermined his arguments. He could not see that Serbia too had rights and that a compromise on the Banat would have yielded international good will and all the other territory Roumania coveted. Whining long-winded sophistries before patronizing Englishmen, moralizing Americans, and the openly hostile Premier Clemenceau of France, Bratianu doctored historical facts, tried to play the Great Powers off against one another, and managed to offend everyone he had come to Paris to woo. Woodrow Wilson refused even to meet him. "No man could have been more foolish, unreasonable, irritating or provocative than Ion Bratianu," said Harold Nicolson, the Balkan expert on the British Delegation to the Conference. Nicolson said that Roumania's Prime Minister "so mishandled the Rumanian case at the Conference that he estranged the most ardent friends of Rumania."

The major point of contention between Bratianu and the leaders of the Conference was the treaty signed in 1916 between Roumania and the Allies. At the beginning of the Conference the Supreme Council rejected the treaty, which had among other things guaranteed Roumania's status as a primary power in the peace negotiations. Bratianu, who arrived in Paris expecting a seat on the Supreme Council, was pushed aside; Roumania was allotted only two delegates to the Conference, while even Belgium and Serbia were given three. Furious at what he considered a personal assault on his ego, Bratianu planted his feet firmly on "the treaty of 1916, the whole treaty and nothing but the treaty," while the Peace Conference slipped away around him, leaving him stranded on a document that only he recognized.

It must be added that Bratianu's frustrations with the Supreme Council were shared by representatives of other small countries at the Conference. Decisions about lesser nations were often reached without consulting their emissaries. A delegate who asked to plead his country's cause had to do so standing in front of Clemenceau, who was seated at the head of the conference table surrounded by envoys from the other Great Powers—gentlemen whose state of attention or somnolence too often depended on a faulty knowledge of pertinent geographical data. Thus the British Prime Minister, David Lloyd George, was quoted by the *Daily Mail* asking, "Where the hell is that place [Transylvania] Rumania is so anxious to get?"

Regardless of the injustices of the process, Bratianu was a difficult diplomat, and within weeks of his arrival in Paris, he had reached an impasse with the Supreme Council. It soon became clear that the Roumanian Delegation needed outside reinforcement—someone more at home in the hushed Aubusson-carpeted salons of the Quai d'Orsay, someone who spoke in the quiet, bell-like tones of the Occident. Who better than the beautiful, fair-haired cousin of England's own George V?

The idea of sending for Marie originated with the French Minister to Roumania. Champion of the Roumanian cause, the Count de Saint Aulaire watched sadly as his wily friend Bratianu lost his credibility and, with it, his diplomatic sangfroid. Realizing that Roumania's territorial future was in danger of being sacrificed to Bratianu's pride, Saint-Aulaire suggested that Queen Marie be brought to Paris to "try her philtres" on old Clemenceau. There was little else the Roumanian Premier could do.

The Paris assignment took Marie completely by surprise. Up to her mid-forties, the Queen had been given opportunities to exercise her charms only on comparative small fry—politicians in little countries like her own or military and diplomatic types posted to the backwaters of history. Suddenly she was offered a chance to practice her wiles in the main arena of world politics.

The King approached her one morning early in 1919 to ask if she would "have the courage... to go on an unofficial mission for which we think you are the only right person?" Marie was ecstatic. "It is actually found useful that I should go abroad!... I'm flattered that they all think I can help. What is more... I feel that I *can* help." When Prince Stirbey came to confirm her assignment, the Queen expressed her concern that the visit must be an unofficial one. Stirbey told her "not to protest against the word 'unofficial' or even 'incognito' for once there," he promised, knowing Marie, "it would turn into an official reception." She regretted that Barbo could not come with her, but, as she wrote in her diary, "Nando needs him even more than I do."

The Queen was meticulously prepared for her role. Coached at length in facts and figures, she was told to get in touch with all the leaders of the Conference in order to persuade them to honor the Treaty of 1916 and impress upon them the validity of Roumania's claims. Since England was the most outspoken anti-Roumanian power at the Conference, she was instructed to go home to speak to her cousin, George V.

She asked to be allowed to take her daughters with her, explaining that life in postwar Bucharest was still too disorganized to leave them at home. Actually, she meant to prepare the two older girls for the royal marriage market; Elisabetha in particular was in no condition to win any hearts worthy of her lineage. As the Queen wrote Elisabetha's former governess, Leile Milne, "The moment I can get abroad I want Lisabetta to make a cure, her nerves are certainly not all right and she is tremendously fat... it is only in a sanatorium or something of that kind that she could be obliged to do the necessary for her health and figure... In spite of all my observations, her dresses are nearly up to her knees and she WILL not understand how fat she is. She sits in adoration before the beauty of her face and considers it sufficient to go through life with... only more normal, more severe, more European surroundings would be able to open her eyes."

Worse than narcissistic, Elisabetha was cruel. During the war Mignon had gained a good deal of self-respect working in the army hospitals away from her siblings. At nineteen, easy in her manner and unselfconscious, Mignon was a far more attractive candidate for marriage than her older sister.

If, by some lucky chance, Mignon should appeal to her cousin's son, the Prince of Wales, Queen Marie knew that Elisabetha was mean enough to try to stand in her way. "I would only bring Mignon [to England]," she wrote Miss Milne; "the child would have a better chance in every way if she was without her elder sister...It is sad to say that one sister could harm the other, but in this case I KNOW it is a fact. Of course I have not mentioned this to either of my daughters."

Marie also asked to take her young Russian houseguest, the Grand Duchess Marie, with her to Western Europe. When word came back that she would not be welcomed by the court in England, the Roumanian government denied the Queen's request. Marie broke down in tears of anger, telling Barbo Stirbey that even "if all the world meant to behave like selfish beasts," she would never deny her exiled Russian relatives; "it is not in my nature to behave shabbily or like a coward. I simply cannot & will not do so."

To her credit, Marie did not forget less fortunate relatives in her moment of glory. She sent Joe Boyle into Russia twice to rescue the surviving Romanovs, and in the case of the Grand Duchess Marie, the Queen offered her and her husband a home in Roumania as well. "Of all the royal families still in possession of their thrones," the Grand Duchess wrote later, "and all more or less related to us, it was only from them [the Roumanians] that we met with real sympathy and understanding."

Queen Marie left Roumania for Paris on March 1, 1919. So many people crowded the station that she could not get through to shake hands with Barbo Stirbey. Along with all the ministers and generals there were dozens of aristocratic ladies with knowing smiles on their faces, pleased that they guessed the purpose of the Queen's trip. "On the whole a degree of hope surrounds my journey that makes me somewhat nervous, they expect too much of it..." Marie wrote in her diary. "My Roumanians have an almost mystic belief in my powers which flatters and upholds me but which makes me a bit anxious. One woman's word cannot change the face of such big events."

Nonetheless, with an enthusiasm that would have embarrassed her fellow monarchs, Marie of Roumania set out to talk the Western Powers out of Transylvania, the Bukovina, the Dobruja, and the Banat. This was not a sphere in which kings and queens normally functioned, certainly not openly or with zest. Reserved, discreet, withdrawn from the fray, they might put in a word here and there through trusted envoys or drop a veiled hint, but to rush headlong into the mêlée was not in keeping with royal dignity. In spite of the criticism she was sure to encounter, Queen Marie entertained few doubts about the rightness of her undertaking. If she and her family were not to be overthrown by their subjects—hungry, half-clothed, teetering on the brink of Communism, demanding the territories they had died for—she must take risks.

The mission gave new meaning to the Queen of Roumania's life. When she was young she had yearned for love; now, in her middle years, it was power. The object of Marie's affections was territory. The means were men, and men had always been susceptible to her charms.

Chapter *21*

I am said to be the most beautiful woman
in Europe. About that, of course, I
cannot judge because I cannot know. But
about the other queens, I know. I am the
most beautiful queen in Europe.

—*QUEEN MARIE OF ROUMANIA*

*P*aris in the winter of 1919 was the center of the
political universe, a whirling vortex of national ambitions, international
pretensions, private resentments, and public secrets. From the scions of
deposed dynasties haunting the corridors of seedy hotels to self-satisfied pleni-
potentiaries speeding through the Étoile in limousines, everyone with a
mission from every corner of the civilized world had converged on the capital
of France. Anti-Semitic aristocrats found themselves thrown with impeccably
dressed Jews, who had come from America to demand or buy religious
tolerance for their East European cousins. International newsmen jostled
France's ex-soldiers, who crowded the sidewalks queuing up for sugar and
other luxuries they could no longer afford. The city had gone mad with
profiteering, and the cost of living rendered even the basics of room and
board unattainable to all except their countries' most favored representatives.
Of these, Queen Marie of Roumania immediately took her place at the top
of the diplomatic pyramid.

• • •

On Wednesday morning, March 5, 1919, the French writer Colette out-flanked other reporters by boarding the royal train to interview the Queen before her official arrival in Paris. Justifying her presence with an armful of orchids, she was led through a corridor of watchful servants into the royal compartments at 7:45 A.M. Marie's effect on Colette boded well for her mission.

"She is magnificent..." Colette wrote in *Le Matin* the next day. "The morning was gray, but Queen Marie carried light within her. The glitter of her golden hair, the clarity of her pink and white complexion, the glow in her imperious yet soft eyes—such an apparition renders one speechless."

Marie grasped hold of the reporter's hand with the proffered orchids: "Flowers, oh what joy! Such beautiful flowers! How long has it been since we in our country have seen rare flowers?... Please sit down! How did you get on my train?... Well, here I am near Paris... I cannot tell you how happy I am. Paris... Do you realize that I have only been here one time before and that was when I was ill?"

"How Paris will love you, Majesty!"

"Really? Do you think so? Ah, I am happy!... My country is so little known, so badly known by the outside world, I want people to know it, to love it, to help it. Help me, all of you. Everyone must help me!... My beautiful country trampled by the Germans... I was never afraid of those people! All the time they were there I was... a sort of banner raised for my country... Are you going to call me a sister of charity? I am not a nurse, I have never been one. I simply went, My God! I simply went wherever they called for me, and they needed me everywhere. I was—how should I say it!—an encourager, that's it, an encourager! I don't know if there is such a word, but that's the word I choose."

An interviewer's dream, Marie spoke without prompting. She was easy, voluble, and sure of her effects—a passionate patriot, "alive, concise, illus-trating her words with graceful gestures." Amazed at how Marie managed to smile for the photographer without losing the thread of her story or her charm, Colette was captivated. "Happy the city of Paris, Majesty, who can welcome such a beautiful Queen," the great writer murmured as she left the royal presence.

Colette with her tribute of orchids was only the first of hundreds who responded to Marie's well-publicized love of flowers. Nervous young girls holding spring bouquets stood alongside the reporters, photographers, per-sonal friends, and civil and military dignitaries who thronged the Gare de Lyon to welcome the Queen to Paris. They all cheered as the train pulled in and Marie appeared in the door of the royal coach. For her first postwar appearance in Western Europe, she chose a claret wool coat, a silk hat bordered in gold, and many of her famous pearls. She smiled at the reception committee and inclined her head. Premier Bratianu boarded the train to pay his respects. As the Queen stepped down, she was nearly "buried" by a gigantic basket of orchids tied with ribbons in the Roumanian national colors of red, yellow, and blue. Marie kissed the young girls who offered more bouquets and said she was delighted with her trip. Followed by her three daughters, a large suite, and numerous officials, Marie walked along the quai, nodding and smiling to the curious Frenchmen who had crowded into the station to see her.

As the Queen checked into a suite of twenty rooms at the Hotel Ritz, more flowers appeared. "Conversations," Marie wrote, "were carried on while the door was continually opening and ever more flowers were brought, whole woods of lilacs, roses, callas, orchids, irises, daffodils, freesias, violets." There were so many that the Ritz had to send out "all over Paris" for vases to hold them. Down below on the Place Vendôme, the Roumanian tricolor floated over the entrance to the hotel, while around the doors a squad of uniformed gendarmes waited, detailed to protect the Queen. After months of defeat and deprivation, Marie suddenly emerged in Western Europe as the brightest luminary in the City of Light. It was hard not to relish the role.

"Everybody fusses about me; I am treated as a sort of heroine... All the journalists of the globe seem to be circling round me... I smilingly pass through the rush, noise, confusion, doing my best to remain calm and not lose my head... I am interviewed, photographed, pressed, honoured, invited here, there, everywhere and all this, so to speak 'unofficially.'"

Popularity offered inconveniences as well. Groups of admiring spectators waited around the Place Vendôme hoping to catch a glimpse of Marie or her daughters. In spite of the twenty-four-hour police guard, the Queen could not leave the hotel to shop without being instantly mobbed. In its enthusiasm the crowd, surrounding her car on the way to the Opéra, picked it up and terrified its occupants. Every time Marie set forth she left behind a human wake of the needy—importunate remnants from dethroned royal families ("so much sadness") and pushy dressmakers ("preposterous frocks for a Queen!"). Shopkeepers, vying with one another for publicity, loaded her hotel suite with the latest baubles; her dressing table spilled over with the newest scents; her rooms bulged with dresses, hats, and shoes sent in by couturiers eager to replace the Queen's old-fashioned prewar outfits.

Her wardrobe, Marie decided, did need refurbishing, particularly since her jewels had been expropriated by the Communists. She must try to give herself "a queenly air" without their help. The Queen selected her gowns carefully with specific statesmen or occasions in mind. She chose yellow silk for the Chinese Ambassador's party in her honor, point de Milan lace for a reception at the Italian Embassy, heavily embroidered cloth of gold for the President of the United States, and blue silk over silver brocade for the President of France. She found a gown of mousseline de soie with hand-painted roses. "As soon as I glimpsed it at Jenney's I felt it would be just what Mr. Lloyd George would like." In all some sixty gowns, thirty-one coats, twenty-two fur wraps, twenty-nine hats, and eighty-three pairs of shoes jammed the armoires and garderobes of her suite. "I feel that this is no time to economize..." she explained. "Roumania...has to have Transylvania...Bessarabia too. And what if for the lack of a gown, a concession should be lost?"

Marie soon transformed her royal suite into an Oriental seraglio, complete with brocades and Indian embroideries. "She might well have been in ancient Alexandria instead of in modern France," sniped the Spanish Infanta Eulalia, mother-in-law of Marie's youngest sister, Beatrice. "It was a confusion of barbaric colours, flowers, perfumes and subdued lights, and 'Missie' received me sitting in State on a throne-like seat, reminiscent of Theodora."

The Grand Duchess Marie, on her way to London as an ordinary tourist, was surprised by the metamorphosis of the Queen. "Dressed in new Parisian gowns, imbued with her own importance, beautiful, beaming all over with happiness, the Queen was a different person from the one I had known at the palace of Kotrocheny [sic]. She swept in and out, received guests, gave audiences, entertained, was entertained herself both officially and privately. She was photographed, featured in the papers, interviewed, flattered outrageously, taken advantage of, and talked about everywhere. The Paris public was delighted."

This was not the way Marie thought of herself. Looking in the mirror over her dressing-table, she did not see the royal darling of press and society. The person who smiled back at her was a totally rational being unaffected by ballyhoo, interested only in furthering the cause of her country, aware of her own diplomatic and political inadequacies. "Luckily," she said, "I did not lose my head, but I kept my eyes and ears wide open, I listened, watched, trying to plumb the different currents whirling round this new Europe arisen from flame and ashes...I had no real training, my reactions were entirely spontaneous and unconventional. I never deluded myself into believing I was a great intelligence, but I could learn to understand."

For all her vanity, Marie was at least as honest as other sovereigns about her own abilities and more realistic about her value in a democratic world. She was, she realized, born well, educated poorly, and ensconced in twenty rooms at the Ritz on sufferance of the masses. Because she knew this, she was willing to pay for her privileges. And if she did not express it in these words, it was because royal training had disposed her, like all of her relatives ruling or dethroned, toward permanent circumlocution.

It was just this elegant and studied imprecision of the royal tongue that was required at the Peace Conference. But it must be buttressed with solid facts. Toward that end, Roumania's hardheaded Bratianu, accompanied by the modest Misu, appeared at exactly 9 A.M. every morning to feed the Queen statistics on population distribution, economic and social conditions, education, health, and persecution. Her first test came the day after her arrival at a press conference with forty reporters from England, France, Italy, America, Poland, and Japan. The Queen, dressed in blue, wearing the Croix de Guerre and all her other medals, was "thrust into their midst as into a cage, all forty hanging over me, asking every imaginable sort of question." Acutely aware of the Gallic predilection for patronization and ridicule, she immediately disarmed them by offering to shake hands all around. "I only hope I really kept my wits about me," she said afterward, "and that my French was not too English."

She need not have worried. The Roumanian Minister to France was overjoyed with the comments of the French press. One journalist spoke of the "luminous intensity of her eyes... her grace, her beauty and her simplicity"; another called her "the most beautiful of all the flowers" in her salon. "The atmosphere, so I am told, is not favourable to Roumania," the Queen said, "but is certainly favourable to me."

In her diary the Queen admitted that it was "lucky" she was forty-three or she "really might imagine myself quite irresistible." She was having, she realized, "what Barbo wished for me 'un succès de jolie femme!' [the success of a pretty woman!]." She wrote to tell him so. He was not surprised, only sorry not to be watching her enjoy it. They corresponded often while she was in Paris, as they had corresponded, when they were apart, for more than ten years. She reported her triumphs and promised to try to control her irrepressible humor. He wrote about the darkening international situation and his gallops through the woods, which reminded him of her. He added bits of political advice and gossip about mutual friends. Like Marie, Barbo was an amused observer of the social scene. Beneath the chronicle of local events was his adoration, discreetly hidden by courtly courtesies appropriate to her rank. An interceptor could have found nothing out of the ordinary in these letters except for an unusual acronym. Although he wrote in French, Prince Stirbey always included the letters *i l y m m* (I love you, my Marie?) at least once in every letter to the Queen throughout their lives.

The guest register at the Ritz Hotel reflected Marie's enormous popularity. The Queen received at the opera, where she was given a loge between columns draped in the Roumanian tricolor and decorated with flowers. At the Comédie Française she was cheered during the intermissions. "The cry 'vive la Reine' has become quite usual in Paris," she noted.

But meetings with old friends and public acclamation were not the reasons for the Queen's trip to Paris. Marie's second ordeal, an encounter for which she was lengthily and nervously prepared by Bratianu, was a confrontation with Clemenceau himself, the short, round-shouldered, bushy-browed man known as "The Tiger," who loathed Roumania, her Premier, and her separate peace. Accompanied by a lady-in-waiting, the Roumanian Minister to France, and her A.D.C., Queen Marie set out across the Seine to the Quai d'Orsay, where she was greeted with full military honors and her national anthem. Clemenceau astonished the Queen by running down the steps to greet her before escorting her upstairs to a tête-à-tête in his private office.

"I always imagined I would like Clemenceau and I did," wrote Marie.

"He looks the old man he is, but otherwise there is nothing old about him, and not the smallest little corner of his brain is old or stiff. . . He has certain grievances against Roumania to which he sticks like a leech, and at certain moments we glared at each other like two fighters; I quite enjoyed it, but he certainly had no intention to be convinced. He attacked me *de front* about Roumania:

"'You have treated with the Boches in 1918 before the armistice.'

"'Yes, but we were encircled by our enemy and our Allies as well, who went Bolshevists. We were tracked like game.'

"'Don't tell me those stories, you were for the Resistance—you yourself!'" he countered, staring at the Queen "ferociously in the eye."

"This was a knockout," Marie admitted.

The Queen recovered quickly if weakly: "'Yes, but being a woman I had a passionate *point de vue*, and being at that time so near events, I had no *recul* [perspective] from which to see the situation as a whole. I believed in the allied victory; so I was ready to hang on by the skin of my teeth, but if this was wise, is for the others to judge. However, now I have not come to speak about myself but to modify your attitude towards Roumania and this I mean to fight now as I have fought my battles during our tragic war years.'"

Having prepared the way, the Queen launched into the gist of her argument. "I cannot say how far I convinced him, but I know I did not bore him, because when once I half rose to leave, so as not to steal his precious time, he impatiently waved me back to my seat: 'I have plenty of time for you; you do not whine. . . as some do, you speak up. I like that.'"

She brought up the "delicate subject" of frontiers. Clemenceau, knitting his brows and biting his lip, was hard to break down: "'You think Roumania's revindications are just. Others have equal claims. The Serbians, for instance, who fought so valiantly. . . want part of the Banat, inhabited by them, and they are supported by the English.'

"'Yes, but the English point of view is much more detached. I do not think they understand much about our small countries, nor that they are very well up in the geography of the Balkans. We want the whole Banat to have the Danube as our national boundary.'

"'What! Your Majesty desires the whole Banat as far as the Tisza River—but it's the lion's share!'

"'This is just why I came to see his first cousin, the Tiger,'" said Marie, ending the interview with laughter.

There was no doubt that Marie made measurable headway with the French Premier. Clemenceau later told the Roumanian Minister to France, "We should only receive a Queen like yours with full military honors, Marshal Foch [Supreme Commander of all the Allied Armies] in the lead." President Poincaré told the Queen herself that "Clemenceau has much changed towards Roumania since Your Majesty has given a face to Her Country." Even Bratianu admitted that Marie had "done more. . . in a few days than he in a month or six weeks."

Having dealt as best she could with the French, Marie set out to charm the patrician members of the British Delegation. Although they did not share Clemenceau's natural antipathy toward Roumania, they had been irritated by Bratianu's performance, and persisted in citing the treaty of May 1918 between Germany and Roumania to avoid obligations incurred in the treaty of August 1916 between Roumania and her allies. Along with Clemenceau and Woodrow Wilson, David Lloyd George was one of the three most important men at the Peace Conference. Queen Marie first met him at a luncheon given in her honor by his Foreign Secretary, Arthur Balfour. Present were the lively Prime Minister, his rather more philosophic host, and a small group that included Lord Derby, Lord Robert Cecil, Marie's daughters, ladies-in-waiting, and Colonel Ballif; "conversation at table was general and flowed pleasantly..." noted the Queen. "Mr. Lloyd George," she observed, "loved talking, company stimulated him; he was full of fun and wit; thoroughly enjoying his own jokes. I let myself be carried away by his undeniable charm, all in wondering how much he really understood about Europe, outside the British Empire."

The Queen was pulled in two directions. It was deceptively easy to slip back into the role of Queen Victoria's granddaughter, a person whose birth, rather than current position, entitled her to the consideration of those delegated to reapportion Eastern Europe. She was at home with these men; she understood their outlook, appreciated their witticisms. "In their pleasant, easy company... I was dangerously tempted to take a rest from 'patriotism,'" she acknowledged. But this would have been tantamount to treason. "I must shut away all temptation to understand too well their side of the question. To walk in the middle of the road could not be indulged in, unless everybody was ready to do the same! and no one was willing to compromise." Aware that she was being honored not as the representative of an insignificant little country, but as the cousin of their King, Marie chose her verbal entrances carefully.

"My conversation had to run along and fit in with theirs, but occasionally, all in amusing them with some quaint anecdote, lightly told, I could catch their interest and lead the conversation over towards those nearest my heart. It was no easy task and needed much tact... I had an uncomfortably clear perception of how indifferent my hosts and table companions really were to the anxious hopes of 'those Balkan countries,' which is certainly the name they gave us when we were not in the room!... We, small countries, were but pawns in their great game."

Bratianu had planned for the Queen to revisit the country of her birth to enlist British public opinion on the side of Roumania, and within a few days the awaited invitation arrived. Marie stayed in Paris about a week, just long enough to review a French Guard of Honor at the Élysée Palace (the first queen to be so honored), to accept the Grand Cordon of the Légion d'Honneur from President Poincaré, and to attend her induction as a corresponding member into the Académie des Beaux Arts. The only woman thrown in among men like the philosopher Henri Bergson, Marie was "somewhat bewildered" by the praises heaped on her accomplishments in art and literature. "I was not entirely convinced that I deserved these . . . honours, whilst I had accepted the military tribute paid to me without a blush."

Explaining to the world that Elisabetha "did not want to tear herself away from her many French friends," the Queen arranged to leave her eldest daughter in Paris in the exacting care of Elise Bratianu. She then gathered up Princess Mignon, Princess Ileana, and the most appropriate of her new Paris gowns for the trip across the Channel.

Before leaving for Britain, the Queen granted a private audience to a special correspondent of the London *Times*. She used the interview to say things she could not say to Lloyd George by speaking directly to the English people: "I hope to arouse the interest of your people in my people . . . You English—I can say so, though I, too, am English in a sense—have a way of regarding distant Continental peoples with a sort of superior aloofness. You must really take a serious interest in European affairs, and must see how much your own interests are bound up with . . . other peoples."

As if in answer to her appeal, on the day of her arrival in London *The Times* carried an editorial entitled "The Resurrection of Rumania"—a panegyric to the suffering, bravery, and good common sense of the Roumanians. Recapitulating Roumania's "heroic but hopeless struggle" against the Central Powers, its "desertion" by Bolshevik Russia, and the rape of its resources by the Germans, *The Times* said that the people of Roumania had proved that they deserved British help by their commitment to land reform and their loyalty to their monarchy. The editors of *The Times* welcomed Marie, who was, in their words, "not only a niece of KING EDWARD VII, but the QUEEN of an Allied State, who has done her full woman's part in sharing the sorrows and the sufferings of her adopted country."

"It was a tremendous emotion to arrive in London," Marie wrote, "and to be greeted at the station by George and May [Queen Mary] . . . As in a dream I saw familiar faces smiling at me, faces from out of the past and faces belonging to the near present."

Arriving at Buckingham Palace in time for late supper, Marie caught her first glimpse of the adult Prince of Wales, the future Duke of Windsor. "David is the most attractive boy I have ever seen," she commented wistfully, remarking on his "child's face" and "hair the colour of ripe corn . . . he is so nice and has an enchanting smile. To me he is irresistible!"

While the twenty-five-year-old Prince of Wales fascinated Queen Marie, Princess Ileana at ten nonplussed the British sovereigns with her matter-of-fact recitals of the horrors of deprivation and disease. As did her mother: "The war years had brought me face to face with a reality which had been spared my cousins. I seemed to know too much of the outside world, and I did not want to disturb their peaceful conception with my cruel experiences."

During her first day in England, the Queen paid her son Nicolas a visit at Eton. She was delighted with the routine of quiet discipline, so different from the adulation and agitations at home, and hoped he would benefit from the experience. With his interest in sports, Nicky was more outwardly English than her other children, but Marie worried about his character. Nicolas could "become anything," his mother admitted; "there was both good and bad in his nature: I hope the good predominated."

Marie had left England too young to have learned to conform to the rigorous blandness of the English court. Now, when she needed to enlist the aid and sympathy of her British relations, she saw just how far she had strayed from English ways. "I was a royal guest and had to be very careful not to overstep any of the established conventions. Although so closely related, we had in fact never been much together... I felt that my relatives were watching me, a little anxious as to what surprises I might bring into their well-ordered existence."

When the subject of Grand Duchess Marie came up, Queen Marie was told that George, a "strictly constitutional" monarch, had been "obliged, because of public opinion" to shun her and other Romanov relatives. Marie refused to understand. More than public outcry, she sensed George's fear of "what Russia's blood-curdling example might instigate in quiet, steady England. Everybody seemed to tread lightly, carefully, so as not to awake sleeping forces which would be difficult to control," said the Queen, who lived with these forces every day of her life.

Faced with different problems than George and May, Marie realized that she had changed in ways that were bound to unnerve her cousins. Living in a small country where public servants were often the most corrupt of her subjects, Marie had not been able to delegate active political work. While her English cousins could trust others to run the country, Marie had to take on herself many mundane functions of government. Beset by the day-to-day frustrations entailed in such work, she had lost much of the objectivity and serenity cherished by the Windsors. She was hardworking, quick thinking, and impatient—a touch too eager for her class. Flouting centuries of tradition, she not only accepted publicity but had learned to actively court the press. "Try not to be shocked at me..." she begged George as she launched into her mission. "Forgive me if I am different from what you think a queen ought to be."

Bound by the traditions of Buckingham Palace, Marie found it difficult to conduct her political business. "Everything is so restricted and one is always afraid of upsetting their conventionalities," she wrote in her diary. She was aware of the havoc her nonconformity wreaked around her, even in the back halls of the palace. Marie gave breakfast parties at 9 A.M. in order to present her country's needs to busy statesmen and tycoons brought to the palace by Waldorf Astor and Joe Boyle. Sensing the disapproval of the palace servants, the Queen called them together to explain the urgency of her mission. Although the staid old retainers gave way on the surface, she knew that they, like George and May, deplored her ways.

The Queen took on representatives of the government, the military, and big business; "with never-flagging enthusiasm," she proudly reported, "I demonstrated that our country needed immediate help, as we had our back to the wall." The English press was on her side. The *Daily Mirror* called her an "Irresistible Ambassador." The *Illustrated London News* published a full-page cover picture of Marie dressed in her Red Cross uniform reading to a dying soldier; the caption, which referred to the "tribulations" of Roumania during the war, pointed out that Her Majesty was closely related to England's own beloved King. *Punch* ran a cartoon in which Roumania was portrayed as a starving old peasant woman forced to watch transports of food being sent to countries of the Central Powers while she, the ally, was dying of starvation.

One evening Lord Curzon, acting Secretary of State for Foreign Affairs, gave an official dinner in Queen Marie's honor so that she could plead Roumania's cause with those who were in a position to help. "I did so with an eloquence I did not realize I possessed," she claimed, "sweeping my audience along with me, till each man promised to do what he could for my suffering country." Although Lord Curzon himself was "too ceremonious to inspire any feelings of warmth," one of the other guests, Winston Churchill, Secretary for War and Air, was most sympathetic. His responsiveness was sentimentally appropriate, for he and Marie had entertained a "sneaking liking for each other" when they were children, and on a visit to the Isle of Wight he had announced that when they grew up he would marry her. Marie was grateful for the admiration and support of one rebel for another.

There was no job she didn't tackle. She had arranged for Bratianu to follow her to England so that she herself might present him to King George "to wipe out any ill feeling that may be between him & the English." For this meeting Marie slid gracefully into the role of interpreter. Better than anyone else, the Queen remembered that George's French was not as good as it might have been. Moreover, she knew that the King of England would take the erudite Roumanian Prime Minister better filtered through the moderating voice of a nonintellectual British princess.

Another test of the Queen's diplomacy came during a formal reception of all the foreign ambassadors and ministers, a promenade that Marie dreaded. "All the Countries of the world lined up in a row," she wrote, "and to have to find something not too idiotic to say to each in turn, whilst the last spoken to always hears what I am saying to his neighbor!" was a difficult task. Her final trial was a press conference, urged by the Roumanian Minister to the Court of St. James's and held at the Roumanian Legation. Everywhere she went the Queen received honors. From many she elicited promises. Aware of the chasm between drawing-room etiquette toward a granddaughter of Queen Victoria and territorial realities, Marie grew impatient: ". . . we want action," she insisted, "not just fine words."

In between tedious receptions and humbling appeals, Marie managed to see old friends like Waldorf Astor and his sister, Pauline Spender-Clay. Marie and Waldorf still shared many views on things. "He is advanced, and God knows I am an advanced Queen. He regrets that the court shuts itself off so much in the same old circle," she noted in her diary. She dined at the Astors' and was, as always, impressed by Lady Astor's gifts as a skillful and witty hostess. Marie, who got along better with the Prince of Wales than did her daughter Mignon, often took him to parties with her. "David... is simply delicious in every way [,] he makes my heart melt inside me."

In accompanying Queen Mary on ceremonious tours of her pet institutions, Marie "could not repress a certain feeling of envy" when she compared the well-ordered hospitals in London with the impoverished ones at home. Never entirely comfortable with King George's wife, Marie was more drawn to her predecessor, Dowager Queen Alexandra, the beloved Aunt Alix of Marie's childhood. Clinging to Marie, a "link with unfortunate Russia," Queen Alexandra showed her letters received before the Revolution from her favorite sister, the Dowager Empress of Russia, still in danger in the Crimea in spite of Marie's and Joe Boyle's efforts to bring her to safety. They also talked about Marie's mother; "both our eyes," Marie said, "were full of tears."

While she was in London, Marie received a year-old letter from Ducky. Still stranded in Finland, hounded by revolutionaries, the Grand Duchess, her husband, and three children had no idea when they might be able to escape to friendlier surroundings. Marie arranged to send provisions—food, soap, and a few little luxuries—which King George and Queen Mary guaranteed would reach her.

There was not much time for family business; a great deal remained to be done on the other side of the Channel. After official appearances at a House of Commons tea and a luncheon hosted by the Lord Mayor of London, the Queen returned to France, leaving Ileana, sick with the flu, to be nursed by her English family and brought to Paris by "Uncle Joe" Boyle.

Back in the Paris maelstrom, Marie discovered that she had lost none of her standing with the public, a phenomenon for which she took full credit. "That keen, alive interest I took in everything had much, I think, to do with my popularity. I never looked bored or resigned as many royalties do; time was my only enemy; the hours slipped too quickly through my fingers; exert myself as I would, time could not be found for everything."

She was determined, however, to see both Herbert Hoover and Woodrow Wilson. Hoover had the power to ease the famine in Roumania. Although Marie referred to him as "the one man I mean to thaw out," they did not get along. "Mr. Hoover had no sentimentality about the countries he was helping and had no special sympathy for Roumania and her queen," she concluded after their meeting.

She was even less effective with Woodrow Wilson. The President of the

United States had developed a strong antipathy to Roumania's Prime Minister and had no desire to waste time on her Queen. "The world had selected him as the great Arbiter of peace," Marie commented. "Wherever he went, he was being received as a sort of Messiah... So much indeed had his head been turned... that he wondered if, being 'Democracy's Saviour,' it was not under his dignity to pay a visit to the Queen of Roumania—a mere Queen!" Nonetheless, urged by letters from Barbo Stirbey, who had infinite faith in her ability to change Wilson's attitude, Marie sent a message on her arrival in Paris to say that she would like to receive the President of the United States at his earliest convenience. Sure that he had found a formula for sliding out of an unwelcome audience, Wilson sent back word that he would be "delighted to pay his respects," but being exceedingly busy, he had no free time any day after 9 A.M. The Queen replied that being an early riser, she would be pleased to receive him at any time he chose, say 7 A.M.? They compromised on 8:30.

On the morning of April 10, 1919, the President of the United States arrived, according to Queen Marie, "with his wife and the smile he has on his photographs." For their interview she had chosen a gown of demure gray. Knowing her time was limited, she hurried into a recital of Roumania's territorial claims. "Permit me to assure Your Majesty," countered the President, "that all this was conveyed to me through dispatches long before I left the United States, and it has been thoroughly considered by the Conference. Also your Prime Minister, M. Bratianu, has faithfully presented Rumania's case. So it is useless for me to claim more of your time regarding it." Hoping to appeal to Wilson's Puritanism, Marie launched into "a few savoury details... which he did not know" on Communism and the new Russian laws on free love and female emancipation. Realizing she was shocking him, she switched quickly to the theme of hope that Wilson now offered small countries like her own existing on the edge of the Russian menace, nations for which he had presented himself as champion. This led quickly to the subject of the League of Nations.

"He began by proclaiming the excellency of his pet idea, pointing out how it would be specially beneficial to the smaller countries. All in admiring the beauty of the thought, I could not, however, abstain from drawing his attention to the way great ideas were often marred by the future followers and partisans who gradually corrupted the initial thought... What horrors had not been perpetrated in the name of Religion?"

As Wilson rose to end the audience, the Queen put her hand on his arm to keep him on the sofa beside her. When that failed, she took a photograph of Princess Ileana off the mantel. "This, Mr. President," she said, "is a picture of my youngest daughter, Ileana. My love child I call her. Is she not lovely? My other girls are blonde, like me; but she—oh, she is dark and passionate." As the presidential party headed with some haste for the elevator, Marie knew that she had failed to raise Wilson's opinion of either herself or her country. "Well," said Admiral Grayson, the President's physician, who had accompanied Wilson and his wife, "in all my experience I have never heard a lady talk about such things. I honestly did not know where to look, I was so embarrassed."

Edith Wilson had met Queen Marie the day before the audience at an exhibition at the Grand Palais. As predisposed as her husband to dislike the Queen, Mrs. Wilson had been impressed with Marie's beauty and charm. "What day can you and the President come to dinner with me?" the Queen of Roumania asked the President's wife. Mrs. Wilson replied that they never dined or lunched out. "Then I will propose myself to lunch with you," said Marie. "You can't be so rude as to tell me not to come. Shall it be tomorrow?"

"No. There is a long and important conference for my husband tomorrow; let us say the following day at one o'clock."

"Good," said the Queen. "I will be there with my two girls, my sister [Infanta Beatrice], and one or two of my gentlemen."

According to Mrs. Wilson, the Queen of Roumania came to lunch with a party of five men and five women and was thirty-five minutes late. Nevertheless, she said that "lunch went off very pleasantly." The President's wife dismissed the Queen's two older daughters as "very shy, uninteresting, and German in type." Mrs. Wilson's secretary was less kind; she referred to Elisabetha and Mignon as "fat and dull—little lumps."

During luncheon the Queen "encouraged" the President to "expound his theories. . . . He is a born preacher . . ." Marie observed. "Very convinced of always being right, there is something slightly patronizing about him, but at the same time he is quite 'un homme du monde,' polite, amiable, even somewhat ceremonious. Very ready to argue, he is, however, certain that he will always have the last word, always entrenched in his superior, detached attitude, which makes him soar above the average mortals."

Queen Marie's reaction to Woodrow Wilson was not unlike that of other contemporaries. Clemenceau said the American President believed himself to be "the first man who for 2,000 years had known anything about peace on earth." This attitude led to one argument during lunch in which the President told the Queen of Roumania how she and her countrymen ought to treat their minorities. "He spread himself out at great length upon this topic," wrote Marie, "becoming unctuous and moral as he warmed to his subject, treating me the while as a rather ignorant beginner who could profit of his advice. No doubt I could, but he struck me as being rather too fond of the sound of his own voice, so finally, when he paused to take breath, I mildly suggested that he was evidently well acquainted with these difficulties because of the Negro and Japanese question in the United States. Upon this he bared his rather long teeth in a polite smile, drew up his eyebrows and declared he was not aware there was a Japanese question in America!"

For all his pomposity, Wilson had touched on a sore point. The Jews of Roumania had been abominably mistreated throughout the war. To complaints that Jewish soldiers were being taken out of their regiments and placed in the front lines to be killed first, Bratianu responded that many of the Jews were deserters and German spies. When Ferdinand repeated this complaint to the American Ambassador, Vopicka "suggested that if they were given equal rights it might not be so."

Early in November the American Ambassador had heard that there was a pogrom planned for the day after the Armistice; he warned the Roumanian government that "if Roumania should start killing the Jews, she should not expect anything from the Peace Conference." The Roumanians claimed that the pogrom was the work of Germans seeking to discredit Roumania before world opinion. Two pogroms that subsequently broke out were immediately put down by the military, although the problems of the Roumanian Jews continued to fester and grew into a cause célèbre of the Peace Conference.

When she was not expected to attend an official function, Marie spent time with her sister, the Infanta Beatrice of Spain, who had come to Paris to see her. She also entertained friends at dinner. From Lady Astor, who that year became the first woman to sit in the House of Commons, to Loie Fuller, the dancer who had made her name at the Folies Bergère, an odd assortment took their places around the Queen's dinner table. Away from the pressures of official duties, Marie and her friends grew "very talkative, occasionally even a little boisterous" over the issues of the day.

These evenings were a stimulating respite from the Queen's frustration over the "ghastly" peace terms currently being forced on the Germans; "it is a systematic and complete destruction & ruining of Germany," she said. Having recently labored under unduly harsh conditions in her own country, the Queen of Roumania "shuddered, remembering the feeling of overwhelming indignation and hatred" that had overtaken her. She despaired over the probable repercussions. "I thought of the hideous suffering which would follow, of the seething hatred which would make many million hearts fester with an undying desire of future revenge... I could not help feeling that it was unwise to go so far—too far."

Having charmed as best she could a number of politicians and financiers, Queen Marie was encouraged to leave Paris at the height of her success while the Conference leaders, with the notable exception of President Wilson, still basked in the glow of her beauty and wit. Already the French press, never prone to glorify anyone for long, had labeled her "the Business Queen."

Before she left, Queen Marie arranged for Mignon to attend finishing school in England. Marie hoped her daughter would "get thin and keep in touch with royal potentials." Elisabetha was to be left in Paris to attend art school. She would live with the Duchess de Vendôme in a household with other girls from good families—a situation which "cannot but do her good."

With Nicky still at Eton, Queen Marie was returning home with only ten-year-old Ileana. President Poincaré and Marshal Foch attended their official sendoff, which was complete with national anthems, truckloads of flowers, and cheerful hysteria. As the train pulled out of the station, it was already being said that Queen Marie at the Peace Conference had "put Roumania on the map"—a flattering judgment in which the Queen herself wholeheartedly concurred.

"I was tired, but I felt that I had done my best, bravely, relying entirely on my own intuition. I had shunned no fatigue, had allowed no doubt or discouragement to sap my energies. I had endeavored to grasp situations, to face difficulties, occasionally, even, hostility, intent upon lessening any prejudices held out against Roumania. I had brought forward the needs and aspirations of my people. I had pleaded, explained, had broken endless lances in their defense. I had given my country a living face."

So she had. Unfortunately, the glow of good will faded fast and was replaced with mutual distrust. During the next phase of Roumania's relationship with the Great Powers, the polite exchange of views in Paris degenerated into hostility and name-calling. As Lenin's followers took advantage of the dissolution of the Austro-Hungarian Empire to spread the Russian Revolution, the new Hungarian Communist Party, bent on expansions of its own, came into direct and open conflict with the Roumanians.

Chapter 22

I hope God will help the Roumanians—I
cannot.

—*HERBERT HOOVER*

*D*uring the weeks Queen Marie was in Western Europe trying to extend Roumania's borders, a vast military buildup was taking place at home. King Ferdinand looked to his wife to find the means to restock Roumania's depleted supplies. In response to his frantic wires, Marie invited Marshal Foch, the Supreme Commander of the Allied Armies, to dinner at her hotel on March 31, 1919.

Unlike Clemenceau, Foch and the members of the French military establishment were naturally sympathetic to Roumania, regarding her as a trustworthy bulwark against Communism in Eastern Europe. This attitude was based partly on Roumania's strategic position and partly on reports from passionate Roumanophiles like General Berthelot and the Count de Saint Aulaire. Envoys sent from Paris to Bucharest, whether on diplomatic or military missions, invariably "developed a strong admiration" for their hosts and ended by supporting Roumania's cause in world councils. This phenomenon was based largely on the personality of the Queen.

Marie pleaded with Foch, outlining Roumania's needs and calling the Marshal's attention to France's geographical stake in the preservation of monarchical Roumania. The Bolshevik threat, she announced, is "too real not only to us but to the whole of Europe. . . . Can't France help us with her overstocked *dépots*? . . . By helping us, you are helping yourselves."

The dinner party was a success. As Marie rode out of Paris aglow with a sense of her powers of persuasion, clicking along behind her sleek blue-and-silver coach were a number of freight cars loaded with French armaments and Red Cross supplies. One hundred engines, sent to swell Roumania's skeletal transit system, would arrive in Bucharest later.

The reason for Roumania's hurried buildup of arms was a new military campaign that followed almost immediately the end of World War I. Throughout the entire period of the Peace Conference, Roumania waged war against Hungary, thus complicating and often negating the negotiations taking place in Paris. These were tense months in the life of Roumania's Queen, who was fighting a two-front war—on the international political scene and within the walls of the palace. If Roumania did not get Transylvania, the people would overthrow the dynasty; if the Crown Prince abdicated the succession, the dynasty would be seriously, if not fatally, weakened. During this period, Marie's personal drama was played out against a hostile international backdrop.

Shortly after the Armistice, Prime Minister Bratianu ordered Roumanian troops to advance through Hungary toward the Tisza River, the frontier promised Roumania in the Treaty of 1916 but not yet officially assigned to her. Unable to stop the Roumanians and to protest the Allied decision to award Transylvania to Roumania, Count Karolyi, leader of the Liberal-Socialist government that ruled Hungary after the war, resigned. On March 21, 1919, one of Lenin's disciples, Bela Kun, seized power in a Bolshevik coup, began the liquidation of the enemies of Communism, and within a week invaded Czechoslovakia. Ignoring Kun's aggressive behavior, the Supreme Council of the Peace Conference sent a commission to Budapest headed by General Jan Smuts to determine if Kun was politically stable enough to negotiate the peace.

Serving as a member of the Smuts mission was Harold Nicolson, a member of the English Delegation to the Peace Conference and one of its Balkan experts. Nicolson allowed his prejudices to taint his political judgment, dismissing Bela Kun as nothing more than an insignificant Jewish revolutionary with "little pink eyes," "puffy white face and loose wet lips." The deputation returned to Paris, where it advised the Supreme Council to temporize, since it expected Kun to be replaced shortly. Nicolson expressed his "conviction that Bela Kun and Hungarian Bolshevism is not a serious menace."

This was written on April 9, 1919. On April 10, Kun's soldiers moved into Transylvania, slaughtering well over a hundred people and abducting two members of the governor's family. Although the Roumanians and the Saxons of Transylvania had voted for union with the Old Kingdom shortly after the Armistice, all Bratianu's requests to the Supreme Council for permission to occupy Transylvania had been refused. This confirmed the Roumanian belief that the Peace Conference based its decisions more on distrust of the Roumanian Prime Minister than recognition of the expansionist nature of Communism. In answer to Bela Kun and in defiance of the Conference, Bratianu ordered the Roumanian Army to march against the Hungarians. The Roumanians drove Bela Kun back across Hungary, and by May 1, 1919, Roumanian soldiers were encamped on the western (Hungarian) side of the River Tisza, about eighty miles from the Hungarian capital of Budapest.

To underscore their approval of Bratianu's policies and celebrate the union with Transylvania, King Ferdinand and Queen Marie left Bucharest on a Transylvanian tour. The Queen invited members of the American Red Cross to join the royal party in order to demonstrate to them how happy the former Hungarians were to be living under Roumanian rule. The enthusiastic peasants did not let her down. Queen Marie hailed the royal progress as "the ultimate realization of the great dream...for which so many had died." Allied leaders censured it as just another example of Roumanian violation of borders yet to be officially defined by the Peace Conference.

A few weeks earlier, Marie had basked in the niceties of Parisian receptions. Now she responded with equal delight to the cheers of Transylvanian peasants who had come to ogle her on alpine meadows. Rhapsodizing over "grand parades of carts drawn by magnificent white wide-horned oxen," the Queen of Roumania set herself to capture the hearts of their occupants while the Peace Conference deliberated the disposal of their bodies. Careful to dress in the traditional garb of each province through which she was led, Marie treated her American guests to glimpses of breathtaking scenery, picturesque village life, and manifestations of the Sovereigns' popularity.

Although the Americans were impressed with what they saw, the Supreme Council in Paris ordered Bratianu to halt all military operations against the Hungarians. Meanwhile, Lenin announced formal support of Bela Kun and, on May 18, 1919, officially declared war once again in the name of Soviet Russia on Roumania.* Encouraged by what Seton-Watson called the Supreme Council's "strange tenderness toward him," Bela Kun took advantage of a May quietus to reorganize his army with the help of some German officers who had escaped to Hungary. This was in accordance with Lenin and Kun's plan to launch simultaneous attacks from Russia and Hungary on Roumania, conquer her, and declare her a Communist state.

At the end of May, Bela Kun overran the new state of Czechoslovakia.

---

*The previous declaration of war, issued on January 31, 1918, had been abrogated by the peace treaty procured by Joseph Boyle.

The Slovakian Delegation in Paris protested, and the Roumanians offered to "make order." The Supreme Council, ever distrustful of Bratianu and on guard against Roumanian reprisals against the Hungarians, refused to allow the Roumanian Army to advance. Instead, Paris ordered Kun to evacuate Czechoslovakia, promising him that Roumania would be compelled to withdraw her forces as well. To calm Roumanian fears of Hungarian aggression in their direction, the Council informed Bratianu that if Kun failed to follow orders, Allied troops would be sent to occupy Budapest.

Like everyone else, the Roumanians knew that the Council talked about sending forces into Hungary, but no one was ready to provide the soldiers. As one member of the American staff to the Peace Conference noted in his diary: "They have talked for days about sending an Allied army to Hungary... They are quite enthusiastic... until it comes to the questions of what nation or nations is to furnish the troops and foot the bills... Then they all look blankly at each other until a bright idea occurs to someone who proposes that they send a telegram to Kun calling him a liar and a thief—at which they brighten up immensely, order the telegram sent, and then pass on to something equally inane and futile."

Unable to produce an Allied army or budge the Roumanians, who refused to withdraw their troops from the banks of the Tisza River, the Supreme Council finally authorized Marshal Foch to organize an offensive with Roumania against Kun to be launched on July 20, 1919. Twenty-four hours before, in a last attempt to revitalize his waning popularity at home, Kun threw an army of eighty-five thousand men against the Roumanians. Forced initially to withdraw, the Roumanian Army recovered the offensive in less than a week and defeated the Hungarians. Queen Marie was jubilant. Bela Kun, she said, "played into our hands and gave us our chance. We have strengthened ourselves more with that move on our own hook than with all the so-called help that was being grudgingly given us by our so-called friends.... We have the only army still mobilized."

While Kun and some of his supporters escaped to Vienna, the Roumanian Army took possession of Budapest, ignoring an avalanche of protestations and threats from Paris. What followed was exactly what the leaders of the Peace Conference had feared—the unconscionable rape of Budapest and the surrounding countryside. Bratianu, who could have controlled the situation, made no effort to moderate the behavior of his soldiers. Left on their own, the Roumanians commandeered everything they could transport—corn, fodder, cattle, engines, and railway cars. Private homes were plundered, factories dismantled. "The Roumanian army," Herbert Hoover wrote, "looted the city in good old medieval style. They even took our supplies from the children's hospitals. Many children died. They looted art galleries, private houses, banks, railway rolling stock, machinery, farm animals—in fact, everything movable which Bela Kun had collected."

Hoover admitted that the Roumanian soldiers had "in Eastern European morals, some justification" for their behavior. During the occupation, the Central Powers had taken from Roumania 2.5 million tons of wheat, 1 million tons of oil, hundreds of thousands of head of cattle, and more than one thousand engines, as well as most of the contents of factories and private homes. The Germans were joined in this by the Hungarians, who on one occasion sent "a squad of eighty men, working to order" to sack the house of Take Jonescu. Roumania's requests for reparations and restitutions of property like those awarded to France had been denied. Therefore, given the opportunity, they took what they wanted, while the Supreme Council threatened to oust them from the community of Allied nations.

Pressed by more important problems and uninformed about the area, the leaders of the Peace Conference had authorized a Roumanian Territorial Commission to deliberate Bratianu's claims. But by the time the Supreme Council got around to examining the findings of the Commission in May of 1919, the Roumanian Army had taken the decisions on frontiers nearly out of their hands. In contrast to the personal antipathy of Wilson, Clemenceau, and Lloyd George, the recommendations of the Territorial Commission were highly favorable to Roumania. Broadly sketched, the Commission recommended awarding the entire province of Transylvania, all of Bukovina, and two-thirds of the Banat to the Roumanians. Bratianu complained that this fell short of the promises of the Treaty of 1916.

The proposed enlargement of Roumania had its price. On May 31, 1919, Bratianu and the representatives of the other small countries were invited to a plenary session of the Peace Conference to discuss the terms of the Austrian Peace Treaty. Coming only two days before the formal presentation of the treaty to Austria, the meeting was obviously no more than a formality. Nevertheless, the Roumanian Prime Minister seized the occasion to deliver a diatribe objecting to the so-called Minorities Clause of the treaty. This was an article written in by the Great Powers specifically to protect the persecuted Jews of Eastern Europe. Although the Poles, Serbs, and Czechs expressed mild objections to the Minorities Clause, only Bratianu, a highly vocal anti-Semite, refused to accept its terms.

Three days before the plenary session, the Roumanian government had passed a law giving Jews full rights of citizenship, but it was clear that the measure had been enacted purely to placate world opinion. Certainly Roumania had never felt compelled to honor her commitments to the Jews signed some forty years before in the Treaty of Berlin (1878). Continued persecution of Roumanian Jewry had resulted in what the American Delegation called "the enforced emigration" of Roumanian Jews to America. The Peace Conference, led by the Americans, now determined that the cost of expanding Roumania's frontiers at the expense of ally and enemy alike must be automatic citizenship and decent treatment for her Jews.

Along with the Minorities Clause, there were other, less savory price tags placed on the enlargement of Roumania, such as oil concessions to England,

France, and the United States. These resulted partly from Allied greed and partly from the continual scheming of the Roumanian Prime Minister. Although Bratianu intended to eventually nationalize Roumanian oil, he purposefully pitted the American, British, and French interests against one another, auctioning promises of petroleum concessions in return for famine relief, hefty loans, and sympathy toward Roumanian irredentism. When things did not go his way, he exposed the game, publicly denounced the players, and claimed that it was the "American Jews, bankers and big businessmen" who "seem to think that our country is to be turned over to them for exploitation." This kind of distortion was supported by Ferdinand, who blamed the Jews as "the cause of economical and financial crisis" after the war.

Whatever Bratianu's motivation—oil concessions he had no intention of honoring, a Minorities Clause that clashed with his prejudices, frontiers that did not conform exactly to the Treaty of 1916, Allied demands for the withdrawal of the Roumanian Army, or the high-handed manner in which the Austrian Peace Treaty was presented for his rubber stamp—the Prime Minister of Roumania announced that he would not sign the treaty and walked out of the Peace Conference in early July (1919).

In Budapest, the war and the looting raged on. A trade-union government, which ousted Bela Kun on August 1, 1919, was itself overthrown within a week by another Habsburg, Archduke Joseph, trying to reinstate the monarchy with the support of the Roumanians. Herbert Hoover recommended that the Supreme Council demand the Archduke's resignation, which it did, installing a caretaker government under four Allied generals. When the fall harvest alleviated the worst of the famine, Hoover returned to the United States, leaving the four generals in Budapest to fight with the Roumanians.

As soon as Hoover arrived home, he received a letter from Queen Marie. Written against the advice of Barbo Stirbey, it was twelve hundred words long and penned in a firm black script. "The ink itself," Hoover said, "sputtered her indignation." It was not Marie's finest literary effort, nor did she take into account the cool, Puritanical nature of the recipient. In fighting for Roumania, Marie had finally come to identify completely with its goals. No longer able to distinguish between the interests of her country and objective morality, the Queen blamed Hoover for treating Roumania "as the enemy whilst the enemy was treated as a friend" and argued that in looting Budapest her soldiers were only taking back what was stolen from them during the war. "If you are indeed the man Col. Boyle told me to go to if anything happened to him," she wrote, "then you will not misunderstand the spirit which has moved me to write these lines. Whatever happens I shall never forget how you have helped me to feed thousands and thousands of hungering children, nothing will ever be able to efface that, for that my heart will always remain grateful to you."

The concluding sop was wasted on the irate benefactor. Disillusioned by the rape of Budapest, Hoover would not be mollified. The Roumanian Army on the rampage signified for him "the weakening of that decency which we so hoped would be the reward for America's sacrifice." Like Woodrow Wilson, Hoover was appalled when his own good example did not turn the corrupt from their godless ways. He never forgave the Roumanians or their Queen.

On September 23, 1919, the Council of Four of the Peace Conference (England, France, the United States, and Italy) ordered a blockade of Roumania until she agreed to withdraw her troops from Budapest. Bratianu resigned his premiership in protest, assuming that the Hungarian victory and his artificial majority in Parliament would return him to office. They did not. This election, held according to the 1917 reform laws establishing universal suffrage and proportionate representation, drastically reduced the strength of the Prime Minister's Liberal Party in Parliament and brought to power a new coalition of Transylvanians and peasants called the National Peasant Party. Required to choose a Prime Minister from the elected majority, King Ferdinand postponed the inevitable appointment for three weeks while a Roumanian puppet government, under orders from Bratianu, infuriated the Peace Conference by holding firm to his rigid line. "Hypnotized by Bratianu" was the phrase used by the British Foreign Office to describe the King.

If Roumania's allies expected Ferdinand to throw off the Bratianu yoke, they were discounting history. Like his uncle before him, the King spoke glowingly of the Roumanian peasant but in reality feared him, particularly since Roumania had begun to look like a monarchical island in a proletarian sea. It was the Liberal Party that had brought in the dynasty fifty-three years earlier and had continued, father to son, Bratianu I to Bratianu II, to succor it. Now that the old Conservative Party had died of pro-Germanism and land reform, the Liberals were all that was left to hold aloft the banner of privilege.

Although Bratianu was, according to the King, "the best hated man in the country," it was his brother-in-law, Barbo Stirbey, who was finally sacrificed to the political forces demanding the blood of the old guard. For nearly a year, Stirbey, realizing that his presence as Head of the King's Household was endangering support for the dynasty, had tried to convince Marie that her husband should accept his resignation. In June of 1919 the Roumanian Prince took his family on a short, self-imposed exile in Western Europe "so that no one could accuse the King of being influenced by me." It was an unhappy summer for Stirbey, who suffered deeply over the separation from Marie. On his return in the fall, he gave up his position in the King's house.

Marie was devastated, personally and politically. "Nando and I would not be now where we are, if Barbo Stirbey had not stood at our side..." she wrote in her diary. "Perhaps his country will never know what he did for it, because he is a modest man... Those who send him from us will live to regret having done so." The Queen cried all morning before joining the King for the opening of the first Parliament of Greater Roumania on November 28, 1919; standing in her place at the ceremonies, she deeply resented the fact that "the man who has built up this event with us, should not be there, behind us today, to rejoice over the result."

Ferdinand finally asked Dr. Alexander Vaida-Voevod, the newly elected President of the Chamber of Deputies, to assume the post of Premier. Although Vaida-Voevod belonged to the victorious National Peasant Party, he had served on Bratianu's delegation to the Peace Conference and could be counted on to follow in the footsteps of his predecessor in negotiating the peace. His mission in Paris was helped enormously by the fact that the American Delegation was due to leave for home the day after the Roumanians presented a compromise treaty. Frank Polk, the new head of the American Delegation, allowed himself to be convinced by General Berthelot that the Minorities Clause of the Austrian treaty had been rendered superfluous by the Roumanian law of May 28, 1919, granting Jews the right to apply for Roumanian citizenship. Pressured by homesick colleagues, Polk voted to delete the Minorities Clause, substituting a feeble statement of Roumanian intent. On the evening of December 9, 1919, with their limousines waiting to take them to the station, the Americans signed a treaty modified along Roumanian lines.

The treaty was a complete triumph for Roumania. It was, according to one historian of the Peace Conference, "the Allies, not Rumania" who "capitulated in the end." While representatives of other countries worried about pleasing their electorates at home, King Ferdinand and Queen Marie had made it possible for Bratianu to manipulate in Paris without losing power in Bucharest. With the Queen smoothing his way and Lenin looming in the background, the Roumanian Prime Minister was able to capture an unwarranted share of the spoils of war. Roumania's final gains included all of Transylvania, nearly all of Bukovina, Bessarabia, the southern Dobruja and two-thirds of the Banat—more territory than was even promised in the Treaty of 1916. Her area more than doubled, from approximately 53,000 to almost 114,000 square miles. Her population increased more than 100 percent as well. She became the fifth-largest country in Europe after France, Spain, Germany, and Poland.

King Ferdinand's support of Bratianu did not extend to his successor, Vaida-Voevod. While the new Prime Minister was in Western Europe negotiating the peace settlements and trying to rebuild Roumania's shattered international prestige, the boyars used the King's suspicion of the National Peasant Party, to which Vaida-Voevod belonged, to frighten Ferdinand into getting rid of him. On March 13, 1920, in what Seton-Watson called "the most questionable act of King Ferdinand's reign," the King dismissed Vaida-

Voevod from office. In his place he appointed General Averescu, a war hero turned reactionary demagogue and violent anti-Communist. Averescu called for new elections, and since "elections in Roumania are always won by the Government that makes them," he and his hastily organized People's Party emerged victorious. Averescu was quietly supported by the Liberals, who preferred that someone else take the onus for repression. He applied himself vigorously to stamping out ethnic differences in the new provinces with the excuse that they represented leftist unrest. It was clear that Ferdinand would remain a tool of the vested interests, and it must be assumed that Marie, who based most of her political thought after World War I on fighting Communism, acquiesced in this policy.

Throughout this period of international upheaval, Marie continued to wrestle with the problems of Crown Prince Carol. She had hoped that while she was in Paris and London during the spring of 1919, the Crown Prince would have tired of his morganatic wife. When she came home in April, however, she found Carol just as attached as ever to Zizi. His first demand upon his mother's return was to be permitted to abdicate the succession, remarry Zizi, and move away from Roumania with her and their unborn child. A fortune bequeathed to him by Carol I would enable the Crown Prince to live in comfort. Before leaving for Transylvania, Marie spent hours arguing with her son, trying to get him to change his mind. While she and the King were away, she put the Crown Prince in charge of the Old Kingdom, hoping that serious duties might engage him where words had failed. When she asked him to participate in the triumphal ceremonies on their return, Carol tried to injure himself by throwing himself off his horse.

Refusing to face the fact that Carol was not the stuff of which responsible monarchs are made, the Queen continued to blame Zizi for Carol's defection. Although Zizi's ambition cannot be denied, she was not the siren Marie made her out to be. Her predicament was at least as bad as the Queen's. Young and frightened, she had thought she could turn society upside down by the brilliance of her marriage; instead, she had become a social outcast, dependent on an unstable man who seesawed between blustering protestations of power and temper tantrums.

Toward the end of May, the King asked Carol to serve on a mission to the Far East. The Crown Prince responded by shooting himself in the leg with his revolver. The wound was not serious, just bad enough to make him miss the journey. "For the first time I nearly hated my son," Marie, who had arranged the trip, wrote in her diary.

Accepting temporary defeat, the Queen sent Prince Stirbey to the Crown Prince with an offer: "Her Majesty... agrees to allow you to leave the country where you can lead your own life. But she asks you to wait three months in order to obtain legal and constitutional dispositions and to prepare public opinion." In the meantime Carol and his ex-wife were to vacation at Monastirea in the Danube delta, a humid marshland of reeds, bamboo, aquatic plants, and exotic birds. The young couple moved into what Zizi considered an unprincely house, where they were served by an A.D.C., an attendant, a chauffeur, and fifteen domestics. Pregnancy did not suit Zizi. She did not look well, and the hot, wet climate made her listless. The Crown Prince dressed her hair so she would not have to tire her arms, put on her shoes so she wouldn't have to stoop over, and got up several times each night to bring her something cool to drink.

At the end of July 1919, Carol's regiment was mobilized for the joint attack of Roumania and her allies on Bela Kun. The Queen sent Colonel Boyle and the Minister of War to Monastirea to fetch the Crown Prince. Carol erupted in fury. "Banging his fists on the table" and screaming that "the order to mobilize in this purely political expedition" was simply a trap to ensnare him, he refused to go to the front.

Joe Boyle's visit was followed by a letter from the Queen, begging Carol "in the name of all that was once sacred to him" not to let his regiment go to Hungary without him. "Is it possible that you have so lost all sense of honor and duty..." his mother asked. "Wouldn't it be better to die, a bullet in your head, to be buried in the good Roumanian earth than to betray your country?"

Carol insisted that he could not desert "the woman I have chosen for life." He offered to go to Hungary on condition he be permitted to remarry Zizi first. The King and Queen refused; "of course we do not want him under such circumstances," Marie said as she and Ferdinand left for their own tour of the front lines.

On their way into Transylvania, Ferdinand and Marie heard that Carol's train had passed theirs during the night. Pleased that her son finally had been persuaded to go to his duty, the Queen soon learned that the price of victory came high. Before joining his regiment, the Crown Prince had renounced the succession, consulting with Marghiloman and Jonescu, the two statesmen least sympathetic to the King and Queen, over the form his abdication should take to be legal. He adopted Marghiloman's version and made seven copies, one of which was addressed to his father:

> Sire:
> In light of a natural right implicitly recognized in article 83 paragraph 2 of the Constitution, I renounce my right of hereditary prince to the Crown of Roumania, for me and for my heirs as well as all those rights which are given me by the Constitution as heir to the throne. I remain the servant of my country and, in putting my sword at your service, I beg Your Majesty to give me a place among the soldiers fighting on the front.

Carol's letter of abdication, which was dated August 1, 1919, seemed like the final blow to the dynasty. Its acceptance by Parliament would mean that his younger brother would succeed to the throne, and Ferdinand and Marie knew that Prince Nicolas was not serious enough to make a good king. The Queen called in Joe Boyle, who approached the other six recipients of Carol's letter, asking them to keep it temporarily in abeyance. Meanwhile, the Queen hoped that Carol's tour of duty might change his mind.

But there was little for the Crown Prince in the way of military diversion in Hungary. By the time he had written his will and left for the front, the fighting was over. Undaunted, he marched among his soldiers, airing anti-monarchical views that were immediately quoted by the enemies of the dynasty back in Bucharest. At the same time the Crown Prince boasted to drinking companions at a banquet in Budapest that he meant to become King of Hungary "to show his father he would yet be a king and that there would be no difficulty in handling the situation."

On his return to Roumania, Carol wired his mother asking why they continued to "torture" him by not allowing Zizi to join him at his army camp at Bistritza. "All we ask of you is to do your soldier's duty and keep the promise you gave us not to forsake your country before it is out of its trouble," the Queen replied. "Your happiness, like the happiness of many another, must wait till your duty is accomplished. This is not too much to ask of a man & a prince." In reply, Marie received a spate of "nasty... ugly letters."

Marie held to her conviction that the best way to bring Carol to his senses was to keep him completely away from Zizi. Touched by her son's misery over the first separation from his ex-wife, she had arranged for them to live together, but had been quickly disenchanted by the results. According to Marie, it was the "fetid, demoralizing, degrading atmosphere" created by Zizi and the people around her that caused Carol's hostility; "a Crown Prince who leads half his life amongst such people... with such a woman... will do *none* of his duties," she said.

Separated from Zizi throughout the late summer and fall, Carol sent heartrending letters to his mother, pleading with her to send his ex-wife to him. "Have a little pity for me, don't make me suffer... Take pity, I implore you on my knees, I implore you with all my tears. Pity me," said the love-sick Prince. Marie held firm, encouraged by news from Boyle that in spite of what he said, Carol's separation from Zizi had changed his feelings for her.

During the Christmas holidays a veritable parade of dignitaries, family, and friends made its way to Bistritza to beg the Crown Prince to reassume his birthright before it was too late. Of these the most effective was Carol's close friend, a young officer named Mugur. Mugur, who adored Carol and considered him the hope of the country, finally obtained the Crown Prince's promise that he would give up Zizi for the sake of Roumania if she could be persuaded to do the same.

Two days later the Queen went to Bistritza. She had arranged to meet the Crown Prince on her train to discuss his future. Waiting for him to arrive, she focused on "those who were thinking and praying for me, of Barbo, incredulous but passionately loyal, of Boyle just as passionately loyal, but full of belief." She dimmed the lights and asked for a cup of tea to steady her nerves. The King appeared in her carriage, asking "almost timidly" if he could be present for the interview. When Carol arrived, Marie told him she had heard from Mugur that he was ready to make the "great sacrifice." Carol said that he was. He promised his parents to have nothing more to do with the socialist factions using his name to undermine the dynasty and not to see Zizi again except in the presence of Mugur. "It was the most calm interview, very loving and sober," wrote his mother, who went to bed that night "with a heart full of ardent gratitude."

The next day, January 8, 1920, Zizi gave birth to a son. "The fight with her will be deadly," commented the Queen, who heard the news en route to Bucharest on her train. The baby was named Mircea after Carol's dead brother and Roumania's national hero. "The anxiety is still that they should get Carol to recognize the child as his," Marie wrote in her diary a few days later. "All this sounds so ruthless, would be so ruthless, if the woman were not quite such a beast." The baby was registered under the name of Lambrino; "another danger overcome," wrote the Queen.

Within less than a month Marie's worries were over, and Carol's relationship with Zizi was at an end. Although the Crown Prince wrote his ex-wife after the birth of their child, promising that the three of them would "soon be the happiest and most united family possible," the letter, signed "Yours for life," was quickly followed by another, written at the same time, informing Zizi that they could not marry in Roumania and "if they went away together it would be *la misère noire* [black misery]." Shortly thereafter, Mugur came to tell the Queen that Carol had completed the rupture with a letter to Zizi and one to his father declaring his intention of reassuming his royal status and duties. Taking no chances on another change of heart, the King and Queen sent the Crown Prince on an eight-month cruise around the world. Before he left, his mother promised she would try to "make things possible" for Zizi and his child.

"I quite realized," the Queen wrote later, "that for some I must seem a tremendously ambitious woman who got her way, destroying my son's happiness because of my formidable pride, crushing another woman, casting her out into darkness..." Marie's rancor toward Zizi certainly contrasts with the kindness she showed another castoff of Carol's life, the little milliner of Bucharest. While the Crown Prince fought to abdicate for the woman he said he loved, his mother was quietly picking up the pieces of his still unbroken liaison with the other girl by arranging support for her and her offspring. But the milliner had not presumed to poach on royal territory; an affair was not a marriage. "Each mother has the right to fight for her child's life," Marie said, "and in this case the Queen was fighting for her country as well."

• • •

It was Joe Boyle to whom Marie gave most of the credit for Carol's return to the fold; "he and I alone believed *really* that we would win," she wrote in her diary. For Boyle, saving Carol for the dynasty had been a crusade like feeding the starving peasants or rescuing the Queen's relatives from Russia. He had visited the Crown Prince in Hungary, bargained with Zizi, and kept constant surveillance on the girl's friends, who threatened to publish Carol's love letters. Boyle had lobbied with parliamentary leaders to keep them from acting on Carol's abdication. Roundly resented by the politicians for his intrusion into governmental affairs, he had stormed ahead with his mission, mindful of no one but Marie, whom he loved.

But the triumph over Zizi signaled the end of Boyle's sojourn in Roumania. In April of 1920, just two months after Carol's departure on his world tour, Marie told Boyle that he must leave. Roumanian politicians, she said, were jealous of his place at court. In later years the Queen admitted that there was also a more personal reason, that she was "torn between two loyalties and two affections. It was unbearable to me to hurt anyone and yet I was hurting them and myself even more."

Joe Boyle had never really understood Marie's feelings for Stirbey. He had chosen to believe that the Roumanian Prince was a political opportunist and often chastised the Queen for her dependence on him. Confronted by the truth, Boyle was deeply hurt but gentlemanly. He had once promised Marie that he would not leave Roumania until the Carol business was settled; he stuck to his word, arranging support for Zizi's child and dealing with the financial demands of the young milliner. This was hardly "a man's work" in the lexicon of Klondike Boyle, but he stayed on for a few months, mopping up after Marie's son and trying to be "properly thankful for having been allowed a glimpse of what real happiness is." In spite of his attempts at gallantry, he wrote the Queen in June of 1920 that he was "going through the worst mental trouble of my life. I don't think that in my whole manhood I actually knew what fear was until that night at Sinaia that you told me I must go."

On leaving Roumania, Boyle went to work for Royal Dutch Shell; he returned to Roumania only once more, in 1921. Marie and Boyle continued to correspond. She wrote him long letters about her children, wishing her "dear big pal" were there to share the good things with her. He wrote about his broken heart: "it became impossible for you to keep your old friend and me," he said a year later. "I am gone, do not let me be a shadow on your life. You never owed me anything, always you gave and I am grateful and love you, remember only that."

In the fall of 1919 Marie saw her mother for the first time since the war. The Queen had been trying to visit the Duchess of Coburg ever since the Armistice, but she was not allowed to enter Germany. Their reunion was arranged by Prince Stirbey, who had spent the summer of his political exile in Western Europe tending to family matters for the Queen. Along with doctors for Ileana and a possible Italian husband for Elisabetha, Stirbey found a reliable escort to bring the Duchess to Zurich, where Marie met her in September.

The autocratic daughter of the Tsar, once the richest princess in Europe, had lost nearly everything. Her Russian family had been murdered; Germany, her beloved adopted country, had been vanquished. Her Russian income, the mainstay of her wealth, was in the hands of the Communists. The former resident of gilt and marble palaces had moved to a shabby annex of the Hotel Dolder Grand, the Waldhaus, "an awful little *pension*..." according to one of the Duchess's granddaughters, "very refugee-like."

The meeting was not easy for Marie. During the war her mother had lost both weight and conviction. She was bent forward and walked with uncertainty. Her hands, formerly plump and sure, had become "thin and rather trembling." She still blamed Marie for her role in the war and accused her of rejoicing over the devastating peace terms forced on the Germans. Shocked to be powerful when her mother was not, Marie hesitated to fight back or even express her love. "I want to take her in my arms and let her cry & cry myself, but it is the one offense she would never pardon me... There is the old autocrat in her, slumbering beneath all her outward humility... that is the part I must leave alone & not touch."

Prince Stirbey joined Marie in Switzerland, where they could stroll the streets incognito. "When people are not particularly amiable I try to thaw them with my own personal 'charm' to see how far it can go without my royalty," Marie said. "I discover it goes a good way and that flatters my 43 years." There was no better companion than Barbo. "Never have I seen a man more patient than he with women," the Queen once wrote in her diary.

From Switzerland Marie, accompanied by Stirbey and Elisabetha, took the Duchess for a vacation in Florence. The Queen returned home saddened by her mother's state of mind, promising to visit again the following summer. She continued her practice, begun immediately after the war, of sending money and gifts to her mother and sisters, and she wrote King George on the slim chance that he could get the Soviet government to fulfill the financial obligations of the Duchess of Coburg's Russian marriage contract.

The Duchess was not much better when the Queen visited her the following year, lashing out in her frustration at her eldest daughter for "God knows what far-off lapses" and "certain half hours in my life when I did wrong." The old woman went so far as to list Marie's transgressions for Prince Stirbey. Reminding her that she was speaking to one of the Queen's subjects, Stirbey defended Marie by saying that whatever her mother thought of her, she was "one of the most loved queens" of history and "a worthy and dignified" sovereign. "I am not such a complete failure," Marie wrote a friend, "but [she] continues to bicker, bicker about quite forgotten things I did or left undone. She never admitted that I had any intelligence, only a certain smiling good nature & a sunny face that bamboozled the world. Poor dear, stormy old Mama!"

In spite of this, Marie's summer journey of 1920 was a happy one. She took Ileana and Elisabetha to Paris with her to see Mignon, who had been away in school in England for the past year, and they were all joined by Nicky. She brought her sister Ducky to France for a vacation and saw Baby Bee. She was in Paris for the premiere of Loie Fuller's ballet *The Lily of Life*, based on one of the Queen's own fairy tales.

This trip to Western Europe was a prelude to what seemed like a series of fortunate developments in Marie's family. Soon after her return to Roumania, her two elder children, long a great worry, took on appropriate spouses, starting a trio of marriages that would earn their mother new respect and the nickname "Mother-in-law of the Balkans."

Chapter *23*

> The affairs of the royal house form a
> subject of conversation for those who,
> as a rule, would have no conversation.
>
> —*MARTHE BIBESCO*

*P*rincess Elisabetha of Roumania first met Crown
Prince George of Greece when she was sixteen and he was twenty-one. Three
years later he proposed to her. Marie and Ferdinand were anxious to settle
their eldest daughter in marriage: "... we had hoped that an engagement
would be forthcoming," Ferdinand wrote his brother Wilhelm. "That this
did not happen was mainly Aunt Elisabeth's fault." In 1914 Queen Elisabeth
told her namesake that she could do far better than George, and young
Elisabetha agreed. By 1920, at the age of twenty-five, Elisabetha had been
forced to retire her more extravagant fantasies.

Crown Prince George of Greece was a solid young man. Dark, short, his
erect figure buttoned tightly into an army tunic, a monocle glistening in his
eye, he reminded contemporaries of a proper Englishman—courteous, benign, and rather dull. "God started him but forgot to finish him off," said
Elisabetha. Whereas loving relations pointed to George's honesty, decency,

and infectious laugh, historians dismissed him as a royal cipher with no talent for politics.

George's romantic perceptions were on a par with his political acumen. No one could say that he had not known Elisabetha long enough to gauge that she would never be the comfort of his old age. Nevertheless, when they met in Switzerland after World War I, he asked her again to marry him. Elisabetha could not make up her mind. The Duchess of Coburg, with whom she was staying, said that George "ought to beat her, then she would like him!" Marie shared her mother's concern over Elisabetha's "slumbering depths" and realized that her daughter had a "brutal, almost cruel, reckless" side to her. She was delighted when Elisabetha finally accepted George's proposal in the fall of 1920.

Marie could not have asked for a better family for her eldest daughter. George's father, King Constantine of Greece, was the younger brother of Dowager Queen Alexandra of England; his mother, Queen Sophie, a sister of the Kaiser, was Marie's first cousin. Beyond lineage, George had little to offer Elisabetha, as his political future was bleak. The diplomatic machinations that accompanied the entrance of the smaller nations into World War I had nearly destroyed the Greek royal family. Struggling to keep Greece neutral, King Constantine had been outmaneuvered by his pro-Entente Prime Minister, Eleutherios Venizelos, who brought Greece into the war on the side of the Allies. Constantine was forced to abdicate for himself and his eldest son, George. Since 1917, George's younger brother, Alexander, had been serving as a figurehead King in Athens, while the rest of the family lived in exile in Switzerland.

Marie was nonetheless delighted with the proposed marriage. Although she knew that a match with a homeless, penniless George would be unpopular with the Roumanians, she had assured Elisabetha that she would "stand by her whatever comes, unless she wants to run away with someone not of our class!" Marie invited George to accompany Elisabetha back to Roumania for the announcement of the engagement. Along with George, she invited his two sisters, Helen, aged twenty-four, and Irene, aged sixteen.

As the Queen was ordering the royal train, Crown Prince Carol arrived in Switzerland from his trip around the world. Although Carol had written during the voyage about his "constant and burning sadness" over Zizi, he seemed to be in a surprisingly good mood and announced that he would like to accompany his future brother-in-law back to Roumania. The train carrying the party of young people traveled straight to Sinaia, where the Greeks were installed at the Pelisor, Marie's summer castle.

The Queen was gratified with the change in her elder son. She was nearly as pleased with herself for having invited the Greek Princesses to Roumania; "this idea of having a cheerful company of his class in the house on his return was decidedly a clever move," she reported in a letter to Joe Boyle. Marie arranged all sorts of amusement for her visitors, sending them out on excursions into the countryside in order to give "the young ones occasion to become really acquainted with each other." It was obvious that Carol was attracted to Helen, the older of the two Princesses; "she is just the right sort of girl for attracting," said Marie, who had been impressed by the girl's prettiness and charm when she first met her in Switzerland.

A tall brunette, elegant, slim, and fine-boned, Princess Helen of Greece, who was known in the family as Sitta, was even more innocent of the world than most princesses of her day. She had been jolted out of an insular family life by her father's abdication and suffered deeply over the family's humiliations in exile. Whisked off with her sister to Roumania, fussed over by Queen Marie, and entertained by the attentive Crown Prince, she soon "lost her heart" to Carol.

Their country idyll was shattered by the sudden news that Sitta's childhood companion, King Alexander, had been bitten by a pet monkey in the gardens of the family residence near Athens and had died of blood poisoning. The young woman was desolated by the death of her favorite brother and asked to return immediately to her parents in Switzerland. The next day, before she could leave, word came of the death of the Duchess of Coburg. Marie's mother had died in her sleep in the annex of the Hotel Dolder Grand in Zurich.

The Queen prepared to leave at once for Switzerland with the two Greek Princesses. Prince Stirbey would escort her, while George and Elisabetha stayed in Sinaia with the King. Carol said he wanted to accompany his mother. As he left, Ileana put her arms around his neck and whispered that he should "bring Sitta back" with him. On the train the Queen noted with pleasure that her son and the pretty young Princess seemed to be "coming to an understanding."

When she arrived in Zurich, Marie discovered that she could not follow Ducky and Baby Bee into Germany to bury their mother at Coburg or see her German sister, Sandra, without provoking an international incident. Heartbroken, she wandered around Zurich, taking long walks in the woods with Barbo while waiting for her sisters to return. Although Marie had adored her difficult mother, she did not regret her passing; the humbling circumstances under which the Tsar's daughter had lived at the end made her life far more tragic than her death. "She was profoundly religious," Marie wrote a friend. "I hope God will not disappoint her as most things & beings did in this life."

When Ducky and Baby Bee finally appeared, the three sisters sat down to read their mother's memoirs. They were touched by the picture of the Duchess as a sulky child at the mercy of her tormenting governess. The Queen's principal inheritance from her mother was a fabulous set of pearls that the Duchess had brought out of Germany and placed in a bank in Switzerland along with comparable sets of jewels for each of her other daughters. Marie took the pearls to be appraised; one alone was worth 400,000 Swiss francs.

Within a few days of their arrival in Switzerland, Carol asked Sitta to marry him. Marie was overjoyed. "I feel that I have quite saved my boy," she said, adding only that she wished her mother were still alive to share her delight. She thought of Joe Boyle, the man who "fought this great battle with me...God bless him & my young couple," she wrote happily in her diary. The Queen had a talk with King Constantine, who agreed to his daughter's marriage providing Carol had "quite finished" with Zizi. Marie assured him that she and Ferdinand would not permit their son to marry unless he had.

On the surface it looked like an excellent match for the Greek royal house. At twenty-seven, Crown Prince Carol of Roumania stood something over six feet tall; he was broad-shouldered with a head of wavy dark-blond hair and a thick, clipped moustache. His face would have appeared childlike were it not for an angry flicker in his pale-blue eyes and a scowl that drew his brows together. But what would have been considered ordinary looks in a commoner passed for handsomeness in a future king. Playing over the strings of a tragic and stormy past, the Crown Prince of Roumania convinced the Greek Princess that she in her innocence could provide him with gentle salvation.

Unlike Elisabetha, who was settling for a loveless union, Carol and even Sitta, ordinarily restrained, displayed a strong attraction for each other. "They were madly in love," said one of Carol's younger sisters, recalling the days of their engagement; "he was *wildly* in love." "She is quite the follower, he the leader, impetuous, tyrannical... but he is desperately in love," the Queen wrote Elisabetha's old governess.

Whatever the pleasures of his new passion, Carol still had accounts to settle in the matter of the old one. Remembering how she had been kept in the dark about her husband's first love, the Queen urged her son to tell his fiancée about Zizi. He must have expressed himself very well, for his mother said that after their talk, they seemed to be even better friends than before.

As to Zizi, Carol refused to see her, communicating instead by mail: "Do not believe I was disarmed without a struggle. I resisted up until the last extremity, and it was only at the moment when I saw I was alone that I declared myself beaten. Yes my poor little one, it is true that I am engaged and engaged to a princess. That is so against my principles that I am myself even the most astonished... I have found someone who can understand me and who in theories of life has the same ideas as I. She has agreed to be the consolation of a heart profoundly bruised. I would have wished to wait, to let a little time blur things, but circumstances independent of our will caused us to act more quickly. Yes, such is life."

As a settlement, Zizi said she wanted Carol's property at Monastirea or five million French francs and a title for their son. When she was asked to return the jewels Carol had given her on the ground that they had belonged to Queen Elisabeth and were the last family jewels left outside Moscow, she refused. Prince Stirbey was sent to change her mind. He told Carol's ex-wife that she would be given the income from a specified amount of capital placed in a Paris bank to support her and her child, a sum from which the value of the disputed parure would be deducted. When Carol was told of the incident he refused to become involved. "The affair is out of my hands," he said. "What she [Zizi] cannot get over and which from a woman's point of view I quite understand," Queen Marie wrote in her diary, "is that Carol never came to see the child."

While Carol's family settled with his ex-wife, the fortunes of his fiancée and her family were dramatically improving. The death of Sitta's brother Alexander precipitated a plebiscite, held to determine if Greece wanted to restore Constantine to the throne. The King had always enjoyed great personal popularity, and in spite of Allied denunciations, the Greeks voted overwhelmingly to recall him. In December of 1920, King Constantine, Queen Sophie, and their children returned to Athens in glory; "every royal heart, even if it does not care for the man, beats more quickly because it is a great triumph in the cause of kings," Marie wrote Joe Boyle.

Carol followed his fiancée and her family to Athens after the first of the year. It was spring in the south; the roses were blooming and oranges were hanging from the trees. The Crown Prince had his own car and drove Sitta around the countryside. They visited ancient monuments, where Carol endeared himself to the Greeks with his intellectual curiosity and knowledge of their ancient civilization. "I'm feeling very happy," he wrote his mother, "and feel that we understand each other every day better."

On February 27, 1921, in the first of two ceremonies linking the Roumanian and Greek dynasties, Princess Elisabetha of Roumania married Crown Prince George of Greece in Bucharest. The Queen was delighted by her new son-in-law's change of status; "although they were engaged when he was a homeless, countryless, fortuneless Prince, he is again Crown Prince and has both house and position to offer her." Marie dressed carefully for the wedding in subdued gray and gold so as not to outshine the bride.

As a wedding gift, Ferdinand and Marie gave Elisabetha a chain of diamonds with a huge sapphire pendant, which Marie had bought from Ducky. She was furious that the King and Queen of Greece sent nothing to her daughter: "Not the smallest tiniest little atom of anything... Sophy has *all* her jewels, I lost *all* mine, yet we have made tremendous efforts to send her daughter a beautiful diadem!"

No one loved jewels more than the Queen of Roumania, and the Russian expropriation of the Roumanian crown jewels had left her bereft. Although the Kremlin offered to recognize Roumania's right to Bessarabia if Roumania gave up the claim to its gold and Marie's crown jewels, the Queen refused. "My jewels were my dowry... my father died with debts, my mother died ruined by the Russian revolution... my only reserve would have been those jewels." In former days, she said, she would have been happy to buy secure frontiers for her country. But having seen the eclipse of monarchy in Europe and aware of the capricious nature of her position, Marie felt she dared not relinquish even the claim to her jewels. To replace them, King Ferdinand had given her money to buy Ducky's jewelry, inherited from Kirill's mother. Although Marie felt uncomfortable taking the last of her sister's beautiful things, she realized that it was fortunate for Ducky that she could buy them at full value and pay immediately.

As soon as Elisabetha and George's wedding was over, the entire Roumanian royal family except the King traveled to Athens for Carol's wedding to Helen of Greece. There is a law in the Orthodox Church that when brother and sister marry sister and brother, the ceremonies must take place within the same hour. Since Marie did not intend to miss her son's wedding, she petitioned the Church for dispensation to allow the second ceremony to follow the first within two weeks. Greek peasants shook their heads over the flouting of tradition, predicting it would bring bad luck to both couples.

The superstitions of peasants did not phase the Queen but the attitude of the Western countries did. Britain and France could hardly be expected to approve a double alliance between their Roumanian ally and a dynasty they had hounded off the throne. Marie had tried to forestall the inevitable Allied objections by writing King George immediately after the announcement of Carol and Sitta's engagement, proclaiming "the great joy for us and the country after all the cruel trouble we had with him a short while ago." But for all Marie's efforts, rumors of international disapproval filtered back to Roumania. The Queen shrugged them off. The past few years had taught her one unforgettable lesson in international relations: although Britain and France were ever ready with moral directives for their small allies, they were no help when it came to saving their dynasties. In a letter to Leile Milne, the Queen of Roumania justified her brand of diplomacy: "I know that these marriages are looked upon as unfortunate by some... but little countries cannot always sacrifice themselves to the frowns and smiles of their big cousins, they MUST live their own lives and work out their own fate. For us the important thing was that Carol should be saved and for that I thank God with every breath of my life."

To ensure his continued salvation, the Queen wrote Carol a week before his wedding. "I fought a mighty battle for you to put you back on the straight road," she said, "now it lies before you to walk straight upon it."

Declaring himself madly in love, Crown Prince Carol of Roumania married Princess Helen of Greece in Athens. Like Elisabetha, Helen was the first princess of her country to be married there, and the crowds, dressed in their best and lined several deep on the streets, cheered loudly as she drove by in the state coach with her new husband. Musing over the events of the day in her diary that evening, Marie thought again of Joe Boyle, to whom she owed "my faithful thanks and a thought of warm gratitude this day." She wished that Nando had been able to attend Carol's wedding, "but," she wrote, "it was especially *my* right to be there because it was *I* who saved my son."

Carol and his bride honeymooned for a week at the family home of Tatoi outside Athens, then returned to her family before going home to Roumania. During the hiatus between her son's wedding and his return, Marie traveled around Greece, savoring its glories with typical exuberance. In "a trance of beauty and revelation," she visited ancient sites, collecting marbles, statues, amphorae, and the crowns of ancient stone capitals for her Roumanian palaces. She returned home laden with treasures in time to greet Carol and his bride, who arrived in Roumania at the beginning of May. The Queen learned with joy that her new daughter-in-law was already pregnant.

Helen was now the third Roumanian Crown Princess to make a formal entry into Bucharest. She and Carol came by train from Constantza and descended at the station into the waiting arms of the King, the Queen, and the rest of the royal family. Observing that the crowds were not particularly enthusiastic, Queen Marie attributed their lack of fervor to her son's amorous past. Nevertheless, she felt she had provided a perfectly orchestrated, highly organized reception, shortened as much as possible in the interests of her daughter-in-law's delicate condition.

Princess Helen, who had been unwell since the onset of her pregnancy, brought her old family doctor with her to Roumania. Marie was pleased. "I for one know what it is to be homesick and to have no one from the old country near one," she wrote a friend, recalling her own introduction to Roumania twenty-eight years before, "though her case is a little different than mine, she knows her husband better than I knew mine, she also knows her mother-in-law, and her father-in-law is not a severe man—and above all there is less difference between Greece and Roumania, than between England and Roumania... besides she is 24 and I was 17."

The new Crown Princess was remarkably good-natured about being thrust into the wake of such an overwhelming mother-in-law. The force of the Queen's personality completely dominated the life of the court, which was far more sophisticated than the one in Greece. In Athens the family dined alone and struggled for conversation. At Cotroceni Palace Queen Marie led both family and guests in lively discussions of current affairs and palace improvements. One topic of interest in the spring of 1921 was the Queen's garden, severely damaged during the war and now under reconstruction. While Marie planned new terraces and flower beds, fussing at the high cost of court life and the niggardliness of politicians, Carol's wife marveled at what seemed to her the "greater luxury of the Roumanian Court" compared with the one in Greece.

Although Marie did everything she could to make her son and his bride comfortable, Carol was anxious to move out of Cotroceni Palace. Since the newlyweds returned to Roumania in late spring, it was not long before they could escape to Sinaia. There they took up residence in the Foisor, a neglected and musty Swiss chalet built by Carol I as a temporary residence on the grounds of Castle Peles.

The Crown Princess had already begun to guess that in the first flush of attraction, she might have misjudged her husband's basic nature. When she questioned the Crown Prince about a damaged alarm clock on the shelf of his study, he explained casually that he had thrown it "at Zizi's head." If she was surprised by his displays of temper, he was stunned by her lack of intellectual curiosity. Carol loved to read; his bride was more interested in clothes and interior decoration. He had a passion for music; she accepted it as a cultural propriety. When he sat down to work on his stamp collection, she crawled into his lap. She didn't understand why he grew impatient, although it soon became apparent that they had little in common.

With Carol and his bride settled in Sinaia, Queen Marie took a trip to Transylvania to inspect an old fortress recently given to her by the citizens of the city of Brasov. The fortress was then and is still called Castle Bran. One of the seven strongholds built by the Knights of the Teutonic Order, its foundations date back to the Crusades; until Marie took it over, Bran had never been inhabited. Covering the entire wooded spur of a hill, it appears from the road as a jumble of turrets, towers, and parapets, irregular, thick whitewashed walls with heavy hewn timbers and balconies; once inside, it is no less picturesque, with oddly shaped corners, tiny rooms on many levels, quaint fireplaces, and beautiful old tiled stoves. The Queen made it habitable. She filled the castle with dark Renaissance and baroque furniture and planted elaborate gardens on the flat ground below.

Well suited to Marie's extravagantly romantic taste, Castle Bran quickly took on the look of a Slavic fairy tale. "Everything," she said as she ransacked forgotten corners of Castle Peles for Persian pottery and old silver, "must be quaint and old in Bran." "The whole effect achieved," said Sacheverell Sitwell fifteen years later, "is of that adapted Byzantinism which is associated with its Royal owner." Untitled visitors, Marie soon discovered, found Bran more enchanting than did other royalties. "Missy, not at YOUR age!" sniffed Queen Sophie of Greece when Marie, an indefatigable guide, took her up and down all the stairways of her Transylvanian fantasy.

From Transylvania Queen Marie traveled to France to visit Ducky, who had made her way to Western Europe and was living in a small house she had leased on the coast of Brittany. Her husband, Grand Duke Kirill, had just proclaimed himself "Guardian of the Throne," an honor over which there were heated arguments in the Russian emigrant community. The aristocratic survivors of the Revolution did not all agree with Kirill's assumption of the mantle of the Tsars. They pointed out that his uncle, Grand Duke Nicholas, former Commander in Chief of the Russian Army, offered better credentials of age and experience, while his young cousin, Grand Duke Dimitri, who had taken an active part in the murder of Rasputin, deserved more than just loyalist gratitude. Since the Dowager Empress, matriarch of the Romanov clan, refused to believe the story of her son's death, she claimed there was no dynastic question at all.

Marie, who had heard much of the muttering and grumbling of the *société émigrée*, was not particularly enthusiastic about Kirill's new status, although she realized that Ducky encouraged her husband as a means of his regaining confidence. Kirill had suffered a nervous breakdown the previous year; he had been unable to cross the street without holding Ducky's hand or sleep unless she sat up next to him. Now the Grand Duke rose promptly every day at sunrise. He withdrew into his study to issue Orders, offer Imperial Thanks, sign Promotions, and send out Imperial Directives. Since the recipients of these pronouncements and documents were often taxi drivers, waiters, and titled gigolos, Marie questioned their significance. While Kirill acted the part of the Tsar, Ducky worked in their garden and worried about their future. Marie found her sister badly lined, overworked, and too tired to think about her personal appearance. "No home, no fortune... no hope—trying to keep things together, to make both ends meet, with a family accustomed to live in utmost luxury" was how she described her sister's predicament.

Toward the end of Marie's stay in France, Joe Boyle arrived to see what he could do to help the struggling Grand Duchess. "Perhaps for her they will let him work, they won't let him work for me..." Marie wrote bitterly in her diary; "they all consider me a blind fool in my trust of this dear big man who has been like a father and elder brother to me ever since I knew him."

While Marie was in Brittany with her sister, Ferdinand met his older brother, Wilhelm, Head of the House of Hohenzollern-Sigmaringen, for the first time since 1914. The reconciliation was important to the King, whose family had not until then forgiven him for his role in the war. The Queen was delighted for her husband. She was also pleased that Nando visited the family castle at Weinburg without her. "[Wilhelm] seems to prefer it like that," she noted. "I am so relieved as I was dreading the encounter."

Ferdinand's welcome by the Head of his House was preceded by a partial pardon from the Catholic Church. Ever since 1900, the King of Roumania had been refused Communion because he had allowed his children to be christened in the Orthodox faith. It was not until the spring of 1920, a year after Prince Stirbey visited Rome on his behalf, that Ferdinand was allowed to take Holy Communion once again. "Being a true believer," Marie said, "this means much to him."

After Marie's return in the fall, on October 25, 1921, Crown Princess Helen gave birth to a son. The confinement was complicated, and for some time the lives of both mother and baby were in danger. The Crown Princess was attended by her family doctor, her mother's nurse sent from Athens, and the Queen. "It was a terrible battle... the room looked like a slaughterhouse," said Marie, who herself administered chloroform and helped the doctors. As soon as she could leave the room, the Queen hurried to tell Carol about his son, indulging in a quiet weep on his shoulder before rushing off to inform the rest of the family. The baby was named Mihai (Michael) for the hero who had united Wallachia, Moldavia, and Transylvania in the sixteenth century.

Within a few weeks of the birth of the heir to the throne, a house on the Chaussée Kisselev was found for the Crown Prince and his new family. Harrods of London was engaged to do the decoration. With renovations still in progress, Carol and Sitta moved in during December with their infant and household. Faced with months of domestic unheaval, put off by Carol's ardor, which she did not feel well enough to reciprocate, and concerned about her father, who was ill and again in political trouble, Sitta asked King Ferdinand for permission to take her baby home for a visit.

The Crown Princess spent the next four months in Greece with her family. Her absence, coming within less than a year of her wedding, was destructive to the marriage. When she finally returned to Bucharest in April of 1922, Helen found her new home ready for occupancy and her husband amusing himself elsewhere.

Chapter 24

There is no politician in Europe whose brain could offset the workings of Queen Marie's womb.

—ANONYMOUS EUROPEAN POLITICIAN

While Queen Marie was celebrating the continuation of the dynasty, a third Balkan king, Alexander of Yugoslavia,* had begun looking for allies and a wife. Of medium height, narrow-shouldered, pale and myopic, Alexander looked like the least prepossessing monarch of the twentieth century. His appearance was deceiving. Highly intelligent, ambitious, and politically skillful, Alexander had taken over the reins of the Serbian government from an ailing father and a mad older brother at the beginning of World War I. While still in his twenties, serving as his country's Regent, Alexander personally led his soldiers in the heroic struggles of the war. He emerged from the Paris Peace Conference with his original territory

*From the end of World War I until 1929, what we now call Yugoslavia was known officially as the Kingdom of the Serbs, Croats, and Slovenes. For purposes of simplification the name Yugoslavia is used here.

plus Croatia, Slovenia, bits of Macedonia, and the whole of Montenegro. In 1921 King Alexander was a major power in the Balkans.

He had not been born to rule. The son of an impoverished pretender, Alexander grew up in Geneva. In 1903, following one of the bloodiest coups in the history of Eastern Europe, Alexander's father, Peter Karageorgevich, mounted the Serbian throne. Peter proved an honest ruler and led his country to victory in the Balkan Wars. During that time Alexander, who was a student in the St. Petersburg Military Academy, fell in love with one of the daughters of the Tsar. World War I interrupted his suit, and in 1918 the Bolsheviks murdered his childhood sweetheart. He never fell in love again. Turning to the practical matter of building a dynasty, he started discreet inquiries regarding Princess Mignon of Roumania.

By the spring of 1921 both Yugoslavia and Roumania had signed treaties of alliance with Czechoslovakia; in June of that year Yugoslavia and Roumania signed their own alliance, completing the tricornered Little Entente, dedicated to protecting their newly acquired territories from Hungarian revisionism. Take Jonescu, long a proponent of Balkan unity and currently Foreign Minister, came to ask Queen Marie if she would give Mignon to the Yugoslav King. Marie made no promises. "Speak to my daughter. We will never force her. If you can succeed in convincing her, so much the better."

At twenty-one Mignon was no different than she had been as a child— easygoing and unselfish. "I always said about Mignon," the Queen wrote in her diary, "that if she had been poor, she would have been the one who would have kept the household together. She would have cooked and would have tended the children, nursed the sick, run the messages, carried in the wood, dug up the potatoes." As a young princess, Mignon had been happiest playing the role of go-between, running from her new friend Sitta to her brother Carol, from her sister Elisabetha to George of Greece. She had declared at the time of the others' weddings that she would never marry.

Jonescu knew enough about the Queen's second daughter not to discuss the political alliance dear to his heart, but to talk about a lonely young man with no parents and an insane brother, a poor little rich king in an empty palace who needed a queen to cheer his life and give him a family. Mignon was moved, and Alexander was invited to Sinaia for the Christmas holidays, "the time of all the year," according to the Princess, "when it must be most sad to be alone without family." A week or so after New Year's, Mignon took her suitor through the snow-covered forests on a tour of Castle Peles. They were gone some time. When they returned, she was leading him by the hand. The King of Yugoslavia spoke no English. "Mother, we have arranged it," said Mignon, who burst into tears and ran quickly out of the room.

Queen Marie was concerned. Although she knew Alexander had an excellent personal reputation and that the alliance would be extremely popular in both countries, he was, in her words, "an outsider of unsure race." Shy, uncommunicative, the King of Yugoslavia volunteered nothing about himself. Marie could not understand how her daughter could have accepted him so readily without knowing him better: "... what does Mignon know about married physical obligations, my good, dear, fat, unselfish, good-natured Mignon who is more like a full-blown peony than anything else... It reminds me rather dreadfully of myself... I hated marriage, and my mother encouraged me to hate it, which, of course, I shall not do to Mignon."

The Princess herself seemed to have no anxieties, announcing her new status with pride to everyone around and insisting upon telegraphing government officials herself. The most enthusiastic reaction of all came from the exiled Tsar Ferdinand of Bulgaria, who pronounced his niece Queen Marie "a genius."

Shortly after the official engagement, Marie traveled to Belgrade to inspect her daughter's future home. The capital of an uneasy patchwork kingdom, Belgrade had none of the cultural sophistication of Bucharest and no aristocracy. King Alexander lived the life of a simple soldier, sleeping on a cot and working at an old camp table in a small house across from the royal palace. After the wedding he planned to move with his bride into the old palace, an elegant but uncomfortable home where the bedrooms for the royal couple were at opposite ends of the building "with a kilometre between," separated by armed guards. Marie made arrangements for Alexander and Mignon to live together in one wing of the palace with interconnecting suites, and she ordered all the "stiff and excessively rich" Louis XVI furniture removed from their quarters. She was shocked to find that the entire personnel of the palace was male, "not even the laundry being done by women."

On her return to Bucharest, Marie attempted to wreak a transformation in this placid, plump daughter, pushing her into fine dresses that showed up an incipient prettiness and befitted her new station. But Mignon did not jump easily from background to foreground. "I cannot get her to hold herself upright and she loves to sit with her knees far apart and her toes turned inward," the Queen complained. When Alexander was not around, her mother caught Mignon back in her old shapeless hand-me-down dresses from Elisabetha. Reprimanded by the elegant Queen, Mignon was unashamed. "Oh! Mamma, do let me be ugly for one hour a day. It is such a rest!"

Undaunted, Marie planned her daughter's wardrobe. Although the future Queen of Yugoslavia was "still actually very stout," she was also "very sweet looking" with her innocent cherub face, long blond hair, and pink complexion. For her entry into Belgrade, Mignon would wear a gown of white crepe de chine, a hat of pink roses, and a pink crepe de chine cloak to match. For the wedding she would be gowned in white crepe georgette with a silver court train. "When she holds herself well," Marie said, "she can look tall and stately."

It had been decided that Mignon would enter her new country by water. Early in June, Marie, her daughter, and other members of the family boarded the royal yacht, which took them up the Danube to the port of Belgrade. As they sailed up the river, Yugoslavian peasants gathered on the shores to wave banners and cheer. A steamer carrying young girls in white dresses came to meet them; the girls sang and threw flowers into the water. Marie made Mignon stand away from the other members of the family so that "the crowds should realize which was their future Queen." The bride's mother savored this sort of tribute, giving it more significance than it warranted. "Really a sight for Kings," she exclaimed, as they drew into Belgrade where brilliantly colored bunting streamed from the masts of ships, church bells were pealing, and guns boomed deafening salutes.

In striking contrast to his bachelor frugality, King Alexander had bought fantastic jewels to decorate his Queen. "Everything was there," gasped Marthe Bibesco, "that the kings of old could have found to adorn their chosen brides." The most beautiful of these were a diadem and matching necklace of emeralds; they had belonged to Mignon's maternal great-grandmother, the wife of Tsar Alexander II—"imperial stones, the like of which I hadn't seen since Russia," said Marie as she arranged them on her daughter for the gala banquet the night before the wedding.

During the ceremony the bride impressed the guests with her simple dignity. To receive the crown of Yugoslavia, Mignon lifted her head, and those close to her were struck with her resemblance, never noted before, to Queen Victoria. At about the same time a Yugoslav officer, standing in the cathedral next to one of Marie's ladies-in-waiting, pointed to another section of the church. "See that column, Madame?... Well, that was where I was on duty the night when that other Alexander [Obrenovich, the unfortunate object of the coup of 1903] was butchered twenty years ago, and thrown out of the window with his Queen."

Not long after Mignon was settled on the Yugoslavian throne, Queen Marie received word of the unexpected if not unwelcome advancement of her eldest daughter, Elisabetha, to the throne of Greece. As they had five years earlier, the enemies of King Constantine succeeded in overthrowing the old and popular monarch in 1922 and replacing him with one of his sons, always easier for the Venizelists to manipulate. On September 27, 1922, Constantine's oldest son ascended the throne under the name of George II of Greece, and Marie's eldest daughter became his Queen.

Elisabetha was in Bucharest at the time, recovering from a nearly fatal case of typhoid that had been followed by pleurisy. A brave patient, the new Queen of Greece was a difficult convalescent. Forced to cut her hair because it was falling out, she dyed it red, stained her eyebrows pitch black, powdered her face white, and applied dark makeup to accentuate the black circles under her eyes. "She absolutely cultivated her tragic, ghostlike appearance,"

Queen Marie complained. Marie was even more concerned with Elisabetha's state of mind. "She seems to me in every way utterly unprepared for such an event. She has as yet neither interest nor love for the country. She has studiously refused to have a child, she knows no one, she cares for no one, she trusts no one."

Elisabetha did not have to play the role of Queen for long. George II wore the crown for only fifteen months.* Totally under the control of Venizelos and a military junta, he complained with justification that he was king in name only. Although her mother hoped Elisabetha's difficult life would improve her, the new Queen of Greece showed little interest in her husband or her new country, expending most of her efforts in sending frantic cables to Prince Stirbey and Prince Paul of Yugoslavia (King Alexander's cousin) to come rescue her.

However precarious her position, Elisabetha of Greece and her sister, Mignon of Yugoslavia, were now perched on two of the few remaining thrones in Europe, while Marie herself sat on a third. In a few months Marie of Roumania had procured for her family a near monopoly on the Balkans. In so doing she had made herself a target for the international press. Journalists, who only a few years before were falling all over one another to praise Queen Marie's wartime valor, now aimed at shooting her down. Whereas the benign American *Review of Reviews* said that Marie had succeeded in creating "a peace factor of no small potency" in her part of the world, other publications hinted that she was building a consortium to rival that of the Habsburgs. Speculation started as to whom Queen Marie would pursue for Princess Ileana, aged thirteen. Among the most prominently mentioned prospects was twenty-eight-year-old Tsar Boris of Bulgaria. Another possible bridegroom, favored by those who saw Marie spreading her ambitions out over the British Empire, was the Prince of Wales.

Whatever the realities of her imperialist designs, the Queen of Roumania felt she had some justifying to do. To Mabel Potter Daggett, a contemporary biographer, she said she would "not marry Ileana even to a King, unless she loves him," adding, however, that "princes without thrones for Ileana to sit on, need not apply." "I know," she said elsewhere, "I have been considered an ambitious, intriguing woman, with vast plans and a desire to play a predominant part, even in the world of politics. I read these descriptions of myself with astonishment, because they certainly do not correspond with the truth."

She could never have admitted openly to blatant ambition. But having reached the apex of a rather astonishing career, she could and did admit good cheer and good luck. "I am in very high spirits," she told her new

---

*He was recalled to the throne twice again, in 1935 and 1946, but by then he and Elisabetha were divorced.

Foreign Minister, Jean Duca; "it probably suits me well to be called Mother-in-Law of the Balkans!" And to the adoring Miss Daggett she crowed, "I am a winner in life. Somebody has to lose. But I am a winner in life."

One of Marie's sins in the eyes of other royalties was that she enjoyed her highs so thoroughly and trafficked on her lows. It was Marie's theatricality, far more than her ambition, that vexed her fellow monarchs. As an example, they pointed to her Coronation at Alba Julia.

The idea of a Coronation to commemorate the symbolic birth of Greater Roumania came about soon after the peace settlements. It was started by Prime Minister Averescu, anxious to take the mind of the people off his new campaign of repression. Since none of the political parties but his own would support the venture and since economic conditions in the country were very bad, the King and Queen refused to participate. This left the government with an expensive but unused Coronation Church, constructed in Alba Julia in Transylvania, and a huge Triumphal Arch in the middle of Bucharest. Queen Marie liked neither, saying that they "cost a ridiculous lot of money without being worthy monuments."

In 1922 Bratianu returned to power, and since he was the man primarily responsible for Greater Roumania, the King agreed to be crowned under his Administration. The Transylvanians, who hated Bratianu as much as his predecessor, refused to join in the celebration. Ferdinand and Marie found themselves in the "absurd position" of taking part in a Coronation in Transylvania boycotted by Transylvanian politicians. There was little the Queen could do beyond trying to make the celebration as impressive as possible. Her first move was to invite foreign princes. "If our own people cannot have the grace to surround us on such a solemn occasion," she said, "if their hatred against Bratianu is greater than their loyalty towards us, then we must at least show them that we are solidly with the countries of Europe." In spite of her bravado, she was shaken. "I do not like the whole thing," she wrote in her diary. "It is sad and rather humiliating."

Political troubles were followed by religious ones, for the Catholic Church refused to allow King Ferdinand to be crowned in a Roumanian church by a Roumanian Orthodox priest. "It is very difficult for me to put myself into the shoes of a Catholic," the Queen said. "Being a fighter I feel of course like casting their religion in their face and turning Orthodox straight off." After hours of consultation with Nando and Barbo, Marie suggested that the King be crowned outside the church "on the pretext that it should take place" before all their people. No one, the Queen said, need know the real reason. When the King agreed to put the crown on his own head out in the open air, the Queen felt she had turned thorny problems into glorious happenstance.

With no Coronation precedents to hamper her, Marie of Roumania surrendered guiltlessly to her inborn sense of drama. Although she had always been impressed by the dignified solemnity of such events in Westminster

Abbey, she turned to the barbaric splendor of Nicholas and Alexandra's Coronation in Moscow for inspiration. She asked all the royal women in the procession to wear gold and the others to wear mauve and silver. "I want nothing modern that another Queen might have. Let mine be all medieval." Her daughters, the Queens of Greece and Yugoslavia, and other royal princesses wore gowns in various shades of gold with brightly colored velvet mantles—orange, crimson, and royal blue. As the centerpiece, the Queen dressed herself in reddish-gold with a golden mantle embroidered with local crests and sheaves of wheat, "the chief richness of our land." Over her long, straight dress she hung an extravagant chain of diamonds ending in a gigantic sapphire that the King bought for her at Cartier as a Coronation present. Her crown was copied from one worn by Princess Despina, the wife of a sixteenth-century Wallachian hospodar (prince). Set with rubies, emeralds, turquoises, and giant moonstones, the gold crown weighed four pounds and had huge gold and jeweled pendants that hung down over Marie's ears. The Queen wore it in the Byzantine fashion, as her attendants wore their diadems, over a delicate veil of gold mesh. "I carry off the huge golden-incrusted crown and overpowering mantle splendidly," she said, comparing herself to the figures of the Virgin, robed and jeweled, carried through the streets of Catholic countries on feast days.

Since there were no appropriate accommodations in Alba Julia, Marie dressed for the ceremonies on the royal train. The guests preceded the King and Queen in a formal march to the church, where a Mass was held inside before the participants emerged for the public ceremony. Led by the Metropolitan and the bishops in Oriental robes, Ferdinand in red velvet and ermine, and Marie in gold and jewels, the procession advanced to a platform erected in the center of the public square.

The King and Queen stepped onto a dais swathed in colorful carpets under a huge canopy, swagged, tasseled, and held aloft by six enormous spears. A mantle of royal purple was placed on Ferdinand's shoulders, while the gold mantle was put on Marie. The King made a short speech, took the iron crown that had been made for Carol I, and crowned himself. The Queen knelt down before him. He put the gold crown on her head, bent down to raise her from her knees, and embraced her before a crowd of more than 300,000 wide-eyed peasants. Cannons roared, bells chimed, military bands struck up the national anthem, and the people cheered. "I think it must have been a fine sight and I hope that H.M. and I did our part well and looked as well as we could in our somewhat overwhelming getup," Marie said.

The festivities cost Roumania around a million dollars. "King Ferdinand's and my coronation," Marie said later, "was a modest ceremony in comparison with others I have known." "So very picturesque" was the comment of the future George VI of England, sent by his father to represent his country. "Yes," answered Marie, "and also intensely moving."

Marie seldom confused the public Queen with the private woman. When

Marthe Bibesco, who was unable to attend the Coronation, asked Marie to describe the proceedings, the picture the Queen drew for her was, she said, "full of drollery and good humor." Marie explained to Marthe what she wore, what "Poor Nando" wore, and how she had to kneel down in front of him to receive the crown on her head. "Imagine!" she said. "Me, me kneeling before him!" The King readily acknowledged the absurdity of the situation. It was, he agreed, a "very painful moment."

After nearly thirty years of marriage, Marie and Ferdinand had settled into habits of kindly tolerance and devotion toward each other. She bowed to his superiority as King and male in public. He deferred to her in private because he knew she dealt with the world better than he. But aside from rank, Roumania, and offspring, they had little more in common at their Coronation in 1922 than they had had at their wedding in 1893.

Rejected by his wife soon after the marriage, Ferdinand had turned his attentions elsewhere. In the King's mid-fifties, the Queen still felt justified remarking to her plumpish, aging landscape gardener, Mrs. Martineau, "You are the only woman I can trust the King with." Even so, Ferdinand remained curiously detached from the opposite sex, successfully separating his passions from his affections; he was comfortable with women who, for social or economic reasons, demanded nothing beyond sharing a king's bed.

Marie was just the opposite. A product of nineteenth-century romanticism, she had launched her search for refined ecstasy early in the marriage. She was looking for a man who could engage her imagination and sense of style— a role for which her husband was comically unsuited. If the three most important men in her life—Barbo Stirbey, Waldorf Astor, and Joseph Boyle— had anything in common, it was that they too were all dedicated if diverse romantics, men who knew how to provide the lady in their lives with a white marble, vine-covered, dramatically situated pedestal.

Oddly enough, it was Marie who became the undeserving victim of tales of sexual license—stories that haunted her during her lifetime and have survived into the present. These were started by her jealous predecessor and kept alive by her countrymen, who could not imagine that their Queen was not as unrestrained as they themselves. Later, Marie's relationship with Barbo Stirbey was used by her enemies and his to fuel the rumors.

In fact, Marie was not a sexually passionate woman, although she was high-spirited, flirtatious, and seemingly incapable of verbal restraint. "The moment one is a little different, a little original, they enjoy you, but they tear you to pieces..." she wrote an American friend in 1929, "they imagine that the 'animal' in me must play a big part. They cannot understand 'spirits'... without an underground of something more lurid. It always astounds me the enormous importance people give to a certain part of life; they uglify and degrade everything by it. I suppose it plays a much bigger part than I realize. My royal life has in that way isolated me from that form of brutal reality. It is only through books and certain things that have been said of me that I realized that such immense importance was given to that one thing which has played little part in my life, that chase after 'sexual excitement,' if that is the right technical expression?"

Marriage taught Marie to hate obligation and coercion. As she wrote a friend in later years: ". . . it was so hard to have to eternally keep a so-called master in good humour, just because being a husband, he had nominally the right to order about and control." For her the perfect relationship would be based "on absolutely equal footing . . . absolute spontaneousness." Was she advocating "free love"? No, "but free companionship, yes—if mixed with physical love or not would be entirely according to what we would feel for each other." In her day and caste, a relationship based on mutual affection and spontaneity was rarely found in a marriage of state, and the mere mention of equality between the sexes was enough to destroy a good name.

The closest Marie ever came to her ideal was her relationship with Barbo Stirbey. He adored her for more than thirty years, and if she did not return his love with quite the same passion, their alliance sustained her from the age of thirty-one until her death. Even in middle age the Queen and the Prince presented "a magnificent team," casting the sort of romantic image that stirred the admiration of the young son of one of her ministers who observed them at a concert at Cotroceni Palace one night in the early 1920s. "She had a dress, a very long dress with a train in black velvet with all her magnificent pearls. She was in a corner of the throne room, and Barbo Stirbey was next to her discussing something. They were not looking at each other, they were looking at the crowd. It was an extraordinary sight . . . They were such a magnificent pair. She was so beautiful and he was so handsome. They had such extraordinary allure and grandeur and distinction. . . . The best proof is that after more than fifty years I can still see them as if it happened last night."

Chapter 25

What man would renounce a throne for a woman?

—*KING CAROL II OF ROUMANIA*

*A*fter her Coronation, the Queen settled down to a more peaceful routine than any she had known since before the war. Although she was in her late forties, she still galloped her horses nearly every day, accompanied by whatever members of the younger generation could keep up with her. In Sinaia Marie led her family, guests, and a pack of Russian wolfhounds on long tramps through the woods; in Bucharest she paid frequent visits to the famous Cismigiu Gardens, rising as early as 4:30 A.M. to catch the peonies and roses at their freshest. She still wrote in the early morning—tales of extravagant imagination, articles for magazines, and the beginnings of an autobiography. The rest of her day was filled with audiences and charities.

There were usually young visitors at the palace, relatives like Baby Bee and her husband, Sitta's sisters, or Ducky's and Sandra's children. In the evening everyone including Carol and Sitta joined the Queen for supper and, if there was no formal entertainment, played silly games, danced, or dressed up in outrageous clothes. One evening when the Queen was already in bed, she was surprised by Baby Bee, Mignon, Ali, Prince Paul of Yugoslavia, and Nicky—the girls disguised in the men's uniforms and the men dressed up as "unmentionable ladies."

Along with the younger generation, there were old friends and would-be palace intimates, people who attached themselves to the Queen and whom she could not bring herself to dismiss. Both men and women became infatuated with Marie and had to be eased gently and smilingly out of her life. There was Peter Jay, the American Ambassador to Roumania; only his good manners saved them both from an embarrassing diplomatic situation. More difficult was Roxo Weingartner, the wife of the conductor, a tyrannical admirer who tried to take over the Queen's life. People like Roxo, led on by Marie's casual familiarity, did not realize that they were, as the Queen put it, "singing both voices in the duet."

There was also a constant stream of journalists around the palace. These writers, sent to Roumania to get the inside story on the Queen, invariably returned to their editors and publishers dazzled by Marie's charm and complimented by her frankness. Whoever was at Cotroceni was included in the Queen's daily routine of work, household luncheons, and intimate family dinners. They were treated to palace concerts, movies, and state dinners; taken on excursions to the King's shooting lodge or the royal farm; and invited into Marie's boudoir to hear her latest story.

It was a good life, geared to include everyone, particularly the Crown Prince and his wife. The Queen realized that her elder son chafed at being kept on the political sidelines, but, having publicly allied himself with one party, the National Peasants, he had alienated other politicians and destroyed his chances of working with other Administrations. During the King and Queen's sojourns outside Roumania, the heir to the throne was not even included in the Regency Council that ruled in their absence. Marie was determined to change this. "I am not going to allow them [the politicians] the luxury of being offended... Carol is the future... he must... be brought together with those he will have to work with later on." This, the Queen conceded, was not easy, as her elder son was "both gruff and obstinate."

Carol's *bête noire* was Bratianu, whom he blamed for his father's lack of independence, and the Crown Prince spoke out in public against the leader of the Liberal Party. Marie continued to invite the Bratianus to the palace in hopes of bringing about an eventual rapprochement. Meanwhile, she watched as the Crown Prince expended his energies and organizational gifts on the only areas allowed him—the Roumanian Air Force and Boy Scouts, both of which he started, and the Federation of Sports. Like generations of crown princes before him, Carol combated the frustrations of minimal authority with female recompense, while his mother assumed that he was satisfied to remain at home with the lovely Sitta.

The Queen herself admired the new Crown Princess and thought her "a worthy follower." Sitta had exquisite manners. She conducted her official duties with graceful dedication learned in Greece and transferred to her new country. An excellent horsewoman, she performed with panache in ceremonial parades despite her nearsightedness, which often made it difficult for her to find the King or his generals.

Marie discovered that her daughter-in-law had a wicked sense of humor and an unexpected gift of mimicry, which the Queen loved to turn on herself. She cajoled the Crown Princess into imitating her way of walking through cheering crowds and laughed "at the sight until she cried." Often in the middle of solemn and ceremonious occasions, the Queen would turn to the Crown Princess and whisper, "Now watch me, you must do this later."

Marie did remark that her daughter-in-law seemed "in no hurry" to have a second child, but this she attributed to the difficulty the Crown Princess had experienced in giving birth to the first. She did not resent Sitta's extended visits to her parents in exile and preferred to ignore the fact that during the first two years of her marriage, the Crown Princess spent a total of nine months outside the country, away from the Crown Prince.

In reality, Carol and Sitta's marriage had started to deteriorate soon after Michael's birth. Unable to satisfy her demanding husband, the Crown Princess, like generations of royal wives before her, accepted his adventures and held her head high. The breach between husband and wife was aggravated by the death of Sitta's father, King Constantine, which brought her widowed, exiled mother and younger sisters to live in Bucharest near her. Thereafter, the Crown Princess was rarely seen alone with her husband. "There come Carol and his wives!" said the palace wags, mocking the Crown Prince and his entourage of women. Even the Queen referred privately to her son's ménage as "Carol & Co."

It was some time before Marie realized the seriousness of the situation in her son's home. Shocked when gossips hinted at divorce, she vigorously denied the stories adrift on the Chaussée. "A happier, more united, contented couple it were difficult to find," she wrote Leile Milne in England. "ABSOLUTE harmony reigns between them and she and I really LOVE each other. She is ALL my heart desires."

While Marie was disclaiming the rift between Carol and his wife, a young redhead named Elena Lupescu,* having heard of the availability of the Crown Prince, set out to catch him. It wasn't easy for her. However accessible Prince Carol was to aristocratic young women, to Mme. Lupescu, the divorced wife of a Roumanian Army officer, it meant passing from one world into another, from the demimonde of girdled soldiers swaggering down the Corso bragging about their latest conquests to the discreet palaces of the landed gentry and the court.

---

*Elena Lupescu has often been referred to as Magda. According to her biographer, this is due to the error of an Italian journalist who mistook her for someone else.

Elena's parents had already made one gigantic social leap. Her mother, a good-looking Viennese, had early on exchanged her Judaism for a more convenient Roman Catholicism. Her father, a Jewish druggist in a small Moldavian town, had changed his religion to Roumanian Orthodox at the time of his marriage in order to satisfy his wife and obtain the right accorded only to Christians, to own his own shop. Elena herself had parlayed flaming red hair, green eyes, white flesh, and sauntering hips into marriage with an artillery lieutenant named Tampeanu. When Tampeanu objected to her affairs with his fellow officers, she left him, taking back her father's name of Wolff, which he had Latinized and de-Semitized into Lupescu.

There are many stories of how Elena Lupescu met the Crown Prince. The most plausible, told by Mme. Lupescu's biographer* and confirmed in substance in the memoirs of Prince Nicolas, explains how the young woman from Moldavia used a photographer friend named Posmantir, the only social bridge between her world and that of the Prince, to thrust herself into Carol's consciousness.

Posmantir, whom Carol had met on his world tour, worked for the Carol I Foundation, a charitable organization for students. Since the Crown Prince was the honorary head of the Foundation and had to appear at its programs, Elena asked the photographer to take her to a Foundation-sponsored afternoon of peasant dances. "She was always capricious," he is quoted as saying, "so I didn't suspect anything when she made a big fuss about sitting in just the right place, and I didn't argue when she chose the worst spot from which to see the dancing. It was only later that I found out that all she wanted was to be in Carol's line of vision."

Elena managed to extract invitations for two Foundation functions, each time seating herself where Carol could not miss seeing her, feeling certain that he would ask to meet her. He did, calling on one of his friends, a ship's captain named Tautu, to arrange a meeting. On the appointed evening Lupescu arrived, her milk-white skin dazzling in a virginal white gown, painstakingly decorous in her behavior. When the Crown Prince offered to take her home, she acknowledged the honor but demurred: "What would the neighbors think if they saw me returning in Your Highness' car?"

Captain Tautu was flabbergasted. Instead of simply warning Carol that Elena Lupescu was not the lady she seemed to be, he staged an elaborate charade at his next party to demonstrate Lupescu's easy virtue to the Prince. Posing as Lupescu's lover, he picked a fight with her in the middle of the evening, throwing a nightgown at her head and shouting, "Get out of here, you——— and take your dirty rags with you!" If the Captain hoped to save his Prince, he forgot to reckon with Lupescu. Raising her shoulders in horror, Elena countered, "Is there no gentleman here to protect the honor of a helpless woman?" Carol offered himself, and together they swept out of the Captain's house and into the history books.

*Alice-Leone Moats.

The story, if not true, at least shows something of Lupescu's determination and quickness of wit. It also explains why, since their social circles never intersected, it took so long for reports to reach Queen Marie that her son was involved with the ex-wife of an army officer.

To today's dabbler in old photos and stale gossip, Elena Lupescu's pictures conjure up little of the *femme fatale*. Her coloring was her major asset. Her features were heavy. Her eyelids rivaled those of the Hanovers for length and weight; her nose arched and sprawled across her face; and her lips were fleshy and loose. A tall woman, Lupescu held herself well. Whereas Carol must have found her walk sexy—she swung her hips in an exaggerated manner—another might have thought it lumpish, for Elena was overweight. What attracted the Crown Prince was probably her self-assured vulgarity. The opposite of the slim, ladylike Crown Princess, Mme. Lupescu had complete confidence in herself as a desirable woman. She came to the Crown Prince with a history of successes, and she had no reason to think she couldn't handle him as well, whatever his peculiarities. Even when young, they made a distinctly unappetizing couple.

Unaware of her son's other life, Queen Marie traveled extensively during the early twenties. In August of 1923 she made a pilgrimage to Joe Boyle's grave in England. The soldier of fortune had died in April of heart disease. Less than six months before his death, he defied doctors' orders to make one last foray into Soviet Georgia to rescue an old employee from a Communist jail in Tiflis. When he returned to England, his huge frame reduced to skeletal proportions, he dropped from sight, refusing to see anyone.

Marie had known that he was ill for two years, and they corresponded until a week before his death. He wrote to her of his desire to go home to the Klondike, and in one of his last letters, he said goodbye. The Queen asked him to come to Roumania, but he was too proud. "I want you to remember me as the man I was. I am no more Joe Boyle," he wrote back. He died at Wayside, a little house near London where he lodged with a friend. Marie was shocked; "he had such a mighty will, it was as though by sheer force he would keep death off," she wrote.

Joe Boyle was buried at Hampton Hill.* Old cronies like Captain Hill came out of retirement to mourn him. The press called him "a cross between Don Quixote and a playboy of the Western World" and "the last of the d'Artagnans." Even the conservative London *Times* published a long, laudatory obituary, referring to Boyle's "romantic career" and "his independent and chivalrous character." The Dowager Empress of Russia sent a wreath to his funeral, and one of Boyle's friends laid four lilies on his grave in the name of Marie of Roumania. When Marie herself visited the

---

*In accordance with his belated recognition as a national hero, his body was recently moved to Canada.

peaceful English churchyard, she brought an ancient stone incised with her name to lay on his grave and an antique cross from an old Roumanian monastery.

From England Marie traveled to Yugoslavia for the birth of Mignon's first child—a son named Peter, born September 6, 1923. Six weeks later she went back for the christening. One of the baby's godfathers was the young Duke of York (Britain's future George VI). Marie thought his bride of six months, Elizabeth,* "one of the dearest, sweetest, most gentle... and most agreeable women I have ever met." One of the baby's godmothers was Queen Elisabetha of Greece. Elisabetha, who had preceded her mother to Belgrade, was not delighted to see her younger sister propped in bed, adored, and showered with jewels. By the time Marie returned, she found Mignon sick and Elisabetha flirting with her sister's husband, King Alexander; "she wants everything, everything I have!" the young Queen of Yugoslavia told their mother.

The day after the christening, while festivities continued for the wedding of Prince Paul of Yugoslavia and Princess Olga of Greece, Marie arranged to get Elisabetha out of Belgrade. Shortly thereafter, Elisabetha's husband was toppled from the Greek throne, and George and Elisabetha moved into a wing of Cotroceni Palace. "Lisabetha is one of the griefs of my life," said Marie, who blamed Elisabetha's attempt to wreck her sister's marriage on the humiliation of her exile and lack of material possessions. She was thrilled when Elisabetha's mother-in-law, Queen Sophie, gave Elisabetha a fabulous collection of emeralds. "Now neither Mignon nor I have finer jewels," Marie said, knowing that Elisabetha loved jewelry more than anything else. Marie watched sadly as her eldest daughter surrendered to discontent, spending whole days over the mah-jongg table and ordering rich cakes from the city. She felt sorry for her son-in-law George, living in exile with a wife who did not love him. Years later George told Marie, "You were the only one who made my life supportable."

In April of 1924, Queen Marie left her problems with her children to join King Ferdinand on a good-will tour of Western Europe. Designed as an official renewal of personal ties with heads of state, it was the sort of venture in which the Queen of Roumania reveled and at which she excelled. Their first stop was Paris, where the Conservative newspaper Le Figaro had been touting their arrival for several days. One hundred planes, the paper announced, would be sent to welcome these "sincere friends of France." While the French Air Force was revving up its engines, Marie, on board the royal train approaching the station, discovered that the King had chosen for his official entrance into Paris the uniform of the Royal Guard, a costume topped by a pointed helmet unquestionably German in its origin and in-

*H.M. Queen Elizabeth, the Queen Mother.

spiration. Knowing Nando's obstinacy when crossed, she devised an accident whereby a portly young secretary, traveling as part of their entourage, fell on the offending headpiece, rendering it unwearable. For his entry into Paris King Ferdinand was reduced to the uniform of a Hussar with its inoffensive fur shako.

Ferdinand and Marie's visit to Paris was a success. "I am the sort of Queen they understand and appreciate," Marie wrote in her diary. "There is always plenty to say and think about me... good & bad, but nothing dull!" The Queen took time from parades and state luncheons to visit the House of Chanel with her former houseguest, the young Russian Grand Duchess Marie. The Queen was "frightfully tempted" by Chanel's clothes, but having gained a great deal of weight, could not bring herself to try current fashions.

After the official functions were over, Marie left her husband in Paris to join Ducky for three weeks in Nice at their mother's villa, Château Fabron. The villa was an ongoing problem to the sisters; none of them could afford to keep it up, and all were naïve in business matters. Marie summoned Barbo to help them. Meanwhile, she enjoyed shopping for old copper for her palaces and new varieties of flowers for her gardens, meeting old friends, and driving into the mountains above the Riviera. Happy to be away from "officialities and all the tittle-tattle," the Queen was surprised by a visitor from the Roumanian Legation in Paris who came to tell her that His Majesty had been enjoying himself in Paris, but, according to the members of the Roumanian community there, was seen "much too much" with Marthe Bibesco. Marie was philosophical: "...how could Nando resist Marthe in Paris, what arms could he have against her charm & her knowledge of Paris, Nando who always waits to be led."

The Queen was to join the King in Switzerland. On her way she returned to Paris, where she met Helene Vacaresco for the first time. "We were utterly sweet with each other," Marie noted in her diary. She thought Helene was just as ugly as everyone said but delightful company and a wonderful conversationalist. She was happy when Mlle. Vacaresco came to the station to see her off and knew that the pleasure was mutual. Helene, she said, was "awfully delighted to count now in the inner circle again for which [she] had so long pined!" A year later Marie brought Helene and Ferdinand together for the first time in more than thirty years.

After an official appearance at the League of Nations in Geneva, Ferdinand and Marie traveled to Belgium for a reunion with Ferdinand's first cousin, King Albert, and Queen Elizabeth. Both Belgium and Roumania had been martyred in the war; both Queens had played heroic roles during their countries' occupations; and both Kings, German by birth or extraction, had emerged ennobled in the eyes of the world. The two men embraced warmly as Ferdinand and Marie departed for England.

This visit in London was entirely different for Marie from her journey of five years before. In 1919 the Queen of Roumania was an unofficial guest and, however important her mission, she was free to move about as she wished. On this occasion Marie and Ferdinand were official guests of state, and from the moment of their arrival, their days were filled with presentations and receptions. From laying the traditional wreath on the Tomb of the Unknown Soldier to the Lord Mayor's banquet for 850 guests, they moved in carriages in stately procession, watched and cheered by the crowds that lined up each day in accordance with a published program to see them. There was a traditional state dinner for 150 guests at Buckingham Palace and, to reciprocate, dinner and a concert at the Roumanian Legation. Queen Marie worried that the music, planned and played by Georges Enesco, was "one degree too classical" for her cousin, and she hastily arranged to have the program shortened.

At a Court Ball given in their honor, Marie learned compassion for Queen Mary. All of the royalties were required to sit on a dais, and King George was "very particular" that no one step down except to dance. Marie had quit dancing after the death of Mircea, but once or twice she tried to escape to chat with friends. Each time she was immediately brought to heel by one of the King's gentlemen-in-waiting. "King George lets Her Majesty know that if she wishes to speak to anyone, he or she can be brought up to where she is sitting." "May does not dare budge," said Marie. "George is a real tyrant & stickler at form like his father, but without his father's renowned ease of manner."

Marie continued to find the Prince of Wales (the future Duke of Windsor) "quite irresistible with that delicious face, that short child's nose, that lovely honey-coloured hair and blue eyes. Later if he goes it too hard, his eyes will get tired, the bloom will fade, but for the moment he is 'le Prince Charmant'..."

Until this visit, Marie had always considered Queen Mary stiff in personality and dress, but now was impressed with her "magnificent and monumental" style. Marie, who continued at nearly fifty to dress like a romantic young girl, was not at her most attractive during the trip. Her draped, flowing gowns and unusual jewels required the slim figure she no longer possessed. For the Court Ball Marie wore a Moroccan caftan embroidered in silver and made for the occasion. One guest* thought she looked "ridiculous" and described the caftan as a "green sea-foam crepe-de-chine saut-de-lit [dressing gown] spotted with goldfish she had painted on herself. Her double chins," he added, "were kept in place by strands of pearls attached to an exotic headdress."

The official part of Ferdinand and Marie's visit to England was cut short by the imminent arrival of the King and Queen of Italy. Ferdinand took his diplomatic cue and left at once, but Marie stayed on in an unofficial capacity,

---

*Chips (Sir Henry) Channon, the American-born chronicler of English and European society.

her presence in the country no longer acknowledged by the court. In order not to prove an embarrassment, she retired to her sister's home in Esher. Banished from Spain, the Infanta Beatrice had moved to England with her husband and their three sons. While Marie was at Esher, Barbo Stirbey arrived on business. "We were very happy to meet once in England, it had always been one of our dreams," Marie wrote in her diary. "I took him out into the woods to look at the bluebells." From Esher Marie visited the Astors at Cliveden and Plymouth before returning to Roumania.

Whatever her personal pleasure in revisiting the home of her youth, Marie could not comprehend England's antagonism toward regional pacts, particularly the tricornered Little Entente (Roumania, Czechoslovakia, and Yugoslavia) on which her country counted to defend itself from Russia. In Marie's opinion, the major menace in Europe was Communism, which posed both a national and a personal political threat to her. The Russians had never accepted the decision of the Peace Conference to award Bessarabia to Roumania, and they continued to try to unseat the dynasty. "In the Bolshevik question," Marie wrote, "the world seems still smitten with ...blindness...It even makes me occasionally regret being a woman or anyhow makes me regret that I have not the LEGAL right to put myself at the head of a movement to bring about a COMMON understanding of all civilized countries to protect their civilization."

If the Queen of Roumania could no longer get a hearing in the political councils of the world, she had, by this time in her life, found an audience for her fiction and her pronouncements on many other subjects. "I feel my power augmenting, my style sobering and becoming concise," she said. "Perhaps I could have become a real writer had I been able to develop that side to the detriment of other things," she had written in her diary a few years before. "But being a Queen it is more important that I should always be at my post, punctually, conventionally, patiently, smilingly...There are many artists, writers, poets in the world, but a Queen has a sacred charge." Nevertheless, Marie adored writing, especially fiction: "...it simply pours from my pen....I see everything I relate, it all rises in pictures before me."

On August 4, 1924, *Time* magazine issued a cover story on the Queen, based on the publication of her new book, *The Voice on the Mountain*. In this story the young female protagonist rides a chestnut horse, wields a star-tipped spear, and draws mysterious powers of healing and prophecy from a stricken warrior whom she tends but refused to love; at his death she loses her goddesslike gifts and descends her mountain to a younger, less demanding lover. As might be expected, the book was dismissed by *Time* as "the out-pourings of a gushing schoolgirl." But the Queen herself, whom the magazine referred to as "a real power, abroad and at home," was treated with respect.

If Marie's writing was not as sleek as she imagined nor as bad as *Time* indicated, it was good enough to secure syndication with the North American

Newspaper Alliance. In sixteen articles, published in 1925 in England and America under the general heading A Queen Looks at Life, Marie treated an eager public to her views on royalty, men, clothes, and marriage. Titles like "Can a Woman Make Herself Beautiful?," "Changing Ideas of Marriage," and "My Experience with Men" promised the reader glimpses into the life and mind of Europe's most famous royalty. Aimed at a public that worshiped from afar and wanted to know how a real queen lived and what she felt, the articles were filled with just enough unconventional wisdom to delight American readers and embarrass Marie's relatives. The major theme was the need for more equality between the sexes. When Marie wrote that she did not believe in pandering to the man of the house, that husbands should not exercise their traditional rights over wives, and that temptation was the same for both sexes, there was consternation in royal circles. The last article, "Making Marriage Durable," was dangerously close to a plea for open marriage: "... fidelity does not seem to have been decreed by nature..." Marie wrote. "When passion has died down in both hearts, why not like two good friends be forgiving and lenient?" The New York World, which had promised that the series would be "the sensation of the year in European court circles," was right. After spending her vacation in England justifying herself to the royal family—with whom the offending articles "loom over me like a black mark!"—Marie came to the sad conclusion that "frankness can be called indiscretion."

During her lifetime Marie published more than fifteen books including fairy tales, allegorical romances, travelogues, and, in later years, memoirs. Neither the mystical subject matter nor the high-flown style of her early works is likely to appeal to the modern reader. It was not until the publication of her autobiography in the 1930s that the Queen found her voice and emerged as a writer of consequence.

Beginning in early 1925, Ferdinand's health began to deteriorate. In January the King was operated on for a hernia. Two months later he was put back to bed with what was diagnosed as an embolism that had traveled to a lung. His convalescence was long, but Marie was not worried and sent for Mignon. "H.M. was always supposed to love his eldest daughter best, but Mignon was his chum, his companion, the one who... made his life pleasant," the Queen said, happy to have her second daughter back in the palace.

During his illness the King was kept absolutely quiet, and no one outside the family was allowed to see him. One of the people who haunted the palace but was forbidden access to the King was his beloved Aristitza Dissescu. Mme. Dissescu was the wife of a university professor. Described by one of her husband's pupils as an elegant woman, "like a very handsome, pedantic British governess," she adored Ferdinand. "He is the love of her life," said Queen Marie.

One day during the King's isolation, Marie saw the door of her lady-in-waiting's room shut quickly at her approach, but not before she caught a glimpse of Mme. Dissesscu slipping behind it. Acting on impulse, the Queen opened the door and took the woman by the hand: "... certainly we are obliged to keep him absolutely quiet," she told Mme. Dissesscu, "but you are so devoted to him that I know it will do you good to see him for a moment. If you will come with me, no one will dare bar his door to you. . . ." She led the woman past a phalanx of disapproving guards into the King's room. "I know that visits are not permitted," Marie told the King, "but when someone is this devoted, she at least has the right to look at you for a moment to see that you are really all right."

On her return from England in 1925 Queen Marie started construction on the last and most exotic of her country retreats—a Turkish pavilion on the Black Sea near the town of Balcic. Balcic is located in the part of the Dobruja that the Bulgarians had been forced to cede to the Roumanians at the end of World War I. Marie was first brought there by a group of painters who established an artists' colony on one side of the round blue bay. On the other side was a poor village of Tatars and Turks, a collection of tiny orange, yellow, and green houses perched precariously on chalky cliffs. Marie fell in love with the remains of an old millhouse with a huge poplar tree hanging out over the water, and she convinced an old friend to sell her the property around it. A ramshackle make-believe environment, the brightest "green spot" on the arid Dobrujan coastline, it was a romantic oasis on which to locate a fantasy.

"My strange little house on the Black Sea..." she wrote a friend, "will give me occasion to allow my imagination fair play... The little oddity I will call Tenya-Yuvah—the Solitary Nest—as all names about there are Turkish. I confess that the creation of these harmonious little corners to which I add the gardens, is the craze of my middle age. Which does not prevent my indulging in my dear old hobby and bringing back two horses from England which I paid for with my own earnings." The Queen was now making a great deal from her writing—enough, in fact, to build and furnish this entire project.

She ordered Tenya-Yuvah built entirely à la turque with heavy white walls and few rooms. Inside, the rough white texture served as a pleasantly stark background for Turkish divans, enormous candelabra, and bearskin rugs. Upstairs she built herself an octagonal bedroom with two wide windows overhanging the lower floor and looking out over the sea. The bed, a couch covered with cushions and coverlets, was placed in a raised recess opposite the windows. Low carved and painted doorways opened into a dressing room, a miniature Turkish steam bath, and a porch, where Marie often slept outside.

Next to the bedroom was a hazardous circular stairway winding up to a minaret with a wind harp. The harp tinkled cheerfully over gardens whose luxuriant foliage half hid tiny guesthouses, homes for the Queen's servants, and, in later years, a miniature Byzantine chapel dedicated to Marie's ecumenical faith. Her flower beds were terraces cut out of the hillside and ornamented with huge Greek amphorae, old stone benches, and decapitated columns culled from her travels. A romantic panoply of hidden waterfalls, stone stairwells, and reflecting pools, the gardens of Tenya-Yuvah took advantage of ancient trees and shrubs, which shaded its meandering paths and tumbled over low retaining walls down toward the sea below.

Balcic was to become Marie's favorite retreat. It was a lush if primitive artist's lair (there were mice in her bedroom), where she could indulge her passion for lilies and roses, delphiniums and hollyhocks, away from the demands of official life. She spent as many weeks there as she could during the warm months, arriving in time for the first flowering of spring and returning to catch the last autumn roses. Marie had planted gardens before, but none in such a temperate climate; she greeted each new floral display with wonder and was considerably put out if public duties kept her in the city during the height of the blooming season. As she began to spend more time in Balcic, the Queen offered property around Tenya-Yuvah to her friends, who built more practical villas around her own.

In August of 1925 Queen Marie returned from a holiday in Western Europe to find the marriage of the Crown Prince and Princess disintegrating. Carol, she said, was "a changed man, an ill man, a haunted man." Sitta seemed cool and withdrawn. When Marie cornered her daughter-in-law, the Crown Princess broke down and told her about Carol's adventures, which he had described to his wife, and about his serious involvement with Elena Lupescu. "It makes me sick at heart," Marie wrote after discussing the situation with Barbo Stirbey in early October. "It is one of those intimate troubles which might become a public one."

Nevertheless, the Queen went on with family celebrations, Carol's thirty-second birthday and her fiftieth. Surrounded by her troublesome brood and most of the Greeks as well, Marie seemed younger than her years, although she was distracted by the "heavy atmosphere" of Carol's sulkiness and Sitta's pain. The day started with a telegram of congratulations and two thousand iris bulbs from Barbo and finished with *tableaux vivants* arranged by Carol.

Only a week before his mother's birthday, the Crown Prince had spoken to the King about Lupescu, and the next day he came to talk to the Queen. Marie found him "very inarticulate." "I had to say rather terrible things..." she wrote in her diary, "was not hard & merciless, but tried to make him see how he is bringing misfortune down upon us all." The King, it was said, threatened to exile his son's mistress to some faraway province. Ferdinand had the power to carry out such a threat, and Elena Lupescu seems to have disappeared quickly from the streets of Bucharest.

On November 7, 1925, the Crown Prince and Princess of Roumania appeared together in public for the last time. The occasion was a flower show in Bucharest. In spite of the stories of Carol's affair, now common knowledge in the capital, Sitta preserved a cordial smile for the exhibitors and Carol observed all the outward courtesies.

To his mother, however, the Crown Prince seemed "utterly broken down both in health and nerves." He told his parents that if they would permit him to go abroad, he thought he might be able to "pull himself together." When news of Queen Alexandra's death came from England, Marie and Ferdinand decided to send him as the King's representative to the funeral. "Carol has the permission to remain away for a little holiday till Xmas," Marie wrote in her diary. "But I am anxious. May our boy come back safely and in a better frame of mind."

Queen Alexandra's funeral took place in a whirling snowstorm on November 27, 1925. Carol joined the formal procession, following the gun carriage directly behind the Kings of England, Norway, Sweden, and Belgium and the Prince of Wales. He remained in England one week as the guest of the British royal family; during his stay he did nothing to offend his relatives or to indicate anything out of the ordinary. The first hint of defection came from Ileana, who was at school in England. Carol had promised to escort her home for the holidays. On the day he was due to meet her, he telephoned to say that he was leaving for Paris. There he met Elena Lupescu, and they set off for Italy. In Milan, Carol registered at the Hotel de Ville, cautioning the management not to reveal his presence; Elena registered under the name of Princess Lupescu.

Four days before Christmas, Sitta appeared at Cotroceni Palace with letters from Carol for his mother and herself, along with an official renunciation, addressed to his father, of his right to the throne. "Carol had repeated the first desertion . . ." the Queen wrote in her diary. "Carol is not coming back!" As he had done when he eloped with Zizi, the Crown Prince neglected to mention the reason for his flight, casting himself in the role of victim and misrepresenting the facts to justify his actions. "Cold-bloodedly, lovelessly he writes to his mother & to his wife that he is abandoning everything, that he is misunderstood, misjudged, looked down upon and therefore he has decided to give everything up & to disappear . . . no regrets, only accusations of being misunderstood, persecuted, humiliated. . . . We sent for H.M.—all three we sat there as though struck by lightning. I was expecting Barbo. He came. When we told him he nearly collapsed. Bratianu . . . came at 10½."

They decided to tell no one until the Marshal of the Court, General Angelescu, could be sent to Milan to speak personally with the Crown Prince and give him a letter from his mother, asking him to return. On Christmas Day the Queen received word from Angelescu that the situation was "hopeless" and that the Crown Prince would "hear no sort of reason." Carol's old friend Lieutenant Mugur tried for an entire week to get the Crown Prince to open the door of his hotel suite. Carol's response to Mugur's pleas was a note saying, "You will only bring me home in my coffin."

The Crown Prince's reply to his mother's letter was equally irrational. His explanation for his desertion was that he had "often found life difficult." He was, he said, saddened by her unhappiness and her concern for his future, but told her, "I'm young enough ... I'll manage to make a life for myself.... One should find a way of declaring that I've been killed in a motor accident.... Say drowned in the Lago Maggiore ... I'll know how to disappear without leaving a trace."

The Crown Princess was "desperate" according to Queen Marie, "tormenting herself ... with the idea that she might have saved him had she perhaps ... been different with him." Sitta offered to go to Milan to try to talk to her husband, but she was refused permission. "You are going through this for the first time," she was told. "For us it is the second time. Before, he escaped the death sentence only because of the Queen's intervention. Now, nobody must intervene."

On December 31, 1925, King Ferdinand called a special meeting of the Crown Council at Sinaia to present his son's statement of abdication. He proposed a Regency Council to take over in the event of his death before the majority of his four-year-old grandson, Prince Michael. It was, the Queen said, an "inhuman agony" for the King to be "the one who had to insist upon condemning his own son." Premier Bratianu proposed three names for the Regency Council: Prince Nicolas, the Patriarch of the Roumanian Orthodox Church, and the Chief Justice.

An official communiqué, the result of the emergency session of the Crown Council, announced to a bewildered Roumania that King Ferdinand had accepted Crown Prince Carol's "irrevocable renunciation to the succession to the throne and of all prerogatives appertaining to that rank, including membership in the Royal Family." On January 4, 1926, the decision of the Crown Council was ratified by Parliament, and Michael took his father's place on the ladder of succession.

That should have ended the matter, but it didn't. Carol's renunciation of the throne threw the royal family and the Liberal government on the defensive. The international press leaped in, clucking over the defection of the Crown Prince and positing all kinds of Byzantine plots and family jealousies to explain his actions. They seized upon Carol's defection as a protest against everything from anti-Semitism to government inefficiency.

International rumors were easier for Marie to bear than the suspicions of the Roumanian people themselves, who had always trusted her. Their volte-face, stronger and more painful for the strength of the love that preceded it, stung deeply. But Marie did not take into account the fact that the average Roumanian, carefully shielded by the Queen and her advisers from the antics of the Crown Prince, could not now be expected to comprehend what on earth could have led to his renunciation of the crown. It was easy for Bratianu's enemies to insinuate that the Prime Minister was personally responsible, that he had forced the King and Queen to get rid of their son, who was opposed to him, and that he was paying Lupescu to keep Carol out of the country.

Closer to home and more distressing to Marie was a rumor that Carol was the victim of a personal fight with Barbo Stirbey, in which the Crown Prince tried to throw Stirbey out of the palace and was, in consequence, cut off from the succession and banished by his mother. Gregory Filipescu, son of the fiery Conservative whom Marie had worked so hard to win over before the war, started a newspaper with the express purpose of destroying Stirbey. Filipescu printed Stirbey's portrait over the title "This Is the Man Who Governs," and published a denunciation of him. Stirbey, he said, was the "moral author of all the evils which have fallen on the country and recently on the crown: Every citizen is the victim of the occult influence and the intrigues of Barbo Stirbey." Shaken by the fact that people could use such tactics to make "a hero & martyr" out of her son, Marie did not realize that this story, started by Filipescu, would be repeated and embellished over the years until one day it would be accepted as historical fact.

To counter rumors like these, Marie wrote Carol asking him to send an open letter to the Patriarch of the Roumanian Orthodox Church, explaining the circumstances of his defection. Although Carol would not admit why he renounced the succession, he did try to clear the King with the least possible damage to himself. "Many people think I was the victim of a plot...I could assure Your Holiness that I acted upon my own will and fully aware of my deed. Thus, they who intend to make my dear father responsible for my action commit a great sin before God," said Carol, whose letter was published in the papers. As to Elena Lupescu, she claimed total innocence. "I have no responsibility in what has occurred," she told a reporter. "When everything is known it will be seen that the guilty one is not myself."

The former Crown Prince, who complained about having to stay in his room for nine days to avoid the press, sent word out from behind closed doors that "everything except the official communications are extravagant and damnable lies. I am astonished," he said, "that serious newspapers should publish such fantastic news, which is nothing else but subversive propaganda against my family and myself." When he finally gave an interview, it was as curious and disconnected as the Prince himself:

"I have the highest esteem for Princess Helen, who is an exemplary wife and mother. I am very indignant at the infamous insinuations that have been made against her. As for my son, I adore him. I categorically deny all stories about my future. I will continue to love and serve my country. What I desire is silence. Another thing is painful to me—the allusion made to a certain plot. Say quite clearly that there is absolutely no political reason for my act. My fidelity as prince and my loyalty as a soldier are proof enough in my favor to make it unnecessary to refute such absurdities. The anti-royalist attitude with which I am credited doesn't even deserve a denial on my part. I remain a loyal subject and shall never be an obstacle for my country."

Nevertheless, Carol's abdication was a windfall for the enemies of the dynasty. They seized on his desertion to cut down his mother and succeeded in planting serious doubts about her in the minds of her people. In the desperation and near loss of faith that followed, Queen Marie turned to the teachings of the Baha'i religion, which she discovered a month or so after Carol's flight. The Baha'i call for the unification of humanity under one faith was vastly appealing to the Queen, who had always rebelled against the rigid distinctions separating her immediate family into three religions, and the Baha'i goal of universal peace and its warnings of social upheaval seemed prophetic to the distraught woman. Although she continued to attend the Protestant Church, she said that she prayed "better at home with my Baha-u-llah books and teachings... For the first time I have *felt* religion," said the woman who had tried and failed throughout her life to find the unquestioning belief she thought she ought to have and now needed for support.

Another influence during that unhappy winter was Frank Buchman, an American evangelist and self-styled "soul surgeon," founder of the Oxford Group movement and his own religion, A First Century Christian Fellowship. Sent to Marie by American friends living in Turkey, Buchman spent some weeks at Cotroceni Palace, reading from the Bible with the Queen and her children and "spreading his kind, uniting atmosphere over us all."

Carol's defection left Roumania reeling, and in the backlash, Bratianu was swept out of office. Required by law to reinstate or replace him, Ferdinand turned to Bratianu's own choice of successor, General Averescu, to form a new government. Marie, who did not believe that the people's choice, Juliu Maniu and his National Peasant Party, could overcome the current crisis, pushed the King toward Averescu. Averescu's following was the smallest in Parliament, numbering only five deputies, not enough to staff even a Cabinet. In summoning him, Ferdinand and Marie ignored the agitation for representation from the citizens of the New Kingdom, like the Transylvanians and Bessarabians, as well as the expressed preference of the general electorate of the Old Kingdom. Averescu was logrolled into office in the spring of 1926 amid seething anger and discontent. Seeing in the reactionary Prime Minister just another

Bratianu puppet and convinced by the enemies of the Liberal Party that Bratianu was to blame for Carol's abdication, the public was prevented from demonstrating only by the presence of large numbers of troops patrolling the capital.

The King's actions can be most charitably explained in terms of failing health and the corresponding need to keep the trusted Bratianu in power. By 1926 Ferdinand may well have suspected that there was something seriously wrong with him. Added to his physical malaise was his agony over Carol and the fact that his successor was now a four-year-old boy. As to Marie, she had lost her faith in changes of government. For more than thirty years she had watched politicians come and go, each one ranting about the dishonesty and mismanagement of the previous party before falling into the same practices.

The Queen was worried about her husband. To give him a rest she took him on a three-week trip on the royal yacht through the quiet canals of the Danube delta, a shimmering marshland of islands and lakes. She hoped that cruising through the reeds in search of new specimens to add to his herbarium would cure Nando of his ills, both physical and emotional.

Before they left, Ferdinand agreed to speak with a correspondent from the Associated Press. "The country is completely calm," announced the shaken King. "There is not the slightest indication of revolution. The peasants were never better off or more contented... Our dynasty is as secure as ever."

> We who are placed above the crowd are not climbing... so we are never out of breath.
>
> —*QUEEN MARIE OF ROUMANIA*

*T*he political impact of Carol's flight began to die down during the spring of 1926, and Marie was able to make plans toward the realization of a long-standing dream, a visit to the United States. She had always wanted to travel in the new world, where her wartime valor and outspoken writing had made her a well-loved figure. She hoped to do in America what she had done at the Peace Conference—give Roumania "a living face," which would generate some much-needed loans. She probably also wanted to renew her personal heroic image, fading in the light of her son's misbehavior. There was nothing wrong with the idea of such a journey, only the auspices under which the Queen proposed to make it.

Twenty-four years earlier, when she was still Crown Princess, Marie had attended a dance performance by Loie Fuller at the Roumanian National Theater. Deeply moved by the presentation, the twenty-seven-year-old Princess left a photograph of herself gowned in delicate white lace and signed, "One of your most ardent admirers, in memory of a delicious evening with which you rejoiced all my love of art." On the back of the photo, Loie, whose literary style was even more inventive than her dancing, added, "My mind's eye looked so hard that tears came to my soul, tears of gladness and of joy, to be remembered ever. In remembrance of an artist's soul I met in the wilderness and saw in the sunshine of truth, THE Maria!"

Loie Fuller was not exactly what she appeared on stage. Strip off the undulating veils, turn off the multicolored lights, and the spinning blond wraith unfurled into a pug-nosed farm girl from Illinois with a penchant for celebrities and a naïveté to rival Marie's own. Loie's art, which was based on innovation in costume and lighting, was not difficult to imitate, and to sustain her popularity she needed patrons. Her friendship with Marie was sealed when the Crown Princess helped her over one of her lifelong financial embarrassments a few days after her performance. They corresponded for the rest of their lives, and during the war, Loie, whose career was over, organized aid for Roumania and came to Jassy as a Red Cross nurse.

After the war Marie saw Loie whenever she was in Paris. During the twenties they collaborated on a ballet based on Marie's "The Lily of Life," which Loie later made into a film, and Marie signed papers giving her friend exclusive rights to the production of her stories for stage and screen. The Queen entrusted Loie with state business as well, allowing her to speak for Roumania with Frank Polk, head of the American Delegation to the Peace Conference. "I have a blind faith in Loie," she said; "the difficulty is to get others to have the same faith." With Marie's help, Loie evolved plans for a "mighty organization" that would help Roumania "in a thousand ways." She worked tirelessly if unsuccessfully for Marie and her country, bringing the President of International Harvester, a Senator who helped draft the Farm Loan Act, and sugar heiress Alma Spreckels to Bucharest to talk to the Queen about how to improve Roumania's economy.

Loie also presented her friend Samuel Hill to the Queen. Hill had made and lost a fortune in railways and road construction. Referring to himself as "Farmer Hill" and twirling his Phi Beta Kappa key, this strangely ceremonious American claimed to have gone around the world seven times and served in both the German and the Russian Armies. He was a large man with powerful shoulders and a huge head, bushy white brows over intense blue eyes, and a very low voice. Marie called him "the White Lion." He was given to building edifices honoring peace and the heroes of war.

Marie of Roumania was not Sam Hill's first royalty. "Mr. Hill..." she wrote in her diary after the war, "has singled out Albert [King Albert of Belgium] and me as the two sovereigns that are worthy of upholding, and he is going to uphold us with his tremendous power of great financier and idealist combined. There are... curious and magnificent beings upon this earth, and sometimes, one suddenly, most unexpectedly, stumbles upon them."

In 1926 Loie convinced Marie that it would help Roumania if she made an unofficial tour of the United States. The excuse was an invitation from Sam Hill to dedicate his new building, the Maryhill Museum of Fine Arts, located in the state of Washington. Maryhill was conceived of by Hill as a monument to peace, Hill's dead divorced wife, and the Queen of Roumania. Although he started it as a fortress, Loie persuaded him to turn it into a museum.

As soon as Marie agreed to come to America to perform the dedication, Loie began to make plans for the trip. With a commitment from the Queen of Roumania, it was not hard for Loie to form a committee to sponsor the tour. But the dancer was soon dismissed by the members of her own committee, practical citizens who considered themselves more qualified to work with chambers of commerce, society matrons, charitable organizations, and provincial mayors. Begging, crying, threatening to cancel her friend's projected trip, Loie sent off long, weepy letters to Bucharest while the social establishment took Marie's tour completely out of her hands.

Although "broken-hearted" for her friend, Marie was busy at home confronting a distinct lack of enthusiasm for her voyage. The King had just undergone another operation, this one very minor, but his series of indispositions over the past year had people quite worried. Assured by the doctors that Ferdinand was fine, Marie herself was not concerned about his health; he had, in fact, recovered particularly quickly and painlessly from his latest indisposition. The King did not discourage her trip, nor did Prince Stirbey. Although Marie knew that "every parting" filled Barbo "with nameless anguish," he wanted her to go as a reward for years of hard work. "Be happy!" he wrote, "because Your Majesty deserves it."

Bratianu and the Liberals, out of office only a few months, were opposed to the journey, citing the exaggerated publicity sure to accompany the Queen, as well as her well-known tendency toward "dangerous enthusiasms." But Averescu, currently in power, judged that Marie would generate good will and, with luck, some American dollars.

While the Queen denied any motive for the journey beyond curiosity and friendship, the New York *World* asked, "Is the object of Marie's visit pleasure, or is it business? If it is pleasure, why the elaborate political discussions in Roumania, and the elaborate diplomatic preparations throughout the better part of the civilized world? If it is business, would it be too much to ask just what that business is?"

This sort of question did not disturb Marie, who, with her usual enthusiasms (the ones that worried Bratianu), filled twenty-one packing cases with bronzes, marbles, statuary, costumes, and furniture, earmarked as gifts for Sam Hill's Maryhill Museum. The Queen asked to take Prince Nicolas and Princess Ileana with her. Their good looks and charm, she felt, would add to her overall effect, and she was afraid to leave them behind in the care of their absentminded father. Just before her departure, Nando gave her an elaborate watch for her birthday, which would be celebrated while she was away. "He was so touching about it, had chosen it with such care and yet was afraid I might not like it! dear old thing, so full of kindliness. May God keep him safe whilst I am far," she wrote in her diary.

The small railway station at Sinaia was overrun with family, friends, and politicians the evening of Marie's departure. It was, the press noted, a highly emotional leave-taking at which the King, the Queen, and Princess Ileana were all in tears. In response to a bouquet of flowers presented to her by the Minister of the Interior, the Queen offered her farewell message to the Roumanian people:

"I depart taking in my heart the love of my country and carrying it to America with the thought that there I shall represent and thus serve Rumania. It is my wish that my country will keep until my return the same warm remembrance of me which I now take with me, and will follow my travels with the thought that I shall always try to help it."

These bland generalizations hit the front pages of *The New York Times* on October 4, 1926, and from that day until the end of the month, the Queen was off page one of New York's most prestigious newspaper only twice. Her arrival in Paris was hailed in the American press with almost the same fervor as her subsequent debarkation in New York.

RUMANIA'S QUEEN
BUYS PARIS GOWNS

Slender, Bobbed-Haired and
Chic, Marie Creates Sensation
in the French Capital.

PREPARES FOR VOYAGE HERE

Will Be One of Most Beautifully
Dressed Women Ever to
Visit Us, It Is Said.

Although the Queen's sojourn in Paris served nothing more politically significant than the couture industry, she was met at the station by several members of the French government. Presented with an armful of roses and surrounded by a battery of photographers, the fifty-year-old Marie beamed widely and remarked that it was "a trial for any one to be photographed so early in the morning after such a long journey."

The Queen had promised her government to grant no interviews until she reached New York, and the press, unable to quote her, filled its columns with lengthy paragraphs on her clothes. During her first day in Paris, she was described in minute detail in three separate outfits, all of them covering her calf, as befitted her age and station, and worn with the current style of close-fitting hat, quite unbecoming to her. Although it was noted that Marie attended the theater five evenings in a row and the movies at least once, that she lunched with the Maharajah of Kapurthala, received the Aga Khan and Mrs. Woodrow Wilson, the big news in the papers centered on the three sports outfits and innumerable dinner gowns she purchased for her trip abroad. Thirty trunks, it was reported, stood in the corridors of the Ritz Hotel waiting to be filled.

The night before her departure, Marie saw Carol, who was living in Paris. She had been contemplating this reunion with "dread and emotion." Carol had leased a villa for himself and Elena Lupescu in the Parisian suburb of Neuilly. He was in the process of fighting a ten-million-franc suit brought against him by Zizi for damages incurred by grief over their divorce. Zizi, her lawyer claimed, had been forced to submit to the divorce on the grounds of state and dynastic interests, which were invalidated by Carol's subsequent abdication. With no throne to inherit and Mme. Lupescu at his side, the former Crown Prince of Roumania was just another ordinary deserter, leaving one woman for another.

Caught up in personal problems, Carol complained to his mother that the Roumanian Legation in Paris did not treat him with sufficient respect and that he was "offended" because they had not formally announced the Queen's visit to him. He was seemingly unconscious of the political chaos he left behind in Roumania and blamed his wife for his decision to leave. He told the Queen that he and Sitta had planned his flight together because they were incompatible and he, being a gentleman, wanted to give her an excuse to divorce him. Marie did not know what to think. She wanted desperately to believe her son. She found him "astonishingly well informed" about Roumania, including details about the palace. She believed his indignation was genuine when she repeated rumors that he was planning a *coup d'état* on behalf of the National Peasant Party. "I am certainly loyal to Papa and you," Carol assured her, "nothing would ever induce me to be dragged into a political intrigue. When people want to come and talk politics with me, I keep them at arm's length." Carol asked his mother's permission to come to the station the next day to see her off: "You know, Mama, that they say you are against me; if you let me come to the station, they'll all see you are not!"

The Queen, Prince Nicolas, and Princess Ileana were late next day arriving at the Gare St. Lazare for the boat train, and when the royal cars finally sped into the station, the reason for the delay was apparent. Carol, "his arms full of flowers," was in the first car with the Queen. "It was," according to the press, "a much worried, pale young Prince who walked nervously down the platform beside his mother" and who "impulsively embraced Queen Marie...as she was about to board her private car for Cherbourg to sail for America. Firmly grasping the youth's hand the Queen returned the salute and with a smile hurried up the steps to her private salon."

It was a painful and confusing scene. Relatives like Ducky, Baby Bee, and Princess Alice of Greece did not know "where to look" or "what to do." Aware that the press was bound to jump to conclusions, Marie announced that although she and Carol had been personally reconciled, there was no change in the political situation and that it was not within her power to alter it. She said it, but no one believed it. "Today's demonstration before the representatives of the President of the French Republic and the Government of France," *The New York Times* alleged, "was Queen Marie's melodramatic method of announcing to the world that the Rumanian royal household was again united. The Queen chose this open manner of telling the world so that there could not be any doubts."

The Queen traveled with a party of seventeen and an entire railway car of luggage—168 pieces, 109 of which belonged to the royal family itself. Marie's "American trousseau," as it was called, filled more than fifty trunks. The newspapers took great delight in describing the last-minute hysteria at the Ritz Hotel as bellmen and midinettes ran through the corridors and up and down the great staircase in their hurry to add last-minute purchases to the huge steamer trunks and flowered hatboxes presided over by the Queen's maids. Marie's departure from Cherbourg was as confusing and colorful as her exodus from the Ritz. Everything susceptible to redecoration had been renovated in her honor, from red velvet curtains hung in the railway station to a completely refurbished royal suite on board the S.S. *Leviathan*.

Once on board and at sea, Marie delighted her fellow first-class passengers with the democratic nature of her activities. The Queen walked freely among them on deck; dined frequently in the main dining room; entertained the four-year-old son of a New York garment manufacturer in her suite; swam in the mornings in the ship's pool, returning to her cabin in her bathrobe and cap; and engaged in soul-searching discussions with her old mentor, Frank Buchman, also on the *Leviathan*. Marie was both considerate and generous with the crew, dispensing handsome gifts, including a gold watch with the royal crest, numerous gold- and silver-crested pens, and many large autographed pictures to those who served her.

The Queen's only problem on board was the press. Before her departure, she had agreed to write a series of articles on her trip, entitled *My Impressions of America*, for the North American Newspaper Alliance. An agent for N.A.N.A. threatened to cancel her contract if she gave interviews to the American journalists traveling with her. Since she had already "drawn considerable sums in advance" for the articles she intended to write—most of which she had signed over to Loie Fuller—Marie was forced to forgo the interviews. Besides the agent for N.A.N.A., there was a representative of a second syndicate for whom the Queen had recently written a series of articles; he claimed that her old contract was still in force and that his company owned exclusive control over her output for the next six weeks. Marie of Roumania on tour, said the Associated Press, was assuming the posture of an opera star with rival managers.

Even before the Queen's arrival in New York, the retail clothing firm of Abraham & Straus ran an advertisement with radioed sketches of her gowns designed by Redfern of Paris, duplicates of which, Madame was assured, were "now on the ocean en route to us for quick reproduction." Another store, catering "exclusively to the woman who wears her clothes with an aristocratic air—but pays a modest price," promised daily bulletins with "authentic information about Her Majesty's wardrobe!" From this, it was intimated, cheap copies might be extrapolated.

By the time the *Leviathan* neared New York, everyone who could find an angle had claimed his share of the Queen except Loie Fuller. Withdrawn into silence in a suite at the Plaza Hotel, shrouded in resentment and old veils, Loie authorized a friend to issue her statement of defeat. "I have nothing whatever to do with the visit and mission of Her Majesty the Queen of Roumania except to manifest a lifelong devotion to one whom I consider the noblest woman in the world and any statement to the contrary is false and unfounded."

Ignoring the commercial hullabaloo she had aroused, Queen Marie entered the United States under the official auspices of the American government, and her visits in New York and Washington, D.C., preserved the sort of dignified hysteria acceptable for a granddaughter of Queen Victoria and the Tsar of Russia. When the *Leviathan* docked at quarantine early in the morning of October 18, 1926, a municipal steamer and a Coast Guard cutter, bearing members of the Mayor of New York's Welcoming Committee, arrived to take the Queen and her party to The Battery. Waiting for Marie were two handpicked battalions from the Army and the Navy, three batteries of coast artillery, a crack infantry war unit, and a company of Marines. Seven hundred and fifty policemen had also been pressed into service.

Led by a platoon of mounted police, the Queen's twenty-car motorcade set out from Battery Place exactly at noon, the hour always chosen by the Mayor's Welcoming Committee to ensure enough workers on the streets. Proceeding up Broadway under a shower of ticker tape and torn paper, Marie smiled graciously at tens of thousands of applauding New Yorkers. "I was not prepared for the American custom of throwing papers of every size, shape and description from the thousands of windows of the extraordinary buildings, whose tops I could hardly see. The air seemed alive with fluttering wings, as though swarms of birds had been let loose in the streets."

Dressed in a burgundy velvet, sable-trimmed coat and a gold turban, Marie was officially received at New York City Hall by Mayor Jimmy Walker. The Queen and the handsome, debonair Mayor liked each other immediately. When Walker hesitated before pinning the gold medal of the City of New York to Marie's bodice, the Queen encouraged him: "Proceed, Your Honor," she said, smiling. "The risk is mine."

"And such a beautiful risk it is, Your Majesty," acknowledged the Mayor.

Responding to Walker's welcoming speech, the Queen gave her first radio address and climbed back into her car with Jimmy Walker at her side for the trip to Pennsylvania Station. There was a nasty wind blowing, and the Mayor leaned over to place the limousine lap robe over Her Majesty's knees. Just at that moment the motorcade passed a building under construction. An ironworker caught sight of the gesture.

"Hey, Jimmy," he yelled, "you made her yet?"

The Mayor, not known for blushing, turned purple-red.

"Everyone seems to know you in this great city," temporized the Queen.

"Some of them know me very well indeed," mumbled Walker.

Grover Whalen, Chairman of the Welcoming Committee, said that the Queen "saved the day." Marie, he reported, quick to sense Walker's embarrassment, looked the Mayor of New York straight in the eye and smiled. "Tell him yes," said the Queen, who obviously had no idea what the workman meant.

This was typical of Marie, who sailed through presentations, embarrassing moments, and even confrontations shielded by a singular artlessness. Looking neither right nor left, advancing along the path laid out for her, she was comfortable with her own performance and unaware of her judges. Ebullient and enthusiastic, she never lost her composure or her good humor, even with the often cynical representatives of the press.

During her first few hours in the United States, the Queen gave three interviews. Since questions put to royalty were normally limited to polite inquiries about their good health, these press conferences broke diplomatic precedent, delighted the journalists, and unhinged the nerves of those sent along to protect Marie's image. She fielded questions on her journalistic ventures, the persecution of Jews in Roumania, and Carol's position vis-à-vis the throne. She enchanted both reporters and photographers with her smiles and seeming candor. In braving what the *Times* called "probably the most relentless camera bombardment that anyone has ever been called on to face in the world's history," the Queen amazed photographers with her knowledge of camera angles, admonishing Princess Ileana to stop ruining the pictures by waving her hand in front of her face when acknowledging the applause of the crowd.

Not everyone, of course, was flattering. A Socialist candidate for Governor of New York castigated national and local officials for "undue zest in groveling before the Queen of the most corruptly governed country of Europe." And from London the *Evening Standard* scoffed, "We have not yet heard that by some marvel of engineering the Statue of Liberty, which guards New York Harbor, has been made to curtsy as Queen Marie of Roumania passes, but nothing else seems lacking to show how dearly a republic can adore a regular royal Queen."

As soon as her motorcades and receptions were over, Marie boarded a train for the nation's capital, traveling in the private car of the President of the Pennsylvania Railroad, nodding and smiling to curious factory workers whose grimy windows backed on the Penn's tracks. Several thousand civilians waited at the station to see her, and her motorcade, the third of the day, traveled slowly through the brightly lit boulevards of the nation's capital so that eager Washingtonians could get a good look at her.

Since precedent called for visiting rulers to make the initial overture to the Chief Executive, Queen Marie arrived at the White House at 4 P.M. the following afternoon to call on President and Mrs. Coolidge. Used to welcoming their guests themselves or being met at the door by fellow royalties, the Queen and her children were bewildered by the phalanx of A.D.C.s gathered to greet them; "the President," Marie noted in her diary, "behaves ever so much more royally than any King ever would... he does not himself receive his guests, but comes in after they are there and goes away first leaving them to his military household. In fact *we* would not consider this a polite way of receiving guests, but this is their ceremonial and is strictly adhered to."

Led into the mansion through the lobby and into the Green Room by seven presidential aides, the royal party was left there while word of their arrival was sent upstairs to the President. Coolidge, his wife, and the Secretary of State descended to the Red Room. When assured that all was in order, they moved into the Oval Blue Room, into which the Queen was then escorted. "I have the honor," announced Mr. J. Butler Wright, Assistant Secretary of State, "to present Her Majesty the Queen of Roumania to the President of the United States and Mrs. Coolidge."

Immediately all extraneous persons withdrew, leaving the three principals and the Secretary of State, Frank B. Kellogg. The Americans conducted the Queen back to the Red Room for a chat. In due course, Mrs. Coolidge introduced the subject of children, and word was relayed back via the lineup of aides stretched from the door of the Red Room through the Blue Room to the Green Room, where Prince Nicolas and Princess Ileana had been deposited. Marie's children were produced and presented and a few further politenesses were exchanged before the President and his wife rose to indicate that the interview was over. The formal part of the visit was clocked at four minutes. The time consumed from the moment the Queen entered the White House until she left it—thirteen minutes exactly.

"The President is a thin, dry, waxy-faced little man..." Marie noted. "He talks in short sentences as though words were a pain to him. His mouth is a slit which he keeps tight shut, his nose is long and thin, his hair a sort of golden-red. He is the dryest... most unemotional thing ever made but... he has a sort of twinkle in his keen little eyes & something of a far-off cousin to a smile occasionally at the corner of his relentless-looking mouth.... in spite of all this the President was somehow sympathetic to me."

The feeling was not reciprocated. Wary of the Queen's trip from the beginning, Coolidge had not been consulted as to whether her visit would be welcome. Terrified of being engulfed in the frenzied publicity accompanying Marie's tour, the President had purposely delayed scheduling their meeting until nearly twenty-four hours after the Queen's entry into the capital. During the morning the Queen had committed a social gaffe by allowing one of her ladies-in-waiting to respond to flowers sent her by the First Lady. Not only was there a specific social slight to be weathered, but the air hung heavy with presidential dread of exposure to distasteful and contagious display. Nonetheless, as soon as the White House limousines had whisked Marie back to the Roumanian Legation, they returned to take the presidential party for their obligatory return call.

This time the presentation was made in reverse—the President and First Lady to the Queen—but as before, everyone else withdrew so the principals might chat. This exchange may have offered something better than the first conversation, for it was reported that those outside the drawing room actually overheard one or two bursts of laughter. In accordance with the tradition which says that visits of this sort must last the same amount of time, the President and his wife excused themselves four minutes after their arrival.

"According to the somewhat absurd custom... hardly were we back to our own legation, than the President and his wife drove up to our door to pay back our call..." Marie wrote. "This visit, however, ended upon a humorous note. The never-to-be avoided photographer claimed his rights— that tyrant against whom neither King nor President can stand up. The President, who had already put on his hat and coat, took them off again and patiently sat down with a resigned face between Mrs. Coolidge and myself and submitted to the camera."

In the White House version, the Queen of Roumania caught President Coolidge unawares by hiding the photographers behind the drawing-room curtains, producing them at just the moment when the Coolidges were preparing to leave and forcing him to pose with his hostess. According to Mrs. Coolidge's social secretary, the President's "anger and annoyance increased when he later viewed the unwelcome proof that this clever woman had outwitted him. Queen Marie," said the secretary, "is a most determined lady and was not to be outdone by a mere President of the United States."

Next morning's papers, emblazoned with reproductions of a grim-faced Coolidge and a triumphant Queen, did little to smooth the atmosphere for the formal dinner in Marie's honor that evening at the White House. The occasion had already upset the President. With every society matron in the capital angling for an invitation, he finally reduced the dinner to an official function of state with only forty-six guests, all of whom represented the governments of America, Roumania, or Britain. It was a dismal, rigid affair.

At one minute to 8 P.M. the Queen appeared at the White House, glistening from head to toe. She had put on her diamond-and-pearl diadem and a Patou gown of white crepe embroidered in silver and rhinestones and trailed by a long, one-shoulder train. On her feet she wore rhinestone-encrusted slippers. Jeweled with three strands of her famous pearls, Marie wore a satin blue sash over her breast to signify the highest Roumanian

Order. Her skirt had been designed with side panels strategically placed to hide the fact that it, unlike all her other gowns, was made in the current knee-length fashion. Why she wore it to the White House, no one knows, unless it was an act of pure mischievousness. The Queen must have been briefed on the official attitude toward the new styles; she must have known that Mrs. Coolidge continued to wear floor-length gowns, as the President did not like the sight of ladies' knees. (This may have been due to priggishness or the fact that, as Grace Coolidge's biographer phrased it, the First Lady's legs "were her least graceful feature.") For this particular evening Mrs. Coolidge had chosen a subdued white gown brocaded in pastel velvet flowers with a train lined in mauve chiffon, "modest" pearls, and matching earrings.

"The ceremony at the White House, which is a noble building," said Marie, "was if anything a degree stranger than our first contact. I was ushered in with all ceremony and every honour due to a Queen but the President & his wife came afterwards arm in arm, received me as well as his guests and afterwards left the room again first with his wife, leaving me to the care of his 'suites' in a way that certainly a King would not leave a Queen. At dinner they sat on high chairs different to ours and were served *first*."

Everyone watched while Marie failed to engage Coolidge in small talk. The silence between the consommé and the lobster Newburg made the guests squirm. Dinner, which was usually clocked at one and a quarter hours, lasted just fifty minutes. After dinner the President took the gentlemen to his study for coffee and cigars while the ladies withdrew to the Red Room. The Queen annoyed the White House staff by engaging Alice Longworth in animated conversation, thus precluding other presentations, and both ladies shocked the assembly by lighting up cigarettes. When the men arrived to escort the women back to the Blue Room, the President bade the Queen a hasty good night. By 9:45 Marie found herself and her children on their way out of the White House and back to the Roumanian Legation.

The following day the Queen returned to New York, where she was installed at the old Hotel Ambassador on Park Avenue. For six months preparations had been underway to receive her. "The fourth floor of the hotel had been transformed into a miniature palace," raved one reporter, who estimated the value of the furnishings at something just under a million dollars. The soft-green walls were hung with priceless Gobelin tapestries; Louis XV and XVI furniture, ancient bronzes, and period porcelains were brought in for the Queen, along with the inevitable masses of flowers from friends and admirers. A final touch was the removal of American telephones and the installation of French ones with glass mouthpieces that could be disinfected daily. For the royal safety, there were thirty detectives; for the royal calls, a special telephone operator; for the royal ascents and descents, a private elevator. In charge of the royal suite was a special housekeeper with twelve assistants and chambermaids; in charge of the royal table, a chef formerly in the employ of the Kaiser.

On the evening of the Queen's first day in New York, William Nelson

Cromwell, founder of the Society of the Friends of Roumania, gave a reception for seven hundred. "We had a queen from a medieval legend that night," said Constance Lily Morris, Marie's American hostess. The Queen's gown, designed by Redfern, was silver embroidery over black velvet, worn with a train of peacock-blue. Under her Russian diadem of diamonds and walnut-size sapphires, Marie had placed a cap of pearls, from which cascaded ropes of pearls that she caught under her chin and allowed to hang down to her waist. She also wore the diamond chain from her Coronation with its huge egg-shaped sapphire. Seated on a carved and gilded wooden throne under the flags of America and Roumania, Marie received guests brought up to her by footmen in blue satin livery encrusted with gold.

The morning after the reception she was sick with a cold. Only "royal training," she said, kept her on her feet giving speeches "with an aching throat." She found a doctor who agreed to treat her without putting her to bed. "I explained to him: I CANNOT be sent to bed. But it certainly took every inch of my energy not to collapse." As one of her hostesses put it, "Cold or no cold, Queen Marie had not voyaged this far to be quiet or unseen."

On Marie's second day in New York she gave three major speeches. Although the Queen concentrated on personal anecdotes of her life, a representative of the Banque Chissoveloni accompanied her to the Bankers Club. He reminded Marie's audience that the entire debt of Roumania ($342 million) was roughly equivalent to only a quarter of the resources of one New York bank, an officer of which was in the room at the time.

For the next few days Marie plowed through an unremitting succession of luncheons, dinners, receptions, visits, honors, and speeches. "I was never left breathing space to open a letter, to put my flowers in water, to comb my hair, to wash my hands or to explain to my breathless maids what I intended to wear." ". . . often have I been obliged to put a screen before my bath, so as to be able to continue talking to people during my ablutions."

The object of uncontrolled social lust, the Queen was annoyed by the "fearful competition" among her sponsors for her attention. Her principal host was Nelson Cromwell, a man frequently in his cups. "Old Cromwell & the Legation have their knife in Loie," Marie complained. Another source of strife was Frank Buchman. Pressed by their official hosts to push Buchman aside, Marie and her children balked. Public repudiation of an old friend, the Queen said, was against their royal "creed."

In spite of jealousies and frantic scheduling, no one enjoyed popping flashbulbs more than Marie, and no one delighted more in charming industrial tycoons and dressing for their wives. Unfortunately, no one was more blindly unaware of what would set in motion a potentially hostile press. The apogee of Marie's foolishness—Loie Fuller's performance of *The Lily of Life* at the Metropolitan Opera House—brought the Queen's stay in New York to a dismal conclusion.

The evening was billed as a benefit for a Motherhood Memorial to be erected in Washington, D.C., by the Women's Universal Alliance. The first outcry went up over the price of tickets. A second objection was raised over Loie Fuller's fee; with Loie demanding 50 percent of the box-office take, it could hardly be called a charitable event. When Loie published a list of patrons without their permission or that of the Queen, New York society's biggest gala of the season shriveled overnight. The crowd was sparse. Many orchestra seats remained empty, while speculators outside the Opera House tried to ditch tickets for fifty cents. Although the controversy preceding the event was, in Marie's words, a "nightmare," she wore her best diadem in honor of Loie and concentrated on a charming informal dinner preceding the ballet, given by Mrs. Averell Harriman, at which she met Nancy Astor's sister, Irene Gibson.* By the time the press broke the story of Loie's fizzled gala, the Queen and her party were already on board their train for a journey across the continent.

The *Royal Roumanian*, the train that carried Marie and her party on a tour of the United States, was called by *The New York Times* "one of the most beautiful and elaborate trains ever placed on rails." It was composed of seven private cars, donated by officials of various railway companies, each with its own dining room, chef, and porters; three compartment cars; two sleepers; a general diner, changed every time the train switched railway companies; and baggage cars. Marie's coach alone contained a bedroom with a brass bed, a bath fitted with porcelain and marble fixtures, a second bedroom for Princess Ileana, and an office; at one end was a drawing room; at the other, a private dining room and kitchen. At the end of the train itself was a glass observation car, used by the Queen as a reception room.

The *Royal Roumanian* was none too large for the eighty-five travelers on board. The Queen's entourage included two ladies-in-waiting, Princess Ileana's governess, a representative of Prime Minister Averescu, a gentlemen-in-waiting, and an A.D.C. Other members of the party included Ira Nelson Morris, the Roumanian Counsul General in charge of programs and official entertainments, and his wife, Constance Lily Morris. Major Stanley Washburn, a former journalist and old war friend, now said to be suffering from shell shock and too much alcohol, had been named the Queen's personal aide. The chief executive and official host for the journey was Colonel J. H. Carroll. As the representative of the railroad companies that had agreed to give the Queen free transcontinental passage, Colonel Carroll brooked no schedule changes or dissension in the ranks.

Announcing that she was tired of top-hatted officials and formal receptions and wanted to see "real Americans," Marie set off for Albany, Utica, Syracuse, and Buffalo. To win back a disenchanted press, she gave two informal interviews to journalists traveling on her train. The effect on the

*The original Gibson girl.

reporter from *The New York Times* was dazzling. Pronouncing the occasion "free and frank and jolly," he effervesced over his newfound friends: ". . . the Queen, and for that matter the Prince and Princess, enjoy nothing more than to have those with whom they are visiting talk and act with full freedom. Very likely today's joint discussion by royalty and the press set a precedent in the world in the relations between sovereigns and the public. . . Palaces ceased to be formidable edifices, inhabited by remote personages divinely appointed to wear crowns, but residences of families with servant problems, in which the children plague their 'mommies' and their 'grannies' and fall into ponds and get their faces dirty and want to eat things which are not good for them."

As further proof of the Queen's graciousness, the reporter quoted the servants on the train. "I don't know anything about Queens," said the porter of the observation car, Samuel Williams, "but this one's certainly a lady. We're used to carrying wealthy people, of course, and usually, although they pay us for our services, we don't get a word of appreciation, but every request the Queen, or the Prince or the Princess, makes is made with a smile, and they say 'thank you so much' when we do anything for them." Dora Lee Johnson, a maid on the *Royal Roumanian*, chimed in. "Everything he says is true. I've been curling the hair of the Queen and the Princess and giving them waves, and I know. The Queen and the Princess are just well-bred ladies who treat us with more courtesy than any passengers we have ever had."

Marie further delighted the press by planning one whole day free of government pomp—a day devoted to the farmers of North Dakota, men whose lives, she wrongly supposed, paralleled those of her Roumanian peasants. Although the poorest farmers found to converse with the Queen plowed some eight hundred acres and drove their fashionably dressed wives to the station in up-to-date cars, Marie enjoyed speaking with them. "An American handshake and a friendly greeting put us at our ease," said one of the farm women, a Mrs. Smith. "She is a wonderful hostess and seemed really interested in us. There was nothing regal about either her or her manner." The Queen wore a plain brown dress for the occasion and no jewelry. "She said she wanted to talk with North Dakota farmers because they are somewhat similar to those in Roumania," Mrs. Smith commented, adding, "She did most of the talking."

After the farmers came the cowboys and Indians. The Queen was the honored guest at a rodeo and was adopted into the Sioux nation as a "war woman." She was carried on a buffalo rug into the tepee of Chief Red Tomahawk, the man who had killed Sitting Bull. As a symbol of her bravery, her finger was pricked with a sharpened flint, and a drop of blood was withdrawn.

On November 3, 1926, the *Royal Roumanian* arrived at the station at Maryhill, where the Queen was scheduled to dedicate Sam Hill's memorial museum. But the goal of Marie's odyssey turned out to be nothing more than a small western town of a few frame buildings, the largest of which was the general store. Modern roads, the contribution of Sam Hill, were the major feature of the rocky countryside. One of them ran from the railway station up a steep hill and along a mountain ridge to Hill's half-built Museum of Fine Arts. As a matter of fact, it ran right through it.

The building had been started during the war, but left unfinished. Not even the windows had been put in place. Of white concrete, resembling a garage more than a museum, the strange skeletal edifice loomed above the sagebrush like a symbol of every criticism leveled at the Queen throughout her tour. Had she, the granddaughter of an empress and a tsar, crossed an ocean and a continent to dedicate this?

Two thousand guests and scores of reporters gathered in front of the gaudily decorated construction for the dedication. The Queen appeared "nervous and strained" as she sat through the long, overblown speeches preceding her own, but when she stood up to speak, "her head was high and her voice rich and full." Only too aware of the absurdity of Hill's unrealized vision, Marie determined to make spirit triumph over architectural fact.

"As I stand here today in this curious and interesting building, I would like to explain why I came. There is much more than concrete in this structure. There is a dream built into this place—a dream for today and especially for tomorrow. There are great dreamers and there are great workers in this world. . . . Samuel Hill is my friend. He is not only a dreamer, but he is a worker. Samuel Hill once gave me his hand and said that if there was anything on earth I needed I had only to ask. Some may even scoff, for they do not understand. But I have understood. So when Samuel Hill asked me to come overseas to this house built in the wilderness, I came with love and understanding. . . ."

Enumerating some of the gifts she had brought "to this house that will one day be a museum," the Queen finished her speech standing "dominant and proud in front of the scarlet-draped throne." Her sincerity shook her audience. "Those of the crowd who understood the significance of the Queen's declaration," said one reporter, "stood in astonishment and admiration." "It was," said another, "one of the most dramatic and magnificent things this chronicler ever witnessed, and it is doubtful if any American public official could have the wit and courage to seize a disaster as she did and turn it into a triumph."

Marie stepped forward to the edge of the little rostrum and extended her hand toward Sam Hill, who had been waiting off at the side of the crowd. He walked over to her, took off his Stetson hat and bowed his great head, kissed her hand, then clasped it in both of his. Many in the audience were moved to tears.

Marie's moment of glory was short-lived. Controversy and bad publicity followed the path of the *Royal Roumanian* as a fight developed between Sam Hill and the Queen's personal aide, Major Washburn. "With two such devoted admirers of Her Majesty's charm as are aboard," one member of the party observed, "there is bound to arise some melée." When Hill threatened Washburn with a pistol in the presence of the press and Washburn barricaded himself in his compartment, Colonel Carroll, the representative of the railways, took over and uncoupled Hill's private coach from the train.

It was obvious even in Bucharest that matters had gotten out of hand. The next announcement from the royal party came from Professor Nicolas Petresco, the man representing the Roumanian government on the tour. Petresco called in the traveling correspondents to tell them that henceforward he would be the sole conduit through which news of the royal family would be channeled and that he would in the future be present at those delightful get-togethers between the Queen and the reporters. This "quasi-censorship," Petresco readily admitted, was invoked to prevent Marie from making statements that might have a harmful effect on the volatile political situation at home.

What was happening in Roumania was not exactly clear, but there was growing concern that a confrontation might be developing between Bratianu and the supporters of the former Crown Prince. Marie's all-too-public reconciliation with her son in Paris had, in spite of her denials, encouraged Carol's partisans to believe in the possibility of his restoration. The King appeared to be in failing health, which naturally brought forward the question of the succession. With many people convinced that popular sentiment would back Carol in a struggle for supremacy, Petresco had been instructed by the government to place himself between the Queen and the reporters.

For several days stories about Ferdinand's poor health had been making the rounds of the train and Marie had been growing "more and more anxious." She received a ciphered telegram from Barbo Stirbey, but no one could find the key to the cipher. More ciphered cables appeared, but they could not be decoded. Meanwhile, the Queen fulfilled appearances in Nebraska, Iowa, and Missouri. Finally, when she reached Chicago, she heard from both Prince Stirbey and Prime Minister Averescu that the King was definitely ill and she must not prolong her trip. A few days later word arrived that she must come home at once. Marie broke the news at a banquet in Indianapolis and cried when she said goodbye.

The Queen's aides spent the entire night sending telegrams to cancel her appearances and book passage home. Her last stop was a pilgrimage to Lincoln's log cabin. "A weary and depressed Queen" gave gifts and attended Colonel Carroll's farewell dinner on board her train, now racing back to New York. In spite of official statements from Bucharest, assuring her that the King's condition was not serious, and a cable from Mignon saying, "Papa better, do not worry," it was a sad group that marked off the last of its 8,750-mile journey.

The *Royal Roumanian* arrived with no fanfare back in Jersey City late on the afternoon of Saturday, November 20. Reporters asked Marie for her reactions to America. "This time America has seen me," she answered. "The next time I intend to see America... The official functions were strenuous of course," she added, "but I've met some lovely Mayors." No reference was made to Ferdinand's illness.

If the world expected Marie to shroud herself and withdraw into worried seclusion until her departure, it did not understand her training. Having made plans, the Queen felt obligated to carry them out, and her last three days in New York were crammed with activities. She took a boat trip to the Standard Oil plant at Bayonne; she visited Teddy Roosevelt's grave at Oyster Bay and his home at Sagamore Hill; she inspected the Dugout, a canteen for veterans; and she attended two or three luncheons, teas, and dinners every day. A sentimental populace was aghast. According to one disillusioned reporter, "a public which had been struck with sympathy for a woman eager to see her sick husband read each morning of how she had rushed from this function to that, and thought the less of her; and in cities she had stricken from her list when she decided to hasten home, people who had made effort and outlay to receive her heard about these things and must have felt defrauded."

Marie was aware of the criticism of the press, and at 5:30 the evening of her departure, she broadcast an emotional farewell address from the home of the President of the Friends of Roumania. That night she attended a dinner at Mrs. Astor's and from there boarded her ship. She sailed next day on the *Berengaria*. The only official commemoration of her departure came from the twenty-one-gun salute as the *Berengaria* passed Governors Island. Although Marie still appeared tireless, America had obviously wearied of the Queen.

PART FIVE

The Queen Mother

Chapter *27*

Power is a companion it is not easy to part with; when it goes, the zest of life goes with it. With dry eyes and clenched fist, one stares after it, jealous of the next one it will single out.

—*QUEEN MARIE OF ROUMANIA*

" *I* am sorry that my visit to America raised such unkind criticism," Marie wrote George V, whose opinion she treasured and who disapproved of her latest adventure. "I did what I thought right for my country.... I am not a conventional Queen, I admit, I must often make your dear old royal blood curdle, but my heart is in the right place, Georgie dear."

Even as Marie fretted over her reputation, the international press, satiated with her American odyssey, turned its attention to the dynastic crisis facing her country. For the working reporter, news on that subject was difficult to pry loose. Censorship in Roumania was so tight that the most direct reference to King Ferdinand's terminal cancer was a terse line in the democratic paper *Dimineatza* announcing the arrival in Bucharest of a famous Parisian X-ray specialist, Dr. Rigaud of the Curie Institute, with no explanation of why he was there.

The West was understandably anxious to fill the news void. The probable ascendance to the Roumanian throne of a baby King presaged frightening instability in an area of the world that had already given birth to one world war. Without a responsible adult on the Roumanian throne, Russia might well try to recoup Bessarabia or Hungary might make a bid for Transylvania. "What," asked *The New York Times*, "would be the attitude of certain neighboring nations towards a Roumania governed by a five-year-old King and a board of three persons totally inexperienced in the complicated politics of Southeastern Europe?... something must be done and done quickly to clear up the dynastic impasse now facing Roumania."

Because of her influence on the King and her reconciliation with the former heir to the throne, Marie looked like the pivot around which the dynastic crisis would turn. Her trip from New York across the Atlantic was timed by squadrons of reporters who were waiting for her in a blinding wind and rain storm when she arrived in France on November 30, 1926. The expectations of the press had been foreseen in Bucharest. As soon as the *Berengaria* docked at Cherbourg, the Marshal of the Court, General Angelescu, came on board to escort the Queen off the boat, keep her away from reporters, and make sure she did not see her Carol.

The sudden appearance of Angelescu "astonished" Marie. She was upset at being prevented from seeing her son. The General brought letters from the King and Prince Stirbey. Nando's letter was very brave; it made light of his illness and asked her to look for Christmas presents for their daughters. The letter from Barbo was "full of alarm."

Since the Queen arrived in Paris too late to catch the *Simplon Express* for Bucharest, she spent the following day filling the King's requests. When Carol tried to reach her, she sent him a gift and a letter explaining why she could not see him. "Haunted" by her son's need for her and "not quite sure" she was doing the right thing, the Queen ran from shop to shop, determined to finish Nando's list, dogged at every street corner by photographers and reporters. Near dusk she emerged from one store ahead of her suite only to find herself face-to-face with Carol, a bunch of flowers and a letter in his hand. He was "pale, haggard," and "unshaven." He gave his mother a kiss, pushed the flowers at her, mumbled a few words about sending something to Ileana, and disappeared. It was, in Marie's words, "a nightmare day."

Her homecoming was worse. She was met at the station by the King, her children, members of the government, and the usual crowd. "People tried to cheer," she noted, "but one saw that a big fear was hovering over everything." In spite of his "skeleton-like" face and difficulty in walking, Ferdinand was the most lighthearted person present. He was highly indignant at the fuss over his health, said it was ridiculous for Missy to have hurried home, and asked innumerable questions about her trip. In the car on the way to the palace she had a chance to observe him out of the public eye. "There is the worst news written on his face," she said.

An immediate consultation with the doctors confirmed her suspicions.

Ferdinand was suffering from an inoperable cancer of the lower intestine that was spreading rapidly. The doctors could not say how long he might live; they hoped for a year at the outside, depending on the effect of the treatments. These started within two days of the Queen's return and consisted of the insertion of silver tubes into the King's intestine to draw out poison. In constant pain before and after the treatments, Ferdinand remained his modest and uncomplaining self, dragging his body in a baggy robe and oversized slippers through the palace corridors among the colorful steamer trunks.

Although the Queen broke the news of their father's condition to her children, the doctors had decided not to tell the King himself, and Marie spent much of her time trying to protect him from the truth. She rose early in the mornings to get two hours of work in before her husband awoke. Around 9 A.M. she joined him for breakfast in his rooms. The rest of the day was consumed by conferences with teams of doctors and audiences with a worried constituency. Her major relaxation was a short gallop on one of her horses. Stirbey came every day, but even he could not help her "face the inevitable." Within a few weeks of her return, Marie noted that she and Ferdinand were starting their thirty-fifth year together: "May God allow that it be not our last..." she wrote in her diary; "we have lived to become firm and faithful friends, two wildly different characters that have managed to produce harmony out of what might have been something quite else... we have lived for the country & for our children and always knew how to keep passion sufficiently under so as never to harm these two loves of our lives."

Ferdinand started radium treatments in late January. Soon after, Marie suggested that he make a list of his personal possessions with instructions for their eventual disposal. "I insinuate little by little one name after another who will be so happy if something is left to them," Marie confided to her diary. "At first he protests, but I generally win him over, and he is half amused half shy when I tell him to put down things for his different flirts: Titi, Julie, Valentine, the Robescus and of course as first and chief poor old Aristitza who has loved him so faithfully, also Maruka, we had quite fun over it. It would never come into his mind to do this alone but he likes to do it with me, and I make it all appear a huge joke!"

Although she managed to preserve an outward cheerfulness for Ferdinand, Marie was haunted throughout his illness by the image of Carol. The news from Paris was not good. No sooner had the Queen returned to Roumania than Lupescu had issued a statement saying that she would give Carol up on condition that he was reinstated in the succession. Marie was incensed: "... as if she were giving up a thing she rightly owned," wrote the Queen.

Lupescu's presumption did not disturb her as much as her son's lack of character. She realized that Carol had simply grown bored with his new existence. "Spoilt, accustomed to soft-living and to be treated as master and prince... he does not know how to fit into a simple man's life." The former

Crown Prince had begun to besiege his mother with letters pleading for her to arrange his reinstatement with his father, swearing that only she could help him now: "... don't turn away from me or I shall go down completely," Carol wrote, insisting as before that he had left Roumania with Sitta's knowledge and approval. Marie found herself embroiled in an argument between husband and wife during which she was shown letters from both sides, personal letters that embarrassed her and proved that Carol was lying.

While her son plagued her from Paris, the Carlists attacked her at home. One by one they demanded audiences to tell the Queen that Carol was "a changed man," that his morality was not at issue, and that an adult king, even a wayward one, was a more viable future sovereign than a five-year-old boy. Caught between mother love and national duty, Marie admitted the truth to herself in her diary. "I have *lost all* belief in Carol... I do not believe in his 'fundamental change'... he does not see the... difference between right and wrong, honour and dishonour, truth & lies."

Still she did not know what to do. Bratianu was unalterably opposed to Carol's return; he considered the volatile Prince a danger to the country. Barbo Stirbey, who believed in the sanctity of the law, felt that Carol's return would deal a major blow to the dynasty and the principle of monarchy in general. He shared his brother-in-law's assessment of Carol, but his devotion to Marie made it difficult for him to say so. Desperate for outside opinions, Marie turned to her brother-in-law, the Infante Alfonso, and her old friend Waldorf Astor. Accused by the Carlists of keeping Carol away so she herself might remain in power, the Queen sent out two letters during the winter of 1927 that attest to her desire to reinstate her eldest son.

The Infante Alfonso, Carol's favorite uncle, was vacationing in Paris. Marie asked him to see Carol and try to talk some sense into him. "There is not the smallest little hope for his coming back before he has purged himself of all that atmosphere of sin and degradation he is living in..." Marie wrote Ali. "Tell him I send you to him because I... want to help him at least to become a man again. ... It needs a man of his own class to make him realise what the world thinks of him. And because you are the dear clean creature I know you are, you will perhaps be able to find something by which he can be pulled out of the mire in which he is drowning."

Ali's meeting with Carol was a failure. When the Infante asked his nephew if he wanted to return to Roumania, Carol said he would "like to go back" but "only... on certain conditions." Alfonso was startled. "My dear Carol, I fear you completely misunderstand your position. It's not you who can ask for conditions, but your father and mother, your King and Queen, who will put forward conditions under which perhaps they might soften their hearts and let you return. Let me tell you this: there is not one person in a royal family, not one person who has monarchical principles who does not look with horror and sadness at the harm you have done monarchy in general, and who does not look upon your present life with anger and contempt."

After Ali, Marie turned to Waldorf Astor to ask if she should support her son's bid for power. Lord Astor was as blunt as good manners would allow. "You can have a Republic or you can have a Monarchy," he wrote the Queen. "One of the advantages of a Monarchy is that the rules are quite simple—heredity—primogeniture—certainty. Now if an heir renounces his rights the system is probably not much affected. But if the same man reverses his decision then it seems to me that you verge on chaos in your system and that you seriously endanger the whole structure. Quick changes for love are all very well as plots for novels or opera, but they are unsuited for real kingdoms in an epoch of revolutions."

The people who were pressing Marie to help reinstate her son were confused about the man they hoped to put on the throne. Carol was not the classic profligate many thought (or even wished) him to be. He was not a glamorous ladies' man, but a princely Milquetoast, tied to his mistress like an adolescent to an indulgent mother. Even Marie did not understand this; what she mistakenly referred to as the "atmosphere of sin and degradation" surrounding her son was hardly worth the name.

Carol's pleasure dome—a partially furnished rented home—was plebeian, for he was tightfisted and undemanding in his tastes. His major indulgence was fast cars, while Mme. Lupescu, famous for shedding tears to get what she wanted, bought jewels and furs. Periodically they appeared at a concert or nightclub in Paris or in the casinos on the Riviera. Most of all, Carol loved his Duduia (his pet name for Lupescu), his liquor, his Wagner on the phonograph, his evening card games, and his hearty meals. His mistress provided him with the sensual pleasures, and he gave her full sway over his life. She ran his home like a frugal French housewife, and the former Crown Prince, who considered himself a brilliant political tactician, wrote his mother more than once to complain about the servant problem.

A third person soon entered Carol's household—a Roumanian in his early twenties named Constantin Dimitresco and called Puiu for short. Originally a student in Paris, Puiu was a parody of the Latin lover and adventurer, boasting of his conquests, setting intrigues into motion. At first only a visitor, he gradually ingratiated himself into the household and finally achieved the rank of Carol's personal secretary and valet. But Puiu dreamed of being more than a flunky to an exiled Prince. From the time he wormed his way into Carol's life, he counted on his employer returning to Roumania.

In the beginning of April 1927, Ferdinand suffered an attack of flu which he was not expected to survive. For a week Marie stayed by his bedside day and night, and at one point he received the last rites of the Catholic Church. When, much to everyone's surprise, he showed signs of recovering, the Queen moved him to the Crown Estate of Scroviste near Bucharest. There, in a quiet villa overlooking a lake and surrounding forests, the King passed the spring and early summer, shuffling between his bed, his sitting room, and an outside terrace. For a while he improved enough to have visitors. Marthe Bibesco came to see him, as did Aristitza Dissesscu and another old friend, Titi Mignano. "She [Titi] of course saw the horrible change and even she the dearest of flirts hardly got a smile," said Queen Marie. As Ferdinand's strength gave way, he submitted himself quietly to the inevitable, but gave no indication that he knew he was dying.

The King's condition and his absence gave Prime Minister Averescu, a devotee of Mussolini and his methods, an opportunity to organize a coup that would bring him to power in a military dictatorship modeled on that of Il Duce. Backed by a number of regiments under orders to enter Bucharest secretly, Averescu lost his bid for control when Ferdinand, warned about the troops, promptly relieved him of his position. In his place the dying King named his old friend Barbo Stirbey. Marie was taken completely by surprise. There was an understanding between the King, the Queen, and Prince Stirbey that Stirbey would accept the position of Prime Minister only in case of "absolute need." Although she realized that the situation must have warranted Nando's action, Marie knew she would be blamed for the appointment: "...who on earth would ever believe that I* did not get rid of Averescu to put our man in!" she asked. "No one," she concluded.

On the night of June 4, 1927, Stirbey was sworn in by the King from his bed. The Roumanian Prince was enthusiastic about his opportunity to pacify the warring political parties and create a bona fide coalition government. He almost succeeded, uniting for the first time the two most important parties, the Liberals and the National Peasants, in his Cabinet. But the artificial amity broke down over elections, and three weeks after his nomination, Stirbey was forced to hand in his resignation. "Barbo and I were very sad to bury for the moment our ideals and our hopes," Marie wrote in her diary. "I thanked him and our parting handshake was a covenant to try again when the next occasion arose."

The King turned to Bratianu to form a government. It was the fifth time Bratianu had served his country as Prime Minister. At sixty-two he appeared hale and hearty. At sixty-one Ferdinand was a spent man. When the claustrophobic heat of summer descended into the plains, Marie moved her husband to the fresh mountain air of Sinaia. She had a tent erected outside his bedroom on the lawn of Pelisor Palace. There she watched him slip away from life. When the end seemed imminent, she sent for the children, all except their elder son. Ferdinand had not asked for Carol since the onset of his illness.

The Queen was in the habit of spending the nights on a sofa in the King's salon "with doors open so that I could hear every sound." Toward midnight of July 19, 1927, Ferdinand, restless with pain, tried to get out of bed. Although the doctor gave the King an injection, he did not calm down. "I

---

*Underlined twice in the original.

am so tired," he complained to Marie. Standing by the side of his bed, she took him in her arms, his head resting on her shoulder so that he might breathe more easily. The doctor took his pulse and warned her that the end was near. The nurse ran to get the family and a priest, but before they arrived, Ferdinand was dead. "His head fell against my shoulder [,] his already cold hands became limp, his face quite small... it was over—he was no more tired but at rest," she said.

The next morning Premier Bratianu asked Marie's daughter-in-law to take Michael, aged five years and nine months, to Bucharest to be formally proclaimed King before Parliament. Dressed in white knickers and a white silk shirt, he stood, pudgy and unsmiling beside his black-veiled mother, to receive the acclamation of the Chamber of Deputies. Later, seated in a throne-like chair fifteen steps above his ministers, the baby King watched while Prince Nicolas, the head of the Supreme Court, and the Patriarch of the Church laid their hands on a huge golden Bible to be sworn in as Regents. Left in Sinaia, Marie took comfort in memories of the day thirteen years before when she herself became Queen. "I still hear their many voices crying, shouting Regina Maria, Regina Maria, and all their faces looking at me with hope in their eyes and also something of love and trust."

King Ferdinand lay in state for four days on a red velvet pall. Marie had given orders that black was not to be used, and she herself arranged the red flowers around his body. She was moved by his face in repose. "Such a beautiful face with his noble features frozen into a stillness which gave him a grandeur which was not his in life," she said. "In life he was too modest, too timid, he always seemed to be excusing himself for everything he did. Now, without any more gestures he was calmly... accepting all the honours paid, all the flowers, prayers, tears."

There were not as many honors as there might have been. Worried about Carol and the Carlists, Premier Bratianu sped up the funeral proceedings. The date set for the ceremonies did not allow time for Ferdinand's and Marie's relatives to gather from around Europe; the only male royal mourners following the casket were the King's second son, Prince Nicolas, and his son-in-law King Alexander of Yugoslavia. His other son-in-law, the exiled King George of Greece, did not arrive from England until the day after the funeral.

Like his great-uncle before him, Ferdinand was buried at Curtea de Arges. Four trains made the ninety-five-mile journey across the dusty plains to the town hidden away in the mountains. There, a colorful procession of family, priests, war veterans, and diplomats from Bucharest, augmented by a thousand peasants in fanciful native dress carrying tapers, followed the King's body to the church. The coffin itself, relieved of all its ceremonial trappings, bore only a small bunch of faded pink roses with a card inscribed "Marie." The Queen had laid similar roses on the King's deathbed in memory of the first bouquet of flowers he had brought her when she was sixteen.

"It was a long life we lived side by side with the ups and downs as is the way of married life, with storms sometimes and struggles, but with faith and trust mostly and especially with patience. . . . Patience . . . to go beyond the day of struggle . . . not lovers but friends, respecting each other's particularities, patient, both of us, patient, trusting hand in hand until the end."

After a short outdoor service, Ferdinand's coffin was carried inside the church and placed in the open vault. Marie returned to Sinaia. "One volume shut forever," she wrote in her diary, "and now forward with courage, and with what remains to me of health and strength and hope & faith—"

The Queen had wired her elder son immediately to inform him of his father's death, but it was Elena Lupescu who reacted most violently to the news. On hearing of the King's death, she is said to have begun wailing loudly, claiming to have seen the "white lady" just the night before. (According to Hohenzollern legend, the "white lady" is the ghost who appears to members of the Hohenzollern dynasty when one of its men is about to die.) A month later Carol wrote his mother that Mme. Lupescu was still ill "with despair" and "cried so much and is in such a state of anemia . . . she went nearly blind and the doctor had to stay all night."

As to Carol, he claimed that word of his father's death "broke" him completely. "Nobody," he wrote, "felt as much as I did the terrible loss we all suffered." His request for permission to attend his father's funeral in Bucharest was denied by Bratianu, and he retaliated in a letter to his mother. "For me more than for you all these moments were much harder because I was prevented to be near the one I so tenderly loved. Till the last moment . . . I did not stop hoping that I would be able to see Papa once more, or at least be allowed to kneel next to his deathbed. With the greatest sorrow I see that other considerations than those of pure family relations were the strongest."

On the day of his father's funeral, the former Crown Prince put in a showy appearance at the King's memorial service, held in the Roumanian church in the Latin Quarter of Paris. Carol wore a Prince Albert coat, dark trousers, and a top hat; all his royal decorations and ribbons were lined up across his chest. Since the Prince had never before appeared with his medals in public, the reporters took it as a sign of his intention to fight for the throne. Certainly he did not appear displeased with cries chanted by supporters outside the church of "Vive le Roi!"

For the Dowager Queen the first month of widowhood was lived "in a sort of daze." The King had left no instructions, political or financial. "I think he had no anxiety," Marie said, "he felt I would carry on." She herself showed remarkably little concern about her personal future or her finances. "I never worried about that nor anything else," she said. "I have a sort of blind faith that those I am left to would treat me well." To make sure, Prince Stirbey stayed in Bucharest after the funeral to represent Marie's interests in the reorganization of the court and the Civil List. Ferdinand had left Castle Peles to Marie until his grandson Michael came of age; Marie gave it to Sitta to redecorate and use for herself and her son.

A few days after the funeral Marie's sisters arrived. When they left, Marie took Ileana to Balcic for three weeks at the seaside. Returning to Sinaia she said she was "slowly picking up the threads of life again . . . planning how to carry on . . . I am still the very heart of the country. . . . The father has gone but the mother is still there for everybody." She announced that she was starting her memoirs, as she had "so often" been asked to do. But however cheerfully she phrased it, however carefully she covered her feelings, it quickly became clear to Marie and to the world at large that she was left with little to do *but* write. "The truth," said the press on the day of Ferdinand's funeral, "is that Marie becomes merely a spectator about the throne of Roumania which for so many years bowed to her commands."

Marie always said that she did not want a seat on the Regency for herself, and she had tried, since the onset of the King's illness, to prepare Prince Nicolas to represent the family in the governing body. But Nicky had never been easy to direct or control. Charming, amusing, his mother's favorite companion among her children, he was still irresponsible. "All good and bad slumbers in Nicky . . ." his mother wrote. "Since my experience with Carol I no more dare say that the good is stronger than the bad." To save Nicolas from the corrupting atmosphere of the Roumanian *haut monde*, the Queen had arranged for him to join the British Navy. Nicky loved it and deeply resented having to give up his naval career to prepare for his position on the Regency. His skills were mechanical, not political. After his father's death, his mother and Prince Stirbey had a difficult time keeping him at his job of Regent.

Marie was also ambivalent about her daughter-in-law, whom she pitied and resented in turns. Although she admired Sitta's dignity in a humiliating situation, the younger woman's perfectionism began to irritate Marie. "Outside things count too much . . . a tidy house, perfect dress, unruffled hair, punctuality, excessive politeness, good manners, form, procedure." She admired Sitta's taste, but deplored the money she spent redecorating her home, remarking rather uncharitably that the Princess Mother had "fallen materially into a soft nest at an early age."

For Marie the third generation of her family was turning out as disappointing as the second. Six-year-old King Michael, isolated from his peers by his overprotective mother and English governess, was distrustful and overweight. His royal manners were impeccable; he never failed to return the salutes of his army on parade or solemnly kiss the hands of the ladies at court. But he invariably entered a room with a fixed smile on his face and never altered his expression. Slow to learn verbal skills, the baby King, like the other men in the family, showed mechanical talent and could drive a car at six.

Marie agreed with her daughter-in-law's determination to keep the child out of the public eye and away from the scandal that followed Carol, but disagreed with Sitta's policy of never allowing Michael's father's name to be mentioned in front of him. She resented the fact that the Greeks continued to swarm around her daughter-in-law's house, creating two royal camps and turning Michael, the future King of Roumania, into a little Greek. It was clear that Marie was being kept away from her grandson. "Sitta has rather separated him from us in her eagerness to bring him up better than his father," she wrote Sister Sandra.

Pushed into unwanted retirement by the government and her family immediately after Ferdinand's death, Marie was suddenly thrown into the foreground four months later. At 2:30 on the morning of November 24, 1927, she was awakened by a telephone call informing her that Prime Minister Bratianu, who had contracted a throat infection twenty-four hours before, was dying. She hurried to his bedside. In agony from an incision in his throat, scarcely able to make a sound, Bratianu greeted her in a whisper. "How good and gracious it is of you to come here at such an hour," he said. By 6:45 A.M. he was dead.

This was the "first time" Marie said she regretted not being a member of the Regency. "I mean something abroad. The knowledge that I am still 'officially' there would give a feeling of continuity, whilst [with] Bratianu gone no one knows *who* still really counts in this hard-hit country." Her appraisal of the situation was accurate. Bratianu had always refused to delegate authority, and his choice of Regents indicates that even at the end of his life the old politician worried less about Roumania than his ego.

Serving in the Regency with Prince Nicolas was Miron Christea, the Patriarch of the Orthodox Church. The Patriarch was an imposing-looking Transylvanian priest with a long silver beard, social ambitions, and an eye for women. The third Regent, the only responsible one, was George Buzdugan, President of the High Court of Cessation (Chief Justice). Experienced in politics and law, he might have given meaning to the Regency had the other two Regents been more willing to do their jobs.

To fill Bratianu's position as Prime Minister, the Regency appointed his brother, Vintila, who had held the portfolio of Finance Minister in Ion's many Cabinets. Faced with a poor economy and under pressure from the National Peasant Party, Vintila tried to secure loans from abroad. On his way to a vacation in Switzerland, Prince Stirbey stopped in Paris and London to test Roumania's borrowing power with Western banks. "What's holding back credit," he wrote Marie, "is the fear of political upheaval... it is the question of Carol."

After his father's death, Carol begged his mother to stay in touch with him, and they corresponded frequently. "The tiniest kind word from him makes me believe in him again, makes me idiotically grateful," Marie admitted to herself. Over the objections of the Liberals in power, she sent Nicky, then Ileana to see Carol, and she herself visited with him in St. Briac in the spring of 1929. Marie and her son exchanged presents on birthdays and holidays. Carol asked his mother to help Mme. Lupescu's parents obtain passports, and when he bought his mistress a Louis XVI château in the French countryside, he wrote for her advice on relandscaping the gardens. "Oh Mama dear," he wrote the year after his father's death, "let us have only loving relations between us."

His political activities belied his words. The Queen learned of these through various emissaries, usually military men or members of her European family. "Now he suffers perhaps but... just in his personal love for you and occasionally when he thinks that he is not treated with enough importance..." Baby Bee wrote after seeing her nephew. "He is blindly in love, he has fallen into a gang which evidently tells him he is a splendid fellow greatly wronged by certain politicians in his own country." Those outside the family complained about Lupescu's undue influence over the former Prince and mentioned new faces around Carol's household, men in league with the Carlists to put Carol back on the throne.

Toward this end Lupescu published her memoirs, a series of newspaper articles that were sent to Marie by an American friend. Lupescu's story was a saccharine confection, whipped up out of Carol's political plans for the future and Elena's desire for an aristocratic past. In it the druggist's daughter denied her Jewish parentage, alleging that she had first met Carol when her father took her to tea with Queen Elisabeth. She also claimed that the Crown Prince had been forced to abdicate by Bratianu and his party. Called by the publisher a "human document of unforgettable emotion," the series is interesting primarily for the forewarning it gives of Carol's determination to raise his status at home by demeaning that of the Queen. "There are dreadful tales in circulation—old slanders about her Majesty's love affairs, long since discredited but brought out every now and then... by the Queen's enemies," wrote Carol's mistress, carefully planting the first seed of her lover's campaign to destroy his mother in the eyes of the Roumanian people.

Carol made his first attempt at a coup less than a year after his father's death. The scheme was said to have been devised by Sidney Harmsworth, the first Viscount Rothermere. Rothermere, the British newspaper owner and Hungary's chief exponent after World War I, had taken on himself the mission of returning Transylvania to the Hungarians. Whether Rothermere intended to destabilize Roumania or whether he had made an actual agreement with Carol for Transylvanian lands, he remained in the background, working through an expatriate Roumanian named Barbo Jonescu. Jonescu was an ambitious, self-made food tycoon living in London, delighted to be in league with important people and to have the former Roumanian Crown Prince as a guest at his Surrey estate.

The take-over was planned to coincide with a protest meeting of peasants set for May 6, 1928, at the historic site of Alba Julia. Two planes were chartered in England and thousands of leaflets were printed with a message from Carol to the people of Roumania. In his bid for the throne, the former heir declared that he had left Roumania "unwillingly," forced out by a "misunderstanding about the way in which the country was ruled" and "sad matrimonial conflicts." If his father had lived, Carol told the people, he felt "sure" that King Ferdinand "would have called me back home." To prepare the international public for his move, Carol gave an interview that appeared in Rothermere's *Daily Mirror*. In it he vehemently denied the fact that he had renounced his claim to the succession; his exile, he said, had nothing to do with Mme. Lupescu, but was based on his impotence in the face of the Bratianu government. "I did not leave Rumania on account of her, and any statement to that effect is an absolute lie," said Carol.

On the appointed day two planes stood revved up, waiting on the field, their pilots ready in their cockpits. But the minute the former Roumanian Crown Prince approached the gangway, officials from the British Home Office stepped up to inform him that because of the friendly relations existing between England and Roumania, His Majesty's government could not permit a mission of this sort to take off from England.

Carol returned to sulk at Jonescu's elegant estate, while Carlists smuggled his proclamation out of England. Two days later, officers from Scotland Yard appeared to inform Carol that he was *persona non grata* in England. The following week the Home Secretary stood up in Parliament to report that the Roumanian Prince's undesirable activities on British soil had ceased, as the Prince had been expelled.

Marie was deeply shamed by the incident and wrote King George to apologize for her son. The London *Times* castigated Rothermere for his Hungarian campaign and Carol for his "incredible folly in allowing himself to be identified" with it. Carol took out his humiliation on his mother. A Roumanian General, who brought him a letter from Marie, returned to Bucharest reporting that the former Crown Prince was "rude" and "foaming at the mouth." Carol swore that "what happened in England was an intrigue of the [Roumanian] government" and claimed that the entire fiasco was "the fault of 'those filthy swines' who are ruling at home and ruining the country."

In reply to his mother, Carol sent a letter spattered with crossed-out words and inserted threats. He accused Marie of purposely misinterpreting the actions of the British government and of not backing him from Roumania as she ought to have done. "My time will come," he warned her, "and on that day there will be many who will be sad that they did not see the reality as it really was. I've had enough of all these things every step that is taken against me I know it and if till now I have not responded it is that I was always hoping that some honest person would take measures to stop the dilapidating of the country's money for filthy things and the first person who ought to have realised this was you."

. . .

The failure of Carol's coup did not strengthen the fortunes of his enemies in the Liberal Party. Since the Great War, the incorporation of Bessarabia and Transylvania had cast a harsh light on Liberal policies. Marie granted a number of audiences to Constantine Stere, an old revolutionary leader of the Socialist Peasant Movement in Bessarabia, who complained bitterly about the repressive measures taken by the government there. She also received General Averescu, who was responsible for the crackdown. Averescu warned her that Roumania was heading for revolution. "Bessarabia is being mismanaged," said Marie; "being politicians... they prefer proving another's guilt or incapacity."

The situation in Transylvania was no better. The Magyars, formerly the businessmen, professionals, and intellectuals of the province, had been removed from government posts. Where the Roumanians had once bewailed the Magyarization of the population, they Roumanized it with ferocity. Rural properties belonging to "foreign landlords" were systematically expropriated. The Liberals and their allies under Averescu robbed Hungarians and Jews in the name of nationalism and agrarian justice; to justify these crimes, both groups were lumped with the Communists as enemies of the state. Since some prominent Communists were in fact Jewish, the oligarchy of the Old Kingdom was able to rationalize its traditional anti-Semitism, and reactionary politics paraded through Transylvania in the guise of feudal reform.

This is not to say that Ion Bratianu and the oligarchy had not contributed significantly to the growth of Roumania. Between 1923 and 1928, a period of general European prosperity preceding the Depression, the Roumanian economy grew apace, disproportionately to that of other small burgeoning European countries. Roumania, of course, did have the natural resources to develop—seemingly inexhaustible sources of oil, timber, and fertile farmlands that Bratianu protected with government subsidies and favorable taxes. But the primary need was agrarian reform. The peasants opposed mechanization and modern farming methods, and the regime did not care to educate them. The fact that throughout this period in Roumanian history Ferdinand held on to his image of "King of the Peasants" must be attributed in large part to Marie's popularity as well as Bratianu's political skill.

With the deaths of King Ferdinand and Bratianu, however, the Liberal Party reached the end of a long run. In November of 1928, just a year after Bratianu's death, the National Peasant Party under Juliu Maniu came into power. Charged by the Regency with forming a new government, Maniu and the National Peasants were affirmed by 78 percent of the vote in elections untainted by coercion. The new regime lifted repressive laws passed by the nervous Liberals in the face of peasant agitation and set Roumania's course for equality and reform. Even the Jews were protected from anti-Semitic demonstrations.

This about-face in a country known for repressive politics was largely due to the character of Juliu Maniu himself. Referred to by one historian as the "self-styled guardian of national morality," Maniu was aloof and sanctimonious, but sincere. Born in Transylvania in 1873, raised in the austere discipline of the Jesuits, Maniu had turned to politics with the same selfless dedication required by the Church. With his broad face and austere ways, Maniu grew quickly to be the spiritual leader of all the oppressed Roumanians of Hungary before World War I. After the war, having united the peasants from the new provinces with their brothers in the Old Kingdom, Maniu emerged as the leader of the National Peasant Party, the major force opposing the Liberals.

Before his victory in 1928 Maniu had paid yearly visits to Marie, who resented his prophecies of gloom but admired his dignity and the fact that he told her that she should be the sole Regent of Roumania. Marie was pleased when he became Prime Minister, not because she agreed with him that he could change things, but because she thought he ought to be given a chance to try. "Personally I would like them [the National Peasant Party] to come in once, so that they can see for themselves that they... cannot at one stroke make a Paradise out of Roumania," she said.

In October of 1929, a year after Maniu assumed power, Chief Justice Buzdugan, the only responsible member of the Regency, died. The obvious person to replace him was Marie. "I would choose myself if asked who ought to be chosen," she wrote in her diary. But Maniu, who felt that two members of the royal family in the Regency was "too much," offered Marie the position only on the proviso that she arrange for her son Nicolas to step down. Although Maniu had a point and Prince Nicolas was no asset to the ruling body, Marie rejected his offer in foolish anger. She resented the fact that Maniu tried to bargain with her over a job that she called her "most superlative dread." She for one did not need more honors or positions. "A monarchy does not exist for the ego satisfaction of the sovereigns," she told Maniu, "but for the good of the state."

To fill the third position, Maniu nominated Constantine Saratzeanu, the brother-in-law of his Finance Minister and a judge of no consequence. In the storm of national protest that followed the appointment, the Finance Minister was forced to resign and Maniu's own position was threatened. The Regency turned into a public embarrassment. "The country has no leader," the Patriarch told Marie in a burst of self-justification; "Prince Nicolas passes his time smoking cigarettes; Saratzeanu, the new Regent, passes his playing patience; and I, a priest, must confine myself to appeasing conflicts."

While no one was surprised at the incompetence of the Regency, Juliu Maniu's failure to live up to expectations disillusioned the most cynical Roumanians. Maniu assumed the role of Premier just as the Great Depression was spreading across Europe to Roumania. The peasants were unable to sell their crops; hundreds of banks closed their doors; and foreign capital dried up. In the face of the world economic situation, Maniu's dream of modernizing the agrarian economy and cleaning up the corrupted bureaucracy evaporated, as did his mandate from the Roumanian people. The Liberal

Party lost no chance to foment unrest, and as conditions deteriorated, Roumanians began to look back fondly at the days of the traditional monarchy. As the sworn enemy of the Liberal Party, Carol was the natural ally of the National Peasants. Desperate to stay in power, Prime Minister Maniu sent an emissary to Paris to negotiate with the former Crown Prince.

Without any official position to keep her at home, the Dowager Queen traveled extensively during the years following her husband's death. In the spring of 1929 she took Ileana to visit Baby Bee and Ali in Spain. During the visit, the Prince of Asturias, the invalided and hemophilic heir to the Spanish throne, fell in love with Ileana and said he wanted to marry her. The Spanish court was delighted. At twenty, the Roumanian Princess was a superb match. Brown-haired with bright blue eyes, slim and athletic, she projected a sense of exuberant life. At the same time her early experiences with death and disease had given her a sense of royal duty and a desire to devote herself to the common good. Given her penchant for self-sacrifice and falling in love, it is not surprising that she was touched by the Prince's interest and undeniable charm. Marie was upset. "The greatest argument against such a marriage would be Alfonso [King Alfonso XIII], much more even than the invalid husband...Alfonso...makes up to every woman & then has a way of declaring that they threw themselves at his head. A pretty daughter-in-law, wife of his invalid son would in no wise be safe from him," she said.

The Dowager Queen spoke from family experience. Baby Bee, a former object of the King's attentions, had been banished from Spain when she was young for just this reason. Now, even the fifty-three-year-old Dowager Queen found the King of Spain difficult to handle. "One has...to be exceedingly careful with him...age, position, attitude, nothing stops him...it would be quite impossible for a young woman to have anything to do with him."

Much to Marie's relief, the romance soon died down. Unfortunately, however, the next candidate for Ileana's hand caused her mother even more worry, and Ileana, genuine heartbreak. This sad interlude started at the end of 1929 when Marie received a copy of the memoirs of her old friend Daisy, Princess of Pless, a beautiful Englishwoman who had married a German Prince. Writing to thank the author, Marie complimented Daisy on her three handsome sons, whose pictures appeared in the book, and sent photos of her own children. Daisy's middle son, Lexel, tall, blond, and blue-eyed, shortly thereafter arrived in Roumania to ski.

The young German Prince came just in time for Ileana's twenty-first birthday party, a fancy dress ball given at Cotroceni Palace. Ileana fell in love at first sight. Lexel of Pless proposed within a few days, and Ileana accepted. They planned their wedding and picked out a house. Marie was thrilled. Her favorite child married to a minor and rich German princeling could settle in Roumania near her mother.

Lexel's father, the old Prince of Pless, arrived in Bucharest, but Prime

Minister Maniu warned Queen Marie not to enter into any agreements before he was able to investigate the boy. Barbo Stirbey explained to Marie the Premier's concerns, which were soon validated. At eighteen Lexel had been implicated in a homosexual scandal. Although nothing was proved at the time, Maniu told Marie that the Roumanian government would not permit the marriage.

Ileana was forced to break off the engagement, but not before someone in the palace leaked the reason to the press: "... being royal our griefs, sorrows, joys, triumphs or humiliations are public property..." Marie said; "the Press rules the world." She and a friend, Cella Lahovary, took Ileana to Egypt to escape the reporters and recover from the shattering experience. By the time Marie returned home in April of 1930, the uproar over Lexel of Pless had been superseded by issues far more vital to the country's welfare.

Depressed economic conditions, the obvious impotence of the government, and the inadequacy of the Regency had combined to create serious political unrest during the winter and spring of 1930 following the Regency crisis. Angry leaders of opposition parties demanded audiences with the Dowager Queen, but their partisan schemes only increased her sense of personal frustration. Prince Stirbey was traveling in Western Europe when she arrived home from the Middle East. His letters, filled with enigmatic warnings, became more circumspect as the weeks wore on. He reproached himself for leaving her alone. He needed to speak to her, he said, because his letters were opened by others. All he could do from afar was beg her to stay out of party politics, not to compromise the crown, and to assume the utmost prudence. There are enemies all around, he told her, "even in the immediate entourage of the Court."

With Barbo away and no one to listen to her complaints, Marie's resentment at her daughter-in-law blossomed. Sitta, she said, had succeeded so well in separating her from her grandson that she had completely lost interest in him. When Independence Day rolled around on May 10, the Dowager Queen went to Balcic rather than participate in the annual parade in Bucharest. "I had no heart to drive through the streets beside a fat over-educated unresponsive little boy who... is almost a... stranger."

Worse than her grandson was her son Nicolas. Angry at being thrust into a job for which he was unsuited, subject to violent outbreaks of temper, Prince Nicolas had become a "real danger" to the dynasty. He started fistfights with drivers in the streets and was no better at home. "He... raises his voice & feels himself a fine fellow when he insults the servants, the gentlemen [-in-waiting], all those around him," his mother said. People suddenly started cautioning Marie about Nicky's A.D.C., a man named Alexandru Manolescu. Manolescu was originally recommended to her by Carol, who said he would be a good influence on Nicky. Now she heard that Manolescu was turning her second son against her. When Prince Stirbey returned in the middle of May, he warned Marie that her two sons might be planning to overturn the government. Certainly Nicky had become very secretive. On June 2 Marie heard that he was going abroad; rumor had it that he was planning to meet Carol. Marie begged him to give his fellow Regents assurances that he was not plotting a coup with his brother. Nicky promised he would.

Marie herself had made plans to leave Bucharest in early June for a trip through Central Europe with Ducky and Mignon. Now that she was again permitted to travel in Germany, Marie was going to visit her mother's grave; she would also go to Langenburg to see Sandra, to Munich to see Baby Bee's new house, and to Oberammergau for the Passion Play. Marie worried about leaving Roumania. There was "treachery in the air," she wrote in her diary. Nevertheless, assured by her A.D.C. that she could "trust them all," Marie boarded her train for Vienna on the morning of June 6, 1930. The following day, as she was leaving Vienna for Munich, the Roumanian Minister to Austria brought her a telegram from Prince Nicolas. From it, Marie learned that twelve hours after her departure, Carol had returned to Roumania.

Chapter 28

Vulgarity in a king flatters the majority of
the nation.

—*GEORGE BERNARD SHAW*

*T*he coup that brought Carol home without his mother's
knowledge was accomplished with the help of Prime Minister Maniu. At
opposite ends of the political spectrum, Marie and Maniu had always agreed
about Carol; they both believed that if the prodigal would admit his sins,
give up Elena Lupescu, and agree to reign in a constitutional manner, he
would be a viable occupant of the throne. The summer before Carol's coup
the Prime Minister and the Dowager Queen had talked about the former
Crown Prince quite openly, going so far as to discuss the possibility of
restoring his royal title to him in exile. But three months later Marie and
Maniu quarreled over the Regency crisis, and when the Prime Minister
decided to bring Carol back, he did it without telling Carol's mother.

Maniu had not changed his mind about Carol, and the Prime Minister
outlined three conditions to be satisfied before the Prince would be allowed
to come home: first, that Carol should take over only as Regent, leaving his
son Michael as titular King; second, that Carol break completely with Elena

Lupescu and leave her behind; third, that he reconcile with Princess Helen. From Mme. Lupescu he obtained the comforting assurance that on the "day that H.R.H. is restored to the throne for the happiness of the country, I shall disappear forever."

With Lupescu's promise and a corroborating pledge from the Crown Prince, the Prime Minister made preparations for Carol's return. He informed Prince Nicolas and his Cabinet of the date and arranged with Saratzeanu to give up his place on the Regency to Carol; he ordered the Minister of War to prepare the troops to receive their former Crown Prince.

Carol's greatest partisans were in the army. In his early days as a soldier, he had committed to memory the file of the officers' corps and could identify many officers by name as well as reel off their dossiers. This feat along with his interest in things military, particularly uniforms, had earned Carol a special niche in military hearts. Since the death of Ferdinand, the army had been neglected. The soldiers were underpaid, poorly fed, and badly clothed; the Regency did nothing to improve their lot. The soldiers hoped for better things from their old friend Prince Carol.

In Paris, Carol's secretary, Puiu, obtained false passports for Carol and himself and chartered a plane at Le Bourget. At 10:30 on the evening of June 6, 1930, the former Crown Prince landed in Bucharest. While Nicolas waited for him at Cotroceni Palace, Carol paid a visit to his old barracks. When he finally appeared at the palace, he made a dramatic entrance, accompanied by music and cheering soldiers. The brothers embraced happily, and Carol settled down to receive members of the government, starting with Prime Minister Maniu.

Carol's first act on returning home was to renege on the first of his three promises to Maniu, that he would accept the position of Regent. Carol told the Prime Minister that he would not take a secondary seat, even for an interim period. He announced that he expected to occupy the throne at once.

"Immediately?" asked Maniu in a state of shock.

"Yes, immediately," Carol answered, "and with the legal proviso that I have reigned since my father, King Ferdinand, passed away in 1927."

"Then," countered the Prime Minister, "I must resign, for I have sworn allegiance to the Son, not to the Father."

Over Maniu's objections both the Regency and the Cabinet voted to accept Carol as King. While the Liberal Party took vehement exception to the restoration on the grounds of Carol's instability, his supporters claimed that Carol had been only "the victim of discreditable intrigues" perpetrated by Barbo Stirbey and the late Ion Bratianu. The following day Parliament took the crown away from Michael to proclaim his father King Carol II. Maniu temporarily resigned.

On the afternoon of June 8, 1930, Carol II made a triumphal drive in an open carriage from Carol I's palace on the Calea Victoriei to Parliament.

Not since his parents' return from Jassy after the war had there been such enthusiastic crowds lining the streets. By 4 P.M. less than two days after his return, the man who had twice abdicated the succession had succeeded in having himself proclaimed King. He received a wild ovation lasting fifteen minutes, a reception that old parliamentarians said had seldom been equaled. In a short speech the new King claimed that although his exile had been "inflicted" on him by others, he had not come home "to take vengeance against anybody." He assured his new subjects that with his ascendance to the throne, his beloved father's "last wish was fulfilled."

The news that her son had taken over in Bucharest took Marie completely by surprise. "In the very bottom of my heart," she admitted after the first shock was over, "I am glad that Carol is back." The succession was re-established, the future of the dynasty secured. Marie's only concern was that her son's return had been purposely timed to coincide with her absence "so that it should appear to the world as though I had left because I will not forgive him!"

By the time her train reached Munich, the reporters were lined up at the station. Queen Marie refused to speak with them, asking her suite only to make it clear to the press that she had neither fled Roumania nor been expelled. At Oberammergau there was a telegram from Bucharest announcing that Carol had had himself proclaimed King. She thought that he had made the right move politically in seizing the crown while public sentiment was with him. "They were right not to mix me in the whole thing," she decided. "I could not have consented as I was bound to what had been decided by H.M. . . . it was not I who could upset the order of things."

Marie sent the new King a "carefully worded" telegram from Oberammergau designed to make it clear that she did not oppose him. She received an answer the next day. "It was very important that he should telegraph to me," she wrote in her diary, "so that there should be a warm feeling between us from the beginning." She was concerned about Prince Stirbey; ". . . it is sad to think that we will not be united in this. He so absolutely believes that Carol will be the last disaster of the Dynasty."

There was also the question of Princess Helen, for whom Carol's return spelled catastrophe. "I got back my son, but she loses everything," said Marie, who was not wholly sorry that her daughter-in-law, who had been "lording it over us all just because she held the future in her hands," would now be required to share Michael with the rest of the family. Personal pique aside, Marie felt great sympathy for the young woman.

She decided to cut her trip short and go home immediately. Carol sent a special train to the frontier to pick her up and guards of honor and officials to greet her in every station along the way. As they neared Bucharest, Marie could scarcely wait for the train to reach the red carpet and come to a stop before jumping off into Carol's arms. Next to him stood Nicolas and Elisabetha. All three children embraced her warmly. Marie bent down to kiss her grandson Michael, a forlorn and chubby little boy standing shyly next to his father, confused by the absence of his mother. Both Marie and Carol were "pale" with "tears in their eyes." She was surprised by the frenzied cheers of the crowds gathered outside the station as she, King Carol II, and Michael drove away in her car. "Carol was proud and a little shy," she said, "Mikey was dumb."

On her arrival at Cotroceni, Marie found a touching letter from Stirbey, announcing that he would no longer be in Bucharest when she arrived home. "It costs me a great deal to say this," he explained, "but I feel that it is in the best interests of Your Majesty." She understood that in distancing himself from her, Barbo hoped to spare her from sharing Carol's resentment toward him.

Stirbey's absence did not help Marie. Within a few days of her return, the Head of her Household, the liaison between her court and the government, was forced to resign. Two weeks later her first A.D.C. was transferred from Cotroceni Palace to a regular army regiment. Marie suddenly found that her household had been reduced to one aide, Colonel Zwiedinek, who was stripped of his royal epaulets and put in the uniform of an ordinary artillery officer. When she complained, she was sent a second aide who turned out to be a spy for the King. She tried to remain calm, assuring herself that the "best policy is no opposition of any kind, a smiling acceptance of his authority, a willing surrender. When the hour of 'drunkenness' is over," she told herself, "he will have to settle down. . . . For the moment it is a real 'orgy' of orders, clearing up, setting right, putting into place. One must let him do it & not interfere."

Matters did not improve. "I am never asked my opinion," Marie complained in reference to the changes taking place at Cotroceni, "things are only burst upon me and I do not see who he has beside him who could give him wise gentlemanly advice." Certainly not "the indispensable Puiu, our *bête noire*," as Marie referred to her son's secretary, a man whom she claimed she could not look at "without flinching." Describing Puiu in a letter mailed outside Roumania to her friend Roxo Weingartner, Marie struggled for an appropriate metaphor: ". . . the creature's face is the face of the oily fiend in a film whom the moment he appears, you know is the one who is going to seduce the young girl & steal the father's money." Puiu bragged to Marie's A.D.C. about the "marvelous spying system" he had installed at Cotroceni Palace to report on the King's mother; he also read Marie's letters and arranged to deliver them to Carol before they were mailed.

It had been Marie's practice to blame Carol's behavior on bad influences, but in the question of money, she admitted that her son was wholly responsible for the difficulties that soon beset her. Marie's annual government stipend did little more than cover the running of her palaces and her charities. Her personal income had stopped with World War I; after 1918, it was Marie who sent money, clothing, and travel expenses to her mother and sisters. Concerned about his wife's financial comfort after his death, Ferdinand had added a codicil to his will leaving the income from Sinaia to his widow. On his return to Roumania, Carol broke his father's will, expropriating his mother's income for himself. Afraid of arousing public opinion against the new King, Marie said nothing.

Shortly thereafter, the King asked Parliament to cut 25 percent off the Civil List, the appropriations that provided Marie's income from the government. Marie did not disagree in principle with the measure. "It is quite just that this should be so," she wrote in her diary, "but as unlike him [King Carol II] I have no private fortune to fall back upon, I do not know how we are going to pull through." The King also delayed his mother's payments by a few months, collecting the interest on the money himself. With Prince Stirbey away, Marie had no one to turn to for financial advice and was too proud to ask her son for relief. "I cannot plead for myself when it is a question of money," she wrote in her diary. "I simply *cannot*."

Marie was too popular to attack openly, but Princess Helen was not, and she soon became the principal target of the King's vengeance. Sitta was no longer Carol's legal wife. She had obtained a divorce two years earlier. One of Maniu's conditions for Carol's return, however, was a reconciliation between them. In bringing Carol back from exile, the government had not hesitated to make political capital of a reunited royal family, and since his arrival the Roumanian public had been "in a state of chronic enthusiasm and sentimentality," waiting breathlessly for Carol and Sitta to "fall into each other's arms."

Maniu, who had failed in his rather crude efforts to reunite the King and his former wife, counted on Marie to patch things up between them. She visited her daughter-in-law as soon as she reached Bucharest, but there was little she could do on either side. Already subjected to intense government pressure, Sitta resented her mother-in-law's attempts to advise her. The new King would scarcely allow his mother to mention Sitta's name in his presence. Carol said that any accommodation with his ex-wife would be "downright immoral, we hate each other too completely."

Sitta did eventually break down and agree to a public reconciliation. Carol remained adamantly against it, although he tried to bribe her into taking the blame with the government on herself. When Sitta refused, there was a "dreadful scene" between them, and Carol, who had been trying to make her life uncomfortable, redoubled his efforts.

The King prohibited his ex-wife from any contact with politicians and refused to allow her to show herself on public occasions. He surrounded her home on the Chaussée with a police guard instructed to report the names of all those who signed her guest book. He had her portrait removed from the officers' mess of the Ninth Hussars, and she herself was relieved of her appointment as its Honorary Colonel. Only his fear of public opinion prevented Carol from completely removing Michael from his mother as well. As it was, every morning after breakfast the boy was taken from Sitta's home and delivered to Carol's palace, from which he was not returned until bedtime.

To the public, the King characterized his ex-wife as a cold, heartless woman who had refused to accept a repentant husband. He portrayed himself as a man who had made the supreme sacrifice for his country, leaving his beloved mistress to be reconciled with a frigid wife. By doing this, Carol thought he could force his ex-wife to leave the country. But Sitta, who had once said she would never stay in Roumania if her ex-husband returned, now refused to leave her son.

Although it took extraordinary imagination to cast himself in the role of saint—particularly when his martyrdom consisted of defecting to Paris with his mistress—Carol made a bold stab at it. To commemorate his suffering in exile, he instituted a new medal, La Décoration de la Souffrance (The Order of Suffering), a white enamel medallion with two interlocking C's under a royal crown encircled by a wreath of thorns. Among those decorated were Puiu, now Carol's private secretary with a secretary of his own, and Barbo Jonescu. The King issued new stamps and coins picturing himself under a crown of thorns. "I wish that every time anyone uses a coin or stamp, he shall be reminded of my suffering during the years of my Calvary," King Carol II announced.

Although this revision of history infuriated Marie, she did feel sorry for her son under the present lonely circumstances of his life and thought he must be rather lost without his mistress. On a visit to the Foisor in Sinaia, she found photographs of Lupescu everywhere, and above the King's bed, a painting done by her. "I felt a lump in my throat suddenly understanding his loneliness," she confided to her diary at the end of August. Marie might have felt less sorry for her son had she known that Elena Lupescu had returned to Roumania shortly after Carol. Less than two months after his coup, the King broke his promise to Maniu and brought his mistress home. She was comfortably ensconced in the Foisor, hidden from his family and the Roumanian government.

Maniu, who had resigned temporarily over the issue of Carol's status, resigned permanently when he learned that Lupescu had returned. "I am responsible for bringing Prince Carol back to Roumania," he told his associates, "because I sincerely believed in him. But since he has broken his solemn word twice—once about getting reconciled to the Princess, and once about leaving Madame Lupescu for good, I cannot accept to serve such a master." To replace Maniu, the National Peasant Party advanced its second-strongest leader, Ion Mihalache, an agrarian reformer. But Mihalache's high ideals and peasant tunics did not appeal to Carol, who laid greater stress on appearances than convictions. The position of Prime Minister was finally settled on George Mironesco, a man of tact, conservative dress, and wavering beliefs—the sort of politician most likely to survive under Carol II.

From the beginning of his reign, Carol played politician against politician and party against party, thus removing any pockets of strength or resistance to monarchical authority. In this he exhibited what one subject called "a kind of Machiavellian gusto, reminiscent of the Byzantine Emperors of the year one thousand." In 1930, the political situation was eminently suited to the King's purpose.

The Conservative Party had long been dead, and the Liberals were fast losing credibility in their eagerness to attract disparate elements opposed to Carol. An expedient coalition of nationalistic, quasi-democratic, and conservative elements, the Liberal Party knew it stood little chance with its traditional enemy on the throne, and some of its members broke away to join the King. Similarly, opportunists in the National Peasant Party deserted Maniu. The old political hierarchies dissolved into a jumble of splinter groups with no one faction large or strong enough to oppose the King.

It can be argued that in this aspect of his reign, Carol II was no worse than Carol I or Ferdinand I. But Carol I tempered his basic premise of divide and rule with cool rationality, and Ferdinand I sought advisers with a tradition of prudence and judgment behind them. "I see him play his every card wrong..." observed Marie, who realized that in wielding his arbitrary will, her son was putting the fate of the entire monarchy in jeopardy; "it means all the work of two patient generations being smashed up."

In pursuing his course of one-man rule, the new King relegated his Prime Ministers to the position of His Majesty's errand boys and filled other important posts with ill-mannered adventurers in the stamp of Puiu Dimitresco—men whose primary qualification for statesmanship was that Elena Lupescu liked them. The Roumanian people, faced with a palace populated by parvenus and pimps, began to look back fondly to the traditional chicaneries of Bratianu, Stirbey, et al.

The first to withdraw was the aristocracy. The only friend of the previous court who frequented Carol's palace was Marthe Bibesco. Princess Bibesco, who had, in Princess Ileana's words, "dropped Mama for Papa when he became King," now "dropped Mama for the Lupescu." Along with a photograph of herself, Marthe sent obsequious notes to the King's mistress, addressed to "Ma Souveraine." One of these contained a memorable toadyism: "... the moment today when you allowed me to kiss your hand was the happiest of my life."

Roumania had always been known for the welcoming informality of her court, but with the advent of Carol II, this changed. His palace was both garish and forbidding. There was too much marble; the gilding was obtrusively bright; the guards were "alarmingly magnificent." A stickler for form, Carol lost his temper when one of his sisters, who was pregnant, sat in a large chair meant for a visiting king. Uniforms were a fixation with him.

He designed new ones nearly every year, adding cockaded helmets to the bright red and blue, gold-tasseled trappings of the palace A.D.Cs. During his reign Carol created innumerable decorations and medals that he passed out generously on trips to Western Europe. "Carol really *has* an unhealthy passion for the outward showy little signs of royalty which I always induced Nando to ignore," said his mother.

This emphasis on veneer was one of the reasons the King kept Mme. Lupescu very much in the background. However much he loved her, she never appeared at state functions; even at informal palace events, he kept his mistress hidden on a private balcony behind curtains. Lupescu spent her nights at the Casa Noua, Carol's underfurnished and impersonal villa behind the palace, but her official residence was a four-story red-brick mansion in the fashionable Modrogan Park section of Bucharest. A dark house with skimpy windows, it was encircled by a huge walled garden with guardhouses and chicken coops. A "dingy place..." said Countess Waldeck, "crammed with indifferent furniture and bric-a-brac like a secondhand furniture shop."

While the King's Duduia snuggled down in her Modrogan Park nest, his ex-wife struggled for breath in her home on the Chaussée. Sitta's position grew more difficult as the months went by. It was a well-known fact that the King took reprisals against anyone who saw her, and her isolation increased until it assumed the character of house arrest. No one dared go near the Princess except Marie and members of the royal family.

All of Marie's earlier resentment of her ex-daughter-in-law dissolved in the face of Sitta's vulnerability. If there was a family celebration without the King, Marie made sure that she was included; if Carol joined them, she invited his ex-wife for another day. Marie did not understand Carol's "deep and irremediable hatred for Sitta." Although Marie had sympathized with Carol's desire to remove Michael from the cloying atmosphere of Sitta's home, she was horrified at his choice of playmates for his son—nubile little girls like Puiu's daughter—and his lack of supervision when Michael was under his care.

For the first few months of his return, the King remained on superficially good terms with his mother, and Marie kept hoping that power would free him to behave more generously toward his family. Then, on October 29, 1930, her fifty-fifth birthday, Carol asked to speak to her alone. He had tried once before to win Marie to his side by accusing his ex-wife of indiscretions during their marriage. Now he told his mother that she must break off relations with Sitta. Marie's friendship with her ex-daughter-in-law was, he said, a public slap at him. Marie answered that it was against her "code of honour" to "ill-treat the one who is a foreigner amongst us."

From that day forward, Marie's relationship with Carol was never the same. The King ordered the security around his mother tightened; she was followed, and all her conversations, in and out of Cotroceni Palace, were reported to him. He made appointments with her, then sent underlings to cancel them at the last minute. The King tried to prevent Marie from entertaining old friends at her palace because, he said, "he knew that every criticism against him . . . started from Cotroceni" and that everyone who came to see Marie "spread . . . disloyal and disparaging talk about him." At the same time, to disguise the fact that they were no longer on good terms, Carol invited his mother to spend Christmas at Sinaia with Michael and him. Grateful for "small mercies," Marie accepted.

During the vacation nine-year-old Michael came down with a serious case of flu. Against the King's orders, Sitta came to Sinaia with Elisabetha to see him. Carol, who accused his wife of playing a "dirty trick" on him and his sister of being "a traitor," asked his mother not to receive them in her home. Marie ignored his request. The next day the King refused to see his mother and gave orders that when his ex-wife returned to Sinaia to see their son, she not be given any food from his palace. "Refuse food to the mother of his child . . . his former wife. It really makes one long to hide one's face in shame!" Marie wrote in her diary.

In the middle of March 1931, Marie left Roumania with Ileana for a trip to Western Europe. Although she hesitated to leave Sitta "so entirely un-protected and forsaken," she herself needed a respite from Carol. Due to the King's financial restrictions, Marie no longer traveled with a lady-in-waiting. She went to Paris, where she saw Prince Stirbey, "my excellent friend Barbo whom I miss more than anyone else." Stirbey was in the hospital. They had not seen each other for nine months.

Until that winter, Prince Stirbey had been living with his family in Brasov, Transylvania. The King had tried to remove Stirbey from all his boards of directors and positions of financial responsibility, but financiers in Roumania and abroad had refused to carry out his orders. Unable to ruin him financially, Carol encouraged Stirbey's old enemy Filipescu to destroy him through the press. He also had Stirbey followed and his mail censored. Marie had been unable to communicate with him except through friends who were willing to risk reprisal from the King.

When Marie heard that Stirbey needed a hernia operation, she sent word that he must not undergo even the most minor surgery in Roumania. The King, Marie said, had been loudly proclaiming that he had refused to eat at his mother's table when he first returned to Bucharest "because he *knew* that Barbo had bribed" her "servants to *poison* him!" If Carol could prom-ulgate such outrageous lies, "Barbo had certainly better not give himself over defenceless into *any* hands here in the country."

Marie's fears for her old friend's life were not overstated. Just before the Stirbeys' departure for Paris, Puiu told Marie's A.D.C. that he was "launch-ing . . . attacks against Prince Stirbey & that they meant to stamp him out of existence." They nearly succeeded. On the *Orient Express* en route to West-ern Europe, an attempt was made on Stirbey's life.

When Marie saw Barbo in Paris, the fifty-eight-year-old Prince was still recuperating from his operation. Barbo and Nadeje joined Marie a few days later in St. Briac, where Marie went to visit Ducky. They saw each other every day for two weeks. The parting was painful. Stirbey fretted about his inability to protect Marie. "Dear Barbo," she wrote in her diary. "We tried to be as unsentimental as possible, but our grief though wordless was great."

From St. Briac Marie traveled to Umrich, near Freiburg, Germany, to join Ileana, who was visiting her Hohenzollern cousins. Ileana's trip had been planned to coincide with that of Archduke Anton of Austria, a young man whom she had met in Spain in 1929. The meeting had been arranged by Carol.

Ileana had always been close to her elder brother, and after his coup Carol assumed that his youngest sister would support him in his feud with his ex-wife. When she took Sitta's part, Carol retaliated by removing her from her favorite positions, the presidency of the Y.W.C.A. and the Girl Scouts. The King told his sister that she could no longer tour the country for her organizations because she was spreading "propaganda against him."

Looking for a way to rid himself of this "aching thorn" in his side and remembering Anton of Austria, Carol decided to marry Ileana off. He contacted Prince Friedrich, Head of the House of Hohenzollern-Sigmaringen, and his wife and asked them to invite Ileana and Anton to Umrich. "We found that there were many things we had in common," Ileana recalled many years later. "We liked flying and we got on very well. It was sort of a rebound thing... I never realized the trap I was walking into, or else I might have thought twice about it."

When Ileana said she wanted to marry the Austrian Archduke, Marie was concerned. She could not fault Anton's pedigree. On his father's side he was a great-nephew of Emperor Franz Josef, and on his mother's, a Bourbon of Spain. But Anton was a penniless exile; after the family fled Austria, he had earned his living working in a gas station in Spain. Marie felt that of all her children, Ileana was best suited to wear a crown. A decent, kindly young man, more comfortable in workman's overalls than formal dress, Anton had had little time or opportunity for an education. "So there are great lapses in his knowledge of art, literature and... history," Marie said. "But he is an expert engineer and electrician, and a first-rate pilot. Big, solid, trustworthy, he has not a penny except what he earns with his own hands."

Marie wrote to ask the King's consent for his sister to marry her Archduke and for the young couple to take up residence in Roumania. "I have no objection to the proposed match..." he answered. "Unhappily I cannot consent to the plan that once married they should establish themselves in Roumania." Carol's scheme had worked perfectly. Having arranged to tie his sister to an offshoot of the Habsburgs, he now used the connection to push her out of the country. The Roumanians, he contended, would never stand for a Habsburg living within their borders.

Marie's intention to return home immediately to plan the wedding was overturned by the King, who wired telling her to stay out of Roumania for three more weeks. When she heard that Carol was conferring with her old friend Jean Duca, now head of the Liberal Party, she understood why. It would have been embarrassing for the King to make overtures to the Liberals while continuing to excoriate Barbo Stirbey. With her money running out, she did not know where to go. Whereas the government had formerly paid her traveling expenses, Carol now required that she pay them herself. As a public figure the Queen could not hide herself in a second-class hotel, and the deluxe hotels were now beyond her means. She finally accepted an invitation from an Italian acquaintance who offered her his villa outside Rome. Marie heard that Carol, who had had her followed in Western Europe, was "furious" because she had seen Stirbey. In doing this, the King said his mother had "declared" herself his enemy.

Carol's ferocious hatred of Stirbey cannot be explained merely on the basis of political differences—particularly in light of his accommodation to the Liberal Party—or simply as the jealousy of a son who never overcame his obsession with his mother. Like his attitude toward the members of his own family, Carol's antagonism to Stirbey seems to have been based on a desperate need to control or remove anyone uncontrollable. If you did not fawn on Carol, you were his enemy. Unlike Nicolas and Elisabetha, Stirbey could not be seduced away from Marie to Carol's camp; unlike Ileana and Sitta, he was strong. Moreover, Stirbey was the only person outside the royal family who was intimately familiar with the details of Carol's two desertions. In assuming the role of innocent victim hounded into exile by his political enemies, Carol had created a myth he could not afford to have exploded. The mere existence of Barbo Stirbey, the man who knew the truth about him, was an offense in the eyes of the King.

Shortly after Marie's return from Western Europe, Princess Helen left Roumania. In Marie's absence, Carol's increased persecution of his ex-wife had succeeded in arousing several quiet but public demonstrations of sympathy for the Princess. Fearing more violent expressions of loyalty, the government proposed a plan whereby it agreed to maintain Sitta abroad and assure her of financial security. The agreement provided for Michael to visit his mother twice a year and for her to return to Roumania each year for his birthday.

Marie took her former daughter-in-law to the railway station. Only a handful of foreigners came to bid Sitta goodbye; Roumanians were forbidden to appear. Marie walked with Sitta and a few family members through the empty station to the train, which had been drawn up on the farthest track. "It was unbearable to see her get into the train, without anyone there of all those who yesterday bowed down before her every smile or frown," Marie said.

Carol was anything but consistent, and within a month of Marie's return home he had once again assumed the pose of a loving son. With his mother successfully isolated from other sources of affection, he could afford to be solicitous. Marie was touched. Carol, she wrote happily in her diary, was "nice & kind and said that he hoped I would look upon him as my best friend ready to help me and make my life easy. That when Ileana was gone (I think he also meant Sitta, but her name was not mentioned) I would be lonely & he hoped I would let him fill in the emptiness as best he could."

On July 27, 1931, ten days after Sitta's departure, Marie attended the wedding of her youngest and best-loved child at Sinaia. The King, who was superb at arranging ceremonial events, masterminded the formal presentations of gifts, the reception of gawking deputations from the provinces, a great court ball, the formal signing of the civil contract, and lastly, a solemn religious service. The newlyweds were paraded in an open carriage through the streets of the mountain resort, which had been decorated for the occasion.

After the wedding, the mother of the bride, suffering from ill health and depression, took to her bed. "It all ended up in a sort of breakdown this summer," she wrote; "the Rolls-Royce needed overhauling, a little garage and tinkering." It was, she said, the separation from Ileana that caused her "final collapse." The doctors prescribed total rest.

Hearing that his sister-in-law was "very run-down," the Infante Alfonso wrote Marie a letter, exhorting her to pull herself together for the sake of royalty everywhere. "I have always looked to you as one of the throwbacks to old times..." Ali said. "I know your spirit cannot break. I can see you licking your... wounds & gathering strength again. I know you will fight to a finish."

Chapter *29*

To commit violent and unjust acts, it is
not enough for a government to have the
will or even the power; the times must
lend themselves to their committal.

—*ALEXIS DE TOCQUEVILLE*

*W*ith Ileana gone and her activities drastically curtailed by the King, Marie's life deteriorated into periods of distracted wandering. Relieved to be out from under the repressive dominion of her son, Marie traveled anywhere anyone invited her—to her daughters' homes in Yugoslavia and Austria, her sister's house on the seacoast of northern France, and the homes of family and friends in England.

To ensure his mother's continued absence from the country, Carol decreed that after her marriage Ileana was to be allowed no more than one month a year in Roumania and only with permission of the King. Having rid himself of his youngest sister, Carol now turned on his brother.

When Marie first heard about Carol's coup, her initial pique at not being told of Nicky's role in it had been more than offset by the joy of finding her two sons working hand in hand for the good of their country, or so she thought. In reality, Carol had used Nicolas only as a stepping-stone to the throne. Irrationally jealous of the popularity of other members of his family, he determined early in his reign to stand alone in the limelight.

As a reward for helping him get back into the country, the King named Nicolas Commander of the Roumanian Armed Forces. The title was a mere formality. Nicky, as Carol well knew, was not a worker but a bon vivant. His passion was a young Roumanian divorcée named Jeanne Doletti. The King encouraged his brother's love for the pretty commoner in hopes that Nicky's involvement would get him into political trouble.

Nicolas wanted to marry Jeanne. But as in the cases of Ferdinand and Helene, Carol and Zizi, and Carol and Elena Lupescu, the Roumanian Constitution expressly forbade princes of the dynasty to marry their subjects. In the first flush of brotherly enthusiasm, Carol had promised Nicky that when he became King, he would arrange for his younger brother's marriage. In his own personal interest, the King did try to push a law through Parliament that would legalize morganatic marriages for princes of the royal house, but, as Marie put it, "Even the Roumanians have some principles they stick to."

A year later, confronted by Nicolas' request to contract a morganatic marriage, the King tried an experiment. If Roumania refused to accept Jeanne Doletti, Carol had found an unassailable motive for getting Nicolas out of the country; if, by some strange chance the Roumanians tolerated Jeanne, they might swallow Elena Lupescu as well. "Put me before a *fait accompli*," Carol told Nicky. Prince Nicolas did just that. On October 28, 1931, he and Jeanne eloped to the small village of Tohan. When he returned with his bride, the King stripped him of his military rank and declared that in contracting an illegal marriage, Prince Nicolas had forfeited his rights as a member of the royal family and citizen of Roumania. Marie was not impressed with Carol's sudden infatuation with the law. "Living as he does," she said of the King, "he cannot expect Nicolas to honour him."

Nicolas soon left the country with his bride. When he tried to return in the spring of 1932, the King had him arrested and exiled for a year. Before he left Roumania, Nicolas spoke to his mother about money. Having spent a fortune on his wife, a new-minted connoisseur of antiques and old silver, Nicky worried about what would happen if the King suddenly cut him off from his income. Could Barbo Stirbey help him? Since Nicolas had followed Carol's line in denouncing Stirbey, Marie suggested he write a letter to Barbo, now living in Switzerland, asking for forgiveness and financial assistance. Stirbey promised to help. Both he and Marie begged Nicolas not to openly oppose his brother. "It is only through dignity, *bonne tenue* [good bearing] and work that you can prove to the world that you have been persecuted, you cannot rehabilitate yourself by screaming against the King," Marie wrote her younger son, explaining that in publicly attacking Carol he was undermining the dynasty and the country. Although Marie managed to see Nicolas whenever she was outside Roumania, she refused for a long time to receive his wife, whom she dismissed as "a hardhearted, painted little hussy whose one idea is money and luxury."

Shortly after the King exiled Nicolas, Marie accepted an invitation to Yugoslavia. It was the fourth time in the two years since Carol's coup that she had taken refuge with Mignon and Alexander. Although the King of Yugoslavia was erratic—warm and personable one moment, withdrawn the next—Marie trusted him. He was, in her words, "what my sons failed to be—son, brother, friend, upholder." Alexander sympathized with Marie when she received a letter from Carol accusing her and Nicolas, whom she met in Belgrade, of "plotting together to overthrow him."

During her sojourn in Yugoslavia, Marie traveled with her daughter and son-in-law into Macedonia. Later, to conform to Carol's demands that she stay out of Roumania, she journeyed with Mignon to Istanbul. These were Marie's sorts of excursions, all quaintness and exotica. In the mountains of Macedonia she found "incredibly costumed people, Turks, Albanians, Montenegrins, Serbs, each with their special dress, so wild-looking and so picturesque, so that each man, woman and child we met seemed to have dressed up for our special enchantment." Friends, aware of her persecution at home and struck by her seemingly indestructible capacity for enjoyment, wondered how long she could hold up this way: "As long as my health lasts out, for the spirit will not weaken," she answered. But when they asked why she did not leave Roumania for good she said she was "too proud to take residence abroad, it would be to admit my life has been a failure."

Ileana was expecting her first baby, but King Carol refused to allow her to have the child in Roumania. Since Anton, an exiled Habsburg, was a man without a country and Ileana had not relinquished her Roumanian passport, the child would be born a Roumanian citizen. Whether the King's opposition was based, as he claimed, on the political repercussions of bringing a Habsburg into the world within Roumania's borders or whether he worried that Ileana's child might figure someday in the succession, Carol II was adamant about keeping his sister out. "The government wills it, and I absolutely cannot go against their wishes," he said, although his mother knew that he alone was now the government.

For a brief moment Marie relaxed family pride. In a letter asking George V to stand as godfather to the expected child, she allowed herself to complain to her cousin about her son. "I have never written to you lately as my life has been very difficult & very sad. . . . I have struggled for over two years, swallowing every unkindness, every setback, but all in vain . . . all mother's rights are denied me, even the right of being loved. . . . Lately I have been living in a world which I no more understand & which has become very lonely. Ileana married, Sitta gone, Nicky banished, but I struggle on . . . I was always a good fighter you remember. But fight against one's own flesh and blood?"

George answered from aboard his yacht at Cowes. Although his Protestant faith prohibited him from becoming the godfather to a Catholic child, he was deeply touched by Missy's unhappiness: "What a terribly sad letter yours is. In reading it the tears came into my eyes . . . I have seen Sitta and George, and they have both told me of the many insults and unkindnesses that have been heaped upon you; even this last cruel act, that Ileana was forbidden to enter the country to have her baby in your house is cruel and disgraceful. I do hope that some day soon we may meet and then you will be able to pour your heart out to me. . . . I cannot help thinking that he is mad . . . one wonders what he will do next."

Marie arrived in Austria for the birth of Ileana's child with a retinue that included her A.D.C., the Queen of Yugoslavia, and two Roumanian doctors. The house was small, and Marie was installed in a room opening into the young couple's bedroom. The proximity, if uncomfortable, created an opportunity for the education of Anton: "Ileana and I, with combined tact and very much love are teaching him in tiny, imperceptible doses how a civilised 'pater familias' and a self-respecting Archduke is supposed to live and behave," Marie wrote to a friend. She had brought a pot of earth to place under Ileana's bed so the child could be born on Roumanian soil. After a difficult labor of three days and nights, a boy, Stefan, was born.

Word had traveled to Vienna that King Carol II had refused his sister permission to come home for her confinement. Determined to make up for the slight and anxious to celebrate the first archducal birth on Austrian soil since World War I, the Austrians made a great fuss over the new infant. Guns boomed on the outskirts of the city and bells were rung in all the neighboring churches. Marie and her daughter could scarcely wait for news of the reception to reach the King of Roumania. Carol responded with unexpected graciousness, inviting his sister to spend a few weeks with their mother in her native land.

Marie's joy in bringing Ileana back to Roumania was tempered by a new family problem. Princess Helen suddenly broke through her accustomed ladylike reserve with a public attack on Carol. In a series of articles published in the London *Daily Mail*, the King's ex-wife denounced his persecutions of her, calling on the English public to "help . . . preserve for me the rights which I claim as a mother who has been treated with cruel heartlessness."

The articles, which were suppressed in Roumania, grew out of an absurd incident over young Michael's attire. Allowed to visit his mother for one month twice a year, Michael had arrived in London with two A.D.C.s and instructions from King Carol that he was not to wear long pants. But when Sitta and her son were invited to Buckingham Palace for tea, the Princess, knowing that short pants would be considered deep discourtesy, took him to the palace in a regular dark suit. The senior A.D.C., a Roumanian colonel, telephoned Bucharest to report the breach of commands to the King. Carol ordered that Michael be taken away from his mother at once. Instead of the prescribed month, the visit lasted just three days.

In her disappointment Princess Helen followed her son back to Roumania, where she continued her angry denunciations of the King and broadened her accusations to include Marie. "This after having stuck up for her against my own son . . . bringing his wrath down on my head," Marie complained to her diary.

During the holidays Marie had a chance to observe eleven-year-old Michael, now entirely in his father's care. An English biographer, who undertook the Augean task of whitewashing Carol II, once quoted the King as saying that if he had not been born a Prince, he would have liked to have been a schoolmaster. Trying his theories on his son, Carol established classes for Michael with half a dozen boys his age imported from different social classes and provincial districts along with one or two sons of Lupescu's friends. Dressed in blue uniforms of the King's design, Michael and his schoolmates were drilled in military science, government, history, mathematics, philosophy, and languages. To underscore his devotion to Roumania and his hatred of the boy's mother, the King removed all traces of English influence instituted by her. Michael was forbidden to speak English or wear English clothes. His English governess was replaced by a cadre of A.D.C.s.

Jealous even of his son, Carol II seesawed between overweening expressions of affection and arbitrary attacks on the boy. Michael, who "hated his father's entourage, especially Puiu," quickly learned to disguise his feelings. "I take good care to whom I speak," he told his grandmother. "I have learnt to hold my tongue, and I even smile at Puiu because I must."

There was little the Dowager Queen could do at home for her children, her grandson, or her country. Abroad, she was less frustrated, and the King, delighted to be rid of her, encouraged every journey. Soon after the holidays Marie left for a few weeks in Austria, then moved on to Belgrade. Upon her return to Bucharest she received an invitation to make an extensive tour of Morocco as an official guest of the French government. She accepted immediately and left Roumania again.

From Morocco Marie continued straight to St. Briac to see Ducky. Although she managed to spend part of every summer bathing at the seaside home of her favorite sister, this journey was purely an errand of mercy. Ducky, Marie explained in a letter to a friend, "has had an overwhelming soulgrief which has shattered her conception of life and humanity." The trouble, "which no one was allowed to mention," remains a mystery, and Marie, sworn to secrecy, never divulged it. It had to do with Ducky's husband, Grand Duke Kirill, and from the day she discovered it until the day she died, the Grand Duchess avoided further physical contact with him.

It would seem that a case of simple infidelity, particularly on the part of a Russian Grand Duke, would not justify the violence of the Grand Duchess's reaction. Whatever it was, Ducky took some sort of perverse pleasure in her misery, and it was several weeks before Marie could convince her sister to come back with her to Balcic to be nursed back to health. When she finally sent Ducky home to France, Marie was still worried enough to write Waldorf and Nancy Astor to keep an eye on her from England.

After Ducky's departure, Marie picked up Ileana and her husband, Anton, for a cruise to Scotland, Ireland, Spitsbergen and the fjords. In August they returned to Bran. Every time she came home, Marie experienced afresh the frustration of being forced to watch her son destroy the dynasty.

"My voice has become a small voice because I have been set aside from all power, and I could only make my voice heard in accusation..." she wrote an American correspondent. "I could become chief accuser. But it is just the power that I, as mother, cannot use.... But it's terribly hard for me to let them think that I am blind.... But my word of disapproval, said publicly, could set fire to the house.... I see the danger coming nearer & nearer.... Whichever way I turn, there is danger...whilst I remain silent, the danger grows."

By the fall of 1933, Carol II had made marked headway in undermining the strength of the National Peasant Party through the cunning seduction of its leaders. The great experiment in reform of 1928 deteriorated rapidly after 1930, as the King escorted Prime Ministers, one by one, in and out of office. Unable to overcome agricultural and industrial problems brought on by the worldwide Depression and the need for agrarian reform, Maniu's successors succumbed to the easy solutions of repression and Jew-baiting. Encouraged by the King, they set new records for dishonesty and police brutality, trampling the rights of the peasants and workers, the people who had brought them into office.

As Maniu's National Peasant Party faded from power, a new personality, purporting to represent another kind of reform, appeared on the scene. Corneliu Zelea Codreanu was the founder of the Legion of the Archangel Michael. The Legion, a fanatical right-wing movement, was the Roumanian answer to the rising tide of fascism and anti-Semitism emanating from Hitler's Germany. It was not easy to be accepted into the Legion; most applicants were refused, and the chosen had to serve a three-year apprenticeship. From its inception, the Legion was composed of the elite of young toughs. In 1930 it became the backbone of the infamous Iron Guard, a terrorist organization dedicated to anti-Communism, anti-Semitism, raving Orthodoxy, and romantic suicide.

Codreanu was supported financially and spiritually by Hitler's Nazis and Mussolini's Fascists, who recognized in him the makings of a mystical spellbinder, an agent provocateur in the garb of a saint. When the handsome young Codreanu, dressed in dazzling white, galloped into the provincial villages brandishing an icon, the peasants believed he was the earthly representative of the Archangel Michael. By 1933 the Iron Guard, fed by the grievances of an economically depressed populace looking for scapegoats, had become a major political force.

Thinking he could manipulate Codreanu to further his own plans, Carol II supported the young terrorist through various of his subject politicians. When Marie was told that the Iron Guard was a healthy revolt against "old-fashioned reaction, bankrupt capitalism, political graft and international Semitism," she did not agree. "It is a dangerous game," she warned. "The King should not encourage nationalistic demagogues who, in spite of their blatant nationalism, get their inspiration from foreign ideologies."

It would be nice to say that the King's mother, who was ecumenical in her religious outlook, was equally tolerant of the Jews. Certainly, Marie was not anti-Semitic by conviction. "I try hard to feel towards them as I do to other nationalities," she wrote in 1920, "but ever again I am appalled by their extraordinary physical hideousness." The Queen's aesthetic sensitivities had been compounded by dynastic worries. By the 1930s the Jews had come to represent two things to her—Elena Lupescu and Communism, the dangers she most feared in the preservation of the monarchy. Marie had read *The Protocols of the Learned Elders of Zion,** sent to her in 1920 by Loie Fuller, but she did not subscribe to the Nazi polemic. Nonetheless, she frequently referred to Elena Lupescu as "the Jewess," although she based her hatred of her son's mistress on moral and financial issues rather than religious ones.

The early thirties, which were financially disastrous years for the Roumanian people, were highly lucrative for their King and his mistress. While Ferdinand and Marie had struggled to overcome traditional graft in government circles, Carol simply took over the lion's share of the profits. Not content with the sizable fortune left him by his great-uncle and his father, nor the money he expropriated from his mother, the King looked to Mme. Lupescu's friends for ways to increase his nest egg. He developed profitable associations with men like Max Aushnit, founder of the largest steel trust in Roumania, and Nicolae Malaxa,** an armaments tycoon and major supporter of the Iron Guard. As he amassed his fortune, the King arranged to deposit money outside Roumania, and it is estimated that he sent between $40 million and $50 million out of the country between 1930 and 1940.

Marie knew that her son was dishonest but not to what degree. "Decidedly today I must not look too closely into things or I would die of grief," she wrote in the fall of 1933. Some months earlier, when one of Carol's ministers came to Cotroceni to smooth matters out between Carol and his mother, Marie told him that she had "not much left but... the right to keep clean hands," and that they "could only remain clean by having absolutely nothing to do with anything that was going on" at the King's palace.

In 1931 Ernesto Urdareanu, a cavalry officer, joined the group of A.D.C.s attached to Carol's palace guard. From there he rose quickly, profiting from a scandal around Puiu to replace him as Lupescu's general factotum and

---

The Protocols of the Learned Elders of Zion: A Russian forgery published in the early 1900s and translated into many languages, purporting to outline a Jewish plan to dominate and destroy the world. It was a major tool of the Nazis.
**In 1946 Malaxa fled with a large fortune to the United States. Although he was a known Nazi collaborator, corporate partner of Hermann Goering, and supporter of the Iron Guard, he was helped to enter the United States, where he remained until his death in 1965, by high-ranking U.S. officials. Among these was Richard Nixon, then the Junior Senator from California, who wrote a letter to the Defense Production Administration urging the approval of Malaxa's application for permanent residency. Nixon's efforts in Malaxa's behalf are documented in the *Congressional Record* of October 5, 1962.

eventually, when Puiu was thrown out, as the King's personal secretary. Short and smooth, with tiny feet, Urdareanu easily grasped the formalities demanded by the King and within two years rose to the position of Lord High Chamberlain of Carol's palace. Considered the most powerful man in Roumania, he was courted and bribed by businessmen, politicians, and diplomats alike.

By November of 1933 the King had run through all the leaders of the National Peasant Party, and he turned to Jean Duca, his onetime enemy and leader of the Liberals, to form a government. The resurgence of the Liberals looked on the surface like a major defeat for Carol II. Some historians suggest, however, that in setting Duca up in opposition to Codreanu and the Iron Guard, the King purposely pitted the last two strong men left in power against each other, hoping that they would kill each other off. Although this would have been in character for Carol, no one has ever explained why he did not try to strengthen the hand of the adversary least opposed to his wobbly dynasty. Codreanu had become the loudest and most forceful critic of Carol's regime. Schooled by the Nazis in the tactics of anti-Semitic propaganda, raving about God and country, Sodom and Gomorrah, his attacks on the King's Jewish mistress and her friends daily grew more shrill.

Jean Duca, on the other hand, was an anachronism in the power structure of the 1930s. A slight aristocrat with a pince-nez, a beautifully trimmed moustache, and a great appreciation of elegant women, Duca was a gentleman of culture and wit and an aristocratic orator of subtle eloquence. Unlike most of his predecessors, he was incorruptibly honest, and he based his political beliefs on principles of Western democracy. He was an old friend of Marie's, whose primary objection to his assuming power was that in so doing he compromised himself by accepting Elena Lupescu.

During the elections of November 1933, Codreanu and his Iron Guard launched a campaign of vilification against Duca, greeting his subsequent accession to the premiership with rioting and acts of terrorism. "I cannot govern Roumania with the Legionnaires out of hand and anarchy rampant," he told the King. "The law must be enforced."

Duca asked the King's permission to outlaw the Iron Guard. The government split on the issue, and Carol hesitated on the grounds that serious reprisals might ensue. "Then, Sir," said the new Premier, "I shall sign myself the decree of dissolution, taking the whole responsibility upon my shoulders."

Duca declared war on the Iron Guard, and in so doing, signed away his own life. On December 9, 1933, some eighteen thousand followers of Codreanu were arrested, although Codreanu himself escaped. Within three weeks the Iron Guard took its revenge. Standing on a platform at the Sinaia railway station after a visit to the King, Prime Minister Duca was shot down by three members of the Guard. Although it was common knowledge that Codreanu ordered the assassination, he was acquitted of complicity. The man who actually fired the shots told the foreign press with "complete calmness and satisfaction" that he had no regret for having killed the "friend of the Jews." This blatant flouting of the law did not affect the King's subsidies to the Iron Guard, which continued as before, and during the trial of Duca's assassins, Codreanu was hidden in the home of a cousin of Mme. Lupescu.

The Dowager Queen was in Austria visiting Ileana when Duca was murdered. She was grief-stricken at the violent death of her old friend and could scarcely believe it when she heard that her son was too frightened to attend his Prime Minister's funeral. "I am sick with sadness," she wrote in her diary, "and also with humiliation for my own son!" Oblique consolation came in the form of a letter from Barbo Stirbey, one of Jean Duca's oldest friends. "Perhaps we ought to think of him [Duca] as the chosen one," Barbo wrote Marie, "the one who was taken before greater disillusions set in."

Chapter 30

Are all ends of life so sad?

—*QUEEN MARIE OF ROUMANIA*

 *W*hat little that was left of Carol II's credibility plummeted in the aftermath of the Duca assassination. After three and a half years on the throne, the only sphere to which the King could point with pride was foreign affairs. In February of 1934, Nicolae Titulescu, Carol's Foreign Minister, concluded the Balkan Pact. A Balkan counterpart of the Little Entente and a safeguard against territorial encroachment from larger nations, the Balkan Pact was signed by Roumania, Turkey, Greece, and Yugoslavia.

Titulescu was the only man of talent left in the government. He was a true physical oddity—tall, hermaphroditic, with curiously shiny skin and a hairless face. John Gunther said he resembled a "mongoloid monkey." Titulescu was also witty, lively, and a superb orator. An associate of Take Jonescu's before World War I, he had taken over as Roumania's leading voice in international affairs after Jonescu's death in 1922. Like Jonescu, Titulescu advocated strong cooperation between the countries of Eastern

Europe. Wielding influence far beyond his country of origin, he was a strong champion of the League of Nations and was the only man to be twice elected as its President. He also served as President of the Little Entente and the Balkan League.

As Carol grew more unpopular at home, Titulescu's international prestige became more important to him. After Duca's death, Titulescu refused to re-enter the Cabinet until the King rid himself of the infamous Puiu. Marie was delighted when her nemesis fell from power. Without Puiu, Carol— lonely, floundering in the rising tide of condemnation—sought out his mother's company.

Among the angry rumblings in Bucharest in the spring of 1934 was a rumor that an attempt would be made on the King's life during the national Independence Day parade. To protect himself, Carol brought out his mother. "...in spite of all false modesty," Marie had written a friend the previous month, "I am still a beautiful woman. I feel a sort of vibration of appreciation shudder through a crowd or assembly when I appear...a sort of new beauty has come to me. I can see it myself, so when I am told about it, I know it is true."

If not her beauty, certainly her popularity proved itself on May 10, 1934. Dressed in a red tunic, fastened with elaborate frogged closings, a white skirt, and her hussar's helmet with aigrettes, Marie created a sensation. Cheering, shouting Roumanians stretched and strained to catch a glimpse of the lady who had not recently been on display. Even diplomats forgot their dignity and waved their silk top hats in the air as her horse pranced down the Calea Victoriei. The happy madness caused by Marie contrasted painfully with the barely polite reception given the King.

Although Titulescu's war on Puiu earned Marie's gratitude, his subsequent rapprochement with the Soviets infuriated her. During the summer of 1934 Roumania renewed diplomatic relations with Russia. Marie wept on the day she heard the news and nearly refused to shake hands with Titulescu when he arrived expecting congratulations. "We are so terribly near to them, and I think it is a huge and dangerous mistake..." she wrote an American friend. "I certainly do not mean to receive in my house those who murdered all my mother's family." She begged Carol to "keep his eyes open about the Bol- shevik propaganda...Bigger and wiser countries than ours have blown up, so why should we...hold out against those world destroyers." It was the Communists who had driven her mother's family into exile. "Will I also live to be uprooted and to become an exile one day, just at an age when one dreams of harvest and rest?"

Perceptive about the threat of Communism, Marie, like many others of her class, was undiscerning about Hitler. In the mid-thirties Hitler was still wooing European monarchs, and he had always been known to respect the Hohenzollern dynasty in Roumania. Sister Sandra had succumbed early to the Führer's promises of a regenerated Germany, and Ducky too was said to be an admirer. "What a curious figure Hitler is..." Marie wrote an American correspondent. "I withhold every judgment, but mostly everybody is virulent against him abroad." After the bloody purge of June 30, 1934, and the assassination of Dollfuss in Austria the following month, Marie commented on Hitler's "fearful brutality," but seemed unwilling to draw the logical conclusions.

In the spring of 1934, Marie received an invitation to come to London for the publication of her autobiography. She was overjoyed. It was nearly ten years since she had set foot in England; her return was a triumph and a much-needed ego boost. Cassell had just published *The Story of My Life*, which was already running into two and three printings. In America *The Saturday Evening Post* had offered her fifty thousand dollars for the serial rights, and her agent had told her that her characterizations were "as good as Galsworthy at his best." "This might have been merely fine words to a queen," she commented, "but the number of dollars offered was rather more convincing."

By the time Marie arrived in London, everyone she knew was reading or had read her book. "Even an old highbrow like Lady Oxford [Margot Asquith], who writes herself, is enthusiastic about it, and she has a tongue for ten!" Marie gleefully reported. "Old England is glad to have me back.... It is well managed that I and my book should appear together."

The reviews of the critics were nearly as flattering as those of her friends. Some faulted Marie for lack of historical depth and breadth, but most praised her lavishly for the portraits of her relatives and her vivid re-creation of a lost world. Writing in the prestigious literary monthly *The Forum*, Mary Colum called Marie a "female counterpart" of H. G. Wells, and compared her gift for portraiture to his. Although Colum criticized Marie's lack of personal psychological insight, she readily admitted that the world in 1934 would not "take very seriously a disinterested valuation of her own personality from any woman." It was clear that in tackling the autobiographical form, Marie had finally found a hospitable framework for her romantic imagination and fanciful powers of description, as well as her penchant for irreverent characterization.

In London Marie divided her time between publicity forays and parties with old friends like the Astors. In Scotland she visited the royal family, and in a letter to an American correspondent, she described herself and her hosts.

"George has always kept an especial affection for me. I stimulate him, my uncrushable vitality makes the blood course more quickly through his veins. May [Queen Mary] feels it also. She likes being with me, and then I am never heavy on their hands. I know so perfectly how to look after myself and be happy over everything, finding interests everywhere...

"May... is fundamentally tidy, orderly, disciplined. She likes possessing, collecting, putting things in order... She looks into things in detail and is an excellent and vigilant housewife. She has excellent appetite, excellent health, and sleeps beautifully. . . . Both she and he are scrupulously polite, but their demonstrations of pleasure or affection are always restrained and decorous. You can think, as contrast, impulsive, uncalculating, unconventional *me*. I am always astonished that they really like me, but they do!"

One of Marie's great pleasures while in Scotland was a visit to the Duke of York (the future George VI) and his family. The Dowager Queen was enchanted by his daughters, who sang and acted out nursery rhymes for her; "little Elizabeth* . . ." she wrote in her diary, "is just as adorable as she was always said to be. A quite perfect child, friendly, polite, unselfconscious, amiable & intelligent and into the bargain pretty. Little Margaret Rose is a replica in small and is also a delicious child. I fell in love with the whole family."

Marie returned to London, where she had planned two more weeks of pleasure for herself. On the afternoon of October 9, she attended the Chelsea Flower Show and at 5 P.M. stopped for tea at the home of an old friend. While they were talking, the telephone rang. It was the Roumanian Ambassador reporting that Marie's son-in-law, King Alexander of Yugoslavia, had been assassinated in Marseille by a Macedonian terrorist. Mignon was a widow. Marie's grandson Peter, aged eleven, was now King of Yugoslavia.

"We were just speaking of the importance of Sandro's visit. . ." Marie wrote in her diary. "I felt as though I had been hit between the eyes. *Nothing* could be more horrible, horrible, horrible—for us all, for Europe [,] for the world! He was the steadiest of them all, the best, the most needed, the most important, the one who counted most. . . . The anguish was not to be able to get into contact with Mignon . . . it was a fearful thought, her all alone there . . . unsustained by any of the family."

The Queen of Yugoslavia, who was suffering from a gall-bladder ailment, had taken the train to Lyon, where she had been scheduled to meet her husband. Her carriage was rerouted to Marseille, and Marie asked Baby Bee, already in Paris, to meet Mignon there. Avoiding the reporters crowding around the Ritz Hotel, Marie sent for her grandson, young King Peter, for the sad trip to Paris. The boy, who had been at school in Surrey, seemed "curiously little moved" by his father's death. Both the Infante Alfonso and Waldorf Astor insisted upon accompanying them on the trip, and Lord Astor kept the young King amused on the train with magic tricks.

The following day the Dowager Queen went to the station in Paris to receive her widowed daughter. President Lebrun of France led her to Mignon's carriage. Draped in black, her blond head heavily veiled, the Queen of Yugoslavia tried to smile. "She was very calm & marvelously dignified, but her hands were trembling," said Marie, who was intensely proud of her daughter's equanimity in the face of tragedy. "Mignon's royal blood showed

*H.M. Queen Elizabeth II.

in the terrible ordeals," her mother said. The next day the royal party was escorted with great pomp to the *Arlberg Express* bound for Belgrade.

King Alexander's funeral was attended by everyone from the President of France to Hermann Goering. On his arrival in Belgrade, the King of Roumania made a great fuss about staying in his brother-in-law's palace, where Alexander's body lay in state. Carol said he "could not bear being under one roof with the dead!" Marie was stunned by her "big grown healthy" son's fear. "What an extraordinary attitude to take!... I could *sleep* in the room where Sandro's body lies if I were asked to!" she wrote in her diary.

With the departure of the guests, Marie turned to her widowed daughter and family. Mignon seemed incapable to her mother of acting on her own. Over the years since her marriage to the moody Alexander, the young Queen of Yugoslavia had built up a history of dependence on other women. Her most recent attachment was to an English nanny, who had completely taken over raising Mignon's three sons; Marie lost no time in firing the woman. To counteract young King Peter's indifference to his father's death, Marie encouraged the boy to prepare an altar of flowers and candles under Alexander's portrait. Convinced that the new Regent of Yugoslavia, Prince Paul, needed the benefit of her experience in the Balkans, Marie offered advice to him as well. Although she admired Paul's refinement, she said he was "too much an Occidental.... This is where I can help..." she wrote in her diary. "I shall try and broaden him."

It was two months before Marie could tear herself away from the satisfactions of dispensing wisdom to return to her own country, where she was usually ignored. Having fallen into the habit of advising, however, she took advantage of the Christmas holidays to tackle some difficult questions with Carol. She told the King that Mme. Lupescu was said to be making a profit on all government munitions orders and that "huge sums" of money were being transferred in his name from the Roumanian National Bank to banks in other countries. She asked Carol to please give his mistress a message that if "she really loved him she should find means of stopping these hideous reports." "This is the first conversation we have had on these subjects," Marie wrote in her diary, adding that the exchange was "exceedingly friendly and never once did either of us lose our calm or get angry."

The winter of 1934–1935 seemed long and lonely to Marie, who was increasingly isolated from family and friends. It was nearly four years since she had seen Barbo Stirbey. After their reunion in France, they had decided not to meet anymore so as not to give the King a chance to accuse his mother of disloyalty. They did not speak on the telephone unless Marie was outside the country, and they corresponded only when their letters did not have to pass through the hands of Carol's minions.

In September of 1934, the King had formally banished Stirbey from Roumania. He also applied financial sanctions, making it increasingly difficult for Stirbey to take money out of Roumania to support his wife and himself in exile in Switzerland. No doubt Carol had heard what more and more people were saying—that Ion Bratianu and Barbo Stirbey had been right about him, that he never should have been permitted to come home.

Although his letters to Marie were no longer read by curious intermediaries, Stirbey continued to maintain a respectful distance between himself and the Queen. At the same time, he managed to convey undiminished love in every word. "It is so sweet to hear you speak as you do of your recollections of other times when one had the right to be happy," the exiled Prince wrote in answer to one of Marie's letters. Neither time nor distance, Barbo told Marie, could "efface the freshness or the intensity" of his own memories.

Left alone much of the time, Marie took consolation in her lifetime passion for reading. She stopped eating a formal supper and had a cup of hot soup brought to her rooms so she could continue enjoying her books. Reading kept her from dwelling on the problems of her children. She was worried about Mignon, isolated in her palace in Belgrade. "She is very young to have no more . . . love in her life & being placed as she is there is no possibility for her ever to have any male company except of the most official kind," Marie wrote a friend.

She also felt sorry for Nicky, who brought his wife back to Roumania in 1935 after more than two years in exile. Nicolas was an embittered man; "he is nasty and unkind about everybody," his mother said. She resented the fact that Nicolas was "entirely & sinfully indifferent to his duties" as a Prince of Roumania. Marie also looked askance at his wife's mania for buying antiques. "Jeanne," she said, "can only sit upon historical chairs or eat off tables that ought to be in a museum and drink out of historical glass & eat off historical china."

Marie was even more embarrassed by Elisabetha, who had fallen in love with a Greek businessman and was in the process of divorcing George. Marie thought her eldest daughter was "helping to destroy the prestige of the dynasty." Elisabetha, who had already bought the most valuable country estate in Roumania and was building a huge palace in town, was "not too proud to dirty her hands" working for her brother, according to their mother, nor was she averse to accepting "personal profit" for her efforts.

Marie found it sadly ironic that Carol, Elisabetha, and Nicky, the three children who ignored their duty to their country, were the three who had remained in Roumania, "whilst Mignon & Ileana, the two believers in 'Noblesse Oblige'" lived elsewhere. Marie said she hated to talk about these three children with other people: "I feel I arouse pity and I do not wish to be pitied," she explained.

The publication in the spring of 1935 of the second volume of Marie's autobiography prompted some adverse reviews. "Some readers," said the critic for the *Illustrated London News*, "may find the extremely personal character of the memoirs a little embarrassing, the consciousness of royalty they every-where confess a little overwhelming."

Marie blamed the critics for not trying to understand her position and her mission and resented the attacks on her writing as personal attacks on herself. According to Marie, the world simply did not understand the royal condition.

Worse than the impersonal criticism was a scathing review that appeared in France by Marthe Bibesco. The venom with which Bibesco belittled the author and her work stemmed from Carol's court, where it was mandatory to denigrate the King's mother. "After all, who was Queen Marie?" Bibesco asked. "Nothing more than the wife of Ferdinand I and the mother of Carol II. She was there so the dynasty could go on. She was nothing but a cow."

The Story of My Life was translated into Roumanian the following winter, and compliments from the Queen's other subjects made up for Bibesco's attack. The book was also translated into French, German, Polish, Czech, Swedish, Italian, and Hungarian; even the Japanese requested a translation. "I feel rather like a hen who has hatched ducklings!" Marie said. Moreover, she was invited to return to England in May to preside over the 145th Annual Banquet of the Royal Literary Fund—the first woman so honored.

Marie's 1935 visit to England coincided with George V's Jubilee. Comparing her lot with that of her cousins, she found "something comforting, reassuring, touching about the reception the King received. . . . No matter that he has no special personality, that she is stiff and sometimes conventional—they were emblems—flags—the kindly father, the benevolent mother." Accustomed to angry masses of discontented peasants barely kept under control by the repressive forces of Carol II, Marie marveled at the good will of the crowds and the polite bobbies.

On a visit into the countryside to see the home where she was born, Marie was struck by the changes in English country life and surprised to find the chatelaines in old dresses and maids serving at table instead of powdered footmen. She still admired the dignity of these houses and their inhabitants, their quiet manners and secure traditions. "It was all mine once but I left it," she said, "and when I come back, I have no place there anymore, it belongs to others."

The romance between the Prince of Wales and Wallis Simpson was the major topic of conversation in England that year. "The difficulties his parents are having with him make them a little more understanding for my difficulties with my own son," Marie wrote a friend. "David . . . kicks against traditions and restrictions, without realizing that tradition made him, is his *raison dêtre*."

From England Marie traveled to Austria and Yugoslavia. Left at last with nowhere to go but home, she was upset by the conditions she found there. In spite of a good harvest and high prices, there was open unrest throughout the country, and the heavily guarded streets of Bucharest were abnormally quiet. During the spring, Maniu had attacked Mme. Lupescu openly on the floor of Parliament; now in the fall, a pamphlet appeared that suggested that if Carol II did not reform, Roumania might be better off without the monarchy. Nevertheless, as Marie wrote a friend, her son continued "to dance his mad dance." "I have to sit by and look on knowing that when the hour of reckoning will strike, I shall be swept away with all the rest and be an outcast-beggar because, having lived for my people, I have never put anything by for myself. The other, however, is fabulously rich as for years her hands have been deep in the chests of the State."

On her return, Marie was notified that the Roumanians wanted to celebrate her sixtieth birthday with deputations and a gala parade in Bucharest. She was delighted and returned from her gardens at Balcic a week ahead of time, stopping in Sinaia for a more private celebration planned by the King. "The whole country is celebrating this 60th. birthday with special fervour..." she wrote in her diary. "...all my virtues are being raked together... Suddenly all my faults have disappeared and it seems I am a very wonderful person, *le bon génie* [the good fairy] of the country, the luck-bringer, the angel of charity... the good soldier, the supreme spirit of our Roumanian unity."

Carol did not share his mother's enthusiasm. Afraid that the larger demonstrations planned for Bucharest might detract from his wilted prestige, the King instructed his Prime Minister to inform the Head of Marie's Household that he was canceling the festivities in Bucharest. Accustomed to Carol's habit of sending other people to transmit disagreeable orders, Marie insisted upon confronting her son directly. There had to be "some misunderstanding somewhere ..." she said. "This tampering with my liberty was laughable. But alas," she learned, "it was *not* laughable." The King told his mother that everything that was going to be done to honor her had already taken place "under *his* roof," and no public manifestations would be allowed.

Torn between accepting Carol's decision and coming to an open break with her son, Marie submitted, quietly swallowing her resentment. She was too proud to beg Carol for the honors she felt she deserved. But when she appeared a few moments later at a family lunch, her face, according to one of her children, "had become small, like a little lemon."

The winter of 1935–1936 was foggy and bleak. Christmas, celebrated at Sinaia, was empty, full of official pomp created by Carol to mask an absence of good will. The only bright note was a growing relationship with her grandson Michael, who was allowed to spend more time with her than before. The teen-age boy lunched once a week with Marie and took her for a drive afterward. Marie thought this favor had been granted because she had learned to control herself; she had grown "less impetuous, and so awake less apprehension."

Shortly after Christmas the King approached his mother to see if she would be willing to receive Mme. Lupescu. It was a "painful moment" for Marie. Although it would have been "a relief to say yes," Marie felt she must refuse, as she knew Lupescu would use the meeting for political ends: ". . . if I had seen her, I would have played into her hands and into the hands of her associates," Marie wrote in her diary.

At 3 A.M. on January 21, 1936, the King called his mother to tell her that George V had died. It was a deep and personal blow to Marie: ". . . so much goes with him to the grave. . ." she wrote, "the dear comrade of my youth, the one who kept in his heart, the same happy remembrances of sunny Malta, the one who also gave one a feeling of reassurance, out there in the big world."

For the first time in many years Carol consulted his mother about the proprieties. He came to Cotroceni to say that he wanted to attend the King of England's funeral. Marie agreed that he ought to go. Carol had not been in England since his attempted coup in 1928, when he had been unceremoniously asked to leave. Marie thought this was "perhaps the only moment" when "the ice could be broken." She asked the King to take the Head of her Household, Colonel Zwiedinek, to represent her, since she thought it best not to go herself; "widowed queens, even if they are loved are difficult personages to place at official occasions and it is good they should remember this themselves, without having to be told." More important, Marie did not want it to look as though she were "leading" her son "by the hand."

Marie wrote Queen Mary to express her condolences and explain her actions. "It is very hard to remain away from you all just now. . . all my instinct was to rush off to London so as to accompany the dear friend of my youth to his last resting place and to be able to tell you personally how I grieve for you. You were such wonderful companions. . . . You will be very lonely now. . . I follow your every feeling with almost painful understanding, may much be spared you which I had to endure. . . I hope you will never forget what a warm, loving friend you have in me. I am far off, can mean nothing real to you, but don't forget me. . . May you have the quiet strength you always have to bear all these sad ceremonies and the cruel loneliness which will follow, and may your children be a comfort to you as some of mine have been to me—"

A few weeks later Marie received word that her sister Ducky was dying. The Grand Duchess Kirill had gone to Germany for the birth of a grandchild and had suffered a stroke there, which paralyzed one side of her body and left her unable to speak. Marie left Bucharest immediately. "I had the consolation that she just realised that I had come," she said, joining the bedside vigil with Ducky's husband and children, Sandra, and Baby Bee.

After twelve days of anguish, with the family praying for her to go quickly but "seeing her die by inches," Ducky died. The three remaining sisters wrapped her body in a long, white robe, and Marie placed white lilacs around her head and shoulders. They took her body to Coburg and buried her beside their parents and brother, Alfred. The day was icy cold with half snow and half rain falling. It was hard for Marie to leave the graveside. Ducky, she said, "always hated being alone."

Marie returned home in time for the Independence Day celebrations of May 10, 1936. "It is a good show, with a lot of bluff in it," she remarked. "Carol thrones on a huge white horse with the attitude of Kaiser Bill [Wilhelm II of Prussia]—he is surrounded by brilliant uniforms & busy syco-phants... he is dancing on a volcano!" From Bucharest she traveled to Balcic to set out a memory garden for Ducky. Her daily horseback rides, her best antidote to depression, had been reduced to every other day. There was little left to take her mind off "the sad mess our leaders have got the country into, and my own impossibility to help or even prevent... mistakes amounting to crimes."

By the summer of 1936, fascism and anti-Semitism were definitely in fashion. Early in the year the anti-Semitic Christian League and the National Christian Party joined one wing of the National Peasant Party to form a solid reactionary bloc whose platform nearly mirrored that of the Iron Guard. In August, under mounting pressure from right-wing groups, the King uncer-emoniously removed Titulescu from office. The Foreign Minister, who represented close relations with France and the Little Entente against Ger-many, had become a liability. The fanatic right-wing elements within Rou-mania found further encouragement outside the country that year as Mussolini completed his conquest of Ethiopia and Hitler occupied the Rhineland.

Six years of political frustration had taken its toll on Marie. Her focus on international affairs had narrowed to exclude those events that did not touch her personally. She was disturbed that the Little Entente had taken a stand against the Habsburgs in Austria, and she did not dare ask the King to allow his sister to come home for her annual visit; "who knows how many days I may have left to be with the child I love," she wrote a friend. In order to see her daughter, Marie invited Ileana and Anton to accompany her to England in July, where they visited the Astors and the royal family. Edward VIII was now seen openly with Wallis Simpson, who was on her way toward divorce. Marie had the satisfaction of noting that May's problems with David's mistress cast her own difficulties with Mme. Lupescu in a new light.

The trip to England was a respite from the many irritations that assailed Marie throughout 1936. New restrictions from Carol's palace curtailed her independence and put her under the thumb of Urdareanu, now Lord High Chamberlain. Marie received an order that required her to send her baggage to Carol's palace for inspection, instead of being allowed to pass freely through Customs as she had for more than forty years. She was prohibited from dedicating the new wing of her favorite hospital. And she was accused of plotting with Princess Helen against the King.

None of these petty provocations hurt Marie as much as the ceremonies celebrating the opening of the Triumphal Arch in Bucharest in early December. The Arch, begun after World War I to welcome King Ferdinand and Queen Marie on their return from Jassy, had only recently been completed. For the dedication ceremony, Carol II wore "his latest invention," a dramatic white cape with a huge blue cross signifying his new Order of Michael the Brave. The procession engendered little enthusiasm from the crowd. "Carol with all his new rules and tremendous police, has certainly made things more tidy," Marie remarked, "but he has also... ruled out every contact with his subjects." The King gave a long speech in which he praised everyone connected with World War I. "As I listened, and it rolled on and on," his mother wrote in her diary, "I kept thinking, now will come a word for me, after all, everyone there connected me with this arch." But Carol never mentioned his mother's name. "And as he had not allowed anyone else to speak, no one said a word in remembrance of me... I felt almost a fool for being there," wrote Marie, who had been asked to stand next to her son throughout the entire ceremony.

On December 11, 1936, Edward VIII abdicated the throne of England. "I hardly dare wish you a happy Xmas," Marie wrote Queen Mary a week later, "knowing all you have gone through. Perhaps no one can more completely understand your pain and grief than I, who have so suffered through my sons. It was even because of this that I have not written sooner.... But my thoughts were with you in intense sympathy and with an understanding only possible to me who has been hit in the same way."

For the Duke and soon-to-be Duchess of Windsor, Marie had less sympathy. "Personally I am too royal not to look upon David as a deserter..." Marie wrote a friend. "Also I can work up no feelings for Mrs. Simpson.... She has too much to do with cocktails and night clubs.... Do you think David will never hanker back to all he kicked aside? Do you think Mrs. Simpson in great spoonfuls will replace all he gave up? He is forty-two. Is it luck at that age to have no duties, no work, no obligations, no outlook—only night clubs, bars, rowdy society, sport.... Is this a career, an end for the golden-headed prince? I could weep over him and my feelings towards Mrs. Simpson are none too charitable. She, like Lupescu, will remain in history—but will their memory be blessed?"

Chapter 31

> It has been said of her [Queen Marie]
> that she formed a whole generation—
> every man was in love with her, every
> artist inspired by her, every woman
> wished to look like her.
>
> —*LESLEY BLANCH*

*D*uring the winter of 1936–1937, King Carol invoked the final humiliation—a restriction that snapped Marie's last powers of restraint. Under her son's new orders, the Queen was prohibited from direct communication with the Roumanian government and ordered to make all future requests through the King's household. In undercutting Marie's sense of herself as an independent, if silenced, factor in the country, Carol slashed at his mother's royal pride. Now her every need had to be funneled through the upstart Urdareanu, and Carol's Lord High Chamberlain was only too ready to frustrate Marie's wishes.

In an undated letter written sometime during that winter and scrawled over twenty pages, Marie fought back at her son: "Every mortal bourgeois has the right to address himself to the authorities, and suddenly, after forty-three years I am put under tutelage... nothing could make me accept this."

At first she tried to appeal calmly to Carol's reason: "I want this to be a quiet talk between two friends, no accusations... I want today to quietly sum up the accumulation of all those things which finally brought about my cry of protest."

Her complaints constituted a sad list.

Number One: The King had taken away the income that his father had left for her support. She had been forced to rearrange her household under stringent economic restrictions. "Although I lived thirty-five years with your father, not a penny of his fortune came to me . . . I raised no protest, but I never forgot that my son could be so unloving."

Number Two: "You hated me [for the way I behaved towards Sitta], treated me as an enemy whilst on the contrary, knowing the world's opinion, it was the act of a friend."

Number Three: "You wished all honours, all rights for yourself exclusively. An immense mistake. A King's family is the wood which protects the central tree. . . . Roumanians consider your family part of yourself—we all together are the Dynasty, and in honouring me they are still honouring you. Have you not enough honours? Can it make you shine less because . . . some still remember and love your mother?"

Number Four: Without her knowledge, Marie later discovered, she had been demoted from Queen to Queen Mother. "I was Queen of this country and have my definite position recognised by parliament, it is my right also to the title of Regina Marie which Papa wished me to have."

"In general," she charged, "I swallowed every insult and never complained, considering it not dignified . . . with the hope that one day you would become kinder and more thoughtful of my feelings. . . .

"Conclusion: I may be forced to accept your rules and orders, but I do so under protest and this protest I shall not silence. I consider it as an attack against my personal dignity. . . . Therefore, what I ask, even demand . . . as my right: give my house the position of independence it had before . . . you can do it, I have deserved this. . . . Give me your hand my son and let us live in good peace and content, it CAN be if you leave my house alone, respecting my rights and treating me with all the respect you owe to the one who was a builder a long time before you! I am a peaceful being, but I am not a slave and shall never consent [to] being one!"

There is no evidence that the King ever answered the letter.

In early March of 1937, at the age of sixty-one, Marie's fabulous health broke down. She lay in bed for more than a month with internal hemorrhaging. Unable to pinpoint the cause of the bleeding, the court physician, Dr. Mamulea, and his associates suggested the possibility of cirrhosis of the liver, although how this could be with a woman who had scarcely ever touched alcohol, they did not know. Meanwhile, Marie was kept immobile on a starvation diet of cold liquids.

While his mother lay ill, Carol sent his brother Nicolas into permanent exile, blaming his decree on Nicky's morganatic marriage. It was a hard blow for Marie, already weakened from illness. "Both my sons, at this late hour, after having so cruelly abandoned me, are now most assiduous, and I am torn to pieces between them," she wrote in her diary. Frightened by his mother's illness, Carol had grown very solicitous of her and telephoned every day, while Nicky visited frequently to complain about his brother. Toward the end of April, Nicolas came with his wife to say goodbye.

Before he left, Prince Nicolas wrote a former Prime Minister and historian, Nicolas Jorga, that he "never had and never will" renounce his Roumanian titles or his rights as a Roumanian citizen. The result of this public flouting of the King's decree was a confrontation between the two brothers. A rumor started that a gun fight had taken place in the presence of their mother, giving rise to whispers that Marie's sickness came from a stomach wound incurred when she threw herself between her sons. The story was, of course, a total fabrication, although it has persisted to this day.

It was only one of many rumors that materialized to fill the vacuum left by the King's silence about his mother's poor health. "If Carol had wanted to give no importance to my illness, by forbidding a bulletin, he produced the contrary result," said Marie, who reported with satisfaction that the "whole country" had gone "mad with anxiety" over her poor health.

Both Mignon and Baby Bee hurried to Bucharest. To quiet rumors in the capital, the Queen of Yugoslavia drove around the city, smiling and attending various functions at which her mother was to have presided. Mignon and Baby Bee convinced Carol that he must send for Ileana, and the Austrian Archduchess was allowed to spend a week with her mother as well.

Marie's condition continued throughout the month of May with little improvement. Forced to remain immobile, Marie said she preferred to be laid up at Sinaia than in a hospital, and on June 1 Mignon arrived to drive her there. Mignon asked her brother's permission to call in a specialist, Dr. Hans Eppinger, from Vienna. Ileana disagreed with her sister's choice; her doctor had warned her that although Eppinger was an excellent physician, he cared little for his patients.* Eppinger said he could not diagnose Marie properly at home and wanted to take her to a clinic, but the King refused.

Throughout his mother's illness, Carol exhibited the same strange ambivalence toward her that he had shown when she was well. He was anxious about her, but oddly reluctant to bring in the best medical help from abroad or send her to a first-rate hospital outside the country. There are several possible explanations for this. By 1937–1938, the King was extremely unpopular, and his jealousy of his mother was common knowledge. Carol may have retained the services of the Roumanian doctors simply to protect himself against possible accusations of malfeasance. He may also have made a conscious decision to bow to national pride. Or, as two of his sisters later suggested, he was not particularly interested in prolonging his mother's life.

---

*This assessment of Eppinger proved tragically correct. Within a few years the specialist who saw Marie was conducting medical experiments on Jews for the Nazis.

Whatever the King's motives, Mignon finally prevailed upon him to ask the Prime Minister to call in other specialists under the auspices of the Roumanian government. Three more doctors—a Frenchman, a Swiss, and an Italian—were brought to Sinaia. They all agreed that the liver trouble had left Marie anemic and that she must be built up with food and injections. Mignon insisted that a doctor be sent from Vienna to supervise her mother's care, as the court doctor resented outside specialists and could not be relied on to follow their prescribed treatments.

For a while Marie seemed to be on her way to recovery, and by the end of June she was out of bed. At the end of July Eppinger returned and announced that her liver was "*cured*" and that she might "more or less live a normal life." In August she moved to Bran. Although she could no longer run up and down the steep steps of her fairy-tale castle, she enjoyed the change and spent her days reading biographies of historical figures or being read to by her A.D.C., Colonel Zwiedinek.

At the end of September, Marie left for her home in Balcic on the Black Sea. On the way, the court doctor took blood tests; the results, which were very bad, indicated the need for immediate treatment. Instead of telephoning or wiring Dr. Eppinger in Vienna, Dr. Mamulea sent the findings by mail; since Eppinger was not in Vienna when the letter arrived, the information was further delayed in reaching him. Within a short time of her arrival at Tenya-Yuvah, Marie started to hemorrhage again. Added to the bleeding were fainting spells and blurred vision. Her visit to her beloved gardens was cut short as she was moved down to Bucharest for better medical care.

Marie's arrival coincided with festivities at Sinaia celebrating Michael's coming of age, but she was not well enough to attend. On October 29, 1937, her sixty-second birthday, Marie was forced to admit that she was "more or less an invalid" and received her guests sitting down. Of all her gifts, the one that most delighted her was the return of one of her own Fabergé walking-stick handles, made of blue enamel encrusted with diamonds. Originally a gift from her cousin Boris, it had been stolen by the Bolsheviks during the First World War and was found in London by Carol. Marie was ecstatic. It had been one of her favorite possessions, she said, "the remembrance of which often haunted me."

Four days later, on the anniversary of Mircea's death, Marie felt well enough to kneel briefly in the morning at his crypt in Cotroceni Chapel and even managed to walk to her stables. The Crown Prince of Sweden, who lunched at the palace that day, was "dazzled" by the Dowager Queen, who was feeling "in high spirits." That night she suffered another relapse.

The intestinal hemorrhaging started again. Marie was in serious danger. This time it was the King who insisted that the four specialists be brought back from Paris, Vienna, Zurich and Italy. They recommended that Marie be sent to a convalescent home in Merano, Italy, as soon as she was able to make the trip. Ileana, who had made plans to take her mother to Vienna for treatment, was unhappy with the decision. While the young Archduchess wrangled with her brother, Marie suffered a major gastric hemorrhage, so severe that the foreign physicians, on their way home, had to be called back a second time. There was nothing they could suggest beyond complete rest, severe diet, and mental relaxation. Marie could not be moved.

She remained in bed the next two months. Although she fought against being kept quiet and indoors, Marie enjoyed her bedroom at Cotroceni, which she had redecorated only a few years before. She thought of it as a "sober" room, "churchy" and "mellow." To others it looked like a golden lair with gold church gates at the entrance and massive gold-leaf furniture, fur rugs, icons, and old silver everywhere. Although her large bed had been replaced by two smaller ones to accommodate a nurse, Marie lay against lace pillows and was surrounded by dozens of Venetian glass vases filled with seasonal flowers. She was now too weak to continue her writing, but amused herself with hundreds of letters that poured in from all over the world offering consolation and medical advice.

Her children were kind. Even Elisabetha managed to visit her mother nearly every day, and Carol came as often as his duties would permit. Marie was most grateful for his attention, although she still deplored his despotism. Her great consolation was the fact that he, unlike the Duke of Windsor, was still a bona fide King with a country and a job to do.

Christmas was celebrated early on the twenty-fourth so that Carol could go to Sinaia for the official festivities. Marie was wheeled in to the tree. She could "hardly believe her eyes" when she opened her gift from Ileana and Anton—an ermine cape that she had admired at Revillon on her last trip to Paris. "I *do* think they made a too great effort for their modest means," she said, "but it was awful sweet and generous of them & I was deeply touched."

On December 29, 1937, she suffered another relapse, and world headlines announced her imminent demise. This time the bleeding continued almost uninterruptedly for six days. Marie had begun to worry about her treatment. Eppinger was no longer in evidence, and the court physician, Dr. Mamulea, whom she distrusted, had been put completely in charge of her. "I need to get into other hands..." she wrote in her diary. "I *do* feel that perhaps Mamulea, although so dead sure of himself, is not quite *à la hauteur* [up to] his task." She was furious when told that two more specialists were on their way. "I am dead sick of doctors and have no wish to accumulate more in my life, who will say yea, yea to the Court doctor who will get them to sign undigested documents which will allow him to go on keeping me in bed indefinitely."

In the middle of February, Dr. Mamulea pronounced Marie well enough to travel to the San Martino Sanatorium in Merano, Italy. Elisabetha accompanied her mother to the four-story eaved and turreted building nestled in the mountains of the Italian Tyrol, where Marie's brother, Alfred, had died in 1899. Ensconced in a small room with pristine bed and two understuffed chairs, Marie enjoyed her views of snow-capped mountains and the huge bouquets of flowers sent by Mussolini and the Italian royal family. Most of all she relished the peace of being away from family and political conflicts. Marie hated being a source of contention among her children, who continued to argue about her treatment in the absence of a clear diagnosis of her ailment. At the same time, she did not want to stay away from Roumania for too long a period of time: "... my very existence is for many a reassurance," she wrote an American correspondent; "simply to know that Cotroceni is not empty, that their faithful Regina Maria is breathing behind its walls helps them, gives them courage."

While the Dowager Queen was fighting for her life, her son's inept political juggling had brought his countrymen to yet another point of crisis. The King had grown increasingly frightened of the Iron Guard and its denunciations of himself, his Jewish mistress, and their friends. Before the elections of November 1937, which were supposed to confirm the King's choice of a Liberal government, Carol tried to make a deal with Codreanu, the leader of the Iron Guard. He failed. Taking advantage of extra funds that the King's supporters had poured into the Guard in hopes of buying peace, Codreanu redoubled his efforts against Carol and the Liberal Party. Even former Prime Minister Maniu, head of the National Peasant Party, signed a pact with Codreanu and donated his good name to the surging forces of fanaticism, fascism, and anti-Semitism.

At election time, with gangs of thugs from all the parties offsetting one another at the polls, the Liberals earned the dubious distinction of being the first party in power in Roumanian history ever to lose an election. Although they required only 40 percent of the vote to be confirmed, the Liberals fell short; Maniu's National Peasants polled 22 percent, and Codreanu's Iron Guard, 16 percent.

The King panicked. Terrified of the Guard, infuriated with Maniu, he dissolved Parliament before it had a chance to convene and appointed Octavian Goga, leader of the fanatical National Christian Party (which received only 9 percent of the vote), to form a government. With Goga as his own in-house fascist-racist, Carol thought he could outdo the Iron Guard.

In his three months in office, Goga brought Roumanian anti-Semitism to a new high. Jews were beaten up, and their businesses were closed. When the French and English Ministers protested the effect on the Roumanian economy, Goga was summarily dismissed by the King. Parliamentary rule, said Carol II, was no longer viable in Roumania. He would scrap the Roumanian Constitution and dissolve all existing political parties.

In February of 1938, as his mother was leaving for Italy, Carol II declared himself Royal Dictator. To steal Codreanu's religious thunder he named Miron Christea, the lecherous old Primate of the Orthodox Church, his Prime Minister. The Roumanian people and the world outside, appalled by Goga, seemed almost relieved that the King had taken over.

When Carol presented his solution to his mother as a "coalition government," she was pleased. But when it became apparent that the King had changed the ground rules and given himself "almost dictatorial rights," she drew back. "Many things were rotten in our country, but have Carol, & those he works with clean enough hands to become real reformers; that is where the horrible doubt remains in my mind. . . . I wish I could have more confidence in him. I so terribly mistrust those he intimately works with & now that he has ruled out all opposition will he not more and more abuse. . . the rights he has taken to himself?" she wrote from her bed in Merano.

Since he was no longer permitted to enter Roumania, Nicolas came to see his mother while she was in Italy. He and Jeanne had moved to Venice. Nicolas told Marie that the King had cut off his allowance, which made it difficult for him to buy Jeanne a home. "I have full sympathy at his desire to buy a house and settle down," Marie wrote in her diary, "but there is no reason why in the same year you must buy pearl solitaires and pictures by Velasquez and silver which. . . belonged to Napoleon."

Marie had met her daughter-in-law once before in Roumania, when Nicolas was ill. Although she never approved of her, particularly because Jeanne tried to turn Nicolas against his family, she received her again in Merano. In later years, Nicolas' wife talked about "what a wonderful woman" Marie had been. "She forgave me in the end," Jeanne said, "and I really did behave very badly to her."

Another visitor was Princess Helen, who obtained King Carol's permission to see his mother. Marie had not met her ex-daughter-in-law for almost seven years. "We both had tears in our eyes," said Marie, who thought that Sitta was "looking awfully pretty, more admirably got up than ever."

A third visitor was Waldorf Astor. He made the long trip to Italy at the behest of Ileana, who thought a visit from him would cheer her mother. Nancy agreed and urged him to go alone. He was with Marie for just over forty-eight hours. She was deeply moved by his visit and wrote sometime later to Nancy to express her gratitude. It may have been her last letter. "I cannot say how touched I was that Waldorf flew down to see me," she wrote, "he really is an angel and both of you are beyond words precious friends. He will tell you all about me, not an overcheerful report, but I am still patient. . . . Bless you all and keep you."

In the middle of March, Prince and Princess Friedrich (Friedel) of Hohenzollern-Sigmaringen arrived in Merano. As Ferdinand's nephew and Head of the House of Hohenzollern-Sigmaringen, Friedel was concerned about Ileana and Anton, who were visiting Marie at the time. Their home had been taken over by the Nazis, but if they left Austria, they had nowhere to go. Marie, whose attitude toward Hitler was changed by Ileana's plight, was pleased by Friedel's concern for his cousin. "Friedel. . . unlike Carol has a very keen family feeling & a real and heartfelt desire to help all those who are in difficulties. . . whilst Carol. . . finds a perverse pleasure in dominating & crushing those dependent on him, beginning. . . [with]. . . his mother."

Although Marie did not know it, her nephew was trying to help her as well. He and his wife had visited Marie with Professor Warnerkrose, a gynecologist from Dresden, who told them after only a few minutes' conversation with her that Marie was dying. They must, he said, "do something immediately" to save her. Warnerkrose recommended that the Hohenzollerns send for his colleague, Professor Stoermer, from the Weisser Hirsch Clinic in Dresden. Stoermer, who arrived on May 1, 1938, was "horrified" by Marie's condition. "The moment she can be moved," he said, "she must be brought to Dresden where I can look after her properly."

Marie's trip to Dresden was postponed by another outbreak of bleeding, and it was the middle of May, three months after her arrival in Merano, before she could be moved by stretcher to Germany. Meanwhile, Stoermer treated her as best he could with diet and injections, but without the facilities of a hospital. Marie was relieved: "... at last we have found a doctor who takes me energetically in hand and has every intention to... discover the cause of my bleeding," she wrote in her diary, adding that Professor Stoermer's presence was "a great comfort to Zwiedy," who had been left alone to care for her.

Although Zwiedinek was devoted to Marie, it is clear that he would never have been allowed to stay with her if he had been loyal *only* to her. Whatever accommodation the Head of Marie's House made with the King, he weathered eight years of changes in her household and in 1936 was promoted by Carol from colonel to general. Although Zwiedinek later gained a reputation for cowardice under duress, this does not diminish the comfort he was to Marie during the last, difficult years of her life. He organized her houses, her finances, and her trips, smoothed her way, and when she was ill, he read to her and tended her like a child.

The trip to the Weisser Hirsch Clinic was a difficult one, but once there, Marie was made extremely comfortable. She occupied a bright bedroom with bay windows and window seats in one of twelve private villas. At the Weisser Hirsch it was possible for the first time since the onset of the illness to make extensive X rays, which led to a proper diagnosis. According to several German specialists, Marie was suffering from esophageal varices (dilated blood vessels that encroached on the esophagus) resulting from the liver disease. The cirrhosis of the liver was an extremely rare type, not caused by alcohol. Professor Stoermer said he would do "everything within his power, but there was nothing he could do to save her." His associate, Warnerkrose, complained about Marie's treatment up to her arrival in Dresden: "... she's been given the wrong treatment from the beginning. I can only say that the doctor who did that had to have done it purposely. He can't have been that stupid."

As Marie was about to leave for Dresden, she received orders from Bucharest saying that the King could not "for the sake of national feeling" permit her to proceed for treatment without the "sanction or at least presence of two Roumanian doctors." Furious, Marie replied that she was acting on her "own responsibility" for the first time. She "ought to have been in a Sanatorium or rather a real clinic ages ago," she told Carol, but she had been left "alone to get well as best" she could at Merano, where she had made no progress toward recovery. Now she wanted to go somewhere where she could be helped. In spite of this outburst, the King delayed his mother's trip until the arrival of the Roumanian doctors.

Although she was losing strength by the hour, Marie did not give up hope. "I resign myself as uncomplainingly as possible, decided to obey the most disagreeable orders, patient in the hope of recovery. I feel that something is being done for me," she wrote in her diary shortly after her arrival in Dresden. By the middle of June, she had noticed some improvement: "I am no more breathless and can with help go from one room to another, though of course my legs are leaden and shaky. My eyes also seem to see more clearly, & I am less depressed." Even when the doctors decided to send her home, Marie did not admit the possibility that the end was near. "They all want to patch me up as well as possible to transport me back to Sinaia, as here the air is becoming oppressive and mountain air would be beneficent."

Only to Barbo Stirbey did Marie try to say goodbye. She had written him when she first fell ill, giving the letter to one of the Viennese doctors to post outside the country for her, and she had received an answer, written the previous July from Switzerland. "My thoughts are always near you . . ." Prince Stirbey said. "I am inconsolable at being so far, incapable of being any help whatsoever to you, living in the memory of the past with no hope for the future. . . . Remember my longing, my nostalgia, the prayers which I constantly offer up for your health and never doubt the boundlessness of my devotion. Ilymmily [I love you my Marie, I love you?]."

Before she left Dresden, Marie wrote Stirbey a last letter. Even now she knew she must leave "so much unsaid, which would so much lighten my heart to say: all my longing, my sadness, all the dear memories which flood back into my heart. . . . The woods with the little yellow crocuses, the smell of the oaks when we rode through those same woods in early summer—and oh! so many, many things which are gone. . . . God bless you all and keep you safe. . . ."

Marie had written her will in 1933. She divided her homes among her children and designated the distribution of her jewels among her daughters, reserving the Duchess of Coburg's fabulous diamond-and-sapphire tiara for Ileana. There was little else to be done. Her will had provided for the two people she loved best and who most needed money—her youngest daughter and her sister Ducky, whom she had entirely supported during the last years of her life. Now that Ducky was gone, she hoped her demise would ease the financial strain on the young Archduchess.

Marie left the sanatorium in Dresden on July 15, signing the register with a flourish. But a picture taken of her in the carriage with Dr. Stoermer and

General Zwiedinek shows the face and body of a ravaged woman. Her eyes had grown piercingly sad, her graceful frame unwieldy.

Although the doctors advised transporting Marie by plane, Carol objected to the cost. The trip through the mountains by train was so rough that she began almost immediately to hemorrhage again. Dr. Stoermer, who was traveling with her, was forced to administer oxygen constantly, and by the second day, he ordered the train stopped in the little town of Cernautzi in Bukovina. The summer sun blazed down mercilessly on the steel coach. As soon as the local people heard she was there, they cut down huge trees which they carried down to the tracks, constructing a makeshift pergola to protect the Queen from the unrelenting heat. All day long the peasants brought buckets of water to wash down the hot steel. But the temperature inside did not drop, and after twelve hours Marie begged for the train to proceed.

They dared not refuse her. The train started up again, very slowly. As it wound through the mountains and foothills across the country, stationmasters doffed their hats and little clumps of people waited at railway crossings to catch a glimpse of the blue-and-silver coach with drawn curtains. "Regina is dying," they chanted. When the train finally arrived at the little station at Sinaia at 8:45 in the evening, only the Dowager Queen's family and special members of her household were permitted on the platform.

Since Marie refused to be carried from the train on a stretcher, the officers of her regiment fashioned a portable chair in which they could lift her—painstakingly, one step at a time—out of the station. For her last public appearance Marie chose a loose robe of pearl gray, a gown that floated around her misshapen body rather than embracing it. She tried gallantly to smile at those who came forward to kiss her hand.

She lingered for nearly a day in the nursery at the Pelisor, attended by Carol and Elisabetha—the children she loved least—the Patriarch Miron Christea, her grandson Michael, and four doctors. When she asked to say goodbye to Zwiedy, the King refused.

Marie lay watching the door of the old nursery, waiting for Ileana to appear, but Carol had not telephoned his sister in time. Rather than call the Archduchess when his mother arrived at Sinaia, the King waited until the next day to notify her. "I think Elisabetha finally put her foot down," Princess Ileana said many years later. *

The dying Queen asked for the Lord's Prayer to be recited in English and whispered to Carol to be "a just and strong monarch" before lapsing into a

*The Queen's youngest daughter was not notified until the morning after her mother's arrival in Sinaia. She and her husband drove all night from their home in Austria. "We reached the Roumanian frontier in the early morning, and I asked what the news was. They said they had only been told that I would be coming and should pass through quickly. Afterward, when we passed the border after the funeral, they said, 'We knew, but we hadn't the heart to tell you.'" Princess Ileana realized her mother was dead when she saw the flags flying at half-mast.

coma. She died eight minutes later, at 5:38 P.M. on July 18, 1938. The death was announced to the Roumanian people within the hour. "A moving silence," one reporter said, "reigned in the streets."

Marie's private secretary assured friends that the end had been peaceful and without a struggle. "She slipped into eternity without any pain. No agony, no consciousness of death. Just a slow soaring into the world beyond."

Indeed, Marie's face in death again reasserted its claim on its old beauty. Dressed in a simple white robe, the Queen of Roumania seemed to have sloughed off the recent years of pain and disappointment, and her features radiated the loveliness of a trusting young woman. With an icon of the Virgin and Child in her hands, her body was borne in an open coffin by six officers of her regiment from the Pelisor to Castle Peles.

On July 20 Marie's body was taken to Bucharest, where she lay in state in the white drawing room at Cotroceni. The coffin was surrounded by flowers and glowing tapers and was guarded by four officers of the Fourth Hussars. Thousands of people filed by the bier during the three-day lying in state. At the end of the third day the palace was opened to factory workers who came to pay their respects to their beloved Mama Regina, filing through the white room in a continuous gray stream from dusk to dawn the next morning.

Before her death, Marie had requested that no one wear black for her funeral, but rather "my favourite colour—mauve. All flowers placed on the coffin," she added, "should be red." In accordance with these wishes, the Roumanians decorated the streets of Bucharest in mauve. Lavender flags and bunting floated from windows over the route of the cortege, where 250,000 people gathered to pay their last respects to Mama Regina.

If Carol did little for his mother during her life, he organized a magnificent display of pomp and protocol for her funeral, which he postponed for three days to allow members of other royal houses to reach Bucharest. The night before, Marie's coffin was closed, sealed, and moved from Cotroceni to the new throne room of the King's palace. Draped in mauve and bearing the Queen's standard and crown, it was attended by her sons and two of her nephews.

At 8:30 in the morning there was a private service for the family, foreign royalty, and members of the diplomatic service. This was followed by a march down the marble stairs Marie had climbed for the first time almost forty-six years before. Her exit was accompanied by music from Wagner's *Götterdämmerung*, played by the Bucharest Symphony Orchestra. The body, borne out by six officers of the Fourth Hussars beneath a mauve silk canopy, was placed on the traditional gun carriage, draped in mauve and drawn by the traditional six black horses. The honor guard presented arms, the standards were lowered, there was a fanfare of trumpets, the army band played the national anthem, and amid the tolling of bells of all the churches in

Bucharest and the roar of low-flying planes, the cortege moved slowly forward.

The procession was led by the members of Marie's regiment, the Fourth Hussars, carrying lances tied with mauve crepe, and one hundred crippled veterans, accompanied by white-robed sisters of the Red Cross. Following them came the Orthodox clergy in their spectacular Byzantine robes and one hundred priests with high black headdresses bearing lighted tapers and swinging censers of incense. King Carol added the Knights of the Order of Michael the Brave to the cortege; these men wore their white cloaks flung dramatically over one shoulder. The catafalque itself was preceded by the Minister of the King's Court, carrying a lavender velvet cushion on which rested the medieval crown that Marie had designed for her own Coronation. The gun carriage was accompanied by four ex-Prime Ministers holding mauve ribbons. Observers were struck by how small Marie's coffin appeared. Behind the bier pranced one of her favorite horses with its eloquently empty saddle.

King Carol II, dressed in his dramatic white cloak and a plumed helmet, marched alone behind his mother's casket. His shoulders, according to the press, were "bowed," his face, "pale and heavily lined," his eyes, "red-rimmed." The King was followed by Prince Friedrich of Hohenzollern-Sigmaringen, Crown Prince Michael, the Duke of Kent, and a man listed in the official program only as "Queen Marie's second son." Prince Nicolas was permitted by his brother to return for their mother's funeral, although he was required to leave his wife at home. At the Arch of Triumph, the symbol of Roumania's victory in World War I, there was a slight pause while the King gave a sign for the gun carriage to pass under the Arch. He himself walked deliberately around it.

When the cortege reached the station, Marie's body was placed on an open car for the journey to Curtea de Arges. It was normally a two-hour journey from Bucharest across the Wallachian plains to the ancient village in the foothills, but the train had to stop so many times that it took six hours to cover the distance. Thousands of peasants, lighted candles in hand, accompanied by their village priests, knelt by the side of the tracks to pay their last respects. It was said that so many flowers were thrown over the bier in its open carriage that the soldiers of the honor guard, standing at attention, were in danger of being suffocated.

It was 4 P.M. before the funeral train finally reached Curtea de Arges. Bells tolled; seventy-five guns gave their salute; the guard of honor presented arms; and the national anthem was played. As the procession left for the church both King Carol and Prince Nicolas were said by reporters to be crying. The five-mile route was lined with delegations of peasants from all over the country in their embroidered costumes; the streets themselves had been hung with carpets and bunting in crimson, purple, and yellow; except for the tears on the faces of the peasants, an English visitor said he would have thought the town was dressed for a triumphal celebration.

A last, short service for Marie of Roumania took place outside the church in the fading light of dusk; the coffin was then moved into the brightly painted Byzantine interior, shimmering in the candlelight, and was placed in the vault next to her husband. According to Marie's instructions, her heart had been taken from her body, put in a small gold casket embellished with emblems of the provinces of Greater Roumania, and sent to the little Orthodox chapel in the gardens of her home in Balcic overlooking the sea. * Unlike the crypts of Carol I, Elisabeth I, and Ferdinand I, whose stones were incised with their lineage and accomplishments, the stone that was laid over Marie's coffin was absolutely plain, a pristine slab of white marble, unidentified and unadorned except for a large cross. It is unthinkable that in death Marie did not wish to be allied with those who had also devoted their lives to the dynasty and the country, and it must be assumed that this was one of several ways in which Carol II tried to deny his mother's role in the history of Roumania.

Before Marie's death she wrote a letter to her countrymen. It was a long document, touchingly overstated, exactly the sort of letter one might have expected her to leave. "When you read these lines, my people, I shall have crossed the threshold of the eternal silence. . . . And yet because of the great love which I have pledged to you I wish to speak to you again. . . . I have become yours for joy and sorrow. When I look back, it is difficult to say which was greater, the joy or the sorrow. I believe that joy was the greater," she said, "but too long was the sorrow."

*When the Bulgarians took over the Dobruja in 1940, General Zwiedinek moved the casket containing Marie's heart to a wooden church at Castle Bran in Transylvania. In recent years the Roumanian government, concerned about the value of the jeweled casket, has removed it to a safe place (unknown) in Bucharest.

Epilogue

The year of Queen Marie's death, 1938, was pivotal in the history of Eastern Europe. In the spring Hitler invaded and annexed Austria. In the fall England and France acquiesced while the Führer expropriated one-third of the citizens and territory of Czechoslovakia, establishing Germany as the dominant power on the Continent and destroying the Little Entente. Roumania soon fell to the Fascists and, when World War II was over, to the Communists.

A leader in transit from the Victorian Age to the Communist Expansion, Marie understood that one price of royal survival in an age of democracy is personal contact. She loved being a queen. She gave herself to the Roumanians with exuberance and played her role with drama and humor. At times she overplayed it. But it was style, not substance, which separated her from her fellow monarchs.

Born into a world in which her grandmother reigned over the British Empire and her grandfather ruled Imperial Russia, Marie was sustained throughout her last years by her fervent belief in the value of kings. One of the last of the royal innocents offered up on the altar of dynasticism, she spent her life justifying the sacrifice, determined to keep monarchy alive in her part of the world. At her death the London *Times* spoke glowingly of her "great personal beauty" and tallied a list of virtues which recalled the English Princess as much as the Balkan Queen—her superb horsemanship, her grace, her literary gifts, her bravery during wartime, and her cheerfulness under stress. Across the Atlantic *The New York Times*, once a source of mindless copy on Marie's wardrobe and hairdos, treated the Queen of Roumania with great respect. "No public figure in Roumania was more patriotic than this Queen of alien blood," said the *Times*. "Like King Albert of the Belgians, she earned for herself a regard from her people that amounted to idolatry."

But the strongest testament to Queen Marie's efficacy as a monarch was Roumania's long-standing resistance to Communism. The Russians themselves acknowledged Marie's power in a curious way. A week after her death *Time* magazine reported that a mass was held in honor of the Queen of Roumania in an Orthodox church in Moscow—the only tribute of its kind paid since the Russian Revolution to any member of any royal house in the world.

Marie's accomplishments were all the more poignant for the dingy failures of her son. A few months after his mother's death, Carol II made a highly publicized trip to Western Europe in an effort to keep Roumania out of World War II. In England he called on family connections to fortify Roumania's relations with the Allies; in Germany he promised economic cooperation to appease Hitler. But the Nazi-Soviet Pact of August 1939 destroyed him. Forced by Hitler to give Bessarabia and northern Bukovina to Russia, northern Transylvania back to Hungary, and the southern Dobruja to Bulgaria, the King lost face and was hounded off the throne in September of 1940.

Carol II fled the country with Mme. Lupescu. They took Ernesto Urdareanu and nine railway cars crammed with valuable possessions. Carol appealed to Hitler for refuge, but the Führer refused to take Mme. Lupescu because she was Jewish. They wandered through Europe, eventually crossing the Atlantic to Mexico. After World War II they went south to Brazil, where the deposed King finally married his mistress. Seemingly on her deathbed at the time of the ceremony, Carol's new wife made an immediate recovery. He bestowed on her the title of Her Royal Highness Princess Elena of Roumania before they moved on to Portugal, a haven for ex-royalty.

In the spring of 1953 Carol received a wire from Mircea, his son by Zizi Lambrino. Zizi's income from Carol's family had stopped five years earlier when the Communists took over Roumania. The wire read, "Mother died, have no money for funeral." Carol sent no response. A few weeks later he himself died and was buried with the Kings of Portugal (the ancestors of his paternal grandmother) at the Monastery São Vicente. His wife, in possession of the treasures of the Roumanian royal family as well as vast sums of money taken out of the country, survived him by nearly twenty-five years.

Carol's son by Helen became King Michael I for the second time on September 7, 1940, a few weeks before his nineteenth birthday. Roumania was being ruled by General Ion Antonescu, who assumed dictatorial powers after Carol's abdication. Antonescu took Roumania into the war on the side of Nazi Germany in June of 1941. In a coup in August of 1944, Michael had Antonescu arrested and declared Roumania on the side of the Allies. In doing this the young King hoped to preserve his country from Russian occupation and help the Allies. Although his action saved many Allied lives, it was impossible to prevent the Soviet occupation of Roumania. Russia disarmed over 100,000 Roumanian soldiers and confiscated much of the Roumanian fleet and merchant marine, railway stock, automobiles, and oil-field supplies. Within less than a year, Andrei Vishinsky arrived in Bucharest, where he staged a Communist coup (February–March 1945). From then on King Michael, the last monarch left in the Eastern bloc, was virtually a prisoner of the Communists.

In November of 1947 the twenty-six-year-old King traveled to London for the marriage of Princess (now Queen) Elizabeth. His government, which expected him to take the opportunity to escape to the West, was shocked when he returned voluntarily. Michael was forced to abdicate on December 30, 1947. A few days later he and the remaining members of the royal family were sent into exile. King Michael married Anne, Princess of Bourbon-Parma, in the summer of 1948 and moved to Switzerland; he went to work as a test pilot and later as a technical consultant. When his father died in 1953, Michael did not attend the funeral.

Michael's mother, Queen Helen, who came back to Roumania after Carol's abdication, left with Michael in 1948. She moved back to Florence, where she lived until shortly before her death in 1982. Elisabetha, who remained in Roumania during the reigns of Carol II and Michael, went into exile at the same time. Although she is reported to have escaped Roumania with a fabulous collection of jewels, by the time she died in Cannes in 1956 she was penniless. Queen Marie's second daughter, Mignon, the widowed Queen of Yugoslavia, was in England when her son, King Peter, was forced out by the Germans. She died in 1961 and is buried in the Windsor family mausoleum of Frogmore in Windsor Park. Nicolas, who remained an exile after his brother's abdication, died in Madrid in 1977. He was the only member of the immediate family to attend Carol II's funeral. "I came because I felt it was my duty," he said. "Although I hated Carol more than I ever hated anybody in my life, he was my brother and my King." Ileana, who returned to Roumania after Carol's flight and ran a hospital there during World War II, left in 1948 with the rest of the family. She settled eventually in the United States with her six children. Later, she became a nun, founding a monastery in Pennsylvania, where she still lives.

Another person who went back to Roumania after Carol's abdication was Barbo Stirbey. During World War II he was one of the leaders of an underground movement supporting the Allies. In February of 1944 he traveled to Cairo on behalf of the Liberal and National Peasant parties to discuss the possibility of Roumania's surrendering to Great Britain and the United States. King Michael sent him to Moscow to sign the armistice with the Allies in September of 1944. The following February, the King nominated Stirbey as Prime Minister, but the Communists refused to accept him, substituting Petru Groza, a non-Communist who was acceptable to the Soviet Union and whose advancement marked the end of parliamentary democracy in Roumania. A year later Stirbey died at Buftea at the age of seventy-three.

Until World War II there had always been a distinct lack of enthusiasm on the part of the Roumanian people for the Soviet way of life, and at the end of the war there were only one thousand members of the Communist Party in the entire country. King Michael's armistice with the Allies brought a resurgence of support for the traditional political parties, the Liberals and the National Peasants, whose power had been usurped by Carol II and General Antonescu. But Churchill's decision in October of 1944 to give Stalin "ninety per cent predominance in Roumania" brought the Roumanians completely under the control of the Soviet Union and its occupying army of one million soldiers. In spite of King Michael's agitation for free elections and charges by England and the United States that the Communist government was not representative of the will of the people, the election of November 1946, conducted by the Communists, established them permanently in power. In August of 1947, the Liberal Party and the National Peasant Party were formally dissolved. Along with the right to freely choose their leaders, the people lost the opportunity to know their history.

Few Roumanians born since 1948 have heard of Queen Marie. Over the last thirty-five years, the good deeds of the Hohenzollern dynasty have been expunged, their failures have been exaggerated, and nearly a century has been deleted from the history books. The family that brought Roumania from Turkish suzerainty to modern times, that led her successfully through one world war and got her honorably out of another, is referred to, if at all, as an "alien dynasty," brought in purely for self-enrichment. In this, historical revisionism has been helped by the character of King Carol II.

Queen Marie's worries about her son were realized with his enforced abdication two years after her death. Her worst fears about the Communists came to pass eight years later. It might be said that she died just in time.

NOTES

The following abbreviations are used in the notes:

B-L: Letters from the collection of the Hon. Lady Bowes-Lyon.

HH: Herbert Hoover Presidential Library.

HI: Hoover Institution on War, Revolution, and Peace.

H-L: Letters from the collection of H.S.H. the Prince of Hohenlohe-Langenburg.

IR: Letters and papers from the collection of H.R.H. Princess Ileana of Roumania.

KE: Letters from the Estate of Lee Keedick.

KSU: Kent State University Library.

MM: Maryhill Museum.

RU: Reading University Library.

RA: Roumanian Archives.

RAWC: Royal Archives at Windsor Castle.

SA: Sigmaringen Archives.

Chapter 1

pp. 23–24

"Affie would... charming.": Roger Fulford, ed., *Dearest Mama*, p. 53.

p. 24

"In confidence... years.": *Ibid.*, p. 213.

"heavy blow... frame": *Ibid.*, p. 107.

"The young... ugly...": *Ibid.*, p. 56.

"very good... skin,": *Ibid.*, p. 258.

"very pretty... eyes,": *Ibid.*, p. 262.

"sickly-looking, ... feet!": *Ibid.*, p. 265.

"very plain, ... complexion.": *Ibid.*, pp. 177–8.

p. 25

"she does... well-bred.": Roger Fulford, ed., *Dearest Child*, p. 290.

"She has... ladylike.": *Ibid.*, p. 224.

"She is... loud.": *Ibid.*, pp. 311–12.

"I saw... Affie?": Fulford, *Dearest Mama*, p. 344.

"If he... Affie.": Roger Fulford, ed., *Your Dear Letter*, p. 147.

p. 26

"the tables... occasion.": Brian McKinley, *The First Royal Tour*, p. 141.

"I fear... do!": Fulford, *Your Dear Letter*, p. 205.

Late that summer [of 1868]: Sources cite the summers of both 1869 and 1871 as the date the Duke of Edinburgh and Grand Duchess Marie first met. Neither can be correct. In the summer of 1869, the Duke was cruising on the *Galatea* between Tahiti and Japan. Since the Queen was already questioning Gladstone on the exigencies of Marie's Orthodox faith in July of 1869, they had to have met before then. That leaves 1868, when he returned home to recover from his gunshot wound, as the only summer the Duke spent in Europe between 1867 and 1871.

p. 27

"the Tsar... them.": Count Egon Corti, *The Downfall of Three Dynasties*, p. 212.

"There is... objectionable.": Philip Guedalla, *The Queen and Mr. Gladstone*, p. 246.

p. 28

"*half Oriental... notions.*": Elizabeth Longford, *Queen Victoria*, p. 394.

"We implore... hand.": E. M. Almedingen, *The Emperor Alexander II*, p. 262.

"The murder... out.": Longford, *op. cit.*, p. 393.

"Silly old fool!": Corti, *op. cit.*, p. 214.

"Sovereign &... shocked.": Longford, *op. cit.*, pp. 394–5.

p. 29

"You know... God.": Hector Bolitho, ed., *Further Letters of Queen Victoria from the Archives of the House of Brandenburg-Prussia*, p. 198.

pp. 29–30

"all the... so.": Dean of Windsor and Hector Bolitho, eds., *Later Letters of Lady Augusta Stanley*, pp. 204–29 *passim*.

p. 30

"The Grand-duke... man.": Longford, *op. cit.*, p. 116.

"very kind... worthy.": George Earle Buckle, ed., *The Letters of Queen Victoria*, Second Series, Vol. II, pp. 337–8.

p. 31

"Between you... belief.": Corti, *op. cit.*, p. 216.

p. 32

"rare intelligence... well.": Mrs. George Cornwallis-West, *The Recollections of Lady Randolph Churchill*, p. 238.

"too good": E. E. P. Tisdall, *Marie Fedorovna, Empress of Russia*, p. 72.

"wonderful diamonds.": Meriel Buchanan, *Queen Victoria's Relations*, p. 116.

"an abominable... tact.": Charles Morris and Murat Halstead, *Life and Reign of Queen Victoria*, p. 268.

"Papa... him.": Marie, Queen of Roumania, *The Story of My Life*, p. 245.

p. 33

"No officer... him,": Giles St. Aubyn, *Edward VII, Prince and King*, p. 291. (Sir Henry Ponsonby is quoting Sir Henry Keppel, Admiral of the British Navy, when he says, "No officer... it—" The rest of the quote is Ponsonby himself speaking.)

"Uncle Alfred... liquor.": H.R.H. Princess Alice, Countess of Athlone, *For My Grandchildren*, p. 86.

"thoroughly English... degrading": RA V, 1787/1895, Dec. 10, 1895, Duchess of Coburg to Queen Marie.

"amounted to... disease.": Longford, *op. cit.*, p. 398.

p. 34

"with *extraordinary*... character.": Corti, *op. cit.*, pp. 241–4.

p. 35

"that Russia... triumphant.": Longford, *op. cit.*, p. 414.

Chapter 2

p. 39

"Her Royal... well": London *Times*, Oct. 30, 1875.

pp. 40–43

"I still... tremble.": Marie, *The Story of My Life*, pp. 4–69 *passim*.

p. 43

"you only... horns.": Count Egon Corti, *The Downfall of Three Dynasties*, p. 243.

"the sole... domineer.": Charles Morris and Murat Halstead, *Life and Reign of Queen Victoria*, p. 267.

pp. 43–45

"She dazzled... know.": Marie, *op. cit.*, pp. 6–90 *passim*.

p. 45

"Herald of Death": H.R.H. Prince Nicholas of Greece, *My Fifty Years*, p. 53.

pp. 45–46

"I can . . . dear little,": Marie, *op. cit.*, pp. 40–145 *passim*.

p. 47

"kind, honest . . . true.": Harold Nicolson, *King George the Fifth*, p. 37.

"like a . . . mother": RA V, 1005/1920, Dec. 12, 1920, King George V to Queen Marie.

"beloved chum . . . whatever.": Marie, *op. cit.*, p. 127.

"I am . . . mine.": RA V, 980/1888, Jan. 2, 1888, King George V to Queen Marie.

"You are . . . Missy,": RA V, 983/1888, June 26, 1888, King George V to Queen Marie.

"a great . . . face.": RA V, 989/1889, Oct. 25, 1889, King George V to Queen Marie.

pp. 47–48

"simple burghers . . . Germans.": Marie, *op. cit.*, pp. 144–69 *passim*.

p. 48

"rejoiced": RA III, 124:83.

pp. 48–49

"eager, blundering . . . servant.": Marie, *op. cit.*, pp. 153–83 *passim*.

p. 49

"*der Lieber . . . Ernst*": H.R.H. Princess Alice, *For My Grandchildren*, p. 85.

p. 50

"because it . . . hours!": Marie, *op. cit.*, p. 157.

"if indeed . . . Coburg.": Corti, *op. cit.*, pp. 141–5 *passim*.

"Russia . . . it.": RA III, 141:42.

p. 51

"We too . . . altogether.": Marie, *op. cit.*, p. 200.

Chapter 3

pp. 52–53

"I quite . . . young.": Harold Nicolson, *King George the Fifth*, p. 43.

p. 53

"I quite . . . church.": James Pope-Hennessy, *Queen Mary*, p. 240.

"I simply . . . you.": RA V, 1740/1893, June 28, 1893, Duchess of Coburg to Queen Marie.

p. 54

"How he . . . professor.": Princess Marthe Bibesco, "Ferdinand of Roumania," *Saturday Evening Post*, Aug. 27, 1927, p. 150.

p. 55

"poor little . . . romance": Marie, *The Story of My Life*, p. 249.

"Your Royal ... matter.": Princess Anne-Marie Callimachi,*Yesterday Was Mine*, p. 146.

"the manifold ... heartaches": SA, Dec. 12/27, 1891, King Ferdinand to Prince Leopold and Princess Antonia.

pp. 55–56

"quickly ... tomorrow.": SA, Nov. 30/Dec. 12, 1891, King Ferdinand to Prince Leopold.

p. 56

"interfere ... kind": SA, Jan. 24/Feb. 5, 1892, King Ferdinand to Prince Leopold.

pp. 56–57

"there was ... life,": Marie, *op. cit.*, pp. 203–7 *passim*.

p. 57

"would for ... influence": RA V, 2036/1907, Feb. 12, 1907, Duchess of Coburg to Queen Marie.

"What fun ... danced,": RA V, 990/1890, Jan. 3, 1890, King George V to Queen Marie.

"... it is ... Georgie.": RA V, 992/1891, Jan. 7, 1891, King George V to Queen Marie.

"he must ... Malta.": HI, George Duca, *Maria Regina*, Chap. 2.

p. 58

"Georgie lost ... waiting.": Richard Hough, ed., *Advice to a Grand-daughter*, p. 120.

p. 58n

"It was ... decision": Terence Elsberry, *Marie of Roumania*, p. 25.

pp. 58–59

"they begin ... fate.": Marie, *op. cit.*, pp. 188–209 *passim*.

p. 59

"We have ... Oct:!": Hough, *op. cit.*, p. 117.

"Missy's engagement ... life....": Pope-Hennessy, *op. cit.*, p. 241.

pp. 59–60

"Disgusted to ... bitter.": Pope-Hennessy, *op. cit.*, pp. 232–42.

p. 60

"a great ... pitied.": RA V, 1740/1893, June 28, 1893, Duchess of Coburg to Queen Marie.

pp. 60–64

"Papa had ... understood.": Marie, *op. cit.*, pp. 212–27.

p. 64

"in the ... fashion.": Elsberry, *op. cit.*, p. 44.

pp. 64–65

"He was ... land.": Marie, *op. cit.*, pp. 228–39 *passim*.

p. 65

"in general ... one.": SA, Dec. 22, 1892, King Ferdinand to Prince Wilhelm.

"My mother ... everything.": Marie, *op. cit.*, p. 241.

"I will ... separated.": RAWC, Nov. 21, 1892, Queen Marie to Queen Victoria.

pp. 65–66

"loved each . . . happy,": RA V, 880bis/1892, Nov. 3, 1892, King Ferdinand to Queen Marie.

"good and . . . children.": SA, Dec. 27, 1892, King Ferdinand to Prince Leopold.

"You write . . . myself.": RA V, 866/1892, Sept. 29/Oct. 11, 1892, King Ferdinand to Queen Marie.

"It will . . . rooms.": RA V, 880bis/1892, Nov. 17/29, 1892, King Ferdinand to Queen Marie.

"jumping around . . . sentimental.": SA, Dec. 7, 1892, King Ferdinand to Princess Antonia.

pp. 66–68

"*Ach*! my . . . did not come.": Marie, *op. cit.*, pp. 252–66 *passim*.

p. 68

"I married . . . it.": RA V, 3900/1921, Mar. 3, 1921, Queen Marie to Joseph Boyle.

p. 69

"We both . . . Mamma!": Marie, *op. cit.*, p. 267.

Chapter 4

p. 74

"vain and . . . gasbag.": R. W. Seton-Watson, A *History of the Roumanians*, p. 370.

"The table . . . light.": Marie, *The Story of My Life*, p. 276.

"You sent . . . mad . . .": Walpurga, Lady Paget, *Embassies of Other Days*, p. 546.

p. 75

"It is . . . throne.": Charles Morris and Murat Halstead, *Life and Reign of Queen Victoria*, pp. 265–6.

Dracula: These were actually two different men, Vlad Dracul (the Devil) and Vlad IV, the Impaler. See Seton-Watson, *op. cit.*, pp. 35–41.

p. 76

"the land . . . blood.": Mrs. Will. Gordon, *Roumania Yesterday and Today*, p. 56.

"What is . . . fate.": Seton-Watson, *op. cit.*, pp. 130–4.

p. 78

"The Roumanian . . . founded.": Gordon, *op. cit.*, p. 62.

"Gentlemen, I . . . me.": Seton-Watson, *op. cit.*, p. 301.

p. 80

"Proceed at . . . Palace?": Sidney Whitman, ed., *Reminiscences of the King of Roumania*, pp. 18–30.

p. 81

supported by Emperor Franz Josef: This was through the Compromise of 1867, a document signed by the Hungarians and Franz Josef after his defeat by Prussia in the Seven Weeks' War (1866). Through the Compromise, the Austrian Emperor formally recognized the dual nature of his empire, conceding virtual independence to the Hungarians and allowing them to persecute the Roumanians of Transylvania as they liked.

"My sole... persuasions": Seton-Watson, *op. cit.*, pp. 321–3 *passim*.
pp. 81–82
"I was... curiosity.": Elizabeth Burgoyne, *Carmen Sylva*, pp. 65–72.
p. 82
"I believe... thrones?": Roger Fulford, ed., *Your Dear Letter*, p. 277.
"access to... manger": Count Ottokar Czernin, *In the World War*, p. 81.
p. 83
"turned a... enemy.": Seton-Watson, *op. cit.*, p. 343.
p. 84
"The lips... her.": Blanche Roosevelt, *Elisabeth of Roumania, A Study*, p. 98.

Chapter 5

p. 87
"It was... duties.": Marie, *The Story of My Life*, pp. 273–9.
p. 88
"Rather bewildered": RA V, 2285/1893, undated (winter, 1893), Queen Marie to the Duchess of Coburg.
"simply embowered... flowers,": Maude Parkinson, *Twenty Years in Roumania*, p. 182.
pp. 88–89
"glass case... dinner....": Marie, *op. cit.*, pp. 283–4.
pp. 89–90
"get a... mind.": RA V, 2251/1893, Feb. 9, 1893, Queen Marie to the Duchess of Coburg.
p. 90
"hideous lot... waistcoats.": RA V, 2285/1893, undated (winter, 1893), Queen Marie to the Duchess of Coburg.
"So at... anymore.": RA V, 2284/1893, undated (winter, 1893), Queen Marie to the Duchess of Coburg.
p. 91
"disastrous rococo... what?": Marie, *op. cit.*, pp. 292–3.
"This condition... unpleasantnesses.": SA, Mar. 12, 1893, Queen Marie to Princess Antonia.
"uniform, grey... depressing.": Marie, *op. cit.*, p. 294.
p. 92
"It is... us.": RA V, 2283/1893, undated (winter, 1893), Queen Marie to the Duchess of Coburg.
"... we generally... Nando,": RA V, 2290/1893, undated (winter, 1893), Queen Marie to the Duchess of Coburg.

"It is . . . here.": RA V, 2283/1893, undated (winter, 1893), Queen Marie to the Duchess of Coburg.

"dressing too tight.": SA, June 21/July 3, 1893, Queen Marie to Princess Antonia.

"You will . . . you?": RA V, 2283/1893, undated (winter, 1893), Queen Marie to the Duchess of Coburg.

". . . you must . . . complain.": RA V, 2258/1893, Mar. 19, 1893, Queen Marie to the Duchess of Coburg.

pp. 92–93

"Give yourself . . . health.": Marie, *op. cit.*, pp. 295–300.

p. 93

"'Your Royal . . . it?'": Mabel Potter Daggett, *Marie of Roumania*, p. 114.

"it does . . . church.": SA, Mar. 31, 1893, Queen Marie to Princess Antonia.

p. 94

"hideous, dirty-looking . . . garlic,": RA V, 2275/1893, June 4, 1893, Queen Marie to the Duchess of Coburg.

"I sensed . . . land,": Marie, *op. cit.*, p. 304.

"An agreeable . . . acquainted.": Ethel Greening Pantazzi, *Roumania in Light and Shadow*, p. 133.

"It is . . . close.": E. O. Hoppe, *In Gipsy Camp and Royal Palace*, p. 59.

"gimcrack affair . . . building.": Arthur Gould Lee, ed., *The Empress Frederick Writes to Sophie*, p. 173.

p. 95

"true works . . . art.": SA, Nov. 23, 1886, King Ferdinand to Prince Wilhelm.

"Everything seemed . . . sun,": Marie, *op. cit.*, p. 310.

"For Uncle . . . large.": Lee, *op. cit.*, pp. 150–2.

"I hope . . . permission.": SA, June 8, 1893, Queen Marie to Princess Antonia.

p. 96

"doctors, wet . . . rooms.": Marie, *op. cit.*, p. 314.

"I had . . . have.": RA V, 1745/1893, July 17, 1893, Duchess of Coburg to Queen Marie.

pp. 96–97

"We want . . . salutes.": Marie, *op. cit.*, pp. 234–315 *passim*.

Chapter 6

p. 98

"thin as . . . thread.": SA, Apr. 1, 1894, Queen Marie to Princess Antonia.

"One feels . . . it.": RA V, 2253/1893, Feb. 29, 1894, Queen Marie to the Duchess of Coburg.

pp. 98–99

"You will . . . ministers.": RA V, 1763/1894, Feb. 23, 1894, Duchess of Coburg to Queen Marie.

p. 99

"Life has . . . people.": SA, Apr. 1, 1894, Queen Marie to Princess Antonia.

"Nando looks... Mamma.": RA V, 2434/1900, Aug. 8/21, 1900, Queen Marie to the Duchess of Coburg.

"had it out": Richard Hough, ed., *Advice to a Grand-daughter*, p. 120.

"Your and... proposal.": George Earle Buckle, ed., *The Letters of Queen Victoria*, Third Series, Vol. II, p. 342.

p. 100

"I had... her.": RA V, 1764/1894, Mar. 8/20, 1894, Duchess of Coburg to Queen Marie.

"I never... many,": David Duff, *Hessian Tapestry*, p. 233.

"Little Missy... thin.": Arthur Gould Lee, ed., *The Empress Frederick Writes to Sophie*, p. 170.

p. 101

"Poor Elisabeth!... her.": Sir Frederick Ponsonby, ed., *Letters of the Empress Frederick*, p. 445.

"furiously angry": KSU, George H. Huntington, *Diary of Visit with Her Majesty Queen Marie*, p. 51.

"Aunty, overcome... later.": Marie, *The Story of My Life*, pp. 322–3.

p. 102

"It was... more.": Marie, Queen of Roumania, *Crowned Queens*, p. 116.

"... you must... it.": RA V, 2353/1895, Dec. 21, 1895, Queen Marie to the Duchess of Coburg.

"Everyone feels... times,": SA, undated (winter 1894–5), Queen Marie to Prince Leopold.

"It is... pieces!": Marie, *op. cit.*, p. 325.

pp. 102–3

"... with Uncle... you.": RA V, 1752/1893, Dec. 7, 1893, Duchess of Coburg to Queen Marie.

p. 103

"Yesterday evening... suppose.": Lee, *op. cit.*, p. 159.

pp. 103–4

"... in the... given.": Marie, *op. cit.*, pp. 254–349 *passim*.

p. 104

"in affectionate... lookers-on.": RA V, 2559/1905, Mar. 20, 1905, Queen Marie to the Duchess of Coburg.

"certain regal magnificence": Meriel Buchanan, *Queen Victoria's Relations*, p. 193.

p. 105

"the most... specimen": RA V, 1836/1898, Oct. 22, 1898, Duchess of Coburg to Queen Marie.

pp. 105–6

"more like... festivities.": Marie, *op. cit.*, pp. 331–9 *passim*.

p. 107

"Princess Marie... night.": Prince Felix Youssoupoff, *Lost Splendour*, p. 44.

"a waist... gratitude.": Marie, *op. cit.*, pp. 340–1.

"I rejoice... to.": Mabel Potter Daggett, *Marie of Roumania*, p. 135.

pp. 107–8

"I certainly... loathsome.": RA V, 2375/1896, undated (summer/fall, 1896),

Queen Marie to the Duchess of Coburg.

p. 108

"...how will...encouraged,": RA V, 2374/1896, undated (fall, 1896), Queen Marie to the Duchess of Coburg.

"not as...yawns.": RA V, 2368/1896, Oct. 2, 1896, Queen Marie to the Duchess of Coburg.

"very different": RA V, 2364/1896, July 2, 1896, Queen Marie to the Duchess of Coburg.

"Perhaps I...you.": RA V, 2377/1896, Nov. 11, 1896, Queen Marie to the Duchess of Coburg.

"...all intimate...liberty.": RA III, 131:20.

"My husband...you!": RA V, 2376/1896, undated (fall, 1896) Queen Marie to the Duchess of Coburg.

p. 109

"always had...frivolous.": Marie, *op. cit.*, pp. 344–6.

"Young Light": KSU, Huntington, *op. cit.*, p. 51.

"God of...bear.": Elizabeth Burgoyne, *Carmen Sylva*, p. 180.

pp. 109–10

"Riding played...home.": Marie, *op. cit.*, pp. 358–65.

Chapter 7

p. 112

"It was...music.": Marie, *The Story of My Life*, pp. 485–93.

"infectious": *Ibid.*, p. 367.

p. 113

"It was...vitality.": H.R.H. Nicholas, Prince of Greece, *My Fifty Years*, p. 177.

"the fighting...Duchess"; footnote: "the little spitfire.": David Duff, *Hessian Tapestry*, pp. 260–1.

p. 114

"the term...intricate": Princess Anne-Marie Callimachi, *Yesterday Was Mine*, pp. 48–9.

"It is...drawing-room!": Ethel Greening Pantazzi, *Roumania in Light and Shadow*, p. 81.

pp. 115–16

"She was...allowance.": Callimachi, *op. cit.*, p. 64.

p. 116

"every shining...eye,": Pantazzi, *op. cit.*, p. 77.

"Ducky and...attire.": Marie, *op. cit.*, pp. 369–70 *passim*.

"...you are...noble.": RA V, 1796/1897, Mar. 21, 1897, Duchess of Coburg to Queen Marie.

pp. 116–17

"wee churches...true,": Marie, *op. cit.*, pp. 373–4 *passim*.

p. 117

"I feel... delirious.": H–L, June 15, 1897, Queen Marie to Princess Alexandra.

pp. 117–18

"Sickness had... hands.": Marie, *op. cit.*, pp. 384–7.

p. 118

"pale and... cured.": Princess Marthe Bibesco, "Ferdinand of Roumania," *Saturday Evening Post*, Aug. 27, 1927, p. 6.

"terribly, terribly disappointed": RA V, 2388/1897, June 15, 1897, Queen Marie to the Duchess of Coburg.

"I am... exercise!": RA V, 2390/1897, July 1, 1897, Queen Marie to the Duchess of Coburg.

pp. 118–19

"After the... pieces.": Marie, *op. cit.*, pp. 390–1.

p. 119

"this absolutely... person.": RA V, 2729/1899, Nov. 8/20, 1899, King Carol I to the Duchess of Coburg.

"To my... quietly.": SA, undated (winter, 1897–8), Queen Marie to Prince Leopold.

"safe guardians... content.": Marie, *op. cit.*, pp. 394–8.

p. 120

"If you... him,": RA V, 1821/1898, Feb. 15, 1898, Duchess of Coburg to Queen Marie.

"feed him... spirits.": RA V, 1824/1898, Mar. 20, 1898, Duchess of Coburg to Queen Marie.

"simply enchanted... Nice.": RA V, 1827/1898, Apr. 30, 1898, Duchess of Coburg to Queen Marie.

"I think... fire!": Arthur Gould Lee, ed., *The Empress Frederick Writes to Sophie*, p. 308.

"... the moment... exterior.": Marie, *op. cit.*, p. 401.

pp. 120–21

"with the... encounter.": SA, undated (fall/winter, 1899), Queen Marie to Prince Leopold.

p. 121

"pale and... away.": Marie, *op. cit.*, p. 404.

"He hardly... boy,": H–L, Feb. 1899, Queen Marie to Princess Alexandra.

"the boy... society.": Marie Mallet, *Life with Queen Victoria*, pp. 157–8.

"It is... him.": Lee, *op. cit.*, p. 156.

"not one... office.": Mallet, *op. cit.*, p. 156.

"May God... son,": SA, May 29/June 10, 1899, King Ferdinand to Princess Antonia.

p. 122

"God bless Mamma": Mabel Potter Daggett, *Marie of Roumania*, p. 153.

"Aunt asked... her,": Interview, H.R.H. Princess Ileana.

pp. 122–23

"We of... mother.": Daggett, *op. cit.*, pp. 140–2. (Nandó is spelled Nanda in Daggett.)

p. 123

"I pray . . . Nando.": SA, Oct. 31, 1899, Queen Marie to Prince Leopold.

"serious and . . . passions.": RA V, 2716/1889, Nov. 15, 1899, Duchess of Coburg to King Carol I.

"as a . . . fact.": RA V, 2712/1899, Nov. 25, 1899, Duchess of Coburg to King Carol I.

"I can . . . procedures,": RA V, 2716/1899, Nov. 15, 1899, Duchess of Coburg to King Carol I.

"*very feeble*": RA V, 1863/1899, Nov. 27, 1899, Duchess of Coburg to Queen Marie.

p. 124

"was permitted . . . Holland,": RA V, 2712/1899, Nov. 25, 1899, Duchess of Coburg to King Carol I.

"Your old . . . you,": RA V, 1861/1899, Nov. 9, 1899, Duchess of Coburg to Queen Marie.

"You have . . . woman.": RA V, 1867/1899, Dec. 7, 1899, Duchess of Coburg to Queen Marie.

"the whole . . . behavior,": RA V, 1862/1899, Nov. 17, 1899, Duchess of Coburg to Queen Marie.

"I could . . . hope.": Marie, *op. cit.*, p. 403.

"I hope . . . him,": RA V, 900/1900, Mar. 5/18, 1900, King Ferdinand to Queen Marie.

"You forget . . . obedience,": RA V, 901/1900, Mar. 6/19, 1900, King Ferdinand to Queen Marie.

"Your Nando . . . it,": RA V, 904/1900, undated (spring, 1900), King Ferdinand to Queen Marie.

"large enough, . . . infantry.": H.R.H. Princess Alice, *For My Grandchildren*, p. 89.

p. 125

"It was . . . life,": Marie, *op. cit.*, p. 404

"Her only . . . child.": Elizabeth Burgoyne, *Carmen Sylva*, p. 189.

"Mamma had . . . her,": Marie, *op. cit.*, p. 405.

"The education . . . King,": RA V, 2729/1899, Nov. 8/20, 1899, King Carol I to the Duchess of Coburg.

"had at . . . Aunty.": Marie, *op. cit.*, p. 405.

Chapter 8

p. 126

"*never* would . . . himself!": RA V, 2422/1900, Apr. 29, 1900, Queen Marie to the Duchess of Coburg.

"Nando will . . . to.": RA V, 2424/1900, May 26, 1900, Queen Marie to the Duchess of Coburg.

pp. 126–27

"At first... punished,": RA V, 2422/1900, Apr. 29, 1900, Queen Marie to the Duchess of Coburg.

"Yes, I... days.": RAWC, GEO. V, AA43–107, Nov. 26, 1901, Queen Marie to King George V.

p. 127

"would only... more.": RA V, 2431/1900, July 7, 1900, Queen Marie to the Duchess of Coburg.

"Oh, God, ... eighty-one!": Elizabeth Longford, Queen Victoria, p. 558.

"quite dreadfully... me.": RA V, 2451/1901, undated (spring, 1901), Queen Marie to the Duchess of Coburg.

"barely recovered": SA, July 15/28, 1900, Queen Marie to Prince Leopold.

p. 128

"after what... life.": James Pope-Hennessy, Queen Mary, pp. 363–4.

"I arranged... again.": Muriel Buchanan, Queen Victoria's Relations, p. 34.

pp. 128–29

"God had... this.": B–L, Nov. 27, 1903, Queen Marie to Pauline Astor.

"the marble man.": Princess Marthe Bibesco, Some Royalties and a Prime Minister, p. 160.

p. 129

"I don't... people.": B–L, Nov. 6, 1903, Queen Marie to Pauline Astor.

"the idol... men.": Alexander, Grand Duke of Russia, Always a Grand Duke, p. 144.

"Nando shuts... jailors.": RA V, 2460/1901, Sept. 11/24, 1901, Queen Marie to the Duchess of Coburg.

"Marie Remained Here": Elizabeth Longford, Louisa, Lady In Waiting, p. 98.

pp. 129–30

"My dearest... life.": Marie, The Story of My Life, p. 435.

p. 130

"The keynote... gloom.": Christopher Sykes, Nancy: The Life of Lady Astor, p. 103.

"not a... live.": Virginia Cowles, The Astors, p. 148. In her biography Lady Sackville, Susan Mary Alsop says that Astor's heirs deny that he made this remark (Avon Books, p. 187), but it is commonly attributed to him.

"I had... knew.": Terence Elsberry, Marie of Roumania, p. 73. I am indebted to Terence Elsberry for this story concerning Marie and Pauline Astor as well as the information on Pauline Astor's relationship with King Carol. Mr. Elsberry had interviewed Pauline Astor (Spender-Clay).

pp. 130–31

"A more... happiness.": Marie, op. cit., pp. 435–8 passim.

p. 131

"I thought... Adonis.": Consuelo Vanderbilt Balsan, The Glitter and the Gold, pp. 145–7.

p. 132

"My father, ... risk.": Interview, the Hon. David Astor.

"This enormous... amusement": Marie, *op. cit.*, pp. 437–62 *passim*.

p. 133

"I'm *sure*... fact,": RA V, 3715/1906, undated (winter/spring, 1907), Waldorf Astor to Queen Marie.

"he played... nobody.": Princess Marthe Bibesco, *Royal Portraits*, pp. 52–3 *passim*.

"Ferdinand was... admiration.": Interview, George Duca.

"Prince (later King)... ones.": Princess Anne-Marie Callimachi, *Yesterday Was Mine*, p. 63.

p. 134

"no vices... fornication.": William Rodney, *Joe Boyle, King of the Klondike*, p. 307.

"Being the... repute.": Interview, George Duca.

"In those... say.": Bibesco, *op. cit.*, pp. 49–54.

"And so... typical.": Interview, George Duca.

p. 135

"Framed in... Queen.": Callimachi, *op. cit.*, pp. 64–98 *passim*.

pp. 135–36

"I am... conversation.": B–L, Aug. 4, 1903, Queen Marie to Pauline Astor.

p. 136

"Delicate": Marie, *op. cit.*, p. 437.

p. 137

"who through... Hohenzollern.": RA V, 3736/F.D. undated, Waldorf Astor to Queen Marie.

"sentiment laid... spatula.": Interview, Lady Bowes-Lyon.

"be very... this.": B–L, Oct. 5, 1904, Queen Marie to Herbert Spender-Clay.

"it is... flatteries.": RU (Nancy Astor papers), Feb. 2, 1906, Queen Marie to Nancy Astor.

p. 138

"How full... else.": RU (Nancy Astor papers), Apr. 8, 1906, Queen Marie to Nancy Astor.

"I longed... me.": RU (Nancy Astor papers), June 2, 1906, Queen Marie to Nancy Astor.

"You have... alone,": RU (Nancy Astor papers), Feb. 27, 1906, Queen Marie to Nancy Astor.

"not to... notes,": RA V, 3693/1906, Apr. 26, 1906, Waldorf Astor to Queen Marie.

pp. 138–39

"... it was... *more*....": B–L, Feb. 16, 1907, Queen Marie to Pauline Astor.

p. 139

"I won't... meet.": B–L, Mar. 12, 1907, Queen Marie to Pauline Astor.

Chapter 9

pp. 140–41

"A sudden . . . friendless.": H–L, Feb. 6, 1907, Queen Marie to Princess Alexandra.

p. 141

"Once I . . . thing.": H–L, Feb. 25, 1907, Queen Marie to Princess Alexandra.

"never sang . . . presence.": Princess Anne-Marie Callimachi, *Yesterday Was Mine*, p. 127.

"I liked . . . did.": Marie, *The Story of My Life*, p. 444.

pp. 141–42

"strikingly handsome . . . city.": Callimachi, *op. cit.*, pp. 99–101.

p. 142

"She *had* . . . was.": Interview, George Duca.

pp. 142–43

"I have . . . original,": Elizabeth Burgoyne, *Carmen Sylva*, pp. 211–12 *passim*.

p. 143

"both a . . . perfection.": Callimachi, *op. cit.*, p. 124.

"beloved church bedroom": H–L, Jan. 9, 1907, Queen Marie to Princess Alexandra.

"very pleased . . . lead,": B–L, Oct. 13, 1905, Queen Marie to Pauline Astor.

p. 144

"as seriously . . . Parliament.": RA V, 2039/1907, Mar. 10, 1907, Duchess of Coburg to Queen Marie.

pp. 144–45

"Not an . . . wife.": Callimachi, *op. cit.*, pp. 122–4.

p. 145

"I don't . . . husband.": RA V, 2487/1902, Sept. 18/31, 1902, Queen Marie to the Duchess of Coburg.

"At least . . . missing.": RA V, 2592/1906, Mar. 18, 1906, Queen Marie to the Duchess of Coburg.

"Certainly there . . . Nando!": H–L, May 10, 1907, Queen Marie to Princess Alexandra.

"We know . . . come!": B–L, Sept. 27, 1907, Queen Marie to Pauline Astor.

p. 146

". . . when one . . . armchair.": RA V, 2534/1904, Apr. 11/24, 1904, Queen Marie to the Duchess of Coburg.

"because of . . . horses,": RA V, 2609/1907, Jan. 26, 1907, Queen Marie to the Duchess of Coburg.

"You can't . . . future!": RA V, 2611/1907, Feb. 11, 1907, Queen Marie to the Duchess of Coburg.

"disappointment . . . humiliation": RA V, 2482/1902, July 30, 1902, Queen Marie to the Duchess of Coburg.

"I had . . . that.": RA V, 2038/1907, Feb. 2, 1907, Duchess of Coburg to Queen Marie.

p. 147

"There seemed... humiliation": B–L, Apr. 12, 1907 (incomplete), Queen Marie to Pauline Astor.

"I have... over.": Marie, *op. cit.*, pp. 530–1.

p. 148

"With male... quality": Callimachi, *op. cit.*, pp. 138–9 *passim.*

p. 149

"In a... modesty.": Interview, George Duca.

"long for... away]!": H–L, May 10, 1907, Queen Marie to Princess Alexandra.

"His speech... pride.": Marie, Queen of Roumania, *Crowned Queens*, p. 18.

Chapter 10

pp. 150–51

"I hated... instruct.": Marie, *The Story of My Life*, pp. 516–18.

p. 151

"absolutely convinced... general.": Princess Marthe Bibesco, *Royal Portraits*, p. 105.

"fits of... anger.": SA, Jan. 1/14, 1903, Queen Marie to Prince Leopold.

p. 152

"two old maids,": H–L, May 10, 1907, Queen Marie to Princess Alexandra.

"profoundly moral... here.": H–L, July 19, 1907, Queen Marie to Princess Alexandra.

"filling his... remorse,": Marie, *op. cit.*, pp. 563–4 *passim.*

"I found... wits.": RA V, 292/1911, July 27, 1911, Infanta Beatrice to Queen Marie.

p. 153

"Since she... marble,": Bibesco, *op. cit.*, pp. 105–6.

"I feel... now.": H–L, Feb. 18, 1908, Queen Marie to Princess Alexandra.

"Mamma thinks... dull,": H–L, Aug. 22, 1907, Queen Marie to Princess Alexandra.

"deeper, more... nature.": RA III, 148:189.

"It is... master.": KSU, Oct. 28, 1907, Queen Marie to Leila Milne.

p. 154

"Lisabetha is... way,": B–L, June 4, 1908, Queen Marie to Pauline Astor.

"... young men... statue.": RA V, 2689/1912, June 20, 1912, Queen Marie to the Duchess of Coburg.

"I used... others.": Marie, *op. cit.*, pp. 403–519.

"She is... minute.": Bibesco, *op. cit.*, p. 112.

p. 155

"She is... justified": Marie, *op. cit.*, pp. 412–527 *passim.*

"The ladies... over.": RA V, 1947/1903, June 5, 1903, Duchess of Coburg to Queen Marie.

p. 156

"What of... worse.": B–L, June 5, 1903, Queen Marie to Pauline Astor.

"very much... will.": Marie, *op. cit.*, pp. 414–16.

"With this... Carol,": RA V, 2556/1905, Feb. 15, 1905, Queen Marie to the Duchess of Coburg.

"blind furies": H–L, Feb. 18, 1908, Queen Marie to Princess Alexandra.

"quite the... alive.": H–L, Oct. 8, 1907, Queen Marie to Princess Alexandra.

p. 157

"Here as... soul,": Marie, *op. cit.*, pp. 520–7 *passim.*

"like a... all,": H–L, May 30, 1909, Queen Marie to Princess Alexandra.

"Ileana was... knew.": Marie, *op. cit.*, p. 521.

"the more... table": RA V, 2719/1916, July 6/19, 1916, Queen Marie to the Duchess of Coburg.

Stirbey's letters: I cite one letter in particular, dated July 20, 1937 (RA V, 5300/1937), in which Stirbey compares Ileana with her older siblings. "She [Ileana] is really her mother's daughter! One recognizes in her the virtues of the mother without the faults which tarnish them in her brothers and eldest sister." An old-fashioned gentleman, Stirbey would never have compared Ileana favorably with her brothers and sister if she were his child.

p. 158

"a very... opinion": RU (Waldorf Astor papers), Apr. 28, 1909, Queen Marie to Waldorf Astor.

pp. 158–59

"I was... swords.": Marie, *op. cit.*, p. 480.

p. 159

"with great... everywhere,": Prince Von Bulow, *Memoirs* (1903–09), p. 28.

"the face... best.": B–L, May 2, 1908, Queen Marie to Pauline Astor.

"I can't... me...": RA V, 2637/1908, May 2/15, 1908, Queen Marie to the Duchess of Coburg.

pp. 159–60

"Queen Alexandra... rise.": Marie, *op. cit.*, pp. 459–534.

p. 160

"He was... him.": Interview, George Duca.

"had a... companion": Marie, *op. cit.*, pp. 422–3 *passim.*

"my severe... lady.": Interview, H.R.H. Princess Ileana.

pp. 160–61

"Because I... lazy!": Marie, *op. cit.*, pp. 377–8.

p. 161

"I don't... more.": H–L, Apr. 17, 1907, Queen Marie to Princess Alexandra.

"I never... current.": Interview, George Duca.

"No doubt... murdered!": RA V, 2578/1905, Nov. 12, 1905, Queen Marie to the Duchess of Coburg.

"all that... Alliance.": Marie, *op. cit.*, p. 531.

p. 162

"No admirer... Ferdinand.": Princess Anne-Marie Callimachi, *Yesterday Was Mine*, p. 139.

Chapter 11

p. 163

"place of . . . round.": Marie, *The Story of My Life*, pp. 546–7.
"historical rival . . . enemy": R. W. Seton-Watson, *A History of the Rouman-ians*, p. 455.

p. 164

"must in . . . will": Marie, *op. cit.*, p. 513.
"I am . . . visitors.": RA V, 2647/1909, June 16/29, 1909, Queen Marie to the Duchess of Coburg.
"I feel . . . timid.": RA V, 2617/1907, May 7, 1907, Queen Marie to the Duchess of Coburg.
"almost royal . . . bewildered": Marie, *op. cit.*, p. 512.
"Always afterwards . . . charm.": Count Ottokar Czernin, *In the World War*, p. 79.
"occasionally allowed . . . understanding": Marie, *op. cit.*, p. 513.

p. 165

"The Bulgarians . . . Balkans,": B–L, June 29, 1913, Queen Marie to Pauline Astor.
"I only . . . horribly.": B–L, Jan. 29, 1913, Queen Marie to Pauline Astor.
"Bucharest went . . . delight": Marie, *op. cit.*, p. 549.

p. 166

"For Roumania . . . walkover.": Princess Anne-Marie Callimachi, *Yesterday Was Mine*, p. 243.

pp. 166–67

"I saw . . . keeper,": Marie, *op. cit.*, pp. 551–4 *passim*.

p. 167

"unnecessarily sentimental . . . use.": RA V, 2710/1914 (date incorrect), Aug. 30, 1913, Queen Marie to the Duchess of Coburg.
"paddling about . . . beds,": Marie, *op. cit.*, p. 555.
"my life . . . person.": RA V, 2710/1914 (date incorrect), Aug. 30, 1913, Queen Marie to the Duchess of Coburg.
"in 1913 . . . understand.": Marie, *op. cit.*, p. 560.

p. 168

"Uncle is . . . enemy,": RA V, 2708/1913, Aug. 1, 1913, Queen Marie to the Duchess of Coburg.
Albania was granted independence: Albanian independence accorded with Austrian demands that Serbia not be given a seaport on the Adriatic, an outlet the Serbs had long and ardently sought.

p. 169

"underwent certain . . . question.": Marie, *op. cit.*, pp. 566–7.
the Danube question: The greatest obstacle to navigation of the Danube was the rapids at the Iron Gates, a gorge where the river breaks through the Transylvanian Alps into Roumania. In 1878 the Congress of Berlin gave Austria the right to execute the work to provide passage down river and levy taxes to cover the expenses. Austria transferred its mandate to Hungary. In

1905 Hungary built a glaringly inadequate canal: it was not deep enough, and even the most powerful steamer could not negotiate the current. Hungary imposed taxes which were not only prohibitive but varied depending on the shipper, "the burden," according to a Viennese newspaper, falling on the countries of the lower Danube like Roumania, while advantageous rates were assigned to Austria and Hungary. (*Rumania*, A Confidential Handbook Prepared Under the Department of the Historical Section of the Foreign Office, No. 21, December, 1918.)

"Although this... go.": Marie, *op. cit.*, p. 568.

"is not... Cross.": SA, July 13, 1913, Queen Marie to Prince Wilhelm.

pp. 170–72

"as though... terms.": Marie, *op. cit.*, pp. 570–83 *passim*.

p. 172

"Who could... her!": Pierre Gilliard, *Thirteen Years at the Russian Court*, p. 96 footnote.

"Her character... Roumanians!": Seton-Watson, *op. cit.*, pp. 469–71.

Chapter 12

p. 174

"Aunty... mute.": Marie, *The Story of My Life*, p. 585.

"*his honour... Mérite.*": Count Ottokar Czernin, *In the World War*, pp. 90–1.

pp. 175–76

"a house... house.": Take Jonescu, *Some Personal Impressions*, pp. 48–52.

p. 176

"a boiling... intrigue.": Princess Anne-Marie Callimachi, *Yesterday Was Mine*, pp. 259–60.

"policy of sentiment,": R. W. Seton-Watson, A *History of the Roumanians*, p.475.

"May God... victory,": SA, Aug. 1/14, 1914, King Ferdinand to Prince Wilhelm.

"We all... Highness,": Princess Marthe Bibesco, *Royal Portraits*, p. 63.

p. 177

"Gentlemen, you... impossible.": Seton-Watson, *op. cit.*, pp. 476–7.

pp. 177–78

"like a... heart.": Marie, *op. cit.*, pp. 588–91.

p. 178

"irresolute, shifting... surroundings": Leonard A. Magnus, *Roumania's Cause and Ideals*, pp. 81–2.

p. 179

"hope for... Christmas.": Marie, *op. cit.*, p. 593.

"I was... Queen.": Terence Elsberry, *Marie of Roumania*, p. 111.

pp. 179–80

"Have no... it.": Marie, *op. cit.*, p. 594.

p. 180

"I need... friends.": RA III, 102:6.

"red," "unsteady.": Bibesco, *op. cit.*, p. 67.

"It was... later.": RA III, 102:4–5.

"Regina Maria... loved.": Marie, *op. cit.*, p. 596.

"As Crown... loved,": Callimachi, *op. cit.*, p. 263.

"Poor Nando... master.": H–L, Oct. 23, 1914, Queen Marie to Princess Alexandra.

"legacy which... enemy.": SA, Jan. 25/Feb. 7, 1915, King Ferdinand to Prince Wilhelm.

"was given... regret.": Callimachi, *op. cit.*, p. 262.

p. 181

"not even... man.": H–L, Oct. 23, 1914, Queen Marie to Princess Alexandra.

"so rich... enormous": H–L, Jan. 11, 1915, Queen Marie to Princess Alexandra.

"Think of... dead!": Princess Marthe Bibesco, *Some Royalties and a Prime Minister*, p. 88.

pp. 181–82

"I... hand.": Marie, *Ordeal: The Story of My Life*, pp. 11–12.

p. 182

"I know... duty.": Comte Charles de Saint-Aulaire, *Confession d'un Vieux Diplomate*, p. 311.

"Oh, I... can't—": Elizabeth Burgoyne, *Carmen Sylva*, pp. 284–93.

"the great... times.": SA, May 19/June 1, 1916, King Ferdinand to Prince Wilhelm.

Chapter 13

pp. 186–87

"every word... success.": Marie, *Ordeal*, pp. 22–42.

p. 187

"Queen Marie... enjoyed.": Princess Anne-Marie Callimachi, *Yesterday Was Mine*, p. 266.

"Prince Stirbey... day.": Marie, *op. cit.*, p. 42.

pp. 187–88

"If no... friends.": Interview, George Duca.

p. 188

"Who knows... cowards!'": H–L, Mar. 16, 1915, Queen Marie to Princess Alexandra.

"It never... Bessarabia,": SA, Jan. 25/Feb. 7, 1915, King Ferdinand to Prince Wilhelm.

pp. 188–89

"The Emperor... share.": Marie, *op. cit.*, p. 23.

p. 189

My dear... cousin...: RAWC, GEO. V, Q1550/XVII–125, Mar. 13, 1915, Queen Marie to King George V.

p. 190

"very kind... begged": Marie, *op. cit.*, p. 25.

"these geographical... war.": RAWC, GEO. V, Q1550/XVII–126, May 22, 1915, Queen Marie to King George V. (Note: This letter, which is reproduced in *Ordeal*, pp. 26–28, differs slightly in wording. The phrase "the places can..." is taken from the book.)

pp. 190–91

"dearest Missy... you!": Marie, *op. cit.*, pp. 28–34 *passim*.

p. 191

"Missy is... politics,": SA, Jan. 7/20, 1916, King Ferdinand to Prince Wilhelm.

"exceedingly hazy... go.": Marie, *op. cit.*, p. 44.

"enough of... atmosphere": Charles J. Vopicka, *Secrets of the Balkans*, p.79.

p. 192

"harsh": SA, Jan. 7/20, 1916, King Ferdinand to Prince Wilhelm.

"overjoyed": SA, May 19/June 1, 1916, King Ferdinand to Prince Wilhelm.

pp. 192–93

"what a... Germans?": Marie, *op. cit.*, pp. 9–10.

p. 193

"Performing like... bazaar,": Sherman Spector, *Rumania at the Paris Peace Conference*, p. 29.

"belle odalisque... advantage.": Comte Charles de Saint-Aulaire, *Confession d'un Vieux Diplomate*, pp. 319–36.

pp. 193–94

"military promenade": R. W. Seton-Watson, *A History of the Roumanians*, p.489.

p. 194

"What he... in.": Marie, *op. cit.*, pp. 43–8.

"best ally,": Saint-Aulaire, *op. cit.*, p. 332.

"Only I... through.": Marie, *op. cit.*, p. 49.

"Thank God... me.": RA III, 102:28.

"I like... myself!": RA V, 2719/1916, July 6/19, 1916, Queen Marie to the Duchess of Coburg.

pp. 194–95

"I would... change.": RA V, 2721/1916, Aug. 20, 1916, Queen Marie to the Duchess of Coburg.

p. 195

"there was... material.": Seton-Watson, *op. cit.*, p. 490–1.

"I simply... changed.": Marie, *op. cit.*, p. 50.

Chapter 14

p. 196

"every sentence... instinct.": Marie, *Ordeal*, pp. 46–50.

p. 197

"ravaged by... trembling.": Comte Charles de Saint-Aulaire, *Confession d'un Vieux Diplomate*, p. 448.

"think and... Roumanian.": SA, July 11/24, 1916, King Ferdinand to Prince Wilhelm.

"Although I... to...": Charles J. Vopicka, *Secrets of the Balkans*, p. 86.

"May Roumania... myself.": Mrs. Will. Gordon, *Roumania Yesterday and Today*, p. 144.

"If things... help.": R. W. Seton-Watson, *A History of the Roumanians*, p. 492.

"It is... myself!": Saint-Aulaire, *op. cit.*, p. 448.

"Gentlemen, no... be.": Mabel Potter Daggett, *Marie of Roumania*, p. 224.

"the Chief... lost.": *Current History* (monthly magazine of *The New York Times*), Oct. 1916, Vol. V, No. 1.

pp. 197–98

"It's all... side!": Ethel Greening Pantazzi, *Roumania in Light and Shadow*, pp. 145–6.

p. 198

"embraced war... religion.": Saint-Aulaire, *op. cit.*, p. 399.

"I was... mad.": RA III, 102:38.

"advance a... yard.": Vopicka, *op. cit.*, p. 95.

p. 199

our people... Missy: Marie, *op. cit.*, pp. 53–4.

pp. 199–200

"the sacrifice... anxiety.": RAWC, GEO. V, Q1550/XVII–136, Oct. 7, 1916, King George V to Queen Marie (wire).

p. 200

"everybody talks... appearances,": RA III, 102:52–3.

"fat daughters,": RA III, 103:20.

"holy war... Roumanians!": RA V, 2725/1916, Sept. 19/Oct. 2, 1916, Queen Marie to the Duchess of Coburg.

pp. 200–201

"Why should... eyes.": Marie, *op. cit.*, pp. 55–6.

p. 201

"little vices... action.": RA III, 103:42–50.

"I think... favourites!": RA III, 102:93. Note: in her diary the Queen put parentheses around (to try it with favourites). Judging from several phrases treated in this way, she may have been indicating possible deletions for Roumanian publication.

"Oh! he... country!": RA III, 104:106–7.

"People begin... wonder,": RA III, 103:77.

"half-hearted and... offensive.": Seton-Watson, *op. cit.*, p. 493.

pp. 201–2
"The bulk . . . Roumania.": Vopicka, *op. cit.*, pp. 94–6.
p. 202
"made all . . . retreats,": Marie, *op. cit.*, p. 62.
"Poor Roumania . . . lost.": Vopicka, *op. cit.*, p. 100.
pp. 202–3
My Dear . . . Missy: Marie, *op. cit.*, pp. 62–3.
p. 203
"If only . . . name!": RA III, 103:69–70.
"has time . . . done.": RA III, 103:85.
"for amiable . . . money.": RA III, 102:67.
"solid military . . . point.": Marie, *op. cit.*, p. 65.
"furiously angry . . . saved!": RA III, 103:78.
p. 204
"fierce and . . . stubbornness,": Gordon, *op. cit.*, p. 168.
"as much . . . rotundity.": Saint-Aulaire, *op. cit.*, p. 378.
"calm, smiling . . . will": Seton-Watson, *op. cit.*, p. 501.
"Tell King . . . succeeding.": Saint-Aulaire, *op. cit.*, pp. 349–50 *passim.*
pp. 204–5
"I am . . . last . . .": Marie, *op. cit.*, pp. 64–9.
p. 205
"holy taper,": RA III, 104:8.
pp. 205–6
"after a . . . sinking.": Marie, *op. cit.*, pp. 70–2.
p. 206
a"the end . . . grave.": RA III, 104:35–9.
"We carried . . . dead.": Marie, *op. cit.*, p. 73.
"Not a . . . political treason": Saint-Aulaire, *op. cit.*, pp. 351–2.
p. 207
"Cruel news . . . rest.": Marie, *op. cit.*, p. 78.
pp. 207–8
"although [the] . . . heavy.": RA III, 104:104–12.
p. 208
"I can . . . King,": RA III, 115:180.
"As things . . . to!": RA III, 104:113.
"the house . . . time.": Marie, *op. cit.*, p. 84.
"The hardest . . . lost.": RA III, 104:116–8.
"The last . . . despair.": Marie, *op. cit.*, p. 85.

Chapter 15

p. 209
"endless, endless . . . foresees,": Marie, *Ordeal*, p. 86.
p. 210
"indescribable confusion . . . heads,": Frank Rattigan, *Diversions of a Diplomat*, p. 187.

"panic...groundless.": Charles J. Vopicka, *Secrets of the Balkans*, pp. 102–3.

p. 211

"the man...sledge-hammer,": Mrs. Will. Gordon, *Roumania Yesterday and Today*, p. 178.

"taste every...Germans.": Marie, *op. cit.*, p. 82.

"I am...adventuress.": RA III, 103:68–86 *passim*.

"One can...meals.": Vopicka, *op. cit.*, p. 116.

p. 212

"You are...you.": Comte Charles de Saint-Aulaire, *Confession d'un Vieux Diplomate*, p. 359.

pp. 212–13

"Everybody came...mountains.": Marie, *op. cit.*, pp. 87–98.

p. 213

"an excessively...hand.": RA III, 105:63–5.

"to my...administration,": RA III, 106:18.

pp. 213–14

"After a...beans.": Rattigan, *op. cit.*, p. 192.

p. 214

"clearly wishing...unpalatable.": Interview, H.R.H. Princess Ileana.

"there was...death.": *Literary Digest*, "Marie, Queen of Conquered Roumania, Defies the Kaiser," June 8, 1918, p. 56.

p. 215

"only the...wire.": Saint-Aulaire, *op. cit.*, pp. 362–4.

"determined not...Entente.": RA V, 2180/1916, Nov. 4, 1916, Duchess of Coburg to Queen Marie.

pp. 215–16

"Can she...humiliated.": Marie, *op. cit.*, pp. 96–111 *passim*.

p. 216

"...something uncanny...enthusiasms.": RA III, 106:35.

"too strained.": Marie, *op. cit.*, p. 113.

p. 218

"He is...capabilities.": RA III, 103:95–6.

"inspecting, inquiring...loved.": Marie, *op. cit.*, pp. 134–48.

"with all...work.": RA III, 108:10.

"Am very...done!": RA III, 107:56–69.

"devoured...anticipated.": Marie, *op. cit.*, p. 137.

Chapter 16

p. 220

"Some disorders...serious.": Edmond Taylor, *The Fall of the Dynasties*, p. 256.

"heartening news.": Joachim Remak, ed., *The First World War: Causes, Conduct, Consequences*, p. 41.

"What would...Rasputin.": Marie, *Ordeal*, pp. 142–6 *passim*.

"the Rasputin . . . Roumania.": Terence Elsberry, *Marie of Roumania*, p. 83.

"from above": Robert H. Johnston, *Tradition Versus Revolution, Russia and the Balkans in 1917*, p. 73.

p. 221

"Sons of . . . affairs.": R. W. Seton-Watson, A *History of the Roumanians*, pp. 503–4.

"persuaded . . . over.": RA III, 108:177–8 *passim*.

"Prince Stirbey . . . misery.": Marie, *op. cit.*, pp. 147–58 *passim*.

"shot to pieces": RA III, 110:17.

"I really . . . rubber!": Marie, *op. cit.*, p. 177.

p. 222

"martyrs to . . . cause.": Johnston, *op. cit.*, p. 75.

p. 223

"strengthened by . . . generosities,": Comte Charles de Saint-Aulaire, *Confession d'un Vieux Diplomate*, p. 373.

"This makes . . . over.": RA III, 108:15.

"bundled off . . . misery,": RA V, 2183/1917, Aug. 16, 1917, Duchess of Coburg to Queen Marie.

pp. 223–24

"breakdown . . . hope?": Marie, *op. cit.*, pp. 208–23 *passim*.

p. 224

"one of . . . Europe.": Charles J. Vopicka, *Secrets of the Balkans*, p. 144.

". . . a boy . . . advice.": RA III, 109:46.

pp. 224–25

"I did . . . allies.": Marie, *op. cit.*, pp. 192–208.

p. 225

"full disintegration . . . position.": Seton-Watson, *op. cit.*, p. 502.

Chapter 17

p. 227

"They came . . . manner.": Marie, *Ordeal*, p. 234.

p. 228

"to the . . . despair": RA III, 111:44.

"death-day.": Marie, *op. cit.*, pp. 243–4.

"We were . . . hearts.": RA III, 110:153.

"the last . . . not.": RA III, 111:56.

"Part of . . . vote.": Marie, *op. cit.*, pp. 258–9.

"We know . . . get [to Russia]": Comte Charles de Saint-Aulaire, *Confession d'un Vieux Diplomate*, pp. 416–7.

p. 229

"very warm": Marie, *op. cit.*, p. 266.

"with all . . . hospitality.": RAWC, GEO. V, 1550/XVII–152, Dec. 11, 1917, Queen Marie to King George V.

"violently remove": Charles J. Vopicka, *Secrets of the Balkans*, p. 148.

"I cannot . . . him.": Saint-Aulaire, *op. cit.*, p. 428.

p. 230

"an island... exhausted.": Frank Rattigan, *Diversions of a Diplomat*, pp. 194–5.

pp. 230–31

"I was... way.": Marie, *op. cit.*, pp. 268–83.

p. 231

"Roumania, having... her.": Saint-Aulaire, *op. cit.*, p. 440.

"a simple... news": Marie, *op. cit.*, pp. 274–86.

p. 232

"I wonder... hope.": RA V, 2733/1918, Jan. 12, 1918, Queen Marie to the Duchess of Coburg.

"Nando and... situation,": Marie, *op. cit.*, pp. 290–4.

p. 233

"punishment for treachery": R. W. Seton-Watson, A *History of the Roumanians*, p. 512.

"instead of... soldiers.": RA III, 112:32.

pp. 233–34

"I began... stake!": Marie, *op. cit.*, pp. 305–10 *passim*.

p. 234

"barely polite": *Ibid.*, p. 310.

"an honourable peace": Count Ottokar Czernin, *In the World War*, p. 260.

pp. 234–35

"The peace... him.": Marie, *op. cit.*, pp. 310–12.

p. 235

"terrible scene... cowards!": RA III, 112:94–8 *passim*.

pp. 235–36

"to express... honourable.": Marie, *op. cit.*, pp. 314–17.

p. 236

"Nando *cannot*... abdicate,": RA III, 112:107–8.

"The character... slavery.": Vopicka, *op. cit.*, p. 188.

"model of... England!": Seton-Watson, *op. cit.*, pp. 516–18.

pp. 236–37

"We all... iron.": Marie, *op. cit.*, pp. 312–25 *passim*.

p. 237

"À *bientôt*... *bientôt*": Saint-Aulaire, *op. cit.*, p. 444.

pp. 237–38

"even if... together.": Marie, *op. cit.*, pp. 326–7.

p. 238

"formal assurances... give.": Saint-Aulaire, *op. cit.*, p. 446.

"very ordinary men.": Vopicka, *op. cit.*, p. 188.

"could hardly... Russia.": Marie, *op. cit.*, pp. 324–32.

"Marie, Queen... Germany.": *Literary Digest*, "Marie, Queen of Conquered Roumania, Defies the Kaiser," June 8, 1918, p. 56.

p. 239

"carrying off... to!": RA III, 113:18–9.

"The annexation... Government.": Marie, *op. cit.*, p. 338.

"Vice-Roy": RA III, 112:156.
"a very... nature.": Marie, *op. cit.*, pp. 333–45 *passim*.

Chapter 18

p. 240
"I have... it.": Kim Beattie, *Brother, Here's a Man*, pp. 106–7.
p. 241
Order of St. Vladimir: Later changed to the Order of St. Anne.
p. 242
"surging around... lives.": G. A. Hill, *Go Spy the Land*, p. 8.
"He was... since.": Hill, *ibid.*, p. 89
"an elderly... reassuring.": Marie, *Ordeal*, p. 343.
"marked the... place.": Beattie, *op. cit.*, p. 233.
p. 243
"He [Boyle] had... port.": Marie, *op. cit.*, p. 344.
"People had... dead,": Ethel Greening Pantazzi, *Roumania in Light and Shadow*, p. 259.
p. 244
"systematic robbery... enemy.": Charles J. Vopicka, *Secrets of the Balkans*, pp. 211–13 *passim*.
pp. 244–45
"I stood... watchdog.": Marie, *op. cit.*, pp. 348–52 *passim*.
p. 245
"not to... first.": RA III, 114:12.
"I mean... guests.": Marie, *op. cit.*, pp. 347–53.
"No one... help.": RA III, 115:51.
pp. 245–46
"made all... aware.": Marie, *op. cit.*, pp. 354–66.
pp. 246–47
"I am... woman.": RA III, 114:36–78 *passim*.
p. 247
"royal duties... horrid!": Marie, *op. cit.*, p. 396.
"... he has... energy.": RA III, 114:198.
"central figure": RA V, 3820/1918, Nov. 27–29, 1918, Joseph Boyle to Queen Marie.
"I who... you,": RA V, 3830/1919, Sept. 5, 1919, Joseph Boyle to Queen Marie.
p. 248
"Poor Nicky!... demands.": Marie, *op. cit.*, pp. 366–8 *passim*.
"crying like... him.": RA III, 114:7–215.
"cold-blooded... her,": RA III, 113:68–74.
"Poor child... moment!": RA III, 114:81.
pp. 248–49
"She really... smiled.": RA III, 114:136.

p. 249
"a certain . . . predicament": Marie, *op. cit.*, pp. 375–7 *passim*.
"quite like . . . Roumanians.": RA III, 113:198.
"It is . . . troops,": Vopicka, *op. cit.*, p. 234.
p. 250
"an almost . . . unprepared.": Marie, *op. cit.*, p. 386.

Chapter 19

pp. 251–53
"charming anarchy . . . rule.": Jeanne Lambrino, *Mon Mari Le Roi Carol*,
pp. 16–81.
p. 253
"unable to . . . Boches [Germans],": RA III, 114:213–7 *passim*.
pp. 254–55
"all eyes . . . her,": RA III, 115:2–80 *passim*.
p. 255
"there was . . . wished.": Lambrino, *op. cit.*, p. 98.
"After a . . . war [came about].": Comte Charles de Saint-Aulaire, *Confession
d'un Vieux Diplomate*, p. 469.
pp. 255–56
"Cambrai has . . . news": Marie, *Ordeal*, pp. 388–9.
p. 256
"almost giddy . . . us.": RA III, 115:64.
pp. 256–57
"ready . . . pieces.": Marie, *op. cit.*, pp. 394–7.
p. 258
"Nando cannot . . . whatever.": RA III, 115:90–119 *passim*.
"squarely in . . . reforms,": Marie, *op. cit.*, pp. 390–401.
p. 259
"Germany seems . . . is.": RA III, 115:128.
"We realized . . . effect.": Charles J. Vopicka, *Secrets of the Balkans*, p. 276.
"Perhaps it . . . us.": RA III, 115:135.
"I, for . . . success.": Marie, *op. cit.*, pp. 403–4.
"Why are . . . twice,": Saint-Aulaire, *op. cit.*, p. 474.
p. 260
"In the . . . stormy": RA III, 115:142–181.
pp. 260–61
"I would . . . touched": Marie, *op. cit.*, pp. 407–16.

Chapter 20

p. 262
"difficult to . . . Germany.": Herbert Hoover, *Memoirs*, pp. 406–7.

p. 263

"Disorder, dirt... porridge.": Ethel Greening Pantazzi, *Roumania in Light and Shadow,* pp. 275–6.

"During the... possible.": Charles J. Vopicka, *Secrets of the Balkans,* pp. 287–9.

pp. 263–64

"It is... failure.": RA V, 3883/1919, Feb. 2, 1919, Queen Marie to Joseph Boyle.

p. 264

"Duke of Bucharest": Kim Beattie, *Brother, Here's a Man!,* p. 291.

"would rather starve": Hoover, *op. cit.,* p. 407.

"... he is... men.": RA V, 1002/1918, Dec. 28, 1918, King George V to Queen Marie.

"All day... once.": *Literary Digest,* "Marie, Queen of Conquered Roumania, Defies the Kaiser," June 8, 1918, p. 56.

p. 265

"... it was... approach.": HI, George Duca, *Maria Regina,* Chap. 1.

"Rumania was... life.": Marie, Grand Duchess of Russia, *A Princess in Exile,* p. 30.

"wall of... inertia,": RA V, 3884/1919, Feb. 12, 1919, Queen Marie to Joseph Boyle.

pp. 265–66

"would let... passion": Marie, Grand Duchess of Russia, *op. cit.,* pp. 18–35 *passim.*

p. 266

"My daughters... house.": KSU, Feb. 7, 1919, Queen Marie to Leile Milne.

"but seemed... fondness.": Marie, Grand Duchess of Russia, *op. cit.,* p. 31.

"He is... job,": RA V, 3883/1919, Feb. 2, 1919, Queen Marie to Joseph Boyle.

"a shadow... honeymoon": Jeanne Lambrino, *Mon Mari Le Roi Carol,* p. 107.

p. 267

"The more... describing.": Marie, Grand Duchess of Russia, *op. cit.,* pp. 30–1.

"Marie of... century.": Terence Elsberry, *Marie of Roumania,* pp. 172–3.

"the most... indulgence,": HI, George Duca, *Queen Marie,* unpublished monograph.

"I never... talking.": KSU, George H. Huntington, *Diary of Visit with Her Majesty, Queen Marie,* p. 51.

"protruded in... desired,": Marie, Grand Duchess of Russia, *op. cit.,* pp. 15–17 *passim.*

p. 268

"his chief... rival,": R. W. Seton-Watson, *A History of the Roumanians,* p. 536.

"*un grand Européen,*": Dr. E. J. Dillon, *The Inside Story of the Peace Conference,* p. 84.

"the only... abroad": RA V, 3883/1919, Feb. 2, 1919, Queen Marie to Joseph Boyle.

"... disquieting rumours... helpless.": RAWC, GEO. V, Q1550/XVII–184, Jan. 11, 1919, Queen Marie to King George V.

p. 269

"No man... Rumania.": Harold Nicolson, *Peacemaking 1919*, pp. 136–7 *passim*.

"the treaty... treaty,": Seton-Watson, *op. cit.*, p. 539.

"Where the... get?": Dillon, *op. cit.*, p. 63.

p. 270

"try her philtres": Comte Charles de Saint Aulaire, *Confession d'un Vieux Diplomate*, p. 485.

"have the... person?": Duca, *Maria Regina*, Chap. 1.

"It is... help.": RA III, 116:56–7.

"not to... reception.": RA V, 5195/1919, Feb. 27, Mar. 12, 1919, Barbo Stirbey to Queen Marie.

"Nando needs... do.": RA III, 116:92.

pp. 270–71

"The moment... daughters.": KSU, Feb. 7, 1919, Queen Marie to Leile Milne.

p. 271

"if all... so.": RA III, 116:84–5.

"Of all... understanding.": Marie, Grand Duchess of Russia, *op. cit.*, p. 13.

"On the... events.": RA III, 116:93.

Chapter 21

p. 274

"She is... Queen,": *Le Matin*, Mar. 6, 1919.

p. 275

"buried... violets.": Queen Marie of Roumania, "My Mission, I. In Paris" in *Cornhill Magazine*, Oct. 1939, pp. 437–8.

"all over Paris": RA V, 5317/1919, Mar. 3–5, 1919, Queen Marie to Barbo Stirbey.

"Everybody fusses... 'unofficially.'": Queen Marie of Roumania, *op. cit.*, pp. 437–8.

("so much... Queen!"): HI, George Duca, *Maria Regina*, Chap. 1.

"a queenly air": RA III, 116:167.

pp. 275–76

"As soon... lost?": Mabel Potter Daggett, *Marie of Roumania*, p. 269.

p. 276

"she might... Theodora.": H.R.H. The Infanta Eulalia of Spain, *Courts and Countries After the War*, p. 236.

"Dressed in... delighted.": Marie, Grand Duchess of Russia, *A Princess in Exile*, pp. 64–5.

"Luckily, I... understand.": Duca, *op. cit.*, Chap. 1.

p. 277

"thrust into . . . English.": Queen Marie of Roumania, *op. cit.*, pp. 441–2.

"luminous intensity . . . simplicity": *Le Petit Journal*, Mar. 7, 1919.

"the most . . . flowers": *Le Journal*, Mar. 7, 1919.

"The atmosphere . . . me.": Queen Marie of Roumania, *op. cit.*, p. 438.

"lucky . . . femme!": RA III, 116:109.

"The cry . . . Paris,": RA III, 116:138.

pp. 277–78

"I always . . . Country.": Queen Marie of Roumania, *op. cit.*, pp. 444–57.

p. 278

"done more . . . weeks.": RA V, 3886/1919, Mar. 10, 1919, Queen Marie to Joseph Boyle.

pp. 279–80

"conversation at . . . blush.": Queen Marie of Roumania, *op. cit.*, 452–5 *passim*.

p. 280

"did not . . . friends,": Queen Marie of Roumania, "My Mission, II. At Buckingham Palace" in *Cornhill Magazine*, Nov. 1939, p. 578.

"I hope . . . peoples.": London *Times*, Mar. 10, 1919.

"heroic but . . . country.": *Ibid.*, Mar. 12, 1919.

pp. 280–81

"It was . . . be.": Queen Marie of Roumania, "My Mission, II. At Buckingham Palace," *loc. cit.*, pp. 580–4 *passim*.

p. 281

"Everything is . . . conventionalities,": RA III, 116:153.

p. 282

"with never-flagging . . . wall.": Queen Marie of Roumania, "My Mission, II. At Buckingham Palace," *loc. cit.*, p. 588.

"Irresistible Ambassador.": London *Daily Mirror*, undated (clipping from Queen Marie's diaries).

"tribulations": *Illustrated London News*, Mar. 15, 1919.

"I did . . . warmth,": Queen Marie of Roumania, "My Mission, II. At Buckingham Palace," *loc. cit.*, p. 599.

"sneaking liking . . . other": Marie, *The Story of My Life*, p. 32.

"to wipe . . . English.": RA V, 3886/1919, Mar. 10, 1919, Queen Marie to Joseph Boyle.

"All the . . . neighbor!": Queen Marie of Roumania, "My Mission, II. At Buckingham Palace," *loc. cit.*, p. 598.

". . . we want . . . words.": Duca, *op. cit.*, Chap. 1.

p. 283

"He is . . . me.": RA III, 116:153–68 *passim*.

"could not . . . tears.": Queen Marie of Roumania, "My Mission, II. At Buckingham Palace," *loc. cit.*, pp. 592–3 *passim*.

"That keen . . . everything.": Queen Marie of Roumania, "My Mission, III. Paris Again" in *Cornhill Magazine*, Dec. 1939, p. 723.

"the one . . . out,": RA III, 116:118.

"Mr. Hoover... queen,": Queen Marie of Roumania, "My Mission, I. In Paris," *loc. cit.*, p. 452.

p. 284

"The world... photographs.": Queen Marie of Roumania, "My Mission, III. Paris Again," *loc. cit.*, pp. 727–30.

"Permit me... it.": Edith Bolling Wilson, *My Memoir*, p. 258.

"a few... Religion?": Queen Marie of Roumania, "My Mission, III. Paris Again," *loc. cit.*, p. 730.

pp. 284–85

"This, Mr. President... type.": *Wilson, op. cit.*, pp. 258–60.

p. 285

"fat and... lumps.": Alden Hatch, *Edith Bolling Wilson, First Lady Extraordinary*, p. 182.

"encouraged... mortals.": Queen Marie of Roumania, "My Mission, III. Paris Again," *loc. cit.*, p. 731.

"the first... earth.": Sherman David Spector, *Rumania at the Paris Peace Conference*, p. 280.

"He spread... America!": Queen Marie of Roumania, "My Mission, III. Paris Again," *loc. cit.*, pp. 731–2.

p. 286

"suggested that... Conference.": Charles J. Vopicka, *Secrets of the Balkans*, pp. 271–2.

"very talkative,... boisterous": Queen Marie of Roumania, "My Mission, III. Paris Again," *loc. cit.*, p. 747.

"ghastly... Germany,": RA III, 117:133.

"shuddered, remembering... far.": Queen Marie of Roumania, "My Mission, III. Paris Again," *loc. cit.*, pp. 736–7.

"get thin... potentials.": RA III, 117:27.

"cannot but... good.": KSU, June 10, 1919, Queen Marie to Leile Milne.

p. 287

"put Roumania... map": Duca, *op. cit.*, Chap. 1.

"I was... face.": Queen Marie of Roumania, "My Mission, III. Paris Again," *loc. cit.*, p. 750.

Chapter 22

p. 288

"developed a... admiration": Sherman David Spector, *Rumania at the Paris Peace Conference*, p. 302, note 85. Another reason for France's support of Roumania, according to Hugh Seton-Watson (*Eastern Europe Between the Wars*), was her fear of Germany and the desire to create a *cordon sanitaire* of small states between Germany and Russia.

p. 289

"too real... yourselves.": Queen Marie of Roumania, "My Mission, III. Paris Again" in *Cornhill Magazine*, Dec. 1939, p. 739.

"little pink... menace.": Harold Nicolson, *Peacemaking 1919*, pp. 298–307 *passim*.

p. 290

"the ultimate... oxen,": HI, George Duca, *Maria Regina*, Chap. 1.

pp. 290–91

"strange tenderness... order.": R. W. Seton-Watson, A *History of the Roumanians*, pp. 544–5.

p. 291

"They have... futile.": Spector, *op. cit.*, pp. 294–5.

"played into... mobilized.": RA III, 118:184.

pp. 291–92

"The Roumanian... justification": Herbert Hoover, *Memoirs*, pp. 400–4.

p. 292

"a squad... order": Seton-Watson, *op. cit.*, p. 546, note 3.

"the enforced emigration": Edward Mandell House and Charles Seymour, eds., *What Really Happened at Paris*, p. 220.

p. 293

"American Jews... exploitation.": Stephen Bonsal, *Suitors and Suppliants*, p. 170.

"the cause... crisis": SA, Mar. 1, 1920, King Ferdinand to Prince Wilhelm.

"the ink... indignation.": Hoover, *op. cit.*, p. 404.

"as the... you.": HH, AC 88, Aug. 30, 1919, Queen Marie to Herbert Hoover.

p. 294

"the weakening... sacrifice.": Hoover, *op. cit.*, p. 404.

"Hypnotized by Bratianu": Spector, *op. cit.*, p. 199. Original phrase is "still hypnotized."

"the best... country,": RA V, 924/1919, Oct. 24, 1919, King Ferdinand to Queen Marie.

"so that... me.": RA V, 5220/1919, Barbo Stirbey to Queen Marie.

pp. 294–95

"Nando and... result.": RA III, 119:69–73v.

p. 295

"the Allies... end.": Spector, *op. cit.*, p. 219.

"the most... reign,": Seton-Watson, *op. cit.*, pp. 550–1.

p. 296

"elections in... them,": Hugh Seton-Watson, *Eastern Europe Between the Wars*, p. 200.

"For the... son,": RA III, 117:149.

pp. 296–97

"Her Majesty... country?": Jeanne Lambrino, *Mon Mari le Roi Carol*, pp. 110–19.

p. 297

"the woman... life.": RA V, 487/1919, July 25, 1919, King Carol II to Queen Marie.

"of course... circumstances,": RA III, 118:105.

Sire: In... front.: Lambrino, *op. cit.*, pp. 122–3.

p. 298
"to show . . . situation.": Spector, *op. cit.*, p. 307, note 3.
"torture . . . letters.": RA III, 118:181–205.
"fetid, demoralizing . . . duties,": RA III, 120:42–3.
"Have a . . . me,": RA V, 489/1919, Dec. 24, 1919, King Carol II to Queen Marie.
p. 299
"those who . . . overcome,": RA III, 120:17–72 *passim*.
"soon be . . . life,": Lambrino, *op. cit.*, pp. 137–8.
"make things possible": RA III, 121:51.
"I quite . . . well.": RA III, 128:54.
p. 300
"he and . . . win,": RA III, 120:63.
"torn between . . . more.": RA III, 122:133.
"a man's work": RA V, 3842/1921, Joseph Boyle to Queen Marie.
"properly thankful . . . is.": RA V, 3840/1920, Apr. 25, 1920, Joseph Boyle to Queen Marie.
"going through . . . go.": RA V, 3844/1920, June 20, 1920, Joseph Boyle to Queen Marie.
"dear big pal": RA V, 3894/1920, Nov. 2, 1920, Queen Marie to Joseph Boyle.
"it became . . . that.": RA V, 3856/1921, Oct. 28, 1921, Joseph Boyle to Queen Marie.
p. 301
"an awful . . . refugee-like.": Interview, H.R.H. Princess Ileana.
"thin and . . . trembling.": RA III, 119:2.
"I want . . . touch.": RA V, 3887/1919, Oct. 25, 1919, Queen Marie to Joseph Boyle.
"When people . . . years.": RA III, 118:226.
"Never have . . . women.": RA III, 134:41.
"God knows . . . wrong.": RA V, 3890/1920, Aug. 21, 1920, Queen Marie to Joseph Boyle.
"one of . . . dignified": RA III, 123:89–90.
pp. 301–2
"I am . . . Mama!": RA V, 3890/1920, Aug. 21, 1920, Queen Marie to Joseph Boyle.

Chapter 23

p. 303
". . . we had . . . fault.": SA, Mar. 1, 1920, King Ferdinand to Prince Wilhelm.
"God started . . . off,": Interview, H.R.H. Princess Ileana.
p. 304
"ought to . . . him!": RA V, 3893/1920, Oct. 14, 1920, Queen Marie to Joseph Boyle.

"slumbering depths... reckless": RA V, 3903/1921, Feb. 9, 1921, Queen Marie to Joseph Boyle.

"stand by... class!": RA V, 2739/1919, Dec. 13, 1919, Queen Marie to the Duchess of Coburg.

"constant and... sadness": RAV, 489/1919, Mar. 3, 1920, King Carol II to Queen Marie.

pp. 304–5

"this idea... heart": RA V, 3893/1920, Oct. 14, 1920, Queen Marie to Joseph Boyle.

p. 305

"bring Sitta... understanding": RA V, 3894/1920, Nov. 2, 1920, Queen Marie to Joseph Boyle.

"She was... life.": MM, Oct. 31, 1920, Queen Marie to Loie Fuller.

p. 306

"I feel... finished": RA III, 125:26–31.

"They were... love.": Interview, H.R.H. Princess Ileana.

"She is... love,": KSU, Apr. 14, 1921, Queen Marie to Leile Milne.

pp. 306–7

"Do not... hands,": Jeanne Lambrino, Mon Mari Le Roi Carol, pp. 147–51.

p. 307

"What she... child.": RA III, 127:10.

"every royal... kings,": RA V, 3894/1920, Nov. 2, 1920, Queen Marie to Joseph Boyle.

"I'm feeling... better.": RA V, 492/1921, Jan. 21, 1921, King Carol II to Queen Marie.

"although they... her.": RA III, 126:51.

"Not the... diadem!": RA III, 126:40.

pp. 307–8

"My jewels... jewels.": RA III, 137:51.

p. 308

"the great... ago.": RAWC, GEO. V AA43–314 (extract), Nov. 29, 1920, Queen Marie to King George V.

"I know... life.": KSU, Jan. 14, 1921, Queen Marie to Leile Milne.

"I fought... it.": RA V, 3900/1921, Mar. 3, 1921, Queen Marie to Joseph Boyle.

pp. 308–9

"my faithful... son.": RA III, 127:15.

p. 309

"a trance... revelation,": HI, George Duca, Maria Regina, Chap. 2.

"I for... 17.": RA V, 3899/1921, May 1, 1921, Queen Marie to Joseph Boyle.

"greater luxury... Court": Arthur Gould Lee, Helen, Queen Mother of Rumania, p. 88.

p. 310

"at Zizi's head.": Terence Elsberry, Marie of Roumania, p. 173.

"Everything must... Bran.": Duca, op. cit., Chap. 2.

"The whole ... owner.": Sacheverell Sitwell, *Roumanian Journey*, p. 25.
"Missy, not ... age!": Duca, *op. cit.*, Chap. 2.
p. 311
"No home ... encounter.": RA III, 129:24–78.
"Being a ... him.": RA III, 121:136.
p. 312
"It was ... slaughterhouse,": RA III, 130:19–21.

Chapter 24

p. 314
"Speak to ... better.": Princess Marthe Bibesco, *Royal Portraits*, p. 117.
"I always ... potatoes.": RA III, 131:21.
"the time ... family.": Bibesco, *op. cit.*, p. 117.
"Mother, we ... it,": Mabel Potter Daggett, *Marie of Roumania*, p. 171.
p. 315
"an outsider ... Mignon.": RA III, 131:20–4.
"a genius.": RA V, 318/1922, Feb. 8, 1922, Infanta Beatrice to Queen Marie.
"with a ... between,": RA III, 132:61.
"not even ... women.": HI, George Duca, *Maria Regina*, Chap. 2.
"I cannot ... inward,": RA III, 132:105.
"Oh, Mamma ... rest!": Bibesco, *op. cit.*, p. 120.
"still actually ... stately.": KSU, May 7, 1922, Queen Marie to Leile Milne.
p. 316
"the crowds ... Queen.": RA III, 133:47.
"Really a ... Kings,": Duca, *op. cit.*, Chap. 2.
"Everything was ... brides.": Bibesco, *op. cit.*, p. 120.
"imperial stones ... Queen.": Duca, *op. cit.*, Chap. 2. The last of the Obrenovich dynasty, King Alexander and his wife, Queen Draga, were butchered by conspirators who broke into the palace on the night of May 29, 1903, and threw their mutilated bodies out of the window.
"She absolutely ... appearance,": KSU, Feb. 24, 1923, Queen Marie to Leile Milne.
p. 317
"She seems ... one.": RA III, 135:120.
"a peace ... potency": Charles H. Sherrill, "Are Kings Useful?" in *Review of Reviews*, May 1923, p. 509.
"not marry ... apply.": Daggett, *op. cit.*, p. 172.
pp. 317–18
"I know ... Balkans!": Duca, *op. cit.*, Chap. 2.
p. 318
"I am ... life.": Daggett, *op. cit.*, p. 297.
"cost a ... place": RA III, 135:75–81.
p. 319
"I want ... medieval.": Daggett, *op. cit.*, pp. 294–5.

"the chief... land.": Duca, *op. cit.*, Chap. 2.

"I carry... getup,": RA III, 136:10–28.

"King Ferdinand's... moving.": Duca, *op. cit.*, Chap. 2.

p. 320

"full of... moment.": HI, July 28, 1975, Marthe Bibesco to George Duca.

"You are... with.": Terence Elsberry, *Marie of Roumania*, p. 180.

pp. 320–321

"The moment... expression?": KE, Aug. 8, 1929, Queen Marie to Lavinia Small.

p. 321

"... it was... other.": HI, Sept. 4, 1934, Queen Marie to Lavinia Small.

"a magnificent... night.": Interview, George Duca.

Chapter 25

p. 323

"unmentionable ladies.": RA III, 136:41.

"singing both... duet.": RA III, 156:86.

"I am... obstinate.": RA III, 152:33.

pp. 323–24

"a worthy follower.": RA III, 140:82.

p. 324

"at the... later.": Arthur Gould Lee, *Helen, Queen Mother of Roumania*, p. 102.

"in no hurry": H–L, Jan. 15, 1924, Queen Marie to Princess Alexandra.

"There come... wives!": Interview, H.R.H. Princess Ileana.

"Carol & Co.": RA III, 138:116.

"A happier... desires.": KSU, Feb. 24, 1923, Queen Marie to Leile Milne.

p. 325

"She was... woman?": Alice-Leone Moats, *Lupescu*, pp. 34–9.

p. 326

"I want... Boyle,": Toronto *Star*, Nov. 1, 1926.

"he had... off,": RA III, 139:4.

"a cross... d'Artagnans.": Kim Beattie, *Brother, Here's a Man!* p. 309.

"romantic career... character.": London *Times*, Apr. 17, 1923.

p. 327

"one of... have!": RA III, 144:6–10 *passim*.

"Lisabetha is... life,": RA III, 148:162.

"Now neither... jewels,": RA III, 145:62.

"You were... supportable.": Interview, H.R.H. Princess Ileana.

"sincere friends... France.": *Le Figaro*, Apr. 5, 1924.

p. 328

"I am... tempted": RA III, 147:164–8.

pp. 328–29

"officialities and... monumental": RA III, 148:8–84 *passim*.

p. 329

"ridiculous... headdress.": Kenneth Rose, *King George* V, p. 283.

diplomatic cue: King Ferdinand and Queen Marie's itinerary originally included visits to Rome and Madrid. The trip had to be changed at the last moment when Benito Mussolini, angered by Roumania's ties with Yugoslavia, arranged with Primo de Rivera of Spain to withdraw the invitations to both those countries. Under these conditions the Roumanian monarchs could not afford to run into the King and Queen of Italy in England.

p. 330

"We were... bluebells.": RA III, 148:125.

"In the... concise,": HI, George Duca, *Maria Regina*, Chap. 2.

"Perhaps I... charge.": RA III, 119:98.

"... it simply... me.": RA III, 126:33–4.

"the outpourings... home,": *Time*, Aug. 4, 1924.

p. 331

"... fidelity does... lenient?": New York *World*, June 15, 1925.

"the sensation... circles,": New York *World*, May 28, 1925.

"loom over... indiscretion.": RA III, 152:141–3 *passim*.

"H.M. was... pleasant,": RA III, 151:125.

"like a... governess,": Interview, George Duca.

pp. 331–32

"He is... right.": RA III, 151:119–20.

p. 332

"green spot... earnings.": Duca, *op. cit.*, Chap. 2.

p. 333

"a changed... all,": RA III, 154:7–144 *passim*.

p. 334

"utterly broken... together.": RAWC, GEO. V, AA43–235, Jan. 5, 1926, Queen Marie to King George V.

"Carol has... mind.": RA III, 154:108.

There he met Elena Lupescu: Prince Nicolas claimed that Mme. Lupescu left for Paris with Bratianu's consent twenty-four hours after Carol's departure and that, in allowing Mme. Lupescu to go, the Prime Minister "showed... his hand... certain there would be no return." (H.R.H. Nicolas, Prince of Roumania, unpublished memoirs, p. 19.)

"Carol has... reason.": RA III, 154:143–59.

p. 335

"You will... coffin.": RA III, 155:6.

"often found... trace.": Duca, *op. cit.*, Chap. 2.

"desperate... him.": RA III, 154:163.

"You are... intervene.": Lee, *op. cit.*, pp. 654–5.

"inhuman agony... son.": RA III, 154:162.

"irrevocable renunciation... Family.": Duca, *op. cit.*, Chap. 2.

p. 336

"This Is... Stirbey.": *New York Times*, Feb. 14, 1926.

"a hero... martyr": RA III, 155:22.

"Many people . . . God,": RA III, 155:74v. (The article from the newspaper was inserted in Queen Marie's diary.)

"I have . . . myself.": *New York Times*, Jan. 6, 1926.

"everything except . . . myself.": *New York Times*, Jan. 4, 1926.

pp. 336–37

"I have . . . country.": Moats, *op. cit.*, pp. 73–4.

p. 337

"better at . . . religion,": RA III, 155:82.

"soul surgeon,": *New York Times*, Oct. 16, 1926.

"spreading his . . . all.": RA III, 155:87.

p. 338

"The country . . . ever.": *New York Times*, May 23, 1926.

Chapter 26

pp. 339–40

"One of . . . Maria!": HI, George Duca, *Maria Regina*, Chap. 3.

p. 340

"I have . . . faith.": RA III, 120:19.

"mighty organization . . . ways.": RA III, 119:9.

"the White Lion.": RA III, 159:16.

"Mr. Hill . . . them.": RA III, 117:73–4.

p. 341

"broken-hearted": Duca, *op. cit.*, Chap. 3.

"every parting . . . anguish,": RA III, 133:41.

"Be happy! . . . it.": RA V, 5244/1926, Sept. 3, 1926, Barbo Stirbey to Queen Marie.

"dangerous enthusiasms.": Duca, *op. cit.*, Chap. 3.

"Is the . . . is?": *Literary Digest*, quoting the New York *World*, "Why the Queen of Roumania Is Here," Oct. 30, 1926, p. 10.

p. 342

"He was . . . far,": RA III, 158:19.

"I depart . . . it.": *New York Times*, Oct. 4, 1926.

RUMANIA'S QUEEN . . . " . . . journey.": *New York Times*, Oct. 6, 1926.

p. 343

"dread and . . . flowers,": RA III, 158:48–65 *passim*.

"It was . . . salon.": *New York Times*, Oct. 13, 1926.

p. 344

"where to . . . do.": Interview, H.R.H. Princess Ileana.

"Today's demonstration . . . doubts.": *New York Times*, Oct. 13, 1926.

"American trousseau,": *New York Times*, Oct. 12, 1926.

"drawn considerable . . . advance": *New York Times*, Oct. 16, 1926.

p. 345

"now on . . . wardrobe!": *New York Times*, Oct. 15, 1926.

"I have . . . unfounded.": *New York Times*, Oct. 16, 1926.

"I was . . . streets.": Duca, *op. cit.*, Chap. 3.

pp. 345–46

"Proceed, Your . . . indeed,": *New York* magazine, "The First of the Celebrity Mayors," Vol. 2, No. 45, Nov. 10, 1969, p. 41.

p. 346

"saved the . . . yes,": Grover Whelan, *Mr. New York,* p. 98.

"probably the . . . Queen.": *New York Times*, Oct. 19, 1926.

p. 347

"the President . . . to.": RA III, 158:92–3.

"I have . . . Coolidge.": *New York Times*, Oct. 20, 1926.

"The President . . . me.": RA III, 158:93.

p. 348

"According to . . . camera.": New York *World, Impressions of America* ("The Home of Washington") by H.M. The Queen of Roumania.

pp. 348–49

"anger and . . . modest": Ishbel Ross, *Grace Coolidge and Her Era*, pp. 196–8.

p. 349

"The ceremony . . . *first.*": RA III, 158:95–6.

"The fourth . . . palace,": *New York Times*, Oct. 18, 1926.

p. 350

"We had . . . night,": Constance Lily Morris, *On Tour with Queen Marie*, p. 43.

"royal training . . . collapse.": Duca, *op. cit.*, Chap. 3.

"Cold or . . . unseen.": Morris, *op. cit.*, p. 70.

"I was . . . wear.": Duca, *op. cit.*, Chap. 3.

". . . often have . . . ablutions.": New York *World, Impressions of America* ("The Bankers' Lunch") by H.M. The Queen of Roumania.

pp. 350–51

"fearful competition . . . nightmare" (*cauchemar* in the original), RA III, 158:113–44.

p. 351

"one of . . . rails.": *New York Times*, Oct. 21, 1926.

"real Americans,": *New York Times*, Oct. 27, 1926.

p. 352

"free and . . . them.": *New York Times*, Oct. 30, 1926.

"I don't . . . had.": *New York Times*, Oct. 27, 1926.

"An American . . . woman.": *New York Times*, Nov. 2, 1926.

p. 353

"nervous and . . . admiration.": *New York Times*, Nov. 4, 1926.

"It was . . . triumph.": Harold Norman Denny, "Mr. Babbitt Draws a Queen" in *The Forum*, Vol. 77, Mar. 1927, p. 352.

pp. 353–54

"With two . . . melée.": Morris, *op. cit.*, p. 133.

p. 354

"quasi-censorship,": *New York Times*, Nov. 10, 1926.

"more and . . . anxious.": RA III, 159:77.

"A weary... Queen": *New York Times*, Nov. 20, 1926.
"Papa better... worry,": RA III, 159:106.
p. 355
"This time... Mayors.": *New York Times*, Nov. 21, 1926.
"a public... defrauded.": Denny, *op. cit.*, p. 353.

Chapter 27

p. 359
"I am... dear.": RAWC, GEO. V, AA43 (extract), Feb. 24, 1927, Queen Marie to King George V.
p. 360
"What would... Roumania.": *New York Times*, Nov. 21, 1926.
"astonished... face,": RA III, 159:139–47.
p. 361
"face the... joke!": RA III, 160:34–114 *passim*.
"... as if... owned,": RA III, 159:158.
pp. 361–62
"Spoilt, accustomed... lies.": RA III, 160:67–99.
p. 362
"There is... contempt.": Terence Elsberry, *Marie of Romania*, pp. 214–15. (Author's note: Although I have not been able to find the source of these letters, Marie refers to them in her diary and the wording is typical of her style.)
p. 363
"You can... revolutions.": RA V, 3722/1927, Feb. 23, 1927, Waldorf Astor to Queen Marie.
p. 364
"She of... smile,": RA III, 162:27.
"absolute need... one,": RA III, 161:164.
pp. 364–66
"Barbo and... faith—": RA III, 162:43–111 *passim*.
p. 366
"white lady": Alice-Leone Moats, *Lupescu*, p. 89.
"with despair... night.": RA V, 505/1927, Aug. 27, 1927, King Carol II to Queen Marie.
"broke": RA V, 503/1927, July 27, 1927, King Carol II to Queen Marie.
"Nobody felt... strongest.": RA V, 504/1927, Aug. 20, 1927, King Carol II to Queen Marie.
"Vive le Roi!": *New York Times*, July 25, 1927.
"in a... on.": HI, George Duca, *Maria Regina*, Chap. 4.
"I never... well.": RA III, 162:114.
p. 367
"slowly picking... everybody.": KE, Oct. 19, 1927, Queen Marie to Lavinia Small.
"so often": Duca, *op. cit.*, Chap. 4.

"The truth . . . commands.": *New York Times*, July 25, 1927.

"All good . . . bad.": RA III, 162:51.

"Outside things . . . procedure.": KE, Feb. 25, 1928, Queen Marie to Lavinia Small.

"fallen materially . . . age.": RA III, 172:100.

p. 368

"Sitta has . . . father,": H–L, Nov. 20, 1928, Queen Marie to Princess Alexandra.

"How good . . . hour.": *New York Times*, Nov. 25, 1927.

"first time . . . country.": RA III, 164:16.

"What's holding . . . Carol.": RA V, 5250/1927, Dec. 10, 1927, Barbo Stirbey to Queen Marie.

"The tiniest . . . grateful,": RA III, 163:115.

p. 369

"Oh Mama . . . us.": RA V, 508/1928, Sept. 19, 1928, King Carol II to Queen Marie.

"Now he . . . country.": RA V, 362/1927, Jan. 4, 1927, Infanta Beatrice to Queen Marie.

"human document . . . emotion": *The Sunday News*, Oct. 9, 1927.

"There are . . . enemies.": *ibid.*, Oct. 23, 1927.

p. 370

"unwillingly . . . home.": RA III, 166:67v. The quotations from Carol's appeal are from copies of an article from a London paper inserted in the Queen's diary for May 1928.

"I did . . . lie.": London *Daily Mirror*, May 5, 1928.

"incredible folly . . . country.": RA III, 166:68–79. The quotations from the *Times* are from a copy of the editorial inserted in the Queen's diary for May 1928.

"My time . . . you.": RA V, 514/1928, undated (May–June 1928), King Carol II to Queen Marie.

p. 371

"Bessarabia is . . . incapacity.": RA III, 169:74.

p. 372

"self-styled guardian . . . morality,": Stephen Fischer-Galati, *Twentieth Century Rumania*, p. 43.

"Personally I . . . Roumania,": RA III, 164:57.

"I would . . . state.": RA III, 172:75–83v.

"The country . . . conflicts.": Duca, *op. cit.*, Chap. 5.

p. 373

"The greatest . . . him.": RA III, 170:100–3.

p. 374

". . . being royal . . . world.": RA III, 174:91.

"even in . . . Court.": RA V, 5270/1930, Apr. 9, 1930, Barbo Stirbey to Queen Marie.

"I had . . . stranger.": RA III, 174:116.

"real danger . . . him,": RA III, 166:114.

p. 375

"treachery in . . . all,": RA III, 174:171.

Chapter 28

p. 377

"day that . . . forever.": John Gunther, *Inside Europe*, p. 385.

"Immediately . . . Father.": HI, George Duca, *Maria Regina*, Chap. 5.

pp. 377–78

"the victim . . . fulfilled.": *New York Times*, June 9, 1930.

p. 378

"In the . . . him!": RA III, 174:171–2 *passim*.

"They were . . . hands,": RA III, 176:5–14 *passim*.

p. 379

"pale . . . eyes.": H–L, June 15, 1930, Simone (Simky) Lahovary to Princess Alexandra.

"Carol was . . . dumb.": RA III, 176:6–19.

"It costs . . . Majesty.": RA V, 5273/1930, June 10, 1930, Barbo Stirbey to Queen Marie.

"best policy . . . advice.": RA III, 176:22–64.

"the indispensable . . . *noire*": RA III, 177:101–2.

"without flinching.": RA III, 178:84.

". . . the creature's . . . money.": RA V, 5702/1931, Mar. 19, 1931, Queen Marie to Roxo Weingartner.

pp. 379–80

"marvelous spying . . . through.": RA III, 178:29–158 *passim*.

p. 380

"I cannot . . . *cannot*.": RA III, 176:65.

"in a . . . arms.": H–L, June 15, 1930, Simone (Simky) Lahovary to Princess Alexandra.

"downright immoral . . . completely.": RA III, 177:6.

"dreadful scene": RA III, 176:150.

p. 381

"I wish . . . Calvary,": Arthur Gould Lee, *Helen, Queen Mother of Roumania*, pp. 144–5.

"I felt . . . loneliness,": RA III, 176:158.

pp. 381–82

"I am . . . up.": Duca, *op. cit.*, Chap. 5.

p. 382

"dropped Mama . . . Lupescu.": Interview, H.R.H. Princess Ileana.

"Ma Souveraine . . . life.": Countess R. G. Waldeck, *Athene Palace*, p. 208.

"alarmingly magnificent.": A. L. Easterman, *King Carol, Hitler, and Lupescu*, p. 89.

p. 383

"Carol really . . . ignore,": RA III, 184:86.

"dingy place... shop.": Waldeck, *op. cit.*, p. 205.
"deep and... us.": RA III, 177:3–106.
p. 384
"he knew... shame!": RA III, 178:14–87 *passim.*
"so entirely... forsaken,": RA III, 179:24.
"my excellent... country.": RA III, 177:102–43.
"launching... existence.": RA III, 178:158.
p. 385
"Dear Barbo... great.": RA III, 179:76.
"propaganda against him.": RA III, 178:10.
"aching thorn": Duca, *op. cit.*, Chap. 5.
"We found... it.": Interview, H.R.H. Princess Ileana.
"So there... hands.": Duca, *op. cit.*, Chap. 5.
"I have... Roumania.": RA V, 531/1931, Apr. 6, 1931, King Carol II to Queen Marie.
p. 386
"furious... declared": RA III, 179:108.
pp. 386–87
"It was... could.": RA III, 180:61–109 *passim.*
p. 387
"It all... collapse.": Duca, *op. cit.*, Chap. 5.
"very run-down... finish.": RA V, 1967/1931, Aug. 13, 1931, Infante Alfonso to Queen Marie.

Chapter 29

p. 389
"Even the... to.": RA III, 181:70.
"Put me... *accompli,*": RA III, 182:23.
"Living as... him.": RA III, 184:132.
"It is... King,": IR, May 16, 1932, Queen Marie to Prince Nicolas.
pp. 389–90
"a hardhearted... upholder.": HI, George Duca, *Maria Regina*, Chap. 5.
p. 390
"plotting together... him.": RA III, 183:54–5.
"incredibly costumed... weaken,": Duca, *op. cit.*, Chap. 5.
"too proud... failure.": IR, H.R.H. Nicolas, Prince of Roumania, unpublished memoirs, p. 43B.
"I have... blood?": RAWC, GEO. V, AA43–403, July 23, 1932, Queen Marie to King George V.
pp. 390–91
"What a... next.": RAWC, GEO. V, AA43–404, July 27, 1932, King George V to Queen Marie.
p. 391
"Ileana and... behave,": KE, Aug. 29, 1932, Queen Marie to Lavinia Small.
"help... heartlessness.": *Daily Mail*, Oct. 4, 1932.

"This after... head,": RA III, 184:167.
p. 392
"hated his... must.": RA III, 185:92.
"has had... humanity.": HI, June 19, 1933, Queen Marie to Lavinia Small.
"which no... mention,": Duca, *op. cit.*, Chap. 5.
pp. 392–93
"My voice... grows.": HI, Aug. 24, 1933, Queen Marie to Lavinia Small.
p. 393
"old-fashioned reaction... ideologies.": Duca, *op. cit.*, Chap. 5.
p. 394
"I try... hideousness.": RA III, 122:85.
"Decidedly today... grief,": RA III, 188:5.
"not much... on": RA III, 185:20.
p. 395
"I cannot... shoulders.": Duca, *op. cit.*, Chap. 5.
p. 396
"complete calmness... Jews.": *New York Times*, Dec. 30, 1933.
"I am... son!": RA III, 189:52.
"Perhaps we... in.": HI, Jan. 14, 1934, Queen Marie to George Duca.

Chapter 30

p. 397
"mongoloid monkey.": John Gunther, *Inside Europe*, p. 387.
p. 398
"... in spite... true.": HI, Apr. 2, 1934, Queen Marie to Lavinia Small.
"We are... family.": KSU, July 18, 1934, Queen Marie to "an American friend." In 1934 Queen Marie began corresponding with a young American man whom she never met. He allowed her letters to be published (A *Biographer's Notebook*, by Hector Bolitho), provided his name never be used. These extracts are from the typescript of the letters in the Queen Marie Collection of Kent State University.
"keep his... destroyers.": RA III, 197:163.
"Will I... rest?": KSU, Aug. 31, 1934, Queen Marie to an American friend.
p. 399
"What a... abroad.": KSU, Aug. 7, 1934, Queen Marie to an American friend.
"fearful brutality,": RA III, 191:5.
"as good... convincing.": HI, Nov. 6, 1933, Queen Marie to George Duca.
"Even an... together.": KSU, undated (Sept.–Oct. 1934), Queen Marie to an American friend.
"female counterpart... woman.": Mary M. Colum, "The Queen and Mr. Wells" in *The Forum*, p. 86.
pp. 399–400
"George has... do!": KSU, Jan. 8, 1935, Queen Marie to an American friend.

p. 400

"little Elizabeth... family.": RA III, 191:137.

"We were... trembling,": RA III, 192:4–13.

pp. 400–401

"Mignon's royal... ordeals,": HI, George Duca, *Maria Regina*, Chap. 5.

p. 401

"could not... angry.": RA III, 192:24–128 *passim*.

p. 402

"It is... happy,": RA V, 5289/1934, Nov. 26, 1934, Barbo Stirbey to Queen Marie.

"efface the... intensity": RA V, 5299/1936, Oct. 6, 1936, Barbo Stirbey to Queen Marie.

"She is... kind,": HI, Feb. 11, 1935, Queen Marie to Lavinia Small.

"he is... china.": RA III, 195:38–9.

"helping to... dynasty.": RA III, 190:8.

"not too... profit.": RA III, 196:20.

"whilst Mignon... pitied,": RA III, 197:26.

pp. 402–3

"Some readers... overwhelming.": *Illustrated London News*, Apr. 6, 1935, p. 582.

p. 403

"After all... cow.": Interview, H.R.H. Princess Ileana.

"I feel... ducklings!": Duca, *op. cit.*, Chap. 5.

"something comforting... mother.": KSU, May 25, 1935, Queen Marie to an American friend.

"It was... others.": HI, May 30, 1935, Queen Marie to Lavinia Small.

"The difficulties... *d'être*.": KSU, May 25, 1935, Queen Marie to an American friend.

p. 404

"to dance... State.": HI, undated (summer 1935), Queen Marie to Lavinia Small.

"The whole... roof,": RA III, 195:98–106.

"had become... lemon.": Interview, H.R.H. Princess Ileana.

"less impetuous... apprehension.": KSU, Jan. 8, 1936, Queen Marie to an American friend.

pp. 404–5

"painful moment... broken.": RA III, 196:29–62.

p. 405

"widowed queens... told.": Duca, *op. cit.*, Chap. 5.

"leading... hand.": HI, Jan. 18, 1936, Queen Marie to Lavinia Small.

"It is... me—": RAWC, GEO. V, CC45–1003, Jan. 24, 1936, Queen Marie to Queen Mary.

"I had... inches,": HI, Mar. 6, 1936, Queen Marie to Lavinia Small.

p. 406

"always hated... alone.": Duca, *op. cit.*, Chap. 5.

"It is... volcano!": RA III, 197:67–8.

"the sad... love,": HI, May 30, 1936, Queen Marie to Lavinia Small.

p. 407

"his latest... there,": RA III, 199:124–6.

"I hardly... way.": RAWC, GEO. V, CC45–1064, Dec. 19, 1936, Queen Marie to Queen Mary.

"Personally I... blessed?": Duca, *op. cit.*, Chap. 6.

Chapter 31

pp. 408–9

"Every mortal... one!": HI, George Duca, *Maria Regina*, Chap. 6.

p. 410

"Both my... them,": RA III, 200:101.

"never had... will": KSU, May 6, 1960, Prince Nicolas to Hector Bolitho.

"If Carol... anxiety": RA III, 200:99.

p. 411

"*cured... life.*": RA III, 201:62.

"more or... me.": RA III, 202:4.

"dazzled... spirits.": H–L, Nov. 10, 1937, Christine Galatzi to Princess Ileana.

p. 412

"sober... mellow.": H–L, Dec. 29, 1929, Queen Marie to Princess Alexandra.

"hardly believe... indefinitely.": RA III, 202:29–41.

p. 413

"... my very... courage.": KSU, Feb. 14, 1938, Queen Marie to an American friend.

pp. 413–14

"coalition government... Napoleon.": RA III, 202:48–63.

p. 414

"what a... her.": Interview, H.R.H. Princess Ileana.

"We both... ever.": RA III, 202:103.

"I cannot... you.": RU (Waldorf Astor papers), July 14, 1938, Queen Marie to Nancy Astor.

"Friedel... mother.": RA III, 202:96–7.

p. 415

"do something... properly.": Interview, H.R.H. Princess Ileana.

"... at last... Zwiedy,": RA III, 202:119.

"everything within... her.": Interview, H.R.H. Princess Ileana.

"... she's been... stupid.": Terence Elsberry, *Marie of Romania*, p. 279. Verified in interviews with H.R.H. Princess Ileana.

pp. 415–16

"for the... beneficent.": RA III, 202:123–48.

p. 416

"My thoughts... Ilymmily.": RA V, 5300/1937, July 20, 1937, Barbo Stirbey to Queen Marie.

"so much... safe....": Duca, *op. cit.*, Chap. 6. The author assumes this letter was written to Prince Stirbey. In his unpublished manuscript, *Maria*

Regina, Duca says only that it was addressed to "one of her oldest and most trusted friends."

p. 417

"I think...down.": Interview, H.R.H. Princess Ileana.

"a just...monarch": *Time*, July 25, 1938, p. 18.

p. 418

"A moving...streets.": *Le Moment*, No. 1021, July 20, 1938, p. 3.

"She slipped...beyond.": KSU, Aug. 3, 1938, Christine Galatzi to Queen Marie's American friend.

"my favourite...red.": Hector Bolitho, A *Biographer's Notebook*, p. 63.

p. 419

"bowed...son.": *New York Times*, July 25, 1938.

p. 420

"When you...sorrow.": KSU, Marie, Queen of Roumania, "À *Mon Pays et à Mon Peuple*."

Epilogue

p. 422

"great personal beauty": London *Times*, July 19, 1938.

"No public...idolatry.": *New York Times*, July 19, 1938.

"Mother died...funeral.": Interview, Prince Mircea Hohenzollern.

p. 423

"I came...King.": Alice-Leone Moats, *Lupescu*, p. 216.

p. 424

"ninety per...Roumania": Ghita Ionescu, *Communism in Rumania*, p. 92

Selected Bibliography

In addition to books and periodicals, the following archives, personal collections, and libraries were consulted:

Archives and repositories: The Coburg Archives; The Hoover Institution on War, Revolution, and Peace: letters and papers from the collection of George Duca and his unpublished manuscript *Maria Regina*; The Kent State University Library: letters and papers from the Queen Marie Collection; Maryhill Museum; The Reading University Library: letters from the files of the Second Viscount Astor and Lady Astor; The Roumanian Archives (Arhivele Statului Bucuresti, Romania fond Casa Regala, Regina Maria Memoires, Regina Maria Correspondence); The Sigmaringen Archives (Staatsarchiv Sigmaringen).

Personal Collections: letters from the collection of the Hon. Lady Rachel Bowes-Lyon; letters and papers of Eleanor Harris; letters from the collection of H.S.H. the Prince of Hohenlohe-Langenburg; letters and papers from the collection of H.R.H. Princess Ileana of Roumania; letters from the Estate of Lee Keedick;

letters and papers from the collection of John N. Rosekrans, Jr.

Libraries: Bibliothèque Nationale; The British Museum; The British Newspaper Library; Harvard University Libraries; The Library of Congress; The London Library; The New York Public Library; The New York Public Library Newspaper Annex; The New York Society Library; Yale University Library.

Of the titles and authors listed below, several were particularly important in the preparation of this book. They are: R. W. Seton-Watson's definitive survey, *A History of the Roumanians*; Elizabeth Longford's *Queen Victoria*, on which I based the characterization of the Queen; Egon Corti's *The Downfall of Three Dynasties*, consulted for the portrait of the Russian court; Anne-Marie Calli-machi's *Yesterday Was Mine*, a firsthand portrayal of aristocratic Roumanian life before 1914; Alice-Leone Moats's *Lupescu*, a picture of the daily life of King Carol II; William Rodney's outstanding biography, *Joe Boyle*; Dr. E. J. Dillon's *The Inside Story of the Peace Conference*, a study of the dilemma of the small countries at Versailles; Sherman David Spector's *Rumania at the Paris Peace Conference: A Study in the Diplomacy of Ioan I. C. Bratianu*, a minute dis-cussion of its topic; and Terence Elsberry's *Marie of Romania*, an earlier bi-ography of the Queen which pointed the way for this one. Without the work of these authors, my job would have been much more difficult.

Alexander, Grand Duke of Russia. *Always a Grand Duke*. New York: Farrar and Rinehart, Inc., 1933.

———. *Once a Grand Duke*. Garden City, N.Y.: Garden City Publishing Co., Inc., 1932.

Alice, Princess of Great Britain. *For My Grandchildren*: Some Reminiscences of H.R.H. Princess Alice, Countess of Athlone. Cleveland: World Publishing Co., 1967.

Almedingen, E. M. *The Emperor Alexander II*. London: The Bodley Head, 1962.

———. *An Unbroken Unity*: A Memoir of Grand Duchess Serge of Russia, 1864–1918. London: The Bodley Head, 1964.

Alsop, Susan Mary. *Lady Sackville*: A Biography. Garden City, N.Y.: Doubleday, 1978.

Argyll, John George Edward Henry Douglas Sutherland Campbell, Ninth Duke of. (The Marquis of Lorne). *V.R.I. Queen Victoria, Her Life and Empire*. New York & London: Harper & Brothers, 1901.

Armstrong, Hamilton Fish. *The New Balkans*. New York: Harper & Brothers, 1926.

———. *Peace and Counter-Peace*: From Wilson to Hitler. New York: Harper & Row, 1971.

———. *Where the East Begins*. New York: Harper & Brothers, 1929.

Baedeker, Karl. *Austria–Hungary, including Dalmatia and Bosnia*: Handbook for Travellers. Leipzig: Karl Baedeker; New York: Charles Scribner's Sons, 1905.

Bagger, Eugene S. *Eminent Europeans:* Studies in Continental Reality. New York: G. P. Putnam's Sons, 1922.

Balfour, Neil, and Sally Mackay. *Paul of Yugoslavia, Britain's Maligned Friend.* London: Hamish Hamilton, 1980.

Balsan, Consuelo Vanderbilt. *The Glitter and the Gold.* New York: Harper and Brothers, 1952.

Barbusse, Henri. *I Saw It Myself.* Trans. Brian Rhys. New York: E. P. Dutton & Co., 1928.

Battiscombe, Georgina. *Queen Alexandra.* Boston: Houghton Mifflin, 1964.

Beal, Erica. *Royal Cavalcade.* London: Paul & Co., 1939.

Beattie, Kim. *Brother, Here's a Man!* The Saga of Klondike Boyle. New York: Macmillan, 1940.

Bell, T. P. *Our Nuptial Ode and Welcome:* In Honour of the Marriage of H.R.H. the Duke of Edinburgh with H.I.H. the Grand Duchess Marie of Russia, 23 January, 1874. London: Hamilton, Adams & Co., 1874.

Benger, G. *Rumania in 1900.* Trans. A. H. Keane. London: Asher and Co., 1900.

Bennett, Daphne. *Vicky, Princess Royal of England and German Empress.* New York: St. Martin's Press, 1971.

Benson, E. F. *Queen Victoria's Daughters.* New York: D. Appleton–Century Co., Inc., 1938.

Bercovici, Konrad. *That Royal Lover.* New York: Brewer and Warren, 1931.

Berkson, Seymour. *Their Majesties!* New York: Stackpole Sons, 1938.

Bernardy, Francoise de. *Albert and Victoria.* Trans. Ralph Manheim. New York: Harcourt, Brace and Co., 1953.

Bibesco, Marthe Lucie (Lahovary), Princess G. V. *Royal Portraits.* New York: D. Appleton and Co., 1928.

————. *Some Royalties and a Prime Minister.* New York: D. Appleton and Co., 1930.

Blanch, Lesley. *Pavilions of the Heart:* The Four Walls of Love. New York: G. P. Putnam's Sons, 1974.

————. *Under a Lilac-Bleeding Star:* Travels and Travelers. New York: Atheneum, 1964.

Bocca, Geoffrey. *Kings Without Thrones. The Uneasy Heads:* A Report on European Monarchy. London: Weidenfeld and Nicolson, 1959.

Bolitho, Hector. *A Biographer's Notebook.* New York: Macmillan, 1950.

————, ed. *Further Letters of Queen Victoria from the Archives of the House of Brandenburg–Prussia.* Trans. Mrs. J. Pudney and Lord Sudley. London: Thornton Butterworth, Ltd., 1938.

————, ed. *Letters of Queen Victoria: From the Archives of the House of Brandenburg–Prussia.* Trans. Mrs. J. Pudney and Lord Sudley. New Haven: Yale University Press, 1938.

————. *Roumania Under King Carol.* London: Eyre and Spottiswoode, 1939.

Bonsal, Stephen. *Suitors and Suppliants:* The Little Nations at Versailles.

New York: Prentice-Hall, 1946.

Brook-Sheperd, Gordon. *Uncle of Europe:* The Social and Diplomatic Life of Edward VII. New York: Harcourt Brace Jovanovich, 1976.

Buchan, John, ed. *Bulgaria and Romania:* The Nations of To-Day, A New History of the World. London: Waverly Book Co., Ltd., n.d.

Buchanan, Meriel. *Queen Victoria's Relations.* London: Cassell, 1954.

Buckle, George Earl, ed. *The Letters of Queen Victoria:* A Selection from Her Majesty's Correspondence and Journal between the Years 1862 and 1885. Second Series. Vol. II: 1870–1878. London: John Murray, 1926.

––––––, ed. *The Letters of Queen Victoria:* A Selection from Her Majesty's Correspondence and Journal between the Years 1886 and 1901. Third Series. Vol. II: 1891–1895. London: John Murray, 1931.

Bulow, Prince von. *Memoirs 1903–1909.* Vol. II. Trans. F. A. Voight. London: Putnam, 1931.

Burgoyne, Elizabeth. *Carmen Sylva:* Queen and Woman. London: Thornton Butterworth, 1940.

Buxhoeveden, Sophia, Baroness. *The Life and Tragedy of Alexandra Feodorovna, Empress of Russia:* A Biography. New York: Longmans, Green and Co., 1928.

Callimachi, Anne-Marie, Princess. *Yesterday Was Mine.* London: Falcon Press, 1952.

Carol the Second and the British Press: A Scrap-book of Articles Written on the Occasion of the Royal State Visit to England of the Roumanian Sovereign in November 1938. London: E. T. Heron and Co., 1939.

Cartland, Barbara. *The Scandalous Life of King Carol.* London: Frederick Muller, 1957.

Catalogue of The Collection of Porcelain, Bronzes, Arms, Japanese Lacquer and other Specimens of Oriental Art, formed by H.M.S. The Duke of Edinburgh, K.G., during His Cruise in H.M.S. 'Galatea.' London: William Clowes and Sons, 1875.

Clarke, Elizabeth Dodge Huntington. *The Joy of Service:* Memoirs of Elizabeth Dodge Huntington Clarke. New York: National Board of the Young Women's Christian Association, 1979.

Clary, Prince. *A European Past.* Trans. Ewald Osers. New York: St. Martin's Press, 1978.

The Collection of European China, Marbles, Bronzes, Pictures, Water-colours, Drawings, and other Objects of Art and Vertu at Clarence House, St. James. London: William Clowes and Sons, 1875.

Constantine, King of Greece. *A King's Private Letters.* London: Eveleigh Nash & Grayson, Ltd., 1925.

Cornwallis-West, Mrs. George. *The Reminiscences of Lady Randolph Churchill.* New York: The Century Co., 1908.

Corti, Egon, Count. *The Downfall of Three Dynasties.* Trans. Marie Sieveking and Ian F. D. Morrow. 1934; rpt. New York: Books for Libraries Press, 1970.

––––––. *The English Empress.* London: Cassell, 1957.

Cowles, Virginia. *The Astors.* New York: Alfred A. Knopf, 1979.

————. *The Romanovs.* New York: Harper & Row, 1971.

————. *The Russian Dagger.* New York: Harper & Row, 1969.

Cox, J. Charles. *The Marriage of the Duke of Edinburgh:* The Cost of the Royal Household, Royal Annuities and Crown Lands. London: E. Truelove, 1873.

Cunliffe, Marcus. *The Age of Expansion: 1848–1917.* Springfield, Mass.: G. and C. Merriam Co., 1873.

Cyril, H.I.H. the Grand Duke. *My Life in Russia's Service—Then and Now.* Ed. H.S.H. Prince Leonid Lieven. London: Selwyn and Blount, 1939.

Czernin, Ottokar, Count. *In the World War.* London: Cassell, 1919.

Daggett, Mabel Potter. *Marie of Roumania:* The Intimate Story of the Radiant Queen. New York: George H. Doran, 1926.

Daisy, Princess of Pless. *Better Left Unsaid.* New York: E. P. Dutton, 1931.

Dewhurst, Jack. *Royal Confinements:* A Gynaecological History of Britain's Royal Family. New York: St. Martin's Press, 1980.

Diesbach, Ghislain de. *Secrets of the Gotha.* Trans. Margaret Crosland. New York: Meredith Press, 1967.

Dillon, E. J. *The Inside Story of the Peace Conference.* New York: Harper and Brothers, 1920.

Duff, David. *Hessian Tapestry.* London: Frederick Muller, 1967.

————. *Victoria and Albert.* New York: Taplinger Publishing, 1972.

Easterman, A. L. *King Carol, Hitler, and Lupescu.* London: Victor Gollancz, Ltd., 1942.

Edinburgh, K.G. Duke of. *A Guide to the Works of Art and Science Collected by Captain His Royal Highness The Duke of Edinburgh, K.G., during his Five-Years Cruise Round the World in H.M.S. 'Galatea'* (1867–1871). London: John Strangeways, 1872.

Elsberry, Terence. *Marie of Romania:* The Intimate Life of a Twentieth Century Queen. New York: St. Martin's, 1972.

Eulalia, H.R.H. Infanta of Spain. *Court Life from Within.* London: Cassell and Company, Ltd., 1915.

————. *Courts and Countries After the War.* New York: Dodd, Mead and Co., 1925.

Fenyvesi, Charles. *Splendor in Exile:* The Ex-Majesties of Europe. Washington, D.C.: New Republic Books, 1970.

Fischer-Galati, Stephen. *Romania.* New York: Frederick A. Prager, 1956.

————. *Twentieth Century Rumania.* New York: Columbia University Press, 1970.

Forbes, Nevill, Arnold J. Toynbee, D. Mitrany, and D. G. Hogarth. *The Balkans:* A History of Bulgaria, Serbia, Greece, Rumania, Turkey. London: Oxford, 1915.

Forter, Norman L., and Demeter B. Rostovsky. *The Roumanian Handbook.* London: Simpkin Marshall, Ltd., 1931.

Fox, Frank. *The Balkan Peninsula.* London: A. & C. Black, Ltd., 1915.

Fulford, Roger, ed. *Dearest Child: Letters between Queen Victoria and the Princess Royal, 1858–1861.* London: Evans Brothers, Ltd., 1964.

————, ed. *Dearest Mama: Letters Between Queen Victoria and the Crown Princess of Prussia, 1861–1864.* New York: Holt, Rinehart and Winston, 1969.

————. *Hanover to Windsor.* New York: The Macmillan Company, 1960.

————, ed. *Your Dear Letter: Private Correspondence of Queen Victoria and the Crown Princess of Prussia 1865–1871.* London: Evans Brothers Ltd., 1971.

Fuller, Loie. *Fifteen Years of a Dancer's Life* with Some Account of Her Distinguished Friends. n.d.; rpt. New York: Dance Horizons, n.d.

Gernsheim, Helmut and Alison. *Victoria R.* New York: G. P. Putnam's Sons, 1959.

Gilliard, Pierre. *Thirteen Years at the Russian Court:* A Personal Record of the Last Years and Death of the Czar Nicholas II and His Family. Trans. F. Appleby Holt. New York: George Doran, 1921.

Giurescu, Constantin C. *Transylvania in the History of Romania:* An Historical Outline. London: Garnstone Press, n.d.

Gordon, Mrs. Will. *Roumania Yesterday and Today.* With two chapters and an introduction by H.M. the Queen of Roumania. London: John Lane, The Bodley Head, 1919.

Gore, John. *King George* V: A Personal Memoir. London: John Murray, 1941.

Graham, Stephen. *Alexander of Jugoslavia:* The Strong Man of the Balkans. London: Cassell and Co., 1938.

Guedalla, Philip. *The Queen and Mrs. Gladstone.* Garden City, N.Y.: Doubleday, Doran and Co., 1934.

Gunther, John. *Inside Europe.* New York: Harper and Brothers, 1938.

A *Handbook of Roumania.* Naval Staff Intelligence Department, I.D. 1204, London: 1918.

Hardinge, Arthur, Sir. A *Diplomatist in Europe.* London: Jonathan Cape, n.d.

Hatch, Alden. *Edith Bolling Wilson:* First Lady Extraordinary. New York: Dodd, Mead and Co., 1961.

Heathcote, Dudley. *My Wanderings in the Balkans.* London: Hutchinson & Co., n.d.

Hill, George A., Captain. *Go Spy the Land:* Being the Adventures of I.K.8 of the British Secret Service. London: Cassell and Co., 1932.

Hoover, Herbert. *The Memoirs of Herbert Hoover:* Years of Adventure 1874–1920. New York: Macmillan Co., 1952.

Hoppé, E. O. *In Gipsy Camp and Royal Palace:* Wanderings in Rumania. New York: Charles Scribner's Sons, 1924.

Hough, Richard, ed. *Advice to a Grand-Daughter: Letters from Queen Victoria to Princess Victoria of Hesse.* London: Heinemann, 1975.

House, Edward Mandell, and Charles Seymour, eds. *What Really Happened at Paris:* The Story of the Peace Conference, 1918–1919; by American Delegates. New York: Scribner's Sons, 1921.

Hurst, A. Herscovici. *Roumania and Great Britain.* London: Hodder & Stoughton, 1916.

Ileana, Princess of Roumania and Archduchess of Austria. *I Live Again.* New

York: Rinehart and Co., 1952.

Ionescu, Ghita. *Communism in Rumania 1944–1962*. London: Oxford University Press, 1964.

James, Robert Rhodes, ed. *Chips:* The Diaries of Sir Henry Channon. London: Weidenfeld and Nicolson, 1967.

Johnston, Robert H. *Tradition Versus Revolution:* Russia and the Balkans in 1917. East European Monographs, No. XXVIII. Boulder: East European Quarterly; dist. New York: Columbia University Press, 1977.

Jonescu, Take. *Some Personal Impressions*. London: Nisbet and Co., Ltd., 1919.

Judd, Denis. *Eclipse of Kings:* European Monarchies in the Twentieth Century. London: Macdonald and Jane's, 1976.

Kedward, H. R. *Fascism in Western Europe 1900–1945*. New York: New York University Press, 1971.

Kennard, Dorothy Katherine (Barclay) Lady. *A Roumanian Diary, 1915, 1916, 1917*. New York: Dodd, Mead and Co., 1917.

Kirke, Dorothea. *Domestic Life in Rumania*. London: John Lane, 1916.

Lambrino, Jeanne. *Mon Marie Le Roi Carol*. Paris: Calmann-Levy, 1950.

Lee, Arthur Gould. *Crown Against Sickle:* The Story of King Michael of Rumania. London: Hutchinson and Co., Ltd., n.d.

———, ed. *Empress Frederick Writes to Sophie, Her Daughter, Crown Princess and later Queen of the Hellenes: Letters 1889–1901*. London: Faber and Faber Ltd., 1955.

———. *Helen, Queen Mother of Rumania:* Princess of Greece and Denmark. An Authorized Biography. London: Faber and Faber, 1956.

Lloyd George, David. *War Memoirs*. 2 Vols. London: Ivor Nicholson and Watson, 1933.

Longford, Elizabeth, ed. *Louisa, Lady in Waiting:* The Personal Diaries and Albums of Louisa, Lady in Waiting to Queen Victoria and Queen Alexandra. London: Jonathan Cape, 1979.

———. *Queen Victoria:* Born to Succeed. New York: Harper & Row, 1964.

Loti, Pierre (pseudonym), (Viaud, Julien). *Carmen Sylva and Sketches from the Orient*. Trans. Fred Rothwell. New York: Macmillan, 1912.

Magnus, Leonard A. *Roumania's Cause and Ideals*. London: Kegan Paul, Trench, Trubner and Co., Ltd., 1917.

Magnus, Philip. *King Edward the Seventh*. London: John Murray, 1964.

Malcolm, Sir Ian. *Trodden Ways, 1895–1930*. London: Macmillan & Co., Ltd., 1930.

Mallet, Victor, ed. *Life with Queen Victoria: Marie Mallet's Letters from Court 1887–1901*. Boston: Houghton Mifflin, 1968.

Manning, Olivia. *The Balkan Trilogy*. New York: Penguin, 1981.

Marie, Grand Duchess of Russia. *Education of a Princess:* A Memoir. Trans. under supervision of Russell Lord. New York: Viking, 1931.

———. *A Princess in Exile*. New York: Viking, 1932.

———. *Things I Remember*. Trans. under supervision of Russell Lord. London: Cassell and Co., 1931.

Marie, Queen of Roumania. A *Christmas Tale*. Privately Printed for friends by Aldus Printers. New York, 1957.

———. *The Country That I Love*: An Exile's Memories. London: n.p., 1925.

———. *Crowned Queens*. London: Heath Cranton Ltd., 1929.

———. *The Dreamer of Dreams*. London: Hodder & Stoughton, 1915.

———. *The Magic Doll of Roumania*. New York: Frederick A. Stokes Co., 1929.

———. *Masks*. New York: E. P. Dutton & Co., Inc., 1937.

———. *My Country*. London: Hodder & Stoughton, 1916.

———. *Ordeal: The Story of My Life*. New York. Charles Scribner's Sons, 1935.

———. *The Queen of Rumania's Fairy Book*. New York: Frederick A. Stokes Co., 1926.

———. *The Story of My Life*. New York: Charles Scribner's Sons, 1934.

———. *The Story of Naughty Kildeen*. New York: Harcourt, Brace and Co., 1926.

———. *Why? A Story of Great Longing*. Stockholm: Svenska Tryckeriaktie-bolaget (private printing), 1923.

Marie-Louise, Princess. *My Memories of Six Reigns*. New York: E. P. Dutton and Co., 1957.

Martineau, Mrs. Philip. *Roumania and Her Rulers*. London: Stanley Paul and Co., Ltd., 1927.

Massie, Robert K. *Nicholas and Alexandra*. New York: Atheneum, 1967.

Mavrogordato, John. *Modern Greece*: A Chronicle and a Survey 1800–1931. London: Macmillan & Co., Ltd., 1931.

McKinley, Brian. *Royal Tour*. Adelaide: Rigby Limited, 1970.

Miller, William. *The Balkans*: Roumania, Bulgaria, Serbia, and Montenegro. 1896; rpt. London: T. Fisher Unwin, 1923.

Moats, Alice-Leone. *Lupescu*. New York: Henry Holt and Co., 1955.

Morris, Charles, and Murat Halstead. *Life and Reign of Queen Victoria*. Chicago: International Publishing Society, 1901.

Morris, Constance Lily. *On Tour with Queen Marie*. New York: Robert M. McBride and Co., 1927.

Morris, Ira N. *Heritage from My Father*. New York: private printing, 1947.

Negulesco, Gogu. *Rumania's Sacrifice*: Her Past, Present, and Future. Trans. Mrs. C. de S. Wainright. New York: The Century Co., 1918.

Nicholas, H.R.H. Prince of Greece (Prince of Denmark). *My Fifty Years*. London: Hutchinson and Co., Ltd., 1926 (?).

Nicolson, Harold. *King George the Fifth*: His Life and Reign. London: Constable and Co., 1952.

———. *Peacemaking*. New York: Grosset and Dunlap–Universal Library, 1965.

O'Connor, Harvey. *The Astors*. New York: Alfred A. Knopf, 1941.

Oprea, I. M. *Nicholae Titulescu's Diplomatic Activity*. Bucharest: Publishing House of the Academy of the Socialist Republic of Romania, 1968.

Packard, Edward H. "Queen Marie's Visit." In *New England Essays*. Cambridge, Mass.: n.p., 1926.

Paget, Walpurga Ehrengarde Helena (von Hohenthal), Lady. *Embassies of Other Days and Further Recollections*. 2 vols. New York: George H. Doran, 1923.

Pantazzi, Ethel Greening. *Roumania in Light and Shadow*. Toronto: The Ryerson Press, n.d.

Parkinson, Maude. *Twenty Years in Roumania*. London: George Allen and Unwin, 1921.

Parrot, Cecil. *The Tightrope*. London: Faber and Faber, 1975.

Patmore, Derek. *Invitation to Roumania*. London: Macmillan & Co., Ltd., 1939.

Peter II, King of Yugoslavia. *A King's Heritage*. New York: G. P. Putnam's Sons, 1954.

Politics and Political Parties in Roumania. London: International Reference Library, 1936.

Ponsonby, Arthur. *Henry Ponsonby, Queen Victoria's Private Secretary*: His Life from His Letters. New York: Macmillan, 1943.

————, ed. *Letters of the Empress Frederick*. New York: Macmillan, 1930.

Pope-Hennessy, James. *Queen Mary: 1867–1953*. New York: Knopf, 1960.

Pridham, Francis, (Vice-Admiral), Sir. *Close of a Dynasty*. London: Allan Wingate, 1956.

Queux, William Le, ed. *The Secret Life of the Ex-Tsaritza*: Amazing Disclosures by her Maid-of-Honor and Confidante the Baroness Zeneide Tzankoff. London: Odhams, Ltd., 1918.

Radziwill, Catherine, Princess. *The Intimate Life of the Last Tsarina*. London: Cassell and Co., 1929.

————. *Royal Marriage Market of Europe*. New York: Funk and Wagnall's, 1915.

————, (Count Paul Vassili). *Secrets of Dethroned Royalty*. London: John Lane, The Bodley Head, 1920.

————, (Catherine Kolb-Danvin). *Sovereigns and Statesmen of Europe*. London: Cassell and Co., 1915.

————, (Catherine Danvin). *Those I Remember*. London: Cassell and Co., 1924.

Rattigan, Frank. *Diversions of a Diplomat*. London: Chapman and Hall, Ltd., 1924.

Remak, Joachim, ed. *The First World War*: Causes, Conduct, Consequences. New York: John Wiley and Sons, Inc., 1971.

————. *The Origins of World War I, 1871–1914*. Hindsdale, Illinois: The Dryden Press, 1967.

Roberts, M. Elizabeth. *Outlines of Balkan History*. London: Arthur H. Stockwell, Ltd., n.d.

Rodney, William. *Joe Boyle*: King of the Klondike. Toronto: McGraw-Hill Ryerson, Ltd., 1974.

Roosevelt, Blanche. *Elisabeth of Roumania*: A Study. London: Chapman and Hall, Ltd., 1891.

Rose, Kenneth. *King George* V. London: Weidenfeld and Nicolson, 1983.

Ross, Ishbel. *Grace Coolidge and Her Era.* New York: Dodd, Mead and Co., 1962.

Roucek, Joseph S. *Contemporary Roumania and Her Problems*: A Study in Modern Nationalism. London: Humphrey Milford-Oxford University Press, 1932.

Rudin, Harry R. *Armistice 1918.* New Haven: Yale University Press, 1944.

Rumania, Confidential Handbook. The Historical Section of the Foreign Service, No. 21, London, 1918.

Saint Aubyn, Giles. *Edward VII*: Prince and King. New York: Atheneum, 1979.

Saint-Aulaire, Auguste Félix Charles de Beaupoil, Comte de. *Confession d'un Vieux Diplomate.* Paris: Flammarion, 1953.

Seton-Watson, Hugh. *Eastern Europe Between the Wars 1918–1941.* London: Cambridge University Press, 1945.

Seton-Watson, R. W. A *History of the Roumanians*: From Roman Times to the Completion of Unity. Cambridge: The University Press, 1934.

———. *The Little Entente.* The Garden City Press Ltd., *Contemporary Review*, Dec., 1927.

———. *Roumania and the Great War.* London: Constable and Co., Ltd., 1915.

———. *Sarajevo*: A Study in the Origins of the Great War. London: Hutchinson and Co., Ltd., n.d.

———. "Some Aspects of Dynastic Policy in the Balkans." In *Transactions of the Royal Historical Society*, Vol. XXXII. London: Offices of the Royal Historical Society, 1950.

———. *Transylvania*: A Key-Problem. (essay) London: The Classic Press (private printing), 1943.

Seymour, Charles. *The Intimate Papers of Colonel House.* New York: Houghton Mifflin, 1926.

Sitwell, Sacheverell. *Roumanian Journey.* London: B. T. Batsford, Ltd., 1938.

Spector, Sherman David. *Rumania at the Paris Peace Conference*: A Study in the Diplomacy of Ioan I. C. Bratianu. New York: Bookman Associates, 1962; rpt. Ann Arbor, Michigan: University Microfilms International, 1980.

Spiro, Edward. *From Battenberg to Mountbatten.* London: Arthur Barker, Ltd., 1966.

Stephenson, John, ed. A *Royal Correspondence: Letters of King Edward VII and King George V to Admiral Sir Henry F. Stephenson.* London: Macmillan and Co., Ltd., 1938.

Sulzberger, C. L. A *Long Row of Candles*: Memoirs and Diaries. New York: Macmillan and Co., 1969.

Sykes, Christopher. *Nancy*: The Life of Lady Astor. William Collins Sons, 1972; rpt. London: Panther-Granada, 1979.

Taylor, A. J. P. *The Last of Old Europe*: A Grand Tour. New York: Quadrangle–The New York Times Book Co., 1976.

———. *The Struggle for Mastery in Europe 1848–1918.* Clarendon Press, 1954; rpt. London: Oxford University Press, 1971.

Taylor, Edmond, *The Fall of the Dynasties:* The Collapse of the Old Order 1905–1922. Garden City, New York: Doubleday, 1963.

Tennyson, Alfred. "A Welcome to Her Royal Highness Marie Alexandrovna, Duchess of Edinburgh". London: Henry S. King and Co., 1874.

Tilea, R. V. *The Last Century of Roumanian History.* Cambridge: n.p., 1943.

Tisdall, E. E. P. *Marie Fedorovna:* Empress of Russia. New York: The John Day Co., 1958.

———. *Queen Victoria's Private Life.* London: Jarrolds, 1961.

———. *Royal Destiny:* The Royal Hellenic Cousins. London and New York: S. Paul, 1955.

Tuchman, Barbara W. *The Guns of August.* Macmillan, 1962; rpt. New York: Bantam Books, 1976.

———. *The Proud Tower:* A Portrait of the World Before the War 1890–1914. Macmillan, 1966; rpt. New York: Bantam Books, 1976.

Vacaresco, Helene. *Kings and Queens I Have Known.* New York: Harper & Brothers, 1904.

Vacha, Robert, ed. and trans. *The Kaiser's Daughter:* Memoirs of H.R.H. Viktoria Louise, H.R.H. Duchess of Brunswick and Luneburg, Princess of Prussia. Englewood Cliffs, N.J.: Prentice-Hall, 1977.

Von der Hoven, Helena, Baroness. *King Carol of Romania.* The Authorized Biography. London: Hutchinson & Co., Ltd., 1940.

Vopicka, Charles J. *Secrets of the Balkans:* Seven Years of a Diplomat's Life in the Storm Center of Europe. Chicago: Rand McNally & Co., 1921.

Vorres, Ian. *The Last Grand Duchess:* Her Imperial Highness Grand Duchess Olga Alexandrovna. London: Hutchinson, 1964.

Waldeck, R. G. *Athene Palace.* Garden City, N.Y.: Blue Ribbon Books, 1942.

Walker, Mrs. *Untrodden Paths in Roumania.* London: Chapman & Hall, 1888.

West, Rebecca. *Black Lamb and Grey Falcon:* A Journey through Yugoslavia. 2 vols. New York: Viking Press, 1941.

Whelan, Grover. *Mr. New York:* The Autobiography of Grover Whelan. New York: Putnam, 1955.

White, Leigh. *The Long Balkan Night.* New York: C. Scribner's Sons, 1944.

Whitman, Sidney. *Reminiscences of the King of Roumania.* (edited from the original) New York: Harper & Brothers, 1899.

Whittle, Tyler. *The Last Kaiser:* A Biography of Wilhelm II, German Emperor and King of Prussia. New York: Times Books–Quadrangle–New York Times Book Co., 1977.

Wilson, Edith Bolling. *My Memoir.* New York: Bobbs-Merrill Co., 1938.

Windsor, Dean of, and Hector Bolitho, eds. *Later Letters of Lady Augusta Stanley 1864–1876.* London: Jonathan Cape, 1929.

Youssoupoff, Felix, Prince. *Lost Splendour.* Trans. Ann Green and Nicolas Katkoff. London: Jonathan Cape, 1953.

MAGAZINES AND JOURNALS

Allen, Charles R., Jr. "Nazi War Criminals Among Us." rprt. from *Jewish Currents*, Jan., Feb., Mar. 1963.

American Review of Reviews. "Queen Marie of Roumania." 74:536–7 (Nov. 1926).

Bent, Silas. "The Passing of King Ferdinand of Roumania." *Current History,* 26:974–7 (Sept. 1927).

Bercovici, Konrad. "Royal Intrigue in Roumania." *Outlook and Independent,* 157:526–8+, 558–61+, 592–4+ (April 15, 22, and 29, 1931). 158:16–18+, 50–2+, 80–2+, 114–17, 142–4+ (May 3, 13, 20 and 27, 1931).

Bibesco, Marthe, Princess. "Ferdinand of Rumania, King and Martyr." *Saturday Evening Post,* Vol. 200, No. 9:6–7+ (Aug. 27, 1927).

———. "The Madonna of Rumania." *North American Review,* 226:436–9 (Oct. 1928).

———. "A Roumanian Louis XIV: Brancovan." Trans. Arthur Stanley Riggs. Forward to the issue devoted to Roumanian art and architecture by Marie, Queen of Roumania. *Art and Archeology,* 21:2–3 (Jan. 1926).

Chambe, René. "Marie de Roumanie." *Revue des Deux Mondes,* 46:850–6 (Aug. 15, 1938).

Clark, Charles Upson. "A Queen Comes Visiting." *The Independent,* Vol. 117, No. 3985:438–40 (Oct. 16, 1926).

Collins, Frederick L. "What's Happened to Royalty?" *Woman's Home Companion,* 50:17–18 (May 1923).

Colum, Mary M. "The Queen and Mr. Wells." *Forum,* Vol. 93, No. 2:86–7 (Feb. 1935).

Commeianu, G. "A New Explanation of Roumania's Defeat." (rpt. from *Gazette de Lausanne,* Apr. 7, 1917). *The New Europe,* Vol. III, No. 28:64–4 (Apr. 26, 1917).

Current History (Magazine of *The New York Times*). "Roumania's Intervention." Vol. V, No. 1:57–69.

———. "Ruler of the Balkan Nation Whose Declaration of War on the Side of the Entente Was the Chief Military Event of that Month." Vol. V, No. 1 (Oct. 1916).

Current Opinion. "Queen Marie of Roumania, Whose Ambition Is to Make Her Daughter Princess of Wales." 76:772–3 (June 1924).

———. "The Queen Who Will Pay Us a Visit Soon." 67:90–1 (Aug. 1919).

Denny, Harold Norman. "Mr. Babbitt Draws a Queen." *The Forum,* 77:344–53 (Mar. 1927).

Ellis, William T. "Rumania's Soldier Queen." *Century Magazine,* 96:330–8 (Jul. 1918).

Fischer, Henry W. "The Roumanian Marriage." *Harper's Weekly,* 37:43–4 (Jan. 14, 1893).

Fleming, Thomas J. "The First of the Celebrity Mayors." *New York,* Vol. 2, No. 45:41 (Nov. 10, 1969).

Gibbons, Herbert Adams. "Romance and Reality in Rumania: An Illuminating Story That the Queen Forgot to Tell." *Century Magazine,* 115:527–34 (Mar. 1928).

Hoover, Irwin H. (Ike). "A Queen and Lindy." Ed. Wesley Scout. *Saturday Evening Post,* 207:10–11+ (Aug. 11, 1934).

Iliescu, General. "Explanation of 'A New Explanation of Roumania's Defeat.'" (rpt. of an interview in *Le Matin*, Apr. 3, 1917). *The New Europe*, Vol. II, No. 26:407–9 (Apr. 26, 1917).

L'Illustration. No. 4156:406–11 (Oct. 28, 1922).

Jonescu, Take. "Count Czernin." (rpt. from *La Roumanie*, Dec. 1916). *The New Europe*, Vol. I, No. 11:344–7 (Dec. 28, 1916).

———. "The Greatest Danger." *The New Europe*, Vol. III, No. 31:129–31 (May 17, 1917).

——— (Bessie). "Roumania's Choice." *The New Europe*, Vol. III, No. 39:398–403 (Jul. 12, 1917).

Krabroff, Irina. "Royal Gardens in the Balkans." *Country Life*, 72:76 (Jul. 1937).

Lauzanne, Stephane. "Marie, Queen of Roumania." *Delineator*, 99:7 + (Oct. 1921).

Lengyel, Emil. "The Situation That Made Carol King of Rumania." *Current History*, 32:1085–9 (Sept. 1930).

Literary Digest. "Marie, Queen of Conquered Roumania, Defies the Kaiser." 57:56–9 (June 8, 1918).

———. "Poison or Pie: Queen Marie's Sudden Illness Leads to Speculative Stories." 123:14–15 (Mar. 27, 1937).

———. "A Queen's Among Us Taking Notes." 91:34–40 (Nov. 6, 1926).

———. "Romance, Tragedy and a Boy King." 94:36–42 (Aug. 6, 1927).

———. "Roumania's Melancholy Marie." 95:21 (Dec. 3, 1927).

———. "When Some Daughters Stole a Princess." 62:50–3 (Aug. 9, 1919).

———. "Why the Queen of Roumania Is Here." 91:10–11 (Oct. 30, 1926).

Lupu, Nicolae. "Roumania Irredenta." *The New Europe*, Vol. V, No. 61:274–8 (Dec. 13, 1917).

Marie, Queen of Roumania. "The Fallen Czar." *Woman's Home Companion*, 47:7–8 (Jul. 1920).

———. "Lulaloo—A Fairy Tale Told by a Queen." *Good Housekeeping*, 80:20–3 + (Mar. 1925).

———. "Modern Fashions." *The Living Age*, 324:297–300 (Feb. 7, 1925).

———. "My Mission." *Cornhill Magazine*, Vol. 160, No. 958: 433–57, 578–603, 722–52 (Oct., Nov., and Dec. 1939).

———. "A Queen in a Crisis: 'It Is No Sinecure to Be the Queen of a Country.'" *Ladies' Home Journal*, 35:8 (Dec. 1918).

———. "A Resurrected Army." *Living Age*, 310:131–4 (Jul. 16, 1921).

———. "Some Memories of the Russian Court." *Living Age*, 303:157–60 (Oct. 4, 1919).

———. "The Vanished Tsarina." *Living Age*, 303:16–8 (Oct. 4, 1919).

Merz, Charles. "Marie of Rumania." *The New Republic*, 48:237–9 (Oct. 20, 1926).

Minnigerode, Fitzhugh L. "The King Who Cannot Be a Boy." *New York Times Magazine*, Vol. 78, No. 26090:1–2 (June 30, 1929).

Minnigerode, Patricia. "Queen Marie Transforms a Tiny Domain." *The New York Times Magazine*, Vol. 78, No. 26132:7 + (Aug. 11, 1929).

New York Times Magazine. "Rumania's Boy King Romps in His Kingdom of Toys." Vol. 77, No. 25558:12 (Jan. 15, 1928).

Ogg, Frederic A. "Anti-Semitism in Rumania." *Current History,* 32:1085–9 (Sept. 1930).

———. "The Unsolved Question of the Roumanian Succession." *Current History,* 26:978–80 (Sept. 1927).

Outlook. "Queen Marie Returns Home." 144:455 (Dec. 8, 1926).

Phillips, J. "King Carol of Rumania." *Life,* 8:72–82 (Feb. 19, 1940).

Popescu, Aureliu Ion. "Rumania's Political Unrest." *Current History,* 28:572–9 (Jul. 1928).

Remusat, "Le Mariage du Duc d'Edinbourg." *Revue des Études Historiques,* pp. 464–90 (Oct.–Dec. 1935).

Rohn, Alice. "Queen Santa Claus." *Good Housekeeping,* 69:15–6 (Dec. 1919).

Seton-Watson, R. W. "The Roumanians of Hungary." *The New Europe,* Vol. I, No. 1:20–7 (Oct. 19, 1916).

Severus, Alexander. "The Building of Greater Roumania." *The New Europe,* Vol. IV, No. 41:45–51 (Jul. 26, 1917).

Sherrill, Charles H. "Are Kings Useful?" *American Review of Reviews,* Vol. 67, No. 5:507–9 (May 1923).

The Slavonic and East European Review. University of London. 74:252–5 (Dec. 1951); 75:331–7+ (June 1952).

Stoddard, Lothrop. "The Balkan Flux." *The Saturday Evening Post,* 197:14+ (Jul. 12, 1924).

Time Magazine. "Marie Windsor Hohenzollern." Vol. IV, No. 5:cover + (Aug. 4, 1924).

———. "Rumania: Stalin and Marie." 32:17–18 (Aug. 1, 1938).

Vacaresco, Helene. "Life in Roumania." *The Contemporary Review,* 80:645–56 (Jul.–Dec. 1901).

———. "La Reine Marie de Roumanie." *Revue de Paris,* Vol. 45, No. 16:78–9 (Aug. 15, 1938).

Val, Adio. "A Royal Interior Decorator." *Arts and Decoration,* 18:11 (Jan. 1923).

Whitehead, O. Z. "Queen Marie of Rumania Renowned First Royal Believer." *Baha'i News,* March 1973, pp. 2–6.

Wilson, P. W. "Marie Comes as Her Royal Self." *New York Times Magazine,* Vol. 76, No. 25082:1+ (Sept. 26, 1926).

World's Work. "On the Flanks of the Bulgar." 33:25–9 (Nov. 1916).

In addition to the above periodicals, the following newspapers were consulted frequently:

London: *The Daily Mail, The Daily Mirror, The Illustrated London News, The Times, The Times Literary Supplement.*

New York: *The Times, The World.*

Paris: *Le Figaro, Le Matin, Le Populaire.*

THE ENGLISH ROYAL FAMILY
FROM MARIE'S POINT OF VIEW

VICTORIA
"Grandmama Queen"
(1819-1901)
Queen of England

=== MARRIED ===

ALBERT
"Grandpapa"
(1819-1861)

He died before Marie was born. Prince of Saxe-Coburg-Gotha, later Prince Consort of England. His older brother, Great-uncle Ernst, was the Duke of Saxe-Coburg-Gotha whose title and lands passed to Marie's father in 1893.

VICTORIA
"Aunt Vicky"
(1840-1901)

Princess Royal of England. She married Friedrich, Crown Prince of Prussia, became Crown Princess, later Empress of Germany. Her eldest son was the pompous Kaiser Wilhelm II. Her eldest daughter was the ubiquitous "Cousin Charly" (Charlotte, Princess of Saxe-Meiningen). Another daughter was Sophie, Queen of Greece, whose daughter, Helen, married Marie's son Carol, and whose son, King George II of Greece, married Marie's daughter Elisabetha.

EDWARD
"Uncle Bertie"
(1841-1910)

Prince of Wales, later King Edward VII. He married Alexandra, Princess of Denmark, the beautiful "Aunt Alix." Their second son, George, who became King George V, wanted to marry Marie.

ALICE
(1843-1878)

She married Louis, Grand Duke of Hesse, and died when Marie was only three. Their three children. Their eldest son, Ernst, married Marie's sister Ducky. Their youngest daughter, Alexandra, married Nicholas II, the last Tsar of Russia.

ALFRED
"Papa"
(1844-1900)

Duke of Edinburgh, later Duke of Saxe-Coburg-Gotha. He married Marie, Grand Duchess of Russia, only daughter of Tsar Alexander II.

five other children

ALFRED
(1874-1899)

He should have inherited the duchies of Saxe-Coburg-Gotha, but he died in his twenties, predeceasing his father.

MARIE
"Missy"
(1875-1938)

She married Ferdinand, Crown Prince of Roumania, became Crown Princess, later Queen of Roumania.

VICTORIA MELITA
"Ducky"
(1876-1936)

She married Ernst, Grand Duke of Hesse, and divorced him to marry Kirill, Grand Duke of Russia.

ALEXANDRA
"Sister Sandra"
(1878-1942)

She married Ernst, Prince of Hohenlohe-Langenburg.

BEATRICE
"Baby Bee"
(1883-1966)

She married Alfonso, Infante of Spain.

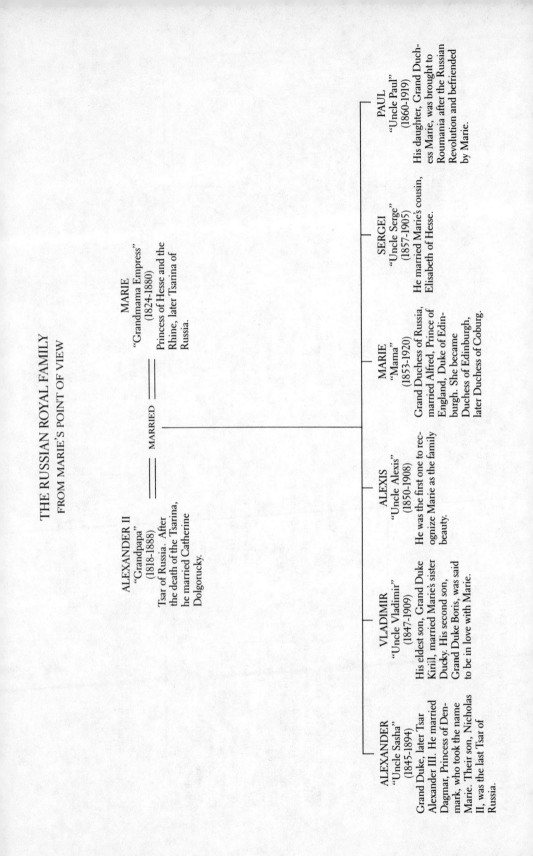

THE RUSSIAN ROYAL FAMILY

FROM MARIE'S POINT OF VIEW

ALEXANDER II
"Grandpapa"
(1818-1888)
Tsar of Russia. After
the death of the Tsarina,
he married Catherine
Dolgorucky.

═══ MARRIED ═══

MARIE
"Grandmama Empress"
(1824-1880)
Princess of Hesse and the
Rhine, later Tsarina of
Russia.

ALEXANDER
"Uncle Sasha"
(1845-1894)
Grand Duke, later Tsar
Alexander III. He married
Dagmar, Princess of Den-
mark, who took the name
Marie. Their son, Nicholas
II, was the last Tsar of
Russia.

VLADIMIR
"Uncle Vladimir"
(1847-1909)
His eldest son, Grand Duke
Kirill, married Marie's sister
Ducky. His second son,
Grand Duke Boris, was said
to be in love with Marie.

ALEXIS
"Uncle Alexis"
(1850-1908)
He was the first one to recognize Marie as the family
beauty.

MARIE
"Mama"
(1853-1920)
Grand Duchess of Russia,
married Alfred, Prince of
England, Duke of Edin-
burgh. She became
Duchess of Edinburgh,
later Duchess of Coburg.

SERGEI
"Uncle Serge"
(1857-1905)
He married Marie's cousin,
Elisabeth of Hesse.

PAUL
"Uncle Paul"
(1860-1919)
His daughter, Grand Duch-
ess Marie, was brought to
Roumania after the Russian
Revolution and befriended
by Marie.

THE ROUMANIAN ROYAL FAMILY

KARL ANTON
Furst* of Hohenzollern-Sigmaringen
(1811-1885)

He married Josephine, Princess of Baden.

three other children

KARL
"der Onkel"
(1839-1914)

Prince of Hohenzollern-Sigmaringen. Became Prince of Roumania, later King Carol I of Roumania. He married Elisabeth, Princess of Wied, who became Queen Elisabeth I of Roumania ("Aunt Elisabeth," "Carmen Sylva" 1853-1916). Their only child died at three.

LEOPOLD
"Papa"
(1835-1905)

Furst* of Hohenzollern-Sigmaringen. Marie's father-in-law.

MARIA II
Queen of Portugal
(1819-1853)

She married Ferdinand, Prince of Saxe-Coburg-Gotha.

ANTONIA
"Mama"
(1845-1913)

Infanta of Portugal. She married Leopold, Prince of Hohenzollern-Sigmaringen. Marie's mother-in-law.

four other children

=== MARRIED ===

FERDINAND
"Nando"
(1865-1927)

Prince of Hohenzollern-Sigmaringen. Became Crown Prince of Roumania, later King Ferdinand I of Roumania.

WILHELM
"Fat William"
(1864-1927)

Furst* of Hohenzollern-Sigmaringen. He refused the Roumanian throne.

one other son

MARIE
"Missy"
(1875-1938)
Princess of Edinburgh.

=== MARRIED ===

CAROL
(1893-1953)

Crown Prince of Roumania, later King Carol II of Roumania. He married three times. His son by Crown Princess Helen, King Michael I, was the last King of Roumania.

ELISABETHA
"Lisabetha"
(1894-1956)

Princess of Roumania. She married George, Crown Prince of Greece, who became King George II of Greece. She divorced him and had no children.

MIGNON (MARIE)
(1900-1961)

Princess of Roumania. She married King Alexander II of Yugoslavia and bore him three sons.

NICOLAS
"Nicky"
(1903-1977)

Prince of Roumania. He married twice, but had no children.

ILEANA
(1909-   )

Princess of Roumania. She married twice. Her first husband, Anton, Archduke of Austria, was the father of her six children.

MIRCEA
(1913-1916)

Prince of Roumania. He died during World War I.

*Furst: the eldest son and head of the family.

PHOTO CREDITS

Arhivele Statului Bucuresti, 12, 50, 51, 52, 54, 55, 60, 63, 66.
The Viscount Astor, 27, 33.
Kim Beattie, 42.
Bettmann, 2, 57, 61, 64.
Bettmann/BBC Hulton, 3, 44, 45, 62.
The Hon. Lady Bowes-Lyon, 32.
The British Library, 75.
George I. Duca, 70.
Reproduced by gracious permission of Her Majesty Queen Elizabeth II,
    1, 4, 5, 6, 7, 8, 10, 11, 15, 17, 26, 28, 29, 30.
Mme. Nadeje Flondor, 34.
Victor Gollancz, 69.
Harper's and Bros., 67.
The Prince and Princess of Hohenlohe-Langenburg, 31, 40, 56, 73.
H.R.H. Princess Ileana, 20.
The Illustrated London News Picture Library, 38, 39, 53.
The Mansell Collection, 9, 14, 16, 22, 23.
H.R.H. Princess Margaret of Hesse and the Rhine, 21, 65.
Mary Evans Picture Library, 36, 41, 46, 48.
Gebr. Metz, Tubingen, 18, 19.
Scribner's, 13, 24, 25, 35, 37, 74.
Stanford University, 68.
Time, Inc., 59.
Wide World, 58, 71, 72.

   The author also wishes to thank Vincent Virga, photographic editor, for his skilled and imaginative work; and Frances Dimond, Curator of the Photograph Collection, the Royal Archives, Windsor Castle, for her help in locating pictures.

Index

(*continued from page 4*)

Le Journal, March 7, 1919.

Le Matin, March 6, 1919.

Le Petit Journal, March 7, 1919.

Literary Digest, 1918, 1926.

Macmillan and Company, Ltd., for *Letters of the Empress Frederick*, edited by the Right Honourable Sir Frederick Ponsonby, copyright 1929.

Robert H. McBride & Company for *On Tour with Queen Marie* by Constance Lily Morris, copyright 1927.

McGraw-Hill and Ryerson, Ltd., for *Joe Boyle, King of the Klondike* by William Rodney, copyright © 1974.

Methuen & Co., Ltd., for *In Gypsy Camp and Royal Palace* by E. O. Hoppe, copyright 1924.

John Murray, Ltd., for *The Letters of Queen Victoria*, edited by George Earle Buckle, copyright 1926, and for *Life with Queen Victoria*, edited by Victor Mallet.

New York magazine for "The First of the Celebrity Mayors" by Thomas J. Fleming, Nov. 10, 1969.

New York World, June 1925, May 1925, Oct. 1926, and Nov. 1926.

The New York Times, copyright 1916, 1926, 1927, 1930, 1933, 1938 by The New York Times Company.

Nigel Nicolson and Constable Publishers for *King George the Fifth: His Life and Reign* by Harold Nicolson, copyright 1952.

Nigel Nicolson and Harcourt Brace Jovanovich for *Peacemaking 1919* by Harold Nicolson, copyright © 1965.

Nisbet & Co., Ltd., for *Some Personal Expressions* by Take Jonescu, copyright 1919.

Prentice-Hall, Inc., for *Suitors and Supplicants: The Little Nations of Versailles* by Stephen Bonsal, copyright 1946.

G. P. Putnam's Sons for *Mr. New York* by Grover Whalen, copyright © 1955, and for *Memoirs* by Prince von Bülow, Vol. II, 1903–1909, copyright 1931.

Rand McNally & Company for *The Secrets of the Balkans* by Charles J. Vopkka, copyright 1921.

Paul R. Reynolds, Inc., and Macmillan Publishing Company for *A Biographer's Notebook* by Hector Bolitho, copyright 1950.

The Ryerson Press for *Roumania in Light and Shadow* by Ethel Greening Pantazzi.

St. Martin's Press for *Marie of Roumania* by Terence Elsberry, copyright © 1972.

The Saturday Evening Post, copyright 1927 The Curtis Publishing Company.

Edward Mandell House and Charles Seymour quoted from *What Really Happened at Paris*, copyright 1921 Charles Scribner's Sons; copyright renewed 1949; reprinted with the permission of Charles Scribner's Sons.

Marie, Queen of Roumania, excerpted from *Ordeal: The Story of My Life*, copyright 1935 Charles Scribner's Sons; copyright renewed © 1963; reprinted with the permission of Charles Scribner's Sons; and Marie, Queen of Roumania, excerpted from *The Story of My Life*, copyright 1934 Charles Scribner's Sons; copyright renewed © 1962; reprinted with the permission of Charles Scribner's Sons.

Rumania at the Paris Peace Conference by Sherman Spector, University Microfilms International, copyright Sherman David Spector.

Toronto *Star*, Nov. 1, 1926.

Time magazine, Aug. 4, 1924, and July 25, 1938.

The Times (London), Oct. 30, 1875, March 12, 1919, and April 17, 1923, copyright Times Newspapers, Ltd.

Viking Penguin, Inc., for *A Princess in Exile* by the Grand Duchess Marie, copyright 1932 Grand Duchess Marie, renewed © 1960 by Count Lennart Bernadotte, and for *The Portable Dorothy Parker* by Dorothy Parker, copyright 1926, renewed copyright 1954 by Dorothy Parker.

John Wiley & Sons, Ltd., for *The First World War: Causes, Conduct, Consequences* by Joachim Remak, copyright © 1971.